INSTRUCTOR'S RESOURCE

Aaron U. Bolin
Arkansas State University

PSYCHOLOGY

TWELFTH EDITION

CHARLES G. MORRIS
ALBERT A. MAISTO

Upper Saddle River, New Jersey 07458

© 2005 by PEARSON EDUCATION, INC.
Upper Saddle River, New Jersey 07458

All rights reserved

10 9 8 7 6 5 4 3 2

ISBN 0-13-189150-2

Printed in the United States of America

This work is protected by United States copyright laws and is provided *solely for the use of instructors* in teaching their courses and assessing student learning. Dissemination or sale of any part of this work *(including on the World Wide Web)* will destroy the integrity of the work and is not permitted. The work and materials from it should never be made available to students except by instructors using the accompanying text in their classes. All recipients of this work are expected to abide by these restrictions and to honor the intended pedagogical purposes and the needs of other instructors who rely on these materials.

Table of Contents

Chapter 1: The Science of Psychology 1

Chapter 2: The Biological Basis of Behavior 31

Chapter 3: Sensation and Perception 63

Chapter 4: States of Consciousness 93

Chapter 5: Learning 118

Chapter 6: Memory 149

Chapter 7: Cognition and Language 184

Chapter 8: Intelligence and Mental Abilities 208

Chapter 9: Motivation and Emotion 235

Chapter 10: Lifespan Development 275

Chapter 11: Personality 313

Chapter 12: Stress and Health Psychology 350

Chapter 13: Psychological Disorders 377

Chapter 14: Therapies 417

Chapter 15: Social Psychology 447

Chapter 1 The Science of Psychology

chapter outline 2

learning objectives 6

lecture suggestions

    Teaching Diversity 7
    Psychology and Common Sense 8
    African-Americans and Psychology 9
    Fact-of-the-Month Club 9
    Deception in Research: The Case Against It 10
    An Historical Perspective on Research Ethics 11

demonstrations and activities

    Perceptions of the Professor 12
    Self-Awareness and Cultural Identity 12
    Misconceptions About Psychology 13
    Are Psychologists Scientists? 14
    Careers in Psychology 14
    Understanding Random Assignment 15
    Wonder Horse Dials 911 to Save Boy's Life 16
    Softens Hands While You Do Dishes 16
    Debate: Is It Ethical to Use Animals in Psychological Research? 16

student assignments

    Exploring Psychology Through Art 17
    Psychology and the Media 17
    Using Sherlock Holmes to Teach Observation and Inference 17
    Keeping a Psychology Journal 18

video 19

multimedia 22

transparencies 29

handout

    Knowledge of Psychology Test 30

chapter outline

I. What is Psychology?
- A. Fields of psychology
    1. Developmental psychology
        a. Mental and physical growth from conception to death
    2. Neuroscience and Physiological psychology
        a. Behavior influenced by physical and chemical phenomena in the body
    3. Experimental psychology
        a. Learning, perception, memory, motivation, and other basic processes
    4. Personality psychology
        a. Individual differences in traits
    5. Clinical and counseling psychology
        a. Clinical: diagnosis, cause, and treatment of psychological disorders
        b. Counseling: "normal" problems of adjustment (family, career, coping)
    6. Social psychology
        a. The influence of people on one another
    7. Industrial and organizational psychology
        a. Psychology applied to the workplace (training, placement, productivity)
- B. Enduring issues
    1. Person-Situation: Behavior caused by interplay of internal and external factors
    2. Nature-Nurture: "Heredity-Environment" remains a perennial issue
    3. Stability-Change: How and when does behavior change? Why does it not?
    4. Diversity-Universality: Behavior across a spectrum of backgrounds and experiences
    5. Mind-Body: Dualism will not die
- C. Psychology as science
    1. Psychologists rely on the scientific method for answering questions of interest
        a. Formulate theories, generate hypotheses, collect data, explain results

II. The Growth of Psychology
- A. The "New" Psychology: A Science of the Mind
    1. Wilhelm Wundt and Edward Bradford Titchener: Voluntarism and Structuralism
        a. In 1879 Wundt founds experimental psychology laboratory at Leipzig
            i. Voluntarism concerned with conscious control of attention
        b. Titchener refocuses Psychology on the study of conscious experience
        c. Structuralism concerned with identifying the units of conscious experience
    2. William James: Functionalism

  a. Philosopher, physiologist, spiritualist James instigates American psychology

    i. Taught first class in 1875 at Harvard

  b. Functionalism concerned with the ongoing use of conscious experience

 3. Sigmund Freud: Psychodynamic psychology

  a. Neurologist Freud introduces psychoanalysis as a method of therapy

  b. Psychodynamic view focuses on the unconscious determinants of behavior

B. Redefining Psychology: The Study of Behavior

 1. John Broadus Watson: Behaviorism

  a. Watson rails against consciousness and "mentalism" as objects of study

    i. Attacks structuralism in particular

  b. Behaviorism concerned with observable, quantifiable, measurable behavior

 2. Burrhus Frederick Skinner: Behaviorism revisited

  a. B. F. Skinner continues Behaviorist tradition after Watson in United States

  b. Skinner's Behaviorism focused on the role of reinforcement

C. The Cognitive Revolution

 1. The precursors: Gestalt and humanistic psychology

  a. German Gestaltists also attack Structuralism, on different grounds

    i. Gestalt school concerned with perceptions of wholes, "good form"

  b. Humanistic psychology concerned with developing potential, maximizing abilities

 2. The rise of cognitive psychology

  a. Current dominant movement in psychology

  b. Concerned with memory, thinking, language, learning, decision making

D. New Directions

 1. Evolutionary psychology

  a. A focus on the adaptive value of mental processes and behavior patterns

 2. Positive psychology

  a. Attention devoted to understanding "the good life"

 3. Multiple perspectives

  a. Psychology embraces a variety of perspectives, methods, and traditions

E. Where are the women?

  a. From the beginning of the discipline women have made significant contributions

    i. Their apparent absence from historical record may reflect larger issues of diversity

III. **Human Diversity**

A. Gender

 1. The terms male and female, men and women, sex and gender are defined

 2. Gender stereotypes

  a. Characteristics assumed to be typical of each sex

  b. Gender roles: Behaviors we expect men and women to engage in

       3. Feminist psychology

           a. Research should move away from the male-dominated model

           b. Gender differences should focus on similarities rather than extremes

           c. "Women's issues" should receive greater research attention

       4. Sexual orientation

           a. APA's Division 44 is helping to advance the field

   B. Race and ethnicity

       1. Race: A subpopulation of a species

           a. Among humans, racial distinctions are difficult to maintain

              i. Interbreeding has spread genetic characteristics widely

              ii. Melanin, or skin pigmentation, is only one categorizing factor

       2. Racial and ethnic minorities in psychology

           a. Underrepresentation in the field remains a problem

   C. Culture

       1. Tangible and intangible artifacts of a society

IV. Research Methods in Psychology

   A. Naturalistic observation

       1. Behavior is studied in its natural environment, without intervention

       2. Advantages: spontaneous; more varied than lab; ideas for future study

       3. Disadvantages: observer bias; one-shot occurrence; multiple behaviors

   B. Case studies

       1. Intensive analysis and description of an individual or small group

       2. Advantages: rich description of behavior; ideas for future study

       3. Disadvantages: observer bias; difficult to generalize beyond single case

   C. Surveys

       1. Asking predetermined questions using an interview or questionnaire

       2. Advantages: lots of information at relatively low cost

       3. Disadvantages: respondents may not be representative; response biases

   D. Correlational research

       1. Used to investigate and clarify the relationships among variables

       2. Advantages: description and prediction are possible

       3. Disadvantages: no causality; cannot explain the relationship

   E. Experimental research

       1. Independent and dependent variables

           a. The effects of the manipulated IV on the DV are measured

       2. Experimental and control groups

           a. Experimental group receiving treatment is compared to control group

       3. Experimenter bias

          a. Psychologists need to maintain objectivity in their measurements
      4. Advantages: conclusions can be drawn about causal relationship
      5. Disadvantages: ethical considerations; behavior constrained in the lab
    F. Multimethod research
      1. Psychologists typically use multiple methods to answer their questions
    G. The importance of sampling
      1. A randomly drawn, representative sample of the population is used

V. Ethics and Psychological Research
    A. Ethics in research on humans
      1. Milgram's obedience studies renewed interest in ethical treatment
      2. Guidelines for ethical treatment
          a. Review boards, informed consent, use of deception, debriefing
    B. Ethics in research on nonhuman animals
      1. Animal models can provide important insights into human functioning
          a. Guidelines have been established for the ethical treatment of nonhuman research participants

VI. Careers in Psychology
    A. Academic and applied psychology
      1. Employment opportunities for master's and doctoral psychologists
    B. Clinical settings
      1. Distinctions among psychiatrists, psychoanalysts, clinicians, counselors, social workers

learning objectives

After reading this chapter, students should be able to:

1. Describe the major fields of psychology including developmental, physiological, experimental, personality, clinical and counseling, social, and industrial/organizational psychology.

2. Summarize five enduring issues of psychology.

3. Distinguish between the five basic methods used by psychologists to gather information about behavior. Identify the situations in which each of the methods would be appropriate.

4. Describe the importance of sampling related to issues of gender, race, and culture in research.

5. Discuss the concerns of ethics in psychology.

6. Describe the history and founders of psychology, early schools of psychological thought, and explain how they contributed to the development of psychological science.

7. Explain the difference between psychiatrists, psychologists, and psychoanalysts.

lecture suggestions

Teaching Diversity

As psychology enters its second century, there is a growing appreciation among researchers, clinicians, and teachers for the great diversity that exists in human behavior. Psychologists increasingly acknowledge that a science of thought and behavior must take into account the social, cultural, and ethnic settings in which thought and behavior take place.

This consideration of diversity extends to the classroom. Classes in colleges and universities have an increasingly rich composition of students who vary in their cultural backgrounds, gender, age, sexual orientation, ethnicity, and life experiences. Instructors are called upon to present information relevant to the experiences of their students, and to capitalize on those experiences to stimulate discussion, reflection, and learning. In short, teaching a diverse group of students can require a diversity of information.

The references given below are excellent sources of ideas for teaching about diversity to a diverse audience. They include both suggestions for integrating diversity issues into classroom presentations and tips for effectively working with students who come from a wide range of backgrounds. Here are a few examples of strategies and topics you might consider:

❖ Schoem, Frankel, Zúñiga, and Lewis (1993, pp. 293-311) offer 15 concrete suggestions for improving multicultural teaching in the college classroom. Presented in the form of answers to commonly asked questions, they include tips on helping students to integrate theoretical material with their personal experiences, empowering "underrepresented voices" in the class, dealing with explicitly racist or sexist remarks made by students, and evaluating teaching and learning throughout the semester.

❖ Five chapters in Clark (1993) offer profiles of African-American, Hispanic/Latino, Asian and Pacific Islander, Native American, and other foreign-born students. Included are comments on demographics, cognitive styles, heterogeneity of the various groups, factors influencing academic success, and other issues surrounding teaching diverse groups.

❖ Joyce Bishop, of Golden West College, suggests assigning projects that involve a fair amount of latitude in their execution, so that students can integrate aspects of their personal and cultural backgrounds with the concepts of psychology. For example, students might write about their experiences with culture shock and the impact it had upon them.

❖ Laura Border and Nancy Van Note Chism (1992, pp. 103-115) provide a list of resources for promoting diversity issues in the classroom. These include journal articles, videotapes, and institutional programs and contact persons.

❖ Mardee Jenrette and J. Q. Adams (M. Adams, 1992) discuss ways in which Miami-Dade Community College and Joliet Junior College were able to successfully meet the challenges of teaching to a diverse student body at the community college level. Diane vom Saul, Debrah Jefferson, and Minion Morrison (Border & Van Note Chism, 1992) also discuss programs at eight universities (such as Stanford, Harvard, and the Ohio State University) that were successful in promoting a wide range of viewpoints in the classroom.

❖ To encourage students to think about diversity issues, Edith A. Lewis (Schoem et al., 1993, pp. 328-329) suggests a "How Ethnic Am I?" exercise. Students reflect on their ethnic group backgrounds, the values they hold, and the forces that shape and influence their experiences. This exercise could be used at the start of the semester to introduce the general concerns of psychology as the study of behavior (of many types, from many perspectives), and it can also be linked profitably to the issues of social identity discussed in Chapter 14.

Throughout this Instructor's Manual you will find lecture suggestions that draw on the experiences of diverse groups of people. To find these quickly look for the globe near the title.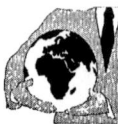

Adams, M. (Ed.) (1992). Promoting diversity in college classrooms: Innovative responses for the curriculum, faculty, and institutions. In R. J. Menges & M. D. Svinicki (Eds.), *New directions for teaching and learning* (Vol. 52). San Francisco: Jossey-Bass.

Border, L. L. B., & Van Note Chism, N. (Eds.) (1992). Teaching for diversity. In R. J. Menges & M. D. Svinicki (Eds.), *New directions for teaching and learning* (Vol. 49). San Francisco: Jossey-Bass.

Bowser, B. P., Auletta, G. S., & Jones, T. (1993). *Confronting diversity issues on campus*. Newbury Park, CA: Sage.

Bowser, B. P., Jones, T., & Young, G. A. (Eds.) (1995). *Toward the multicultural university*. Westport, CT: Praeger.

Bronstein, P., & Quina, K. (Eds.) (1988). *Teaching a psychology of people: Resources for gender and sociocultural awareness*. New York: American Psychological Association.

Clark, L. W. (Ed.) (1993). *Faculty and student challenges in facing cultural and linguistic diversity*. Springfield, IL: Charles C. Thomas.

Scher, D. (1995, January). Teaching to cultures different from your own: What works and what doesn't? Poster presented at the 17th Annual National Institute on the Teaching of Psychology, St. Petersburg Beach, FL.

Schoem, D., Frankel, L., Zúñiga, X., & Lewis, E. A. (Eds.) (1993). *Multicultural teaching in the university*. Westport, CT: Praeger.

Psychology and Common Sense

A common refrain voiced by laypeople and scientists is that most, if not all, of behavioral science "is just common sense." Introductory psychology students are particularly apt to make this claim, given that much of their prior exposure to psychology is likely to have been very common-sensical (though perhaps not well-established) claims by a variety of "professionals" on the talk-show circuit. In a nutshell, it's difficult to counter the "common-sense" belief when so much of behavior seems to be explainable at an intuitive surface level.

Mark Leary shares some suggestions for discussing this issue with your students. It is true that the subject matter of psychology is much more familiar to most people than is the subject matter of subatomic physics or gastroendocrinological biology; we see behavior all around us, but rarely stumble over a gluon. Psychology would be an odd science of thought and behavior if it only considered thoughts and behaviors completely foreign to people's experiences, or if its findings always ran counter to most people's beliefs. But neither greater visibility of subject matter nor popular consensus guarantee greater understanding. Many people believed whole-heartedly in flat Earths and cheese moons only to find their common-sense views dismantled in the face of scientific evidence. Although most people would like to believe that large rewards produce greater liking for a boring task, that the behavior of men and women is determined by their biology, or that absence makes the heart grow fonder, researchers studying cognitive dissonance, sex-role stereotypes, and close relationships would be happy to share their findings to the contrary. In short, common-sense belief may not always be consistent with scientific evidence.

More importantly, psychologists (like all scientists) are primarily engaged in the task of explaining behavior, rather than merely cataloging it. The difference between theory and description--"why" versus "what"--echoes the difference between science and common sense. Common sense certainly helps describe *what* takes place in behavior, but doesn't compel us to understand *why* it takes place. The development of theory in understanding behavior sets science apart from everyday, common-sense accounts.

Leary, M. (1995). *Behavioral research methods* (2nd ed., pp. 24-25). Pacific Grove, CA: Brooks/Cole.

African-Americans and Psychology

Like women, African-Americans faced many obstacles to their education and participation in psychology. Most institutions would not accept African-American students, and when they were able to enroll, they often experienced discrimination. In addition, few undergraduate black colleges offered a major in psychology until after the 1940s. Howard University, the only major black university offering graduate study, awarded 32 Ph.D.s to African-Americans from 1920 to 1950. During the same period, only eight African-Americans earned a Ph.D. from the ten most prestigious universities. Not only was earning the Ph.D. difficult, employment opportunities were scarce for African-American psychologists since neither universities nor organizations in the private sector would hire them. As a result, most African-American psychologists taught at black colleges where opportunities to engage in research were limited, thus restricting opportunities for professional recognition. The situation for African-American students has improved dramatically in recent years. Kenneth B. Clark, best known for his research on the effects of racial segregation, became the first African-American elected as APA president in 1970.

Guthrie, R. V. (1976). *Even the rat was white: A historical view of psychology.* New York: Harper and Row.
Schultz, D. P., & Schultz, S. E. (1992). *A history of modern psychology (5th ed.).* Orlando, FL: Harcourt Brace Jovanovich.
Reprinted from Hill, W. G. (1995). Instructor's resource manual for *Psychology* by S. F. Davis and J. J. Palladino. Englewood Cliffs, NJ: Prentice Hall.

Fact-Of-The-Month Club

The American Psychological Association celebrated its 100th anniversary in 1992. To commemorate this occasion, Warren Street compiled historical citations relevant to psychology for each day of the year. A handful of these are presented below for you to share with your students; a daily citation can be found at: http://www.cwu.edu/~warren/today.html.

January	2, 1925	APA is incorporated
	8, 1902	Carl Rogers' birthdate
	9, 1878	John B. Watson's birthdate
	11, 1842	William James' birthdate
	29, 1954	Gordon Allport's *The Nature of Prejudice* is published
February	1, 1844	G. Stanley Hall's birthdate
	18, 1896	Fritz Heider's birthdate
	28, 1939	Dollard, Doob, Miller, Mowrer, and Sears publish *Frustration and Aggression*
March	4, 1888	Howard Long, early Black psychologist, is born
	7, 1897	J. P. Guilford's birthdate
	18, 1959	Festinger and Carlsmith publish "Cognitive consequences of forced compliance," *Journal of Abnormal and Social Psychology*
	20, 1904	B. F. Skinner's birthdate
	30, 1863	Mary W. Calkins' birthdate
April	14, 1886	Edward C. Tolman's birthdate
	15, 1880	Max Wertheimer's birthdate
	16, 1943	Albert Hoffman "feels odd" after absorbing LSD-25 in his lab
	25, 1968	Darley and Latane publish "Bystander intervention in emergencies" in *Journal of Personality and Social Psychology*
May	6, 1907	Kenneth Spence's birthdate
	8, 1919	Leon Festinger's birthdate
	13, 1893	Henry Murray's birthdate
	15, 1917	Eleanor Maccoby's birthdate

	24, 1884	Clark Hull's birthdate
June	2, 1922	Lange and James publish *The Emotions*
	7, 1890	Karl Lashley's birthdate
	14, 1920	Francis Sumner, first Black Ph.D., Clark University
	26, 1878	G. Stanley Hall, first American psychology Ph.D., Harvard
July	11, 1857	Alfred Binet's birthdate
	16, 1965	Robert Zajonc publishes "Social facilitation" in *Science*
	25, 1871	Margaret Floy Washburn's birthdate
August	5, 1903	Rensis Likert's birthdate
	9, 1896	Jean Piaget's birthdate
	15, 1933	Stanley Milgram's birthdate
	16, 1832	Wilhelm Wundt's birthdate
	25, 1974	*Journal of Black Psychology* published
September	4, 1929	Psi Chi founded
	9, 1890	Kurt Lewin's birthdate
	13, 1890	James' *Principles of Psychology* published
	17, 1904	Oskar Pfungst begins studying Clever Hans, the wonder horse
	26, 1849	Ivan Pavlov's birthdate
October	9, 1981	Roger Sperry awarded Nobel Prize for split-brain research
	11, 1885	Freud leaves to study with Charcot in Paris
	30, 1942	MMPI first published
	31, 1905	Harry Harlow's birthdate
November	6, 1929	E. G. Boring publishes *A History of Experimental Psychology*
	11, 1897	Gordon Allport's birthdate
	20, 1875	Wundt's first lecture at Leipzig
December	1, 1847	Christine Ladd-Franklin's birthdate
	11, 1893	*Psychological Review* published
	22, 1903	Magda B. Arnold's birthdate
	27, 1892	First annual APA convention at University of Pennsylvania

Street, W. R. (1992). *American Psychological Association 1992 centennial calendar.* Washington, DC: APA.
Street, W. R. (1994). *A chronology of noteworthy events in American Psychology.* Washington, DC: APA.

Deception in Research: The Case Against It

The ethical principles of the American Psychological Association allow for the use of deception in research as long as it is justified by the study's prospective value, no alternatives are available, and the participants are given a full explanation of the study as soon as possible. Diana Baumrind, however, argued strongly against any use of intentional deception in psychological research (such as withholding information to ensure that subjects will participate, using deceptive instructions, or using staged manipulations in naturalistic settings). She attributed its justification to the adoption of an act-utilitarianism meta-ethic. That is, a particular action, in this case deception, is perceived as being acceptable if no other action would have better consequences. She criticized act-utilitarianism on the basis that it fails to account for long-range costs, the rights of the minority, and its subjectivity. She argued that deception is morally wrong on the basis of three generally accepted ethical rules in Western society: the right of informed consent, the obligation of researchers to protect the welfare of the subject, and the responsibility of researchers to be trustworthy. Furthermore, she argued that the costs of deception to the research participant (for example, undermining their trust in their own judgment), profession of psychology (loss of community support for their research or suspicion of always trying to "trick" the research participant), and society (the potential that trust in authority will be undermined) outweigh its use in research. Alternatives to using deception proposed by Baumrind included conducting naturalistic rather than experimental research, introspection about the phenomenon by researchers and their confederates rather than experimental manipulations, and detailed debriefing by a skilled and concerned professional.

Baumrind, D. (1985). Research using intentional deception: Ethical issues revisited. *American Psychologist*, 40, 165-174.

Reprinted from Hill, W. G. (1995). Instructor's resource manual for *Psychology* by S. F. Davis and J. J. Palladino. Englewood Cliffs, NJ: Prentice Hall.

A Historical Perspective on Research Ethics

When discussing the ethical treatment of human research participants, several "classic" studies, which would be ethically questionable by today's standards, serve as examples. For instance, many instructors discuss Stanley Milgram's studies of obedience, Philip Zimbardo's prison simulation, or Stanley Schachter's studies of autonomic arousal and attribution. Students often have mixed reactions to these examples. Some find them relatively innocuous, whereas others have strong reactions to the treatments participants were asked to endure. The fact that such studies took place within relatively recent times compounds the issue. Some students see these 1960s experiments as "long ago and of a different time," whereas others see them as examples of the "unethical treatment" psychologists "still foist on people to this day."

To provide a context for these types of issues, your students might be interested in hearing about older examples of ethically questionable research. For example, Carney Landis, a noted psychologist of the 1920s and 1930s, conducted a series of studies dealing with the experience and expression of emotion. In one set of studies he was particularly interested in capturing facial expressions of emotion, and used strong elicitors of emotion to produce them. For example, one situation involved dropping a lit firecracker underneath an unsuspecting subject's chair, whereas another involved showing participants pornographic (for their day) photographs and photos of horribly disfiguring skin diseases.

Although these manipulations may seem harsh, Landis used stronger ones as well. For example, participants were instructed in one situation to plunge their hands into a pail of shallow water that, unbeknownst to them, contained three live frogs. (This manipulation was presumably used to evoke disgust.) To quote Landis, however..."After the subject had reacted to the frogs the experimenter said, 'Yes, but you have not felt everything yet, feel around again.' While the subject was doing so he received a strong...shock from an induction coil, attached to the pail by concealed wiring."

And for the *coup de grâce*:

"The table in front of the subject was covered with a cloth. A flat tray and a butcher's knife were placed on the cloth. A live white rat was given to the subject. He (sic) was instructed, 'Hold this rat with your left hand and then cut off its head with the knife.'...In five cases where the subjects could not be persuaded to follow directions the experimenter cut off the head while the subject looked on."

Although Landis has been singled out for examination here, there certainly are no lack of experiments from the 1920s through the 1960s work mentioned above that can provide examples of ethically dubious research. Discussing such studies, especially in light of current APA standards, should produce spirited discussion among your students.

Landis, C. (1924). Studies of emotional reactions II: General behavior and facial expression. *Comparative Psychology*, 4, 447-509.

demonstrations

Perceptions of the Professor

This activity is both a good "ice-breaker" for the first class and an opportunity to generate some data for a discussion of impression formation. A basic principle of impression formation is that we form our opinions of others from very limited information (for example, physical appearance, tone of voice, age, occupation). In this activity, you'll have the students in your class share their inferences about you. At the start of the first class, enter the classroom and go through the normal routine of stating your name, the course title and number, and then go over the syllabus in detail. Immediately after discussing the syllabus, ask students to take out a blank sheet of paper and tell them that you are going to ask a series of questions about yourself in order to help them get to know you. Explain that it is their task to write down their best guess about what the answers are, and assure them that you will later give them all the "correct" answers. Then, proceed to ask them several questions that relate to concrete behaviors or characteristics or even about more abstract aspects of your personality. Although the questions may vary from class to class (and may depend on what you are comfortable revealing), potential questions include: How old do you think I am? Am I married? What kind of music do I like? What kind of car do I drive? What are some of my favorite TV shows? What are my hobbies or favorite leisure time activities? Do I like sports? Do I play any instruments? Am I liberal or conservative? Am I a Mac user or a PC fan? Am I a vegetarian? Am I an "outdoorsy" kind of person? Did I go to a large university or a small liberal arts college?

You can also give them the opportunity to ask additional questions (with the caveat that you can decline to answer a particular question for personal reasons). Instead of collecting their answers, go through the questionnaire by first asking them to share their answers and then giving them the correct answer. You can then use their answers to discuss impression formation and introduce them to social psychology as a field of study. This exercise, besides being fun for all involved, tends to be effective in "relaxing" the students and encouraging classroom discussion from the outset of the course. Lashley (1987) proposed a similar exercise to the one described above using a personality inventory that is designed to assess the class's perceptions of the professor and illustrate aspects of person perception.

Lashley, R. L. (1987). Using students' perceptions of their instructor to illustrate principles of person perception. *Teaching of Psychology, 14*, 179-180.

Adapted from Hill, W. G. (1995). Instructor's resource manual for *Psychology* by S. F. Davis and J. J. Palladino. Englewood Cliffs, NJ: Prentice Hall.

Self-Awareness and Cultural Identity

Chapter 1 discusses the importance of culture and the role that it plays in our cognitive, motivational, and emotional processes. Despite its broad influence on our behavior, however, many of us are not terribly aware of aspects of our own culture. Carolyn Enns (1994) suggests two exercises that may be helpful in increasing students' self-awareness.

In one exercise, Enns suggests dividing students into small groups and having them discuss the following questions (quoted from p. 209): (a) What is your own cultural/ethnic/racial background? (b) How did your family describe this identity to you as you were growing up? (c) How did this ethnic identity influence the way you and your family related to your community and friends? (d) What is the impact of your racial/ethnic identity on your self-definition, personality style, and/or relationships with others? (Enns reports that even in fairly homogenous groups, students are able to discover diversity.) After students have had approximately 15 minutes for discussion, she suggests conducting a full group discussion to identify themes and commonalties discovered in the smaller groups. According to Enns, students may be less likely to develop faulty stereotypes when they have an increased awareness of the unique life experiences of others.

In another exercise, Enns attempts to help students understand and describe their own culture through the use of symbols rather than words (because much of culture is implicit and difficult to describe). Students are first asked to draw pictures of their culture by using crayons, markers, and symbols. Then, in small groups, students take turns labeling certain aspects of their culture (as depicted) and describing it to the others. According to Enns, students not only gain a better understanding of cultural influences on their own pictures and symbols, but also gain (by comparison with others' pictures) an understanding of how individualistic and collectivist cultures can shape world views in vastly different ways. As an example, Enns reports that American students typically depict separate symbols representing specific aspects of culture such as home, religion, and family values, whereas international students from more collectivist cultures create more unified images with a central theme of interdependence.

Enns, C. Z. (1994). On teaching about the cultural relativism of psychological constructs. *Teaching of Psychology, 4*, 205-211.

Misconceptions About Psychology

One of the most popular and oldest activities for the introductory course is the administration and subsequent discussion of a test of misconceptions about psychology. Although a new 65-item multiple-choice test was developed by McCutcheon (1991), the most popular test is the Test of Common Beliefs developed by Vaughan (1977). Vaughan's test, however, has been criticized for the ambiguity of some of the items (Brown, 1984; Gardner & Dalsing, 1986; Ruble, 1986), the fact that all items have "false" as the correct response, which may lead to a response set tendency (Vaughan, 1977), and the finding that many of the items are not really misconceptions since they are often correctly answered (Gardner & Dalsing, 1986; Lamal, 1979). Griggs and Ransdell (1987) compared responses to Vaughan's Test of Common Beliefs from students that had taken an introductory psychology course in high school to those of several other studies (Lamal, 1979; Gardner & Dalsing, 1986; Vaughan, 1977). Using a criterion of at least a 50% error rate for an item (that is, they were answered as "true"), they identified 15 questions that met the criterion in at least two studies and had not been subject to earlier criticisms of ambiguity. These items are reproduced in Handout 1-1 and are ordered from highest to lowest with respect to their average error rate. You can administer these items to your class and use the responses as a starting point for a discussion on common-sense notions and misconceptions about psychology. You may want to note to your students that many of these items are also answered incorrectly by psychologists and other social scientists (see Gardner & Hund, 1983). You can also tell your students that the correct answers to many of these items are discussed in their textbook.

Brown, L. T. (1983). Some more misconceptions about psychology among introductory psychology students. *Teaching of Psychology, 10*, 207-210.
Brown, L. T. (1984). Misconceptions about psychology aren't always what they seem. *Teaching of Psychology, 11*, 75-78.
Gardner, R. M., & Dalsing, S. (1986). Misconceptions about psychology among college students. *Teaching of Psychology, 13*, 32-34.
Gardner, R. M., & Hund, R. M. (1983). Misconceptions of psychology among academicians. *Teaching of Psychology, 10*, 20-22.
Griggs, R. A., & Ransdell, S. E. (1987). Misconceptions tests or misconceived tests? *Teaching of Psychology, 14*, 210-214.
Lamal, P. A. (1979). College students' common beliefs about psychology. *Teaching of Psychology, 6*, 155-158.
McCutcheon, L. E. (1991). A new test of misconceptions about psychology. *Psychological Reports, 68*, 647-653.
Ruble, R. (1986). Ambiguous psychological misconceptions. *Teaching of Psychology, 13*, 34-36.
Vaughan, E. D. (1977). Misconceptions about psychology among introductory psychology students. *Teaching of Psychology, 4*, 138-141.

Reprinted from Hill, W. G. (1995). Instructor's resource manual for *Psychology* by S. F. Davis and J. J. Palladino. Englewood Cliffs, NJ: Prentice Hall.

Are Psychologists Scientists?

Before introducing students to the various subfields of psychology, make the point that all psychologists, regardless of their area of expertise, are indeed scientists. This brief exercise (adapted from Smith, 1982) also illustrates students' stereotypical view of psychologists as clinicians. First, write the word "psychologist" on the board and ask students to describe some characteristics and traits of the typical psychologist. With encouragement to freely answer with any words or images that come to mind, the following responses frequently come up: caring, patient, warm, lying on a couch, soothing, good listener, giving advice, etc. After erasing these responses, write the word "scientist" on the board and ask students to do the same for the typical scientist. Their responses clearly indicate that their perceptions of "scientists" (which include traits like analytical, brilliant, and achieving, and images of conducting research and wearing lab coats and pocket protectors) are markedly different from their perceptions of "psychologists." Near the end of in the exercise, a few students will invariably catch on and ask, "But aren't psychologists scientists?", which leads the class into a discussion of why their perceptions are so divergent. By this time, the idea that psychologists are *scientists* that study the mind and behavior rather than genes, chemicals, or subatomic particles makes perfect sense. Now, you can describe cognitive psychologists as *scientists* who study human mental processes, developmental psychologists as *scientists* who study changes in capacities throughout the lifespan, and so on. [As a side note, you may also ask students whether the images they conjured up were male or female. Most will confess that their images of both the psychologist and the scientist were male. It may be a good opportunity to bring up gender stereotypes and feminist psychology.]

Smith, G. (1982). Introducing psychology majors to clinical bias through the adjective generation technique. *Teaching of Psychology, 9*, 238-239.

Careers in Psychology

In a mad rush to begin covering the tremendous amount of material in introductory psychology, many instructors overlook more practical issues that would be of interest to introductory students, especially those who think they might major in psychology. It is never too early to introduce students to psychology as a profession, and even students who do not major in psychology are bound to gain a greater understanding and appreciation for the field. After discussing the various subfields of psychology, devote some time (perhaps a class session) to issues pertaining to psychology as a career choice. There are a variety of activities and topics you could introduce, and several suggestions are given here.

To promote early student involvement in psychology, describe the goals and activities of Psi Chi, the National Honor Society in Psychology. Tell students (or better yet, bring in the Psi Chi President to tell students) about the requirements for joining (e.g., psychology major or minor, 3.0 GPA overall and in all psychology courses, completion of three semesters or five quarters of college courses) and the benefits of membership (e.g., interaction with psychology faculty and majors, participation in worthwhile activities related to psychology, an important honor that will be noticed by graduate schools). In addition, Psi Beta is a psychology oriented honor society for students at community colleges and two-year schools. Along the same lines, explain to students how they might become student affiliates of the two biggest professional organizations in psychology, the American Psychological Association (APA) and the American Psychological Society (APS). Both organizations have student application forms that you can make available (Call APA at 800-374-2721; APS at 202-783-2077). Stress to students the benefits of presenting their research (perhaps in their sophomore or junior years) at one of these national conferences or perhaps at a regional one (e.g., Southwestern Psychological Association, Western Psychological Association).

You may also give your students information about graduate school -- how to get in, what it's really like, and what opportunities it affords. Tell students how you got interested in your major field and what life in graduate school was like. Explain degree plans (including how many years it takes, what is expected in the way of course work and research), funding opportunities (many students are surprised that teaching and research assistantships actually cover most graduate school expenses), and research and teaching opportunities. Bring in the latest edition of APA's Guide to Graduate Study in Psychology and give an overview of its purpose. Briefly outline for students what they should be doing during each year of their undergraduate career if they are interested in going to graduate school (e.g., when to study and take the GRE, when to send for applications, when to get research experience, when to ask for letters of recommendation). Encourage students to seek out a close relationship with a faculty member whose research interests coincide with theirs.

Finally, discuss career opportunities in psychology. Bring to class recent issues of the APA *Monitor* and APS *Observer* and show students representative job listings and requirements for consideration. Show either of two excellent APA-produced videos, *Careers in Psychology: Your Options are Open* (a brief, 9-minute segment that features a panel of psychologists from different specialties discussing career opportunities) or *Career Encounters in Psychology* (a longer, 28-minute segment that provides an overview of the diverse specializations and careers in psychology through interviews with several different types of psychologists). Have someone from your career counseling center give a talk on opportunities for psychology majors (he or she may also have data on the current employment status of recent psychology graduates). Better yet, invite to class (a) a psychologist from an applied setting (e.g., a clinician in private practice, an industrial/organizational psychologist, a sports or forensic psychologist) and (b) a psychologist who works in an academic setting (this could be you, another faculty member at your college or university, or someone outside your institution) to talk about career opportunities and experiences.

Understanding Random Assignment: The In-Class Basketball Team

Expand on the text's treatment of research methods by discussing the procedure by which participants are assigned to conditions in an experiment. Explain that *random assignment* involves placing participants in experimental conditions in such a way that every participant has an equal chance of being placed in any condition. Participants can be assigned to conditions by any number of random methods, including flipping coins, drawing slips of paper out of a hat, or by using a random number table. Random assignment is a key feature of experiments because it ensures that the experimental groups are roughly equivalent (e.g., in age, intelligence, personality, attitudes, appearance, and so on) before the independent variable is manipulated. As a result, experimenters can be more confident that differences in behavior at the end of the experiment are due to the effects of the independent variable rather than to any preexisting differences between participants.

David Watson suggests a simple but clever exercise to demonstrate this principle (which can be difficult to understand in the abstract). Tell your class that you have invented a superior new way of coaching basketball and you would like to test the effectiveness of your method in an experimental context. One team (the experimental group) will be trained by your new method and the other team (the control group) will be trained by traditional methods. If your training method is indeed superior, then the team trained by your method should do better than the traditional team in a tournament. Explain to your class that you are worried about controlling for height, a variable that is obviously important in basketball (i.e., if all the tall players ended up, say, on the control team, the experimental team may lose the tournament and the loss might be attributed to failure of the new training method rather than to height, the true cause). Tell the class that you will randomly assign students to two teams by flipping a coin. Watson suggests using only one sex to avoid too much variation in height (he uses females because they are more plentiful in psychology classes). Randomly approach students in the class and flip a coin for each so that "heads" go to Team A and "tails" go to Team B. Ask students to stand on different sides of the room as they are assigned to one of the two teams. After 10 students are assigned to each team, Watson suggests lining up the members of each team (so that Team A is standing directly behind Team B) from tallest to shortest. Randomization should have ensured that the teams are clearly equal in height, and everyone will be satisfied that the height variable is eliminated from your experiment.

Watson, D. L. (1990). A neat little demonstration of the benefits of random assignment of subjects in an experiment. In V. P. Makosky, C. C. Sileo, L. G. Whittemore, C. P. Landry, & M. L. Skutley (Eds.), *Activities handbook for the teaching of psychology: Vol. 3* (pp. 3-4). Washington, DC: American Psychological Association.

Wonder Horse Dials 911 to Save Boy's Life

Jane Halonen (1986) suggests a fun class exercise that tests students' understanding of experimental methodology principles. After you have covered the basics of correlation, experimentation, and causal inference, challenge your students to apply these principles by examining the outrageous claims made in tabloid headlines, many of which imply a causal relationship (e.g., dreaming in black-and-white improves your sex life; garlic diet improves memory...but not breath; large gopher presence precedes volcano eruptions). For this exercise, bring in a variety of headlines from the *Star*, *National Enquirer*, *Weekly World News*, *Globe*, etc. that are psychology-related and causal-sounding (or ask students to bring in examples). Challenge students to design simple studies that will accurately test whether or not the relationship claimed in the headline is a valid one. Halonen reports that students enjoy the opportunity to "think like scientists" in response to humorous and outrageous claims and that this exercise helps stimulate them to scrutinize causal claims from all sources and to design experiments more carefully and creatively (and, if that isn't enough, they can practice their newfound skills in line at the grocery store!).

Halonen, J. S. (1986). *Teaching critical thinking in psychology*. Milwaukee: Alverno Productions.

Softens Hands While You Do Dishes

A variation of the tabloid exercise suggested above encourages students to apply experimental principles to claims they are bombarded with on a daily basis--television and magazine advertising. For this exercise, bring in (or have your students bring in) samples of advertising and have students critique the product claims of success according to principles of experimental methodology. Ads can be critiqued on several grounds, including the problem of personal testimony as unreliable, the absence of a control or comparison group, the presence of extraneous variables, the presence of plausible alternative explanations, unclear or undefined variables, and a lack of supporting statistics. Halonen (1986) reports that students become enthusiastic about experimental methodology when they realize it has the potential to make them smarter consumers.

Halonen, J. S. (1986). *Teaching critical thinking in psychology*. Milwaukee: Alverno Productions.

Debate: Is It Ethical to Use Animals in Psychological Research?

There currently exists a heated controversy over the use of animals in psychological research, and an in-depth consideration of this important issue would make an excellent introduction to the topic of research ethics. This debate raises the question of whether the benefits of animal research outweigh the moral costs. On one hand are animal-rights supporters who allege inhumane treatment of laboratory animals and argue that the welfare of humans should not be placed above that of animals. On the other hand are researchers and scientists who argue that animal research is necessary and beneficial for society and that strict laws and guidelines are in place to protect laboratory animals. Use the debate procedures suggested at the beginning of this manual (or develop your own) and assign students to research and defend both sides of this issue. Excellent background resources for this discussion can be found in *Taking Sides* (Issue 3), *American Psychologist*, *Psychological Science*, and *Newsweek* (full references are given below).

Devenport, L. D., & Devenport, J. A. (1990). The laboratory dilemma: A solution in our backyards. *Psychological Science, 1,* 215-216.
Johnson, D. (1990). Animal rights and human lives: Time for scientists to right the balance. *Psychological Science, 1,* 213-214.
Miller, N. E. (1991). Commentary on Ulrich: Need to check truthfulness of statements by opponents of animal research. *Psychological Science, 2,* 422-423.
Slife, B. (1998). *Taking sides: Clashing views on controversial psychological issues* (10th ed.). Guilford, CT: Dushkin Publishing Group.
Slife, B. (2000). *Taking sides: Clashing views on controversial psychological issues* (11th ed.). Guilford, CT: Dushkin Publishing Group.
Ulrich, R. E. (1991). Animal rights, animal wrongs and the question of balance. *Psychological Science, 2,* 197-201.

student assignments

Exploring Psychology Through Art

Maureen Pierce suggests a unique ice-breaking assignment that encourages students to explore their ideas about psychology through the creation of a piece of artwork. After you have discussed the definition of psychology during the first or second class session, ask your students to create a piece of art that expresses and reflects their own ideas about the definition of psychology, some topic in the field of psychology, or something they hope to learn in the course. Tell your students that as long as the object reflects a psychological theme, the choice of materials and media is up to them. They should also include a short (1-2 page) summary statement that describes how the art reflects their understanding or definition of psychology. They should explain how and why they chose the media and materials used as well as how their creation specifically expresses their unique interpretation of psychology. Pierce reports that students are typically very creative in using a wide variety of media (including fabrics, modeling clay, and paints) to create sculptures, mobiles, and collages. She also notes that in addition to the fact that students are enthusiastic about the assignment, it gives them an opportunity at an early stage in the course to think critically, to explore the textbook, and to carefully consider their ideas about psychology.

Pierce, M. C., & Davis, S. F. (1995). Exploring psychology through the visual realm. Paper presented at the 103rd annual meeting of the American Psychological Association, New York, August.

Psychology and the Media

Do the media present a distorted image of psychology? The answer to this question is explored in a good first-week assignment suggested by Lester Sdorow (1994). Instruct your students to spend a week or two observing and noting any coverage of psychology in the media (including radio and television, newspapers and magazines, and motion pictures). Place a copy of Benjamin's (1986) article on this topic on reserve in the library, and ask students to write a short (2-3 page) paper discussing the "popular" image of psychology from the perspective of their own observations as well as from those noted by Benjamin. Sdorow suggests that students' papers address the following questions: (a) Do the media present psychology more as a science or more as a form of common sense? (b) Do the media present the diverse fields of psychology or only a few? (If only a few, which are overrepresented and which are underrepresented?) (c) Do the media rely more on psychologists or self-proclaimed experts for information? (d) Do the media present psychological information more in a sober manner or in a sensationalistic manner?

Benjamin, L. T. (1986). Why don't they understand us? A history of psychology's public image. *American Psychologist, 43,* 87-94.
Sdorow, L. (1994). The Frankenstein course: Teaching assistants, laboratory exercises, and papers in introductory psychology. Paper presented at the Southwest Regional Conference for Teachers of Psychology, Fort Worth.

Using Sherlock Holmes to Teach Observation and Inference: Elementary, My Dear Watson

Chapter 1 discusses naturalistic observation as a research method as well as the importance of critical thinking in psychology. Halonen (1986) suggests an excellent exercise that incorporates both of these ideals. In this assignment, students are asked to test their critical thinking and observation skills by assuming the identity of detective Sherlock Holmes. The basic premise is that Sherlock Holmes has carefully examined one of the student's personal environments (e.g., home, work, car, health club) and is attempting to find and meet the student based on clues derived from his investigation. Students are asked to write a short paper that consists of the letter that Sherlock Holmes might write to Dr. Watson describing his pursuit in detail, including the reason for it and the specific elements from the environment that justify his leads. This exercise should be assigned after you have talked about naturalistic observation and inference, and Halonen suggests that students read Webb et al.'s (1981) excellent chapter on physical evidence in their *Nonreactive Measures in the Social Sciences*. According to Halonen, students react very enthusiastically to this assignment, as they enjoy the opportunity to disclose about themselves as well as to role-play the clever Holmes. Importantly, students' papers are typically very thoughtful and reveal many instances of critical thinking, such as extensive observations, use of concepts from the Webb chapter (e.g., erosion, garbology), logical but purposefully inaccurate inferences to add humor, and attention to the ethical dilemma of exploring private environments.

Halonen, J. S. (1986). *Teaching critical thinking in psychology*. Milwaukee: Alverno Productions.
Webb, E. J., Campbell, D. T., Schwartz, R. D., Sechrest, L., & Grove, J. B. (1981). *Nonreactive measures in the social sciences* (2nd. ed.). Boston: Houghton-Mifflin.

Keeping a Psychology Journal

In order to increase the personal relevance of material covered in class, you may require students to keep an on-going psychology journal for the duration of the course. The primary purpose of the journal is to encourage students to connect the facts, concepts, and principles that they acquire from the course to their own personal experiences. The journal adds a personal dimension to the course and provides an opportunity to apply course concepts to daily experiences (Hettich, 1990). The following writing prompts are a useful starting point. Additional suggestions for writing prompts are included in other chapters.

1. Why have you decided to study psychology? Name at least one topic in psychology or a question you have about human behavior that you would like to explore over the course of the semester. What is your current understanding of psychology? What do psychologists do? What is psychology all about? Why are you interested in taking this course? What is your opinion of having to keep a journal throughout the course?
2. What is your opinion about knowledge gained from research that violates ethical standards? How do you feel about using animals to conduct painful or damaging research? What is the best way to balance the benefits of knowledge with the rights of research subjects?

Hettich, P. (1976). The journal: An autobiographical approach to learning. *Teaching of Psychology, 3*(2), 60-63.
Hettich, P. (1980). The journal revisited. *Teaching of Psychology, 7*(2), 105-106.
Hettich, P. (1990). Journal writing: Old fare or nouvelle cuisine? *Teaching of Psychology, 17*(1), 36-63.

video

Against All Odds: Inside Statistics, Part 12: Experimental Design (1989, 30 min, ANN/CPB). Distinguishes between observational and experimental research and addresses basic principles of experimental design including comparison, randomization, and replication.

Against All Odds: Inside Statistics, Part 14: Samples and Surveys (1989, 30 min, ANN/CPB). Describes the importance of sampling within the context of administering and interpreting surveys.

Aspects of Behavior (1971, 31 min, IM). Describes subdivisions of psychology. Includes discussion by Stanley Milgram, John Darley, and Bibb Latane.

Behavioral Sciences (23 min, FHS). Social behavior, behavior in the workplace, and innate versus acquired behavior serve as themes in this exploration of why we do what we do. This video may be suitable for introducing students to psychology or for a discussion of genetic and biological influences on behavior.

Black and White America (1988, 26 min, FHS). Five students of different races negotiate their lives based on how they feel about their own race, and how they perceive others feel about theirs.

Career Encounters: Psychology (1991, 28 min, IM). Provides an overview of specializations and careers in psychology through interviews with various types of psychologists, including research, clinical, sports, community, industrial/organizational, school, and health psychologists.

Discovering Psychology, Part 1: Past, Present, and Promise (1990, 30 min, ANN/CPB). Provides a brief overview of the field of psychology, including its history and relationship to several other disciplines.

Discovering Psychology, Part 2: Understanding Research (1990, 30 min, ANN/CPB). Describes the scientific method, data collection and analysis, and the role of critical thinking in research.

Discovering Psychology, Part 26: New Directions (1990, 30 min, ANN/CPB). A discussion of future directions in the field of psychology by prominent psychologists.

Do Scientists Cheat? (1988, 60 min, MICH). Demonstrates that research misconduct can take many forms, "from sloppily done studies and negligence, to flagrant manipulation or fabrication of scientific data." This NOVA production examines why scientific fraud (which is still relatively rare but seemingly on the rise) is difficult to identify and details the many factors that inspire fraud. Analyzes how scientists instill and maintain quality control, and explores the scientific community's reaction to research fraud.

Domino: Interracial People and the Search for Identity (44 min, FHS). Six people of interracial backgrounds discuss how history, family politics, gender roles, and race hierarchies influenced their definitions of who they are.

Experimental Design (Parts I and II, 1989, 30 min each, ANN/CPB). Observation, experimentation, randomization, control groups, and causality are explored in this 2-tape set.

Experiments in Human Behavior (1985, 35 min, IM). This video uses several well-known studies to illustrate concepts such as independent variables, experimenter bias, or the differences between field and lab studies.

The Great Ideas of Psychology (48 parts, 1997, 45 min each, IM). This series includes something for everyone. Daniel Robinson of Georgetown University delivers lectures on the history of psychology, major theories and systems, intelligence, testing, and biological determinism.

Inferential Statistics: Hypothesis-Testing -- Rats, Robots, and Roller Skates (1975, 28 min, MEDIAG). Humorous sketches explain control groups, random assignment, and the formation of hypotheses.

Landmarks in Psychology (1980, 50 min, IM). Highlights the contributions of Freud, Jung, Adler, Pavlov, Horney, Maslow, Watson, and Skinner to the development of psychology using a historical narrative style and dramatizations.

Methodology: The Psychologist and the Experiment (1975, 30 min, IM). Discusses independent and dependent variables, control groups, random assignment. Schachter's "fear and affiliation" study is used as an example.

Protecting Human Subjects: Balancing Society's Mandates (38 min, OPRR/NIH). Illustrates the basic ethical criteria used in evaluating research through following a research proposal through review by an Institutional Review Board (IRB).

Protecting Human Subjects: Evolving Concern (23 min, OPRR/NIH). Examines the historical developments that led to the current federal guidelines and programs to protect human subjects.

Psychology: Scientific Problem Solvers - Careers for the 21st Century (1995, 14 min, APA). This fast-paced video provides a broad overview of psychology, presents interviews with psychologists working in a range of areas, and suggests strategies for pursuing a career in psychology.

Psychology: Understanding Ourselves, Understanding Each Other (1992, 29 min, APA). A walk through the recent popular museum exhibit of the same name. An engaging way to introduce students to psychologists' breadth of interests and laypeople's reactions to psychological information.

Research Methods (1990, 30 min, IM). Presents the basics of conducting sound research. The importance of solid theorizing combined with supporting data is emphasized.

The Scientific Method (1988, 23 min, ANN/CPB). This Blue Ribbon winner at the American Film and Video Festival presents the research process from developing a hypothesis through testing it experimentally.

Sociobiology: Doing What Comes Naturally (1976, 20 min, DOC). The sociobiological interpretation of behavior is presented in this brief film.

Statistics and Psychology (24 min, FHS). This video uses data from the Applied Psychology Unit of Cambridge University to demonstrate correlations and how they are used in the conduct of science.

Teaching in a Diverse Classroom (30 min., CIDR). Four general strategies are described for teaching effectively in a diverse classroom. These include creating an environment of respect and openness, using curriculum choices to recognize diversity, responding to a variety of learning styles, and helping students feel connected to the university.

Two Research Styles (1991, 24 min, IM). Experimentation and observation are compared using profiles of two research programs. A good introduction to the array of research strategies available to psychologists.

Understanding Research (1990, 30 min, IM). This video draws on examples from psychology to present the basics of scientific methodology.

Using Samples (20 min, FHS). The differences between samples and populations, and the differences between different types of sampling, are explored. Confidence intervals, variability, and standard errors are also presented.

Valuing Diversity: Multicultural Communication (1994, 49 min, IM). Although this examination of similarities and differences in communication across cultures could be profitably used in a number of contexts, showing the video early in the semester may set the stage for later discussions of diversity issues.

What Is Psychology? (1990, 30 min, IM). A brief look at some major approaches, historical developments, and methodology in the discipline.

The Way of Science (58 min, FHS). Science and myth are both ways of explaining the world around us. How to choose one path versus the other, and why, are examined in this generalist approach to discussing the workings of science.

World Song (1993, 15 min, PYR). A collection of images from around the world, celebrating the diversity of different cultures. A novel way of introducing the topic of multiculturalism.

multimedia

Live! Psych

Module	Title	Book Page #
1.1	Observational Studies	p. 30

This module describes the two major types of observational research methods. Advantages and limitations of both the laboratory observation and naturalistic observation are provided. Examples of classic observational studies are presented, such as research done by Jane Goodall, Diana Baumrind, and David Rosenhan. Steps that researchers take to minimize limitations of the observational method are discussed. Finally, students' ability to distinguish between laboratory and naturalistic observation is assessed.

1.2	Correlations	p. 34

This module opens by showing positive, negative, and zero correlations. Scatterplots are also introduced. Next, students are shown eight different scatterplots and asked to decide if the correlation is positive, negative, or zero. Then, students are introduced to the correlation coefficient and engage in an interactive exercise in which they change the value of the data to see the effects on the value of the correlation coefficient. A quiz on correlation coefficients follows and the module concludes with reasons why correlations cannot prove causation.

1.3	The Hypothesis	p. 35

The first of these two screens explains that the experiment is the method of choice for drawing conclusions about cause-and-effect. Import this screen to introduce questions that an experimenter may use to form a hypothesis. The second screen defines hypothesis and variables. Import this screen to introduce how the hypothesis is stated in an "if-then" form.

The Independent and Dependent Variables   p. 35

This concept includes five screens. The first screen distinguishes between independent and dependent variables. Screen 2 makes the point that experimenters try to keep all aspects of the experimental situation constant, allowing changes only in the independent variable in order to determine whether the independent variable actually does cause changes in the dependent variable. Screen 3 provides examples of hypotheses with independent and dependent variables. The student scrolls over three pictorial examples to compare independent and dependent variables. Screen 4 defines operational definitions and explains the usefulness of such definitions for replication of an experiment. Screen 5 provides examples of operational definitions of independent and dependent variables. The student scrolls over three pictorial examples to read examples of such definitions.

1.4	The Representative Sample	p. 37

Screen 1 defines a representative sample. Screen 2 defines a random sample. Screen 3 defines a biased sample. Import these three screens to distinguish between a population and a sample, and explain the importance of a representative sample.

Experimental and Control Group   p. 37

Screen 1 introduces the simplest psychological experiment comparing two groups of participants: the experimental and the control group. Screen 2 provides examples of experimental and control groups. The student scrolls over three pictorial examples to compare the different treatments of the two groups. Screen 3 emphasizes the importance of keeping all aspects of the experiment constant with the exception of treatment.

Random Assignment   p. 37

Explains the rationale for random assignment in assigning participants to the experimental or control conditions in such a way that they have an equal chance of being put into either group. Screen 2 introduces the coin flip. In Screen 3, the student interacts with this lesson on random assignment. Using the coin flip, the student assigns 60 participants to either the experimental or control group.

Web Investigations

Caveat Emptor: Evaluating Knowledge Claims

This learning activity, written by Steve Davis, reviews the law of parsimony and presents the case of Clever Hans, Pfungst's remarkable "calculating horse." As students apply the law of parsimony and evaluate knowledge claims, Davis asks them to apply five specific questions in their search for the truth. These questions offer you an opportunity to discuss experimental methodology and statistics. There are also three exercises at the end of the activity that allow students to evaluate product claims and claims made on the Internet. The responses to each exercise can be either emailed to you or printed out for discussion in class. You may also find it helpful to use a computer projector or transparencies to show these questions and exercises as you discuss methodology and the scientific approach during class.

Analyzing Arguments: Deciding What to Believe

Diane Halpern helps your students scrutinize persuasive appeals, identify good reasons and conclusions, and practice the art of analyzing arguments. This demonstration includes exercises that can be completed either as a take-home assignment or as an in-class activity. Use this activity when discussing research methodology and the scientific method.

Critical Thinking: I Know It's a Good Thing, But What Is It?

This short tutorial, also written by Diane Halpern, helps students understand the basic elements of being a critical thinker. Students examine a few scenarios and test their ability to recognize critical thinking in action. This is a good foundational exercise to help hone students' abilities to evaluate the information they'll be reading about all semester.

Making Connections

What Is Psychology?

Q What are the major fields of psychology, and what does each one study?

A The major fields of psychology are developmental psychology, which studies human mental and physical growth; physiological psychology, which investigates the biological basis of human behavior, thoughts, and emotions; experimental psychology, which conducts research on basic psychological processes; personality psychology, which studies the differences among individuals; clinical psychology, which focuses on the diagnosis, cause, and treatment of psychological disorders; counseling psychology, which is concerned with normal problems of adjustment; social psychology, which studies how people influence one another; and industrial and organizational psychology, which is concerned with such practical issues as selecting and training personnel.

Q How do enduring issues hold the field of psychology together?

A Five enduring issues--person-situation, heredity-environment, stability-change, diversity-universality, and mind-body--serve to hold psychology together because all psychologists share a common interest in them regardless of their area of specialization.

Q What does it mean to say that psychology is a science?

A Psychology is a science because psychologists rely on the scientific method when seeking to answer questions: They collect data through systematic observation, attempt to explain what they have observed by developing theories, make new predictions based on those theories, and systematically test those predictions through additional observations and experiments.

Q What is critical thinking, and why is it important?

A Critical thinking is the process of examining information and then, based on this inquiry, making judgments and decisions. It is important because it questions common knowledge, which is often incorrect.

The Growth of Psychology

Q What contributions did Wilhelm Wundt, William James, and Sigmund Freud make toward the development of the new science of the mind?

A Wilhelm Wundt founded the first psychological laboratory and developed ways to study immediate experience. William James developed a functionalist theory of mental processes and behavior. Sigmund Freud developed psychodynamic theory, a comprehensive theory of mental life that emphasized unconscious instincts and urges.

Q What assumptions did behaviorists make about the workings of the mind?

A Behaviorists assumed that all mental experiences are physiological changes in response to accumulated experiences of conditioning and reinforcement.

Q What is meant by the "cognitive revolution"?

A The phrase "cognitive revolution" refers to a shift away from a focus on behavior toward a broad interest in mental processes.

Q What is the difference between positive psychology and other schools of psychological thought?

A Positive psychology differs from other schools of psychological thought in that it emphasizes positive feelings and traits rather than problems.

Human Diversity

Q What are the major contributions of feminist psychology?

A Feminist psychology has questioned research findings based on all-male samples, emphasized similarities between the genders, and called attention to issues of primary concern to women.

Q What is the difference between race and ethnicity?

A Race refers to a subpopulation whose members have reproduced exclusively among themselves and therefore are genetically similar and distinct from other members of the same species. Whereas racial categories are based on physical differences, ethnic categories are based on cultural characteristics. An ethnic group is a category of people who see themselves as distinctive because of a common homeland and history, language, religion, or traditional cultural beliefs and social practices.

Q Why is knowledge of cultural diversity important to psychologists?

A Knowledge of cultural diversity is important to psychologists because in an increasingly multicultural society they increasingly will be dealing with diverse clients, research participants, and students.

Research Methods in Psychology

Q What is observer bias, and how can it affect the results of naturalistic research?

A Observer bias occurs when observers subtly distort what they see to conform to what they were hoping or expecting to see. It can affect the accuracy of research results.

Q Explain how surveys address the shortcomings of naturalistic research and case studies.

A Surveys ask a carefully selected group of people a set of predetermined questions. It is therefore possible to draw general conclusions from the findings, something that cannot be done when using naturalistic observation or case studies.

Q What does it mean to say that "correlation is not causation"?

A Correlation shows how two phenomena are related, but it does not identify the direction of influence. It therefore provides no basis for drawing conclusions about cause and effect.

Q What are some methods that researchers use to avoid introducing bias into experimental results?

A To avoid introducing bias into their results, experimenters create two groups of participants that are equal in all respects except the variable being manipulated; one group is the experimental group and the other the control group. They also avoid experimenter bias by asking a neutral person to score the results.

Q Explain some of the problems that can be caused by unrepresentative sampling.

A If the proportions of participants of different races, ages, genders, and other characteristics in a sample do not match their proportions in the population under study, the results of the research cannot be said to apply to the entire population. It therefore is essential to create a representative sample through techniques such as random sampling.

Q What safeguards are used to protect human experimental subjects?

A Participants must be informed of the nature of the research in which they will take part. Any risks or adverse effects must be spelled out, and participants cannot be deceived about these aspects of the research. Deception about the goals of the research can be used only when absolutely necessary.

Careers in Psychology

Q What are the major kinds of jobs in academic and applied psychology?

A The major jobs in psychology include college and university faculty positions; jobs in school, health, industrial, commercial, and educational psychology; clinical and counseling jobs; research positions; and jobs in health, industry, and education.

Q What is the difference between psychiatrists, counseling psychologists, and psychoanalysts?

A A psychiatrist is a medical doctor who has completed residency training in psychiatry. Psychoanalysts are psychiatrists who have received additional specialized training in psychoanalytic theory and practice.

Counseling psychologists do not have medical training but are trained to help people cope with situational problems.

Mind Matters

The Science of Psychology

This section of the Prentice Hall Mind Matters CD-ROM distinguishes between scientific psychology and common sense, dispelling the myth that the former is nothing more than the latter. Students are introduced to the scientific method and can review the basics of methodology. Several interactive exercises are available, such as a critical thinking task in which students predict the outcome of a psychological study, a video clip of a case study involving a schizophrenic woman, and archival footage of the Milgram obedience study. Students can also test claims of the paranormal and review evidence of psychic abilities. Although this section of the CD-ROM, like pretty much every other section, is highly engaging and should be explored voraciously by your students on their own, you might use some of the clips or interactive exercises during your course presentations. For example, if you have a media projector in your classroom, show the various video clips that illustrate research principles, such as Lewin's leadership study, the interactive correlation generator, the methodology decision tree, or the case study and obedience clips mentioned earlier.

Psychology's Roots

This section highlights the main schools of thought in psychology, such as structuralism, functionalism, psychoanalysis, humanism, behaviorism, and Gestalt psychology. The explanations and demonstrations are humorous and highly interactive. Use some of the pop-ups and images in this section to spice up your lectures.

Recent Trends in Psychology

Cognitive psychology and biopsychology are spotlighted in this section. Students can learn more about these relatively recent areas of study, and can explore material about each subdiscipline in more detail. A video clip on depression among the Amish is used as an applied example of biopsychology. A section on careers in psychology and branches of psychology should prove useful to your students considering this field as a major or profession.

Video Classics

Interview with Konrad Lorenz

SYNOPSIS: Lorenz discusses some basic principles behind experimentation, observation, validation, and the importance of rigorous scientific controls. His remarks are in the context of ethology and unobtrusive observation; however, the principles he outlines apply generally to doing sound psychological research.

Form a Hypothesis

Q What do you think is the purpose of an experiment?

A Experiments evaluate possible cause and effect relationships between variables.

Q In an experiment, any differences in behavior can be logically traced back to what feature of the experiment?

A Differences in behavior between the two conditions are a function of the independent variable.

Q The independent variable is the variable that the researcher manipulates in an experiment. It is "independent" of any other factors. The purpose of an experiment is to test a hypothesis by manipulating the independent variable, keeping other aspects of the experimental situation constant, and observing behavior. Thus, any differences can be traced back to the experiment. What do you think is meant by the term, unobtrusive experiment?

A An unobtrusive experiment is one in which the research participant is unaware that she or he is being observed.

Test Your Understanding

Q What are two essential elements of true experiments?

A Experimental manipulation of the independent variable is one essential element. Two (or more) groups that permit comparison of the various manipulations is the other.

Q What is the basic model of an experiment?

A An experiment ascertains causality by creating two conditions that differ only in the independent variable. Any difference between the two conditions is caused by the independent variable.

Thinking Critically

Q Konrad Lorenz is talking about "unobtrusive experiments". How are these different from the experiments that are discussed in the text?

A Unobtrusive experiments are experiments in which the participants do not know that they are in an experiment. In more traditional or laboratory experimentation, participants are aware of the unique experimental setting or the fact of their observation

Q What are some of the advantages of "unobtrusive experiments" vs. laboratory experiments?

A Keeping participants unaware of their observation is usually accomplished by keeping the experimental setting as close as possible to the settings in which behavior occurs "naturally." Consequently, the behavior of participants in these studies more closely reflects what would happen in the natural environment.

Web Links

1. http://apa.org/about/division.html
The American Psychological Association's links to all of its divisions. Steer your students here to learn more about the major areas of psychology and what psychologists with these specializations do for a living.

2. http://server.bmod.athabascau.ca/html/aupr/history.htm
The Psychology Center's History of Psychology page has many websites to choose from, including broad topics and those specific to the history of psychology. Your students can learn more about psychology's past or investigate the history of a particular topic that interests them.

3. http://www.geocities.com/Athens/Delphi/6061/en_linha.htm
History of Psychology Timeline from early civilization to the present. This is worth a visit by both you and your students. Recommend this to your students as a way of organizing their studying, by placing the right people and the right ideas at the right time.

4. http://www.barnard.edu/psych/museum/b_museum.html
Consists of links to historical psychological documents, photographs, and apparatus. If your classroom is multimedia-equipped, you might link to this site and show some examples of these artifacts as you lecture. A picture is worth...oh, you know.

5. http://pages.slu.edu/faculty/josephme/resguides/psyhist.html
Complete and detailed resource guide to the history of psychology. Useful for preparing your remarks on this subject; fun to explore for your students. Assign a visit here as the basis for a short writing assignment or as a starter for an in-class discussion.

6. http://trochim.human.cornell.edu/kb/
The Knowledge Base: An Online Research Methods Textbook. Pretty much just what it says. If you include any detailed discussion of this topic in your Introductory Psychology course, this would be a worthwhile resource for your students.

7. http://www.apa.org/ethics/code.html
American Psychological Association's Ethical Principles of Psychologists and Code of Conduct. Your students may be required to participate in experiments as part of their introductory course. Introduce them to this website either at the start of the semester (to allay their fears about participating in studies) or at the end (as a "wrap-up" paper comparing their research experiences with the ethical guidelines stated by APA).

8. http://www.psych.bangor.ac.uk/deptpsych/Ethics/HumanResearch.html
This website links to several other ethics-related resources, such as position statements of review boards, guidelines at other institutions, or ethical principles of other organizations (e.g., the American Mathematical Association). Use the guidelines suggested in #8, above, with this resource.

9. http://www.apa.org/students/
A wealth of student resources from APA. Encourage your students to find out more about what psychology has to offer students.

10. http://www.uky.edu/Education/EDP/psyprog.html
Graduate Programs in Psychology. Steer your students to this site to answer the many questions you undoubtedly answer yourself. "What's the GRE?" "What do forensic psychologists do?" and "What's the difference between a PsyD and a Ph.D.?" can be answered here.

transparencies

Series V

1. *Fields of Specialization in Psychology*
This pie chart shows the fields of specialization for members of APA in 1997.

2. *Employment Settings for Psychologists*
This pie chart shows where psychologists work. The data are drawn from over 82,000 APA members.

3. *Basic Methods of Research: Correlational Research*
This transparency defines correlational research and states the advantages and limitations of this approach.

4. *Examples of Actual Correlations from Psychological Research*
Examples of positive, negative, and zero correlations between two variables.

5. *Basic Methods of Research: Experimental Research*
Defines the experiment and lists the advantages and limitations of this method.

6. *Basic Model of an Experiment*
Presents the basic components of an experiment: population, sample, random assignment, experimental and control groups, independent and dependent variables.

7. *Basic Methods of Research: Naturalistic Observation*
The advantages and limitations of naturalistic research are presented.

8. *Basic Methods of Research: Surveys*
The advantages and limitations of this method are presented.

9. *Basic Methods of Research: Case Studies*
The case study method is presented, listing the advantages and limitations of this approach.

10a. *Ethical Principles of Research*
10b. This two-part transparency identifies the basic APA guidelines for conducting research.

11. *Longitudinal and Cross-Sectional Research*
This transparency contrasts these two research designs.

Text Figures

Table 1-1	*APA Divisions*
Summary Table	*Basic Methods of Research*

Handout 1-1

Knowledge of Psychology Test

Instructions: Read each item carefully and then circle whether you believe the statement to be true or false.

T F 1. To change people's behavior toward members of ethnic minority groups, we must first change their attitudes.

T F 2. By feeling people's faces, blind people can visualize how they look in their minds.

T F 3. Children memorize much more easily than adults.

T F 4. Unlike humans, the lower animals are motivated only by their bodily needs--hunger, thirst, sex, etc.

T F 5. "The study of the mind" is the best brief definition of psychology today.

T F 6. The more you memorize by rote (e.g., poems), the better you will become at memorizing.

T F 7. The best way to ensure that a desired behavior will persist after training is completed is to reward the behavior every single time it occurs throughout training (rather than intermittently).

T F 8. Fortunately for babies, human beings have a strong maternal instinct.

T F 9. The ability of blind people to avoid obstacles is due to a special sense that develops in compensation for their absence of vision.

T F 10. By giving a young baby lots of extra stimulation (e.g., mobiles and musical toys), we can markedly increase its intelligence.

T F 11. Psychiatrists are defined as medical people who use psychoanalysis.

T F 12. Boys and girls exhibit no behavioral differences until environmental influences begin to produce such differences.

T F 13. The high correlation between cigarette smoking and lung cancer proves that smoking causes lung cancer.

T F 14. Genius is akin to insanity.

T F 15. In love and friendship, more often than not, opposites attract one another.

Reprinted with permission from R. A. Griggs and S. E. Ransdell (1987), Misconceptions Tests or Misconceived Tests?, *Teaching of Psychology, 14*, 210-214. Copyright 1987 by Lawrence Erlbaum Associates, Inc.

Chapter 2 The Biological Basis of Behavior

chapter outline 32

learning objectives 34

lecture suggestions

    Brain Metaphors 35
    The Cranial Nerves 35
    Would You Like Fries With That Peptide? 36
    Women, Men, and PETs 37
    Would You Like A Smoking Or Non-Smoking Brain? 38
    Understanding Hemisphere Functioning 38
    Psychophysiological Measurement 39
    En Garde! Dualism versus Monism 40
    The Phineas Gage Story 40
    Handedness, Eyedness, Footedness, Facedness 41
    Brain's Bilingual Broca 42
    On Your Mark, Get Set, Go! 43

demonstrations and activities

    Using Dominoes to Understand the Action Potential 44
    Hemispheric Communication and the Split Brain 44
    Hemispheric Lateralization 45
    Demonstrating Neural Conduction 45
    Debate: Are Gender Differences Rooted in the Brain? 46
    The Dollar Bill Drop 46
    Reaction Time and Neural Processing 47
    The Importance of a Wrinkled Cortex 47

student assignments

    The Brain Diagram 48
    Reunited Twins 48
    The Man Who Mistook His Wife For A Hat 49

video 50

multimedia 53

transparencies 60

handout

    Reunited Twins Assignment 62

chapter outline

I. Neurons: the Messengers
    A. The composition of neurons
        1. Neurons, individual nerve cells, composed of axon, cell body, dendrites
            a. A collection of axons bundled together is a nerve
                i. Myelin sheath improves efficiency of some axons
                ii. Motor, sensory, and interneurons are the three types of neurons
        2. Remaining cells in nervous system are glial cells (or glia)
            a. Perform a support function for the neurons
    B. The neural impulse
        1. Ions, resting potential, polarization contribute to transmission of impulse
        2. Absolute and relative refractory periods, all-or-none law govern firing
    C. The synapse
        1. Synapse is space between axon terminal and dendrite
        2. Synaptic vesicles release neurotransmitters into synaptic space
            a. Neurotransmitters find receptor sites in a lock-and-key fashion
                i. ACh, dopamine, serotonin, endorphins, norepinephrine common
        3. Psychopharmacology
            a. Chlorpromazine, clozapine, caffeine, cocaine, MAOI, SSRI, etc.
    D. Neural plasticity and neurogenesis
        1. Neural plasticity: brain's ability to change in response to experience
            a. Enriched environments foster larger neurons, more synaptic connections in rats
            b. Neurogenesis: Adult brains are capable of producing new cells

II. The Central Nervous System
    A. Organization of the nervous system
        1. Central nervous system: Brain and spinal cord
        2. Peripheral nervous system: Nerves connecting brain and cord to every other part of body
    B. The brain
        1. The central core
            a. Hindbrain: Medulla, pons, cerebellum
            b. Midbrain: Hearing, sight, pain registration, eating, drinking, sex, emotion
                i. Above the midbrain: Thalamus, hypothalamus, reticular formation
        2. The limbic system: Hippocampus and amygdala are primary structures
        3. The cerebral cortex
            a. Cerebral cortex is the large, visible surface structure
                i. Occipital, temporal, parietal, frontal lobes, association area
        4. The case of Phineas Gage
            a. Industrial accident sheds light on brain function
    C. Hemispheric specialization
        1. Corpus callosum connects the two hemispheres of cerebrum
        2. Split-brain patients help to illustrate hemispheric specialization
            a. contralateral control, language, emotion, spatial skills
        3. Language: Broca's and Wernicke's areas
        4. Cognitive and emotional style
            a. Hemispheric specialization; also emotional specialization within frontal lobes
    D. Tools for studying the brain
        1. Microelectrode techniques
        2. Macroelectrode techniques
            a. Alpha waves, beta waves, event-related potential, evoked potential
        3. Structural imaging

    a. Computerized axial tomography, magnetic resonance imaging
   4. Functional imaging
    a. Alphabet soup (EEG, MEG, PET, SPECT)
  E. The spinal cord
   1. Complex afferent and efferent system keeps our toes out of the fire
III. The Peripheral Nervous System
  A. The somatic nervous system
   1. Composed of all afferent and efferent neurons
  B. The autonomic nervous system
   1. All neurons connecting CNS to internal organs
    a. Sympathetic nervous system: Quick action in an emergency
    b. Parasympathetic nervous system: Calms and relaxes the body
IV. The Endocrine System
  A. The thyroid gland
   1. Thyroxin to regulate metabolism
  B. The parathyroid glands
   1. Parathormone to control calcium and phosphate
  C. The pineal gland
   1. Regulates activity level during the course of the day
  D. The pancreas
   1. Secretes insulin and glucagon
  E. The pituitary gland
   1. Posterior secretes vasopressin and oxytocin
   2. Anterior is the "master gland"
  F. The gonads
   1. Testes and ovaries produce androgens and estrogen
  G. The adrenal glands
   1. Adrenal cortex
   2. Adrenal medulla
V. Genes, Evolution, and Behavior
  A. Genetics
   1. Study of how heredity (the transmission of traits) takes place
    a. Genes (found on chromosomes) control transmission of traits
     i. DNA codes the genetic information
    b. Dominant genes control the appearance of certain traits
    c. Recessive genes must be paired in kind to produce a trait
    d. Polygenic inheritance responsible for many important traits
  B. Behavior genetics
   1. Animal behavior genetics: Strain studies, selection studies
   2. Human behavior genetics:
    a. Family studies
    b. Identical and fraternal twin studies
    c. Adoption studies
   3. Molecular genetics
    a. The Human Genome Project is a beautiful, beautiful thing
  C. Evolutionary psychology
   1. Adaptive behaviors, rather than structural changes, are the focus
  D. Social implications
   2. Amniocentesis, chorionic villus sampling link psychology to biology

learning objectives

After reading this chapter, students should be able to:

1. Describe the structure of a neuron. Trace the path of a neural impulse and explain how it transmits messages from cell to cell.

2. Explain how neurons communicate. Identify the roles of neurotransmitters and receptors. Describe the effects of drugs on the synapse.

3. Describe the organization of the nervous system.

4. Describe the structures of the brain and explain the role of each structure.

5. Identify the functions of the sensory and motor projection areas.

6. Understand cortical specialization and describe the abilities of the two hemispheres of the cerebral cortex.

7. Identify the divisions of the peripheral nervous system, and the autonomic nervous system and explain how they work together to regulate the glands and smooth muscles of the body.

8. Describe the glands in the endocrine system and their functions. Explain how hormones released by the endocrine system affect metabolism, blood-sugar level, sex characteristics, and the body's reaction of stress.

9. Describe different tools and techniques used to study the brain and nervous system.

10. Summarize the concerns of behavior genetics.

11. Describe the role chromosomes play in inherited traits and characteristics.

12. Explain the concepts of dominant and recessive genes.

13. Identify several approaches to studying heritability of a trait.

14. Discuss some social implications of behavior genetics.

lecture suggestions

Brain Metaphors

Metaphors are powerful tools in psychology, because they help us to understand systems that aren't directly observable through reference to things that are more familiar and perhaps better understood (Weiner, 1991). Our understanding of the human brain and its activity has been helped through a reliance on metaphor. The metaphors used, however, have changed over time.

❖ *Hydraulic models*. Thinkers such as Galen and Descartes described the brain as a pneumatic/hydraulic system, relying on the "new-fangled" plumbing systems dominant during their lifetimes. Galen, for example, believed that the liver generated "spirits" or gases that flowed to the brain, where they then formed "animal spirits" that flowed throughout the nervous system. Descartes expanded on this view, adding that the pineal gland (the supposed seat of the soul) acted on the animal spirits to direct reasoning and other behaviors. In short, the brain was a septic tank; storing, mixing, and directing the flow of spirit gases throughout the body for the purposes of behavior and action.

❖ *Mechanical and telephone models*. With the advent of new technology came new metaphors for the brain. During the Industrial Revolution machine metaphors dominated, and in particular the brain was conceived as a complex mechanical apparatus involving (metaphorical) levers, gears, trip hammers, and pulleys. During the 1920s, the brain developed into a slightly more sophisticated machine resembling a switchboard; the new technology of the telephone provided a new metaphor. Inputs, patch cords, outputs, and busy signals (though no "call waiting") dominated explanations of brain activity. This metaphor, however, faltered by viewing the brain as a system that shut down periodically, as when no one was dialing a number. We now know, of course, that the brain is continually active.

❖ *Computer models*. Current metaphors for the brain rely on computer technology. Input, output, memory, storage, information processing, and circuitry are all terms that seem equally suited to talking about computer chips or neurons. Although perhaps a better metaphor than plumbing or telephones, the computer model still has its shortcomings. As a descriptive device, however, this metaphor can at least suggest limits in our understanding and point the way to profitable areas of research.

McGuigan, F. J. (1994). *Biological psychology: A cybernetic science*. Englewood Cliffs, NJ: Prentice Hall.
Weiner, B. (1991). Metaphors in motivation and attribution. *American Psychologist, 46*, 921-930.

The Cranial Nerves

The textbook discusses various divisions of the nervous system. You may want to add a description of the cranial nerves to your outline of the nervous system. Although the function of the cranial nerves is not different from that of the sensory and motor nerves in the spinal cord, they do not enter and leave the brain through the spinal cord. There are twelve cranial nerves, numbered 1 to 12 and ordered from the front to the back of the brain, that primarily transmit sensory information and control motor movements of the face and head. The twelve cranial nerves are:

1. *Olfactory*. A sensory nerve that transmits odor information from the olfactory receptors to the brain.

2. *Optic*. A sensory nerve that transmits information from the retina to the brain.

3. *Oculomotor*. A motor nerve that controls eye movements, the iris (and therefore pupil size), lens accommodation, and tear production.

4. *Trochlear.* A motor nerve that is also involved in controlling eye movements.

5. *Trigeminal.* A sensory and motor nerve that conveys somatosensory information from receptors in the face and head and controls muscles involved in chewing.

6. *Abducens.* Another motor nerve involved in controlling eye movements.

7. *Facial.* Conveys sensory information and controls motor and parasympathetic functions associated with facial muscles, taste, and the salivary glands.

8. *Auditory-vestibular.* A sensory nerve with two branches, one of which transmits information from the auditory receptors in the cochlea and the other conveys information concerning balance from the vestibular receptors in the inner ear.

9. *Glossopharyngeal.* This nerve conveys sensory information and controls motor and parasympathetic functions associated with the taste receptors, throat muscles, and salivary glands.

10. *Vagus.* Primarily transmits sensory information and controls autonomic functions of the internal organs in the thoracic and abdominal cavities.

11. *Spinal accessory.* A motor nerve that controls head and neck muscles.

12. *Hypoglossal.* A motor nerve that controls tongue and neck muscles.

Carlson, N. R. (1994). *Physiology of behavior* (5th ed.). Boston: Allyn and Bacon.
Thompson, R. F. (1993). *The brain: A neuroscience primer* (2nd ed.). New York: W. H. Freeman.

Reprinted from Hill, W. G. (1995). Instructor's resource manual for *Psychology* by S. F. Davis and J. J. Palladino. Englewood Cliffs, NJ: Prentice Hall.

Would You Like Fries With That Peptide?

Toast and juice for breakfast. Pasta salad for lunch. An orange, rather than a bagel, for an afternoon snack. These sound like reasonable dietary choices, involving some amount of deliberation and free will. However, our craving for certain foods at certain times of the day may be more a product of the brain than of the mind.

Sarah F. Leibowitz, Rockefeller University, has been studying food preferences for over a decade. What she has learned is that a stew of neurochemicals in the paraventricular nucleus, housed in the hypothalamus, plays a crucial role in helping to determine what we eat and when. Two in particular-- Neuropeptide Y and galanin--help guide the brain's craving for carbohydrates and for fat.

Here's how they work. Neuropeptide Y (NPY) is responsible for turning on and off our desire for carbohydrate. Animal studies have shown a striking correlation between NPY and carbohydrate intake; the more NPY produced, the more carbohydrates eaten, both in terms of meal size and duration. Earlier in the sequence, the stress hormone cortisol seems responsible, along with other factors, for upping the production of Neuropeptide Y. This stress ⇨ cortisol ⇨ Neuropeptide Y ⇨ carbohydrate craving sequence may help explain overweight due to high carbohydrate intake. But weight, and craving, rely on fat intake as well. Leibowitz has found that the neuropeptide galanin plays a critical role in this case. Galanin is the on/off switch for fat craving, correlating positively with fat intake; the more galanin produced, the heavier an animal will become. Galanin also triggers other hormones to process the fat consumed into stored fat. Galanin itself is triggered by metabolic cues resulting from burning fat as energy, but also from another source: estrogen.

Neuropeptide Y triggers a craving for carbohydrate, galanin triggers a craving for fat, but the two march to different drummers throughout a day's cycle. Neuropeptide Y has its greatest effects in the morning (at the start of the feeding cycle), after food deprivation (such as dieting), and during periods of stress. Galanin, by contrast, tends to increase after lunch and peaks toward the end of our daily feeding cycle.

The implications of this research are many. For example, the findings suggest that America's obsession with dieting is a losing proposition (but not around the waistline). Skipping meals, gulping appetite suppressers, or experiencing the stress of dieting will trigger Neuropeptide Y to encourage carbohydrate consumption, which in turn can foster overeating. Paradoxically, then, by trying to fight nature we may stimulate it even more. As another example, the onset and maintenance of anorexia may be tied to the chemical cravings in the hypothalamus. Anorexia tends to develop during puberty, a time when estrogen is helping to trigger galanin's craving for fat consumption. Some women (due to societal demands, obsessive-compulsive tendencies, or other pressures) react to this fat trigger by trying to accomplish just the opposite; subsisting on very small, frequent, carbohydrate-rich meals. The problem is that the stress and starvation produced by this diet cause Neuropeptide Y to be released, confining dietary interest to carbohydrates, but also affecting the sex centers nearby in the hypothalamus. Specifically, Neuropeptide Y may act to shut down production of gonadal hormones.

Marano, H. E. (1993, January/February). Chemistry and craving. *Psychology Today*, pp. 30-36, 74.

Women, Men, and PETs

The 1990s have been dubbed "the decade of the brain," and it is true that remarkable advances were made by the neurosciences in discovering how the brain operates. Several recent studies suggest that the operation of men's and women's brains may differ in significant ways.

For example, Ruben Gur and his colleagues at the University of Pennsylvania recorded PET scans of men and women who were asked to think of nothing in particular. That is, the research participants were instructed to relax and let their brains idle as they exerted as little mental effort as possible. The researchers found that for most participants the task was difficult to complete; PET scans revealed that these idle minds nonetheless hummed with activity. The locus of that activity, however, differed across the sexes. Men's brains often showed activity in the limbic system, whereas women often showed activity in the posterior cyngulate gyrus. The meaning of these differences is difficult to interpret; the difficulty is compounded by the 13 men and 4 women who showed patterns of activity characteristic of their opposite sex peers. As an early peek into the brain, however, they hint that the centers of activity for "blank" brains differ for women and men.

In a separate study, researchers at the University of California, Irvine, asked 22 men and 22 women to solve SAT math problems while undergoing a PET scan. Half of each group had SAT math scores above 700, whereas the other half had scores below 540. The temporal lobes of the 700+ men showed heightened activity during the math task, although this was not true for the women; the 700+ women's temporal lobes were no more intensively used than those of the 540-group women. Richard Haier, who helped lead the study, speculates that women in the top group might be using their brains more efficiently than women in the average-scoring group. More generally, although both men and women did well at the task, their brains were operating differently to accomplish it.

Ruben and Raquel Gur also studied men's and women's brains in response to emotional expressions. Shown pictures of either happy or sad faces, both men and women were quite adept at spotting happiness. Women, however, could identify sadness about 90% of the time, regardless of whether it was on the face of a man or a woman. By comparison, men were accurate in spotting sadness 90% of the time on a man's face, but only 70% of the time if the expression was posed by a woman.

Once again, PET scans revealed that women's brains didn't have to work as hard at this task as did men's; in fact, women's limbic systems were less active than the limbic systems of the poor-scoring men.

There are a number of other differences between women's and men's brains. Women tend to have a larger corpus callosum than men, for example. Women may also have a higher concentration of neurons in their cortexes than men. The meaning behind these differences is still unclear.

Begley, S. (1995, March 27). Gray matters. *Newsweek*, pp. 48-54.

Would You Like a Smoking or Non-Smoking Brain?

Most people who have tried to quit smoking report that it is at best a hit-or-miss proposition; a few days off the coffin nails, and the body dearly longs for that wispy blue smoke. Despite claims made by the tobacco industry, the culprit seems to be nicotine, an addictive substance that produces craving and withdrawal. Recent evidence from the Brookhaven National Laboratory suggests that nicotine alone may not be responsible for addiction to smoking. Rather, the action of certain enzymes in the brain may also contribute to the pleasures of cigarettes.

All addictive substances -cocaine, heroin, cigarettes--cause an increase in dopamine (a pleasure-enhancing neurotransmitter). Dr. Joanna Fowler led a research team that studied live images of smokers' and nonsmokers' brains. They found that an enzyme called monoamine oxidase B, or MAO B for short, was 40 percent less active in smokers. MAO B is responsible for breaking down dopamine. Therefore, when MAO B is inhibited, dopamine levels continue to remain high, which in turn allows smoking to remain pleasurable. The trick now is to find the ingredient in tobacco smoke that inhibits MAO B.

Oddly enough, these same findings may account for the fact that smokers are about half as likely as nonsmokers to develop Parkinson's disease, which is characterized by decreased dopamine levels. If smokers' dopamine remains high it may contribute to staving off the onset of Parkinson's. Although this observation is hardly a reason to start smoking, it at least suggests that drugs which are effective in treating Parkinson's disease might be adapted for use in treating smoking addiction.

Leary, W. E. (1996, February 22). Brain enzyme linked to smoking addiction. *Austin American-Statesman*, A5.

Understanding Hemisphere Function

A variation on the rather dubious statement that "we only use one-tenth of our brain" is that "we only use one-half (hemisphere) of our brain." Research suggests that each cerebral hemisphere is specialized to perform certain tasks (e.g., left hemisphere/language; right hemisphere/visuospatial relationships), with the abilities of one hemisphere complementary to the other. From this came numerous distortions, oversimplifications, and unwarranted extensions, many of which are discussed in two interesting reviews of this trend toward "dichotomania" (Corballis, 1980; Levy, 1985). For example, the left hemisphere has been described variously as logical, intellectual, deductive, convergent, and "Western," while the right hemisphere has been described as intuitive or creative, sensuous, imaginative, divergent, and "Eastern." Even complex tasks are described as right- or left-hemispheric because of their language component. In every individual one hemisphere supposedly dominates, affecting that person's mode of thought, skills, and approach to life. One commonly cited, but questionable, test for dominance is to note the direction of gaze when a person is asked a question (left gaze signaling right hemisphere activity; right gaze showing left hemisphere activity). Advertisements have claimed that artistic abilities can be improved if the right hemisphere is freed, and the public schools have been blamed for stifling creativity by emphasizing left-hemisphere skills and by neglecting to teach the children's right hemisphere.

Corballis and Levy explode these myths and trace their development. In reality, the two hemispheres are quite similar and can function remarkably well even if separated by split-brain surgery. Each hemisphere does have specialized abilities, but the two hemispheres work together in all complex tasks. For example, writing a story involves left-hemispheric input concerning syntax, but right-hemispheric input for developing an integrated structure and for using humor or metaphor. The left hemisphere is not the sole determinant of logic, nor is the right hemisphere essential for creativity. Disturbances of logic are more prevalent with right-hemisphere damage, and creativity is not necessarily affected. Although one hemisphere can be somewhat more active than the other, no individual is purely "right brained" or "left brained." Also, eye movement and hemispheric activity patterns poorly correlate with cognitive style or occupation. Finally, because of the coordinated, interactive manner of functioning of both hemispheres, educating or using only the right or left hemisphere is impossible (without split-brain surgery). (*Note*: Suggestions for a student activity on this topic are given in the following *Demonstrations and Activities* section of this manual.)

Corballis, M.C. (1980). Laterality and myth. *American Psychologist, 35*, 284-295.

Levy, J. (1985). Right brain, left brain: Fact or fiction? *Psychology Today, 19*, 38-45.

Reprinted from Whitford, F. W. (1995). Instructor's resource manual for *Psychology: Principles and applications* by S. Worchel and W. Shebilske. Englewood Cliffs, NJ: Prentice Hall.

Psychophysiological Measurement

The text discusses various strategies for measuring activity in the brain, focusing especially on more recently developed techniques such as PET, SPECT, or MRI. There are, of course, other bodily systems and other techniques for measuring them, many of which rely on the electrophysical activity of the body.

- ❖ *EMG - Electromyography.* An electromyogram records the action potential given off by contracting muscle fibers. A common example is the recording of facial EMG, in which either inserted electrodes or surface electrodes record the activity of muscles as they pose various expressions.

- ❖ *EGG - Electrogastrography.* Electrogastrograms provide a record of smooth muscle activity in the abdomen. The contractions of the stomach or intestines, for example, can be measured by comparing the readings from a surface electrode attached to the abdomen with those of an electrode attached to the forearm. In the special case of measuring contractions in the esophagus, surface electrodes are attached to a balloon, which is "swallowed" by the person being measured. EGG may be used successfully to gain information about fear, anxiety, or other emotional states.

- ❖ *EOG - Electrooculography.* Readings from electrodes placed around the posterior of the eyes are the basis for EOG. Electrical signals result from both small saccadic eye movements as well as more gross movements that can be directly observed. EOG can be used for measuring rapid eye movements during sleep.

- ❖ *EKG - Electrocardiography.* EKG records changes in electrical potential associated with the heartbeat. Electrodes are placed at various locations on the body, and their recordings yield five waves that can be analyzed: P-waves, Q-waves, R-waves, S-waves, and T-waves. EKG may be used by psychologists to supplement observations relevant to stress, heart disease, or Type A behavior patterns.

- ❖ *EDA - Electrodermal Activity.* Formerly called *galvanic skin response, skin resistance*, and *skin conductance*, EDA refers to the electrical activity of the skin. As activity in the sympathetic nervous system increases it causes the eccrine glands to produce sweat. This activity of the eccrine glands can be measured by EDA, regardless of whether or not sweat actually rises to the skin surface. The folklore of "sweaty palms" associated with a liar might be measured using this technique.

- ❖ *EEG - Electroencephalography.* As discussed in the text, EEG provides information about the electrical activity of the brain, as recorded by surface electrodes attached to the scalp. EEG has been used in a variety of ways to gather information about brain activity under a wide range of circumstances.

- ❖ *Pneumography.* Pneumographs measure the frequency and amplitude of breathing, and are obtained through a relatively straightforward procedure. A rubber tube placed around the chest expands and contracts in response to the person's inhalations and exhalations. These changes can then be recorded with either an ink pen or electrical signal.

McGuigan, F. J. (1994). *Biological psychology: A cybernetic science.* Englewood Cliffs, NJ: Prentice Hall.

En Garde! Dualism versus Monism

Rene Descartes certainly didn't lack for credentials. As the "Father of Rationalism," "Father of Modern Philosophy," and originator of Cartesian geometry, he had more than enough interests to fill his spare time. But his role as "Father of Skepticism" helped popularize a major change in thinking about the nature of human experience. Dualism, or the doctrine that mind and body are of two distinct natures, is one of the key philosophical problems inherited by psychology. In both philosophy and psychology there have been several attempts to reconcile the mind and body.

On the dualism side of the argument, *psychophysical parallelism* and *psychophysical interactionism* have been advanced as explanations for the workings of mind and body. Parallelism has it that mental and physical events are independent of one another but occur simultaneously. Philosophers such as Leibnitz, for example, held that the activities of the mind and body were predetermined, and that both simply ran their course in a carefully orchestrated, synchronized, yet independent fashion. Interactionists, on the other hand, hold that mental and physical events are related in a causal way, such that the mind can influence the body and vice-versa. Descartes championed this idea with his notion that humans are "pilots in a ship;" mental beings who guide physical bodies through the world. Both psychophysical parallelism and psychophysical interactionism agree that the mind and body are of two different natures, and disagree over how closely those natures may interact.

Monists, by comparison, argue that there is one nature to things, although they disagree about whether it is primarily mental or primarily physical. *Subjective idealism* (or "mentalism," as it is often called), argues that there is only the mental world, and that the reality of the physical world is suspect. George Berkeley, for example, provided numerous arguments as to why the essence of existence is to be perceived; when not in direct perception the physical world cannot support the claim of its existence. (Berkeley, by the way, apparently hated walks in the forest, for fear of all those falling trees that he may or may not have heard.) In contrast, *materialistic monism* takes the position that there is only physical "stuff" to the world, such that ideas, thoughts, and images are actually physical events in the body. Many modern biological scientists would agree with this form of monism, arguing that the brain is primary while the "mind" is either illusory or epiphenomenal.

Add to this mix a handful of specialty doctrines and you've got quite an argument. But why all the fuss? As research on mind and behavior grows to embrace evidence gathered in the neurosciences, what once was a stuffy philosophical issue takes on a new importance. Many thinkers, especially those in the materialist camp, would claim that we are closer and closer to identifying the neural connections and chemical actions that produce our experience of "an idea." Fueled by the boom in neural network modeling, the notion that the circuitry of the brain can be mapped to identify where thoughts, images, memories, creativity, and similar "mental activities" originate seems more like science and less like science fiction. Whether dualism will be completely resolved to everyone's satisfaction seems doubtful, but biopsychologists and neuropsychologists continue to contribute data to address this philosophical puzzle.

Dennett, D. C. (1991). *Consciousness explained.* Boston: Little, Brown, and Company.
McGuigan, F. J. (1994). *Biological psychology: A cybernetic science.* Englewood Cliffs, NJ: Prentice Hall.
Ryle, G. (1949). *The concept of mind.* London: Hutchinson.

The Phineas Gage Story

Recently, the journal *History of Psychiatry* reprinted the original presentation of the case study of Phineas P. Gage. Gage is noteworthy in psychology for surviving after having an iron tamping rod driven through his skull and brain. The case notes, by physician John M. Harlow, reveal aspects of the event that provide greater detail about Gage and his unfortunate accident.

Phineas Gage stood five feet six inches tall, weighed 150 pounds, and was 25 years old at the time of the incident. By all accounts this muscular foreman of the Rutland and Burlington Railroad excavating crew was well-liked and respected by his workers, due in part to "an iron will" that matched "his iron frame." He had scarcely known illness until his accident on September 13, 1848, in Cavendish, Vermont. Here is an account of the incident, in Harlow's own words:

"He was engaged in charging a hold (sic) drilled in the rock, for the purpose of blasting, sitting at the time upon a shelf of rock above the hole. His men were engaged in the pit, a few feet behind him... The powder and fuse had been adjusted in the hole, and he was in the act of 'tamping it in', as it is called...While doing this, his attention was attracted by his men in the pit behind him. Averting his head and looking over his right shoulder, at the same instant dropping the iron upon the charge, it struck fire upon the rock, and the explosion followed, which projected the iron obliquely upwards...passing completely through his head, and high into the air, falling to the ground several rods behind him, where it was afterwards picked up by his men, smeared with blood and brain."

The tamping rod itself was three feet seven inches in length, with a diameter of 1¼ inches at its base and a weight of 13¼ pounds. The bar was round and smooth from continued use, and it tapered to a point 12 inches from the end; the point itself was approximately ¼ inch in diameter.

The accounts of Phineas' frontal lobe damage and personality change are well-known, and are corroborated by Harlow's presentation. Details of Phineas' subsequent life (he lived 12 years after the accident) are less known. Phineas apparently tried to regain his job as a railroad foreman, but his erratic behavior and altered personality made it impossible to do so. He took to traveling, visiting Boston and most major New England cities, and New York, where he did a brief stint at Barnum's sideshow. He eventually returned to work in a livery stable in New Hampshire, but in August, 1852, he turned his back on New England forever. Gage lived in Chile until June of 1860, then left to join his mother and sister in San Francisco. In February, 1861, he suffered a series of epileptic seizures, leading to a rather severe convulsion at 5 a.m. on February 20. The family physician unfortunately chose bloodletting as the course of treatment. At 10 p.m., May 21, 1861, Phineas eventually died, having suffered several more seizures. Although an autopsy was not performed, Phineas' relatives agreed to donate his skull and the iron rod (which Phineas carried with him almost daily after the accident) to the Museum of the Medical Department of Harvard University.

Miller (1993) also briefly notes that John Martyn Harlow himself had a rather pedestrian career, save for his association with the Gage case. Born in 1819, qualifying for medical practice in 1844, and dying in 1907, he practiced medicine in Vermont and later in Woburn, Massachusetts, where he engaged in civic affairs and apparently amassed a respectable fortune as an investor. Like Gage himself, Harlow was an unremarkable person brought into the annals of psychology by one remarkable event.

Harlow, J. M. (1848). Passage of an iron rod through the head. *Boston Medical and Surgical Journal, 39*, 389-393.
Harlow, J. M. (1868). Recovery from the passage of an iron bar through the head. Paper read before the Massachusetts Medical Society.
Miller, E. (1993). Recovery from the passage of an iron bar through the head. *History of Psychiatry, 4*, 271-281.

Handedness, Eyedness, Footedness, Facedness

Although the title sounds like a Dr. Seuss rhyme, it actually denotes something sensible to neuropsychologists. Most people are familiar with the concept of handedness. The human population is distributed across many people who are adept at using their right hands for most tasks, some who have greater skill using the left hand, and a smaller proportion of those who are equally skilled using either hand (or who alternate hands for certain tasks). The concepts of footedness, leggedness, eyedness, and facedness may be less familiar to the layperson, although they stem from the same principle as handedness.

The basis of these distinctions lies in the concept of laterality. Just as the cerebral hemispheres show specialization (e.g., left hemisphere language functions, right hemisphere visual-spatial functions), so too are there preferences or asymmetries in other body regions. The concept of eyedness, then, refers to the preference for using one eye over another, such as when squinting to site down the crosshairs of a rifle or to thread a needle. Footedness and leggedness similarly refer to a preference for one limb over the other; drummers and soccer players will attest to the importance of being equally adept at using either foot, and to the difficulty in achieving that. Finally, facedness refers to the strength with which information is conveyed by the right or left side of the face. It has been suggested that verbal information shows a right-face bias whereas emotional expressions are more strongly shown on the left side of the face, although these conclusions remain somewhat controversial.

Why are these distinctions useful? They play their largest role in the areas of sensation and perception, engineering psychology, and neuropsychology. Studies of reaction time, human-machine interaction, ergonomic design, and so on, take into account the preferences and dominances of some body systems over others. In the case of facedness and emotional expression, researchers are working to illuminate the link between facial expressions and cerebral laterality. Given the right hemisphere's greater role in emotional activities, the contralateral control between the right hemisphere and the left hemiface becomes an important proving ground for investigating both brain functions and the qualities of expression.

Borod, J. C., Caron, H. S., & Koff, E. (1981). Asymmetry of facial expression related to handedness, footedness, and eyedness: A quantitative study. *Cortex, 17*, 381-390.
Ekman, P., Hagar, C. J., & Friesen, W. V. (1981). The symmetry of emotional and deliberate facial actions. *Psychophysiology, 18*, 101-106.
Friedlander, W. J. (1971). Some aspects of eyedness. *Cortex, 7*, 357-371.
McGuigan, F. J. (1994). *Biological psychology: A cybernetic science.* Englewood Cliffs, NJ: Prentice Hall.
Sackheim, H. A., Gur, R. C., & Saucy, M. C. (1978). Emotions are expressed more intensely on the left side of the face. *Science, 202*, 434-436.

Brain's Bilingual Broca

Se potete parlare Italiano, allore potete capire questa sentenza. Of course, if you only speak English, you probably only understand *this* sentence. If you speak both languages, then by this point in the paragraph you should be really bored.

Bilingual speakers who come to their bilingualism in different ways show different patterns of brain activity. Joy Hirsch of Memorial Sloan-Kettering Cancer Center in New York and her colleagues monitored the activity in Broca's area in the brains of bilingual speakers who acquired their second language starting in infancy, and compared it to the activity of bilingual speakers who adopted a second language in their teens. Participants were asked to silently recite brief descriptions of an event from the previous day, first in one language and then in the other. A functional magnetic resonance image (fMRI) was taken during this task. All of the 12 adult speakers were equally fluent in both languages, used both languages equally often, and represented speakers of English, French, and Turkish, among other tongues.

Hirsch and her colleagues found that among the infancy-trained speakers, the same region of Broca's area was active, regardless of the language they used. Among the teenage-trained speakers, however, a different region of Broca's area was activated when using the acquired language. Similar results were found in Wernicke's area in both groups. Although the full meaning of these results is a matter of some debate (do they reflect sensitivity in Broca's area to language exposure, or pronounced differences in adult versus childhood language learning?), they nonetheless reveal an intriguing link between la testa e le parole.

Bower, B. (1997, July 12). Brains show signs of two bilingual roads. *Science News, 152*, 23.

On Your Mark, Get Set, Go!

Biological clocks are handy for keeping track of relatively long time intervals. Even when they're slightly slow (see *Shedding light on biological clocks* in Chapter 4 of this manual) they are still reasonably accurate at ticking off 24-hour cycles. But oh, to have a biological mechanism that would tell us there's enough time to run to the kitchen for a snack during a commercial, or to dart across the street before the light turns green, or to temper our impatience by knowing when "five minutes more" have elapsed. That kind of clock has recently been identified.

The striatum, a structure deep within the brain, seems to function as a kind of interval clock, keeping track of events that have relatively short durations. Warren Meck, of Duke University, and his colleagues performed a simple experiment to observe the action of the striatum. Using magnetic resonance imaging, Meck asked research participants to squeeze a rubber ball every 11 seconds. As they did so, the MRI revealed that their striata were working overtime. That's comforting to know: somewhere between your anterior commisure and your *thalamus opticus* there's a minute/second timer keeping you on track. But it's also handy in other ways. For example, knowing where the interval clock is may eventually allow researchers to develop better treatments for patients who suffer from Alzheimer's, Parkinson's, or other forms of brain damage.

Staff. (1996, February 13). Scientists find brain's stopwatch. *Austin American-Statesman*, A7.

demonstrations

Using Dominoes to Understand the Action Potential

Walter Wagor suggests using real dominoes to demonstrate the so-called "domino effect" of the action potential as it travels along the axon. For this demonstration, you'll need a smooth table-top surface (at least 5 feet long) and one or two sets of dominoes. Set up the dominoes beforehand, on their ends and about an inch apart, so that you can push the first one over and cause the rest to fall in sequence. Proceed to knock down the first domino in the row and students should clearly see how the "action potential" is passed along the entire length of the axon. You can then point out the concept of refractory period by showing that, no matter how hard you push on the first domino, you will not be able to repeat the domino effect until you take the time to set the dominoes back up (i.e., the resetting time for the dominoes is analogous to the refractory period for neurons). You can then demonstrate the all-or-none characteristic of the axon by resetting the dominoes and by pushing so lightly on the first domino that it does not fall. Just as the force on the first domino has to be strong enough to knock it down before the rest of the dominoes will fall, the action potential must be there in order to perpetuate itself along the entire axon. Finally, you can demonstrate the advantage of the myelin sheath in axonal transmission. For this demonstration, you'll need to set up two rows of dominoes (approximately 3 or 4 feet long) next to each other. The second row of dominoes should have foot-long sticks placed end-to-end in sequence on top of the dominoes. By placing the all-domino row and the stick-domino row parallel to each other and pushing the first domino in each, you can demonstrate how much faster the action potential can travel if it can jump from node to node rather than having to be passed on sequentially, single domino by single domino. Ask your students to discuss how this effect relates to myelinization.

Wagor, W. F. (1990). Using dominoes to help explain the action potential. In V. P. Makosky, C. C. Sileo, L. G. Whittemore, C. P. Landry, & M. L. Skutley (Eds.), *Activities handbook for the teaching of psychology: Vol. 3* (pp. 72-73). Washington, DC: American Psychological Association.

Hemispheric Communication and the Split Brain

Even after reading the textbook and listening to your lecture, many students may have difficulty conceptualizing the effects of a split-brain operation on an individual's behavior. Morris (1991) described five activities designed to simulate the behavior of split-brain patients. All of the activities have the same basic setup. You will need to solicit two right-handed volunteers and seat them next to each other at a table, preferably in the same chair. The volunteer on the left represents the left hemisphere, and the other student is the right hemisphere. The students are instructed to place their outer hand behind their back and their inner hands on the table with their hands crossed, representing the right and left hands of the split-brain patient. Finally, the student representing the right hemisphere is instructed to remain silent for the remainder of the activity. In one of the activities described by Morris, both students are blindfolded and a familiar object (Morris suggested a retractable ball-point pen) is placed in the left hand of the "split-brain patient" (the hand associated with the right hemisphere). Then ask the "right hemisphere" student if he or she can identify the object, reminding him or her that they must do so nonverbally. Next, ask the "right hemisphere" to try to communicate, without using language, what the object is to the "left hemisphere." Your more creative volunteers may engage in behaviors that attempt to communicate what the object is through sound or touch. If your "right hemisphere" has difficulty in figuring out how to communicate, ask the class for suggestions. This demonstration can be used to elicit discussion about why only the "left hemisphere" student can talk, the laterality of the different senses, and how split-brain patients are able to adjust their behavior to accommodate. You should refer to Morris's original article for descriptions of the other activities.

Morris, E. J. (1991). Classroom demonstration of behavioral effects of the split-brain operation. *Teaching of Psychology, 18*, 226-228.

Reprinted from Hill, W. G. (1995). Instructor's resource manual for *Psychology* by S. F. Davis and J. J. Palladino. Englewood Cliffs, NJ: Prentice Hall.

Hemispheric Lateralization

Kemble (1987) described three demonstrations designed to illustrate cerebral lateralization. One of these demonstrations explores the cerebral lateralization of language. This demonstration requires a wooden dowel stick (about 1.25 cm in diameter and 92 cm long), a stopwatch, and several difficult verbal problems (for example, reciting the alphabet backwards or spelling a long word backwards). After identifying a student volunteer, he or she is given between 5 and 10 minutes to practice balancing the dowel on the index finger of both hands. Approximately the same amount of time should be spent practicing with each hand. Following the practice period, the student is then asked to balance the dowel eight times, four per hand in a variable order, and the amount of time that he or she balances the dowel is recorded. However, during half of the trials for each hand, the student is asked to perform one of the verbal problems out loud, while the other trials are conducted in silence. Since the verbal task requires a high degree of activity in the left hemisphere, and the left hemisphere controls the right hand, the competition between the verbal and motor activity will consistently result in a decrease in balancing time for the right hand compared to that of the left hand when performing the verbal task. Kemble also suggested comparing the performance of male and female subjects since gender differences are often observed in this demonstration. This can provide an opportunity to discuss how and why these gender differences occur. The other demonstrations described by Kemble illustrate the effects of cerebral lateralization on pattern recognition.

Kemble, E. D. (1987). Cerebral lateralization. In V. P. Makosky, L. G. Whittemore, & A. M. Rogers (Eds.), *Activities handbook for the teaching of psychology*, Vol. 2 (pp. 33-36). Washington, DC: American Psychological Association.

Reprinted from Hill, W. G. (1995). Instructor's resource manual for *Psychology* by S. F. Davis and J. J. Palladino. Englewood Cliffs, NJ: Prentice Hall.

Demonstrating Neural Conduction: The Class as a Neural Network

In this engaging exercise (suggested by Paul Rozin and John Jonides), students in the class simulate a neural network and get a valuable lesson in the speed of neural transmission. Depending on your class size, arrange 15 to 40 students so that each person can place his or her right hand on the right shoulder of the person in front of them. Note that students in every other row will have to face backwards in order to form a snaking chain so that all students (playing the role of individual neurons) are connected to each other. Explain to students that their task as a neural network is to send a neural impulse from one end of the room to the other. The first student in the chain will squeeze the shoulder of the next person, who, upon receiving this "message", will deliver (i.e., "fire") a squeeze to the next person's shoulder and so on, until the last person receives the message. Before starting the neural impulse, ask students (as "neurons") to label their parts; they typically have no trouble stating that their arms are axons, their fingers are axon terminals, and their shoulders are dendrites.

To start the conduction, the instructor should start the timer on a stopwatch while simultaneously squeezing the shoulder of the first student. The instructor should then keep time as the neural impulse travels around the room, stopping the timer when the last student/neuron yells out "stop." This process should be repeated once or twice until the time required to send the message stabilizes (i.e., students will be much slower the first time around as they adjust to the task). Next, explain to students that you want them to again send a neural impulse, but this time you want them to use their ankles as dendrites. That is, each student will "fire" by squeezing the ankle of the person in front of them. While students are busy shifting themselves into position for this exercise, ask them if they expect transmission by ankle-squeezing to be faster or slower than transmission by shoulder-squeezing. Most students will immediately recognize that the ankle-squeezing will take longer because of the greater distance the message (from the ankle as opposed to the shoulder) has to travel to reach the brain. Repeat this transmission once or twice and verify that it indeed takes longer than the shoulder squeeze.

This exercise--a student favorite--is highly recommended because it is a great ice-breaker during the first few weeks of the semester and it also makes the somewhat dry subject of neural processing come alive.

Rozin, P., & Jonides, J. (1977). Mass reaction time measurement of the speed of the nerve impulse and the duration of mental processes in class. *Teaching of Psychology, 4*, 91-94.

Debate: Are Gender Differences Rooted in the Brain?

The text's discussion of gender diversity indicates that although gender differences are not as large as commonly believed, there are nonetheless some psychological differences between the sexes. Males and females, for example, show differences on specific cognitive tasks, emotional sensitivity, aggressive behavior, and conformity. How do we explain such differences? Are they primarily the result of natural differences in biological constitution (*nature*) or are they a product of the cultural and social forces that shape our behavior (*nurture*)? Questions such as these have sparked a heated controversy among psychologists. Although most researchers agree that both nature and nurture play a role in shaping gender differences, many psychologists tend to lean more heavily one way or the other. Ask your students to thoroughly explore this issue by considering the available scientific evidence in a debate format. Assign students to research this issue and to be prepared to defend either side. Issue 1 in *Taking Sides* (1994) presents both pro and con viewpoints on this controversial topic, and students should have no trouble finding more recent sources from journal articles and from the popular media. Because there has been a flurry of recent research reporting sex differences in brain activity you might encourage students to include studies that use brain-scanning technology (see also the related lecture suggestion in this chapter).

Begley, S. (1995, March 27). Gray matters. *Newsweek*, pp. 48-54.
Slife, B. (1994). *Taking sides: Clashing views on controversial psychological issues* (8th ed.). Guilford, CT: Dushkin Publishing Group.

The Dollar Bill Drop

After engaging in the neural network exercise, try following it up with the "dollar bill drop" (Fisher, 1979), which not only delights students but also clearly illustrates the speed of neural transmission. Ask students to get into pairs and to come up with one crisp, flat, one-dollar bill (or something bigger, if they trust their fellow classmates!) between them. First, each member of the pair should take turns trying to catch the dollar bill with their nondominant (for most people, the left) hand as they drop it from their dominant (typically right) hand. To do this, they should hold the bill vertically so that the top, center of the bill is held by the thumb and middle finger of their dominant hand. Next, they should place the thumb and middle finger of their nondominant hand around the dead center of the bill, as close as they can get without touching it. When students drop the note from one hand, they should be able to easily catch it with the other before it falls to the ground.

Now that students are thoroughly unimpressed, ask them to replicate the drop, only this time one person should try to catch the bill (i.e., with the thumb and middle finger of the nondominant hand) while the other person drops it (i.e., from the top center of the bill). Student "droppers" are instructed to release the bill without warning, and "catchers" are warned not to grab before the bill is dropped. (Students should take turns playing dropper and catcher.) There will be stunned looks all around as dollar bills whiz to the ground. Ask students to explain why it is so much harder to catch it from someone other than themselves. Most will instantly understand that when catching from ourselves, the brain can simultaneously signal us to release and catch the bill, but when trying to catch it from someone else, the signal to catch the bill can't be sent until the eyes (which see the drop) signal the brain to do so, which is unfortunately a little too late.

Fisher, J. (1979). *Body Magic*. Briarcliff Manor, NY: Stein and Day.

Reaction Time and Neural Processing

Yet another exercise that illustrates the speed of neural processing is suggested by Harcum (1988). The point made by this simple but effective exercise is that reaction times increase as more response choices become available (i.e., because more difficult choices in responses involve more neuronal paths and more synapses, both of which slow neural transmission). Depending on your class size, recruit two equal groups of students (10 to 20 per group is ideal) and have each group stand together at the front of the room. First, explain that all subjects are to respond as quickly as possible to the name of a U.S. President. Then, give written instructions to each group so that neither group knows the instructions given to the other. One group should be instructed to raise their right hands if the president served before Abraham Lincoln and to raise their left hands if the president served after Lincoln. The other group should be instructed simply to raise their left hands when they a hear a president's name. Ask participants and audience members to note which group reacts more quickly. When all students are poised and ready to go (i.e., hands level with shoulders and ready to raise), say "Ready" and then "Ford." The group with the simpler reaction time task will be obviously faster than the group whose task requires a choice.

Harcum, E. R. (1988). Reaction time as a behavioral demonstration of neural mechanisms for a large introductory psychology class. *Teaching of Psychology, 4*, 208-209.

The Importance of a Wrinkled Cortex

At the beginning of your lecture on the structure and function of the brain, ask students to explain why the cerebral cortex is wrinkled. There are always a few students who correctly answer that the wrinkled appearance of the cerebral cortex allows it to have a greater surface area while fitting in a relatively small space (i.e., the head). To demonstrate this point to your class, hold a plain, white sheet of paper in your hand and then crumple it into a small, wrinkled ball. Note that the paper retains the same surface area, yet is now much smaller and is able to fit into a much smaller space, such as your hand. You can then mention that the brain's actual surface area, if flattened out, would be roughly the size of a newspaper page (Myers, 1995). Laughs usually erupt when the class imagines what our heads would look like if we had to accommodate an unwrinkled, newspaper-sized cerebral cortex!

Myers, D. G. (1995). *Psychology* (4th ed.). New York: Worth.

student assignments

The Brain Diagram

Students often have trouble encoding the location and function of the different parts of the brain, both because (a) they glance too quickly over the colorful textbook illustrations and (b) their eyes tend to glaze over during class discussion of the brain's structure and function. As an easy remedy to this problem, try asking students to draw their own colorful rendition of the human brain, an active learning strategy that ensures that they encode and think about the parts of the brain rather than passively glossing over them in the text. Prior to the class period in which you will be discussing the brain, ask students to read Chapter 2 and to hand-draw a diagram of the brain (in a cross-section, much like Figure 2-6 in the text) on a clean white sheet of unlined paper. For each of the following sections of the brain, students should color (using map pencils) and label the appropriate structure, and also list at least one or two of its major functions: (a) the cerebral cortex, including the four lobes, (b) the thalamus, (c) the hypothalamus, (d) the hippocampus, (e) the amygdala, (f) the cerebellum, (g) the pons, and (h) medulla. Added benefits of this assignment are that it is easy to grade, students enjoy doing it (and it is an easy and fun way for them to get points), and it can be used by students as a study aid for the exam.

Reunited Twins

Chapter 2 points out that although twin studies (particularly studies of identical twins reared apart) seem to confirm genetic links to intelligence, psychological disorder, and some complex personality traits, critics become skeptical when the same research reveals eerie (and ostensibly genetically-based) similarities between twins on such things as aftershave brand, selection of hobbies, attraction to tattoos, and even child name preferences. Although amazing behavioral similarities do indeed turn up between identical twins raised apart (see Rosen, 1987), Wyatt and his colleagues (1994) suggest that, rather than being genetically based, these similarities are merely selected examples of coincidences that are inevitable given the hundreds or even thousands of questions typically asked of reunited twins by eager researchers. In other words, it is likely that similar "amazing" coincidences would be found if genetically *un*related people were asked a large number of questions about their behavior.

To illustrate this point, Lester Sdorow (1994) designed the "Identical Twins Reunited Questionnaire" and accompanying exercise. For this assignment, students should first read the articles by Rosen (1987) and Wyatt et. al (1994); you can put these on reserve in the library. Next, you'll need to distribute one copy of the ITRQ to each student. Handout 2-1 contains the questionnaire (which, as you can see, asks students about their behaviors, relationships, and characteristics) along with instructions for the assignment. After students have completed their surveys, you should collect them and identify pairs of students who are the most similar. [Note: You may want to take the surveys home with you and present the results during the next class period.] Once you have described for your class the "reunited twins" among them, instruct them to write a 2-3 page paper discussing how the results from the class study bear on the rationale for reunited twin studies. Ask students to incorporate into their paper insights from the Wyatt et al. study and an additional reference of their choosing from *Psychological Abstracts*. [Note: This assignment can also be used as part of Chapter 11, which covers personality.]

Rosen, C. M. (1987, September). The eerie world of reunited twins. *Discover*, pp. 36-46.
Sdorow, L. (1994). The Frankenstein course: Teaching assistants, laboratory exercises, and papers in introductory psychology. Paper presented at the Southwest Regional Conference for Teachers of Psychology, Fort Worth. Used by permission of the author.
Wyatt, W. J., Posey, A., Welker, W., & Seamonds, C. (1984). Natural levels of similarities between identical twins and between unrelated people. *The Skeptical Inquirer, 9*, 62-66.

Psychology in Literature:
The Man Who Mistook His Wife For a Hat

Oliver Sacks' (1985) national bestseller chronicles over 20 case histories of patients with a variety of neurological disorders. His compassionate retelling of bizarre and fascinating tales include patients plagued with memory loss, useless limbs, violent tics and jerky mannerisms, the inability to recognize people or objects, and unique artistic or mathematical talents despite severe mental deficits. A reading of this absorbing book will surely increase your students' understanding of the connection between the brain and the mind, and will also give them invaluable insights into the lives of disordered individuals. Ask your students to write a book report focusing on a few of the cases that most interest them, and to apply principles from the text and lecture to the stories. As a more elaborate project, you might consider assigning this book at the end of the semester, as many of the cases are ripe with psychological principles that may be encountered later in the course (e.g., perception, memory, mental retardation).

Sacks, O. (1985). *The man who mistook his wife for a hat.* New York: HarperCollins.

video

ABC News/Prentice Hall Video Library

Born or Bred? (14 min, Series III). Simon Le Vay's research on the biological concomitants of homosexuality have sparked considerable debate among politicians, religious leaders, and members of the gay community. On one side of the issue are those who applaud evidence that sexual orientation might be primarily a biological matter. On the other side are those who fear that biological evidence may spark a move toward eugenics. This *PrimeTime Live* segment focuses on Le Vay and representatives from both sides of the debate.

Building Brains (12:41 min, Series III). The developmental changes that take place during the first three years of life are remarkable, particularly those changes that occur in the brain. This *Nightline* segment focuses on the importance of early stimulation, training, and education for "building" better brains.

Cloning: Dawn of a Brave New World (7:51 min, Series III). The success of Dolly, the cloned sheep that introduced Scotland's geneticists on the rest of the world, has led to an important question: What if it were possible to make an exact copy of a human being? This issue is examined in this *Nightline* segment featuring interviews with bioethicists, physicians, and others concerned with the possibility of human cloning.

Other Sources

The Autonomic Nervous System (28 min, FHS). Describes the role of the autonomic nervous system in controlling the glands and organs. It also addresses how meditation, autosuggestion, and hypnosis can be used to control autonomic functions.

Biology and Behavior (1980, 22 min, PENN). Examines the biological roots of behavior, including close-ups on classic issues such as nature vs. nurture, and basic studies in taste aversion, imprinting, and instinctive drift.

Biology of Behavior (1990, 30 min, IM). This video gives an overview of the nervous system, including material on neurotransmitters, neurons, and the fight or flight response.

The Birth of a Brain (1983, 33 min, CRM). Hereditary and environmental influences on brain development are emphasized. A live birth may make this film unsuitable for less mature audiences.

The Brain, Part 1: The Enlightened Machine (1984, 60 min, ANN/CPB). Gives an overview of the study of the brain from Franz Gall to the present and reviews neurotransmitters functioning at the synapse.

The Brain, Part 6: The Two Brains (1984, 60 min, ANN/CPB). Explores split-brain studies and what they indicate about hemispheric functioning, the relationship between thought and language, and the issues of sex differences in the brain.

The Brain, Part 8: States of Mind (1984, 60 min, ANN/CPB). The limits of our knowledge about the brain are the focus of this program. Research in genetics, artificial intelligence, and medicine are discussed to shed light on this mysterious gray lump.

The Brain (50 min, IM). This BBC program uses animation and models of the brain to tour the structures and functions of the brain.

The Brain (23 min, FHS). This "Brain" begins with an exploration of dreams, follows with a detailed look at the nervous system and how it works, and ends with a discussion of EEG and NMRI as techniques for peering into the brain.

The Brain (28 min, FHS). And <u>this</u> "Brain" takes a cellular approach. The relationship between cell assemblies and complex processes such as hearing, vision, and language forms the focus of this video.

Brain Sex (1993, 3 volumes, 150 min total, IM). Differences between the sexes in areas such as learning, appetite, expectations, and behavior are examined. Parts of this 3-volume set can be profitably used in a variety of contexts.

Discovering Psychology, Part 3: The Behaving Brain (1990, 30 min, ANN/CPB). Provides an overview of brain structure and function through a description of the biochemical reactions involved in thoughts, feelings, and actions.

Discovering Psychology, Part 4: The Responsive Brain (1990, 30 min, ANN/CPB). Explores the interaction between the development of brain structures and function and the environment.

Discovering Psychology, Part 14: The Mind Hidden and Divided (1990, 30 min, ANN/CPB). Examines the influence of the subconscious mind on thought and behavior. The segment on the split-brain phenomenon is relevant to this chapter.

Discovering Psychology, Part 25: A Union of Opposites (1990, 30 min, ANN/CPB). A unique approach to a seldom addressed topic, this program presents "a yin-yang model of complementary opposites," to facilitate an understanding of the basic principles thought to govern human nature and animal behavior. A useful means of addressing the nature-nurture debate.

Endocrine Control: Systems in Balance (1997, 30 min, IM). This video focuses on the endocrine system's role in regulating and controlling other bodily systems.

The Enlightened Machine (1984, 58 min, ANN/CPB). CAT, PET, and EEG are discussed, as is the work of Gall, Broca, and Wernicke. Microphotography takes the viewer inside the brain. Degenerative conditions are also examined.

Epilepsy: Breaking the Barrier (28 min, FHS). Footage of grand mal seizures in progress bring home the often debilitating affliction of epilepsy. Various treatments, including drug therapy and surgical interventions, are described.

Hormones (28 min, FHS). Illustrates the role of hormones in controlling a variety of bodily functions.

The Human Brain (1997, 25 min, IM). The focus of this video is that brain functioning can be enhanced by the proper environment. Recovery from brain injury, brain surgery techniques, and silicon retinas are used as examples.

Inside Information: The Brain and How It Works (58 min, FHS). This award-winning film contains interviews with leading researchers, who discuss how and why the brain works, and works as it does. Pattern recognition, computer analogs, and individual brain structures are also discussed.

Is Your Brain Really Necessary? (1988, 50 min, FHS). This must-see video follows the lives of three people who have undergone drastic brain surgery (e.g., hemispherectomies). Their subsequent levels of functioning should prove illuminating to your students.

Journey to the Centers of the Brain (5 Parts, 58 min each, FHS). This series explores different topics related to the brain. For example, *The Electric Ape* looks at brain structure and function, whereas *Bubble Bubble Toil and Trouble* examines neural circuitry and *Through a Glass Darkly* looks at brain imaging techniques.

Left Brain, Right Brain (1979, 56 min, FLI). Norman Geschwind narrates this intriguing look at hemispheric specialization. Wada tests and split-brain operations illustrate the semi-independent functioning of the hemispheres.

Living With Tourette's (24 min, PENN). Combines case studies of individuals with Tourette's syndrome with an examination of chemical imbalances in the brain associated with the disorder.

The Mind: Development (60 min, PBS). Focusing on particular brain cells, this program (part of a 9-part series) examines brain development from conception to age six.

Nerves (1992, 24 min, IM). As the title suggests, this video is a bundle of nerves. Action potentials, synapses, agonists and antagonists, brain slices and neurons all take a bow.

Nervous System (1993, 14 min, IM). Using animation, this program demonstrates the action potential and neurotransmitter activity. It also discusses disorders of the nervous system including Alzheimer's disease, Parkinson's disease, depression, and anxiety.

The Neural Connection (1997, 30 min, IM). Receptors galore: thermoreceptors, chemoreceptors, mechanoreceptors, nocireceptors, and photoreceptors display their charms to teach about neural connections and neural impulses.

Neuropsychology (23 min, FHS). How a tangled collection of cells produces memory, emotion, language, and thought is the subject of this film. Particular attention is given to recognizing facial expressions and intellectual functioning.

Sex Hormones and Sexual Destiny (26 min, FHS). Examines the role of hormones on "masculine" and "feminine" behavior, sex differences in brain structure, and environmental influences on male and female behavior.

Split-Brain and Conscious Experience (18 min, PENN). Discusses the pioneering work conducted by Michael Gazzaniga on the split-brain phenomenon using epileptic patients with severed corpus callosums.

Teaching Modules from The Brain (30 segments from *The Brain* series, ANN/CPB). These self-contained modules offer brief glimpses into the lives of split-brain patients, the story of Phineas Gage, the brain basis of schizophrenia, REM, and speech, and aspects of stress and health.

Two Brains (1984, 55 min, ANN/CPB). Hemispheric specialization and split-brain surgery is highlighted. A woman with a severed corpus callosum is featured.

Who Are You? (60 min, FHS). Genetic influences on behavior are reviewed through an examination of several twin studies. Also included are case studies of individuals, such as the sober son of an alcoholic who fears taking a drink.

multimedia

Live! Psych

| Module | Title | Book Page # |

2.1   The Nervous System   p. 49

Screen 1 in this concept describes the function of the neurons and the glial cells. Import this screen to show how neurons vary widely in size and in shape.

Three Types of Neurons   p. 49

In Screen 1, the student clicks on each type of neuron to interact with this concept and watch simulations of how the sensory neurons, interneurons, and motor neurons provide communication links. Import Screen 2 to view a simulation of how the three types of neurons work together in reaction to pain.

The Structure of the Neuron   p. 49

Import Screen 1 to examine the basic structure of a neuron. The student clicks on each part of the neuron to learn more about it. Import Screen 2 to introduce the axon terminals and terminal buttons. Import Screen 3 to introduce myelin and nodes of Ranvier and to explain the purposes of myelin. Import Screen 4 to watch a simulation of a myelinated and an unmyelinated axon. Student clicks on each axon to compare the action potential transmission speeds.

2.2   The Neural Impluse   p. 51

Import Screen 1 to view a simulation of a neuron firing. In Screen 2, positive and negative ions are introduced. This screen depicts the cell membrane as separating the inside of the neuron from its surroundings. Screen 3 explains that the cell membrane is semipermeable. Screen 4 explains resting potential and a simulation of depolarization is shown. Screen 5 simulates the all-or-none response of an action potential. Import this screen to show a visual step-by-step of what happens during an action potential.

2.3   The Synapse and Neurotransmitters   p. 52

Import this concept for a simulation showing how a neurotransmitter crosses a synapse. Screen 1 shows action potential. Screen 2 takes a closer look at how the message cross the synapse. Screen 3 provides a closeup view of synaptic vesicles. Screen 4 shows how neurotransmitter molecules bind briefly with receptor sites on the receiving side of the synaptic cleft.

2.4   Neurotransmitters   p. 54

Screen 1 provides a simulation of excitatory and inhibitory neurotransmitters. Import this screen in a discussion of acetylcholine and dopamine.

2.5   The Brain   p. 59

Import Screen 1 to introduce the three major regions of the brain: the brain stem, the limbic system, and the cerebral cortex.

The Brain Stem   p. 59

In Screen 1, an illustration of the structures of the brain stem is shown. In Screen 2, the functions of the medulla and pons are explored. Screen 3 describes the function of the reticular activating system. Screen 4 describes the function of the cerebellum, located at the back of the brain stem.

2.6   The Limbic System   p. 62

Screen 1 introduces the key structures of the limbic system. Screen 2 describes the function of the thalamus. Screen 3 describes the function of the hypothalamus. Screen 4 describes the function of the amygdala and the hippocampus.

2.7   The Cerebral Cortex   p. 64
Import this concept to examine the structures of the cerebral cortex and the functions of each. Screen 1 shows the cerebral cortex and its convolutions. Screen 2 shows the two hemispheres of the cerebral cortex, connected by the corpus callosum. Import Screen 3 to show the four lobes of the cerebral cortex. The occipital lobe and the visual cortex are highlighted here. The parietal lobes and the somatosensory cortex are highlighted in Screen 4. The temporal lobes and the auditory cortex are highlighted in Screen 5. The frontal lobe and the motor cortex are highlighted in Screen 6. Screen 7 has an animation of the association cortex.

2.8   Cerebral Hemispheres and Corpus Callosum   p. 67
This concept explains how the two cerebral hemispheres communicate with each other via the corpus callosum. Import Screen 1 to view a simulation of the cerebral hemispheres pulling apart to reveal the corpus callosum.

2.9   Broca's Area and Wernicke's Area   p. 68
This concept examines cases of brain damage and localization of function. Screen 1 displays PET scans of subjects hearing words, seeing words, speaking words, and generating words. Screen 2 displays the left hemisphere and an animation points to Broca's area and Wernicke's area. Import this screen to explain that people with these aphasias demonstrate that there are at least two distinct cortical centers for language. Explain that if Broca's area is damaged, the aphasia tends to be "expressive." If Wernicke's area is damaged, the aphasia tends to be "receptive." In Screen 3, an animation traces the process involved in saying the written word "psychology."

2.10   Hormones   p. 78
Import this concept to examine how the endocrine system works and to teach about the locale and functions of the major endocrine glands. Screen 1 provides an animation that illustrates how the endocrine system works with the nervous system. Screen 2 provides a simulation of how the nervous system works with the endocrine system to regulate sex hormones. Screen 3 allows the student to interact with the shown diagram. The student clicks on major endocrine glands to learn about its locale and function.

2.11   Genetic Building Blocks   p. 80
Screen 1 morphs one visual to the next to demonstrate the genetic building blocks of life, starting with the human body, to the nucleus, to the chromosomes, to the chromosomes from each parent, to the strands of DNA, to the genes. Import Screen 2 for an animation of the double helix spiraling effect of the DNA molecule. In Screen 3, an interaction asks the student to match a sequence of nucleotides with its corresponding sequence. Screen 4 explains how each gene is the blueprint for a specific type of protein in the body.

            Gregor Mendel: Genes   p. 80
Screen 1 introduces the discoveries of Gregor Mendel in the mid-1800s who cross-pollinated pea plants. These experiments provided the foundation for the study of genetics. Screen 2 illustrates how Mendel began with true-breeding round and wrinkled seeds that produced offspring exactly like their parents. He found that all of the offspring of his experiment, the F1 generation, had round seeds. Screen 3 illustrates how Mendel then planted those seeds and allowed the normal process of self-fertilization to produce the second (F2) generation. Import this screen to distinguish between dominant and recessive genes. Import Screen 4 to distinguish between homozygous and heterozygous traits using the Punnett square and Mendel's F2 generation offspring to illustrate. Screen 5 explains how the genes for certain traits are passed down in families, from parents to their offspring. Screen 6 explains that if a gene is dominant, the expression of that gene will dominate that of the other gene in the pair; and that a characteristic controlled by a recessive gene will be expressed only when both members of the gene pair are recessive. Screen 7 distinguishes between phenotype and genotype. Student clicks on a table to learn about other examples of dominant and recessive traits.

2.12   Exploring Darwin's Theory of Evolution   p. 87
This concept introduces three key elements in Darwin's theory: fitness, adaptation, and natural selection. The student clicks on each element to learn more about it. Import Screen 2 to look at an example of how the process of natural selection creates traits in a species that are adaptive to their environment.

Web Investigations

Action at the Synapse

This four-part activity by John H. Krantz focuses on the action at a synapse and the behavioral consequences of that action. The activity has plenty of animation to illustrate the principles discussed. Any of the sections can be used individually or all four can be used to frame a class presentation on synaptic processes.

Part 1 provides a brief review of the synapse and the action potential. Students can complete a labeling exercise, either on their own or as part of a class activity. In Part 2 (Synaptic Communication) production, storage, and release of the action potential is highlighted, as are removal and postsynaptic effects. An interactive exercise requires students to generate an action potential by balancing excitation and inhibition. Part 3 (Neurotransmitters and Behavior) describes some of the better-understood neurotransmitters (dopamine, serotonin, GABA, endorphins) and provides some vivid images to project during class. The "Test Your Understanding" section is a great exercise for helping students identify each neurotransmitter's effect and location in the brain. In Part 4 (How Drugs Affect the Synapse) students are exposed to the steps of synaptic communication and the various neurotransmitters are brought together. Students should gain a better understanding of neurotransmitter and drug action at the synapse. Part 4 might also be profitably used in Chapter 13 when discussing drug therapies.

Making Connections

Neurons: The Messengers

Q How does a single neuron connect to hundreds, even thousands, of others?

A A neuron is able to receive messages from many other neurons because is has a large number of dendrites, or branches; it can relay messages to many neurons because its axon may also branch out in numerous directions.

Q What regulates the neural impulse so that it doesn't fire at random?

A A neuron can fire only if the impulse it receives is greater than its threshold of excitation. After firing, a neuron goes through an absolute refractory period, during which it cannot fire again.

Q Describe the ways that psychoactive drugs and toxins alter neural transmission.

A Most psychoactive drugs and toxins work either by blocking or enhancing the transmission of chemicals, such as neurotransmitters, across synapses. Others, such as cocaine, work by interfering with the removal of neurotransmitters from synapses, thus prolonging stimulation and heightening arousal. Antidepressants, such as tricyclics, have the similar effect of prolonging the circulation of serotonin.

Q What evidence demonstrates neural plasticity? What are the potential benefits of understanding adult neurogenesis?

A Neural plasticity: A classic series of experiments with rats demonstrates that enriched environments lead to larger neurons with more synaptic connections. Other experiments show that rats raised in stimulating environments perform better on cognitive tests. Musicians who use the left hand increase the size of a corresponding area on the right side of the brain, and in deaf people, an area of the brain responsible for hearing rewires itself to read lips and sign language. Understanding neurogenesis may lead to new treatments for patients with Parkinson's disease, stroke, and spinal cord injury.

The Central Nervous System

Q In evolutionary terms, the central core and limbic system are the oldest parts of our brains. What "vegetative" functions does the core regulate? What "primitive reactions" are controlled by the limbic system?

A The central core regulates breathing, heart rate, and blood pressure (medulla); sleep-wake cycles (pons); balance and coordination (cerebellum); hearing and sight (midbrain); integration of incoming signals (thalamus); motivation (hypothalamus); sending "alert" signals (reticular formation). The limbic system controls formation of new memories (hippocampus); regulates emotions related to self-preservation (amygdala and hippocampus); and coordinates the body's reactions in times of stress.

Q The cerebral cortex is the most recently evolved part of our brain, the seat of many qualities we think of as distinctively human. How does the "division of labor" among the four lobes, large associative areas, and hemispheric specialization enhance our mental capacities?

A The occipital, parietal, and temporal lobes and the association areas within them carry out specific functions related to sensory processing, speech, and movement. The functions of all these areas seem to be monitored and integrated by the frontal lobes, which, in addition, regulate goal-directed behavior and the ability to make mature judgments. Each of the two halves of the brain regulates the activities of the opposite side of the body, and in addition, each half seems to have special responsibility for certain higher cognitive functions in most people: the right half, visual and spatial functions, and the left half, verbal functions. The entire cortex is integrated by billions of interlinked neurons, and the parts work together in complex ways that psychologists are only beginning to understand.

Q What tools do scientists use to study the structure of the brain? Brain activity?

A To study brain structures, researchers use structural imaging, such as CAT scans and MRIs. To study brain activity, they use microelectrode techniques to investigate the functions of single neurons, macroelectrode techniques to study overall functioning of particular regions, EEG imaging to measure ongoing brain activity, MRG and MSI to determine which parts of the brain perform various activities, and PET techniques to map brain activity.

Q Describe the three main functions of the spinal cord.

A The three functions of the spinal cord are to carry motor impulses from the brain to the internal organs and muscles, to carry sensory information from the extremities and internal organs to the brain, and to carry out some simple reflexes.

The Peripheral Nervous System

Q Why is this portion of the nervous system called peripheral?

A This branch of the nervous system is called "peripheral" because it collects and transmits information to and from the peripheral areas of the body (the trunk, extremities, and internal organs) and is not part of the central part of the nervous system--the brain and spinal cord.

Q Describe the system of "checks and balances" in the autonomic nervous system.

A In general, the sympathetic division of the autonomic nervous system signals arousal: it tells your heart and lungs to work faster, your pupils to dilate, your digestion to stop. The parasympathetic division has the opposite effect: it tells the organs to return to their normal functioning.

The Endocrine System

Q If the nervous system resembles a "telephone network," the endocrine system might be described as a "radio broadcast." Explain.

A The nervous system resembles a telephone network because it delivers messages from one neuron to other specific neurons, and all "receivers" are connected through a very complex network of "wires." The endocrine system resembles a radio broadcast because it delivers its "messages"--hormones--throughout the entire body via the bloodstream, to be "heard" by any cells with the proper receptors.

Q How are the endocrine systems of males and females different? How are they alike?

A The endocrine systems of males and females are alike except for the gonads--testes in males and ovaries in females. These produce sex hormones (androgens and estrogens). Both males and females produce both types of hormones, which have a wide variety of effects on the body, but androgens are more prevalent in males and estrogens in females.

Genes, Evolution, and Behavior

Q How do genes provide continuity and variation over generations?

A Genes provide continuity by providing a mechanism for transmission of traits from one generation to the next. They provide for variation by allowing for mutations and crossing over during production of ova and sperm, and of gradual evolution over time.

Q What techniques do behavior geneticists use to assess heritability? How do the results of heritability studies differ from the results of molecular genetics?

A To assess heritability of traits, behavior geneticists use strain studies and selection studies in animals, and family studies, twin studies, and adoption studies in humans. The results of all of these are indirect only--they show what percentage of a trait seems to be attributable to heredity. In contrast, molecular genetic techniques allow scientists to study the human genetic code directly.

Q How are new technologies creating new ethical questions?

A New technologies may soon enable scientists to create new categories of people, so that a government might be able to breed "workers" or soldiers. Advances in genetics allow scientists to predict which babies will be born with genetic diseases, but they also allow parents to select for a child who is the desired sex or who lacks a disability. The potential to identify genes that code for antisocial behavior could lead to government interference in reproduction or increased surveillance over individual activity.

Mind Matters

Physiological Psychology: Neurons and the Endocrine System

A detailed description of neurons is included in this section. Students learn all the various structures and functions of different types of neurons, and can simulate excitation, inhibition, and the graded potential. Interactive demonstrations help make synaptic action more understandable. A review of the endocrine system provides a nice companion to the material on the nervous system. The many interactive exercises and demonstrations included in this section should help your students master this sometimes esoteric material.

Physiological Psychology: The Brain

This section outlines the structure of the nervous system and identifies the various divisions of the brain (i.e., hindbrain, midbrain, forebrain). The Interactive Brain allows students to discover the functions that various anatomical structures in the brain perform. A pop-up on the Phineas Gage story provides a nice application of brain structure and function, as does the pop-up on brain lateralization. Project the slides from this section on a media projector to illustrate basic brain anatomy.

Evolution and Behavior

Students can review a profile of Charles Darwin, understand the assumptions underlying natural selection, and conduct a simulation of the natural selection process using "cyberlemmings." The principles of evolution are applied to human emotions and facial expressions, mate selection, and phobias. Use the materials in this section to illustrate lecture concepts. For example, the demonstration of universal facial expressions of emotion is a handy way to illustrate the expressions and quiz your students. You might also ask your students to conduct the cyberlemming simulation and write a brief report summarizing their findings.

Video Classics

Probing the Cerebral Cortex

SYNOPSIS: This clip contains commentary by Wilder Penfield, a pioneer in mapping the areas of the cerebral cortex. Penfield discusses the work that led to electrode-stimulation of the cortex. He also interviews a brain surgery patient about her experiences during surgery: stimulation of various areas of her cortex produced memories for past events and the perception of music playing.

Form a Hypothesis

Q What happens when Penfield stimulates a small area of the temporal lobe, called the auditory cortex?

A The patient "hears" sounds.

Test Your Understanding

Q What are the four lobes of the cerebral cortex?

A The four lobes of cerebral cortex are occipital, parietal, temporal, and frontal.

Q What are the functions of the somatosensory cortex, motor cortex, and association cortex areas?

A Somatosensory cortex interprets sensations and coordinates the motor behavior of skeletal muscles. Association areas, located on all four cortical lobes, are involved in the integration of various brain functions, such as sensation, thought, memory, planning, etc.

Q What two areas of the association cortex specialize in language?

A Wernicke's area, located towards the back of the temporal lobe, is important in understanding the speach of others. Broca's area is essential to sequencing and producing language.

Thinking Critically

Q What four types of research methods are commonly used in the study of behavioral neuroscience?

A Microelectrode techniques are used to study the functions of individual neurons. Macroelectrode techniques, such as an EEG, record activities of brain areas. Structural imaging, such as computerized axial tomography or CAT scans is useful for mapping brain structures. Functional imaging, in which specific brain activity can be recorded in response to tasks or stimulation, offers the potential to identify specific brain areas and functions.

Web Links

1. http://server.bmod.athabascau.ca/html/aupr/biological.htm
Links to several sites relevant to biological and physiological psychology. A good starting point for a number of assignments, such as writing short papers or assembling study guide terms.

2. http://psych.hanover.edu/Krantz/neurotut.html
Basic Neural Processes Tutorials. A good site for your students to help them learn about basic brain functioning.

3. http://www.neuropat.dote.hu/caud.gif
A cross-sectional image of the human brain. Good to have on hand if you need one. Show your students and help them identify the various structures.

4. http://faculty.washington.edu/chudler/neurok.html
Neuroscience for kids. A great non-technical treatment of neuroscience.

transparencies

Series V

15. Schematic Diagram of the Divisions of the Nervous System
The major divisions of the human nervous system are depicted.

16a. Functions of the Parasympathetic & Sympathetic Nervous System
16b. This two-part transparency shows the functions of these complementary systems.

17. Nerve Cell
The anatomy of a typical motor neuron shows the cell body, dendrites, and axon.

18. Action Potential Transmission
The transmission of an action potential via ion exchange.

19. Synapse
This transparency illustrates a synaptic transmission.

20. The Human Brain
The brain stem, limbic system, and cerebral cortex are highlighted in this transparency.

21. Lobes of the Brain
The four lobes of the cerebral cortex and other structures are illustrated.

22. Broca's Area and Wernicke's Area
These important brain regions related to speech and language are highlighted.

23. Hemispheric Specialization of the Cerebral Cortex
The areas of dominance in the left and right hemispheres are illustrated.

24. Illustration of a Spinal Reflex
The patellar reflex is used to illustrate reflex action across an afferent neuron and motor neuron.

25. The Endocrine System
The chemical communication system of pituitary, pineal, thyroid, parathyroid, adrenal, pancreas, and gonads is presented.

26. The Twenty-Three Pairs of Chromosomes Found in Every Normal Human Cell
Just what it sounds like.

27. Transmission of Eye Color by Dominant and Recessive Genes
The four possible combinations of eye-color genes in a parents' offspring are depicted.

Text Figures

- 2-1. *Parts of the Neuron*
- 2-2. *The Neural Impulse*
- 2-3. *Electrical Changes During the Action Potential*
- 2-4. *Synaptic Transmission*
- 2-5. *Brain Growth and Experience*
- 2-6. *Divisions of the Nervous System*
- 2-7. *Divisions of the Brain*
- 2-8. *The Limbic System*
- 2-9. *The Four Lobes of the Cerebral Cortex*
- 2-10. *The Two Cerebral Hemispheres.*
- 2-11. *Split-brain Research*
- 2-12. *Processing of Speech and Language*
- 2-13. *Brain and Spinal Cord*
- 2-14. *The Spinal Cord and Replex Action*
- 2-15. *The Sympathetic and Parasympathetic Nervous Systems*
- 2-16. *The Glands of the Endocrine System*
- 2-17. *Average Risk of Schizophrenia Among Relatives*

Handout 2-1

Reunited Twins Assignment

Research on identical twins who have been reunited later in life after having been separated in infancy has revealed some amazing similarities. But researchers typically ask the reunited twins hundreds or even thousands of questions. Perhaps their amazing similarities are coincidences and not attributable to their identical heredity. This questionnaire has been designed to assess whether unrelated persons will also be similar in unusual ways or in several not so unusual ways. The results of this questionnaire will be announced in class. For this assignment, you will write a brief paper discussing the findings. Did students show surprising similarities? If so, what are some of the possible explanations? What does this say about research on identical twins who have been reunited?

IDENTICAL TWINS REUNITED QUESTIONNAIRE

Instructions: Give your response to the following questions; if you prefer not to answer a particular question, feel free to leave it blank.

1. Academic major: _____
2. Favorite musical group/performer: _____
3. Mother's name: _____
4. Favorite dessert: _____
5. Boyfriend's/girlfriend's first name: _____
6. Favorite television show: _____
7. Political affiliation: (Dem/Rep/Ind/Other): _____
8. Favorite food: _____
9. Favorite actor: _____
10. Favorite actress: _____
11. Favorite movie: _____
12. Favorite hobby: _____
13. Favorite sport to watch: _____
14. Favorite sport to play: _____
15. Favorite professional sports team: _____
16. Favorite author: _____
17. Father's name: _____
18. Most distinctive habit: _____
19. Favorite politician: _____
20. Favorite professional athlete: _____
21. Most disliked food: _____
22. Favorite automobile: _____
23. Favorite kind of pet animal: _____
24. Professional goal: _____
25. Most recent non-course book read: _____

Sdorow, L. (1994). The Frankenstein course: Teaching assistants, laboratory exercises, and papers in introductory psychology. Paper presented at the Southwest Regional Conference for Teachers of Psychology, Fort Worth. Reprinted by permission of the author.

Chapter 3 Sensation and Perception

chapter outline 64

learning objectives 67

lecture suggestions

    Sniffing Out the Truth About Fragrance 68
    Development of Sensory and Perceptual Processes 68
    Smell Myths 70
    The (Dis)embodiment of Fear 70
    The Perception of Pain 71
    The Perception of Phantom Limb Pain 72
    Sense, Nonsense, and Extra-sense 72
    Setting Thresholds 73
    Noses, Aisle 12 74

demonstrations and activities

    Sensory Adaptation 75
    Sound Localization 76
    The Role of Smell in Determining Flavor 76
    The Effect of Visual Cues on Taste 76
    Saliva and Taste 77
    Odor Identification Test 77
    The Body's Sensitivity to Touch 77
    Expectancy and Perception 78
    Using Escher to Illustrate Perceptual Principles 78
    Goggles That Boggle 79

student assignments

    Field Demonstrations 80
    In Search of Perceptual Illusions 80
    Explaining the Moon Illusion 81
    Keeping a Psychology Journal 81

video 82

multimedia 83

transparencies 91

chapter outline

I. The Nature of Sensation

    A. The basic process

        1. Energy ⊃ receptor cell ⊃ neural signal ⊃ central nervous system

    B. Sensory thresholds

        1. Absolute threshold

            a. The least amount of energy detected as stimulation 50% of the time

                i. Sensory adaptation: Adjustment of the senses to stimulation

        2. Difference threshold (just noticeable difference)

            a. The smallest change in stimulation detected 50% of the time

                i. Weber's Law describes the jnd

    C. Subliminal perception

        1. Stimulation below the threshold of conscious awareness

            a. Evidence under lab conditions, no support in commercial use

    D. Extrasensory perception

        1. Not a lot of solid evidence for telepathy, clairvoyance, precognition

II. Vision

    A. The visual system

        1. Structures: Cornea, pupil, iris, lens, retina, fovea

        2. Receptor cells

            a. Rods (120 million) specialized for light/dark vision, none in fovea

            b. Cones (8 million) specialized for color vision, need bright light

            c. Bipolar cells

                i. Rods and cones connect to bipolar cells

        3. Adaptation

            a. Dark adaptation: Increased sensitivity of rods and cones in darkness

            b. Light adaptation: Decreased sensitivity of rods and cones in light

                i. Afterimage effects are a consequence of these processes

        4. From eye to brain

            a. Rods and cones ⊃ bipolar cells ⊃ ganglion cells ⊃ optic nerve

                i. Blind spot: Ganglion cells join to leave the eye

                ii. Optic chiasm: Fibers separate to connect to each hemisphere

                ii. Feature detectors detect specific stimulus elements

                iv. Blindsight

B. Color vision

1. Properties of color: Hue, saturation, brightness

2. Theories of color vision

    a. Color mixing

        i. Additive color mixing: Mixing lights of different wavelengths

        ii. Subtractive color mixing: Mixing pigments

    b. Trichromatic theory: Red cones, green cones, blue-violet cones

    c. Opponent-process theory: Yellow-blue pairs, red-green pairs, brightness pair

    d. Both theories of color vision are valid

3. Color vision in other species

    a. Primates are trichromats; other species are dichromats, monochromats

III. Hearing

A. Sound

1. Components: Frequency, Hz, pitch, amplitude, decibels, overtones

B. The ear

1. Eardrum ⊃ hammer, anvil, stirrup ⊃ oval window ⊃ cochlea ⊃ organ of corti

2. Neural connections: A circuitous path from ear through brain

C. Theories of hearing

1. Place theory

    a. Brain determines pitch by noting place on basilar membrane

2. Frequency theory

    a. Brain determines pitch by frequencies across basilar membrane

        i. Volley principle modifies original frequency theory

D. Hearing disorders: Any of several structures could be disrupted

IV. The Other Senses

A. Smell

1. Detecting common odors

    a. Odorant binding protein ⊃ olfactory bulb

2. Communicating with pheromones

    a. This aspect of smell is questionable in humans

B. Taste

1. Tongue ⊃ papillae ⊃ taste buds ⊃ sweet, sour, salty, bitter

C. Kinesthetic and vestibular senses

1. Kinesthetic senses: Muscle movement, posture, strain on joints

    a. Stretch receptors and Golgi tendon organs

2. Vestibular senses: Equilibrium and awareness of body position in space

    a. Semicircular canals and vestibular sacs

D. Sensations of motion
   1. Visual + vestibular = nausea
E. The skin senses
   1. Various skin receptors produce cutaneous sensations
F. Pain
   1. Individual differences
      a. Gate control: An explanation of the pain process
      b. Biopsychosocial theory: Pain involves elements of all three systems
   2. Alternative approaches
      a. Acupuncture, hypnosis, placebo effects

V. Perception
   A. Perceptual organization
      1. Figure/ground distinction a guiding principle of all perception
   B. Perceptual constancies
      1. Constancy of size, shape, color
   C. Perceiving distance and depth
      1. Monocular cues
         a. Aerial perspective, texture gradient, linear perspective, motion parallax
      2. Binocular cues
         a. Stereoscopic vision, retinal disparity, convergence of the eyes
      3. Location of sounds
         a. Monaural cues and binaural cues
   D. Perceiving movement
      1. Real movement
      2. Apparent movement
         a. Autokinetic effect, stroboscopic motion, phi phenomenon
   E. Visual illusions
      1. Perceptual illusions

learning objectives

After reading this chapter, students should be able to:

1. Describe the difference between the absolute threshold and the difference threshold.
2. Trace the path of light from the time it enters the eye until it reaches the receptor cells.
3. Distinguish between rods and cones, and list their characteristics and functions with respect to light, color, and how they connect to bipolar and ganglion cells.
4. Describe the process of adaptation, include the phenomenon of afterimages.
5. Describe the three basic properties of color.
6. Describe the two main theories of color vision.
7. Identify the characteristics of sound.
8. Describe the structure of the ear and explain the functions of the various parts.
9. State the two theories of hearing.
10. Summarize the theories that explain how the sense of smell is activated by chemical substances.
11. Explain the processes involved in the sense of taste and name the four primary qualities of taste.
12. Explain the importance of vestibular senses and describe the functions of the two divisions.
13. Discuss the principles of perceptual organization identified by the Gestaltists.
14. Define perceptual constancy and identify four kinds.
15. Describe four observer characteristics that can affect perception.
16. Identify the contributions of both monocular and binocular cues of depth perception.
17. Describe two kinds of visual illusions.

lecture suggestions

Sniffing Out the Truth About Fragrance

Devotees of New Age practices such as aromatherapy claim that various fragrances can have a dramatic impact on one's health, well-being, and psychological state. Makers of the air fresheners claim pretty much the same thing, except that the piece of mind comes from successfully masking offensive odors in the environment. Although both camps agree that aromas can impact behavior and mental states, neither has been that forthcoming with evidence in support of these claims.

Social psychologist Robert A. Baron, of Rensselaer Polytechnic Institute, has risen to the challenge of investigating such claims and has conducted several studies on the effects of fragrance on behavior. For example, participants in one study were angered or not angered by either a male or female confederate. The participants were later given the opportunity to aggress against the instigator under one of three conditions; in the presence of perfume (a very pleasant scent), in the presence of pine-scented aerosol (a mildly pleasant scent), or in the absence of any pleasant scent. When the confederate was a man, results indicated that aggression was enhanced in the perfume condition if the participants had been angered, but reduced in this same condition if the participants had not been angered. When the confederates were women, however, aggressive retaliation was enhanced by the perfume regardless of whether participants had been previously angered. These findings may be attributed in part to the heightened arousal that is often experienced in the presence of fragrances.

In a subsequent set of studies, Baron investigated the effects of pleasant fragrances on the work environment. Participants completed a word task under conditions of either high or low stress, and in the presence or absence of a pleasant fragrance (*Powder Fresh* or *Spiced Apple* air fresheners). In both stress conditions, the presence of the fragrance significantly enhanced performance.

What causes fragrances to have such effects? Baron suggests that pleasant fragrances act as a mild mood enhancer, one at least as effective as other mood manipulations. In an additional experiment, for example, participants complete an anagram task under low or moderate stress and in the presence or absence of a fragrant air freshener (lemon and floral scents were used). In this experiment, a small gift of candy was also presented to some participants. The results revealed that both the fragrances and the small gift significantly improved performance on the word task, under conditions of either moderate or low stress. In short, the effects of the fragrance seemed to match those of the gift (a known positive mood enhancer). In fact, both the fragrance and the gift increased participants' willingness to help the experimenter in this study as an unpaid volunteer.

Baron, R. A. (1980). Olfaction and human social behavior: Effects of pleasant scents on physical aggression. *Basic and Applied Social Psychology, 1*, 163-172.

Baron, R. A., & Bronfen, M. I. (1994). A whiff of reality: Empirical evidence concerning the effects of pleasant fragrances on work-related behavior. *Journal of Applied Social Psychology, 24*, 1179-1203.

Baron, R. A., & Thomley, J. (1994). A whiff of reality: Positive affect as a potential mediator of the effects of pleasant fragrances on task performance and helping. *Environment and Behavior, 26*, 766-784.

Development of Sensory and Perceptual Processes

There is substantial evidence that the adage "Use it or lose it" is relevant to the development of the central nervous system, particularly the areas involved in sensory and perceptual processes. The experiences of the first weeks or months of life can permanently influence brain functions and perceptual capabilities.

Animals deprived of all visual stimulation (reared in the dark) show significant visual defects (blindness, if the deprivation is extensive), and neural activity in the visual cortex is abnormal or absent (Hubel & Wiesel, 1963). Instead of using complete deprivation, Blakemore and Cooper (1970) limited visual experience to one type. Kittens were reared in the dark except for a period each day when they were exposed to lines of one orientation (horizontal or vertical). When their visual behavior was tested after five months, the kittens showed pronounced visual deficits. For example, those exposed to horizontal lines gave no response to a rod held vertically, but they played with the rod when it was horizontal. Those exposed to vertical lines responded in the opposite way.

Examination of visual cortex neurons also indicated striking differences between the two groups of kittens. The visual cortex contains cells that respond selectively according to particular characteristics of a visual stimulus. Line orientation is one such characteristic. Some cells respond maximally to horizontal lines, others to vertical lines, and still others to intermediate orientations. These cells are present even in the inexperienced newborn brain. (There is debate as to whether the cells are as numerous as they are in the adult brain.) After selective visual deprivation, however, kittens did not have the entire complement of cells. Kittens exposed to horizontal lines had few, if any, cells that maximally responded to orientations other than approximately horizontal; those given vertical exposure had cells that responded primarily to vertical lines. Apparently, cells that were not stimulated became permanently unresponsive.

There seems to be a critical period for these deprivation effects; events before and after this period cause little change. The critical period for kittens is between the fourth and eighth week. Kittens given normal experience for four weeks and then deprived of vision for as little as 24 hours show significant modification (Olson & Freeman, 1975). Deprivation starting after eight weeks has little effect, and after four months, no change occurs even with extensive deprivation (Hubel & Wiesel, 1970).

There are parallels in human visual disorders. Severe congenital astigmatism creates a visual environment similar to that of the selective rearing studies. In astigmatism the cornea is distorted, causing the image to be out of focus in one orientation. Extensive blurring eliminates contours, and cells originally responsive to contours of that orientation are not stimulated. Permanent neural changes occur, and vision is impaired in one orientation. At that point corrective lenses help little: They put the image in focus, but vision will remain poor in the affected orientation because deprived cells will be unresponsive (Mitchell, 1980; Mitchell & Wilkinson, 1974). Astigmatism must be corrected before age 5, approximately, to avoid permanent damage.

In strabismus the eyes are improperly aligned, resulting in excessive disparity between the two eyes' input to the brain. Eventually one eye's input is suppressed. Deprivation of normal binocular stimulation results in the loss of binocularly driven cortical cells, and thus perceptual capabilities such as depth perception are impaired. Strabismus is treatable by surgically adjusting the eye muscles, but to be effective in preserving normal vision, the surgery must be performed in infancy. The critical period for binocular vision development begins the first year and peaks during the second year (Banks, Aslin, & Letson, 1975). After age 4, little development occurs, and treatment does not improve binocular vision. Similar damage occurs when one eye is patched early in life (Mitchell, 1980).

Banks, M. S., Aslin, R. N., & Letson, R. D. (1975). Sensitive period for the development of human binocular vision. *Science, 190*, 675-677.

Blakemore, C., & Cooper, G. F. (1970). Development of the brain depends on the visual environment. *Nature, 228*, 477-478.

Hirsch, H. V. B., & Spinell, D. N. (1970). Visual experience modifies distribution of horizontally and vertically oriented receptive fields in cats. *Science, 168*, 869-871.

Hubel, D. H., & Wiesel, T. N. (1963). Receptive fields of cells in striate cortex of very young, visually inexperienced kittens. *Journal of Neurophysiology, 26*, 994-1001.

Hubel, D. H., & Wiesel, T. N. (1970). The period of susceptibility to the physiological effects of unilateral eye closure in kittens. *Journal of Physiology, 206*, 419-436.

Mitchell, D. E. (1980). The influence of early visual experience on visual perception. In C. S. Harris (Ed.), *Visual coding and adaptability*. Hillsdale, NJ: Erlbaum.

Mitchell, D. E., & Wilkinson, F. (1974). The effect of early astigmatism on the visual resolution of gratings. *Journal of Physiology, 243*, 739-756.

Olson, C. R., & Freeman, R. D. (1975). Progressive changes in kitten striate cortex during monocular vision. *Journal of Neurophysiology, 38*, 26-32.

Smell Myths

Human smell has often been characterized as being deficient when compared to the smell abilities of some lower organisms. Summarized below are four myths about human smell that have been contradicted by research.

Myth 1: *Human smell is less sensitive than that of other animals*

Research indicates that the individual smell receptor cells in humans will respond to a single odorant molecule. The difference in overall sensitivity appears to be due to the fact that some lower organisms, such as dogs, have more smell receptors.

Myth 2: *Humans have a relatively poor ability to detect changes in smell intensity*

Although earlier research indicated that the difference threshold for smell was the largest of all the senses, more recent research, carefully controlling the concentrations of the smell stimuli, indicated that difference thresholds were equal to or lower in size than those for other senses.

Myth 3: *Odor identification ability is poor in humans*

Although early research indicated that the ability to recognize previously presented odors was poor, this result may be related to the fact that unfamiliar odors were used as the stimuli. Odor identification accuracy is primarily a function of labeling, not smell. That is, if subjects are given the correct label of an odor when they are first exposed to it, their ability to later identify the odor is significantly improved.

Myth 4: *While many animals use odors to communicate, humans do not*

Several studies have demonstrated that individuals are able to identify correctly about 75% of the time whether odors associated with sweat or breath came from a male or female. Menstrual synchrony, a phenomenon in which women who live in close proximity for a period of time begin to have similar starting times for menstruation, has also been found to be related to smell.

Goldstein, E. B. (1989). *Sensation and perception* (3rd ed.). Belmont, CA: Wadsworth.

Reprinted from Hill, W. G. (1995). Instructor's resource manual for *Psychology* by S. F. Davis and J. J. Palladino. Englewood Cliffs, NJ: Prentice Hall.

The (Dis)embodiment of Fear

Summaries of research on sensation and perception traditionally have focused on vision and hearing as the two "main" human senses, often to the exclusion of an extended discussion of the chemical and motion senses. Although the present chapter provides good examples of the workings and importance of the "other" senses, your students might gain a better appreciation of their significance through a case study.

Oliver Sacks (1985) reported the case of the "disembodied lady," a woman suffering from a total disruption of her proprioceptive system. A day before gallbladder surgery, a young woman of 27 suddenly experienced bizarre symptoms unrelated to her medical condition. She was unable to hold anything in her hands, was unsteady on her feet, and found that her arms flailed about whenever her attention was directed elsewhere. She lay motionless and expressionless in the hospital bed, complaining of experiencing a strange sense of disembodiment. After initial psychiatric opinions of preoperative anxiety and hysterical conversion, it was determined that the woman was suffering from *acute polyneuritis.* An extremely rare condition, it is characterized by a shutting down of the proprioceptive receptors; in short, a lack of muscle, tendon, and joint sense. As a consequence, the young woman lacked position sense, leaving her literally with one hand not knowing what the other was doing. In fact, she didn't know where her hands *were*, or legs, or arms, for that matter. In absence of feedback from the proprioceptive system her parietal lobes, though functioning quite normally, had no data to function on, leaving her in a truly "disembodied" state.

Many senses contribute to the experience of one's body: Vision, vestibular senses, proprioception. With the disruption of one of these the others became more vital. In order to "know" the location and arrangement of her own body parts, the woman had to have them in direct sight. Thus, seeing her hands in front of her face supplied the only information about where her hands were. Similarly, walking, eating, talking, expressing emotion, or performing any of the other simple bodily actions we take for granted required the utmost diligence and concentration. Her sense of disembodiment was just that; she was left feeling much like a lump of clay.

Although this case is rare, and certainly bizarre, it provides food for thought. While we can close our eyes to simulate blindness, or wear plugs to provide hearing or olfactory impairment, it is difficult to imagine how not to experience one's body. But in imagining how this might feel (or, *not* feel, as the case might be), we can better appreciate the importance of these "hidden" senses.

Sacks, O. (1985). *The man who mistook his wife for a hat.* New York: HarperCollins.

The Perception of Pain

The determinants of pain perception have been one of the most elusive problems in psychology. Unlike other sensory systems, the intensity of pain does not correlate well with stimulus intensity. For example, phantom limb pain, a very intense pain, has no external stimulus, whereas soldiers on the battlefield can be seriously injured and feel little discomfort. A theory based solely on stimulus characteristics is clearly insufficient to explain these phenomena.

Melzack and Wall (1965; see also Melzack and Casey, 1968) included a cognitive component in their gate-control theory of pain perception. They proposed that two neural systems are involved in the transmission of pain information. One, the lemniscal tract, consists of large fibers with fast transmission rates and carries heat, cold, touch, and, to a lesser extent, pain input. The second, the spinothalamic system, transmits pain information over slower, smaller fibers. A "gate" in the dorsal horn of the spinal cord controls what is transmitted to the brain. Activity in the large fibers closes the gate and prevents the small fibers from sending pain input to the brain. This may be why rubbing the area of an injury reduces the pain; large fibers for touch are activated, closing the gate. The cognitive factors in pain perception are explained by adding a cognitive gate control. Attitude, expectancy, and attention can cause the brain to send a signal that closes the gate, reducing pain. Enkephalins (endogenous opiates) may be the biological mechanism involved in the cognitive control of the gate. There is evidence that enkephalins are produced in response to placebos and electrical brain stimulation. Enkephalins block the release of substance P, thus closing the gate and reducing pain.

For possibly 80 million people pain is an everyday fact, costing the United States $60 billion a year (Stark, 1985). Standard treatments for chronic pain include electrical stimulation (to activate the lemniscal system and close the gate), acupuncture, drugs, and, in extreme cases, cingulatomy (cutting the nerve tracts connecting the frontal lobes with the limbic system). Unfortunately, for some people these provide only temporary relief. However, Stark (1985) reports that a cognitive behavioral approach is often very effective in managing chronic pain. Patients are taught what factors affect pain and techniques to reduce pain, such as relaxation. Even limited control over the pain can reduce anxiety and tension, which, in turn, reduces the pain. Although the pain is not eliminated, many patients are better able to cope and to lead relatively normal lives.

Melzack, R., & Wall, P. D. (1965). Pain mechanisms: A new theory. *Science, 150,* 971-979.
Melzack, R., & Casey, K .L. (1968). Sensory, motivational and central control determinants of pain: A new conceptual model. In D. R. Kenshalo (Ed.), *The skin senses.* Springfield, IL: Thomas.
Stark, E. (1985). Breaking the pain habit. *Psychology Today, 19,* 30-36.

The Perception of Phantom Limb Pain

As mentioned above, the stimulus intensity-pain perception relationship is an imperfect one. Perhaps more perplexing than explaining "typical" pain (resulting from illness, injury, or accident) is explaining phantom limb pain.

Phantom limb refers to the subjective sensory awareness of an amputated body part, and may include numbness, itchiness, temperature, posture, volume, or movement. In addition to legs and arms there have been cases of phantom breasts, bladders, rectums, and internal organs. Phantom limb pain refers to the specific case of painful sensations that appear to reside in the amputated body part. Patients have variously reported pins-and-needles sensations, burning sensations, shooting pains that seem to travel up and down the limb, or cramps, as thought the severed limb was in an uncomfortable and unnatural position. Many amputees often experience several types of pain; others report that the sensations are unlike other pain they've experienced. Unfortunately, some estimates suggest that over 70 percent of amputees still experience intense pain, even 25 years after amputation. Most treatments for phantom limb pain (there are over 50 types of therapy) help only about 7 percent of sufferers.

A recent study has shed light on the causes of phantom limb sensations. Researchers at Humboldt University in Berlin suggest that the most severe type of this pain occurs in amputees whose brains undergo extensive sensory reorganization. Magnetic responses were measured in the brains of 13 arm amputees in response to light pressure on their intact thumbs, pinkies, lower lips, and chins. These responses were then mapped onto the somatosensory cortex controlling that side of the body. Because of the brain's contralateral control over the body, the researchers were able to estimate the location of the somatosensory sites for the missing limb. They found that those amputees who reported the most phantom limb pain also showed the greatest cortical reorganization. Somatosensory areas for the face encroached into regions previously reserved for the amputated fingers.

Although these findings do not by themselves solve the riddle of phantom limb pain, they do offer avenues for future research. For example, damage to the nervous system may cause a strengthening of connections between somatosensory cells and the formation of new ones. Phantom limb pain may result due to an imbalance of pain messages from other parts of the brain. As another possibility, pain may result from a remapping of somatosensory areas that infringes on pain centers close by.

Boas, R. A., Schug, S. A., & Acland, R. H. (1993). Perineal pain after rectal amputation: A 5-year follow-up. *Pain, 52*, 67-70.
Bower, B. (1995). Brain changes linked to phantom-limb pain. *Science News, 147*, 357.
Brena, S. F., & Sammons, E. E. (1979). Phantom urinary bladder pain - Case report. *Pain, 7*, 197-201.
Bressler, B., Cohen, S. I., & Magnussen, F. (1955). Bilateral breast phantom and breast phantom pain. *Journal of Nervous and Mental Disease, 122*, 315-320.
Dorpat, T. L. (1971). Phantom sensations of internal organs. *Comprehensive Psychiatry, 12*, 27-35.
Katz, J. (1993). The reality of phantom limbs. *Motivation and Emotion, 17*, 147-179.
Shreeve, J. (1993, June). Touching the phantom. *Discover*, pp. 35-42.

Sense, Nonsense, and Extra-sense

Daryl Bem and Ray Hyman recently engaged in a lively debate regarding the demonstrability of ESP. Although both scholars are critical of ESP research, Bem has recently endorsed the work of the late Charles Honorton examining the *autoganzfeld* procedure for measuring psi ability. The procedure requires a sender to concentrate on a picture while the receiver tries to guess what the sender is viewing. Hyman still finds problems with the procedures and at present, like most other aspects of psychic ability, the issue remains unresolved.

But the debate over the demonstration of psychic powers under controlled conditions raged long before the Bem-Honorton/Hyman articles found their way to the pages of *Psychological Bulletin*. For example, the work of J. B. Rhine, who pioneered the study of parapsychology at Duke University, came under repeated scrutiny throughout his career. The most celebrated debate on this issue, however, arose between self-proclaimed Israeli psychic Uri Geller and James Randi, a long-time professional conjurer and semi-professional debunker (also known by his stage name The Amazing Randi, or his given name

James Zwingli). Randi took Geller and parapsychology to task in a series of books, articles, personal appearances, professional demonstrations, and goading challenges over a period of several years.

For example, Geller claimed that his ability to bend spoons or start watches that had stopped running was the result of supernatural psychic abilities that even he himself did not fully understand. Randi was able to demonstrate conclusively that such claims were highly unlikely. Using common conjurer's tricks Randi duplicated each of Geller's feats, without recourse to any claims of psychic power. As an example, the case of starting a stopped watch can be performed by just about anyone. Provided the watch has not been damaged (but has merely stopped running), a simple vigorous shake will get the hands moving in almost all cases. When this action is surreptitiously performed, with preselected watches, in a context of expectancy on the part of observers, and with enough psychic terminology and flash--all conditions that Geller used masterfully, and which Randi exposed--the result does indeed seem impressive.

Geller's theatrical tricks weren't the true source of Randi's complaints. Rather, the claim by scientists that Geller had demonstrated psychic abilities under controlled conditions is what set Randi to his task. Physicists Russell Targ and Harold Puthoff tested Geller in their laboratory in the early 1970s, and published their results in the prestigious journal *Nature*. They enthusiastically concluded that Geller had shown psychic ability under a number of conditions and across repeated tests. What they failed to mention, however, were details of the experimental procedures or, as Randi discovered, the presence of Geller's chief henchman, one Shippi Strang. In most instances during the "controlled" laboratory tests, Strang either had access to the testing materials ahead of time (and sometimes during the testing) or could visibly signal Geller as the tests were carried out. A close analysis of the procedures, equipment, and outcomes revealed that Geller was much more successful in demonstrating polished stagecraft than in demonstrating psychic abilities.

Bem, D. J., & Honorton, C. (1994). Does psi exist? Replicable evidence for an anomalous process of information transfer. *Psychological Bulletin, 115*, 4-18.
Gordon, H. (1987). *Extrasensory deception: ESP, psychics, Shirley MacLaine, ghosts, UFOs...*New York: Prometheus Books.
Hyman, R. (1994). Anomaly or artifact? Comments on Bem and Honorton. *Psychological Bulletin, 115*, 19-24.
Kurtz, P. (Ed.) (1985). *A skeptic's handbook of parapsychology.* New York: Prometheus Books.
Randi, J. (1982). *Flim-flam! Psychics, ESP, unicorns, and other delusions.* New York: Prometheus Books.
Randi, J. (1975). *The truth about Uri Geller.* New York: Prometheus Books.
Rhine, J. B. (1937). *New frontiers of the mind.* New York: Farrar and Rinehart.

Setting Thresholds

The text presents the idea of an absolute threshold for sensations and gives examples of the amount of stimulation needed to trigger the various senses. The methods for establishing such thresholds have a long history to them, dating to the work of the original German psychophysicists.

❖ *Method of limits.* The presentation of a stimulus that is clearly noticeable is followed by the presentation of increasingly weaker stimuli until observers are unable to detect the stimulus. For example, using the method of limits to establish an auditory threshold might involve presenting a clearly detectable tone, followed by tones of decreasing amplitude until the participant reports hearing no tone at all. This method then involves alternating trials of "no detection" with trials presenting increasingly stronger stimuli. In our example, after establishing the lowest level of detection, tones of increasing amplitude would be presented. These *descending* and *ascending series* of trials are typically repeated several times with one observer.

❖ *Method of adjustment.* Observers control the intensity of stimulus until it is just barely noticeable. For example, the channel surfer who commandeers the remote control might turn the volume on the television set down until it is just barely audible. The distinguishing feature of this method is the self-adjustment by the perceiver.

❖ *Method of constant stimuli.* This technique involves presenting a preselected set of stimuli in a random order to perceivers. The stimuli are chosen so that at least one is clearly below the sensory threshold (established previously, perhaps, by the method of adjustment) and at least one is clearly above the sensory threshold. In a hearing test, for example, a set of tones of varying amplitudes might be presented to a perceiver at random, and the perceiver's ability to discriminate among them would be measured.

Fechner, G. T. (1860). *The elements of psychophysics*. Leipzig: Breitkopf & Harterl.

Matlin, M. W., & Foley, H. J. (1992). *Sensation and perception* (3rd ed.). Boston: Allyn and Bacon.

Noses, Aisle 12

Lewis and his colleagues at the California Institute of Technology are at work developing an artificial nose, research motivated partly by the challenge and partly by practicality. The challenge is that smell remains the least studied and least understood of the senses. Although relatively primitive (compared to the sophisticated intricacies of vision), scientists still don't have a complete understanding of the rules governing how smell works. To that end, Lewis and his colleagues have created a variety of artificial noses, ranging from tiny "noselets" to bookcase-size monstrosities. Each is dedicated to the task of detecting various scents, odors, and stinks in the environment.

That's where the practicality comes in. Smell is big business, from truffle-sniffing pigs to deodorant testers to perfume evaluators to rotten food detectors. Currently this work is done by humans (well, not the truffle-finding) whose noses tire quickly and who aren't equally sensitive to all odors. A reliable artificial nose would allow industry to perform a variety of important tasks cheaply and efficiently. What's more, Lewis envisions a day when small artificial noses will detect carbon monoxide in your home, rotting foods in your refrigerator, leaking fluids in your car, or peptic upset from your breath. In fact, John Glenn's recent NASA mission included a prototype of Lewis' artificial nose to sniff space air for potential health hazards.

Here's how it works. Chemists have known for some time that industrial plastics swell when they absorb a chemical odor. This is not earth-shaking; all polymers do that. However, specialized plastics that conduct electricity could be used to create a unique pattern of electrical activity for each chemical scent. By combining different plastics that generate different electrical signals, a fairly accurate "scentprint" would result for each odor. However, there are a finite number of electricity-generating plastics, so Lewis and his team have switched instead to cheap industrial plastics combined with soot particles to generate electric current. When hundreds or thousands of these units are combined in a single detector, the result is a cheap, mass produced, rugged, yet highly sensitive nose.

Some of these developments are years away, but several research and industry teams have joined the search for an artificial nose. Unfortunately, the answer may not be as plain as the…well, you know.

McFarling, U. L. (1999, February 20). Chemist wants to place noses in your car, house. *Austin American-Statesman*, A21, A24.

demonstrations

Sensory Adaptation

According to the text, our senses automatically adjust to the level of stimulation they are receiving so that they can be as sensitive as possible without getting overloaded. As a result, our senses become less sensitive when the overall level of stimulation is high, but more sensitive when the overall level of stimulation is low. This explains, for example, why the tick of a watch is more annoying in a quiet room than on a busy street. This phenomenon of sensory adaptation can be readily illustrated in class with a variety of senses, including touch, taste, and vision. Depending on your class size (e.g., if you have fewer than 30 or 35 students), you could allow all students to participate in the first two exercises or for larger classes you might prefer to select a subset of volunteers.

Touch. Fred Whitford suggests a simple exercise for demonstrating sensory adaptation with touch. Bring to class a number of samples of very coarse sandpaper and distribute them to students. After rubbing their index fingers gently over the paper a few times, they should rate its coarseness on a scale from 1 (*very soft*) to 7 (*very course*). After a minute or two, have them rub the same finger over the paper and again rate its coarseness. Their senses should have adapted to the coarseness and thus the ratings for the second time should be lower.

Taste. A different exercise (suggested by John Fisher) can be used to demonstrate sensory adaptation with taste. You'll need to bring to class (a) a pitcher containing a strong solution of water and sugar, (b) a pitcher containing fresh water, and (c) several Dixie cups. Distribute two Dixie cups to each student and fill one with sugar water and one with fresh water. Instruct students to take a sip of the sugar water and to swish it around in their mouths for several seconds without swallowing it; gradually it should taste less sweet. After swallowing it (or spitting it back into the cup), students should then taste from the cup containing fresh water. Students will be shocked at how incredibly salty the water tastes and will wonder if you didn't spike it with salt when they weren't looking! Explain that when the overstimulated taste buds responsible for sweetness became temporarily less sensitive, the taste buds responsible for salt became more prominent as a result.

Vision. A final exercise (reprinted from Bill Hill) requires a little more effort but powerfully illustrates sensory adaptation in vision. Davis and Grover (1987) first described this activity, a modified version of a procedure developed by Hochberg et al. (1951), that uses a *Ganzfeld* (a homogenous visual field) to demonstrate that the visual system requires varied stimulation to prevent sensory receptor adaptation. To conduct this demonstration you will need to make a Ganzfeld and have a red light source, such as that on a stereo or coffee maker. The Ganzfeld is constructed using a ping pong ball. Cut the ping pong ball in half and discard the side with the writing on it. Then attach cotton around the rim of the remaining half in order to protect the student's eye. Instruct a student volunteer to place the Ganzfeld on one eye, touch the Ganzfeld on the red light, close their other eye, and continue to stare at the red light, reporting any experience that occurs. After a minute or so, although the light is still on, the student will state that you have turned the red light off. Explain to your students that this effect is the result of receptor adaptation because of the Ganzfeld.

Davis, S. F., & Grover, C. A. (1987). And then the lights went out: Constructing a simple Ganzfeld. In V. P. Makosky, L. G. Whittemore, & A. M. Rogers (Eds.), *Activities handbook for the teaching of psychology: Vol. 2* (pp. 49-50). Washington, DC: American Psychological Association.

Fisher, J. (1979). *Body Magic*. Briarcliff Manor, NY: Stein and Day.

Hill, W. G. (1995). Instructor's resource manual for *Psychology* by S. F. Davis and J. J. Palladino. Englewood Cliffs, NJ: Prentice Hall.

Hochberg, J. E., Triebel, W., & Seaman, G. (1951). Color adaptation under conditions of homogeneous visual stimulation (Ganzfeld). *Journal of Experimental Psychology, 41*, 153-159.

Whitford, F. W. (1995). Instructor's resource manual for *Psychology: An Introduction* by C. G. Morris (8th ed.). Englewood Cliffs, NJ: Prentice Hall.

Sound Localization

Just as binocular cues help us to perceive depth in a three-dimensional world, binaural cues (i.e., information that reaches both ears) help us to locate sounds in the environment. When sounds come from anywhere other than straight ahead or straight behind us, the ear nearer to the sound source will perceive the noise slightly sooner and as slightly louder than will the opposite ear. Although the discrepancy in time and relative loudness is extremely small, the brain is able to use this information to accurately locate the sound. John Fisher suggests an amusing demonstration to illustrate the principle of binaural hearing. Ask a volunteer to sit blindfolded in a chair in the center of the room. The volunteer should, while keeping his or her head perfectly still, judge the location of any sounds you make by pointing in the correct direction. Using a pair of coins rubbed together or a noise-making clicker from a board game, create sounds from a variety of positions about the room. Although volunteers should have no trouble locating noises made off to their right or left, they will invariably be way off the mark when the sound comes from the center (e.g., from between their knees, under their chin, or between their eyes).

Fisher, J. (1979). *Body Magic.* Briarcliff Manor, NY: Stein and Day.

The Role of Smell in Determining Flavor

The rich flavor that we sense from our favorite (and not-so-favorite) foods is derived from a combination of taste and smell. According to the text, without smell we can sense the basic tastes (e.g., bitterness, saltiness, sourness, sweetness) but do not experience flavor and thus we cannot identify many popular foods. You can easily replicate the Mozel et al. (1969) study in your classroom by doing the following. Ask for a volunteer (ideally one with no food allergies) who isn't squeamish about tasting a variety of foods while blindfolded (and with a plugged nose). Implore your class to be quiet (you can show them cue cards with the correct answer during each guess), and then present the subject with a variety of foods that he or she should try to correctly identify without the sense of smell. For best results, food should be cut into small, uniform bite-size pieces and placed on toothpicks (you might need to help guide the food into subjects' hands). Without smell, subjects will have a surprisingly hard time identifying (or distinguishing between) foods with similar textures such as carrots, onions, pears, apples, squash, and potatoes.

Adapted from Fantino, B. F. (1981). Taste preferences: Influence of smell and sight. In L. T. Benjamin & K. D. Lowman (Eds.), *Activities handbook for the teaching of psychology* (pp. 29-30). Washington, DC: American Psychological Association.

The Effect of Visual Cues on Taste

Our sense of taste depends not only on olfactory cues but also on visual cues. To illustrate this fact, have a volunteer wait in the hall while you prepare (in full view of your class) a "typical American meal." Start by placing a bagel (or piece of bread) on a plate and by pouring a glass of orange juice and a glass of milk. Prepare the meal by using food coloring to distort its appearance. For example, you might make the milk a vibrant green, the orange juice look like motor oil (by mixing red, green, blue, and yellow), and the bread look moldy (with blue or green spots). Instruct your class to be a quiet audience and not to giggle or to give anything away. Bring the volunteer, blindfolded, back into the class and ask him or her to comment on the meal (e.g., "Does it taste good?" "Do you know what it is?") while eating it. The volunteer will no doubt correctly identify the foods and confirm that they taste good. After a few minutes, remove the blindfold and observe the volunteer's reaction. Asking the volunteer to continue eating will likely result in an emphatic, "No Thanks!" This should spark a lively discussion of the role of vision in taste and students are usually happy to share their personal experiences.

Adapted from Fantino, B. F. (1981). Taste preferences: Influence of smell and sight. In L. T. Benjamin & K. D. Lowman (Eds.), *Activities handbook for the teaching of psychology* (pp. 29-30). Washington, DC: American Psychological Association.

Saliva and Taste

Students may be surprised to learn that food must be dissolved in water in order to be tasted. That is, some kind of liquid must be available to bind solid food to the appropriate taste receptor (e.g., sweet, sour, bitter, or salty). John Fisher suggests a simple exercise that demonstrates the crucial role of saliva in taste. First, have students wipe their tongue dry (the drier, the better) with the back of their hand. Then, walk around the room with a bowl of sugar and have students take a small pinch and place it on the tip of their tongue. They should not be able to taste anything until their mouth gradually moistens--with renewed saliva, the familiar sweet taste should come flooding back.

Fisher, J. (1979). *Body Magic.* Briarcliff Manor, NY: Stein and Day.

Odor Identification Test

The text notes that although people can discriminate among a large number of odors, they have a surprisingly difficult time identifying the source of even the most familiar odors. You can illustrate this fact to your students (many of whom will be skeptical) by conducting a large-scale "smell test." First, gather several (approximately 8-15) dark or opaque containers with lids (empty black film canisters are ideal). Assign a different number to each canister (be sure to make a coding sheet with the correct sources) and place cotton balls in the bottom of each to absorb the smell. Good substances to test include baby powder, coffee, peanut butter, pencil shavings, ammonia, lemon extract, peppermint extract, vinegar, chocolate, coconut, Crayola crayons, Play-doh, soap, bubble gum, and spices (e.g., cloves, pepper, garlic, cinnamon). Instruct the students to lift the lid but to keep their eyes closed when smelling the canisters. Then, pass the canisters around the room and have students mark their responses on a sheet of paper. Your confounded students will have a sense of familiarity ("Oh, I definitely know this one...what is it?") more often than they will have an exact identification. [Note that having students match the smells with a list of possible sources would greatly increase their chances of being successful.] If you have time, tally the number of correct guesses by a show of hands. Do good or poor smellers have any hypotheses about the cause of their abilities (or lack thereof)? Do the results replicate the finding that women generally have better senses of smell than do men?

The Body's Sensitivity to Touch

Chapter 3 notes that although the skin senses in general are remarkably sensitive, various parts of the body differ greatly in their sensitivity to pressure. This is because larger portions of the cerebral cortex are devoted to body areas that, for adaptive reasons, show greater sensitivity. For example, crucial human features such as the mouth, face, and fingers are much more sensitive than are important, but less central, features such as the legs, feet, and back. Both John Fisher and James Motiff have suggested exercises to illustrate this phenomenon. For this demonstration, divide students into pairs and have them take turns experiencing the vast differences in touch sensitivity on different parts of their body.

In Motiff's version, one student in the pair should keep his or her eyes closed while the other person randomly presses from one to four fingers lightly on that person's back, neck, leg, shoulder, forearm, face, and hand. The person being touched should attempt to guess in each case the number of fingers being applied. Students will have a much easier time correctly identifying the number of fingers applied to especially sensitive areas (such as the face and hand) compared to the other, less sensitive areas, which will feel indistinguishably like one point of pressure (i.e., one finger).

In Fisher's version, distribute a single hairpin to each pair of students. One student should pry the hairpin apart (so that its prongs are roughly an inch apart) and press the hairpin against the back of their partner's forearm. The person being touched will report feeling only a single point of pressure. Next, the student should bend the prongs inward so that they are only about 1/16 inch apart and place it this time on their partner's index finger tip. This time (despite the smaller difference between the prongs), the partner will have no trouble differentiating the two points, as the finger tip is much more sensitive than the forearm.

For an eerier demonstration, Fisher suggests dragging the hairpin (with prongs one inch apart) slowly from the crease of the elbow down to the finger tips. Although the spacing between the prongs remains constant, the person being touched will report that distance between the prongs increases the closer the hairpin gets to the fingertips.

    Fisher, J. (1979). *Body Magic*. Briarcliff Manor, NY: Stein and Day.
    Motiff, J. P. (1987). Physiological psychology: The sensory homunculus. In V. P. Makosky, L. G. Whittemore, & A. M. Rogers (Eds.), *Activities handbook for the teaching of psychology: Vol. 2* (pp. 49-50). Washington, DC: American Psychological Association.

Expectancy and Perception

Chapter 3 notes that our expectations (i.e., preconceptions about what we are supposed to perceive) can influence perception. There are several simple, effective exercises to demonstrate this point in class.

John Fisher suggests conducting a "spelling bee in reverse." Ask students to pronounce a word out loud after you write in on the board. Following MAC DONALD...MAC HENRY...MAC MAHON... with MAC HINERY will likely generate a chorus of Scottish-sounding surnames (e.g., MacHinery) rather than the real pronunciation of *machinery*.

For a similar exercise, Martin Bolt suggests adopting an old children's riddle. Ask students to shout out answer to the following questions: "What do these letters spell?" (Write FOLK on the board) "What do these letters spell?" (CROAK) "And these?" (SOAK). Then quickly ask, "What do you call the white of an egg?" Students will scream out "yolk" before they realize they've been had. (You can then inform them of the little known fact that the white of an egg is called the albumin.)

J. R. Corey suggests an exercise that demonstrates the effect of expectancy on anagram solution. This exercise requires that you construct two different lists of anagrams and randomly distribute one to each student. Half of the students should receive anagrams that can be solved to form animals: LULB (bull), CALEM (camel), NUKKS (skunk), SEUMO (mouse), BAZER (zebra), and EAP (ape). The other half should receive anagrams that can be solved to form vegetables: NORC (corn), NOONI (onion), MATOOT (tomato), PREPPE (pepper), TEBE (beet), and EAP (pea). Note that the last anagram, EAP, can be solved in two ways (ape or pea) and thus provides the expectancy test. If students' expectancies are influential, then those who received the animal list should be more likely to solve EAP as ape, whereas those who received the vegetable list should be more likely to solve EAP as pea. According to Corey, the expectancy effect occurs for approximately 80-90% of the students.

    Bolt, M. (1992). Instructor's resources for use with D. G. Myer's, *Psychology* (3rd ed.). New York: Worth.
    Corey, J. R. (1990). Psychological set and the solution of anagrams. In V. P. Makosky, C. C. Sileo, L. G. Whittemore, C. P. Landry, & M. L. Skutley (Eds.), *Activities handbook for the teaching of psychology.* Vol. 3 (pp. 90-91). Washington, DC: American Psychological Association.
    Fisher, J. (1979). *Body Magic*. Briarcliff Manor, NY: Stein and Day.

Using Escher to Illustrate Perceptual Principles

Debra Stein (1995) suggests a group exercise that both stimulates critical thinking and increases student interest in the discussion of perceptual processes. Divide your students into groups of 5 and give each group copies of two different M. C. Escher prints (an example of Escher's work is illustrated in Chapter 3). You might want to purchase a book or calendar so that you'll have a enough prints to go around. Instruct your groups to choose a recorder and a spokesperson, and then give them 20-30 minutes to identify any and all examples of the following perceptual principles from Chapter 3: (a) figure-ground, (b) closure, (c) similarity, (d) continuity, (e) proximity, (f) monocular cues, (g) binocular disparity, (h) superposition, (i) elevation, (j) aerial perspective, (k) linear perspective, (l) texture gradient, (m) convergence, and (n) shadowing. When groups are finished, the spokesperson from each group should briefly present the group's finding to the class by outlining examples on a transparency projection of the print (Note: you'll need to make these out beforehand). Stein reports several positive benefits of this exercise, including: an increased amount of focused discussion about perceptual processes (due to the group discussions as well as the presentations), an increase in students' understanding of perceptual processes as revealed in test scores, and a tendency for greater application of the material (e.g., her students brought other examples from advertisements and art to class; others created illusions on their own).

Adapted from Stein, D. K. (1995). The use of M. C. Escher and N. E. Thing Enterprises prints to illustrate perceptual principles. Paper presented at the 17th National Institute on the Teaching of Psychology, St. Petersburg Beach.

Goggles That Boggle

Students typically take visual sensation and perception for granted. True, in everyday life, they appear to be one seamless action, from sensory world to visual receptors to the brain. You can illustrate the difference between sensation and perception by disrupting those processes, and along the way highlight the basic mechanisms of the visual system.

Jim Matiya can provide you with prism goggles that invert the visual field or displace it at a specified angle. He can be emailed at PSYCHSIGJM@AOL.COM for more information. Buy a pair of inverted vision goggles and ask volunteers to wear them while performing simple tasks, such as catching a ball, picking up an object from a table, or shaking hands with someone. After the initial cries of "Waugh!" "Omigod!" and "Yip!" students should find that they adapt rather quickly to this flipping of the visual world, and are able to compensate for the effects of the goggles. Use their experiences to frame a discussion of visual sensation and perception.

student assignments

Field Demonstrations

As a simple but involving assignment, ask students to go out into the real world and experience instances of perceptual phenomenon that are too difficult to demonstrate in class. Students could, for example, choose 2 demonstrations from among the following and write a short paper describing their experiences and relating them to theory and research presented in the text.

Dark Adaptation. For this demonstration, students should take about 15 index cards and a flashlight that is opaque on all sides (so that light shines only through the front) into a very dark room. After placing all 15 cards over the beam of light, students should slowly remove the cards one at a time until they can barely detect the light. Have them count the number of cards that remain over the light. After a few minutes, the light should begin to look brighter. When this is the case, have students try to add a card and see if they can still see the light. They should repeat this process of gradually adding cards over a 15-minute period. Consistent with dark adaptation, students should be able to detect an increasingly dim light the longer they spend in the dark.

Night Vision and the Fovea. Because rods rather than cones are active in dim light, it is easier to see objects that fall in areas rich with rods (i.e., outside the fovea) than in areas packed with cones (i.e., the fovea). To experience this, students should choose a relatively clear night (with few surrounding bright lights) to observe stars. Specifically, they should locate a relatively dim star so that it is slightly to the right or left of the focal point of their gaze. When students suddenly shift their gaze to look directly at the star, however, it should disappear.

The Autokinetic Illusion. Students can experience the autokinetic illusion (i.e., the apparent motion created by a single stationary object) for themselves by doing the following. Students should first create a very small point of light, either by using a thin, sharp flashlight or by covering a larger flashlight with a piece of cardboard containing a small hole. They should then go into a very dark room and shine the light on the wall about 10 feet in front of them. After a few moments, the light should appear to drift and move around slightly. In a dark room, there are no cues to tell you that the light is stationary. Therefore, the involuntary eye movements that typically go unnoticed in a changing environment cause the stationary object to appear to move.

Temperature Adaptation. Students can easily explore temperature adaptation by locating 3 medium size bowls and filling them with (a) very hot (but not painfully so) tap water, (b) very cold tap water, and (c) a mixture of the very hot and very cold water. Students should arrange them so that their right hand is in front of the cold water, their left hand is in front of the hot water, and the lukewarm water is in the middle. Students should them submerse their hands into the water (right into cold, left into hot) for about 3 minutes. After 3 minutes, they should quickly transfer both hands to the lukewarm (middle) bowl, and they will undoubtedly experience adaptation "first-hand."

Exercises adapted from Matlin, M. W., & Foley, H. J. (1992). *Sensation and perception* (3rd ed.). Needham Heights, MA: Allyn and Bacon.

In Search of Perceptual Illusions

Although the text provides several examples of the most common perceptual illusions, students can often gain a better understanding of them by actively finding their own examples. Possible ways to document examples include taking photos, cutting clippings out of magazines or newspapers, or by describing the illusion in detail if it is not possible to obtain a sample (e.g., if it was seen in a movie). Real world examples of afterimages, stroboscopic motion, perceptual contrast, Gestalt principles, and monocular cues abound, and students will likely enjoy their quest for the ultimate illusion. An added benefit is that students can share their examples with the rest of the class, who can try to identify the illusion portrayed. This way, all students will have had access to numerous examples outside of the text.

As an alternative assignment, ask students to create or develop their own illusion (i.e., by drawing or painting a two-dimensional picture or by assembling a three-dimensional object). Although the illusion should be unique, it should of course be based on principles from one of the major illusions discussed in the text. As an example, students could create their own reversible figure, illustrate one or more monocular cues (e.g., linear perspective, shadowing) in a drawing or painting, or create new examples of Gestalt principles of perceptual organization such as closure or proximity.

Explaining the Moon Illusion

All of us have succumbed to the moon illusion, that is, the feeling that the moon at the horizon is larger than the moon at its zenith (or highest point). According to Margaret Matlin and Hugh Foley, this paradox has been the source of speculation by scientists and philosophers for thousands of years. Although early research has ruled out physical explanations (e.g., light refraction, angle of head or eye elevation), the precise psychological mechanism responsible is still in debate, and at least 8 competing explanations have been offered in the last 20 years. Ask your students to explore these explanations in more detail and to write a 2 to 4-page paper summarizing two or three different perspectives on this illusion. Ask them to identify which of the theories they believe provides the best explanation and why.

Matlin, M. W., & Foley, H. J. (1992). *Sensation and perception* (3rd ed.). Needham Heights, MA: Allyn and Bacon.

Keeping a Psychology Journal

In order to increase the personal relevance of material covered in class, you may require students to keep an on-going psychology journal for the duration of the course. The primary purpose of the journal is to encourage students to connect the facts, concepts, and principles that they acquire from the course to their own personal experiences. The journal adds a personal dimension to the course and provides an opportunity to apply course concepts to daily experiences (Hettich, 1990). The following writing prompts are a useful starting point.

1. Have you ever had a personal experience that could be described as extra-sensory perception (ESP) such as déjà vu, premonitions, prophetic dreams, telepathy, etc.? What is your opinion of ESP: is it real or just wishful thinking? Why do you think you dream?

Hettich, P. (1976). The journal: An autobiographical approach to learning. *Teaching of Psychology, 3*(2), 60-63.
Hettich, P. (1980). The journal revisited. *Teaching of Psychology, 7*(2), 105-106.
Hettich, P. (1990). Journal writing: Old fare or nouvelle cuisine? *Teaching of Psychology, 17*(1), 36-63.

video

Colorful Notions (50 min, IM). Discusses how people see in color and possible theories concerning the evolution of color vision. Also includes illustrations of visual effects such as negative afterimages.

Controlling Pain (23 min, FHS). Chemical agents, massage, and electrical stimulation are discussed as methods for controlling pain. The complex process of pain perception, from skin to brain, is presented as well.

Dealing With Pain (19 min, FHS). Debilitating, constant pain is the focus of this video. Techniques for dealing with serious chronic pain are discussed.

Discovering Psychology, Part 7: Sensation and Perception (1990, 30 min, ANN/CPB). Provides an overview of how information is processed from sensory data to meaningful impressions, including factors that guide and/or bias perception.

Doors of Perception (1996, 58 min, IM). The relationship between the inner world of consciousness and the outer world of reality is the basis for this artistic look at perception.

The Enchanted Loom: Processing Sensory Information (26 min, FHS). Examines the range of sensory experience and how the brain sorts, classifies, and interprets sensory data.

The Mind: Pain and Healing (60 min, PBS). This segment of the 9-part series examines the role of biological and psychological mechanisms in controlling pain and contributing to the healing process.

Mystery of the Senses (5 parts, 1995, 60 min each, IM). Each tape in this series highlights one of the senses, focusing on issues such as how neural pathways transmit visual information or how perfume fragrances are developed.

Sensation and Perception (1990, 30 min, IM). Describes how the brain constructs reality from sensory information, including the role of expectations and emotion. Also addresses biological and psychological factors in the perception and inhibition of pain.

Sight (23 min, FHS). The complex interaction between eye and brain, ultimately producing sight, is explored. Along the way visual problems and research on artificial vision are also discussed.

The Study of Attention (42 min, FHS). Selective attention, divided attention, and automaticity are considered in this video. Examples of visual search and the Stroop effect are also shown.

Taste and Smell (1994, 25 min, IM). The "forgotten senses" are given center stage in this look at allergies, taste buds, food perceptions, and the basics of olfaction and gustation.

Visual Reality (1994, 25 min, IM). The structure and functions of the eye are explored. The entire visual process, from color vision through brain processing, is also given a detailed look.

Visual Space Perception via Motion (1996, 20 min, IM). This presentation looks at how humans perceive motion. Drawing on binocular and monocular cues, depth perception, motion paradox, and global and local optic flows, it presents a broad overview of this topic.

multimedia

Live! Psych

Module	Title	Book Page #
3.1	A Tour Through the Eye	p. 103

Screen 1 introduces how the visual system works. Light enters the cornea. Screen 2 identifies and describes the iris and the pupil. Screen 3 identifies and describes the role of the lens. Screen 4 identifies and describes the role of the retina and the optic nerve. An animation in Screen 5 shows how the retina is made up of different layers of cells: photoreceptors, ganglion cells, and bipolar neurons. Screen 6 identifies and describes the two kinds of receptor cells for vision: rods and cones. Import this screen to show how rods and cones are arranged differently around the fovea. Screen 7 identifies and describes the role of the optic nerve. Screen 8 identifies and describes the role of the optic disc. Import this screen to show how the absence of receptor cells in this part of the retina produces a "blind spot" in the visual field.

3.2	The Mechanics of Sound	p. 110

Screen 1 explains the mechanics of sound. Physically, sound is vibration. First, something has to move. To demonstrate this principle, the student clicks on the tuning fork to set into the motion the mechanics of sound. The vibrating tuning fork sends molecules of air into a wavelike motion. Air molecules alternate between being compressed or rarefied.

3.3	Virtual Tour of the Human Ear	p. 112

In this concept, students take a self-guided tour of the human ear. In Screen 1, the student scrolls over each label to learn more about the structures of the ear. Screens 2 and 3 involve a simulation of how the auditory system converts sound waves into neural impulses.

3.4	Introduction to Gestalt Psychology	p. 129

Screen 1 shows how we automatically focus on some objects in the perceptual field to the exclusion of others. Screen 2 introduces Gestalt psychology, a theory about how we recognize patterns and separate them from other stimuli coming into our senses. Import Screen 3 to show a gestalt. Ask students if they are able to identify the pattern.

	Figure-Ground Relationship	p. 129

Screen 1 begins by introducing the figure-ground relationship. The student clicks on thumbnail pictures to learn about more examples of figure-ground relationship. Screen 2 explains that the relationship between figure and ground is not always clear-cut. Import this screen for interaction involving reversible figures. Ask students if they can see two possible figures. Discuss what factors influence your perception of figure-ground relationship.

	Gestalt Principles of Grouping	p. 129

Import this concept to explain that certain inherent features of stimuli lead people to group them together, more or less automatically, into coherent objects or sounds. Screen 1 introduces Gestalt principles of grouping. Screen 2 identifies and defines the law of proximity. The student interacts with the screen, clicking the move button to move the lines. Screen 3 identifies and defines the law of similarity. The student interacts with the screen, clicking the adjust button to adjust the dashes and dots. Screen 4 identifies and defines the law of continuity. The student interacts with the screen, clicking the modify button to modify the image. Screen 5 identifies and defines the law of closure. The student interacts with the screen, clicking the adjust button to adjust the illustration.

3.5	Depth Perception	p. 132

Screen 1 defines depth perception. Screen 2 shows a colorful map of the United States. This screen explains that the student will take a 3-D cross-country road trip to find out how depth perception works.

Binocular Cues — p. 132
Screen 1 distinguishes between binocular and monocular cues. One binocular cue, retinal disparity, is defined. Import Screen 2 to provide an example of retinal disparity. The student views the map on the screen, one eye at a time, to demonstrate retinal disparity. Screen 3 defines convergence, another binocular cue. Import this screen to view a simulation of convergence by comparing angles for a bee flying nearby and further away.

Monocular Cues — p. 132
Screen 1 defines monocular cues. Screen 2 shows that the starting point on the road trip is the Golden Gate bridge and identifies the monocular cue of linear perspective. In Albuquerque, New Mexico, Screen 3 identifies the monocular cue of relative elevation showing hot air balloons rising in the sky. In Texas, Screen 4 identifies the monocular cue of relative sizes of the oil rigs. Screen 5 identifies the monocular cue of relative brightness at Mount Rushmore in South Dakota. Screen 6 identifies the monocular cue of texture gradients in the cornfields of Iowa. Screen 7 identifies the monocular cue of motion parallax while comparing horses close by and horses further away on a horse ranch in Kentucky. Screen 8 identifies the monocular cue of interposition as the Washington monument overlaps the U.S. Capital. Screen 9 identifies atmospheric perspective while observing the Statue of Liberty monument overlooking the New York harbor.

3.6 Introduction to Illusions — p. 135
Screen 1 defines perceptual illusions, giving the example of a mirage on asphalt. Screen 2 explains that perceptual illusions rely on our own misinterpretation of a situation. Illusions are useful to psychologists because by understanding how we are tricked into perceiving something that is not really there, they can learn more about how our perceptual processes normally operate.

Ames Room — p. 135
Screen 1 shows two people standing in the Ames room, a specially designed room with misleading depth cues, causing two people of equal size to appear very different. Screen 2 explains the reason for this misperception—the construction of the room.

Ponzo Illusion — p. 135
Screen 1 shows the Ponzo illusion which occurs when there are two horizontal lines inside two slanted lines in an inverted V-shape. Even though it appears that the two red lines are different in length, they are actually equal in length. The student interacts in this exercise by using a ruler to measure the horizontal lines. Import Screen 2 to show the Ponzo illusion in real life—railroad tracks. Screen 3 shows a variation on the Ponzo illusion. Again, the student interacts in this exercise by using a ruler to measure the length of each cat.

Penrose Stairway — p. 135
This screen is a simulation of the Penrose stairway. The Penrose stairway is an impossible figure. Import this screen to show that false depth cues create the illusion of a three-dimensional stairway, in the shape of a square.

Web Investigations

Investigating Olfaction: The Nose Knows

Everyone has a funny (or even embarrassing) story to tell about olfaction. But consider what life would be like without a sense of smell. Some people face this challenge daily because they have lost their sense of smell. This condition is called *anosmia*. Anosmia can be the result of a genetic condition, or it may result from a strong blow to the head. In either instance, the olfactory pathway is disrupted and the sense of smell is diminished or even eliminated.

The *Web Investigations* for this chapter begin with an examination of olfactory anatomy. After students understand the anatomy of smell, they can then examine how smell enhances taste and may change moods. Your students can also critically examine claims that smell can enhance sexual desire or be used in a therapeutic intervention.

Making Connections

The Nature of Sensation

Q Neurons all "speak" the same electrochemical language. How does our brain distinguish between sights, sounds, smells, and other sensations? recognize variations in the same sensory mode?

A The brain is able to distinguish between sights, sounds, smells, and other sensations because receptor cells are specialized to respond to only one form of energy, such as light waves (vision) or sound waves (hearing). Because different stimuli affect how many neurons fire, which neurons are activated or inhibited, and the rate at which they fire, the brain receives detailed information about the kind of stimuli the senses have received.

Q What is sensory adaptation, and why is it important?

A Sensory adaptation refers to the ability of our sense to adjust to the average level of stimulation in a given setting. For example, when confronted with a great deal of stimulation, our senses tune much of it out. Sensory adaptation allows our senses to remain attuned to environmental conditions without becoming overloaded.

Q What is the evidence for and against subliminal perception?

A A number of studies indicate that, in controlled laboratory settings, people can process and respond to information they are not consciously aware of. A review of over 50 studies found that subliminal presentations of comforting phrases tend to reduce negative feelings and promote recall of positive memories. However, in another series of studies, about half of a group of volunteers who used self-improvement tapes reported that they felt better about themselves, but objective tests detected no change. Moreover, volunteers who received a tape labeled "Improve Memory" reported improvement, even though they had actually received a self-esteem tape.

Vision

Q What stimuli do our eyes respond to?

A The receptor cells in the retina respond to different intensities of light and dark (rods) and to different wavelengths on the electromagnetic spectrum, or colors (cones).

Q How do specialized receptor cells (rods and cones) contribute to light adaptation?

A The sensitivity of rods and cones varies according to how much light is available. For the first 5 to 10 minutes after you go from a light to a dark place, the cones gradually become more sensitive to dim light. The rods continue to become more sensitive over the next 20 minutes. When you suddenly go from a dark to a light place, your rods and cones adapt to the increased stimulation in about 1 minute.

Q How are light waves encoded (translated into signals our brain recognizes as images)?

A Rods and cones are connected to bipolar cells. Interneurons link receptor cells to one another and bipolar cells to one another. Bipolar cells connect with ganglion cells, whose axons join to form the optic nerves. A single ganglion cell is connected to large numbers of receptor cells. It summarizes the information they collect and sends this coded message to the brain. The optic nerves send the information to different parts of the brain. In the cerebral cortex, are feature receptors, cells that are specialized to respond to particular visual signals, such as horizontal or vertical lines or movement. Information about different aspects of vision, such as movement or shape, goes to different but nearby areas of the visual cortex.

Q How do the trichromatic and opponent-process theories of color vision complement one another?

A Trichromatic theory proposes that the eye contains cones that are sensitive to red, to green, and to blue-violet. It explains how three primary colors can be combined to produce many different hues. It accounts for some types of colorblindness, but it cannot explain afterimages or why people with normal color vision never see colors such as reddish green or yellowish blue. Opponent process theory proposes that there are three pairs of color receptors: yellow-blue, red-green, and black-white. Each pair can relay information about one of the opposing colors at a time: the yellow-blue pair can process yellow or blue, but not yellow and blue together. This also explains colorblindness, as well as afterimages. Psychologists now believe that the two theories are both valid but operate at different stages in the visual process: there are three types of cones, as trichromatic theory proposed, sensitive to violet-blue, green, and yellow. Higher up the visual pathway, color appears to be coded as opponent-process theory suggests: different sets of neurons increase their rate of firing in response to brightness, to red or green, and to yellow or blue wavelengths.

Hearing

Q What properties of sound waves enable us to recognize pitch, loudness, and timbre?

A Pitch is related to frequency-the number of vibrations per second. Loudness is related to the amplitude, or height, of the sound wave. Timbre is related to the overtones produced by the sound wave, or the relationship between the frequency of the original sound wave and the frequency of the additional waves it produces.

Q Explain the two major theories of pitch discrimination.

A Place theory states a specific place on the basilar membrane is sensitive to each particular pitch. Frequency theory asserts that the frequency of vibrations of the basilar membrane as a whole is translated into an equivalent frequency of neural impulses. Because neural impulses are not as rapid as sound vibrations, this is modified by the volley principle, which states that several neurons firing together can send more rapid impulses than any single neurons firing alone.

Q What are the most common causes of hearing loss, and how can they be prevented?

A Major causes of hearing loss are injury, infections, smoking, and long-term exposure to loud noise. Hearing loss can be prevented by regular checkups to detect childhood infections, by use of earplugs or headphones, and by not smoking.

The Other Senses

Q What are the main differences between common odors and pheromones?

A Odors are detected by receptors in the olfactory epithelium. Signals are routed via the olfactory bulb to the temporal lobes and to the brain core. Pheromones are often odorless and are detected by receptors in the vomeronasal organ, which sends messages to a second olfactory bulb as well as to the hypothalamus and amygdala. Pheromones influence endocrine response and behaviors and provide information about another animal's status.

Q How do psychologists distinguish between taste and flavor?

A Flavor refers to the complex interaction between taste and smell. Taste refers to seven specific qualities of food that the taste buds can detect: sweet, sour, salty, bitter, astringent, umami, and fat.

Q What are the functions of our kinesthetic and vestibular senses (and why do we need both)?

A The kinesthetic senses provide information about the speed and direction of our movement in space. The vestibular senses provide information about our position in space (which way is up and which way is down). Both together allow us to be continually aware of our movements in relation to the physical world.

Q How would the gate control and biopsychosocial theories of pain explain alternative approaches to pain control?

A Gate control theory proposes a mechanistic view of pain. It would suggest that alternative approaches work stimulating the large nerve fibers to close the gate that controls transmission of pain signals to the brain. Biopsychosocial theory, which views the experience of pain as multifaceted, would propose that alternative approaches work by promoting the release of endorphins (biological), making people believe that their pain is eased (psychological), or by providing social support.

Perception

Q What is the difference between sensation and perception?

A Sensation is raw sensory data, such as signals for light intensity or sound frequency. Perception is the brain's interpretation of those raw data and their rearrangement into meaningful patterns.

Q Is perceptual constancy "prewired" into the human brain, or does it require experience?

A Perceptual constancy seems to require memory and experience. A person who has had no experience with depth perception will not recognize depth cues. Because we remember what something looks like (such as the shape of a person's face), we perceive that person's features even if other features have been superimposed into an image.

Q How does binocular (or stereoscopic) vision improve perception of distance and depth?

A Because our eyes are set in the front of our heads, the two visual fields overlap slightly. This allows us to perceive a three-dimensional image of the world and makes our judgments of depth and distance more accurate.

Q How accurate is our perception of movement?

A Our perception of real movement, especially movement of other human bodies, is highly accurate, because we perceive movement in terms of how an object's position changes against a background. We can be readily deceived, however, into perceiving apparent movement. Examples are the autokinetic illusion, created when, because of lack of a visible framework, we perceive motion in a single stationary object, and stroboscopic motion, in which we perceive movement in a rapid series of still images.

Q What factors contribute to individual differences in perception?

A Factors that contribute to individual differences in perception include motivation, values, expectations, cognitive style, culture, and personality.

Mind Matters

Sensory Transduction

If a tree fell in the woods and no one was around to hear it, would it still make a sound? Who knows? Who cares? But that's the principle behind transduction: the process by which the physical properties of a stimulus are converted into electrochemical signals that the nervous system can interpret. This section of the Prentice Hall Mind Matters CD-ROM presents transduction and odor, taste, and sound, provides a review of ear structure and function, and gives the basics of sensory thresholds and psychophysics. Along the way students can complete several activities and view movies illustrating the various principles. If you have access to a computer classroom, you might find the simulation of the psychophysics experiment (illustrating thresholds and the just noticeable difference) a worthwhile exercise.

Sensory Adaptation

If lots of trees fell repeatedly in the woods, and you were around to hear them, would the last one sound as loud as the first? Eh. Sensory adaptation is a principle affecting all sensory systems, and this part of the CD-ROM illustrates this with examples color and motion afterimages, and perceptions of intensity of a visual stimulus. This last exercise could be easily performed by your students in a computer lab, or completed at home and summarized in a brief report.

Sensory Coding

Sensory coding is discussed with reference to odor, sound, hearing, and sight. Students will receive a review of place/frequency theory and the structures and functions of the eye. The section on color mixing and color perception is useful for demonstrating the principles of color vision. In fact, you might want to use this material as you discuss these topics. A high-quality media projector should allow you to faithfully reproduce the colors resulting from additive and subtractive mixture.

Introduction to Perception

A review of Gestalt principles introduces the switch from sensation to perception. Students can perform a sound perception task using the audio file on the CD-ROM. Animations illustrating the Gestalt principles of proximity, closure, similarity, and continuity are presented. Ask you students to review these basic perceptual principles, then provide their own examples of each one.

Perceptual Constancy

Perceptual constancy, especially visual constancy, is the focus of this section. Students will be introduced to the principles of color, size, and shape constancy through a series of engaging animations. Students should begin to appreciate the constructed nature of perception. After completing this section, ask them to provide their own examples of each of these principles at work.

Perceptions as Decisions

Perceptions depend both on the stimulus and the response criteria of the perceiver. This is illustrated through a presentation of signal detection theory, response bias, depth perception, and the perception of motion. Lots of great animations accompany this material, such as demonstrations of the phi phenomenon, a simulation of signal detection, binocular and monocular depth cues, and a digital movie showing the perception of motion. These activities can be used profitably during class or during a lab period, setting the stage for class discussion of perceptual principles and leading into a presentation of perceptual illusions.

Perceptual Illusions

The usual suspects have been rounded up: the Ponzo Illusion, the ambiguous woman, the Hermann Grid, and those creepy face-vases. Students love perceptual illusions. Students love them even more when they understand the Gestalt principles underlying them and the constructive nature of perception, which are presented in this section. Include these illusions in your class presentation of this material.

Video Classics

Visual Displacement

SYNOPSIS: Experimenters in striped shirts illustrate a classic study from the days of Helmholtz. A research participant dons goggles that displace her visual field by 14%, then tries to locate an object in space. With a little practice she eventually learns to compensate for the displacement. However, upon removing the goggles, a brief aftereffect lingers. This clip is particularly helpful if you demonstrate this visual principle in class (see *Goggles That Boggle* in the Demonstrations and Activities section of this chapter).

Form a Hypothesis

Q How do you think the subject's responses will change now? How do you think the knowledge of the inaccuracy of her responses will influence her pointing?

A The woman will initially point to a space that her distorted visual perception leads her to believe is correct. Accuracy feedback will improve her ability to point, such that she compensates and points to the rods actual location.

Test Your Understanding

Q How is the person different from participating in this experiment?

A Although previously psychologists believed that distorting goggles change the visual system, Harris concludes that the subject experienced a change in her positional or kinesthetic sense.

Q How does perception develop in the newborn?

A The newborn develops perception through repeated reaching and touching such that the sense of touch is essential to shaping vision.

Q How does our perceptual set influence our interpretation of sensory input?

A A perceptual set influences perception by 'filtering' sensory input through a sieve of perceptual expectations. We perceive in ways consistent with these expectations.

Thinking Critically

Q What is size constancy?

A Size constancy refers to our understanding that something does not change in physical size even though the sensation of it may be altered by distance or orientation. That is, even though it is sensed as larger or smaller, we perceive it as being a constant size.

Q Is the capacity for size constancy present at birth, or do cultural and environmental influences play a role?

A Research indicates that size constancy is greatly influenced by culture and experience. The story of the Mbuti guide Kenge, described in the text, shows that experience with distance is necessary for the development of size constancy.

Web Links

1. http://psych.hanover.edu/Krantz/sen_tut.html

Sensation and Perception Tutorials. These demonstrations and exercises are helpful starting points for familiarizing your students with the basic principles of sensation and perception.

2. http://www.mentalhelp.net/

Sensation and perception websites, described and rated by Mental Help Net. Peruse these for lecture suggestions, images, and other enhancements for your course presentations.

3. http://www.accessexcellence.org/AE/AEC/CC/vision_background.html

How We See: The First Steps in Human Vision. This is a detailed text website complemented by helpful diagrams that explain the nature of human vision. Also, you can use the URL as a vision test in itself. See how quickly your students can decipher the CAPITALS, underscores, and runtogetherwords.

4. http://www.vision3d.com

Contains links to 3-D eye exercises, vision therapy, optical illusions, and those Magic Eye 3-D things that seem to keep hanging around. Also explains some disorders related to vision. Have your students review this site as a starting point for discussing the basic principles of visual perception.

transparencies

Series V

26. *Sensory Thresholds*
The details of how to spot a sensory threshold are revealed. A good introduction to basic concepts of psychophysics.

27. *The Electromagnetic Spectrum*
The range of energy, visible and nonvisible, is depicted.

28. *Cross Section of the Human Eye*
The anatomy of the human eye is shown.

29. *Components of a Sound Wave*
Hertz, vibration, amplitude...the gang's all here.

30. *How We Hear*
The process of hearing, from sound wave to cochlea to basilar membrane, is illustrated.

31. *Human Olfactory System*
The sense of smell and the processes that accompany it are depicted.

32. *Structure of a Taste Bud*
Sensory receptors for sour, salty, and bitter tastes are shown.

33. *Skin Receptors*
The receptors on the skin are represented.

34. *Ambiguous Figure-Ground Relationships*
The typical figure-ground relationship is clouded in these ambiguous figures.

35. *Gestalt Principles of Perceptual Organization*
Proximity, similarity, closure, and continuity are illustrated in this transparency.

36. *The Relationship Between Distance and the Size of the Retinal Image*
The closer an image is to the eye the larger the image cast on the retina.

37. *Monocular Cues for Depth: Interposition, Linear Perspective, and Elevation*
These elements of depth perception are shown in a pair of illustrations.

38. *Monocular Cues for Depth: Texture Gradient and Shadowing*
Texture gradient and shadow provide cues for depth perception.

39. *Monocular Cues for Depth: Motion Parallax*
The differences in relative movements of retinal images as we move are shown.

Text Figures

3-1.	*Determining a Sensory Threshold*	
3-2.	*A Cross Section of the Human Eye*	
3-3.	*Finding Your Blind Spot*	
3-4.	*The Retina*	
3-5.	*The Electromagnetic Spectrum*	
3-6.	*Rods and Cones*	
3-7.	*A Close-up of the Layers of the Retina*	
3-8.	*An Afterimage*	
3-9.	*The Neural Connections of the Visual System*	
3-10.	*The Color Solid*	
3-11.	*Additive Color Mixing*	
3-12.	*Subtractive Color Mixing*	
3-13.	*Experiencing Colorblindness*	
3-14.	*Afterimage*	
3-15.	*Sound Waves*	
3-16.	*A Decibel Scale for Common Sounds*	
3-17.	*How We Hear*	
3-18.	*A Detailed Drawing of a Hair Cell in the Organ of Corti*	
3-19.	*The Human Olfactory System*	
3-20.	*The Structure of a Taste Bud*	
3-21.	*Paradoxical Heat*	
3-22.	*Closeup of a Pointillist Painting*	
3-23.	*Random Dots or Something More?*	
3-24.	*Camouflage*	
3-25.	*The Reversible Figure*	
3-26.	*Gestalt Principles of Perceptual Organization*	
3-27.	*The Relationship Between Distance and the Size of the Retinal Image*	

Chapter 4 States of Consciousness

chapter outline 94

learning objectives 96

lecture suggestions

    Reflecting on Self-Awareness 97
    Life After Death After Life 97
    The Ecstasy and the Agony 98
    Shedding Light on Biological Clocks 98
    Measuring Hypnotizability 99
    Early Birds, Night Owls, and Hypnotic Susceptibility 100
    Swimming in the Stream of Consciousness 101

demonstrations and activities

    Exploring the Stream of Consciousness 102
    Dream Survey 102
    Guest Lecture: Hypnosis 103
    Demonstrating Hypnotic Suggestibility 103
    Brief Meditation Experience 104
    Debate: Is Alcoholism a Disease? 105
    Debate: Should Drugs Be Legalized? 105

student assignments

    Dream Journal 106
    States of Consciousness in Film: *Altered States* 106
    Drug Abuse in Film: *Drugstore Cowboy* 106

video 107

multimedia 110

transparencies 114

handouts

    Recording the Stream of Consciousness 115
    Dream Survey 116
    Student Assignment: Keeping a Dream Journal 117

chapter outline

I. Consciousness Experience
- A. What is waking consciousness?
    1. Our awareness of mental processes
        a. Decision making, remembering, concentrating, daydreaming, sleeping
    2. Explaining waking consciousness
        a. The stream of consciousness, revisited
            i. Recent brain research augments James' poetic notion
        b. "The tip of the iceberg," reanalyzed
            i. Cognitive psychology fleshes out Freud's iceberg metaphor
        c. Consciousness and adaptation
            i. Consciousness has social, adaptive, organizational benefits
- B. Daydreaming and fantasy
    1. The value and meaning of daydreams in daily life is a matter of debate

II. Sleep
- A. Circadian cycles: The biological clock
    1. Daily rhythms of the body are sometimes upset by jet lag, fatigue, other factors
- B. The rhythms of sleep
    1. Stage 1 through Stage 4 constitute non-REM sleep (NREM)
        a. Cycling through these stages throughout a night's sleep
    2. REM sleep (paradoxical sleep) associated with dreaming
        a. Brain activity, heart rate, blood pressure resemble waking state
- C. Sleep disorders
    1. Sleeptalking, sleepwalking, and night terrors
        a. Talking and walking more likely to take place during Stage 4 sleep
        b. Night terrors are more than just bad dreams
    2. Insomnia, apnea, and narcolepsy

III. Dreams
- A. What do we dream?
    1. Dream content varies with gender, age, culture, sleep cycle
- B. Why do we dream?
    1. Dreams as unconscious wishes
        a. Manifest content versus latent content of dreams
    2. Dreams and information processing
        a. Dreamtime allows consolidation and processing of information from the day's events

   3. Dreams and neural activity

     a. Dreams produced by natural neurophysiological processes

   4. Dreams and waking life

     a. Dreams are an extension of our conscious concerns

  C. Do we *need* to dream?

   1. Irritability without dreams; also, REM rebound

IV. Drug-altered Consciousness

  A. Substance use, abuse, and dependence

   1. Abuse: A pattern of use that diminishes ability to fulfill responsibilities

   2. Dependence: Compulsive use that often results in tolerance / withdrawal

     a. Tolerance: Higher drug doses are needed to produce original effects

     b. Withdrawal: Unpleasant symptoms following discontinuance of drug

  B. Depressants: Alcohol, barbiturates, and opiates

  C. Stimulants: Caffeine, nicotine, amphetamines, and cocaine

  D. Hallucinogens and marijuana

  E. Explaining abuse and addiction

   1. Biological factors

   2. Psychological, social, and cultural factors

V. Meditation and Hypnosis

  A. Meditation

   1. Concentration and reflection that reduces sympathetic nervous activity

     a. Explaining effects and mechanisms remains somewhat controversial

  B. Hypnosis

   1. Hypnotic suggestion

     a. A trancelike state in which susceptibility to suggestion is heightened

learning objectives

After reading this chapter, students should be able to:

1. Explain daydreaming.

2. Describe the stage of sleep and dreaming.

3. Explain why REM sleep is also called paradoxical sleep.

4. Explain the theories of the nature and content of dreams.

5. Define the sleep disorders of insomnia, narcolepsy, and apnea.

6. Describe meditation and hypnosis

7. Explain the difference between substance abuse and substance dependence.

8. Explain the effect of depressants, stimulants, and hallucinogens.

9. List two negative effects of each of the following drugs: alcohol, marijuana, amphetamines, barbiturates, the opiates, cocaine, and the hallucinogens.

10. Explain the biological, psychological, social and cultural factors related to addiction.

lecture suggestions

Reflecting on Self-Awareness

A basic question of consciousness focuses on how we come to know ourselves. Advocates of mind-altering substances or devotees of certain mystic rites point to the "expanded consciousness" and greater awareness of ourselves that can be attained, and almost everyone embraces the admonition to "know thyself."

The framework suggested by these examples, however, recruits a rather select group of self-knowers: sentient, rational, adults with long prior experience (from any number of sources) of acquiring self-knowledge. An investigation of the origins and limits of self-knowledge, however, might entail both phylogenetic and ontogenetic approaches. For example, how much self-recognition does an infant have? Certainly a preverbal child cannot describe his or her experience of the self, and if the child could, its vocabulary would probably be inadequate to capture the richness of the self-recognition experience. (Imagine your 2-year-old reporting that she "apprehended the self-as-known in a moment of lucid insight.") To press the point further, to what extent are members of other species self-aware? We can repeatedly ask the 2-year-old child what he or she is experiencing until, with time, a vocabulary capable of describing the experiences is developed. We cannot, however, expect our cat to relate the "reflective experience of comparing the present self to the ideal self," no matter how much we ask it.

Several researchers have been interested in questions of self-recognition, self-awareness, and self-knowledge in other species, and have actively sought ways to gather evidence for these processes. As an example, Gordon G. Gallup, Jr., developed a technique for testing self-recognition among primates that circumvented the barrier produced by lack of a common communication system between species. One marker of self-recognition is the ability to visually identify oneself, such as occurs when looking in a mirror. Gallup capitalized on this facet of recognition in a study using chimpanzees. The chimps were given several days of exposure to a mirror in their environment. Gallup noted that at first the chimpanzees acted as though the image in the mirror was another animal. Gradually, however, they began to respond in a way that suggested they had realized they were seeing an image of themselves. To validate these observations, Gallup anesthetized the chimpanzees and applied an odorless, bright red dye to their faces, in such a location that it could only be seen in the mirror. When the chimpanzees were revived and the mirrors were reintroduced, all the chimpanzees reacted in a way that strongly suggested mirror self-recognition. The chimps reached up to their faces, exploring the marks, while watching their reflections, and did so more often than under control conditions.

This procedure, subsequently dubbed the "mark test," has been used with a number of other species. Gallup contends, however, that although chimpanzees and orangutans can reliably demonstrate self-recognition of this type, the effect has not been reliably demonstrated among gorillas, monkeys, or prosimians. Recently, work has begun testing the phenomenon among bottlenose dolphins.

Gallup, G. G., Jr. (1970). Chimpanzees: Self-recognition. *Science, 167,* 341-343.
Parker, S. T., Mitchell, R. W., & Boccia, M. L.(Eds.) (1994). *Self-awareness in animals and humans: Developmental perspectives.* Cambridge, UK: Cambridge University Press.

Life After Death After Life

A common belief among the religions of the world is that there is some sort of life after death. Raymond Moody has presented evidence that he suggests supports this belief. It consists of experiences reported by people who have been pronounced dead and then revived, or who have come very close to death. These people report continued consciousness and existence after "death." Such reports have been attributed to an afterlife by some researchers because the experiences are described as vivid and real and because certain events are common to many of these near-death reports. The person often hears the pronouncement of death, views the scene from above, hears a very loud ringing or buzzing noise, moves through a tunnel to a very bright light, meets friends, sees a panoramic view of his or her past, and is aware of some point beyond which return is impossible.

Although other researchers agree that these near-death experiences occur, they disagree with Moody's interpretations of their origin and significance. Kastenbaum notes that not all people who have been near death and are revived report the spectacular visions of Moody's subjects. Siegel suggests that the reported events are hallucinations produced by the stress and biochemical changes in the brain that accompany near-death conditions. He notes that the elements in Moody's accounts are also prevalent in the hallucinations of psychotics, mystics, and drug users. In these hallucinations, tunnels, lights, and geometric forms are very common, and the scene can seem very real.

Hallucinations originate from states of central nervous system arousal that can be induced by various drugs, stress, and illness. One theory suggests that the internal activity that produces hallucinations is usually blocked from expression by normal sensory input. When the normal input is reduced, as occurs when a person is dying, enduring sensory deprivation, or in some meditative states, this internal activity becomes salient and produces a hallucination.

The reports of viewing the scene from a detached position above can also be explained as normal experiences. This depersonalization and dissociation are common to drug states and even, to some extent, normal imagery. Siegel suggests a simple exercise to demonstrate this: Recall the last time you went swimming in the ocean. Does your memory include an image of yourself in the water or on the beach? If so, it is the result of constructive memory, because you obviously could not have been looking at yourself at the time.

Alcock, J.E. (1981). Psychology and near-death experiences. In K. Frazier (Ed.). *Paranormal borderlands of science*. Buffalo, NY: Prometheus Books.
Kastenbaum, R. (1979, September). Temptations from the ever after. *Human Behavior*, pp. 28-33.
Moody, R. (1977). *Reflections on life after life*. New York: Bantam.
Siegel, R.K. (1980). The psychology of life after death. *American Psychologist*, 35, 911-931.

Reprinted from Whitford, F. W. (1995). Instructor's resource manual for *Psychology: Principles and applications* by S. Worchel and W. Shebilske. Englewood Cliffs, NJ: Prentice Hall.

The Ecstasy and the Agony   (FDA OKs MDMA 4 PTSD)

The Food and Drug Administration (FDA) has formally approved the hallucinogenic agent Ecstasy (MDMA) for research use in humans. Although the drug was outlawed by the Drug Enforcement Agency (DEA) in 1986, it has continued to remain popular among underground users for the feelings of euphoria, empathy, and contentment it produces. Researchers now believe these effects may be helpful in treating the pain and distress of terminally ill cancer patients or soldiers suffering from post-traumatic stress disorder (PTSD), and generally accelerate the process of psychotherapy. (The FDA has also recently approved marijuana, LSD, and the hallucinogenic root ibogaine for research studies.)

Studies of basic human safety are underway at the University of California, Los Angeles, after which clinical trials can begin. Although MDMA is known to be safer than LSD, there is concern about MDMA's effects on serotonin levels. One study reported that heavy Ecstasy users experienced a 30 percent decrease in serotonin levels, although they did not experience the hostile and impulsive behavior linked to lowered serotonin in other studies.

Staff (1994, May/June). A dose of Generation X. *Psychology Today*, pp. 16-17.

Shedding Light on Biological Clocks

Ticking away like so much metaphorical springwork, our biological clocks help keep our sleep/wake cycles in order. Most of the time they operate unnoticed, bidding us to sleep or rousing us to wakefulness. When we don't feel particularly healthy, wealthy, or wise, however, we may notice that our biological clocks need winding, and look for a reason for our drowsiness. The culprit may be an unexpected one: Industrial advance may have unwittingly turned us into a species of sleep-deprived zombies.

Biological clocks do get out of sync occasionally, and a great deal of previous research has shown that exposure to bright light can reset the body's internal clock. Therapies for seasonal affective disorder, in fact, capitalize on exposure to bright light as a means of treating this form of depression. However, a recent study by Dr. Charles Czeisler, of Boston's Brigham and Women's Hospital, suggests that exposure to normal levels of indoor lighting may have similar effects. Czeisler led a 5-year study on human responses to light in which he and his colleagues found that as little as five hours a day of exposure to normal levels of illumination can alter the biological pattern of sleep and wakefulness. Over time, the phase of peak grogginess gets shifted to just a few hours before waking. The result is a constant feeling of being run-down or jet-lagged.

What's to blame? Well, with the advent of the lightbulb came the ability to accomplish more by using artificial light. No longer constrained to work when the sun was up and rest when it wasn't, humans could now stay up well past their bedtime. In short, the light bulb allows us to read or work or play Parcheesi until late in the night, which significantly slows the ticking of our biological clock. The problem is compounded by the use of heavy shades in the bedroom to block out the dawn's early light, which could serve to help reset the biological clock. Steps toward cleaning the clockwork would be to avoid bright light just before bedtime, as well as setting and maintaining a regular sleeping schedule.

Staff. (1996, February 8). Run-down? Feeling jet-lagged? Blame Thomas Edison. *Austin American-Statesman*, p. A8.
Staff. (1996, February 19). Run down? Blame the light bulb. *U.S. News and World Report*, p. 20.

Measuring Hypnotizability

As the text mentions, people vary greatly in their susceptibility to being hypnotized. Attempts to quantify these differences may at first seem intractable; short of successfully putting someone into a hypnotic state, it might seem difficult to measure the extent of a person's susceptibility. Several efforts have been made, however, to address this issue.

Perhaps the best known measures of hypnotic susceptibility are the Stanford Hypnotic Susceptibility Scale (SHSS) and the Harvard Group Scale of Hypnotic Susceptibility (HGSHS). Both were developed in the late 1950s/early 1960s and in fact the Harvard scale is an adaptation of the Stanford scale. The HGSHS presents a hypnotic induction followed by 12 suggested behaviors. The HGSHS often is used as a prescreening instrument; those participants who record scores in response to the behaviors show signs of hypnotic susceptibility. These candidates may then be tested on the SHSS, a more elaborate test that takes 50-60 minutes to administer and also involves a hypnotic induction, followed by 12 suggestions.

A more recent measure is the Waterloo-Stanford Group C (WSGC) Scale of Hypnotic Susceptibility (Bowers, 1993). It takes approximately 1½ hours to administer and is intended as a follow-up to prescreening on the HGSHS. Like its predecessors, the WSGC presents a hypnotic induction and 12 suggestions. These including lowering one's hand, hallucinating tastes, music, and a mosquito, maintaining arm rigidity, and experiencing an age regression.

Other measures include the Hypnotic Induction Profile (Spiegel & Spiegel, 1978), characterized by its brief administration. A rapid hypnotic induction is used followed by a short series of suggestions; the entire procedure takes about 10 minutes. Similarly, the Stanford Hypnotic Arm Levitation Induction and Test (SHALIT; Hilgard, Crawford, & Wert, 1979) is a rapid technique emphasizing motor behavior, as is the Rapid Induction Susceptibility Scale (RISS; Page & Handley, 1989).

What these measures share in common, besides tongue-defying acronyms, is a focus on assessing a person's likelihood of entering a hypnotic state. This differs from assessing a person's experience of being hypnotized. This so-called "hypnotic depth," or immersion in the hypnotic experience, also has been measured using a variety of instruments.

For example, the Depth of Hypnosis Inventory (Field, 1965) and variants of the Linton-Langs Questionnaire (Linton & Langs, 1962; Ludwig & Levine, 1965) were two early measures of hypnotic experiences. Such early measures typically focused on the dissociative effects of hypnosis and its qualities as an altered state of consciousness. More recent efforts, such as the Hypnotic Experiences Questionnaire (Kelly, 1985), take a multidimensional approach. Factors such as relaxation, rapport, visual imagery, and amount of anxious, ruminative, self-reflective thought, as well as dissociation/altered states, are assessed using a self-report format.

Both sets of instruments--those measuring susceptibility and those measuring hypnotic experience--combine to shed light on what is still a rather murky state of consciousness.

Bowers, K. S. (1993). The Waterloo-Stanford Group C (WSGC) Scale of Hypnotic Susceptibility: Normative and comparative data. *International Journal of Clinical and Experimental Hypnosis, 41*, 35-46.

Field, P. B. (1965). An inventory scale of hypnotic depth. *International Journal of Clinical and Experimental Hypnosis, 13*, 238-249.

Hilgard, E. R., Crawford, H. J., & Wert, A. (1979). The Stanford hypnotic arm levitation induction and test (SHALIT): A six-minute hypnotic induction and measurement scale. *International Journal of Clinical and Experimental Hypnosis, 27*, 111-124.

Kelly, P. J. (1985). The relationship between hypnotic ability and hypnotic experience. Unpublished doctoral dissertation. University of Waterloo, Canada.

Linton, H. B., & Langs, R. S. (1962). Placebo reactions in a study of lysergic acid diethylamide. *Archives of General Psychiatry, 6*, 369-393.

Ludwig, A. M., & Levine, J. (1965). Alterations in consciousness produced by hypnosis. *Journal of Nervous and Mental Disease, 140*, 146-153.

Page, R. A., & Handley, G. W. (1989). The Rapid Induction Susceptibility Scale. *Psychology: A Journal of Human Behavior, 26*, 49-55.

Shor, R. E., & Orne, E. C. (1962). *Harvard Group Scale of Hypnotic Susceptibility: Form A.* Palo Alto, CA: Consulting Psychologists Press.

Spiegel, H., & Spiegel, D. (1978). *Trance and treatment: Clinical use of hypnosis.* New York: Basic Books.

Weitzenhoffer, A. M., & Hilgard, E. R. (1959). *Stanford Hypnotic Susceptibility Scale: Forms A and B.* Palo Alto, CA: Consulting Psychologists Press.

Weitzenhoffer, A. M., & Hilgard, E. R. (1962). *Stanford Hypnotic Susceptibility Scale: Form C.* Palo Alto, CA: Consulting Psychologists Press.

Early Birds, Night Owls, and Hypnotic Susceptibility

"Mornings are primetime for me; 7:00 a.m. comes and I'm ready to go."

"I do my best work between 10 at night and 1 in the morning."

"I like to get up when the sun is warm, around 1:30 or 2:00 in the afternoon."

These statements illustrate the difference between *day persons* and *night persons*, or those of us who are most alert and active during, respectively, morning and early afternoon hours or late afternoon and evening hours. These differences can be seen through casual observation and have been confirmed by a variety of measures of alertness under more controlled circumstances. These peak periods, however, may themselves be a manifestation of an underlying *ultradian rhythm*, or fragment of the 24-hour rest-activity cycle of the human body. Many physiological processes (such as gastric motility or urinary flow) and behaviors (such as vigilance, fantasizing, or responsiveness to perceptual aftereffects) seem to follow spontaneous cycles of highs and lows throughout the day. Being a "day person," then, may in part be a product of responding to these cycles.

These distinctions have been linked to hypnotic susceptibility in a recent study by Benjamin Wallace, of Cleveland State University. Using a within-groups design in two experiments, Wallace identified day persons and night persons, and administered both the Stanford Hypnotic Susceptibility Scale (SHSS) and the Harvard Group Scale of Hypnotic Susceptibility (HGSHS). Regardless of the scale used, patterns were found in the hypnotic susceptibility of the participants. Day persons seemed most susceptible at 10 a.m. and 2 p.m., whereas night persons peaked at 1 p.m. and between 6 p.m. and 9 p.m.

These results hold practical implications for hypnotic induction as well as theoretical import for the study of biological rhythms. First, they indicate that hypnotic susceptibility will differ not only between individuals but also within a single individual, partly as a function of that person's typical cycles of alertness. Second, although the issue remains unresolved, the role of ultradian rhythms suggests a promising avenue for further research. Such rhymes may impact both the day person/night person distinction as well as one's susceptibility to hypnosis.

Wallace, B. (1993). Day persons, night persons, and variability in hypnotic susceptibility. *Journal of Personality and Social Psychology, 64*, 827-833.

Swimming in the Stream of Consciousness

Whether it's William James' stream or your Uncle Jeb's creek that runs down to the fishin' hole, metaphors that describe consciousness as a continuum hold more than a kernel of truth. Our common experiences of drifting from alertness into a daydream, or from pleasant conversation into the hypnagogic state, reveal that consciousness ebbs and flows rather than existing as discrete states. What this suggests, then, is that thoughts and feelings experienced in one state of consciousness could impact other states of consciousness.

Rosalind Cartwright reasoned that conscious wishes about an important personal dimension should impact one's dreams. Drawing on "housekeeping" notions of dreaming and Freudian ideas, Cartwright suggested that drawing a person's attention to a pressing personal problem should make it more likely that the issue would become the focus of a night's dreaming. To test this idea, 17 volunteers identified aspects of their personality (e.g., "poised," "shy," "lazy," "defensive") that they wanted to change. As they fell asleep, participants were instructed to repeat to themselves "I wish I were not so _____," inserting that aspect that they wanted to change. During their REM periods participants were awakened and asked to recount the content of their dreams, which they typically did easily and thoroughly. When the dream content was analyzed, 15 of the 17 participants were found to have dreamt about the target adjective (importantly, they also dreamt about other descriptors they had rated, although these did not appear at significant proportions). Cartwright suggests that dreaming serves not so much as a vehicle for wish fulfillment, in the Freudian sense, but rather as a means of exploring wants and wishes in ways that might not be available to waking consciousness.

Punctuating this approach is the work on *lucid dreaming*, or dreams in which the dreamer knows that he or she is dreaming. Abandoning that word salad definition for the moment, lucid dreamers essentially are able to control the content and outcomes of their dreams. Realizing that the events unfolding to the mind's eye are only a dream, lucid dreamers report deciding to behave in ways that would ordinarily be dangerous or physically impossible. For example, a lucid dreamer falling from a great height might decide to sprout wings and fly to safety, or walk away, Wile E. Coyote-style, from the impact. Studies of this type of conscious control over what has long been presumed a nonconscious process remain somewhat controversial. As with many aspects of consciousness, the answer lies in further research.

Cartwright, R. (1974). *A primer on sleep and dreaming.* Reading, MA: Addison-Wesley.
LaBerge, S. (1985). *Lucid dreaming.* New York: Ballantine.

demonstrations

Exploring the Stream of Consciousness

Chapter 4 notes that there are many natural fluctuations in consciousness and that as a result our awareness of our mental processes ebbs and flows continuously throughout the day. Using a modification of a procedure developed by Klinger (1990), your students can record changes in their consciousness that occur during the class period. At the beginning of class distribute copies of the data sheet provided in Handout 4-1 to your students. Explain to them that at four intervals during the class, you will stop the lecture and ask them to write down what they were thinking about when the interruption occurred. You should emphasize that their recordings should be honest, free-flowing, and accurate and that the sheets will not be collected in order to maintain their anonymity. You should arrange the demonstration so that the last interruption occurs about 15 minutes before the end of class to allow time for discussion of the results. Discuss the results within the context of daydreaming and ask students to relate their data to the descriptions of daydream content described in the textbook. For example, you can ask students how many of their thought records reflected something related to the lecture or class. How many were related to worry, stress, guilt, or hostility? How many daydreams reflected positive, happy thoughts? You can also discuss the relationship between the fantasy-prone personality and creativity, as well as the many positive aspects of daydreaming (e.g., it helps to build cognitive skills, relieve tension, and incorporate new, complex information).

Klinger, E. (1990). Daydreaming: Using waking fantasy and imagery for self-knowledge and creativity. Los Angeles: Jeremy P. Tarcher.

Adapted from Hill, W. G. (1995). Instructor's resource manual for Psychology by S. F. Davis and J. J. Palladino. Englewood Cliffs, NJ: Prentice Hall.

Dream Survey

As an entertaining introduction to the topic of dreaming, begin your discussion by asking students about their own dreams. Handout 4-2 contains a brief dream survey that can be read aloud (students can simply raise their hands in response to questions) or photocopied and distributed to students. Many students will also be willing to share details of their most interesting dreams. A discussion of common themes in dreams should spark a lively discussion about the function of dreams and will provide a nice context for exploring the various theories of dreaming, including Freud's psychoanalytic explanation, Hobson and McCarley's activation-synthesis model, and other recent neurophysiological interpretations mentioned in the text.

Students may also be interested in knowing how their dreams compare to those of over 1000 *Psychology Today* readers who responded to a survey about dreams. In that survey, 95% of those who responded said that they remember at least some of their dreams, and 68% reported having a recurring dream. Popular recurring dreams included falling, being chased, returning to a childhood home, flying, appearing naked in public, and being unprepared for an exam. Thirty-nine percent reported so-called "lucid" dreams in which they claimed to control the course of the dreams. (Some of your students will no doubt recall using control over a dream to end a nightmare, and others may report using strategies in an effort to dictate what they will dream about on a particular night.) Interestingly, 28% of respondents reported dying in a dream, and over 45% dreamed about celebrities at one time or another (e.g., sex symbols and rock stars, such as Tom Selleck or Elvis Presley). [Celebrities featured in current students' dreams are likely to include Michael Jackson, Madonna, Brad Pitt, Tom Cruise, Michelle Pfeiffer, and Michael Jordan.]

Stark, E. (1984, October). To sleep, perchance to dream. *Psychology Today*, p. 16.

Guest Lecture: Hypnosis

As an engaging and informative complement to the text's discussion of hypnosis, consider inviting a trained hypnotist to give a guest lecture. In addition to discussing the rationale behind hypnosis and dispelling common misconceptions, he or she could also conduct a memorable demonstration to help students get a feel for the experience of being hypnotized. Ideally, this should be a serious demonstration of hypnosis--relying on gradual relaxation, focused concentration, and hypnotic suggestion rather than simple stage antics commonly used by comedians or magicians. Volunteers can describe their experiences afterwards, and student questions and comments should be strongly encouraged. If your guest speaker is also a trained hypnotherapist, you might also be treated to a discussion of the various clinical applications of hypnosis, including treatments for overeating, smoking, fears and phobias, grief, migraine headaches, insomnia, and sexual dysfunction.

Demonstrating Hypnotic Suggestibility

If you'd rather not devote an entire class period to hypnosis, consider performing at least one of several easy demonstrations that require the same kind of suggestibility used in hypnosis. John Fisher describes several simple exercises that can readily be used in class. (1) Bring a small, sealed jar of colored but odorless liquid (e.g., water treated with food coloring) to your class, and explain to students that it contains a very exotic liquid made from foreign ingredients. Tell them that you will open the jar to allow the scent to waft around the room and that they should raise their hands as soon as they smell it. To facilitate acceptance of this suggestion, you might wrinkle your nose as you uncork the jar or even arrange for a cooperative confederate or two to raise their hands. (2) Ask your students to close their eyes and to imagine that they are cutting a large, sour, bitter lemon, a lemon so full of juice that it is dripping on the floor. Then tell them to imagine that they are sucking the juice from the same fruit. The majority of your students should be awash in saliva by this point! (3) Create the perception of a bodily itch by making several suggestions to itching and scratching. Start by reminding students how pleasurable it is to scratch an annoying itch, such as a tickle on the back or the ankle or the nose. Suggest that students might be starting to perceive slight itching sensations on various parts of their body, and that these might get progressively stronger so that they soon won't be able to refrain from scratching (scratching yourself unobtrusively at this point helps). The more you play this up (e.g., by describing your itches and scratches in great deal and with emotion), the more students will feel compelled to scratch. Before long, the majority of your audience will be scratching itches on their heads, shoulders, faces, and arms that exist only in their minds. Suggesting a compelling urge to swallow also works well, as does the suggestion of the need to yawn (especially when accompanied by a wide, exaggerated yawn on your part). (4) Tell students to hold their fists in front of them about 15 inches apart with their index fingers pointing towards each other. Then suggest that their fingers are becoming nervous and shaky in this position and that consequently their fingertips are not pointing precisely together. At this point, suddenly and immediately instruct them to bring their fingertips together instantly, without any hesitation ("NOW!"). Although this sounds amazingly easy, the mere suggestion of shakiness and doubt throws most people off just enough to make their fingertips miss.

In complying with these "suggestions," your students will demonstrate the enormous human capacity for accepting an idea and responding to it almost automatically. Note that some students will be more responsive to these suggestions than others, and you can discuss how this variability relates to real individual differences in susceptibility to hypnosis. How do students think they would score on Hilgard's Stanford Susceptibility Scale? Are they surprised by their responsiveness (or nonresponsiveness)? Discuss how hypnotic susceptibility is related to age, childhood upbringing, having an active imagination, hereditary factors, and contextual cues in the hypnotic setting.

Fisher, J. (1979). *Body magic*. Briarcliff Manor, NY: Stein and Day.

Brief Meditation Experience

During your discussion of altered states of consciousness, students will undoubtedly ask about meditation, which most will have heard about from popular sources but will have never experienced. Concentrative meditation can be demonstrated fairly easily in the classroom using the following exercise, which was adapted from exercises suggested by Linda Leal (1990) and Antonio Puente (1987). Before you begin, briefly explain the rationale behind meditation. The primary goal of meditation is to achieve a deep state of relaxation, usually by concentrating on one repetitive stimulus so that all other thoughts and images are blocked out. This narrowing of concentration, accompanied by deep, slow breathing, effectively reduces the activity of the sympathetic nervous system (e.g., by lowering heart rate and respiration rate) and slows down metabolism. Meditation promotes feelings of well-being and relaxation, and has been used to help people cope with stress as well as to treat certain medical problems (e.g., drug addiction).

After you've introduced the idea of concentrative meditation, turn off (or dim) the room lights and make sure the room is free of distractions for 10 to 15 minutes. Instruct students to sit erect in a comfortable position, with their hands either on the desk or in their lap and with their feet uncrossed and touching the ground. After students are in a relaxed position, ask them to close their eyes and to sit quietly and breathe in and out as usual for about 30 seconds. Tell students that they should try to clear their minds by letting go of all random thoughts and by focusing on their breathing. Tell them that each breath should come from the abdomen, and, if possible, they should breathe through their nostrils. Thus, they should concentrate on the rise and fall of their abdomen, saying slowly to themselves "in" and "out" with each inhalation and exhalation. Stress that they should think of nothing else but the rise and fall of their abdomen and the corresponding thoughts of "in" and "out." At this point, you might want to reassure students that although they may have trouble concentrating initially, this problem diminishes with practice. After approximately 10 minutes of this exercise, gently tell students to start focusing on bodily sensations as well as the sounds in the room around them. Give them about a minute of this reorientation period before asking them to open their eyes.

Once students are fully alert, allow them to discuss their experiences. Linda Leal suggests the following questions to guide discussion. (1) *Why does meditation promote feelings of well-being and satisfaction?* Research suggests that the beneficial effects are related to the lowered activity of the sympathetic nervous system. The most common bodily change reporting during meditation, hypometabolism, is characterized by decreased metabolic rate and reflected in lower heart and respiration rates and lower oxygen consumption. It may also be that the concentration required in meditation distracts people away from other concerns. (2) *Why is it difficult to keep distracting thoughts from entering consciousness while meditating?* One possible explanation is that the repeated presentation of a single stimulus leads to habituation, or a general decrease in sensory responding. Another possibility is that the mind is undisciplined and requires practice to achieve deep concentration. (3) *Does meditation lead to heightened states of consciousness, alertness, or creativity?* There is some controversy over whether meditation significantly alters normal states of consciousness. Many proponents claim that it does, but it is a difficult proposition to test scientifically and many reports are based on personal accounts for poorly controlled studies. Although many of the same physiological changes can be obtained simply from deep relaxation, the text notes that a meta-analysis comparing transcendental mediation (TM) with other forms of meditation and relaxation techniques found TM to be superior for reducing anxiety.

Note: If your roster is too large to perform this exercise in class, consider asking students to practice this technique at home (over the course of several different 20-minute sessions) and to write a short discussion paper describing their experiences and relating them to material presented in the text and lecture.

Leal, L. (1990). Concentrative meditation. In V. P. Makosky, C. C. Sileo, L. G. Whittemore, C. P. Landry, & M. L. Skutley (Eds.), *Activities handbook for the teaching of psychology: Vol. 3* (pp. 237-238). Washington, DC: American Psychological Association.

Puente, A. E. (1987). An introduction to meditation. In V. P. Makosky, L. G. Whittemore, & A. M. Rogers (Eds.), *Activities handbook for the teaching of psychology: Vol. 2* (pp. 284-285). Washington, DC: American Psychological Association.

Debate: Is Alcoholism a Disease?

The text discusses the enormous physiological and social costs of alcohol use and abuse. Given these costs, it is not surprising that a major priority of psychologists is to better understand alcoholism and its causes. Despite the large amount of research devoted to the issue, however, there exists a heated controversy over its cause and opinions are sharply divided. The question at the heart of the debate is this: Should alcoholism be viewed as a disease, a physiological defect over which "victims" have little or no control? Those who support the disease model (including Alcoholics Anonymous, which is based on this premise) issue a resounding "yes" and argue that alcoholism is a biological illness stemming from some combination of genetic, metabolic, hormonal, or other physiological factors. Those who say "no" reject the idea that alcoholism is uncontrollable or has biological causes and argue that the disease model discourages alcoholics from taking responsibility for their behavior. Social attitudes are equally divided and mirror those of researchers and practitioners. Some simply view alcoholism as a behavioral or moral problem whereas others see it as a physical problem whose victims deserve treatment rather than punishment.

Your students are likely to have formed strong opinions on this issue from what they have seen or heard in the media. Encourage them to explore this important issue in greater depth by considering the scientific evidence and arguments in a debate format. Is there evidence supporting the disease model of alcoholism? What does biological and genetic research indicate? What implications do answers to these questions have for assigning personal responsibility for alcoholism and its consequences? Using the debate procedures suggested at the beginning of this manual, assign students to research this issue and to be prepared to defend either side. Both *Taking Sides* (see Issue 11) and *Seeing Both Sides* (see Chapter 7) contain excellent articles supporting the pro and con positions on this topic.

Lilienfeld, S. O. (1995). Seeing both sides: Classic controversies in abnormal psychology. Pacific Grove, CA: Brooks/Cole.
Slife, B. (1994). Taking sides: Clashing views on controversial psychological issues (8th ed.). Guilford, CT: Dushkin Publishing Group.

Debate: Should Drugs Be Legalized?

Chapter 4 considers the ways in which a variety of drugs artificially alter our states of consciousness. Interestingly, although the enormous societal and financial consequences of legal drug use (such as alcohol and nicotine) are well-documented, few topics arouse as much public and political concern as does the use and abuse of illegal drugs. Drug abuse emerged as an important public issue in the 1960s with the rise of the counterculture and its experimentation with drugs such as heroin, marijuana, and LSD. In the 80s, the high price of cocaine led to the development of cheap substitutes (such as crack, a highly addictive, smokable form of cocaine), which produced violent disorderly behavior and led to street wars between gangs fighting over control of its distribution. This epidemic of drug use and violent crime led to the current "war on drugs" (declared during the Reagan and Bush administrations), which advocates stiff penalties for drug use and drug-related crimes.

Has the so-called war on drugs improved the drug problem in this country? Opinions are sharply divided. Many experts who argue that the war on drugs has failed have proposed their own controversial solution to the problem: the controlled legalization of drugs. Proponents argue that legalization would diminish crime by driving drug traffickers out of business and would also lead to a savings of several billion dollars each year (through tax revenues and the reduced need for law enforcement), which could be used for education and treatment programs. Critics argue that widespread availability, lower prices, and the elimination of the legal stigma would lead to an enormous increase in drug abuse, which in turn would lead to skyrocketing medical costs and would jeopardize public safety. Ask your students to debate the scientific merit of arguments and evidence on both sides of this volatile issue. Use the debate procedures suggested at the beginning of this manual and assign students to research this issue and to be prepared to defend either side.

Finsterbusch, K., & McKenna, G. (1994). *Taking sides: Clashing views on controversial social issues* (8th ed.). Guilford, CT: Dushkin Publishing Group.

student assignments

Dream Journal

Ludy T. Benjamin, Jr., suggests that having students keep a record of their dreams over a period of time can be a terrific way to generate data for class discussion. Several weeks before you plan to cover states of consciousness, assign students to keep a daily diary or journal of their dreams (Handout 4-3 contains a sample assignment that can be photocopied and distributed to students as is or modified for your class as desired). A long lead time is necessary to give students who have trouble remembering their dreams several extra chances to remember at least some of them, and will also give you enough time to make observations about their dreams before discussing them in class (ideally, the assignment should be due the class period prior to your discussion). In doing this assignment, students should try to keep daily notes about their dreams (preferably, as soon as they wake up); they can then type up a summary from their notes after they have successfully remembered several dreams. Be aware that you might need to make provisions for the fact that, despite great effort, some students may not remember their dreams; perhaps you could give these students an alternate assignment or make this one optional. You should also reassure students that you will keep the content of their dream journals strictly confidential, and you should encourage them to freely edit or omit any details that they don't feel comfortable sharing with you. Finally, be sure to caution students against discussing their dreams during this assignment so they don't unintentionally influence each other. After you have read the journals, you can solicit student volunteers to share the content of their dreams with the class during discussion.

Benjamin, L. T. (1981). To sleep, perchance to dream. In L. T. Benjamin & K. D. Lowman (Eds.), *Activities handbook for the teaching of psychology* (pp. 196-198). Washington, DC: American Psychological Association.

Portions of the assignment handout were adapted from Bolt, M. (1992). Instructor's resources for use with D. G. Myers', *Psychology* (3rd ed.). New York: Worth.

States of Consciousness in Film: *Altered States*

In *Altered States* (1980), William Hurt stars as a research scientist (and self-appointed guinea pig) who uses experimental drugs and an isolation tank in order to explore other states of reality that presumably reside within us. This film builds on the text's treatment of states of consciousness by asking students to imagine the possibility that other bizarre states exist. Ask students in a short paper to consider these possibilities while applying principles from the text and lecture to this provocative film (Warner; 103 min).

Drug Abuse in Film: *Drugstore Cowboy*

In this critically-acclaimed 1989 film, Matt Dillon and Kelly Lynch star in a gritty, intense look at the lives of a junkie couple and their similarly drugged-out friends. It is an honest but not altogether pleasant glimpse into the world of addiction that most of us, thankfully, will never see. This is a real eye-opening film, one that clearly illustrates many of the principles of the text while allowing students to safely step into the shoes of an addict for an hour and half. Ask students to screen the film and then to write a paper discussing principles from the text and lecture. When possible, their discussion should include any specific drugs that they can identify as well as the physical effects of each as they are manifested in the film (Live; 104 min).

video

ABC News/Prentice Hall Video Library

Heroin: The New High School High (39 min, Series III). This lengthy *Turning Point* report looks at a disturbing trend among America's youth; the re-emergence of heroin as a drug of choice. Teenagers are shown discussing the drug's appeal, buying narcotics, and paying the price for using. Aerosmith's Steven Tyler, no stranger to the stable of the white horse himself, comments on addiction and recovery.

Other Sources

Altered States: A History of Drug Use in America (57 min, FHS). From tobacco to alcohol to street drugs, and through all the attempts to limit their procurement, drugs problems are shown to have had a long history in the United States. Reasons for and historical "cycles" of drug use are discussed.

Approaches to Consciousness (4 parts, 1992, 30 min each, IM). Some leading figures in the study of consciousness, such as Robert Ornstein, Oliver Sacks, and Irving Yalom, discuss a variety of aspects of consciousness.

Can You Stop People From Drinking? (60 min, FHS). This highly-regarded video looks at old and new ways of limiting alcohol intake: hypnosis, prohibition, aversion therapy, incarceration, and support groups are among them.

Child Hypnosis with Dr. Perry London (1990, 40 min, PEF). Actual footage of hypnosis, in the context of child psychotherapy, is a highlight of this film.

Chronobiology: The Time of Our Lives (58 min, FHS). The disparity between the time on our watches and the time in our brains is the focus of this video. Taking a biological and cellular approach, the video looks at the ways our biological clocks get reset.

Coca (26 min, FHS). Coca use, from the Andes right through to Coca Cola, is featured in this film.

Cocaine: The End of the Line (58 min, FHS). The origin of cocaine, how it is used, and its effects are presented. A quiz on myths about cocaine may prove enlightening to your students.

Consciousness (58 min, FHS). That quicksilver quality, consciousness, is examined from a variety of perspectives. Neuroscience, computer models, and philosophy combine to make sense of this shared experience that defies definition.

Cracking a Craving (26 min, FHS). The recent specter of crack cocaine is discussed. The hold it has on people, its addictive potential, and ways of combating cocaine addiction are also featured.

Discovering Psychology, Part 13: The Mind Awake and Asleep (1990, 30 min, ANN/CPB). Explores the nature of sleeping, dreams, and other altered states of consciousness.

Discovering Psychology, Part 14: The Mind Hidden and Divided (1990, 30 min, ANN/CPB). Examines the influence of the subconscious mind on thought and behavior. The segment on hypnosis is relevant to this chapter.

Dream Voyage (28 min, FHS). REM sleep, that mysterious state of consciousness, gets a wide-awake treatment. Footage of a cat "acting out" its dreams is a highlight of this film.

Freud's Interpretation of Dreams (23 min, IM). The royal road of the unconscious is traveled through a series of dramatizations and re-enactments of dreams, with Freudian interpretation.

Hooked on Heroin: From Hollywood to Main Street (52 min, FHS). DEA officials, Boy Scouts, Steven Tyler (of Aerosmith), and other luminaries and people-on-the street talk about what they have in common: At one time or another, they all had to feed the monkeys on their backs.

The Importance of Dreams: I Am Dreaming (22 min, 1996, IM). Dream interpretations from various cultural and religious standpoints form the core of this video. The basics of sleep and dreaming are also discussed.

Kids Under the Influence (58 min, FHS). This close-captioned video looks at the number one drug problem among children and teens: alcohol consumption. Peer pressure, advertisements, and the painful process of recovery are discussed.

Language of Dreams (15 parts, 1995, 60 min each, IM). This multi-part series focuses on recording, remembering, and interpreting dreams. The science of some of it may prove useful.

LSD and Ergot (26 min, FHS). Hallucinogens, synthetic and natural, are the focus of this film.

The Opium Poppy (26 min, FHS). Opium and its derivatives are the focus of this film.

The Power of Addiction (19 min, FHS). Chemical and behavioral addiction, and their causes, are discussed. In particular the physiological and psychological mechanisms of cocaine addiction and recovery are featured.

The Power of Dreams (3 parts, 1994, 60 min each, IM). Freud's views, brain functioning, and clinical insights contribute to this examination of dreaming. Highlights include interpretations from Tibetan, Aboriginal, Jewish, Islamic, Christian, and Native-American perspectives.

Power of the Mind (23 min, FHS). Hypnosis, biofeedback, and self-help techniques are examined in this video. Commentary on the effectiveness of subliminal persuasion techniques is also presented.

Sleep (28 min, FHS). Explores a number of sleep-related topics including stages and types of sleep, dreaming, sleep disturbances, and the effects of sleeping pills.

Sleep: A Prerequisite for Health (18 min, FHS). This short video looks at the consequences of fatigue, produced by too little sleep. The Exxon *Valdez* disaster, for example, or the Three Mile Island incident, serve as chilling reminders that drowsiness is next to clumsiness.

Sleep Apnea (24 min, FHS). The dangers of this sleep disorder, and how it can be treated, are examined in this video.

Sleep Disorders (28 min, FHS). Sleep researchers and patients discuss a variety of sleep disorders.

Sleep Problems (19 min, FHS). Examines diagnosis and treatment issues related to sleep apnea and narcolepsy.

Sleeping Well (1996, 28 min, FHS). Insomnia, jet lag, and breathing disorders are discussed and suggestions for combating them are offered in this short film.

Smokeless Tobacco: Breaking Free (1996, 15 min, FHS). This short video looks at what is often perceived as a harmless alternative to cigarettes. Rod Carew reveals his addiction to smokeless tobacco, and graphic images of mouth lesions send a strong message against starting the habit at all.

Substance Abuse Among Latinos (28 min, FHS). Strong cultural and economic factors play a role in substance use and abuse in the Latino community. Strategies for treatment and prevention are discussed.

Substance Misuse (30 min, FHS). Stimulants, hallucinogens, depressants, and opiates are the misused substances featured in this video. The effects of each and the problems they can cause are discussed.

Through the Smoke Screen: Facts About Tobacco Use (1996, 25 min, FHS). Graphic examples of cancer of the larynx, emphysema, chronic bronchitis, and cancerous mouth lesions illustrate the dangers, especially for young people, of tobacco use.

Wake Up, America: A Sleep Alert (24 min, FHS). Why do some people need more sleep than others? What is narcolepsy? What goes on in a sleep lab? Do over-the-counter sleep aids really work? What causes sleep disorders? Find the answers to these questions in this video.

Waking From Coma (51 min, FHS). A British hospital's pioneering program of coma arousal therapy is examined. The dilemmas faced by patients and staff are also explored.

Walking Through the Fear: Women and Substance Abuse (28 min, FHS). Women in increasing numbers are becoming addicted to alcohol and drugs, yet only 1 in 5 people seeking treatment is a woman. Why is this, and what can be done about it?

The World of Abnormal Psychology, Part 6: Substance Abuse Disorders (1992, 60 min, ANN/CPB). Discusses the abuse of alcohol, cigarettes, and cocaine, their health costs and dangers, and techniques for overcoming these addictions.

multimedia

Live! Psych

Module	Title	Book Page #
4.1	Stages of Sleep	p. 154

Screen 1 introduces the five stages of sleep and the four types of brain waves involved in each of these stages. Animations of EEG patterns associated with each stage are shown. Screen 2 shows how sleep researchers record a person's brain activity. A simulation of brain activity when a person is wide awake and alert is shown. Import this screen to compare beta and alpha waves. Screen 3 examines Stage 1 of the sleep cycle. Import this screen to show an animated EEG pattern of theta waves. Screen 4 examines Stage 2 of the sleep cycle. Import this screen to show an animated EEG pattern of sleep spindles and K complexes. Screen 5 examines Stages 3 and 4 of the sleep cycle. Import this screen to show an animated EEG pattern of delta waves. This screen is useful for teaching the concept that as sleep becomes deeper, brain wave activity changes from high-frequency, small-amplitude waves to lower-frequency, large-amplitude waves. Screen 6 examines Stage 4 of the sleep cycle. Import this screen to show an animated EEG pattern of delta waves.

REM versus NREM Sleep   p. 154

Screen 1 describes REM sleep. Import Screen 2 to show that the brain activity of a person in REM sleep resembles that of a person who is wide awake even though the sleeper is in a deep sleep. Screen 3 compares PET scans of a person who is awake, in REM sleep, and in NREM sleep. Import this screen to note the similarity in the level of activity during REM sleep and waking hours, compared to the scan of a person during NREM sleep.

Sleep Cycles over the Course of a Night   p. 154

Screen 1 describes the repetitive sleep cycle. Screen 2 shows how the patterns of sleep changes as the night progresses. Import this screen to show the sawtooth pattern of sleep cycles throughout the course of a night.

4.2   Four Classes of Psychoactive Drugs   p. 175

In Screen I, the major classes of psychoactive drugs are identified. The student clicks on each class to read about substances that fit each class and the range of effects. Screen 2 examines drug use among youths and a bar graph displays the drugs most commonly used by high school seniors in the United States. The student clicks on each drug to see the percentages of high school seniors who have tried and regularly use various drugs.

Web Investigations

Drug Use, Abuse, and Addictions: Focus on Alcohol

Elaine Cassel contributed this exercise on substance abuse and addiction, looking specifically at alcohol. Quizzes, exercises, and a blood alcohol content calculator make this online activity a good resource for an in-class discussion or a take-it-yourself exercise. If you show this activity in class, ask students to work in small groups to answer the various quiz questions or debate whether the drinking age should be lowered to 18. If you assign this activity as an individual exercise, you might ask students to focus on the role-playing activities or "what's the reward" activity. With any use, students should gain a better understanding of how a habit might turn into an addiction.

Making Connections

Conscious Experience

Q What is consciousness?

A In everyday speech, "consciousness" refers to being alert, but to psychologists it refers to awareness of various mental processes, such as remembering and dreaming.

Q What are three possible explanations for our experience of consciousness?

A Consciousness has been explained as a stream of information resulting from the activity of the thalamus, which analyzes and interprets individual pieces of data received from the various sensory modes. Another view is that consciousness represents only a small portion of the activity of the brain, most of which occurs at an unconscious level. In this view, only thoughts to which we are paying attention at a given moment are conscious. A third explanation holds that consciousness is an evolutionary adaptation to the fact that humans are slow and weak compared to other animals. Consciousness enables humans to make use of their intelligence, cultural knowledge, and social organizations.

Q When do daydreams occur? How are they categorized?

A Daydreams occur about every 90 minutes and are most prominent between noon and 2 PM. They are categorized as positive, negative, scattered (fleeting and loosely connected) and purposeful.

Sleep

Q What is a biological clock? How do our biological clocks work?

A The human "biological clock" is a cluster of neurons in the hypothalamus that respond to levels of proteins in the body. When those levels are low, they stimulate production of more proteins. These proteins are the building blocks of chemicals that regulate biological functions such as metabolism and alertness.

Q Explain the characteristics of each stage of sleep.

A The sleep cycle begins with a "twilight" state in which the person loses awareness. The sleeper then enters Stage 1 of sleep, which is marked by a slowing of the pulse, muscle relaxation, and side-to-side rolling movements of the eyes. This is followed by Stage 2, which is characterized by short rhythmic bursts of brain wave activity called sleep spindles, and Stage 3, in which delta waves (slow waves with very high peaks) emerge. In Stage 4 sleep the brain emits very slow delta waves. About an hour after falling asleep, the sleeper ascends from Stage 4 through Stages 3, 2, and 1 and enters a different state known as REM (rapid eye movement) sleep. In this state, which is distinct from all the other (non-REM) stages, the eyes move rapidly under closed eyelids.

Q What are some common sleep disorders? What treatments are available or under development?

A The most common sleep disorders are sleep walking, insomnia, apnea, and narcolepsy. There are some prescription medicines for insomnia, but they can have dangerous side effects.

Dreams

Q How does the content of dreams typically vary by age? By gender?

A Very young children tend to have brief dreams involving animals; narrative, storylike dreams appear between the ages of 5 and 6. In adults' dreams, narratives follow well-developed story lines and other people play important roles. Men more often dream about weapons and aggressive interactions, whereas women are more likely to dream about being the victims of aggression.

Q Describe each of the four theories that explain why we dream: Freudian, information processing, neural activity, and dreams and waking life.

A According to Freud, dreams represent wishes that have not been fulfilled in reality and therefore reflect motives of which the dreamer may not be consciously aware. The information processing explanation holds that dreams reprocess information gathered during the day in order to strengthen the memory of information crucial to survival. A third proposal is that dreams are the result of neurons firing at random, sending signals that higher brain centers attempt to weave into a coherent story. Still another theory is that dreams are an extension of the conscious concerns of daily life.

Q What evidence suggests that we need to dream?

A There is some evidence that we need to dream, but it is inconclusive. People who are deprived of REM sleep show various ill effects, and when allowed to sleep undisturbed they will double the amount of REM sleep they display. However, it is unclear whether these effects are due to the removal of REM sleep or to the lack of opportunity to dream during the REM period.

Drug-Altered Consciousness

Q What behaviors are included in the psychological definition of addiction?

A Addiction, or substance dependence, refers to ongoing abuse of a psychoactive substance, leading to compulsive use of the substance, often in increasingly higher doses.

Q Why does alcohol remain the most frequently abused drug, despite its dangers?

A Alcohol continues to be popular because it calms the nervous system, thus allowing drinkers to relax or enhance their mood and making them feel more courageous and less inhibited.

Q What are the major effects of stimulants on the nervous system?

A Stimulants excite the central nervous system, temporarily increasing mental alertness and reducing physical fatigue.

Q What are the most widely used hallucinogens? What are their effects?

A The most widely used hallucinogens are LSD, mescaline, peyote, and psilocybin. They cause shifts in perception of the outside world or experience of imaginary landscapes, settings, and beings that may seem more real than the outside world.

Q What factors determine whether a person becomes addicted to drugs or alcohol?

A Several factors make it more likely that a person will abuse drugs. They include a possible genetic predisposition, the person's expectations, the social setting, and cultural beliefs and values.

Meditation and Hypnosis

Q What physiological changes occur during meditation?

A Meditation suppresses the activity of the sympathetic nervous system, lowers the rate of metabolism, reduces heart and respiratory rates, and decreases blood lactate, a chemical linked to stress. Alpha brain waves (which accompany relaxed wakefulness) increase noticeably during meditation.

Q Why is hypnosis a controversial subject?

A It's not really that controversial, although there is no simple definition of what it means to be hypnotized. Different individuals believed to have undergone hypnosis describe their experiences in strikingly different ways. Also, some people seem to be more susceptible to hypnosis than others, for unknown reasons.

Video Classics

Interview with Ernest Hilgard

SYNOPSIS: Hilgard responds to the question of whether "ancillary hypnotists" could be trained; that is, people (let's call them "para-hypnotists") with a high degree of skill at inducing hypnosis, whose job it is to assist doctors, dentists, and other professionals in need of hypnotizing clients. Hilgard thinks not.

Web Links

1. http://www.psywww.com/asc/asc.html

States of Consciousness website provides links about hypnosis, out-of-body experiences, and dreams.

2. http://www.rxlist.com/

RxList: The Internet Drug Index. That is, a list of drugs posted on the Internet, not necessarily "Internet drugs," which are different from "television drugs" or "PalmPilot drugs." If you'd like your students to learn more about drugs and their effects, this is the place to go. A brief report might be in order.

3. http://www.well.com/user/woa/

Web of Addictions offers a variety of links to sites associated with addiction facts, meetings, topics, and help. Students can start here to prepare a report about the various options available for help with addictions.

4. http://www.habitsmart.com/

HabitSmart homepage has links to sites for the treatment or coping strategies one may use for an addiction, and it has links to a variety of other addiction-related websites.

5. http://www.nida.nih.gov/

Drug abuse and addiction-related links about prevention and treatment, research on addictions and substance use, and drugs and social policy.

transparencies

Series V

40. *EEG Patterns*
EEG patterns associated with the waking state, drowsy state, stage 1-4 sleep, and REM sleep are shown.

41. *Sleep over the Life Span*
The average amount of sleep time and proportions of REM and NREM sleep over the course of the life span.

42. *The Effect of Blood Alcohol Level on Behavior*
As blood alcohol level increases resulting behavior becomes more dangerous.

43. *Caffeine Levels in Commonly Consumed Products*
The caffeine levels in coffee, tea, and over-the-counter medications are shown.

Text Figures

4-1.	*Waves of Sleep*
4-2.	*A Night's Sleep Across the Life Span*
4-3.	*Changes in REM and NREM Sleep*
Summary Table	*Drugs: Characteristics and Effects*
4-4.	*Teenage Use of Alcohol*
4-5.	*Alcohol-related Traffic Deaths*
4-6.	*The Amount of Caffeine in Some Common Preparations*
4-7.	*Teenage Use of Ecstasy in Past Year*
4-8.	*Teenage Use of Marijuana in Past Year*

Handout 4-1

Recording the Stream of Consciousness

Instructions: During class, the lecture will be interrupted at four random intervals. Whenever the instructor says "stop and record your thoughts," you should immediately write down in the spaces provided below exactly what you were thinking about just before the interruption. Please write down <u>exactly</u> what you were thinking (i.e., do not edit yourself); anything is acceptable as long as it is accurate. These data will not be collected by the instructor.

Interruption 1:

Interruption 2:

Interruption 3:

Interruption 4:

Handout 4-2

Dream Survey

Instructions. Respond to each question below by circling "YES" if the answer is "Yes" and by circling "NO" if the answer is "No." Please note that your responses to these questions are strictly anonymous. This survey will not be collected, and no one will see your responses but you (although you are welcome to share your responses with the class if you wish).

1. Do you typically remember your dreams?   YES   NO
2. Have you ever been able to control what you dream about or how your dream unfolds?   YES   NO
3. Have you ever died in a dream?   YES   NO
4. Do you have a recurring dream?   YES   NO
    Briefly describe it.

5. Have you ever dreamed about doing something impossible (e.g., flying, playing music even though you can't)?   YES   NO
6. Have you ever had a dream in which one person transformed into another?   YES   NO
7. Do your dreams often contain inconsistencies (e.g., you know it's your house or your room but it doesn't look like it's suppose to)?   YES   NO
8. Do you ever dream about celebrities?   YES   NO   Which ones?
9. Do you incorporate outside noises into your dream (e.g., an alarm clock, a telephone ring)?   YES   NO
10. Have you ever dreamed about:
    - a sexual experience?   YES   NO
    - being naked in public?   YES   NO
    - killing someone?   YES   NO
    - finding money?   YES   NO
    - being attacked or pursued?   YES   NO
    - arriving too late for something important?   YES   NO
    - being locked up?   YES   NO
    - war?   YES   NO

Handout 4-3

Student Assignment: Keeping a Dream Journal

Your task for this assignment is to keep a dream journal for several weeks in order to record the content of at least 5 different dreams.

Instructions:

1. In order to best remember your dreams, you should follow several steps. First, place a pen and pad next to your bed before you go to sleep. Before you go to sleep, tell yourself that you'll be able to remember your dreams when you wake up. When you do wake up, keep your eyes closed and replay the dream until the plot and details become clear in your mind. Then, gently sit up, turn on the light, and write down what you remember about your dream. If you typically have trouble remembering your dreams, try setting your alarm clock for 10 or 15 minutes earlier than normal (this should interrupt your last dream of the night).

2. When recording your dream, include whatever information you can remember about:
   - the setting (e.g., indoors or outdoors)
   - characters (e.g., relatives, friends, strangers)
   - nature of the interaction (e.g., friendly, hostile, sexual)
   - activities (e.g., running, speaking, flying)
   - whether or not the dream was in color
   - any relationship to the previous day's events or the next day's planned activities

3. Once you have recorded your dreams on paper, please type them and arrange them as a list of entries according to the date of the dream. When typing your dreams to hand in, feel free to summarize details or to edit material that you would like to keep to yourself; on the other hand, detailed transcripts are fine, too. Regardless of whether you edit your selections or not, be assured that any information that you turn in to me will be kept strictly confidential.

4. Following your final dream entry, spend a paragraph or two noting your observations and feelings about your dreams. Did you notice any major themes or patterns to your dreams? Did you generally dream in color? Did your dreams seem meaningful or were they totally random and bizarre? Did you have any "lucid" dreams (i.e., in which you were aware of dreaming and exerted control over it)? Were there any recurring characters? Were than any specific events (such as drinking alcohol or getting very little sleep) that seemed to influence the content or character of your dreams?

Chapter 5 Learning

chapter outline 119

learning objectives 121

lecture suggestions

    Laws of Conditioning 122
    Pigeon Overhead: Bombs Away! 122
    Bear Boys, Swine Girls, Wolf Children 123
    Lots of Learning 123
    Punishment 124
    The Cat's Out of the Bag...er, Box! 125
    Applied Learning 125

demonstrations and activities

    Defining Learning 127
    Shark Attack! 127
    Classical Salivary Conditioning 128
    Crunch! A Quick Demonstration of Classical Conditioning 128
    Understanding the Elements of Classical Conditioning 129
    Operant Conditioning in Human Behavior 129
    Using Candy to Illustrate Operant Conditioning Concepts 130
    Conditioning a Student "Rat" 130
    Reinforcement vs. Punishment 130
    Schedules of Reinforcement 130
    Human Cognitive Maps 130

student assignments

    Classical Conditioning and the Pupil Dilation Response 132
    Conditioning in Everyday Life 132
    Behavior Modification Project 133
    Behaviorism in Literature: *Walden Two* 133

video 134

multimedia 136

transparencies 143

handouts

    Defining Learning 145
    Elements of Classical Conditioning 146
    Reinforcement versus Punishment 147
    Schedules of Reinforcement 148

chapter outline

I. **Classical Conditioning**
    A. Pavlov's conditioning experiments
        1. Salivary responses in dogs
        2. Pairing of stimuli over time
    B. Elements of classical conditioning
        1. Unconditioned stimulus
        2. Unconditioned response
        3. Conditioned stimulus
        4. Conditioned response
    C. Classical conditioning in humans
        1. Conditioning of phobias
        2. Desensitization therapy
    D. Classical conditioning is selective
        1. Preparedness and contrapreparedness
            a. Conditioned food aversion

II. **Operant Conditioning**
    A. Elements of operant conditioning
        1. Thorndike's research
            a. Cats in a puzzle box: Speed of correct response increases over trials
            b. Law of Effect = Principle of Reinforcement
        2. Operant response
        3. Consequence
            a. Reinforcers
            b. Punishers
    B. Types of reinforcement
        1. Positive and negative reinforcement
            a. Positive reinforcers add something rewarding to the situation
            b. Negative reinforcers remove an unpleasant stimulus
    C. Punishment
        1. Decreases the likelihood that ongoing behavior will recur
        2. Should be swift, sufficient, certain
        3. Generally not as effective as skillful application of reinforcement
        4. Avoidance training is an alternative strategy
    D. Operant conditioning is also selective

E. Superstitious behavior

F. Learned helplessness

G. Shaping behavioral change through biofeedback

III. Comparing Classical and Operant Conditioning

A. Response acquisition

1. Classical conditioning: Multiple trials strengthen US-CS link

2. Operant conditioning: Relevant responses are selectively reinforced

   a. Shaping: rewarding successive approximations to desired end-state

B. Extinction and spontaneous recovery

1. Classical conditioning: Repeated non-pairing of CS and US

   a. spontaneous recovery can nonetheless occur

2. Operant conditioning: Strength, setting, complexity of response determine extinction

C. Generalization and discrimination

1. Classical conditioning: Both processes occur

2. Operant conditioning: Both processes occur here, too

D. New Learning Based on Original Learning

1. Classical conditioning: Higher-order conditioning

   a. an earlier CS becomes the US for further learning

2. Operant conditioning: Secondary reinforcers

   a. Primary reinforcers: Reinforcement rewarding in and of itself

   b. Secondary reinforcers: Value is learned through association

E. Contingencies

1. Classical conditioning: Reliable "if-then" relationship established between the CS and US

2. Operant conditioning: Intermittent versus continuous reinforcement

3. Schedules of reinforcement

   a. Fixed-interval, fixed-ratio, variable-interval, variable-ratio

IV. Cognitive Learning

A. Latent learning and cognitive maps

1. Latent learning is not immediately reflected in behavior

   a. Cognitive maps are the mechanism for latent learning

B. Insight and learning sets

1. Insight reflects Gestalt notions of "A-ha" phenomenon

2. Learning sets: Learning how to learn

C. Learning by observing

1. Social learning theory describes learning by watching

2. Bandura's studies are a classic example

3. Pay attention, remember, ability to perform action, vicarious reinforcement

D. Cognitive learning in nonhumans: Rats, chickens, octopi demonstrate cognitive learning

learning objectives

After reading this chapter, students should be able to:

1. Describe how classical conditioning was discovered. Define: unconditioned stimulus, unconditioned response, conditioned stimulus, and conditioned response.

2. List the factors necessary for the success of learning in classical conditioning.

3. Explain these processes: extinction, spontaneous recovery, inhibition, stimulus generalization, discrimination, and higher-order conditioning.

4. Distinguish between classical and operant conditioning.

5. Explain the principle of reinforcement. Define primary reinforcer and secondary reinforcer and give examples of each.

6. Identify four schedules of reinforcement and the pattern of response associated with each.

7. Define positive reinforcement.

8. Explain how to use punishment successfully.

9. Define negative reinforcement. Explain the process of avoidance training.

10. Distinguish between cognitive learning and traditional theories of conditioning. Explain contingency theory.

11. Discuss social learning theory and its implications for human learning.

12. Define learning set and describe the phenomenon of insight learning.

lecture suggestions

The Laws of Conditioning

Students of learning theory are familiar with Edward Thorndike's *law of effect*. Stating, roughly, that behaviors which are followed by reinforcement tend to be repeated again in the future, the law of effect forms the cornerstone of operant conditioning. Less well-known, however, are other laws that Thorndike formulated, or the revisions that each underwent.

For example, the law of effect as we know it today was originally stated somewhat differently. Prior to 1930, Thorndike emphasized the connection between a stimulus and response, and how the connection could be strengthened or weakened depending on the consequences of the response. His original formulation, then, stated that if a response was followed by satisfaction (i.e., the maintenance of some state that is agreeable to the organism) the strength of the connection would be increased. If the response was followed by an annoyance (i.e., a situation the organism seeks to avoid), the connection between stimulus and response would be weakened. After 1930, Thorndike revised the law of effect after realizing that, in effect, the effect was incorrect. Put simply, it's only half true: Reinforcement increases the strength of a connection, whereas punishment does nothing to the strength of a connection.

Similarly, Thorndike's *law of readiness* and *law of exercise* underwent revision. The law of readiness states that it is satisfying to complete an act once one has prepared to do so, whereas it is frustrating to not be able to perform an act or to be forced to perform when one does not want to. In short, the law of readiness states that interference with goal-directed behavior is aversive, a point that's difficult to argue with. The law of exercise, on the other hand, can be quibbled with; in fact, Thorndike did so himself. Prior to 1930, Thorndike held that connections between a stimulus and response are strengthened as they are used (the *law of use*) and weakened if they are not (the *law of disuse*). In other words, exercising or discontinuing a stimulus-response connection can respectively strengthen or weaken the connection. Thorndike later abandoned the law of exercise entirely.

Hergenhahn, B. R., & Olson, M. H. (1993). *An introduction to theories of learning* (4th ed.). Englewood Cliffs, NJ: Prentice Hall.

Pigeon Overhead: Bombs Away!

Animals have consistently played a prominent role in learning and conditioning experiments, from Edward Thorndike's cats to Edward Tolman's rats to the disobedient menagerie of Marian and Keller Breland. Included in this list are some very famous pigeons who almost helped the national defense.

B. F. Skinner worked at the University of Minnesota during the second World War. Interested in applying the principles of operant conditioning to the war effort, Skinner trained pigeons to peck at discs which had moving pictures of enemy targets displayed on them. The pecking served to close electronic circuits, which in turn formed a self-regulating system. Although this is no great feat in itself--these actions faithfully follow the most basic rules of operant conditioning--Skinner's vision was to install his pigeons, discs, and circuits in gliders packed with explosives. The idea was to have the pigeons peck on cue to manipulate the circuits, which in turn would keep the glider on its kamikaze course toward an enemy target. A neat, tidy bombing run, with no loss of human life.

The Defense Department declined Skinner's help, even though he demonstrated to top scientists that the homing device withstood electronic jamming, the apparatus was inexpensive to build, and the basic set-up could be applied to a range of enemy targets. In the present era of Star Wars weaponry, stealth bombers, and combat guided by virtual reality, perhaps a pigeon bombardier wouldn't seem so far-fetched.

Hergenhahn, B. R., & Olson, M. H. (1993). *An introduction to theories of learning* (4th ed.). Englewood Cliffs, NJ: Prentice Hall.

Skinner, B. F. (1960). Pigeons in a pelican. *American Psychologist, 15*, 28-37.

Bear Boys, Swine Girls, Wolf Children

Cases of feral children can be traced back for centuries, at least as far as the celebrated case of Romulus and Remus. The term *feral*, in its modern usage, refers to a number of situations: Human children raised by animals; children surviving in the wilderness; children raised in isolated confinement; or children raised in confinement with little human contact. Regardless of the circumstances, children reared under atypical conditions present a unique case of learning.

Carlos Linnaeus first documented cases of feral children based largely on anecdotal evidence. Colorful figures such as the Hessian wolf-boy (1344), Lithuanian bear-boy (1661), or Irish sheep-boy (1672) covered both a lot of terrain and much of the animal kingdom, and provided ammunition for thinkers from Jean-Jacques Rousseau to Francis Gall about the contributions of nature and nurture to human development. Other notable cases include the Wild Boy of Aveyron, Kaspar Hauser, and Wild Peter. It wasn't until the well-known case of the wolf-children of Midnapore, Kamala and Amala, that structured psychological study of feral children began. Captured in 1920 by Reverend J. A. L. Singh and a hunting party, Kamala (approximately age 8) and Amala (perhaps 1½) were seen in the presence of a wolf mother and three cubs, and were taken as they tried to leave their den. Amala died after a year apart from the wolves, although Kamala lived until about the age of sixteen. During her eight years living with humans she was able to understand speech, mastered a vocabulary of 45 words, and could form 2- and 3-word sentences, in addition to a wide repertoire of gestural communication. These developments did not take place overnight. For several years Kamala was frightened of humans (uttering shrieks and cries when they came near) and was largely mute. Through therapeutic massage and dedicated attention by Mrs. Singh, Kamala grew to become an active, affectionate member of the Singhs' orphanage.

The case of Anna provides a contrast to Kamala. Born in 1932, Anna was the second illegitimate child of a rural woman. Unwanted by her parents (they tried unsuccessfully to place her for adoption) and hated by her grandfather, Anna was kept locked from sight in the attic of the family home. For 6 years she lived with minimal human contact and subsisted on a diet of cow's milk. She could neither walk nor talk and was malnourished. After a few years of institutional care Anna was able to speak in phrases and short sentences, although her abilities remained in the retarded range. She died August 6, 1942, at the age of ten.

The challenge to learning is clear in these examples. In many cases feral children are quadruped and in most cases they lack speech. Hence, the challenge of restoring some aspects of behavior (e.g., walking upright, not eating from the floor) compound the normal challenges of learning (e.g., speech training, interpersonal skills training). In some cases, previous responses must be replaced by new ones, such as Kamala's learning to eat from a table, whereas in other cases existing cognitive processes need to be modified, such as Kaspar Hauser's rudimentary speech. In all cases feral children provide food for thought about a variety of issues related to learning, development, and cognition.

Candland, D. K. (1993). Feral children and clever animals: Reflections on human nature. Oxford: Oxford University Press.
Davis, K. (1940). Extreme social isolation of a child. American Journal of Sociology, 45, 554-565.
Gesell, A. (1940). Wolf child and human child: The life history of Kamala, the wolf girl. New York: Harper.
Linnaeus, C. (1758). Systema Naturae (10th ed.).
McNeil, M. C., Polloway, E. A., & Smith, J. D. (1984, February). Feral and isolated children: Historical review and analysis. Education and Training of the Mentally Retarded, pp. 70-79.
Singh, J. A. L., & Zingg, R. M. (1941). Wolf-children and feral man. New York: Harper & Bros.
Zingg, R. M. (1940). Feral man and extreme cases of isolation. American Journal of Psychology, 53, 487-517.

Lots of Learning

Learning theories are typically divided into classical and operant conditioning, cognitive learning, observational learning, and a handful of miscellaneous approaches. Edward Tolman alone, however, perhaps true to his iconoclastic ways, proposed six kinds of learning:

❖ *Drive discrimination.* Organisms can discriminate among various drive states, which leads them to adjust their behavior accordingly. For example, rats know that hunger, thirst, sexual, and aggressive drives are not all the same, and so can act to achieve goals appropriate to the particular drive state being experienced.

❖ *Field expectancies.* Organisms learn which events in their environment lead to other events. For example, a chicken may come to expect that when a green light is flashed it will be followed eventually by a shrill whistle. Confirmation of this expectation apparently is the only reinforcement necessary. Field expectancies are similar to cognitive maps in that both address how an organism comes to learn what leads to what.

❖ *Field-cognition modes.* Tolman tentatively held that field-cognition modes were innate strategies, modified by experience, for approaching a problem-solving task.

❖ *Cathexis.* An association formed between a particular drive state and a particular stimulus. For example, the drive state of thirst might become associated with certain stimuli, such as the typical means used to meet it (sugar-free, diet, no-caffeine, cherry cola). When the drive occurs, a person will actively seek out the stimuli that have been associated with the drive's satisfaction.

❖ *Equivalence beliefs.* Tolman thought that previously neutral events could develop the capacity of satisfying a need, as when a meatloaf sandwich comes to reduce a person's need for affiliation. Equivalence beliefs are similar to secondary reinforcers in many ways, although Tolman emphasized social drives rather than physiological drives in this type of learning.

❖ *Motor patterns.* This type of learning refers to the overt behavior patterns an organism must learn in order to obtain a desired goal. For example, a goat might learn to vigorously shake a fencepost in order to loosen the grass beneath it that provides a meal.

In many ways, Tolman's statement of these types of learning reflects his attempt to consolidate the best ideas from Clark Hull, Edwin Guthrie, Gestalt theories, operant conditioning, and his own views into a single system. Aspects of those various schools of thought are either evident or implied in many of the types of learning Tolman proposed.

Hergenhahn, B. R., & Olson, M. H. (1993). *An introduction to theories of learning* (4th ed.). Englewood Cliffs, NJ: Prentice Hall.
Tolman, E. C. (1949). There is more than one kind of learning. *Psychological Review, 56,* 144-155.

Punishment

Students often have difficulty distinguishing between negative reinforcement and punishment. These examples of types of punishment may clarify what it is and when it should be used.

Physical punishment or *aversive punishment* involves administering a stimulus that evokes discomfort. Spankings, electric shock, harsh sounds, or pinches would be included in this category. Aversive punishment its typically used in extreme cases, as it is neither pleasant to administer nor to receive. *Reprimands* are strong verbal commands ("No!" "Stop that!" "Bad!") used when an inappropriate behavior is displayed. They are sometimes accompanied by physical or nonverbal reprimands. Timeout can be exclusionary or nonexclusionary. *Exclusionary timeout* involves removing an individual for a short time from a situation that he or she finds reinforcing. *Nonexclusionary timeout* involves introducing a stimulus that is less reinforcing. For example, children might be given a "good conduct" badge to wear while playing in a classroom. If the child becomes disruptive the badge will be removed, and the child will be ignored by the teacher and not allowed to play with the others. Finally, *response cost* involves removing a specified amount of reinforcement after an undesired behavior occurs. Parking tickets, bank fees, or library fines would be examples of this type of punishment.

As the text mentions, to be effective punishment must be swift, certain, and sufficient. Some guidelines for deciding to use punishment include selecting a specific response to punish (such as spitting out food) rather than a general category of behavior (such as not eating or being finicky); maximizing the conditions for a desirable alternative response and minimizing the conditions for the causes of the undesirable response; selecting an effective punisher (i.e., one that can be delivered immediately and will not be associated with subsequent positive reinforcement).

Martin, G., & Pear, J. (1992). *Behavior modification: What it is and how to do it* (4th ed.). Englewood Cliffs, NJ: Prentice Hall.

The Cat's Out of the Bag!...er, Box!

Edwin Guthrie is chiefly known for one idea in Behaviorism; the principle of one-trial learning. Guthrie held that learning was complete--that is, an association between a stimulus and a response was at its strongest--after only one pairing of the stimulus and response.

The way he set about testing his idea was to use a variant of Thorndike's puzzle box. Guthrie modified the box by placing a long, thin rod vertically in it, wired so that each time a cat rubbed against it the door to the box would spring open, allowing the animal to exit. Guthrie noted that among some 800 cats each had a stereotyped way of rubbing the rod, which was repeated trial after trial, even in absence of reinforcement. He took this as evidence for one-trial learning; the response was full-blown from the first trial, and it was not modified over trials.

Being a good Behaviorist, Guthrie made careful observations of the laboratory animals. Being a good Behaviorist, Guthrie stuck to fairly straightforward, objective testing conditions. But being a good Behaviorist, Guthrie assumed that species-specific behavior would not play a major role in the experiment's outcomes. Like Clark Hull, for example, Guthrie was interested in demonstrating a principle of learning, regardless of whether it was demonstrated by a cat, rat, chimpanzee, or human. Unfortunately, cats exhibit a stereotyped greeting response when in the presence of a conspecific (which, for most domestic cats, includes humans). That is, they rub against their fellow cat as it passes by or, in the case of greater distances, they rub against a more convenient object, such as a tree, furniture, or Uncle Harry's leg. As Guthrie and his laboratory assistants observed the cats, then, it is not remarkable that they all showed highly stereotyped behavior; they did what cats do.

Bruce Moore and Susan Studdard illustrated this point in a simple experiment. Cats were placed in puzzle boxes that had long, thin, vertical rods, but this time rubbing the rods triggered no doors. Moore and Studdard also varied whether a person was present or not as the cats meandered through the box. They discovered, quite simply, that when a person was present the bar was rubbed, and when a person was not present, the bar was not rubbed. As Guthrie observed, the rubbing itself was quite stereotyped, befitting an innate feline response.

Guthrie, E. R., & Horton, G. P. (1946). *Cats in a puzzle box*. New York: Rinehart.
Leahey, T. H., & Harris, R. J. (1993). *Learning and cognition* (3rd. ed.). Englewood Cliffs, NJ: Prentice Hall.
Moore, B., & Studdard, S. (1979). Professor Guthrie and *felis domesticus*, or: Tripping over the cat. *Science, 205*, 1031-1033.

Applied Learning

Behavior modification can be thought of as a technology that developed out of learning theory. Based on the principles of operant conditioning, behavior modification seeks to structure the reinforcement a person receives for his or her actions in order to modify or shape more productive behavior. There are several areas of application, as noted by Garry Martin and Joseph Pear.

❖ *Education*. Behavior modification has been applied to both classroom management and specific learning skills, from preschool through university education. For example, disruptive behaviors such as tantrums, aggressive acts, or leaving one's seat can be modified effectively with the proper program. Content skills, such as reading comprehension, mathematics, or spelling, can also benefit from the application of operant principles.

❖ *Severe mental and behavioral problems.* Perhaps the most visible use of behavior modification techniques is in the management of mental retardation, schizophrenia, and autism. In these instances social skills, vocational skills, and self-care can be established either in an institutional ward or in a private setting.

❖ *Clinical behavior therapy.* Behavior therapy has grown in popularity over the past several decades. In many cases (e.g., the treatment of phobias, obsessive-compulsive disorder) it is the treatment of choice.

❖ *Self-management.* Behavior modification has been used to help people achieve their personal goals, such as overcoming procrastination, maintaining an exercise program, or relieving mild phobias.

❖ *Medicine and health care.* There are several areas related to medical practice that currently rely on operant principles. For example, patient compliance in drug-taking can be increased through appropriate reinforcement, as can stress management or the promotion of healthy lifestyles.

❖ *Community psychology.* Behavior modification techniques have been applied beyond the level of the individual to the level of the community. Community mental health centers, halfway houses, and youth organizations often employ behavioral techniques to promote job skills training or increase compliance with community programs (e.g., recycling, litter removal, decreasing vandalism).

❖ *Business, industry, government.* Positive reinforcement, schedules of reinforcement, fading, and chaining have been used to improve worker morale, reduce shoplifting, decrease absenteeism, and increase worker efficiency.

❖ *Sport psychology.* Behavior modification has been used to improve athletes' skills (such as coordination and execution), to change coaches' behaviors (such as teaching effective managerial strategies), to increase motivation and endurance (such as having athletes keep public records of their fitness training), and to treat athletes' personal problems (such as a behavioral therapist might do).

❖ *Behavioral assessment.* Psychodiagnostic assessment has gained a new partner in behavioral assessment. Identifying problem behaviors and long-standing behavior repertoires at intake can help establish an effective treatment program.

Martin, G., & Pear, J. (1992). *Behavior modification: What it is and how to do it* (4th ed.). Englewood Cliffs, NJ: Prentice Hall.

demonstrations

Defining Learning

Rather than delving immediately into the principles of classical and operant conditioning, consider introducing the topic of learning by devoting class time to a discussion of its definition. Although the psychological definition of learning is a fairly straightforward one, students may initially have trouble with the concept because of their intuitive notion that "learning" is synonymous with "studying" and also because they have difficulty distinguishing behaviors that are truly learned from those that can be attributed to other factors such as instinct or maturation.

Thomas Rocklin suggests an engaging activity that can be used to help your students explore the concept of learning. Handout 5-1 contains a list of events compiled by Rocklin that potentially represent examples of learning. Duplicate and distribute this list (or read it aloud) and ask students to indicate which events are examples of learning and which are not. As students defend their choices, their own intuitive definitions of learning should become evident. During the discussion, be sure to compare and contrast their ideas about learning with the definition presented in the text (i.e., that learning is "the process by which experience or practice results in a relatively permanent change in behavior or potential behavior"). Rocklin notes that although the majority of events yield fairly consistent answers, items related to computers typically generate disagreement and controversy. In addition to enjoying the active participation encouraged by this exercise, students should also come away with a more thorough understanding of the concept of learning.

Rocklin, T. (1987). Defining learning: Two classroom activities. *Teaching of Psychology, 14*, 228-229.

Classical Salivary Conditioning

Dennis and Rosemary Cogan have designed a relatively quick but powerful demonstration of classical conditioning. You'll need a can of sweetened lemonade powder and enough small Dixie-type cups so that each participating student has one. After discussing Pavlov's work, distribute to each student a cup approximately half-filled with lemonade powder. After deciding on a neutral stimulus to serve as the conditioned stimulus (the Cogans suggest "Pavlov"), you are ready to begin conditioning. Instruct students to moisten the tip of their index finger and then to dip it into the powder and then onto their tongues whenever you give a prearranged signal (such as raising your arm). Also inform students that you will occasionally say the words "test trial" instead of giving the signal; when this occurs, students should refrain from tasting the powder and instead close their eyes and concentrate on their own experience.

Present the CS (i.e., say "Pavlov") and then after a delay of .5 to 1.5 seconds, give the signal for students to taste the lemonade powder (i.e., raise your arm). These learning trials should be repeated every 10 to 15 seconds, with test trials (in which you say, "Pavlov...test trial") occurring after every 10 learning trials. After each test trial, ask for a show of hands for those who are salivating (the majority of the students should be salivating by the 7th or 8th trial). When most students show evidence of conditioning, demonstrate extinction by continuously giving test trials (i.e., saying "Pavlov...test" trial over and over) until students no longer salivate. During the next class session, demonstrate spontaneous recovery by saying the word "Pavlov" and asking for a show of hands for those who salivate. The Cogans report that in addition to being enthusiastically received by students, this demonstration facilitates understanding of conditioning principles and generates a discussion of classical conditioning applications to real life problems.

Cogan, D., & Cogan, R. (1984). Classical salivary conditioning: An easy demonstration. *Teaching of Psychology, 11*, 170-171.

Crunch! A Quick Demonstration of Classical Conditioning

Vandendorpe (1988) described a quick demonstration designed to illustrate a conditioned emotional response to the word "crunch." Start the lecture by telling students that the experimental psychology class is studying cognitive associations to various words, and has asked you to obtain some data by getting associations to the word "crunch." Then ask your class to provide some associations that occur to them when they hear the word "crunch" and record them. Continue with your lecture and when you begin discussing phobias, use the narrative developed by Vandendorpe as an example:

Of course, I don't actually have a phobia, but I do have a rather intense dislike that will show you what I mean by a conditioned emotional response. Now, I really don't mind most insects, like ants and tomato bugs. I even think spiders are fine, although most people don't care for them. But what I really can't stand...what really gets my skin crawling are certain kinds of bugs. You know the ones I mean...they creep around at night, when you can't see them, and they like dark places, and hide in sewers. I'm talking about those black water bugs, and cockroaches, too. I really dislike them. Now I understand that they don't carry disease, so that if a cockroach walked over your dinner plate, it wouldn't be that bad a thing, but I still don't like them. And the thing I really hate about them is that they've got these hard shells, so that if you step on them, they go "crunch" (when you say crunch, do so with some dramatic flair and emphasis).

Vandendorpe noted that this demonstration almost never fails to elicit groaning or physical discomfort to the word "crunch." After producing the conditioned emotional response, go back over the original associations produced to the word and discuss why the word did not initially produce the conditioned emotional response and how the response might have been established.

Vandendorpe, M. M. (1988, October). Crunch: Demonstrating the conditioned emotional response. Paper presented at the Mid-American Conference for Teachers of Psychology, Evansville, IN.

Reprinted from Hill, W. G. (1995). Instructor's resource manual for *Psychology* by S. F. Davis and J. J. Palladino. Englewood Cliffs, NJ: Prentice Hall.

Understanding the Elements of Classical Conditioning

Although students have no problem understanding classical conditioning intuitively, they often become confused by the terminology and have difficulty keeping straight the four elements of classical conditioning: unconditioned stimulus (US), unconditioned response (UR), conditioned stimulus (CS), and conditioned response (CR). After lecturing on classical conditioning, consider giving your students extra practice applying these principles by going over Handout 5-2 in class. Correct answers are given below.

	US	UR	CS	CR
Scenario 1	poison	dizziness & nausea (aversion)	sheep	running away (aversion)
Scenario 2	immune suppressing drug	weakened immune response	saccharine flavored water	weakened immune response
Scenario 3	job interview	anxiety/ nervousness	airplane/ flying	anxiety/ fear
Scenario 4	bad weather	unhappiness	weathercaster	unhappiness
Scenario 5	attractive women	desire	automobile	desire

Ader, R., & Cohen, N. (1985). CNS-immune system interactions: Conditioning phenomena. *Behavioral and Brain Sciences, 8*, 379-94. [Example 2]

Cialdini, R. B. (1993). *Influence: Science and practice* (3rd ed.). New York: HarperCollins. [Examples 4 and 5]

Garcia, J., Hawkins, W, & Rusniak (1974). Coyote predation control by aversive conditioning. *Science, 184*, 581-83. [Example 1]

Operant Conditioning in Human Behavior

Because much of the operant conditioning research presented in textbooks is conducted with animals (e.g., rats, pigeons, dogs), students often have difficulty seeing its relevance to human behavior, which presumably is not as susceptible to environmental control. Edward Stork suggests a simple demonstration that can be used to generate a discussion of human operant conditioning. While discussing operant conditioning, interrupt your lecture with a question that you know will elicit a mostly positive response (e.g., "How many of you are planning to major in psychology?" "How many of you live within 5 miles of campus?" "How many of you plan to register for classes next term?"). Most students will raise their hands in response to your questions. Tell them to hold that position, and ask if anyone told them to raise their hands or even mentioned raising hands. After the chorus of groans (from "being caught") dies down, ask students to explain their behavior in terms of operant conditioning, and then use this activity as a springboard for generating other examples of operant conditioning in humans.

Stork, E. (1981). Operant conditioning: Role in human behavior. In L. T. Benjamin, Jr., & K. D. Lowman, (Eds.), *Activities handbook for the teaching of psychology* (p. 57). Washington, DC: American Psychological Association.

Using Candy to Illustrate Operant Conditioning Concepts

After having tricked your students into displaying evidence of operant conditioning in the previous exercise, reward them with this simple (and tasty!) demonstration that uses a candy machine to illustrate operant conditioning concepts. During your lecture on operant conditioning, place a filled candy machine (e.g., containing M&Ms or peanuts) on a table at the front of the room. [A bubble gum machine can be substituted, but because it requires pennies it can be a little more cumbersome to use.] Invite any and all interested students to come inspect the machine and do whatever they want to with it (most will, of course, pull the lever and be rewarded with candy). While students are engaging in this activity, ask them to relate any behaviors they observe to material from the text. You can also prompt them with questions to help them understand additional terms and concepts, such as: (1) What would happen to your behavior if all the candy was gone? (extinction), (2) What if the machine were refilled? (spontaneous recovery), (3) What if there was an empty coffee jar next to the candy machine? (discrimination), (4) What if there was a similar machine (such as a gumball machine) filled, but not exactly like the candy machine? (generalization), (5) What if you do not like candy or cannot eat it for health reasons? (effectiveness of a reinforcer, motivation), (6) What if the machine were filled with money instead of candy? (secondary reinforcer), (7) What if, like a slot machine, money only appeared after a random number of pulls of the lever? (variable ratio schedule), (8) What might happen to your behavior if you are reinforced on a variable ratio schedule instead of a continuous one? (superstitious behavior, extinction would take longer), (9) What would happen if very bad-tasting candy came out of the machine? (punishment). During the course of this exercise, it is likely that students will come up with additional questions or interesting variations of their own.

Adapted from Smith, J. Y. (1990). Demonstration of learning techniques. In V. P. Makosky, C. C. Sileo, L. G. Whittemore, C. P. Landry, & M. L. Skutley (Eds.), *Activities handbook for the teaching of psychology: Vol. 3* (pp. 83-84). Washington, DC: American Psychological Association.

Conditioning a Student "Rat"

A fun demonstration of shaping the behavior of a student "rat" can be used to liven up your coverage of operant conditioning. [This exercise should be done after students are familiar with the concept of shaping by successive approximations.] Ask for a student volunteer to be the rat and send that person outside the classroom. In the meantime, the class should select a target behavior for the rat to perform. Potential target behaviors include turning off the classroom lights, turning on the overhead projector, picking up chalk or an eraser, scratching his or her head, shaking hands with the instructor, and so on. The class should also select its method of reinforcement; smiles (which can be big or small), nods (which can be slight or vigorous), or even pencil tappings should work well. When the "rat" returns, the class should reinforce successive approximations of the goal behavior. That is, they should reinforce the rat when it is close to performing the behavior, and do nothing when it is far from the desired behavior. Alternatively, students can adopt the popular "temperature" version from the childhood game and use "cold," "cool," "warm," "hot" and so on to reflect closeness to the goal.

This exercise can also be modified to include more student "rats" as part of a small-group activity. Depending on your class size, divide students into groups of about 4-6 people and ask for a volunteer "rat" from each group. To keep things flowing smoothly, you should distribute to each group a slip of paper containing the target behavior. These should be simple, personal behaviors (such as having "rats" cover their eyes, clap their hands, stand on one leg, make the "okay" gesture, say a target word, take off a watch, etc.) rather than more expansive behaviors (such as going to a corner of the room) in order to keep the activity coordinated and manageable. If you have time, you may want to let each student have a turn playing the "rat."

Reinforcement vs. Punishment

Although reinforcement (which serves to increase or strengthen a behavioral response) is conceptually the opposite of punishment (which serves to decrease or weaken a behavioral response), students often have a hard time distinguishing negative reinforcement from punishment. Handout 5-3 contains several realistic examples of behavior that can be classified as positive reinforcement, negative reinforcement, or punishment. After you have discussed these principles in lecture, test your students' ability to apply what they've learned by going over this short exercise in class. Correct answers are given below.

1. PR	5. PR	9. PUN	13. PUN	17. PUN
2. PUN	6. PR	10. NR	14. NR	18. PR
3. PUN	7. NR	11. NR	15. PR	19. PUN
4. NR	8. PUN	12. PR	16. PR	20. PR

Schedules of Reinforcement

After you have lectured on reinforcement schedules, test students' ability to apply Fixed Interval (FI), Fixed Ratio (FR), Variable Interval (VI), and Variable Ratio (VR) schedules to everyday behavior. Handout 5-4 contains many real-world examples of these schedules and can be duplicated and distributed to students or given orally if your copying budget is tight. Correct answers follow.

1. FI	5. FR	9. VI	13. FI	17. VI
2. VI	6. VR	10. VR	14. VR	18. FI
3. VR	7. FI	11. FR	15. VI	19. VR
4. VI	8. FR	12. FR	16. FI	20. FR

Examples selected from a compilation by Roig, M., and Greco-Vigorito, C. (1993). Catalog of negative reinforcement and intermittent reinforcement schedule examples. Paper presented at the 101st Annual Convention of the American Psychological Association, Toronto.

Human Cognitive Maps

The text describes Tolman's famous study, which demonstrated that latent learning (i.e., learning not immediately reflected in behavior change) can occur in rats. His study showed that rats left alone in a maze, even when not reinforced for their behavior, formed "cognitive maps" (mental representations of the maze) that allowed them to run the maze swiftly and accurately when later reinforced with food. Humans, too, use a variety of cognitive maps to represent important environments, such as a school, a stadium, an airport, a freeway system, a parking lot, a shopping mall, and so on. You can illustrate this phenomenon easily with students by having them generate a cognitive map for a relevant environment, such as your college campus. After discussing Tolman's study, ask students to take out a blank sheet of paper and sketch a map of the campus. Compare and contrast the features included in (and excluded from) students' maps by either projecting an actual campus map on the overhead or by having a few students with detailed maps sketch their maps on the board. Discuss how and why students' maps differ. What landmarks were central to most maps? Were any features commonly left out? Were there differences between students who live on campus and those who commute? Were there differences related to major of study? Perhaps students' maps were more detailed and/or accurate for areas near their major department. Were there noticeable differences between maps drawn by seniors (who have spent considerably more time on campus) and first-year students? Were there any gender differences? Were there differences between athletes and nonathletes? These and other questions should spark an interesting discussion on the role of experience in developing cognitive maps.

Whitford, F. W. (1995). Instructor's resource manual for *Psychology: An Introduction* by C. G. Morris (8th ed.). Englewood Cliffs, NJ: Prentice Hall.

student assignments

Classical Conditioning and the Pupil Dilation Response

Roger Hock suggests a simple classical conditioning experiment that students can perform on themselves at home. Students will need a bell, a hand-held mirror, and a room that becomes completely dark when the light is turned off. Instruct students to hold the bell while standing in the room near the light switch. Once in position, they should ring the bell and then immediately turn off the light. After waiting in total darkness for about 15 seconds, they should turn the light back on. They should wait another 15 seconds with the light on, and then ring the bell and immediately turn the light back off (again waiting 15 seconds in the dark). Students should repeat this procedure 20 to 30 times, making sure that in each case the bell is rung immediately before the light is turned off. After numerous pairings, students are ready to see the results. With the light on, they should watch their eyes closely in the mirror and then ring the bell. Students' pupils should dilate slightly even without a change in light!

For a simple out-of-class assignment, ask students to perform this demonstration at home and to report on their results as part of a class discussion. For a more elaborate assignment, ask students to write a 1 to 2-page paper explaining the process in terms of classical conditioning. Students should explain that because pupils naturally dilate and constrict according to the amount of light intensity, the darkness in this study is an unconditioned stimulus (US) that leads to the unconditioned response (UR) of pupil dilation. By repeatedly pairing a neutral stimulus (e.g., the bell) with the unconditioned stimulus (i.e., darkness), the bell has become a conditioned stimulus (CS) that elicits the conditioned response (CR) of pupil dilation. As part of their paper, students should also propose another (i.e., original) classical conditioning experiment that they can perform at home. Have students perform their experiment, and then in their papers they should carefully describe the procedure and results in classical conditioning terms. An added benefit of this assignment is that many of the clever ideas generated by students can be used as out-of-class demonstrations for future classes!

Hock, R. R. (1992). Forty studies that changed psychology: Explorations into the history of psychological research. Englewood Cliffs, NJ: Prentice Hall.

Keeping a Psychology Journal: Conditioning in Everyday Life

After having read the textbook, after having been exposed to lecture, and after having completed some of the practice exercises suggested here, students should be well-versed in the theories and principles behind classical and operant conditioning. Students should now be ready to apply what they've learned to everyday life. Ask students to write a journal entry discussing practical extensions of classical conditioning, operant conditioning, or both. There are several variations to this assignment. In one version, students can discuss a variety of examples of conditioning from their own personal experience. A student might, for instance, retell the story of a recent taste aversion experience, note that a pet cat is conditioned to respond to the sound of a can opener, or describe how they reinforce their own study habits. In another version, students can be asked to find examples of how businesses cleverly use these principles in an attempt to influence consumers. Potential examples include magazine or newspaper ads that associate a product with a stimulus that produces positive feelings, letters from polling organizations that include an incentive (such as a crisp dollar bill) for completing a questionnaire, "gifts" (such as personalized address labels) from nonprofit charitable organizations seeking donations, or any of a new crop of "personalized" appeals that get our attention because they use cues associated with friendship rather than outright sales pitches (e.g., a handwritten message on a yellow sticky note attached to what appears to be a vacation postcard from a friend). In still another version of this assignment, students can be asked to locate two or three reports of recent research that apply principles of classical or operant conditioning to real-world problems (e.g., classical conditioning as a treatment for bedwetting, incentives for participating in curbside recycling programs, the revoking by states of teenage drivers' licenses for school truancy).

Behavior Modification Project

An excellent way for students to gain a greater appreciation for learning concepts is to put what they've learned to good, practical use. For this assignment, ask students to apply principles of operant conditioning to modify an existing behavior. Instruct students to identify a target behavior to be modified, either an undesirable behavior that they would like to eliminate or a desirable behavior that they would like to strengthen. By taking a close look at many aspects of their own behavior--such as study habits, sporting skills, health habits, or personal-interaction skills--students should have no trouble selecting a behavior they'd like to change. Examples of potential undesirable behaviors to eliminate include smoking cigarettes, eating fatty foods, watching too much TV, speeding, phobias or anxieties (e.g., fear of flying, test anxiety), and procrastination before exams or papers. Examples of desirable behaviors to be increased include remembering people's names, becoming more punctual with respect to class or social events, outlining textbook chapters while reading, using a turn signal while driving, and increasing a skill in sports (e.g., using a left foot in soccer, increasing free-throw percentage in basketball).

For this assignment, students should propose a program for changing a behavior and then later, after implementing their program, report on its results. This probably works best as a two-part assignment (to ensure that students' programs are carefully thought out and so they don't fudge on their criteria for, or evaluation of, success), but should also work fine as a single final report. After identifying the target behavior, students should monitor their behavior for a few days and try to generate a plausible explanation for why the problem exists. They should also describe why they want to change the behavior and what benefits change will bring. Next, students should carefully design a program for modifying the behavior. Note that the *Highlights* box ("Modifying Your Own Behavior") in Chapter 5 contains suggested steps for an effective behavior modification program. In their program proposal, students should describe all relevant conditioning principles incorporated within their plan, which might include the use of positive and negative reinforcers, punishment, shaping, schedules of reinforcement, modeling, extinction, stimulus discrimination or generalization, primary and secondary reinforcers, and so on. Students should then implement their program and write up an honest report of the results. To what degree was the program successful? Plausible explanations for success or failure should be highlighted. If students failed, they should propose (but not carry out) an alternative plan that might be more successful in the future. If students succeeded, they should propose a plan that to help them maintain the change. In fairness and to encourage students to select important (but perhaps difficult) target behaviors, students should be graded on their understanding and application of learning principles (e.g., as evident in their program design and implementation) rather than their degree of success at modifying the chosen behavior.

Behaviorism in Literature: *Walden Two*

In *Walden Two*, B. F. Skinner describes a utopian community in which major social problems have been eliminated through the use of operant conditioning. This ideal community is free of racism, crime, poverty, and laziness, all owing to it's strict adherence to reinforcement principles as a means of governing behavior. Ask your students to read *Walden Two* and then to write an essay applying the behavioral principles from the text and lecture to the novel. Their discussion should also include a critical evaluation of the community presented in the novel. Would such an approach be feasible? What are the advantages and disadvantages to this system? Would they personally like to live there? Why or why not?

Alternatively, Michael Gorman and his colleagues have suggested contrasting *Walden Two*, which emphasizes the environment as the sole determinant of behavior, with *The Eden Express*, which explores biological roots of behavior (in this case, schizophrenia). See Gorman, Law, and Lindegren (1981) for further details regarding this assignment.

Gorman, M. E., Law, A., & Lindegren, T. (1981). Making students take a stand: Active learning in introductory psychology. *Teaching of Psychology, 8*, 164-166.

Skinner, B. F. (1948). *Walden Two*. New York: Macmillan.

video

ABC News/Prentice Hall Video Library

Building Brains (12:41 min, Series III). The developmental changes that take place during the first three years of life are remarkable, particularly those changes that occur in the brain. This *Nightline* segment focuses on the importance of early stimulation, training, and education for "building" better brains.

Contract to Get Parents Involved in a Child's Education (3:47 min, Series III). ABC's *World News Tonight* looks at a program in Stone Mountain, Georgia, that encourages parents to actively become involved in their children's education. Parents of students at Pine Ridge Elementary sign contracts agreeing to attend parent-teacher conferences, spend a minimum of 15 minutes reinforcing each day's lessons, and volunteer at the school.

Other Sources

B. F. Skinner and Behavior Change (45 min, PENN). Traces the development of modern behaviorism and examines its applications in a variety of settings, as well as its ethical and social implications.

Biological Preconditions of Learning (28 min, FHS). How the senses, nervous system, and brain interact to produce learning. Changes in neural connections during learning are discussed.

Classical and Operant Conditioning (56 min, FHS). This broad overview of Behaviorism presents terminology, applications, and debates surrounding these two types of learning.

Discovering Psychology, Part 8: Learning (1990, 30 min, ANN/CPB). Covers the basic principles of operant and classical conditioning through a focus on the contributions of Pavlov, Watson, Skinner, and others.

Further Approaches to Learning (57 min, FHS). Latent learning, learning sets, social learning, ethology, cognitive theories, and neuroscience get their just rewards in this exploration of "other" types of learning.

Genie (1991, 60 min, PBS). This powerful video recounts the real-life story of "Genie," a young girl living a feral existence in a disturbed home environment. UCLA psychologists and linguists recount the slow process of working with Genie to produce advances in learning and social adaptation. Actual footage of laboratory studies is used. Worth seeing; applicable in a variety of contexts.

Learning (23 min, FHS). Facets of the learning process--a newborn's adaptation to the environment; a young adult's apprenticeship training; use of educational software; the relationship between aging and learning--form the basis of this video.

Learning (1990, 30 min, IM). Provides an overview of classical and operant conditioning, including applications in treating hyperactivity and an interview with Skinner.

Learning Disabilities (19 min, FHS). Diagnosing, evaluating, and treating learning disabilities are the focus of this video. The daily routine of a 9-year-old boy and his problems are featured.

Schools of Thought: Teaching Children in America and Japan (55 min, FHS). A comparison of Japanese and American educational systems forms the basis for answering questions such as why differences in education exist and how personal and cultural goals influence the education process.

Skinner's Keynote Address: Lifetime Scientific Contribution Remarks (1990, 18 min, APA). In Skinner's last public appearance before his death, he emphasizes that psychology's true object of study is the analysis of behavior. In reaching this conclusion he addresses the various paths psychologists have followed, including introspection, natural selection, and variants of conditioning and learning.

Stimulus Response in Animals (1996, 33 min, FHS). A menagerie of animals is shown illustrating the basic principles of operant conditioning. Hens, calves, and pigs display autonomic and learned responses on demand.

multimedia

Live! Psych

Module	Title	Book Page #
5.1	Pavlov's Dogs and Classical Conditioning	p. 187

This concept demonstrates Pavlov's original experiment along with a paradigm of the classical conditioning procedure. Import Screen 1 to summarize Pavlov's original experiment and how he discovered classical conditioning while studying the digestive system in dogs. Import Screens 2 and 3 to show Pavlov's classical conditioning paradigm before conditioning. Import Screen 4 to show what occurs during conditioning in Pavlov's classical conditioning paradigm. Import Screen 5 to review the basic classical conditioning paradigm. The student clicks on each stage to review.

5.2	Everyday Classical Conditioning	p. 190

Screen 1 introduces a prime example of how classical conditioning occurs in many everyday experiences, such as how humans react to a visit to the dentist's office. Import Screen 2 to review the first stage of classical conditioning—what occurs before conditioning. Import Screen 3 to review the second stage—what occurs during conditioning. Import Screen 4 to review the third stage—what occurs after conditioning.

5.3	Principles of Operant Conditioning	p. 197

Screen 1 introduces B.F. Skinner and the basic principles of operant conditioning. Screen 2 defines reinforcement and explains how reinforcers can be either positive or negative, but both result in strengthening a prior response. The student clicks on the positive and negative reinforcement boxes to learn more about each one. Screen 3 defines punishment and explains how punishers can be either positive or negative, but both result in decreasing a prior response. The student clicks on the positive and negative punishment boxes to learn more about each one. Import Screen 4 emphasize that negative reinforcement should not be confused with punishment.

5.4	Shaping Behavior	p. 201

View this animation an operant conditioning procedure called shaping. Screen 1 explains the method of successive approximations. Import Screen 2 to view an animation of the Skinner box in use. Screen 3 demonstrates how to shape a pigeon to peck at a colored light.

Web Investigations

Principles of Learning in the Real World

This activity presents a general introduction to principles of learning and contains four separate modules on its key concepts: habituation and sensitization, classical conditioning, operant conditioning, and observational learning. Buster, a cyberdog, is your host for the module on classical conditioning. By interacting with Buster students can experience the development of a conditioned response. Dexter, a virtual rat, leads students through the section on operant conditioning, where they can explore positive and negative reinforcement and punishment. A worksheet is available on the principles of classical and operant conditioning; students can complete this activity and submit a hard copy or e-mail to you. In the section on observational learning Bobo is your host, as students can review footage from Bandura's classic experiment.

Making Connections

Classical Conditioning

Q What are the four basic elements of classical conditioning?

A The four elements of classical conditioning are an unconditioned stimulus (US) that invariably prompts a certain reaction; that reaction, the unconditioned response (UR); a neutral stimulus, or conditioned stimulus (CS); and the conditioned response (CR), the behavior the subject learns in response to the CS.

Q How can classical conditioning be used to help people "unlearn" anxiety and fear?

A By pairing the feared object (CS) with a pleasant experience (US), people can be taught to associate their fear with pleasant sensations.

Q How does the idea of preparedness help explain why classical conditioning operates selectively?

A Some stimuli naturally serve as CSs for certain kinds of responses (e.g., many people experience fear when they see a snake). Therefore, humans and animals are prepared by their evolutionary heritage to acquire phobias about certain stimuli and not about others.

Operant Conditioning

Q What two factors are essential for operant conditioning to occur?

A The two basic elements of operant conditioning are the operant response, or the particular response the experimenter wants; and the consequence that follows the subject's behavior.

Q What does it mean to say that a reinforcer is negative?

A A reinforcer is anything that increases the likelihood that a behavior will be repeated. A negative reinforcer is one that elicits desired behavior by removing an unpleasant stimulus.

Q In what kinds of situations is punishment effective?

A Punishment is most effective when it is administered immediately after the misbehavior occurs, when it is sufficient without being cruel, and when it is certain. It is most appropriate as a way of changing dangerous or self-destructive behavior.

Q What is the relationship between the principle of preparedness and operant conditioning?

A The principle of preparedness implies that behaviors that are easiest to condition are those that the subject would perform naturally.

Q How does operant conditioning explain the development of superstitions?

A Superstitions arise when people pair random events with lucky or unlucky occurrences, such as wearing a particular shirt when winning a prize.

Q What is learned helplessness, and how does it affect people?

A Learned helplessness is a failure to escape from an unpleasant stimulus because of previous exposure to unavoidable painful stimuli. It affects people because it generalizes to new situations. Thus a child who is treated abusively at home may "learn" feelings of powerlessness.

Comparing Classical and Operant Conditioning

Q Define shaping, and explain how it helps speed responses in operant conditioning.

A Shaping refers to a process of reinforcing successively closer approximations to a desired behavior. It allows the trainer to reward steps toward the desired behavior rather than waiting for the entire behavior to occur.

Q What factors tend to speed up extinction of learned behaviors?

A Placing the learner in a novel situation tends to speed up extinction; in general, the weaker the original learning, the sooner extinction takes place in the absence of reinforcement.

Q Why is discrimination important to learning?

A Discrimination is important because it is necessary to distinguish between noxious stimuli that are harmful or dangerous and those that are not. For example, small children tend to fear all strangers, but as they get older, they realize that some strangers are trustworthy and friendly.

Q What is the difference between primary and secondary reinforcers?

A Primary reinforcers, such as food, water, or sex, are intrinsically rewarding. They serve as reinforcers without any prior learning. Secondary reinforcers, such as money or tokens, require prior learning to make them valuable.

Q What are some practical applications for using different schedules of reinforcement?

A Examples include: being paid on a piecework basis (fixed-ratio schedule); playing a slot machine (variable-ratio schedule); earning a regular salary (fixed interval schedule); watching a football game and waiting for a touchdown (variable interval schedule).

Cognitive Learning

Q What is the major difference between the study of behavioral learning and cognitive learning?

A Behavioral learning involves the study of events (responses) that can be directly observed. Cognitive learning involves the study of internal events that must be inferred from observations of behavior.

Q What is insight learning? What evidence suggests that animals exhibit insight learning?

A Insight learning is learning that occurs rapidly, as a result of understanding the elements of a problem. Chimpanzees display insight learning when they suddenly realize how to use a stick to obtain an out-of-reach banana. Pigeons display insight learning when, after some preliminary training, they push a box below a picture and peck the picture to receive a reward.

Q What does social learning theory tell us about how people learn?

A Social learning theory tells us that people learn not only from direct experience but also from watching others or listening to them recount their experiences.

Q What evidence is there for cognitive learning in nonhuman animals?

A Evidence for cognitive learning in nonhuman animals comes from latent learning studies and research showing that rats can learn from observation, as can chickens and octopi.

Mind Matters

Learning Through Association: Classical Conditioning

There's a wealth of information in this section of the CD-ROM: profiles of Ivan Pavlov and John Watson, and E. L. Thorndike, examples of conditioning and drug addiction, a film clip of Little Albert, a discussion of conditioning and phobias, and an overview of basic classical conditioning concepts. Your students should find this a valuable study tool when reviewing material from the chapter. You might want to use the pop-up profiles of Pavlov, Watson, or Thorndike as a starting point for a more lengthy assignment about the backgrounds of these thinkers.

Learning Through Association: Operant Conditioning

A profile of B. F. Skinner is included here, as is an audio clip of Skinner speaking on reinforcement. This section also covers the distinction between reinforcement and punishment and looks at the interaction between classical and operant conditioning. Your students should find that this is a fine starting point for understanding the basics of operant conditioning.

Opening the Black Box: Cognitive Learning

This section of the Learning Module contrasts the approach of radical Behaviorists with that of cognitive psychologists. The Black Box model is compared to different accounts of the mind. Several problems with Behaviorism, such as biological preparedness, language, social learning, and mental representation, are considered. Students can watch archival footage of Bandura's young research participants whacking the heck out of a Bobo doll. Consider illustrating your lectures with the brief movie clips included here.

Video Classics

Interview with B. F. Skinner

SYNOPSIS: Skinner discusses the various mechanisms of "programming" behavior: shaping, rewarding successive approximations to a desired end state, schedules of reinforcement, and stimulus control. This vintage footage provides students with a chance to learn about these basic principles of operant conditioning from their originator.

Form a Hypothesis

Q How do you suppose you shape a pigeon to do what you want it to do?

A One reinforces successively better approximations of the final or target behavior, a process called shaping.

Test Your Understanding

Q What steps are involved in shaping?

A One defines the terminal behavior and the steps necessary for it. Then, one reinforces the beginning, intermediate, and terminal steps for the behavior.

Q What are different types of programming?

A In the segment, Skinner describes shaping as a type of programming in which one moves from simple behaviors to a complex one by building on each established behavior. Skinner also characterizes discrimination training, in which an organism is reinforced for responding in the presence of a stimulus, but not in its absence. Skinner also describes scheduled reinforcement, in which an organism is gradually shaped to number or rate of responses for a given reinforcer.

Q What is the Skinner box?

A A Skinner box is a device for presenting discriminative stimuli, recording a behavior (such as a bar press or key peck), and delivering a reinforcing stimulus at rates or patterns determined by the experimenter.

Thinking Critically

Q How do you reinforce successive approximations of the target response? What are everyday examples of how our behavior is shaped?

A Ideally, initial approximations are reinforced immediately and reliably. Much of our behavior is shaped, for example, learning how to ride a bicycle, learning cursive script, learning good work habits, etc.

Pavlovian Conditioning

SYNOPSIS: Taken from a vintage Russian laboratory film, this clip illustrates the principles of classical conditioning. A harnessed dog receives electric shock, which becomes associated with a ticking metronome. Look carefully for the original Russian titles flashing briefly between their English translations.

Form a Hypothesis

Q Do you think that a dog can be conditioned to react to a neutral stimulus (a metronome) that has been paired with an unpleasant stimulus, such as electric shock?

A Yes. Students may note this from their experience, e.g., how the family pet cowers at the sight of a rolled-up newspaper.

Test Your Understanding

Q What is the role of the CS, US, CR, and UR in the pairing of electric shock with the metronome?

A The CS is the sound of the metronome after pairing. The US is the shock and the UR is the leg-withdrawal by the dog. The CR is the leg-withdrawal to the sound of the metronome after conditioning trials.

Thinking Critically

Q How can social behavior be influenced through classical conditioning?

A Much like Pavlov's dogs, we can associate individuals with pleasant or painful stimulation. So, we may come to be attracted towards pleasant persons and learn to avoid punishing individuals.

Little Albert

SYNOPSIS: This clip presents John Watson and Rosalie Raynor interacting with Little Albert. Taken from films of Watson's original studies with Albert, the clip shows all the elements of the fear response that was conditioned in the little tyke. In silent movie fashion, narrations appear on the screen describing the various stages of the conditioning process.

Form a Hypothesis

Q Do you think emotions, such as fear, can be experimentally conditioned? In other words, do you think "Little Albert" can learn to fear a white rat when it is paired with a loud noise?

A Yes. The ability to associate emotional reactions to stimuli and situations would have protective value for the individual. Additionally, there are many other analogies in life to the Little Albert demonstration, such as a student coming to fear an overbearing and critical teacher.

Test Your Understanding

Q Fear of a rat may be experimentally set up by stimulating the infant with a loud sound just at the moment the rat is presented. After seven repetitions of pairing the rat with the loud noise, the boy was frightened of the rat. Further, the conditioned fear of the rat generalized to a rabbit, a dog, a Santa Claus mask, and a white fur coat. What are other examples of how emotional responses can be conditioned? What are other examples of how generalization occurs?

A An individual may come to fear riding in all forms of motor-vehicular transportation after a traumatic car accident, an example of generalization. Positive emotions can also be conditioned, such as the sense of warmth and well being that most individuals experience when seeing a picture of their father or mother; such reactions are the result of many 'trials' in which the sight of their parents preceded parental warmth and affection.

Q What is the process of classical conditioning?

A Classical conditioning occurs when a neutral stimulus (one that cannot by itself evoke a response) is paired with an unconditioned stimulus (one that evokes an unconditioned response). After an adequate number of pairings, the previously neutral stimulus (now a conditioned stimulus) evokes a conditioned response. In the Little Albert demonstration, the neutral stimulus was the rat. The unconditioned stimulus was the loud noise and the unconditioned response was Little Albert's discomfort at the noise. After seven trials, the conditioned response was his withdrawal ('fear') of the rat.

Q What are practical applications of classical conditioning?

A There are many. The video demonstrates emotional conditioning, which can be applied in advertising (e.g., the association of pleasant situations or images with a product). Additionally, other stimuli and ideas may become conditioned to establish conditioned relationships ("higher-order conditioning").

Thinking Critically

Q How does this study violate current ethical guidelines for research involving humans?

A Little Albert was not 'deconditioned' from his fear of white fur or hair. Additionally, it is questionable if fear response needed to be conditioned to demonstrate that emotions in general can be classically conditioned.

Web Links

1. http://www.pigeon.psy.tufts.edu/psych26/alinks.htm

The Animal Cognition Home Page offers information about operant conditioning, in addition to information about classical conditioning.

2. http://www.wagntrain.com/OC/

Use of operant conditioning in animal training describes theories of reinforcement and shaping and then gives examples implementing these theories. A helpful source of practical, real-world examples of learning principles.

3. http://www-all.cs.umass.edu/rlr/

The reinforcement learning repository.

4. http://www.brembs.net/learning/drosophila/general_introduction.html

Compares and contrasts operant and classical conditioning. Provides helpful diagrams that your students can use while learning about learning.

5. http://www.has.vcu.edu/psy/psy101/forsyth/zlearn.htm

Forsyth's Learning Page. Lots of resources for further exploration into the psychology of learning.

transparencies

Series V

44. *A Thorndike "Puzzle Box"*
Fun with cats; show your students how to get out of a box.

45. *Apparatus Used to Study Classical Conditioning of Salivation in Dogs*
Fun with dogs; show your students how to spit in a tube.

46. *Pavlov's Procedure for Classical Conditioning*
Pavlov's basic design for studying US and CS is shown.

47. *Possible Sequences for Presenting the CS and US in Classical Conditioning*
Trace conditioning, delayed conditioning, simultaneous conditioning, and backward conditioning are illustrated.

48. *Stimulus Generalization in Classical Conditioning*
This transparency shows how stimulus generalization occurs in classical conditioning.

49. *Stimulus Discrimination Training in Classical Conditioning*
This transparency shows how stimulus discrimination occurs in classical conditioning.

50. *Operant Conditioning Chamber – A Skinner Box*
The apparatus used to study operant learning is shown.

51. *Training Procedures Used in Operant Conditioning*
The outcomes of positive and negative reinforcement, punishment, and omission are depicted.

52. *Characteristics of Schedules of Reinforcement*
Fixed and variable interval and ratio schedules are compared.

53. *Reinforcement Schedules: Typical Response Patterns*
The behavior resulting from learning under fixed interval, fixed ratio, variable interval, and variable ratio schedules are shown.

54. *Evidence for Latent Learning*
Latent learning in rats is illustrated using the Tolman-Honzik study.

Text Figures

5-1.	*Pavlov's Apparatus for Classically Conditioning a Dog to Salivate*
5-2.	*A Paradigm of the Classical Conditioning Process*
5-3.	*A Cat in a Thorndike "Puzzle Box"*
5-4.	*Learned Helplessness*
5-5.	*Response Acquisition*
5-6.	*A Rat in a Skinner Box*
5-7.	*Response Acquisition and Extinction in Classical Conditioning*
5-8.	*Response Patterns to Schedules of Reinforcement*
5-9.	*Graph Showing the Results of the Tolman and Honzik Story*
5-10.	*Bandura's Experiment in Learned Aggressive Behavior*
5-11.	*Observational Learning of Aggression*

Handout 5-1

Defining Learning

Instructions. For each of the following events, determine whether or not it represents an example of learning.

1. The cessation of thumb sucking by an infant.

2. The acquisition of language in children.

3. A computer program generates random opening moves for its first 100 chess games and tabulates the outcomes of those games. Starting with the 101st game, the computer uses those tabulations to influence its choice of opening moves.

4. A worm is placed in a T-maze. The left arm of the maze is brightly lit and dry; the right arm is dim and moist. On the first 10 trials, the worm turns right 7 times. On the next 10 trials, the worm turns right all 10 times.

5. Ethel stays up late the night before the October GRE administration and consumes large quantities of licit and illicit pharmacological agents. Her combined (verbal plus quantitative) score is 410. The night before the December GRE administration, she goes to bed early after a wholesome dinner and a glass of milk. Her score increases to 1210. Is the change in scores due to learning? Is the change in pretest regimen due to learning?

6. A previously psychotic patient is given Dr. K's patented phrenological surgery and no longer exhibits any psychotic behaviors.

7. A lanky zinnia plant is pinched back and begins to grow denser foliage and flowers.

8. MYCIN is a computer program that does a rather good job of diagnosing human infections by consulting a large database of rules it has been given. If we add another rule to the database, has MYCIN learned something?

9. After pondering over a difficult puzzle for hours, Jane finally figures it out. From that point on, she can solve all similar puzzles in the time it takes her to read them.

10. After 30 years of smoking two packs a day, Zeb throws away his cigarettes and never smokes again.

Reprinted with permission from T. Rocklin, 1987, Defining learning: Two classroom activities, *Teaching of Psychology*, 14, 228-229. Copyright 1987 by Lawrence Erlbaum Associates, Inc.

Handout 5-2

Elements of Classical Conditioning

Instructions. For each scenario presented below, identify the four major elements of classical conditioning. Specify for each example (a) the unconditioned stimulus (US), (b) the unconditioned response (UR), (c) the conditioned stimulus (CS), and (d) the conditioned response (CR).

1. To discourage coyotes from attacking their sheep, ranchers feed the coyotes small pieces of mutton tainted with poison that, when ingested, cause the coyotes experience extreme dizziness and nausea. Later, when the coyotes are placed in the pen with the sheep, the mere smell of the sheep causes the coyotes to run frantically away from their former prey.

2. As part of a new and intriguing line of research in behavioral medicine, researchers give mice saccharine-flavored water (a sweet substance that mice love) and then follow it up with an injection of a drug that weakens mice's immune systems. Later, when these mice drank saccharine-flavored water, they showed signs of a weakened immune response. Research is currently underway to see if the reverse is possible (i.e., if conditioning can be used to increase immune functioning), a discovery which would surely have important implications for new medical treatments.

3. A passenger on an airplane was feeling very anxious about an important job interview the next morning, and as a result he was uneasy and nervous throughout the flight. Back at home weeks later, he is contemplating a holiday trip. Though he hadn't previously been afraid to fly, he finds himself suddenly nervous about flying and decides to cancel his plans to visit an out-of-state relative.

4. It's no secret that people become unhappy when bad weather strikes, but what is surprising is that weather forecasters are consistently blamed for weather over which they obviously have no control. Weather forecasters around the country have been wacked by old ladies with umbrellas, pelted with snowballs, and even threatened with death (e.g., "You're the one that sent that tornado and tore up my house...I'm going to take your head off!", or "If it snows over Christmas, you won't live to see New Year's!") by people who mistakenly infer a causal relationship between the forecaster with subsequent foul weather patterns.

5. Why is it that automobile advertisements--especially those for sports cars--often feature beautiful young women? Because smart advertisers know (and research confirms) that new car ads that include an attractive female are rated by men as faster, more appealing, better-designed, and more desirable than similar ads that do not include an attractive female.

Handout 5-3

Reinforcement vs. Punishment

Instructions. For each example presented below, identify whether positive reinforcement (PR), negative reinforcement (NR), or punishment (PUN) is illustrated by placing the appropriate abbreviation in the blank next to the item.

_____ 1. Police pulling drivers over and giving prizes for buckling up

_____ 2. Suspending a basketball player for committing a flagrant foul

_____ 3. A soccer player rolls her eyes at a teammate who delivered a bad pass

_____ 4. A child snaps her fingers until her teacher calls on her

_____ 5. A hospital patient is allowed extra visiting time after eating a complete meal

_____ 6. Receiving a city utility discount for participating in a recycling program

_____ 7. Grounding a teenager until his or her homework is finished

_____ 8. Scolding a child for playing in the street

_____ 9. A prisoner loses TV privileges for one week for a rule violation

_____ 10. A parent nagging a child to clean up her room

_____ 11. A rat presses a lever to terminate a shock or a loud tone

_____ 12. A professor gives extra credit to students with perfect attendance

_____ 13. A dog is banished to his doghouse after soiling the living room carpet

_____ 14. A defendant is harassed and tortured until he confesses

_____ 15. A young child receives $5 for earning good grades in school

_____ 16. A mother smiles when her child utters "Mama"

_____ 17. A child is put into "time out" for misbehaving

_____ 18. Employee of the month gets a reserved parking space

_____ 19. At a party, a husband becomes sullen when his wife flirts with a colleague

_____ 20. A woman watching a football game offers her child candy to play quietly

Handout 5-4

Schedules of Reinforcement

Instructions. Identify the reinforcement schedule illustrated in the following examples by placing the appropriate abbreviation in the blank next to the item. Use the following code:

Fixed Ratio (FR)
Variable Ratio (VR)
Fixed Interval (FI)
Variable Interval (VI)

_____ 1. Getting a paycheck every other week

_____ 2. Pop quizzes

_____ 3. Slot machines at gambling casinos

_____ 4. Calling the mechanic to find out if your car is fixed yet

_____ 5. A factory worker who is paid on piece work

_____ 6. Fly fishing: casting and reeling back several times before catching a fish

_____ 7. Looking at your watch during a lecture until the end of the lecture

_____ 8. A salesperson who gets paid on commission

_____ 9. Calling a friend and getting a busy signal because he or she is frequently on the phone

_____ 10. Signaling with your thumb while hitchhiking

_____ 11. Frequent flyer program: rewards after flying X amount of miles

_____ 12. Collecting bottles, cans, or other recyclables for cash

_____ 13. An athlete's contract specifies salary increases to be renegotiated every three years

_____ 14. Buying lottery tickets

_____ 15. A person refrains from drugs for fear of random drug testing

_____ 16. Checking the refrigerator to see if the JELL-O is ready

_____ 17. Watching for shooting stars

_____ 18. Checking the mail, assuming the mail carrier comes at the same time every day

_____ 19. Playing Bingo

_____ 20. A worker receives $1 for every 100 envelopes stuffed and sealed

Chapter 6 Memory

chapter outline 150

learning objectives 153

lecture suggestions

    Culture and Memory 154
    The Role of Distinctiveness in Memory 154
    Talented, Prodigious, Autistic, and Idiot Savants 155
    Memory Under the Knife 155
    "Your Name Escapes Me, But Your Face..." 156
    Why You Don't Remember Your First Birthday Party 157
    Déjà Vu 157
    Memory Anomalies: Beyond Déjà Vu 158
    Everyday Memory 158
    The Mind(s) of Mnemonist(s) 159
    Mnemonics in Mind 160
    The Inner Workings of Working Memory 160
    Episodic ≠ Semantic 161

demonstrations and activities

    Demonstrating Simple Memory Principles 162
    Decay and Interference in Short-term Memory 162
    Depth of Processing and Memory 163
    Coding in Long-term Memory 164
    Go Fly a Kite: The Effect of Context on Memory 164
    Paddle Your Own Canoe 165
    Organization and Memory 166
    Schemas and Memory 166
    The Self-Reference Effect 167
    Attention and Memory: Forgetting vs. Not Getting 167
    Debate: Are "Recovered" Memories of Sexual Abuse Always Real? 168

student assignments

    Improving Memory 169
    Memory in Film: *Total Recall* 169
    Memory in Film: *Momento* 169
    Keeping a Psychology Journal 170

video 171

multimedia 172

transparencies 178

handouts

    Memory Test Scoring Sheet 179
    Coding in Long-term Memory 180
    Memory for Word Lists (6.3a, 6.3b) 182, 183

chapter outline

I. The Sensory Registers
- A. Visual and auditory registers
  1. Visual icons and auditory echoes
  2. Virtually unlimited capacity, but very rapid decay of information
- B. Attention
  1. Attention selects some information for further processing
     - a. Filter theories describe the selection process
       - i. Cocktail-party phenomenon

II. Short-Term Memory
- A. Capacity of STM
  1. Chunking illustrates STM capacity
     - a. A 5 to 10 item limit
     - b. A 1.5 to 2 second limit
- B. Encoding in STM
  1. Phonological coding
  2. Visual coding
- C. Maintaining STM
  1. Rote rehearsal: Limited benefits to simply repeating information over and over

III. Long-term Memory
- A. Capacity of LTM
  1. Unlike STM, LTM is a large-capacity system
- B. Encoding in LTM
  1. Coding by imagery
  2. Coding by meaning
- C. Serial position effect
  1. Primacy versus recency effects
- D. Maintaining LTM
  1. Elaborative rehearsal
     - a. Linking new information in STM to familiar material in LTM
  2. Schemata
     - a. Organized set of beliefs or expectations based on past experience
- E. Types of LTM
  1. Episodic memory: Personally experienced events
  2. Semantic memory: General facts and information

       3. Procedural memory: Information related to skills, habits, and perceptual-motor tasks

       4. Emotional memory: Learned emotional responses to stimuli

       5. Explicit memory and implicit memory

          a. Explicit: Episodic and semantic

          b. Implicit: Procedural and emotional

       6. Priming: Primes can influence our memory for information

       7. The tip-of-the-tongue phenomenon

IV. The Biology of Memory

    A. How are memories formed?

       1. Long-term potentiation: changes in neurons take place when memories are formed

    B. Where are memories stored?

       1. Short-term memories in prefrontal and temporal cortices

       2. Long-term memories enlist both cortical and subcortical structures

       3. Hippocampus is important in the formation of memories

       4. Semantic and episodic memories in the frontal and temporal lobes

       5. Procedural memories in the cerebellum

       6. Emotional memories rely on the amygdala

V. Forgetting

    A. The biology of forgetting

       1. Decay theory

          a. Information is lost with the passage of time

       2. Retrograde amnesia

          a. Inability to recall events immediately preceding an injury

    B. Experience and forgetting

       1. Interference

          a. Retroactive interference: New information interferes with previous information

          b. Proactive interference: Previously learned material interferes with new information

       2. Situational factors

          a. Cue-dependent forgetting: Learing cues are absent during recall

       3. State-dependent memory

          a. Learning and retrieval in the same psychological state

       4. The reconstructive process

          a. Schemas can influence memory and recall

    C. How to reduce forgetting: Ten tips for better memory

VI. Special Topics in Memory

    A. Autobiographical memory

       1. Personal memories tend to focus on recent events

       2. Many times memories are of formative decisions and consequential experiences

B. Childhood amnesia
- 1. Why you don't remember your 1st birthday party
    - a. The hippocampus may be a key element

C. Extraordinary memory
- 1. Eidetic imagery: The vaunted "photographic memory"
- 2. Mnemonists demonstrate amazing feats of recall

D. Flashbulb memories
- 1. Vivid remembrance of an event and incidents surrounding it

E. Eyewitness testimony
- 1. Prompts during recall may bias memory for events

F. Recovered memories
- 1. This highly controversial area has recently been informed by research evidence

G. Cultural influences on memory
- 1. Oral traditions, cultural significance, influence memory abilities

learning objectives

After reading this chapter, students should be able to:

1. Describe the path that information takes from the environment to long-term memory.

2. Explain the characteristics of the sensory register, short-term memory, and long-term memory.

3. Explain coding in both short-term and long-term memory.

4. Discuss explanations for forgetting.

5. Describe the different types of long-term memory and their characteristic properties.

6. Explain the limits of memory and determine if they can be expanded.

7. Describe how information is stored and how it is organized.

8. Define "schema". Discuss how schemata are used.

9. Discuss how and why memories change over time.

10. Describe and explain the brain structures and regions where memories are stored.

11. Understand and use techniques for improving your memory.

12. Explain the special types of memory: autobiographical memory, childhood amnesia, extraordinary memory, flashbulb memories, eyewitness testimony, and recovered memories.

lecture suggestions

Culture and Memory

All cultures place certain memory expectations on their members. For example, in Western culture we are expected to remember (through honors, ceremonies, observances) significant dates, persons, or activities. The Fourth of July, Thanksgiving Day, Presidents Day, and, most obviously, Memorial Day, are examples of a kind of culturally-shared memory system. Although often there are no explicit guidelines for activities on these occasions and no particularly dire sanctions for not observing them, we will certainly be looked at askance if we don't remember when they are or what they signify. Other cultures and subcultures have similar occasions, such as religious observances (e.g., first Friday of the month) or anniversaries (e.g., the Tiananmen Square demonstration).

Cultures and subcultures also have ritualized reminders for memory events. For example, people in Western cultures automatically know that a string around one's finger or an image of an elephant serve as reminders to do something, just as rosary beads help Catholics remember their prayers or a flag at half-mast helps remind a large group to honor someone's memory. The use and form of these reminders can vary from culture to culture, although like the memory tasks themselves, they typically are learned implicitly within a cultural context.

Beyond these aspects of a "general cultural memory," there is also evidence that gender stereotypes play a role in what gets remembered and by whom. For example, Stephen Ceci and Urie Brofenbrenner (1985) showed that remembering when to terminate an event is better if the event is consistent with gender stereotypes. Boys were better at remembering when to stop charging a motorcycle battery than remembering when to take cupcakes out of the oven, whereas girls showed the opposite pattern. Similarly, Douglas Herrmann and his colleagues (1992) showed that female and male undergraduates had differential memory for an ambiguous paragraph depending on its title. When given a "male-like" title ("How to Make a Workbench"), men remembered more details than did women, although the opposite was true if the ambiguous passage had a "female-like" title ("How to Make a Shirt"). The influence of culture on memory, then, also occurs indirectly through the expectations and stereotypes set up within a cultural context.

Ceci, S. J., & Brofenbrenner, U. (1985). "Don't forget to take the cupcakes out of the oven": Prospective memory, strategic time-monitoring, and context. *Child Development, 56*, 152-164.
Herrmann, D. J., Crawford, M., & Holdsworth, M. (1992). Gender-linked differences in everyday memory performance. *British Journal of Psychology, 83*, 221-231.
Searleman, A., & Herrmann, D. (1994). *Memory from a broader perspective.* New York: McGraw-Hill.

The Role of Distinctiveness in Memory

The use of bizarre imagery is an effective component of several mnemonic techniques. Winograd and Soloway noted that people often report that they are better able to remember information that they have attempted to make distinctive. For example, we often store things in unusual places (such as leaving soccer cleats in the kitchen) in the belief that it will be easier to remember where we put the item at a later time. This is somewhat like using a bizarre image with the method of loci. In order to examine this belief, Winograd and Soloway presented research participants with sentences that described an object stored in a normal location ("The milk is in the refrigerator.") or an unusual location ("The tickets are in the freezer."). Participants were asked to either rate the sentence for the likelihood of using this location to store the item, the memorability of the storage location, or to generate an image of what was described in the sentence and then rate its memorability. Participants were then given a recall test in which they were asked to remember the locations of the objects presented in the sentences. Contrary to what might be expected, items rated low in likelihood (that is, stored in unusual locations) were remembered less often than those rated high, regardless of the rated memorability. Although distinctiveness may be an effective aid for remembering a *particular* item, Winograd and Soloway concluded that it does not appear to be useful for remembering the *association* between two items. This is an important point because when we store an object in an unusual place we need to remember the association between the object and the location. This differs from what occurs in the method of loci, in which we start with a location and use an imaginal representation of the location to store and remember an object. In the distinctiveness situation we are doing the opposite; starting with an object and trying to remember a location that was not established with a strong imaginal representation.

> Winograd, E., & Soloway, R. (1986). On forgetting the location of things stored in special places. *Journal of Experimental Psychology: General, 115*, 366-372.

> Reprinted from Hill, W. G. (1995). Instructor's resource manual for *Psychology* by S. F. Davis and J. J. Palladino. Englewood Cliffs, NJ: Prentice Hall.

Talented, Prodigious, Autistic, and Idiot Savants

What to call someone of clearly impaired abilities who nonetheless exhibits remarkable memory skills? There are many choices, but they all describe a fascinating aspect of memory.

Savant syndrome, as it is commonly called, refers to people with very low general intelligence who show prodigious abilities in one or a few areas of functioning. Originally called *idiot savants* (through a combination of what were once scientifically acceptable terms), such people were thought to be mentally retarded. However, savants are found at a rate of about 1 in 2000 among the mentally retarded, compared to estimates of about 10 percent among the autistic population (Rimland & Fein, 1988). In fact, the term *autistic savant* is used to describe just these cases: Someone who is autistic, yet shows extraordinary skill in a particular area. Contrast this with the term *talented savant* (used to describe someone mentally retarded but able to perform a task at a comparatively high level, given the degree of retardation) or *prodigious savant* (used to describe a mentally retarded person capable of feats that would be remarkable by any standards).

Autistic savants are usually limited to a narrow range of talents. For example, many show fantastic abilities in art or music, or can perform arithmetic or calendar calculations quickly and accurately. Beyond these areas of expertise, however, their abilities are clearly below average. This observation is just one of many curiosities surrounding savant syndrome. For example, it is not at all clear how or why these abilities develop. Explanations invoking left hemisphere damage, heredity, compensatory development, and just plain practice have all been advanced. What is clear is that more research into the abilities of these remarkable individuals is needed.

> Searleman, A., & Herrmann, D. (1994). *Memory from a broader perspective.* New York: McGraw-Hill.

Memory Under the Knife

Most people's script for undergoing surgery runs something like this: You're a little nervous, the anesthesiologist knocks you out, you wake up again in what seems like no time, you don't remember anything about the surgery, and you pay a hefty hospital bill. Most of that is correct, especially the part about the bill. But there's growing evidence that memory during anesthesia can still take place.

The purpose of anesthesia is clear; to reduce the patient's awareness of the events that are about to take place. Under general anesthesia the patient is literally "knocked out;" however, memories may be formed at an implicit, nonconscious level. For example, Goldmann (1986) asked patients who were about to undergo surgery a series of bizarre questions (e.g., "How many teeth does an elk have?"). Under anesthesia half the patients heard the correct answers to these questions and the other half did not. Within a few days of the surgery, patients were retested on these same questions. Those who had heard the answers showed significant improvement on their test scores compared to the other group, although none of the patients could recall hearing anything during surgery.

This possibility of memory formation suggests that statements made during surgery can affect the patient's well-being. This point is illustrated by the "fat lady syndrome" (Bennett, 1988). Several years ago a lawsuit was brought by a rather large woman against her surgeon, who had derisively referred to her during surgery as "a beached whale." The woman suffered postoperative complications for several days and eventually snapped at her nurse, "That bastard called me a beached whale" (Bennett, 1988, p. 204). The matter was settled out of court, although ample anecdotal (and some experimental) evidence attests to this type of "memory without awareness."

Moreover, there is some evidence that positive statements made during surgery can improve recovery rates. For example, Evans and Richardson (1988) played one of two audiotapes for 39 women undergoing hysterectomies. While under anesthesia, some women heard a tape that described normal postoperative procedures, contained direct therapeutic suggestions ("You will not feel any pain"), and presented positive statements ("Everything's going quite well"). During other women's surgeries a blank tape was played. Not only did women in the first group spend less time in the hospital, they also had fewer gastrointestinal problems and were rated by nurses as having a significantly better recovery. Interestingly, although none of the women in either group could recall any events that occurred during the operation, all but one of the women in the positive statement group correctly guessed that they heard the "statement tape," whereas only 50 percent of the "no tape" women correctly guessed their experimental condition.

Bennett, H. L. (1988). Perception and memory for events during adequate general anesthesia for surgical operations. In H. M. Pettinati (Ed.), *Hypnosis and memory* (pp. 193-231). New York: Guilford Press.

Evans, C., & Richardson, P. H. (1988). Improved recovery and reduced postoperative stay after therapeutic suggestions during general anesthesia. *The Lancet, #8609* (II), 491-493.

Goldmann, L. (1986). Awareness under general anesthesia. Unpublished doctoral dissertation, Cambridge University, Cambridge, England.

Searleman, A., & Herrmann, D. (1994). *Memory from a broader perspective.* New York: McGraw-Hill.

"Your Name Escapes Me, But Your Face... Well, It Escapes Me Too."

Memory disruptions often become increasingly prevalent as we age. Beyond the annoyance of forgetting an acquaintance's name, the groceries we need for a new recipe, or someone's face is the annoyance of not quite knowing what to do about it. Memory disruptions could be due to faulty encoding of information, faulty retrieval, or both. A recent study suggests that encoding may be particularly important in successful memory among the elderly.

Researchers led by Cheryl L. Grady of the National Institute on Aging used positron emission tomography (PET) to study the brain activity of young and elderly participants as they took part in a memorization task. (PET scans show areas of heightened blood flow in the brain, which is often an indicator of activity in those areas.) Two groups of 10 volunteers each (one averaging 25 years of age and the other 69 years) viewed 32 unfamiliar faces for 4 seconds each, while PET scans recorded their brain activity. After a short break, PET scans were again obtained as the participants looked at faces from the first session, now paired with distracter faces, and identified which ones they had seen before.

The research team found that the group of younger participants recognized significantly more faces than did the elderly group. What's more, the PET scans revealed that among the younger participants, several brain regions (especially the hippocampus) leapt into activity during the memorization task. By comparison, the elderly participants' PET scans showed no heightened activity during the memorization process. These findings suggest support for the encoding deficit hypothesis of aging. The relatively poorer performance by the elderly participants seems to be due to not sufficiently encoding the information in the first place.

Wu, C. (1995). Brain scans hint why elderly forget faces. *Science News, 148,* 36.

Why You Don't Remember Your First Birthday Party

Humans typically don't remember events in their lives that happened prior to their third or fourth birthday. Explaining why has been somewhat up for grabs. Freudians might suggest that this *infantile amnesia* is due to some murky unconscious process. However, infantile amnesia has been observed in frogs, mice, rats, dogs, and wolves (Spear, 1979), making it difficult to defend an "amphibian theory of repression" or "canine defense mechanisms." Similarly, the sheer passage of time cannot account for this kind of forgetfulness. Many of us can remember quite clearly and accurately events that happened long ago (such as an 80-year-old remembering her first ride in an automobile), and people with extraordinary memories (such as S., V.P., or S.F.) routinely recount incidents from the distant past. Something different must be at work.

A more promising explanation implicates the retrieval process. It's quite likely that information is encoded and organized by infants in a manner that is very different from what an adult might do. For example, adults routinely rely on language to help store information in memory (e.g., through verbal rehearsal, through mnemonics, through the very process of translating experiences into information that can be communicated). Preverbal infants and children clearly would not have this same strategy, or at least not developed to the same extent as an adult. Consequently, when an adult tries to retrieve memories from childhood, his or her schemas would not likely match the schemas used to encode the information in the first place. Much like the reinstatement of context suggested by the encoding specificity principle, an adult retrieval strategy for child-encoded information isn't going to get very far.

Searleman, A., & Herrmann, D. (1994). *Memory from a broader perspective.* New York: McGraw-Hill.

Spear, N. E. (1979). Experimental analysis of infantile amnesia. In J. F. Kihlstrom & F. J. Evans (Eds.), *Functional disorders of memory* (pp. 75-102). Hillsdale, NJ: Lawrence Erlbaum Associates.

Déjà Vu

Students are fascinated by the topic of déjà vu, or the feeling that one is reliving some prior experience. The déjà vu phenomenon has been investigated by psychologists throughout the history of the discipline, and a number of theories--neurological, supernatural, pathological, and otherwise--have been proposed to explain its presumed occurrence.

A team of Dutch researchers, led by Herman Sno, have investigated the topic at length in recent years. Sno and his colleagues argue that the déjà vu experience can be examined using the hologram as a model. In holographic photography, each piece of an image contains the full information necessary to reproduce the image, a property that gives holographic images their three-dimensional qualities. The smaller the fragment, however, the fuzzier the image reproduced. Sno argues that memory may operate in a similar fashion. When a fragment of a current perception is identical to a segment of a previously stored memory, the déjà vu experience will take place. Traced to their original forms the two memories may be quite different, although based on mismatch of fragments from each they seem so similar as to be a relived experience. This idea is in contrast to other explanations, such as that déjà vu results from a micromomentary hesitation in transmitting information across the cerebral hemispheres, or Freud's notions that déjà vu is a manifestation of the unconscious or a type of defense mechanism.

Sno, H. J., & Linszen, D. H. (1990). The déjà vu experience: Remembrance of things past? *American Journal of Psychiatry, 147,* 1587-1595.

Sno, H. J., Schalken, H. F. A., de Jonghe, F., & Koeter, M. W. J. (1994). The Inventory for Déjà Vu Experiences Assessment: Development, utility, reliability, and validity. *Journal of Nervous and Mental Disease, 182,* 27-33.

Memory Anomalies: Beyond Déjà Vu

The déjà vu experience is perhaps the best known anomaly of memory, but it is by no means the only one. Like déjà vu, these anomalies are relatively harmless (unless they occur quite frequently) and may occur in most people's lives at some point.

- *Jamais vu.* The opposite of déjà vu, jamais vu refers to experiencing a lack of familiarity in a particular situation when this should clearly not be the case. For example, someone who insists that they have never before met a fairly well-known acquaintance might be having a jamais vu experience. Clearly, jamais vu needs to be distinguished from the memory disruptions found among Alzheimer's patients (who often fail to recognize familiar objects, people, or settings), from the effects of amnesia (whether physical or psychogenic in origin), or from simply a faulty memory (such as not encoding information about a person in the first place). A defining quality of jamais vu, then, is the feeling of astonishment or incredulity at encountering the object ("Are you *sure* we've met before?!").

- *Time-gap experience.* "I left work, and then I arrived at home. I'm not sure what happened in between." Most of us have shared the experience of doing a fairly complicated task (such as driving a car) and upon completion realizing that we have no recollection of the task at all (such as which turns were made, when we stopped, the route we took, and so on). This time-gap experience can be explained using the distinction between automatic and effortful processing. An effortful task, such as one that is new or unfamiliar, demands our cognitive resources for its completion. Even a fairly intricate task, however, once it has become automatic, can be performed outside of conscious awareness.

- *Cryptomnesia.* Cryptomnesia can be thought of as unintended plagiarism: A person honestly believes that some thought, publication, composition, or other work is an original creation when in fact it is not. Many musicians, for example, seem to fall prey to this memory anomaly. The most celebrated case involved George Harrison's song "My Sweet Lord," which a court ruled was unintentionally based (quite closely, actually) on the Chiffons' "He's So Fine" (Brown & Murphy, 1989). A song by Huey Lewis and the News, "I Want A New Drug," also came under scrutiny as a too-close variant of Ray Parker's "Ghostbusters," and Aerosmith recently came under fire for lifting the line "Mister, you're a better man than I" from the Yardbirds' song of the same name. In each case the similarities were determined to be unintentional, suggesting that cryptomnesia was at work.

Brown, A. S., & Murphy, D. R. (1989). Cryptomnesia: Delineating inadvertent plagiarism. *Journal of Experimental Psychology: Learning, Memory, and Cognition, 15,* 432-442.

Searleman, A., & Herrmann, D. (1994). *Memory from a broader perspective.* New York: McGraw-Hill.

Everyday Memory

The cognitive revolution heralded a return to investigating topics such as memory, mental imagery, language, and cognition, and doing so in a way that was experimentally rigorous. Unfortunately, the memory situations produced in the lab often did not have real-world counterparts, and the cry went out from several quarters for a more ecological approach to memory, one which would embrace the practicalities of everyday memory.

Alan Baddeley and Arnold Wilkins have summarized some of the pros and cons of taking memory research out of the laboratory. Some advantages of studying memory in real-world situations include:

- *Being able to establish generality of memory findings.* Although the lab is well suited to control and precision, the goal of applying findings can only be achieved by broadening the research scope to include natural settings.

- *Being able to give theories a dry run before applying them.* Although practical decisions could be based solely on theory, it is more prudent to test them under fully realistic conditions.

❖ *Using everyday memory as a source for new investigations.* More attention should be given to the phenomena of memory (i.e., what people actually do), rather than testing the aspects of a procedure (e.g., experiments designed to test other experiments).

Some practical considerations in leaving the laboratory include:

❖ *Learning may not be controlled.* Assessing the present memory capabilities of a real-world research participant may give little or no information about the amount of prior learning that has taken place. Differences in amount or type of learning across participants may cloud interpretations of results.

❖ *Retention interval may not be controlled.* The time elapsed between learning and retrieval may vary in natural settings, or may be altogether unknown.

❖ *Retrieval may not be controlled.* A study of "remembering to do things in the future" (quite a realistic memory task) may not afford the researcher any control over or measure of the retrieval process.

Baddeley, A. D., & Wilkins, A. (1984). Taking memory out of the laboratory. In J. E. Harris & P. E. Morris (Eds.), *Everyday memory, actions, and absent-mindedness* (pp. 1-17). London: Academic Press.

The Mind(s) of Mnemonist(s)

We are often awed, sometimes jealous, and occasionally resentful of those who have prodigious memories. Perhaps it is their smarty-pants attitude that *they* can remember the details of an event that escape *us*. Their smugness soon fades, however, in the face of *truly* extraordinary memory.

One person with a truly extraordinary memory was S., also known to his mother as S. V. Shereshevskii. S. was able to recall even the most meaningless drivel with great accuracy and sometimes years after learning it by relying on mnemonics; visualizing the information, forming elaborate associations, capitalizing on synesthetic experiences, and so on. However, S. is not without company. There are several other people who have demonstrated similar abilities.

For example, V. P., a Latvian born in 1934 in a small town coincidentally close to S.'s birthplace, read at age 3½, memorized the street map of a large city at 5, and committed 150 poems to memory at age 10. Both V. P.'s short-term and long-term memory appear impressive. On standard short-term memory tasks, such as recalling three consonants over an 18-second interval while counting backwards by three, V. P. showed virtually no disruption. Similarly, he could remember the War of the Ghosts with the same extraordinary accuracy after 1 hour or after 1 year. The secret to his success, however, appears to be different from that of S. V. P.'s strategy seems to be based on quickly forming verbal associations to information using any of the several languages that he speaks (Latin, English, Estonian, Latvian, Russian, Spanish, Hebrew, French, German). Information that would stump most of us might call up a bawdy Latin verse for V. P., and thus contribute to his memorization.

Rajan Mahadevan's specialty is numbers. Rajan came to the public's attention while a graduate student in psychology, but his memory feats occurred regularly even as a young boy. People in his native Mangalore, India, were astounded by his ability to remember anything numerical. So were the folks at the *Guinness Book of World Records*; in 1981, Rajan was able to recite the first 31,811 digit of pi. Like V. P., Rajan relies on idiosyncratic associations drawn from a vast knowledge base: Like most of us, he remembers "111" because Admiral Nelson had 1 eye, 1 arm, and 1 leg.

Finally, S. F. represents a "manufactured memorist." While an undergraduate at Carnegie-Mellon University in 1978, S. F. embarked on a laboratory project initiated by K. Anders Ericsson and his colleagues (e.g., Chase & Ericsson, 1981) that lasted 2 years. The task was simple enough. S. F. would read a sequence of random digits at one per second, then recall them in the correct order. If successful, the next group would be increased by one digit, and if unsuccessful it would be reduced by a digit. By the end of the training session S. F. had mastered a sequence of some 80 digits, compared to most people's typical performance of about 7. The secret was in S. F.'s avocation. As a long-distance runner he formed meaningful chunks from the digits he read, such as 1076 for an important race in October, 1976, or other sets of digits for best times, typical distances, and so on. Sadly, S. F. died in 1981 from a chronic blood disorder, although others (such as D. D., also a long-distance runner, who commands a digit span of 106) have continued this project.

> Chase, W. G., & Ericsson, K. A. (1981). Skilled memory. In J. R. Anderson (Ed.), *Cognitive skills and their acquisition* (pp. 141-189). Hillsdale, NJ: Lawrence Erlbaum Associates.
> Searleman, A., & Herrmann, D. (1994). *Memory from a broader perspective.* New York: McGraw-Hill.

Mnemonics in Mind

Chapter 6 briefly mentions some tips for improving one's memory, focusing on the use of mnemonics as one effective strategy. Here is a collection of mnemonics, divided into *naive* strategies (i.e., those used regularly and easily by most people, without needing formal instruction) and *technical* mnemonics (i.e., those requiring some training).

Naive Mnemonics

- *Rehearsal*: Simple rote repetition
- *Rhyme*: Constructing a little ditty to keep track of information
- *Chunking*: Restructuring a list into meaningful units
- *Images*: Visualizing a cereal box full of money to remember "Bank and Groceries"
- *First-letter mnemonics*
    - *Acronyms*: Roy G. Biv for the visible spectrum; HOMES for the Great Lakes
    - *Acrostics*: Arithmetic: "A Real Idiot Thinks He Might Eat Turkey In Church"

Technical Mnemonics

- *Method of Loci*: A physical setting is first memorized, then filled in
- *Peg-Word*: First construct a rhyme, then "hang" the information on the rhyme's peg
- *Number-Letter*: A translation scheme matching letters to numbers and vice-versa
- *Link*: A visual image of each item is linked to the following one, forming a chain
- *Story*: Like the link system, but with stories using the to-be-remembered information

> Searleman, A., & Herrmann, D. (1994). *Memory from a broader perspective.* New York: McGraw-Hill.

The Inner Workings of Working Memory

Area 46 could be anywhere; a loading dock, part of a busy airport, or a sector of a computer chip manufacturing plant. But Area 46 of the frontal lobe refers to a specific location that's revealed a specific function. Scientists are heralding Area 46 as the "scratch pad of the brain."

Most models of memory posit a "working memory" or holding area where information is stored before being consolidated (or lost). Recently, two research teams used functional magnetic resonance imaging (fMRI) to pinpoint where that activity takes place. Susan Courtney, a researcher at the National Institutes of Mental Health, led a research project that had volunteers view a face on a computer monitor for 3 seconds. The participants kept the image in mind during an 8-second pause, then saw another face on the screen. If the second face matched the first, the participants pressed a button. The fMRI scans taken during this task showed that areas in the back of the brain were active when the faces first appeared, whereas Area 46 of the frontal lobe became and stayed active during the pause. (The distinction wasn't perfect; some rear areas were slightly active during the pause, and some frontal areas were active when the faces were shown.) In a second study, a research team led by Jonathan D. Cohen of Carnegie Mellon University and the University of Pittsburgh asked participants to recall increasingly long strings of consonants flashed on a screen. As the sequence of letters increased, activity in the frontal lobe increased. Like the previous study, other areas of the brain were also active during these tasks.

Taken together, these results suggest that there is a coordinated effort in brain activity when working memory is activated. The frontal lobe "scratch pad" of Area 46 works in concert with other brain regions to process information and distribute it effectively. Further research, using millisecond-to-millisecond fMRI recording, may reveal with greater accuracy how different types of information get processed.

Bower, B. (1997, April 26). Where in the brain is working memory? *Science News, 151,* 258.

Boyd, R. S. (1997, November 30). Scientists find "scratch pad" where brain sorts memory. *Austin American-Statesman,* A22.

Episodic ≠ Semantic

The daily lives of Beth, Jon, and Kate sound nightmarish. The 14, 19, and 22-year-olds can't remember where they've been shortly after they've been there, can't recall who've they've seen shortly after they've seen them, and can't recognize familiar buildings shortly after they've walked out of them. Each of these young people suffered from brain seizures at an early age that produced extensive damage to the hippocampus. And if the story ended here we'd shake our heads dejectedly, mumbling about the grace of God and knocking on available wood, as the trio walked away under the constant supervision of their parents.

It turns out, though, that Beth, Jon, and Kate all attended mainstream schools, have good speech and language skills, read and spell as well as their peers, and have acquired lots and lots of factual knowledge. Their abilities in these areas, contrasted with their disabilities in others, highlight the difference between semantic memory and episodic memory. What's more, they suggest that the areas of the brain responsible for these types of memory are different. Researchers led by Faraneh Vargha-Khadem of University College London Medical School studied these unusual individuals and concluded that although the hippocampus regulates recall of personal experiences, it plays only a minor role in the storage and acquisition of factual knowledge. In short, while episodic memory has been tragically disrupted for these three, semantic memory has remained largely intact.

Bower, B. (1997, August 2). Factual brains, uneventful lives. *Science News, 152,* 75.

demonstrations

Demonstrating Simple Memory Principles

Wertheimer (1981) described an activity that can be used to demonstrate a number of principles related to memory and forgetting, including the forgetting curve, the effect of meaningfulness, the effect of distinctiveness (sometimes known as the von Restorff effect), the effect of repetition, and the serial position effect. When you start the class, divide the students into four groups by assigning each person a number from 1 to 4. Explain that you are going to read a list of items to them twice and that they will need to memorize the list. Make sure you tell them not to write the items down. Although you may want to construct your own list, the following list is similar to that suggested by Wertheimer (1981): Clinton, ruj, fet, textbook, nav, Bush, fulfill, GEF, mandate, fet, 47, tal. The items should be read slowly, clearly, and at a uniform rate each time they are read. The nonsense syllables need to be both pronounced and spelled. Finally, shout as loudly as possible the nonsense syllable "GEF." Immediately after completing the second reading of the list, ask Group 1 to write down all of the items that they can remember. Continue with your lecture, but after about 3 minutes ask Group 2 to write down the items. Then, after another 5 minutes, ask Group 3 to remember the items. Finally, about 45 minutes after the initial list presentation, ask Group 4 to write as many items as they can remember. Make sure that during and between each retrieval by a group there is no discussion of the items. Once you have scored and recorded the number of items correctly recalled by each group on the board, you should be able to point out the negatively accelerated forgetting curve. In addition, an examination of performance on particular items across groups will indicate the effects of meaningfulness (recall of presidents should be superior to nonsense syllables), distinctiveness (GEF should show superior recall), repetition (fet should be recalled with a higher frequency), and the serial position effect.

Wertheimer, M. (1981). Memory and forgetting. In L. T. Benjamin, Jr. & K. D. Lowman (Eds.), *Activities handbook for the teaching of psychology* (pp. 75-76). Washington, DC: American Psychological Association.

Reprinted from Hill, W. G. (1995). Instructor's resource manual for *Psychology* by S. F. Davis and J. J. Palladino. Englewood Cliffs, NJ: Prentice Hall.

Decay and Interference in Short-term Memory

This simple exercise uses the Brown-Peterson distracter technique to demonstrate the effects of delay and interference on short-term memory. Tell students that you want them to remember a sequence of three consonant letters while counting backwards from a number you provide them. When they're ready, say, "W T K" and then "701." They should then say "701, 698, 695, 692, 689, 686" and so on. After 15 to 18 seconds, say "write" as a signal to students to recall the three letters. According to Peterson and Peterson (1959), students should have a fairly difficult time accomplishing this because the counting task prevents them from rehearsing the letters and thus allows the memory trace to decay. Keppel and Underwood (1962) later argued that the forgetting in the Brown-Peterson task was primarily due to the buildup of proactive interference. As evidence, they pointed to the fact that students could often remember the letters during the first trial or two, but had much greater difficulty remembering letters on any subsequent trials, when proactive interference would develop (i.e., they would have trouble distinguishing between letters presented earlier and on the current trial). Verify this effect with your students by conducting several trials. Examples of potential letter/number combinations might include PZX 317, BVQ 421, LFC 991, JHG 187, and SRN 275. Students will be astonished at their atrocious performance, which, if typical of experiments of this type, should yield about 1 in 10 correct recalls after only 18 seconds of the distracter task!

Keppel, G., & Underwood, B. J. (1962). Proactive inhibition in short-term retention of single items. *Journal of Verbal Learning and Verbal Behavior, 1*, 153-161.

Peterson, L. R., & Peterson, M. J. (1959). Short-term retention of individual verbal items. *Journal of Experimental Psychology, 58*, 193-198.

Searleman, A., & Herrmann, D. (1994). *Memory from a broader perspective.* New York: McGraw-Hill.

Depth of Processing and Memory

This activity, adapted from exercises suggested by James Jenkins (1981) and Donald DeRosa (1987), reliably demonstrates that memory for information depends on the depth at which it is processed. Do this exercise after you have introduced short- and long-term memory but before you have discussed specific encoding strategies (e.g., encoding verbally, by visual images, by meaning, and so on). Have students take out a clean sheet of paper and number it from 1 to 30. Tell students that you are going to read aloud a list of words and that you would like them to make a judgment about each word. [Do not mention that this is a memory experiment or that they will be asked to recall the words later.] Explain that the letter that precedes each word will signal the particular judgment you would like them to make. Specifically, if the letter "A" is presented before the word, you want them to write down the number of syllables that are in the word. If the letter "B" is presented before the word, you want them to judge whether it is pleasant or unpleasant (by writing "P" for pleasant and "U" for unpleasant). You should write this information on the chalkboard as you give it, and you might also encourage students to write it at the top of their papers as a reminder. Stress that they should make their judgments relatively quickly and without hesitation (e.g., for the pleasantness judgment, they choose one or the other, and not something in between).

Then, slowly and clearly read the following list of words at a rate of about 1 word every 4 seconds (you can either count to yourself or use a stopwatch). For example, you would begin by saying, "A" (short pause), "bike" (pause for 4 seconds), "B" (short pause), "month" (pause for 4 seconds), and so on.

1. A	bike	11. B	fire	21. B	trunk		
2. B	month	12. B	trail	22. A	coal		
3. A	magic	13. A	soap	23. B	pipe		
4. B	foot	14. B	pocket	24. A	pitch		
5. A	monkey	15. A	pencil	25. B	coin		
6. B	clock	16. B	train	26. A	hammer		
7. B	paint	17. A	grass	27. A	door		
8. B	bureau	18. A	story	28. B	church		
9. A	bird	19. B	belt	29. B	travel		
10. A	lemon	20. A	kitchen	30. A	fish		

[Note that this is just one potential word list and one potential order. You can do this exercise with any set of common nouns and you can easily generate a new order (with new judgment pairings) by doing the following. Make notecards for each of the words, shuffle them, and then randomly sort them into two boxes or bins (one for A, the other for B). After writing "A" or "B" on each card next to the word (according to which box it landed in), place all the cards in a stack and then shuffle them thoroughly to get a new order.]

After you've read the entire list, ask students to quickly write down as many of the states in the United States that they remember (give them about 2 minutes for this task). Then, ask students to turn their papers over and to write down as many of the words that they can recall from the list you read, in any order that they want. Give them about 3 or 4 minutes for this task, and then have them score their answers by projecting a transparency containing the word list (provided in Handout 6-1). Ask students to write an "A" or a "B" next to each word they recalled according to the scoring sheet (they should cross out any words recalled that were not on the list). Then, they should count the total number of A and B words recalled. You can tally the results by making a frequency distribution on the board (i.e., writing down for each person the number of A and B words remembered) and calculating (or eyeballing) average scores for each condition. If you're pressed for time or have a large class, you can simply ask students to raise their hands if they remembered more A than B words, and compare this to the number of students who remembered more B than A words. Whichever way you score it, students should have recalled many more B than A words.

After scoring, ask students to explain the results. Most will intuitively be able to explain that the B words were more memorable because they had to think more about the words (and their meaning) in order to make the judgment of pleasantness. By contrast, making the A judgment (i.e., number of syllables) required simply saying the word to themselves rather than thinking about what it meant. Thus, this exercise demonstrates the superiority of coding semantically (i.e., by meaning) over coding phonologically (i.e., by sound). That is, the deeper and more elaborate the processing of information, the more likely it is to be recalled. At this point, if students don't already see it, you'll want to highlight the implications of this experiment for their study habits. The importance of studying actively should now be crystal clear, and students will no doubt realize that thinking deeply about--and attaching meaning to (rather than merely rehearsing)--terms and concepts in their courses is the key to effective recall on exams. Also, you might ask students to explain the purpose of the state-listing task (it was a distracter task to prevent any of the words from being held in short-term memory, which lasts for about 20 seconds). Finally, it wouldn't hurt to remind students of the forgetting assignment (if you did it) and how difficult it was for them to forget something that was encoded as meaningful!

DeRosa, D. V. (1987). How to study actively. In V. P. Makosky, L. G. Whittemore, & A. M. Rogers (Eds.), *Activities handbook for the teaching of psychology: Vol. 2* (pp. 72-74). Washington, DC: American Psychological Association.

Jenkins, J. (1981). Meaning enhances recall. In L. T. Benjamin & K. D. Lowman (Eds.), *Activities handbook for the teaching of psychology* (pp. 81-82). Washington, DC: American Psychological Association.

Coding in Long-term Memory

Searleman and Herrmann suggest a simple exercise (adapted from Sachs, 1967) that demonstrates that information in long-term memory is typically coded by meaning rather than by literal content. Tell your students that they should carefully read the story presented on the overhead (see Handout 6-2) and that they should be prepared to have their memory tested for one of its sentences. After students have had time to read (but not study) the story, present the sentences (students should choose which one was presented in the story) and remove the story. Most students will quickly eliminate choice C (which has a different meaning than the other sentences) but will have difficulty deciding among the other three choices (which differ in form and structure but not meaning). Thus, it appears that people quickly forget verbatim information while retaining its general meaning. In actuality, our coding process is a very flexible and adaptive one. When we absolutely need to (e.g., when we must memorize a poem, riddle, or quotation), we can code verbatim information into long-term memory. Most of the time, however, because it is most important that we remember the meaning of events, we code the gist of information rather than its literal content. [*Note:* If your class is too large or you don't have access to an overhead machine, this exercise can be conducted orally as well.]

Sachs, J. S. (1967). Memory in reading and listening to discourse. *Memory & Cognition, 21*, 73-80.

Searleman, A., & Herrmann, D. (1994). *Memory from a broader perspective*. New York: McGraw-Hill.

Go Fly a Kite: The Effect of Context on Memory

Marty Klein (1981) described an activity that is designed to illustrate the effect of meaningfulness on memory. In his demonstration, meaningfulness is manipulated by presenting the same passage with or without a contextual statement. Prior to reading the passage, give half of the class a piece of paper with the statement, "The context is kite flying." Tell those receiving the contextual statement not to discuss it. Then slowly and clearly read the following passage:

> A newspaper is better than a magazine. A seashore is a better place than the street. At first it is better to run than to walk. You may have to try several times. It takes some skill but is easy to learn. Even young children can enjoy it. Once successful, complications are minimal. Birds seldom get too close. Rain, however, soaks in very fast. Too many people doing the same thing can also cause problems. One needs lots of room. If there are no complications it can be very peaceful. A rock will serve as an anchor. If things break loose from it, however, you will not get a second chance.

After completing the passage, ask students to take out a piece of paper and to write down as much of the passage as they can. Then ask the students that received the contextual statement to mark their paper so that they can be identified, and collect the papers. You can either immediately compare the responses of both groups by reading selected papers from each group, or you can score the responses after class and bring a data summary to the next class. Obviously, you should find that those students with a context outperform those without. Klein suggested using these results to discuss the importance of context and how it may relate to study strategies.

Another example, used by Bransford and Johnson (1972, p. 722), should work just as well if you follow the same procedures described above. Note that for this story the context is "washing clothes."

The procedure is actually quite simple. First you arrange things into groups. Of course, one pile may be sufficient depending on how much there is to do. If you have to go somewhere else due to lack of facilities, that is the next step; otherwise you are pretty well set. It is important not to overdo things. That is, it is better to do too few things at once than too many. In the short run this may not seem important, but complications can arise. A mistake can prove expensive as well. At first the whole procedure will seem complicated. Soon, however, it will become just another facet of life. It is difficult to foresee any end to the necessity for this task in the immediate future, but one can never tell. After the procedure is completed, one arranges the materials into different groups again. Then they can be put into their appropriate places. Eventually they will all be used once more, and the whole cycle will have to be repeated. However, that is part of life.

Bransford, J. D., & Johnson, M. K. (1972). Contextual prerequisites for understanding: Some investigations of comprehension and recall. *Journal of Verbal Learning and Verbal Behavior, 11*, 717-726.

Klein, M. (1981). Context and memory. In L. T. Benjamin, Jr. & K. D. Lowman (Eds.), *Activities handbook for the teaching of psychology* (p. 83). Washington, DC: American Psychological Association.

Paddle Your Own Canoe

Michael Wertheimer suggests an entertaining exercise that, like the kite and laundry stories above, effectively makes the point that context can lead to better retention by enabling us to organize information more effectively and meaningfully. For this exercise, you'll need to enlist the help of some confederates during the class period *prior* to the one in which you'll conduct the demonstration. End class that day a few minutes early and when about half the class has left, ask the remaining students to stay behind for a few minutes. Tell them that they will be in the experimental group and that at the beginning of the next class you'll display a set of digits and some French words to be memorized. Explain that the digits and French words will look haphazard and hard to memorize, but that as the experimental group they will be given the following clues: The digits are actually the squares of the numbers 1 through 9, and the French phrase sounds very much like the English phrase, "Paddle your own canoe." At the beginning of the next class, write the following sequence of digits on the board (be sure to hold the space constant between digits so the control group doesn't catch on):

1 4 9 1 6 2 5 3 6 4 9 6 4 8 1

Underneath the digits, write the following French phrase:

Pas de l'y a Rhone que nous

Tell your students that they'll have 60 seconds to memorize both pieces of information. After a minute has elapsed, erase both lists completely and continue with class. About 20 minutes before the end of the session, ask all students to write down all digits and all French words they can remember (give them 2 or 3 minutes for this task). Then, write the digit list and French phrase on the board in the same manner as before and have students score their papers by counting the number of digits and French words they correctly recalled. At this point, you can let the whole class in on the secret (e.g., tell them about the contextual cues) and compare recall between the experimental and control groups by making a frequency distribution on the board. Of course, the mean number of items (both digits and French words) should be higher for the experimental group. Once again, this exercise should reinforce for students the importance of striving to attach meaning to new material rather than trying to blindly memorize it.

Wertheimer, M. (1987). Meaningfulness and memory. In V. P. Makosky, L. G. Whittemore, & A. M. Rogers (Eds.), *Activities handbook for the teaching of psychology: Vol. 2* (pp. 80-82). Washington, DC: American Psychological Association.

Organization and Memory

Several previous exercises have demonstrated the important role that meaning plays in our ability to remember information. Another important factor in memory is organization. George Mandler was an early proponent of the view that the organization of material (i.e., grouping items together based on shared relationships) is crucial to memory because it effectively reduces the amount of material that needs to be processed and stored (Searleman & Herrmann, 1994). Indeed, research shows that subjects will often spontaneously organize items into groups in order to remember them better.

John Fisher suggests a simple exercise that demonstrates the importance of organization in memory. Handouts 6-3a and 6-3b each contain a list of 12 words that students should study briefly and then try to recall. Note that both lists contain the same dozen words but in a different order: The words in list *B* are arranged so that each word has some natural association with the word that precedes it, whereas the words in list *A* are arranged randomly. Photocopy an equal number of each handout and randomly distribute them (face down) to students so that half have one version of the word list and half have the other (do not mention that the lists are different). Instruct students to turn the list over and briefly study the words; give them about 30 seconds for this task and then have them put the list away. Then, distract your students for about a minute (e.g., by talking to them or by having them count backwards from 100) and then have them take out a clean sheet of paper and write down all the words they can recall. After about 45 seconds, have them stop writing and score their recall list (by comparing it to the original word list). Explain that there were different versions of the word lists and ask students which group they would expect to have superior recall. Most will immediately state that the group with the organized word list should perform better. Verify that this is the case by creating a frequency distribution on the board (and listing the number of correctly recalled words for each student in group A and in group B). Discuss these results with your students. What implications do they have for improving recall on exams? What techniques do students currently use to take advantage of this principle? Can they think of new ways to increase organization and recall?

Fisher, J. (1979). *Body magic*. Briarcliff Manor, NY: Stein and Day.
Searleman, A., & Herrmann, D. (1994). *Memory from a broader perspective*. New York: McGraw-Hill.

Schemas and Memory

Chapter 6 discusses Frederick Bartlett's schema theory, which describes how our past experiences and expectations can affect memory. Specifically, Bartlett argues that our schemas (i.e., organized mental frameworks that we rely on to interpret and filter incoming information) greatly influence the retrieval of information stored in long-term memory. To demonstrate this effect in your classroom, replicate an exercise suggested by Drew Appleby. Tell students that you are going to show them a list of 12 words and that they should try to remember them. Then, slowly display (by using index cards or transparencies) the following words one at a time as you read them aloud:

REST, TIRED, AWAKE, DREAM, SNORE, BED, EAT, SLUMBER, SOUND, COMFORT, WAKE, NIGHT

After you've completed the list, distract your class for 30 seconds or so (to ensure that the words are no longer held in short-term memory) and then give them 2 minutes to write down as many words as they can recall. Ask for a show of hands from all those who recalled the word AARDVARK. Your students, none of whom will have mistakenly recalled AARDVARK, will look at you as if you're crazy. Then ask for a show of hands for those who remembered SLEEP. Appleby reports that 80 to 95% of the students typically recall the word SLEEP, and are astonished to discover that SLEEP was not on the list (prove it to them). Asked to explain the effect, most students will intuitively understand that schemas influenced their recall. That is, because all of the words were associated with each other and related to the topic of sleep, their schema for "sleep" was invoked and it seemed only natural that it would be on the list. Thus, this demonstration suggests that schemas can cause us to fabricate false memories that happen to be consistent with our schemas. You might also want to discuss with students the following interesting implication: If people sometimes mistakenly remember information because it is consistent with their schemas, is it possible that they can mistakenly forget information that is inconsistent with their schemas? Ask students to provide examples from their own lives or from cases they've heard about in the media.

Appleby, D. (1987). Producing a deja vu experience. In V. P. Makosky, L. G. Whittemore, & A. M. Rogers (Eds.), *Activities handbook for the teaching of psychology: Vol. 2* (pp. 78-79). Washington, DC: American Psychological Association.

The Self-Reference Effect

An activity described by Forsyth and Wibberly (1993) is effective in demonstrating the self-reference effect on memory. They noted that, based upon studies of constructive processes in memory, schema theories propose that information is arranged within a system of cognitive groupings or schemas such as event schemas, which define and provide a structure for social situations, or self-schemas, which reflect one's individual characteristics. The self-reference effect refers to retrieval superiority for information that is related to a person's self-schema. Forsyth and Wibberly described how this effect can be demonstrated using an incidental memory task. Explain to the class that you are gathering data about which adjectives are most commonly used for self-descriptions. Ask the class to number a sheet of paper from 1 to 20. Tell them that you will be reading a list of 20 adjectives and if they feel that an adjective is self-descriptive of themselves, they are to circle the corresponding number of the adjective on their paper. Next, read the following list of adjectives: forceful, quiet, generous, dominant, tender, loyal, independent, compassionate, adaptable, courageous, cheerful, secretive, principled, romantic, responsible, dynamic, forgiving, and careful. After completing the list, talk about some matters related to class for about a minute, then ask the students to write down as many of the adjectives that they can recall. Then read the original list of adjectives and have the students calculate the number of descriptive and non-descriptive adjectives that they recalled. Forsyth and Wibberly reported that the results of this demonstration are usually robust, with students consistently remembering a higher percentage of self-descriptive adjectives. They indicated that the demonstration is effective in generating discussion of schema and depth-of-processing theories of memory by noting that self-referent items tend to be processed at deeper levels.

Forsyth, D. R., & Wibberly, K. H. (1993). The self-reference effect: Demonstrating schematic processing in the classroom. *Teaching of Psychology, 20,* 237-238.

Reprinted from Hill, W. G. (1995). Instructor's resource manual for *Psychology* by S. F. Davis and J. J. Palladino. Englewood Cliffs, NJ: Prentice Hall.

Attention and Memory: Forgetting vs. Not Getting

Kenneth Higbee (1993) cites a quote by Oliver Wendall Holmes to illustrate the importance of attention in memory. In saying, "A man must *get* a thing before he can *forget* it," Holmes implies that when we think we "forgot" something, it may be because we never actually paid attention to it in the first place. Ask your class to answer this series of questions posed by Higbee (answers follow):

1. Which color is on top of a stoplight? (red)
2. Whose image is on a penny? (Lincoln) Is he wearing a tie? (yes, a bow tie)
3. What four words besides "In God We Trust" appear on most U.S. coins? (United States of America)
4. When water goes down the drain, does it swirl clockwise or counterclockwise? (counterclockwise in the Northern Hemisphere; clockwise in the Southern Hemisphere)
5. What letters, if any, are missing on a telephone dial? (Q, Z)

For a more elaborate example, ask your students to draw the head of a penny from memory. Interestingly, although we've all seen and handled pennies hundred of times, it is extremely hard to reproduce accurately. For example, did your students orient Lincoln's profile correctly (the right side of his face is showing)? Did they remember "In God We Trust" across the top? Did they remember the word to the left of Lincoln (liberty)? Did they remember the date and the minting place (to the right of Lincoln)? Did they mistakenly remember information from the back of the penny (one cent, E Pluribus Unum, United States of America)?

Higbee suggests several interesting implications of the relationship between attention and memory. For example, because we can only pay attention to one thing at a time, we shouldn't try to study when other distracters are competing for our attention (e.g., television, music, people talking). Also, perhaps the reason we forget other people's names so easily when we first meet them is because we're not really paying attention; instead, we're waiting for our own name to be said or concentrating on what we are going to say. Absentmindedness, suggests Higbee, can also be attributed to not paying attention. We forget where we parked our car because we were not paying attention when we did it; thus, to reduce absentmindedness we should focus our attention on what we are doing (e.g., "Notice that I'm parking my car today on the left side of the front lot"). Encourage your students to provide other examples as well.

Higbee, K. L (1993). *Your memory: How it works and how to improve it.* New York: Paragon House.

Debate: Are "Recovered" Memories of Sexual Abuse Always Real?

It is difficult to imagine another psychological issue in recent memory that has garnered as much public attention as has the validity of repressed memories (e.g., sexual abuse memories that surface many years after the fact). There is no doubt that sexual abuse occurs and is a serious and undeniable trauma; what is in question, however, is whether *all* recovered memories are in fact accurate or whether at least some memories are unwittingly but falsely shaped by others. This volatile but important issue has been the subject of television shows, symposia, journal issues, conferences, and has even spawned an organization, the False Memory Syndrome Foundation. Your students may have already formed opinions on this issue from what they have seen or heard in the media. Encourage them to explore this issue in more depth--and from both sides--by considering the scientific evidence and arguments in a debate format. Assign students to research this issue and to be prepared to defend either side. Issue 9 in *Taking Sides* presents both pro and con viewpoints on this controversial topic, and students should be encouraged to find more recent sources from journal articles (see, for example, the *American Psychologist*) and from the popular media. Among other things, this debate should give students insight into the nature of long-term memory, conflict among psychologists from different perspectives, and the relationship between the media and psychological issues.

Slife, B. (1998). *Taking sides: Clashing views on controversial psychological issues* (10th ed.). Guilford, CT: Dushkin Publishing Group.

Slife, B. (2000). *Taking sides: Clashing views on controversial psychological issues* (11th ed.). Guilford, CT: Dushkin Publishing Group.

student assignments

Improving Memory

This exercise, like the behavior modification project suggested in the previous chapter, asks students to put what they've learned to good, practical use. For this assignment, students should target some specific aspect of their memory that they would like to improve and then apply one or more memory principles from the text or lecture to make the improvement. Students might, for example, strive to enhance their performance on exams, to recall important birthdates and anniversaries, to remember people's names following introductions, or to reduce absentminded actions, such as misplacing keys or a wallet. Potential memory strategies include the use of established (e.g., Pegword, method of loci) or home-made mnemonics, eliminating distracters and paying careful attention when studying, meeting new people, or putting keys down, trying to encode material deeply and by multiple methods (e.g., by meaning, by self-referencing, and by encoding visually), making better use of retrieval cues, engaging in active, elaborative rehearsal while reading, applying the SQ3R method, and so on. Students might also be encouraged (but not required) to consult additional sources for ideas. One potential resource for this assignment is an excellent, well-written book by Kenneth Higbee (1993). After implementing their plan, students should write a short paper in which they report on their experiences. Specifically, students should describe (a) the aspect of memory they targeted for improvement (and why), (b) the memory principles or strategies they used (including the rationale behind them), and (c) any results (positive or negative) from applying these techniques. After grading students' papers, you might want to devote some class time to discussion so that students can share their successful experiences with others.

Higbee, K. L (1993). *Your memory: How it works and how to improve it.* New York: Paragon House.

Memory in Film: *Total Recall*

Arnold Schwarzenegger and Sharon Stone star in this futurist tale of a construction worker who takes a "fantasy vacation" to Mars courtesy of an implanted memory chip. When other, darker memories begin to haunt him, however, he discovers that he was once a secret service agent and that memories of that time period have been stolen from him. Spectacular special effects highlight this engrossing film (from 1990), which shows how reality can be invented with implanted memories and also illustrates the difficulty of drawing a line between reality and memory (ideas that are touched upon in the *Controversies* box in this chapter). Ask your students to gather a few recent articles on reconstructed and/or recovered memories and to write a short paper relating ideas from this research and from the text to this provocative film. (Live; 113 min).

Memory in Film: *Momento*

Guy Pearce stars in this unusual film about a man whose wife has been murdered. A murder-mystery is not so unusual; what's odd is that the film is told entirely in reverse. In the first scene we see Pearce's character gunning down his wife's murderer, and each subsequent scene shows the events that took place right before the previous scene. Imagine reading a book from the last page to the first and you'll get the idea. Oh, and complicating matters is the fact that Pearce's character suffers from the inability to form short-term memories. This leads him not only to develop novel ways of keeping track of information, but also hinders his ability to remember who he's after, whom he can trust, and why he's doing whatever he's doing at a given moment. The filmmakers did their research on short-term memory and the biological systems underlying it. They've also constructed a gripping film with more than a few twists to it. Recommended!

Keeping a Psychology Journal

In order to increase the personal relevance of material covered in class, you may require students to keep an on-going psychology journal for the duration of the course. The primary purpose of the journal is to encourage students to connect the facts, concepts, and principles that they acquire from the course to their own personal experiences. The journal adds a personal dimension to the course and provides an opportunity to apply course concepts to daily experiences (Hettich, 1990).

> Discuss your earliest memory or discuss a personal experience with Flashbulb memory. Have you ever had trouble remembering important dates, events, or information? Why do you think some of your memories stick while others just fade away? Is there anything special that you do to improve your memory?

Hettich, P. (1976). The journal: An autobiographical approach to learning. *Teaching of Psychology, 3*(2), 60-63.
Hettich, P. (1980). The journal revisited. *Teaching of Psychology, 7*(2), 105-106.
Hettich, P. (1990). Journal writing: Old fare or nouvelle cuisine? *Teaching of Psychology, 17*(1), 36-63.

video

ABC News/Prentice Hall Video Library

A Pill to Improve Failing Memory as We Age (3:43 min, Series III). This clip from ABC's *World News Tonight* looks at research conducted by Cortex, a California firm. Using animal models, researchers at Cortex have developed a pill that helps information be retained 30 to 40% longer than normal. Human trials are underway in Europe, and work in America with Alzheimer's patients is soon to begin.

Other Sources

Discovering Psychology, Part 9: Remembering and Forgetting (1990, 30 min, ANN/CPB). Examines memory formation, forgetting through decay and interference, and methods for improving memory.

Memory: The Past Imperfect (1994, 46 min, IM). A range of topics is considered, such as long- and short-term memory, amnesia, eyewitness accuracy, retrieval, and memory skills of babies.

Memory Skills: Power Learning (1991, 25 min, LS). Memory techniques such as visualization and mental "pegboards" are explored, and tips for improving one's memory are offered using short vignettes and examples. An accompanying booklet includes summaries of the key points on the tape and suggestions for further activities. This video is very well produced, although the pacing and level of presentation may make it more appropriate for use in a high school or community college course.

Memory, Suggestion, and Abuse (1994, 60 min, IM). How reconstruction, rather than reproduction, guides the memory process is the focus of this "applied" look at memory. The pitfalls of some therapeutic techniques are discussed, as is the fragile susceptibility of memory to disruption.

Mind Games (1995, 30 min, IM). The spooky secrets of the mind are explored, such as near-death experiences and hypnosis. Deja vu is also considered. Deja vu is also considered.

The Nature of Memory (26 min, FHS). Describes the use of computer models to mimic memory processes, research on amnesiacs, the role of emotion in memory, and how memories can become altered.

The Study of Memory (74 min, FHS). Diagrams and real-life examples are used to explain basic memory terminology, Examples of everyday memory, forgetting, and eyewitness testimony are also presented.

multimedia

Live! Psych

Module	Title	Book Page #
6.1	Iconic Memory Experiment	p. 227

Import this concept to learn more about sensory memory. Screen 1 provides instructions for the test for iconic memory using the partial-report technique. The student participates in the task. Screen 2 explains that the iconic memory experiment is based on George Sperling's classic experiment, originally done in 1960. Sperling found that no matter how large the display of letters was, participants could name only four items. Screen 3 explains Sperling's partial-report technique. Import Screen 4 to explain Sperling's findings about the duration of iconic memory.

6.2	The Information-Processing Model of Memory	p. 228

This concept presents an overview of the three-part memory system. The student clicks on each memory store to learn more about the function of sensory memory, short-term memory, and long-term memory. Import Screen 1 to examine the information-processing model of memory.

6.3	Serial-Position Effect Experiment	p. 232

This concept explores factors that influence recall to give the student a better understanding of how short-term and long-term memory operate. In Screen 1, students are asked to recall as many U.S. presidents as they can, in the correct order they served office. Student clicks on SHOW ME to see answers. Screen 2 shows the U-shaped pattern of the serial-position effect. Screen 3 explains the primacy and recency effect. Screen 4 looks at one theory that suggests that the recency effect happens because at the time of recall, items are still sitting in short-term memory and thus are easy to retrieve. The problem with this theory is that recency effects are often found in tasks that do not involve short-term memory, such as the task involving listing the U.S. presidents in order. Screen 5 explains Robert Crowder's 1993 study in which he found the typical serial-position curve, with the exception that President Lincoln was recalled more frequently than would be expected from the middle position. The distinctiveness theory provides one explanation of how both primacy and recency can work in lists that are recalled from long-term memory, as well as lists that are newly learned.

6.4	Levels of Processing Experiment	p. 234

Screen 1 provides instructions for the levels of processing experiment. The student clicks the start button to begin. Twenty words are flashed, one at a time, every 1-2 seconds. In Screen 2, students are to select all of the even numbers displayed on the screen in 30 seconds. In Screen 3, students are to type as many words as they can remember from the list in which they counted the letters in each word. When they are ready to check their answers, students click on CHECK ANSWERS. Screen 4 involves Trial 2 of the levels of processing experiment. In Screen 5, students are to select all of the odd numbers displayed on the screen in the next 30 seconds. In Screen 6, students are to type as many words as they can remember from the list in which they rated the pleasantness of each word. Screen 7 looks at form versus meaning of words and asks the student which exercise was easier. Screen 8 explains that how you process a word when you first see it directly affects how well you will remember it later on. The screen looks at the levels-of-processing model of memory. Screen 9 is an animation of elaborative rehearsal.

6.5	Memory Tasks	p. 245

Screen 1 introduces the memory tasks to the student. The student is instructed to have a pen and paper ready before proceeding to the next screen. Screen 2 provides the directions for a seven-word recall task. The student clicks on the radio to begin the memory task. Screen 3 provides instructions for a retroactive interference task with a similar word list. Again, the student clicks on the radio to begin the memory task. Screen 4 provides instructions for a recall task that involves a dissimilar interference list. The student clicks on the radio to begin.

Retroactive and Proactive Interference   p. 245

This concept explains the results of the three memory tasks and distinguishes between retroactive and proactive interference. Screen 1 introduces the interference theory of forgetting. Screen 2 examines similarity and interference. It is explained that most people find Memory Task #2 to be the most difficult because it involved another list of countries. The second list of similar words interferes with memory of the first list. The list of ice cream flavors in Memory Task #3 interferes less with most people's memories for a list of countries, because the names of the ice cream flavors are not as similar as the names of more countries. Screen 3 defines retroactive inference. Screen 4 defines proactive interference.

6.6   Types of Mnemonics   p. 247

This concept describes various types of mnemonics. Screen 1 defines mnemonic techniques and explains their use in aiding recall. FACE and Every Good Boy Does Fine are shown as examples of mnemonics. Import Screen 2 to describe imagery. Import Screen 3 to describe the method of loci. Import Screen 4 to describe the peg-word technique. Import Screen 5 to show how to use the peg-word technique to remember a grocery list. Import Screen 6 to describe chunking. Import Screen 7 to describe an acronym. Import Screen 8 to describe an acrostic.

Web Investigations

Test Your Memory

In this activity students get a chance to test their memory by playing the role of an eyewitness who is present when an embarrassing event occurs. After they observe the event they are asked some questions about it. This activity is designed to accompany the Scientific American article "False Memories," described below. Students should complete the activity first, then read the article, then contribute to a class discussion on this topic. This activity works particularly well in a computer lab, where students can each experience the event and then discuss it together.

Making Connections

The Sensory Registers

Q What is a sensory register? Based on what you learned in Chapter 3, identify two additional sensory registers not discussed in the chapter.

A A sensory register is the portion of a sensory system that holds new information for a brief period. In addition to visual and auditory registers, we have sensory registers for smell, taste, and touch.

Q What is eidetic imagery?

A Eidetic imagery, or photographic memory, is the ability to create unusually sharp and detailed visual images of objects seen.

Q How does the cocktail party phenomenon illustrate sensory filtering?

A The cocktail-party phenomenon shows that we are aware of all the sensory information coming to us but only pay attention to information that is meaningful to us. Everything else is filtered out.

Short-Term Memory

Q How much information can most people hold in STM at one time?

A Most people can hold 5 to 10 items in STM at one time.

Q How is verbal information encoded in STM?

A Verbal information is encoded phonologically in STM.

Q How is information kept in STM?

A Information is kept in STM by means of rote rehearsal, which consists of repeating information over and over.

Long-Term Memory

Q What is elaborative rehearsal? How could you use it to remember the meaning of, say, elaborative rehearsal?

A Elaborative rehearsal is the act of relating new information to something that we already know. We could remember the term *elaborative rehearsal* by connecting it to the idea of *elaborating on* something.

Q How does your schemata for parties influence your storage of memories about a party?

A Our schemata for parties cause us to store memories about a party according to such characteristics as who gave the party, where it was held, who was there, and whether we had a good time, and not according to irrelevant characteristics such as who was the president of the United States at the time or what we ate for breakfast that morning.

Q How do semantic memories differ from episodic memories?

A Semantic memories are facts and concepts that many people may store in LTM, whereas episodic memories are limited to a particular individual.

Q Which memories can you more easily "call up" if asked: explicit or implicit memories?

A Because we are aware of explicit memories, it is easier to recall them than to recall implicit memories.

The Biology of Memory

Q What is consolidation, and how long does it take?

A Consolidation is the process through which memories are formed. It produces changes in the synaptic connections among neural cells. It can take years for long-term memories to become stable.

Q Where are short-term memories stored?

A Short-term memories are stored primarily in the prefrontal cortex and the temporal cortex.

Q What subcortical organ is especially important in the formation of long-term semantic and episodic memories?

A The hippocampus is especially important in the formation of long-term semantic and episodic memories.

Forgetting

Q What is retrograde amnesia? Why does ECT cause retrograde amnesia?

A Retrograde amnesia is a condition in which a person cannot remember what happened to him or her shortly before a head injury.

Q What is the role of attention in forgetting?

A Lack of attention to critical cues results in inadequate learning and thus makes forgetting more likely.

Q Explain the difference between retroactive and proactive interference.

A In retroactive interference, new material interferes with information already in long-term memory. In proactive interference, old material interferes with new material being learned.

Q What is cue-dependent forgetting?

A Cue-dependent forgetting occurs when cues that were present during learning are absent during recall.

Q Give an example of state-dependent memory.

A State-dependent memory might occur when a person learns something while feeling sad and later can recall that information more easily when feeling sad than when feeling happy.

Q Name three things you can do to reduce forgetting.

A You can do several things to reduce forgetting:

1. Develop motivation.
2. Practice memory skills.
3. Be confident in your ability to remember.
4. Minimize distractions.
5. Stay focused.
6. Make connections between new material and other information already stored in your long-term memory.
7. Use mental imagery.
8. Use retrieval cues.
9. Rely on more than memory alone.
10. Be aware that your own personal schemata may distort your recall of events.

Special Topics in Memory

Q What is childhood amnesia? Summarize one theory that attempts to explain this phenomenon.

A Childhood amnesia refers to the fact that it is extremely rare for people to recall events that occurred before they were 2 years old. One explanation for this is that the child's brain is not fully developed at birth.

Q How did "S" manage to remember so many things so well?

A "S" managed to remember many things well by using a variety of memory techniques, such as coding verbal material visually.

Q What phenomenon does the "now print" theory attempt to explain?

A The "now print" theory attempts to explain the phenomenon of flashbulb memories.

Q What are the implications of research on false memory for judges and prosecutors?

A Research on false memory suggests that mistaken eyewitness testimony can result in innocent people being sent to jail. As a result, courts are increasingly recognizing the limits of eyewitness testimony.

Q How might memory be measured differently in two societies, one with a written language and one without?

A In a society with a written language, memory might be measured in terms of the ability to recall lists of words or numbers. In a society without a written language, memory might be measured in terms of the ability to recite the deeds of heroes or long genealogies.

Mind Matters

The Process of Remembering

Everything you'd ever want to know about memory (at a rudimentary level, at least) is here. This section of the CD-ROM takes the viewer through encoding, sensory, short-term, and long-term storage, chunking, the serial position effect, depth of processing, retrieval, the construction of memory, déjà vu, and point of view and memory. There are ample interactive exercises and demonstrations. Several of the memory experiments and tests on the CD-ROM can be used as in-class demonstrations or as activities during a lab period. These can also be used as a basis for a longer paper or presentation on memory processes. Consider dividing the students by their interests (e.g., encoding, storage, retrieval, memory disruptions), ask them to review the relevant section of the CD-ROM, and report back to their fellow students on their findings.

Video Classics

Short-Term Memory

SYNOPSIS: A kindly experimenter puts a crewcut youth named Drew through his paces on part of a standard intelligence test. The boy tries earnestly to repeat a sequence of digits held in short-term memory, despite his ability to simply look at the testing sheet and read the numbers back in correct order. This clip illustrates one way of testing short-term memory capacity.

Form a Hypothesis

Q What type of memory does Drew rely on to answer the memory items in the Stanford-Binet?

A Drew is relying on short-term memory. If Drew was required to wait longer before recalling and prevented from rehearsing the number lists or sentences, he would have great difficulty recalling the material.

Test Your Understanding

Q What is the capacity of short-term memory?

A Short-term memory is limited to between 5 to 9 individual items, giving rise to Miller's magic number of "7, plus or minus 2."

Q What is the value of chunking?

A Chunking increases our ability to temporarily store information in short-term memory by creating a single memory out of multiple individual pieces of information. For example, a telephone number consisting of seven individual bits (2328894) may be encoded as the prefix 232 (chunk 1) 88 (chunk 2) 94 (chunk 3).

Q What is the duration of short-term memory?

A It is a relatively short-term store, lasting from between 1.5 to 2 seconds.

Thinking Critically

Q What are the functions of short-term memory?

A Short-term memory probably exists as a temporary buffer for information. When information is in short-term memory, we can review it and see if it should be stored in long-term memory. If we need to keep the information for a long period of time, we will rehearse the information using rote or elaborative strategies.

Web Links

1. http://teach.valdosta.edu/whuitt/
This site offers in-depth information about the stage model of information processing, organization of knowledge, and concept formation.

2. http://www.exploratorium.edu/memory/magnani/index.html

This branch of San Francisco's Exploratorium science museum features work by "a memory artist," who paints his childhood home from memory. A novel application of memory principles that your students will enjoy seeing.

3. http://www.selfgrowth.com/memory.html

This site reviews and recommends memory improvement and memory training websites. A service of Self-Improvement Online.

4. http://www.memory.uva.nl/memory_improvement/mnemonics.htm

Online Memory Improvement Course. Basic and advanced mnemonic strategies are discussed on this site. Visit this site during class and use these strategies as a demonstration topic. Ask students to retain the same information using a variety of these techniques.

5. http://www.psywww.com/mtsite/memory.html

Mind Tools: Memory Techniques and Memories. This site introduces the basic principles of memory, along with suggestions for improving memory and tips for using mnemonic strategies.

transparencies

Series V

55. *An Information-Processing Model of Memory*
The flow of information from the sensory register to short-term memory to long-term memory is depicted.

56. *The Serial Position Effect*
Primacy and recency effects are evident in serial learning. This transparency illustrates these concepts.

57. *Encoding Processes and Memory*
This transparency shows levels of processing for a memory task.

58. *Diagram of Experiments Measuring Retroactive and Proactive Interference*
A diagram of procedures used to measure memory interference is shown in this transparency.

59. *Types of Long-Term Memory*
Procedural, episodic, and semantic memory are illustrated.

Text Figures

6-1.	*The Sequence of Information Processing*
6-2.	*The Serial Position Effect*
6-3.	*A Penny for Your Thoughts*
6-4.	*The Biological Basis of Memory*
6-5.	*PET Scanning Image*
6-6.	*Diagram of Experiments Measuring Interference*

Handout 6-1

Memory Test Scoring Sheet

<u>A</u>	<u>B</u>
bike	belt
bird	bureau
coal	church
door	clock
fish	coin
grass	foot
hammer	fire
kitchen	month
lemon	paint
magic	pipe
monkey	pocket
pencil	trail
pitch	train
soap	travel
story	trunk

Handout 6-2

Coding in Long-term Memory

Instructions: Please read the following story, and be prepared to have your memory tested for one of its sentences.

This is an interesting story about the telescope. In Holland, a man named Lippershey was an eyeglass maker. One day his children were playing with some lenses. They discovered that things seemed very close if two lenses were held about a foot apart. Lippershey began experimenting, and his "spyglass" attracted much attention. He sent a letter about it to Galileo, the great Italian scientist. Galileo at once realized the importance of the discovery and set about to build an instrument of his own. He used an old organ pipe with one lens curved out and the other in. On the first clear night he pointed the glass toward the sky. He was amazed to find the empty dark spaces filled with brightly gleaming stars! Night after night Galileo climbed to a high tower sweeping the sky with his telescope. One night he saw Jupiter, and to his great surprise discovered near it three bright stars, two to the east and one to the west.

Instructions: Now, without referring back to the story, decide which one of the following sentences was IN the story.

A. He sent Galileo, the great Italian scientist, a letter about it.

B. A letter about it was sent to Galileo, the great Italian scientist.

C. Galileo, the great Italian scientist, sent him a letter about it.

D. He sent a letter about it to Galileo, the great Italian scientist.

Adapted from Searleman, A., & Herrmann, D. (1994). Memory from a broader perspective. New York: McGraw-Hill.

Handout 6-3 a

Memory for Word Lists

Instructions: Briefly study the following list of words. You will be given approximately 30 seconds for this task, after which time you will be asked to recall as many as you can.

snake

violin

target

terrace

skin

arrow

book

football

worm

nude

goal

bow

Handout 6-3 b

Memory for Word Lists

Instructions: Briefly study the following list of words. You will be given approximately 30 seconds for this task, after which time you will be asked to recall as many as you can.

book
worm
snake
skin
nude
violin
bow
arrow
target
goal
football
terrace

Chapter 7 Cognition and Language

chapter outline 185

learning objectives 187

lecture suggestions

    The Psychology of Mental Control 188
    Don't Believe Everything Your Read ... Except This 189
    Approaches to Decision Making 190
    Tongue-Eye Coordination 191
    Bilingualism 192

demonstrations and activities

    Defining Language 193
    Context and Speech Perception 193
    Learning to Use Nonsexist Language 194
    Problem Representation 194
    Mental Set as an Obstacle to Problem Solving 195
    Representativeness Heuristic 195
    The Conjunctive Fallacy 196

student assignments

    Exploring Bilingualism 197
    Mental Sets in Everyday Life 197
    Language in Film: *Children of a Lesser God* 198

video 199

multimedia 201

transparencies 204

handouts

    Using Nonsexist Language 205
    The Hospital Room Problem 206
    Luchins' Water Jar Problem 207

chapter outline

I. The Building Blocks of Thought
    A. Language
        1. Characteristics of human language
            a. Semantic: meaningful
            b. Displacement: able to represent past, present, future, and hypothetical
            c. Productivity: flexible form and meaning; infinite combinations
    B. The structure of language
        1. Sound and meaning
            a. Phonemes: The basic sounds that make up any language
            b. Morphemes: The smallest meaningful units of speech
        2. Grammar: The rules governing how sounds and words can be combined
            a. Syntax: Rules for arranging words into sentences
            b. Semantics: Criteria for assigning meaning to morphemes
            c. Surface structure: The words and phrases comprising a particular sentence
            d. Deep structure: The underlying meaning of a sentence
    C. Images: Mental representations of a sensory experience
    D. Concepts
        1. Mental categories of people, objects, experiences
        2. Prototypes
            a. A mental representation of the most typical member of a group

II. Language and Thought
    A. Language and cognition
        1. Linguistic determinism: Language determines thinking and perception of the world
        2. Is our language male-dominated?
        3. Culture and cognition: cultural experiences shape thought and language

III. Nonhuman Thought and Language
    A. Animal cognition
    B. The question of language

IV. Problem Solving
    A. The Interpretation of Problems
        1. Problem representation
    B. Producing Strategies and Evaluating Progress
        1. Trial and error
        2. Information retrieval

      3. Algorithms
      4. Heuristics
          a. hill climbing
          b. subgoals
          c. means-end analysis
          d. working backward
   C. Obstacles to Solving Problems
      1. Mental set
      2. Functional fixedness
   D. Experience and expertise

V. Decision Making
   A. Logical decision making
   B. Decision-making heuristics
      1. Representativeness
      2. Availability
      3. Confirmation bias
   C. Framing
   D. Decisions under pressure
   E. Explaining our decisions
      1. Hindsight bias
      2. Counterfactual thinking

learning objectives

After reading this chapter, students should be able to:

1. List and describe the distinguishing characteristics of language: semantic, displacement, and productivity.

2. Define phonemes, morphemes, grammar and grammar's components.

3. Distinguish between the concepts of "surface structure" and "deep structure."

4. Describe the basic steps of problem solving. List and describe four types of solution strategies.

5. Discuss various obstacles to problem solving.

6. Describe four ways in which a person can become a better problem solver.

7. Distinguish between heuristics and algorithms.

8. Summarize the relationship between language and thinking. Explain linguistic determinism and cite criticisms of it.

lecture suggestions

The Psychology of Mental Control

It seems trivially obvious that we should be able to control and direct our own thinking. But as anyone on a diet (who is bedeviled by thoughts of flying pizzas), victim of childhood abuse (who can't fight the recurring thoughts of the trauma), or person dreading an upcoming decision will tell you, sometimes the very thing we try to banish from our minds plagues us without relief. Mental control seems unusually difficult to maintain at times, and frequently becomes a far from trivial issue. To the extent that unwanted thoughts invade our consciousness, we are robbed of peace of mind.

Dan Wegner, at the University of Virginia, has done pioneering work on the nature of mental control. His research indicates that, quite paradoxically, it is not so much the thoughts themselves that yield such power in troubling our consciousness, but rather our attempts at suppressing the thoughts. The very act of thought suppression gives rise to preoccupation with the unwanted thought. In a set of elegant experiments, Wegner and his colleagues (1987) asked research participants to verbalize their stream of consciousness into a tape recorder for a 5-minute period. Some participants were told specifically to try to think of a white bear, whereas other participants were instructed to try to not think of a white bear. Both groups were told to ring a bell whenever the thought of a white bear came to mind. After the 5 minutes elapsed, participants were given the opposite instructions. That is, the initial suppression group (told not to think of the bear) was now instructed to "try to think of a white bear" during another 5-minute period, whereas the initial expression group was now instructed to suppress the thought. Again, whenever such thoughts came to mind, participants were asked to ring the desk bell in front of them.

When examining both verbalizations of "white bear" and bell rings, an intriguing result was revealed. As might be imagined, participants in the initial suppression period had difficulty not thinking of a white bear. However, during the expression period these same people showed significantly more preoccupation with thoughts of a white bear than even those subjects directly instructed to entertain the thought from the outset. In other words, the act of initial thought suppression produced a rebound effect, calling the unwanted thought to mind with even greater frequency. It seemed, then, that attempts at suppression produced obsession with the unwanted thought. Wegner and his colleagues have since investigated this phenomenon in relation to the mental control strategies of depressives, the suppression of thoughts of sex, stress and mental control, individual differences in mental control, psychophysiological concomitants of thought suppression, and a general theory of ironic processes (Wegner, 1994).

But what explains this suppression-obsession link? Wegner suggests several possibilities. First, by never allowing the thought to be entertained in consciousness, we never quite get used to its presence or to what it signifies. As soon as visions of pepperoni dance in the head of a dieter, for example, the immediate reaction is to squelch, suppress, and banish the thought. This is a short-term solution, however, as our suppression attempts fail to keep pace with the insistence of the thought. Each time the thought creeps back into consciousness, then, it does so at full power, eventually resulting in our preoccupation with it.

Second, and more generally, Wegner (1994) proposes that when we attempt mental control, two cognitive processes are at work. An *operating process* promotes the intended changes by searching for mental contents that are consistent with the desired end state. For example, the thought to "not giggle" in the face of a stressful, somber situation would be a desired end state of one's mental control activities. At the same time, however, a *monitoring process* tests whether the operating process is still needed by searching for mental contents that are inconsistent with the desired state. In the present example, the monitor would search for "giggling" and return either a negative or positive value to the operating process. Here's the rub. While the operating process is somewhat effortful, requiring greater cognitive capacity, the monitoring process is more automatic and takes place without effort. When the two work in harmony, the thinker can revel in some measure of mental control. But if the mental system is taxed, or cognitive resources are depleted in some way, it will be the more effortful operating process that gets disrupted. The monitoring process, searching for the to-be-banished-thought, now becomes more pronounced, and serves to heighten the thinker's sensitivity to the unwanted thought.

It is clear that thought suppression, the roots of obsession, and the nature of mental control are fascinating, interacting, complex topics. A great deal is now known about the processes at work, and applications to therapy, stress reduction, pain control, and health are underway.

Wegner, D. M. (1988). Stress and mental control. In S. Fisher & J. Reason (Eds.), *Handbook of life stress, cognition, and health* (pp. 685-699). Chicester, England: Wiley.
Wegner, D. M. (1989). *White bears and other unwanted thoughts.* New York: Viking Press.
Wegner, D. M. (1994). Ironic processes of mental control. *Psychological Review, 101,* 34-52.
Wegner, D. M., & Erber, R. (1992). The hyperaccessibility of suppressed thoughts. *Journal of Personality and Social Psychology, 63,* 903-912.
Wegner, D. M., & Pennebaker, J. W. (1993). *The handbook of mental control.* Englewood Cliffs, NJ: Prentice Hall.
Wegner, D. M., Schneider, D. J., Carter, S. R., III, & White, T. L. (1987). Paradoxical effects of thought suppression. *Journal of Personality and Social Psychology, 53,* 5-13.
Wegner, D. M., Shortt, J. W., Blake, A. W., & Page, M. S. (1990). The suppression of exciting thoughts. *Journal of Personality and Social Psychology, 58,* 409-418.
Wenzlaff, R., Wegner, D. M., & Roper, D. (1988). Depression and mental control: The resurgence of unwanted negative thoughts. *Journal of Personality and Social Psychology, 55,* 882-892.

Don't Believe Everything You Read...Except This

People sometimes believe in things they ought not to, such as flat Earths, cheese moons, or their own invulnerability. But forming and clinging to misbegotten beliefs may itself be a consequence of some fundamental cognitive processes, such as how information gets encoded in memory or what happens to a disrupted attention system.

Dan Gilbert, of Harvard University, has been exploring the problem of "believing what isn't so" for several years. In explaining the process by which such belief takes place he invokes the thinking of Rene Descartes and Baruch Spinoza, both of whom wrote quite a bit about how information is perceived and stored in a mental system. Descartes argued that information is first comprehended, and then in a subsequent step, a truth value is assigned to it: We decide to accept or reject the information as being true. This would suggest, of course, that we can easily entertain ideas (indefinitely, perhaps...putting them up in a mental guest room, so to speak) without necessarily putting stock in them. If comprehension (understanding) of information and endorsement (acceptance or rejection) are two distinct steps, humans should be able to hold an idea without believing it.

Spinoza adopted a different position on the nature of belief, arguing that comprehension and acceptance of information are accomplished in a single initial step, only later to be followed by certification or rejection of the information. This view holds that the very act of receiving information entails assigning a belief to it ["this information is true" (or false, as the case might be)], which only later can be substantiated or "unbelieved," as might be called for. Quite unlike Descartes, then, Spinoza argued that ideas could not be entertained, "beliefless," in a cognitive system, but rather are believed upon first being received into the cognitive system.

How to disentangle these competing predictions? Notice that both, if allowed to run their course, would lead to the same outcome: The acceptance or rejection of information as being true. The difference lies in when the belief is assigned, either in a Spinozan first step or in a Cartesian second step. Gilbert reasoned, then, that disrupting a belief system in action would be the only way to tell which system (Spinozan or Cartesian) was at work. If Descartes was correct, disrupting the system between steps should have no effect on cognition: We would be left holding a collection of ideas that had not yet been assigned truth values. If Spinoza was correct, however, disruption should produce a very pronounced tendency: We should be left believing information to be true (since it was automatically tagged with a truth valued upon entering the cognitive system) when in some cases it is not.

To test these ideas, Gilbert and his colleagues asked research participants in one of several experiments to learn some (fictitious) Hopi language terms. Participants saw a Hopi/English word-pairing flash on a computer screen (such as "A *monishna* is a star," "A *rirg* is a valley," or "A *neseti* is a bee"), which was followed by a brief pause, and then followed by one of three outcomes: The word "True" (signaling that the preceding pairing was accurate), the word "False" (indicating that the preceding pairing was incorrect), or a blank screen. Note that Descartes and Spinoza are still neck-and-neck at this point. Either account of belief would argue that participants could take in the information (untouched, as Descartes would have it, or believed as true, as Spinoza would have it) and then correct it based on the True or False cue later given (which would mean assigning a belief in the Cartesian system, or revising/substantiating an existing belief in the Spinozan system). However, the researchers asked participants to do one additional task. On some trials participants were asked to press a button if they heard a particular tone. This additional task served to tax their available cognitive resources, making it more difficult to perform the correction step of integrating the true/false cues with the prior information. These participants, however, provided an answer to the riddle of belief. When later polled they showed a particular pattern of errors; namely, they were left believing propositions that should have been revised (i.e., those tagged as "False") as being true. Given the controls of the experiment, the only way to account for this outcome is that the information must have been encoded as true upon first being read (just as Spinoza argued). Because these resource-depleted subjects were disrupted from performing Spinoza's second task (certifying or, in these cases, rejecting the previously-believed information), they were left believing what they ought not to.

The implications of this research are startling. For example, as Dan Wegner and his colleagues have shown, it may help explain the workings of innuendo. When presented with information that may or may not be correct, our Spinozan belief system compels us to endorse that information upon comprehension. If our cognitive resources are later disrupted we may be unable to correct our initial comprehension. Similarly, this research may help explain why belief perseverance takes place. If the stage of correcting initial information is subject to disruption, we may be left clinging to beliefs even in the face of clearly disconfirming evidence. Finally, these results fly in the face of what your parents always told you. Far from "not believing everything you read," it seems that we can't escape that fate.

Gilbert, D. T. (1993). The assent of man: Mental representation and the control of belief. In D. M. Wegner & J. W. Pennebaker (Eds.), *Handbook of mental control* (pp. 57-87). Englewood Cliffs, NJ: Prentice Hall.

Gilbert, D. T. (1991). How mental systems believe. *American Psychologist, 46,* 107-119.

Gilbert, D. T., Krull, D. S., & Malone, P. S. (1990). Unbelieving the unbelievable: Some problems in the rejection of false information. *Journal of Personality and Social Psychology, 59,* 601-613.

Ross, L., Lepper, M. R., & Hubbard, M. (1975). Perseverance in self-perception and social perception: Biased attributional processes in the debriefing paradigm. *Journal of Personality and Social Psychology, 32,* 880-892.

Wegner, D. M., Wenzlaff, R., Kerker, R. M., & Beattie, A. E. (1981). Incrimination through innuendo: Can media questions become public answers? *Journal of Personality and Social Psychology, 40,* 822-832.

Approaches to Decision Making

The textbook describes several heuristics, such as representativeness and availability, that impact on the decision-making process. Irving Janis and Leon Mann described some general decision-making strategies that include the use of these heuristics, which are summarized below.

❖ *Optimizing.* An optimizing strategy has as its goal the selection of the alternative that has the highest potential payoff. Therefore, the process of decision making focuses on an analysis of the relative costs and benefits associated with each alternative. Janis and Mann noted that very few people effectively use this approach because the amount of information that is necessary to be processed often exceeds the mental capacity of the individual. In addition, since this approach is costly in time, effort, and money, it is often not adopted due to personal or external time constraints that are placed upon making the decision.

❖ *Suboptimizing.* Because of personal or external constraints on time or one's capacity to process all of the necessary information, individuals will sometimes adopt a suboptimizing strategy.

This strategy focuses on maximizing some aspects at the expense of others. For example, one may choose to take a new job because it represents a significant increase in salary and benefits. However, the job requires extensive travel and late work hours, resulting in less time spent with family and friends.

❖ *Satisficing.* A satisficing strategy is one that focuses on identifying a solution that is acceptable or meets some minimal set of requirements rather than one that maximizes the outcome. Usually this approach involves setting some minimal criteria for a decision and then evaluating each alternative according to these criteria. The first alternative that satisfies the criteria is the one that is selected. Therefore, this strategy often fails to take into account all possible alternatives. It could be argued that many of our major purchases (for example, an automobile) are made by using a satisficing approach. We may initially make a list of the things we want in a new car, and then purchase the first car that meets these criteria.

❖ *Quasi-Satisficing.* Janis and Mann described a quasi-satisficing strategy as one that makes use of a single, simple decision rule to make moral decisions. This rule, however, is not simply considered to be minimally satisfactory, but rather is believed to be the best or only course of action for making moral decisions. Another quasi-satisficing approach is known as *elimination-by-aspects*. This approach utilizes a set of decision rules or requirements that are used in succession to sequentially narrow down a list of alternatives. That is, you would start with the first requirement and eliminate all alternatives that fail to meet that requirement. You would then continue by applying the next requirement to the remaining alternatives. This process continues until only one alternative remains. The danger of this approach is that it does not weigh the relative values of each of the requirements. Thus, an alternative may be eliminated on the basis of what is essentially a minor criterion.

Janis, I. L., & Mann, L. (1977). *Decision making.* New York: The Free Press.

Reprinted from Hill, W. G. (1995). Instructor's resource manual for *Psychology* by S. F. Davis and J. J. Palladino. Englewood Cliffs, NJ: Prentice Hall.

Tongue-Eye Coordination

"Put the apple on the towel in the box." The ambiguity inherent in this sentence can lead to great confusion. Should the apple that's currently on the towel go in the box? Should the towel lying near the apple first go in the box, followed by the apple on top of it? Or should the apple be placed on the towel in the box, rather than on the plate that's in the box?

Until recently, most views of speech comprehension emphasized the decoding of grammar, followed by a search for contextual clues that might aid in following a command. The grammar in this example illustrates that sometimes that can be a tall order. A recent study, however, suggests that visual cues irrelevant to grammar play a prominent early role in influencing message comprehension. A combination of visual and linguistic information helps us to better understand what others tell us.

A research team led by Michael K. Tanenhaus at the University of Rochester tracked the eye movements of volunteers while they listened to a variety of messages. These simple commands asked them to manipulate objects that were visible in the laboratory. The researchers found that people look at targets as soon as they hear words that distinguish the target from other items. As an example, when asked to "touch the starred yellow square" participants took about a quarter-second to look at the correct target (that lay among other unstarred blocks) after hearing the word "starred." However, if the items included two starred yellow blocks, participants looked at the target after hearing the word "square."

But where does the apple go? When presented with either an ambiguous phrase ("Put the apple on the towel in the box") or an unambiguous one ("Put the apple that's on the towel in the box") participants' eye movements differed. As they heard a particular command, participants viewed either a display with an apple set on a towel, another towel without an apple, a box, and a pencil; or a similar arrangement in which the pencil was replaced by an additional apple on a napkin. When faced with only one apple, the ambiguous phrase led participants to glance at the towel after hearing "towel," showing their inclination that the apple should be placed there, then both placed in the box. Those participants given the unambiguous phrase, however, never glanced at the towel. When the two-apple arrangement was presented, however, both ambiguous and unambiguous instructions produced the same patterns of eye movements. Participants looked from one apple to the other upon hearing the word "apple," then looked at the appropriate apple upon hearing the word "towel," and made no further eye movements until hearing the word "box." An apple on a towel in a box illustrates the coordination that takes place between vision and hearing in speech comprehension. But if the apple stays in the box it doesn't do much for the hearing-hunger connection.

Bower, B. (1995). Understanding speech: I see what you mean. *Science News, 147*, 373.

Bilingualism

Bilingualism is the ability to speak two languages that have different vocabulary, syntax, and speech sounds. Although relatively uncommon in the United States, bilingualism is standard in many other countries.

Multiple languages are acquired easily during early childhood because of favorable neural, social, and attitudinal conditions. For example, children are naturally imitative and are not self-conscious about possible mistakes. Also, they are less likely to have negative attitudes such as "Why do I have to do this?"

Early studies of bilingualism reported that language and intellectual deficits were associated with second-language acquisition. However, these studies were seriously flawed. Although children who simultaneously learn two languages in infancy initially intermingle words from both languages, good differentiation rapidly develops. Also, a more recent, properly controlled study of a bilingual education program in Canada (Bruck, Lambert, & Tucker, 1976) found no unfavorable consequences. This seven-year longitudinal study (grades K through 6) compared the abilities of English speakers enrolled in a standard English-language school program, French speakers in a standard French-language program, and English speakers in a French-language immersion program. The immersion program began with all instruction conducted in French and gradually introduced English each year. The immersion group performed as well as the English control group on tests of English, English-based tests of verbal IQ, and mathematics. They also compared favorably with French speakers on tests of French.

Although early childhood is an ideal time for learning a second language, older individuals can attain competency. Quality teaching methods, an aptitude for languages, and good motivation (sorely lacking in many college students) are necessary. Teaching techniques vary from the translation (indirect) method, in which students translate passages (seldom effective for more than reading), to the direct method, which emphasizes oral skills, and the linguistic method, which drills both oral and syntactic skills and results in rapid competency. Motivation depends both on the reason for learning the language and on the perceived status of that knowledge. Even with adequate motivation and instruction, however, some people have more difficulty than others--attitude is important. Aptitude for languages can be predicted on the basis of the Modern Language Aptitude Test or Language Aptitude Battery, school grades ($r = .62$), or the Language Aptitude Battery plus grades ($r = .72$; Taylor, 1976).

Bruck, M., Lambert, W. E., & Tucker, G. R. (1976). Cognitive and attitudinal consequences of bilingual schooling: The St. Lambert project through grade six. *International Journal of Psycholinguistics, 3*, 13ff.
Taylor, I. (1976). *Introduction to psycholinguistics.* New York: Holt, Rinehart, and Winston.
Reprinted from Whitford, F. W. (1995). Instructor's resource manual for *Psychology: Principles and applications* by S. Worchel and W. Shebilske. Englewood Cliffs, NJ: Prentice Hall.

demonstrations

Defining Language

William Hunter (1981) described an activity designed to illustrate the difficulty in defining what we mean by language. On the day you do this activity, enter the class a few minutes late so that there is some amount of conversation going on. Without speaking, communicate to the students that they should be quiet. For example, you could clap your hands together, put your finger to your lips, or write the word "quiet" on the board as a last resort. After students quiet down, start giving them some easy nonverbal instructions such as making some students sit in another desk, getting other students to stand up and join you at the front of the room, and so on. If you are a real performer, Hunter suggests doing a mime routine. Finally, still using nonverbal communication, form the students into small discussion groups and write the following questions on the board: What is communication? What is speech? and What is language? Give the students about 10 to 15 minutes to discuss the questions within their groups, and then get each group to report their answers. Relate the group answers to the description and definition of language given in the textbook. Hunter also suggested that you may want to ask additional questions during the class discussion such as: "Is mime language? Is American Sign Language really a language? Do animals communicate? Do animals have a language?"

Hunter, W. J. (1981). Language and communication: Defining language can leave you speechless. In L. T. Benjamin, Jr. & K. D. Lowman (Eds.), *Activities handbook for the teaching of psychology* (pp. 103-104). Washington, DC: American Psychological Association.

Reprinted from Hill, W. G. (1995). Instructor's resource manual for *Psychology* by S. F. Davis and J. J. Palladino. Englewood Cliffs, NJ: Prentice Hall.

Context and Speech Perception

Margaret Matlin points out that human speech perception is quite flexible: We are active listeners who, instead of receiving speech sounds, use context as a cue to help figure out a word or a sound. One implication of this flexibility is *phonemic restoration*, in which people regularly (and without awareness) fill in missing sounds using context as a cue. Apparently, our skill at reconstructing missing sounds (e.g., hearing the word *peel* in the sentence, "The _eel was on the orange") has evolved because we are accustomed to having phonemes occasionally masked by extraneous noises, such as coughs, whispers, pages turning, etc. Interestingly, it is our ability to perceive words on the basis of context that also allows us to ignore sloppy mispronunciations. To demonstrate this in class, practice reading the following sentences until you can read them smoothly. Then, read them aloud to your class, asking students to identify which sound/word in each sentence was incorrect.

1. In all the gunfusion, the mystery man escaped from the mansion.
2. When I was working pizily in the library, the fire alarm rang out.
3. The messemger ran up to the professor and handed her a proclamation.
4. It has been zuggested that students be required to preregister.
5. The president reacted vavorably to all of the committee's suggestions.

Your students, if consistent with research by Cole, should not notice mispronunciations when they occur in the context of a sentence (although Cole's subjects were able to distinguish syllables such as *gun* and *con* when the isolated syllables were presented). Matlin notes that our tolerance of sloppy speech may cause us to overlook startling pronunciation mistakes made by children, as in the case of the child who sang the following words to a famous Christmas carol, "O come all ye hateful: Joy, Phil, and their trumpet."

Matlin, M. W. (1994). *Cognition* (3rd ed.). Fort Worth: Harcourt Brace.

Learning to Use Nonsexist Language

The *Controversies* box in Chapter 7 discusses how the generic use of *man* and other masculine pronouns excludes women in our language and also contributes to gender stereotyping. As a thought-provoking assignment, have your students try to generate gender neutral alternatives for the words in Handout 7-1 (suggested alternatives are given below). This exercise should not only spark a lively discussion of the importance of gender neutral language, but should also provide students with plausible alternatives that they will then (hopefully) incorporate into their own speech.

Some suggested gender neutral alternatives:

1. business people
2. businesswoman
3. cave dwellers, cave people
4. chair, head, president, leader, moderator, coordinator
5. student
6. representatives, members of Congress, Congress people
7. craftsperson, artisan, craft worker
8. delivery clerk, courier, deliverer
9. ancestors, forebears
10. supervisor, boss, leader, foreperson, head juror
11. laypeople
12. letter carrier, postal worker
13. the human species, humans, humanity, humankind, human beings, people
14. handmade, hand-built, human-made, synthetic, manufactured, constructed
15. personnel, staff, human resources, labor, people power
16. meter reader, meter attendant
17. police officer
18. repairer, repair person
19. salesclerk, salesperson, sales rep (or representative)
20. trash collector

Adapted from Miller, C., & Swift, K. (1988). *The handbook of nonsexist writing* (2nd ed.). New York: Harper & Row.

Problem Representation

According to the text, the first step in effective problem solving is to represent the problem (i.e., to interpret or define it). Challenge your students by presenting them with the hospital room problem (taken from Matlin, 1994). Handout 7-2 contains the details of the problem, which can be projected onto an overhead or photocopied and distributed to students. After students have had a reasonable amount of time to solve the problem, have them discuss their representation of it as well as its correct answer. [Answer: Ms. Anderson has mononucleosis and is in Room 104.]

Matlin, M. W. (1994). *Cognition* (3rd ed.). Fort Worth: Harcourt Brace.

Mental Set as an Obstacle to Problem Solving

It is well known that mental sets (i.e., the tendency to perceive and approach problems in certain ways), which are typically based on past experiences, can become a major obstacle to problem solving. Margaret Matlin suggests using the following two problems to demonstrate these effects to your class.

Luchins' Water-Jar Problem. To introduce this famous problem, tell your students to imagine that they have three jars, A, B, and C. Tell them that for each of seven problems, the capacity of the jars will be listed. Explain that their task is to use these jars (and nothing else) to somehow obtain the target amount of liquid (specified in the *Goal* column). Tell them that they can obtain the goal amount by adding or subtracting the quantities listed in jars A, B, and C. After giving these instructions, present the seven problems by projecting a transparency of Handout 7-3.

Matlin notes that the best way to solve Problem 1 is to fill up Jar B and remove one jarful with Jar A and two jarfuls with Jar C. In fact, Problems 1 through 5 can all be solved in the same manner, which creates a mental set for problem solvers who naturally adopt the same strategy for Problems 6 and 7. For these problems, however, the earlier strategy is unnecessarily complex: Problem 6 can be solved by simply subtracting C from A, and Problem 7 can be solved by adding C to A. Thus, whereas people who start with Problems 6 and 7 at the outset immediately notice and use the direct approach, those who begin with Problems 1 though 5 typically adopt the more indirect, complex approach.

Number Puzzle. A simpler but equally effective demonstration involves challenging students with the following number puzzle. Tell your students that you are going to write a sequence of numbers on the board, and that it is their task to figure out the pattern for the order of numbers. That is, they should come up with a plausible explanation for why the numbers are arranged in the specified order. Write the following numbers on the board:

8, 5, 4, 1, 7, 6, 3, 2, 0

After allowing students a few minutes to struggle with the problem, tell them that the numbers are in alphabetical order. Their mental set likely suggested that the numbers were in some mathematical sequence, rather than a language-based sequence, causing them to head down the wrong track.

Luchins, A. S. (1942). Mechanization in problem solving. *Psychological Monographs, 54* (Whole No. 248).
Matlin, M. W. (1994). *Cognition* (3rd ed.). Fort Worth: Harcourt Brace.

Representativeness Heuristic

Chapter 7 notes that we often rely on heuristics, or mental rules of thumb, to simplify the process of judgment and decision making. One of the most commonly used is the representativeness heuristic, in which we judge the likelihood of an event based on how well it seems to match, or represent, a typical member of a category. Use the following demonstration (based on work by Kahneman & Tversky, 1972) to show that although representativeness enables us to make decisions quickly, it occasionally leads us astray. Tell your students to imagine that you are going to flip a regular coin (i.e., with one head and one tail; not a trick coin) 6 times. Then, ask them to judge which of two outcomes (write these on the board) seems most likely:

H H H T T T   H T H T T H

If your students are like most people, they will choose the latter sequence. Why? Because most people assume that coin flipping should lead to a relatively random pattern, and the latter sequence is more representative of this expected pattern; that is, it is more random looking than the first pattern. In fact, the probability of the two sequences are equal. As Kahneman and Tversky point out, the probability of any particular sequence is 1/64. However, instead of using true probabilities, people use representativeness as a basis for the decision, and they decision is incorrect.

Kahneman, D., & Tversky, A. (1972). Subjective probability: A judgment of representativeness. *Cognitive Psychology, 3*, 430-454.

The Conjunction Fallacy

Tversky and Kahneman (1983) also note that use of the representativeness heuristic can lead people to commit the conjunction fallacy. You can readily demonstrate this error in class by posing the following question to your students:

Steven is articulate, outgoing, artistic, and politically liberal. Is it more likely that he:

(a) is an engineering major, or
(b) started out as an engineering major and switched to journalism?

The majority of students will choose "b", even though it is statistically impossible. According to the conjunction rule, the probability of joint events can never exceed the probability of either individual event. For example, the number of baseball players born in Texas can never be greater than the total number of baseball players, and the likelihood of the Pittsburgh Steelers winning the next two Superbowls cannot be greater than the likelihood of them winning the next one. Why, then, do people prefer conjunctive (joint) explanations? Because they are more representative: A person who is articulate, outgoing, artistic, and liberal is more representative of our category for journalist than for engineer, so we choose the former description despite the fact that it is statistically less likely.

Tversky, A., & Kahneman, D. (1983). Extensional versus intuitive reasoning: The conjunction fallacy in probability judgment. *Psychological Review, 90*, 293-315.

student assignments

Exploring Bilingualism

Although many educators believe that bilingual children should be taught in English and in their native language (both to preserve their culture and because it has cognitive benefits), other educators and members of Congress are pushing to assimilate non-native speakers into U.S. culture by placing them in classes where only English is taught. Because much of the negativity and confusion about this issue may stem from a general fear and dislike for the unknown, your students might gain a fresh perspective on this controversial issue by considering what it's like to be bilingual or multilingual. For this assignment, ask your students to write a short paper that explores the experiences of being bilingual or multilingual; Margaret Matlin (1994) suggests several excellent questions that can be used as the cornerstone for such an essay. If any of your students are bilingual or multilingual, they can answer some of these questions themselves. Otherwise, students should identify someone they know fairly well who they would feel comfortable asking about their experiences. Questions to be addressed include:

1. How old were you when you first exposed to your second language?
2. How did you acquire this second language (e.g., Did you have formal lessons? Were you taught by a parent?)
3. When you began to learn the second language, did you find yourself becoming less fluent in your native language? What kinds of problems did you experience? Can you give examples?
4. What do you think are the advantages of being bilingual? For example, do you think you have any insight into the nature of language that a monolingual person might not have?
5. When you are with another bilingual person who speaks your native language, do you find yourself switching back and forth between the two languages? Are there situations in which you are especially likely to switch from one language to the other?
6. If you had something embarrassing or secret to divulge, in which language would you discuss it?
7. Are there any topics or kinds of conversation for which you prefer one language over the other? For example, are there aspects of your education or job that, because they were derived from American terminology (e.g., psychological concepts), are harder to discuss in your native language? Is it difficult to express American cultural concepts in your native language?
8. Do you feel that the North American culture discourages bilinguals from using their first language?

Matlin, M. W. (1994). *Cognition* (3rd ed.). Fort Worth: Harcourt Brace.

Mental Sets In Everyday Life

Luchins' water jar problem and the alphabetical number puzzle were suggested above as ways to demonstrate how mental sets can create barriers to effective problem solving. After students have been introduced to the notion of mental sets (from the text, lecture, and exercises such as these), you might ask them to write a short paper in which they identify instances of mental sets in everyday life. As one example, students could consider the problem of making the adjustment from high school to college. How might a mental set (i.e., the tendency to approach or respond to a problem in a particular way) learned in high school interfere with the successful solution of problems later on in college? Students should specify how strategies that at one time were adaptive or successful could eventually become undesirable or maladaptive. Traditional-aged college students should have plenty of experience with mental sets related to academic strategies, social life, living away from home, financial responsibilities, and so on. If your students are older, they might consider mental sets related to major life changes (e.g., marriage, divorce, death of a loved one), career changes, or other situations requiring adjustment on their part. An added benefit of this assignment is that--in addition to better understanding the notion of mental sets--your students might also gain valuable insight into their own problem-solving strategies and skills.

Language in Film: *Children of a Lesser God*

William Hurt and Marlee Matlin star in this critically-acclaimed film from 1986 that chronicles the relationship between a dedicated teacher at a school for the deaf and the beautiful but bitter deaf woman with whom he is fascinated. This film makes an eloquent statement about the power of human communication--especially when there are seemingly insurmountable language barriers to overcome. Because the issues in this film go beyond the text's treatment of language, this would make a nice supplemental assignment. Ask your students to write an essay reviewing the film and applying what they have learned about language to the film; it may be helpful for students to get an article or two on American Sign Language to tie into their discussion. Students will no doubt enjoy this sensitive, moving love story for which Matlin won an Oscar (Paramount; 119 min).

video

Biological Basis of Thinking (28 min, FHS). The chemical activity of neurons and how it forms the basis of cognitive activity are explained. The complex interaction of billions of brain cells and the resulting thought, consciousness, and behavior are examined.

Cognitive Development (1990, 30 min, IM). Piaget's views on how children develop and master thinking skills are emphasized in this video. Experts explain how thinking, reasoning, and language develop.

Decision Making and Problem Solving (1990, 28 min, COAST). This video in the series *Psychology: The Study of Human Behavior* presents a look at how both rationality and irrationality influence human thought. Noted cognitive psychologists such as Keith Holyoak and Robert Sternberg discuss deductive and inductive reasoning, the problem-solving process, expert decision making, and decision making under stress. The biases that limit our ability to make sound judgments are also examined.

Discovering Psychology, Part 6: Language Development (1990, 30 min., ANN/CPB). Explores the development and use of language as a means of social communication.

Discovering Psychology, Part 10: Cognitive Processes (1990, 30 min., ANN/CPB). Examines higher mental processes such as problem solving, reasoning, and planning.

Discovering Psychology, Part 11: Judgment and Decision Making (1990, 30 min., ANN/CPB). Describes processes by which we make judgments and decisions through an examination of risk-taking and negotiation.

Discovering Psychology, Part 16: Testing and Intelligence (1990, 30 min, ANN/CPB). Provides an overview of how tests are developed and used to assign values to different abilities and behaviors, with a particular focus on intelligence and personality.

Intelligence (1990, 30 min, IM). Discusses difficulties associated with the definition and measurement of intelligence, the development of intelligence tests, and the question of whether intelligence is fixed or variable.

Language (23 min, FHS). The origins of language, in humans and nonhumans, and the evolutionary development of language skills are explored.

Language (1990, 30 min, IM). Explores the relative roles of learning and innate factors in the development of language, the stages of language development, and how language use is related to brain functioning.

Language and Thinking (1992, 30 min, IM). The acquisition of language and thinking is the focus of this video. Noted researchers discuss how children develop cognitive and communication skills.

Language Development (40 min, FHS). The development of language skills in babies and young children is the focus of this film. The nature-nurture debate, the Whorf-Sapir hypothesis, and chimpanzee communication are also discussed.

May's Miracle: A Retarded Youth With A Gift For Music (28 min, FL). An "idiot savant"--blind, retarded, and suffering from cerebral palsy--nonetheless recreates complex piano pieces from memory.

Men and Women: Talking Together (1993, 58 min, IM). Robert Bly and Deborah Tannen discuss communication and the sexes before a live audience.

The Mind: Language (60 min, PBS). Presents theories and research on the evolution and development of human language capacity.

The Mind: Thinking (60 min, PBS). Focuses on the role of the frontal lobe of the brain and prefrontal cortex in coordinating memory, emotion, and intelligence to produce conscious thought.

Problem Solving and Decision Making (30 min, IM). Describes the fundamental cognitive processes associated with problem solving and decision making as well as applications to coping with chronic illness and international negotiations.

Schools of Thought: Teaching Children in America and Japan (55 min, FHS). A comparison of Japanese and American educational systems forms the basis for answering questions such as why differences in education exist and how personal and cultural goals influence the education process.

See What I'm Saying (1992, 31 min, IM). A deaf child's first year in elementary school forms the basis of an examination of language acquisition, communication, and, incidentally, the maintenance of self-esteem. *Video Rating Guide* gives this film a "Highest Recommendation."

Sexism in Language (20 min, FHS). Carefully analyzed examples of sexism and antisexism in language are the focus of this video.

Valuing Diversity: Multicultural Communication (1995, 19 min, LS). Diversity in gender, ethnicity, physical handicap, age, culture, education, religion, and sexual orientation are examined in this close captioned video. A young grocery clerk filters the behavior of a varied group of shoppers through her own cultural schemas, until she comes to appreciate the diverse viewpoints of those around her. An accompanying booklet includes summaries of the key points on the tape and suggestions for further activities. This video is very well produced, although the pacing and level of presentation may make it more appropriate for use in a high school or community college course.

Washoe: Monkeys and Sign Language (1996, 52 min, FHS). This celebrated chimp is featured in this look at communication abilities among primates.

Why Didn't I Think Of That? Creative Problem Solving (1990, 28 min, LS). This videotape invites audience participation as it presents brainteasers, analytic problems, and anagrams designed to spur creative solutions. Several principles of cognition are presented at an intuitive level, such as priming, mental imagery, and some Gestalt principles. An accompanying booklet includes summaries of the key points on the tape and solutions to the audience participation problems.

multimedia

Live! Psych

Module	Title	Book Page #
7.1	Algorithms	p. 276

Screen 1 distinguishes between algorithms and heuristics. Examples of the use of algorithms are shown. Screen 2 shows how an algorithm can be used to solve anagrams. In Screen 3, the student participates in an exercise. A scrambled word is displayed and the student is instructed to use an anagram to unscramble the word. Screen 4 discusses the limitations of algorithms and defines heuristics. Screen 5 shows an animation of how to unscramble the same word as in Screen 3 using a heuristic.

7.2　　　　　　　Heuristic: Subgoal Analysis　　　　　　　p. 277

Screen 1 introduces the subgoal analysis heuristic. Screen 2 instructs the student to solve a problem using subgoal analysis. This activity allows students to practice generating alternatives as they try to help move a fox, goose, and a bag of corn across a river. Screen 3 shows the solution to the problem. Screen 4 explains that the subgoal analysis strategy is helpful when you need to limit your focus.

　　　　　　　　Heuristic: Means-end Analysis　　　　　　　p. 277

Screen 1 introduces the means-end analysis heuristic. Screen 2 displays the Tower of Hanoi puzzle and instructs the student to solve the problem. Students click and drag the rings on the pegs. Screen 3 shows the solution to the Tower of Hanoi puzzle. Screen 4 explains that the means-end strategy involves comparing your current position with a desired goal and trying to find a means of closing the gap between the two.

　　　　　　　　Heuristic: Working Backward　　　　　　　p. 277

Screen 1 introduces the working backward strategy. Working backward is an effective heuristic to use when the goal state is clearly defined and the original state is not. Screen 2 shows the Multiplying Dandelions problem and the student is asked to solve the problem. Screen 3 shows the solution to the problem. Screen 4 explains that working backward is an effective strategy when there is a very well-defined end point, such as when planning a trip and when solving mazes.

7.3　　　　　　　Representation Failure　　　　　　　p. 277

Import Screen 1 to introduce the concept of representation failure. The student interacts with the screen by trying to solve the nine-dot problem to learn about how representation failure hinders problem solving. Screen 2 shows two solutions to the nine-dot problem. It is explained that most people assume that the lines must be drawn within the square formed by the dots. Screen 3 examines how you can avoid representation failure in real life by considering the assumptions you make about the problems you encounter.

　　　　　　　　Confirmation Bias　　　　　　　p. 277

Screen 1 defines confirmation bias. The student interacts with this concept by trying to solve the vowels and numbers problem to learn how confirmation bias hinders problem solving. In Screen 2, an animated sequence explains whether each card confirms or disconfirms the rule. Screen 3 explains that people are biased to look for confirming evidence because they ignore the possibility of disconfirming evidence. Screen 4 examines applications of confirmation bias in everyday life.

Functional Fixedness   p. 277

Screen 1 defines functional fixedness. The student interacts with this concept by trying to solve Duncker's candle problem. Screen 2 displays and explains the solution to the problem. Screen 3 explains that finding solutions to practical problems often requires us to overcome functional fixedness by thinking of unusual uses for common objects, such as using a dime to turn a screw when a screwdriver is not available.

The Psychology Place

Learning Activities

Understanding Mental Models

This activity by Diane Halpern allows students to discover how faulty mental processing or mental models work, by participating in interactive demonstrations such as a modified version of Piaget's water level test. Halpern suggests that you divide the class into small groups using the questions she poses in the exercise to generate a discussion. The goal of the exercise is to show students how implicit beliefs can influence events and circumstances around us.

Research News
The Growing Popularity of "Emotional Intelligence"

"Emotional intelligence" means different things to different people. Certainly what it connotes to the research community is quite different from what the lay public and popular media have fashioned it into. In particular, claims about the acquisition of "EQ" and its presumed superiority over traditional IQ in predicting various outcomes is questionable. Ask your students to read this article and debate the merits of measuring EQ versus IQ in business, interpersonal, academic, or romantic situations.

How Stereotypes Affect Test Performance

Many people consider women to be "not so good" in math, whereas they consider men to be "darn good" in math. This article explores how both negative and positive stereotypes about math ability may affect the performance of men and women on math tests. This is important reading for your students, to dispel myths and promote confidence among them; remember, you may be seeing some of these students in your Statistic course next semester!

Another Explanation for Differences in Intellectual Performance: Stereotype Threat

Claude Steele and his colleagues have conducted considerable research on stereotype threat, which suggests that negative stereotypes (especially about women and African Americans) may impair their performance on standardized tests and in the classroom. Steele's research also suggests that stereotyped groups may use disidentification in order to protect their self-esteem in the event of poor performance. Like the article above, this is important reading for your students. Use both of these articles as the basis for a classroom discussion, before the first round of exams is administered if possible.

Web Links

1. http://www.surfaquarium.com/
This site highlights Howard Gardner's eight criteria for identifying intelligence. The list of criteria and an explanation of each is provided. Ask your students to review this site and prepare a short report comparing and contrasting what it takes to make "intelligence."

2. http://maple.lemoyne.edu/~hevern/psychref4-11.html

Psychological Testing, Assessment, and Psychometrics. This site focuses on intelligence, and provides links to other worthwhile sites.

3. http://ericae.net/
Offers definitions, descriptions, resources, and other detailed information about a wide range of assessment measures. Use this site as a starting point for a classroom presentation, demonstrating the different ways to assess mental functioning.

4. http://www.Ldonline.org/

LD Online: a resource for questions and answers about learning disabilities. Presents a different, applied look at learning and memory.

5. http://home8.swipnet.se/~w-80790/Index.htm

This site explains IQ and offers the estimated intelligence quotient of several well-known geniuses. Useful for quick examples of the range of intelligence and the problems of estimating intelligence without sound psychometric techniques.

transparencies

63. *Examples of Different Age-Related Tasks from Binet's 1911 Intelligence Test*
This transparency provides examples of tasks to be performed by a child aged 3, 7, and 15.

64. *Items Similar to Those on the Performance Subtests of the Wechsler Intelligence Scale*
These are items similar to those on the performance subtests of the Wechsler Intelligence Scale, particularly Picture Arrangement and Block Design.

65. *Normal Curve of Intelligence Scores*
A depiction of the distribution of intelligence test scores.

66. *Correlations of IQ Scores of Persons of Varying Kinship*
The hereditary and environmental influences on intelligence are revealed in this presentation of IQ correlations.

81. *Fluid and Crystallized Intelligence*
This transparency shows the changes in fluid and crystallized intelligence over the lifespan.

Text Figures

7-1.	*The Direction of Movement in Speech Production and Comprehension*
7-2.	*Examples of Geometrical Patterns Used in Shepard and Metzler's Experiment*
7-3.	*Problem Solving: Measurement*
7-4.	*Problem Solving: Time*
7-5.	*Problem Solving: Defining the Problem*
7-6.	*Problem Solving: Rings Problem*
7-7.	*The Six-Match Problem*
7-8.	*To Test Functional Fixedness*
7-9 to 7-14	*Solutions to Problems*

Handout 7-1

Using Nonsexist Language

Instructions: For each of the following words or phrases below, try to generate at least one alternative word or phrase that is gender neutral. For example, *firefighter* is an appropriate gender neutral alternative for *fireman*, and *anchor* is a suitable substitute for *anchorman*.

1. businessman   _____

2. career girl   _____

3. cavemen   _____

4. chairman, chairwoman   _____

5. coed (as in, "three beautiful coeds") _____

6. congressmen   _____

7. craftsman   _____

8. deliveryman   _____

9. forefathers   _____

10. forelady, foreman   _____

11. laymen   _____

12. mailman   _____

13. man, mankind (as in the human species) _____

14. man-made   _____

15. manpower   _____

16. meter maid   _____

17. policeman, policewoman   _____

18. repairman   _____

19. salesman, saleswoman   _____

20. trashman   _____

Adapted from Miller, C., & Swift, K. (1988). The handbook of nonsexist writing (2nd ed.). New York: Harper & Row.

Handout 7-2

The Hospital Room Problem

Instructions: Use the following information to answer the question posed below.

Five people are in a hospital. Each one has only one disease, and each has a different disease. Each one occupies a separate room; room numbers are 101-105.

1. The person with asthma is in Room 101.
2. Ms. Jones has heart disease.
3. Ms. Green is in Room 105.
4. Ms. Smith has tuberculosis.
5. The woman with mononucleosis is in Room 104.
6. Ms. Thomas is in Room 101.
7. One of the patients, other than Ms. Anderson, has gall bladder disease.

<u>Question</u>: What disease does Ms. Anderson have and in what room is she?

Source: Matlin, M. W. (1994). Cognition (3rd ed.). Fort Worth: Harcourt Brace.

Handout 7-3

Luchins' Water Jar Problem

Instructions: For each of the following seven problems, use some combination of the jars (i.e., by adding or subtracting quantities of liquid) to obtain the target amount listed in the goal column. The capacity of Jars A, B, and C for each problem is listed below.

Problem	Jar A	Jar B	Jar C	Goal
1	24	130	3	100
2	9	44	7	21
3	21	58	4	29
4	12	160	25	98
5	19	75	5	46
6	23	49	3	20
7	18	48	4	22

Source: Matlin, M. W. (1994). Cognition (3rd ed.). Fort Worth: Harcourt Brace.

Chapter 8 Intelligence and Mental Abilities

chapter outline 209

learning objectives 212

lecture suggestions

    Measuring Intelligence in Infants.. 213
    IQ and Juror Selection 214
    Evaluating the SAT 214
    Birth Order and Intelligence 215
    Culture and the School Year 216
    Termites Show Intelligence 217
    Intelligence Testing and Cultural Considerations.. 217

demonstrations and activities

    Defining Intelligence... 219
    Debate: Can Intelligence Be Increased?.. 219
    Debate: Are There Racial Differences in Intelligence? 220
    Insight.. 220
    Remote Associates Test 220
    Mental Hotfoot 221
    What-if?... 221
    Divergent Thinking 221

student assignments

    Constructing a Multiple Intelligences Test.. 223
    Intelligence and Mental Capacity in Film.. 223

video 224

multimedia 225

transparencies... 231

handouts

    Insight.. 233
    Finding Remote Associates 234

chapter outline

I. **Theories of Intelligence**
    A. Early theories: Spearman, Thurstone, and Cattell
        1. Spearman views intelligence as a general factor
        2. Thurstone views intelligence as a collection of abilities
        3. Cattell views intelligence as crystallized versus fluid intelligence
    B. Contemporary theories: Sternberg, Gardner, and Goleman
        1. Sternberg's triarchic model
            a. Componential, experiential, and contextual intelligence
        2. Gardner's theory of multiple intelligences
            a. Logical, linguistic, spatial, musical, bodily, interpersonal, intrapersonal
        3. Goleman's theory of emotional intelligence
            a. Like parts of Guilford's Structure of Intellect model, emphasizes "EQ"
                i. Knowing one's emotions, knowing others' emotions, mood management, etc.
        4. Comparing the theories

II. **Intelligence Tests**
    A. Binet-Simon Scale ⊃ Stanford-Binet Intelligence Scale
        1. Concept of IQ introduced
        2. Verbal, abstract/visual, quantitative, short-term memory
    B. The Wechsler Intelligence Scales
        1. Emphasizes verbal and performance measures
    C. Group tests
        1. SCAT, CTMM, SAT, ACTP, GRE
    D. Performance and culture-fair tests
        1. Performance tests designed to minimize use of language
            a. Seguin Form Board, Porteus Maze, Baylet Scales of Infant Development
        2. Culture-fair tests designed to reduce cultural bias
            a. Progressive Matrices, Culture-Fair Intelligence Test, Goodenough-Harris

III. **What Makes a Good Test?**
    A. Reliability
        1. The dependability or consistency of measurements
            a. Split-half reliability is one type
        2. Correlation coefficient provides an index of how reliable a measure is
            a. Reliabilities of widely-used intelligence tests are acceptable
    B. Validity

1. The accuracy of measurements
    a. Does the test measure what it was designed to measure?
2. Content validity
    a. An adequate sample of skills or knowledge intended to be measured
3. Criterion-related validity
    a. Compare test scores to other independent measures of intelligence
        i. Predictive ability of the measure

C. Criticisms of intelligence tests
1. Test content and scores
    a. A narrow set of skills is measured
    b. Some tests may measure only the ability to take tests
    c. Content reflects Western middle-class values
2. Use of IQ tests
    a. Labeling of test takers a concern
    b. IQ gives little information on motivation, emotion, attitudes, goals
3. IQ and success
    a. Tests scores predict academic performance, job success
        i. Nature of the prediction still questionable

IV. **What Determines Intelligence?**
A. Heredity
1. IQ correlation between identical twins reared apart tends to be high
    a. Environment still a confound in this research, however

B. Environment
1. Stimulation from the environment necessary to spark inherited abilities
    a. Lower-class/middle-class differences
    b. Role of diet and nutrition

C. Heredity vs. environment: Which is more important?
1. Plant analogy: both genetics and environment are important
2. Flynn effect: IQ scores have risen worldwide over the last several decades

V. **Mental Abilities and Human Diversity**
A. Gender
1. Differences in verbal or mathematical abilities are slight, if any
2. Males show better spatial skills, more extremes of intelligence

B. Culture
1. Stevenson's research comparing Japanese, Chinese, American students
    a. Differences in performance, attributions for performance, value placed on education

VI. **Extremes of Intelligence**
A. Mental retardation

       1. Combination of subaverage intelligence and deficiencies in adaptation
       2. Degrees of mental retardation
           a. Mild, moderate, severe, profound
       3. Causes of retardation are often not known
           a. About 25% seem biological in origin
       4. Mainstream education movement: Inclusion
   B. Giftedness
       1. Combination of above average intelligence and demonstrated abilities
       2. Comparison to overall population a matter of debate
           a. Gifted in one area, or superior across multiple domains?
       3. Causes of giftedness are often not known

VII. Creativity
   A. Creativity and intelligence
       1. The threshold theory of creativity and intelligence describes relationship
   B. Creativity tests
       1. TTCT, RAT, Christensen-Guilford, Wallach-Kogan

learning objectives

After reading this chapter, students should be able to:

1. List the characteristics of intelligence as described by both laypeople and psychologists.

2. Summarize the views of Spearman, Thurstone, Cattell, Sternberg, Gardner, and Goleman with respect to what constitutes intelligence.

3. Trace the development of intelligence tests from Binet through Terman, noting the contributions of each. Describe the standard procedure for the Stanford-Binet Scale.

4. Distinguish the Wechsler Adult Intelligence Scale-Revised from the Stanford-Binet. Identify the two parts of the WAIS-R.

5. Distinguish between individual and group tests. Give three examples of group tests. List the advantages and disadvantages of group tests.

6. Describe the purposes of performance tests and culture-fair tests.

7. Define reliability. Identify three techniques for measuring reliability. Explain how psychologists express reliability and know the reliability of intelligence tests.

8. Define validity. Descibe two ways to measure validity.

9. Identify four criticisms of IQ tests. Distinguish between IQ scores and intelligence.

10. Explain the high correlation between IQ scores and academic performance. Understand the relationship between IQ and later occupational success.

11. Summarize Tryon's experiments with rats. Explain how psychologists measure the influence of heredity on intelligence in human beings.

12. Summarize studies of prenatal nutrition and Skeels' investigation of orphanages to document the influence of environment on intelligence.

13. Explain the relationship between gender differences and cognitive abilities.

14. List two criteria used to identify mental retardation. List four causes of mental retardation.

15. Discuss the pros and cons of placing gifted children in special classes or schools.

lecture suggestions

Measuring Intelligence in Infants

Most of the intelligence tests discussed in the textbook are designed to assess intelligence in older children and adults. There are, however, several instruments that are designed to assess intellectual functioning in infants and very young children. These measures may be examining different aspects of intelligence, such as physical, psychomotor, and social and emotional development rather than the verbally based measures typically used by intelligence tests. Although these measures may not accurately predict later intelligence, they can be useful in identifying potential developmental problems.

The Bayley Scales of Infant Development

The Bayley Scales are probably the most often used measure of early infant intellectual development. This test assesses mental (e.g., memory, language usage, attempts at communication) and psychomotor (e.g., coordination and proficiency in motor activities such as sitting, walking, and grasping) development in children between the ages of 2 to 30 months. In addition, it includes a behavior rating scale to assess the child's emotional and social development.

Denver Developmental Screening Test-Revised

This test assesses potential delays in development occurring from birth to 6 years of age. Using direct observation of the child, it is designed to evaluate developmental progress in four areas: language, fine motor movements, gross motor movements, and social behaviors.

Gesell Developmental Schedules

This assessment instrument, originally developed in 1940, uses direct observation to assess development in five areas: adaptation, fine motor movements, gross motor movements, language, and social behavior. This instrument has been shown to be effective in detecting cognitive deficits associated with neurological problems. It is also known as the Gesell Maturity Scale, the Gesell Norms of Development, and the Yale Tests of Child Development.

Brazelton Neonatal Assessment Scale

The Brazelton scale is used with infants from 3 days to 4 weeks of age, and assesses competence in areas such as neurological, social, and behavioral functioning. Factors such as reflexes, startle reactions, hand-mouth coordination, motor maturity, or cuddliness are used to derive 47 scores (20 elicited responses and 27 behavioral ratings). The chief limitation of the Brazelton scale is the absence of norms: Scores are obtained for a single case, but comparisons across infants are not easily made.

Gardner, M. K., & Clark, E. (1992). The psychometric perspective on intellectual development in childhood and adolescence. In R. J. Sternberg & C. A. Berg (Eds.), *Intellectual development* (pp. 16-43). Cambridge, MA: Cambridge University Press.

Kaplan, R. M., & Saccuzzo, D. P. (1993). *Psychological testing: Principles, applications, and issues* (3rd ed.). Pacific Grove, CA: Brooks/Cole.

Adapted from Hill, W. G. (1995). Instructor's resource manual for *Psychology* by S. F. Davis and J. J. Palladino. Englewood Cliffs, NJ: Prentice Hall.

IQ and Juror Selection

A recent California court case (*People v. Pierce* [40 Cal. Rptr. 2d 254]) raises the issue of how intelligent a person must be to serve as a member of a jury in a criminal trial. Ronald Blaine Pierce was convicted of forcible oral copulation, forcible sodomy, and false imprisonment. His conviction was overturned, however, on the grounds that one of the jurors who convicted him was mildly mentally retarded.

During the voir dire process the judge asked prospective jurors to state their names, occupations, occupations of their spouses, and whether they had ever served on a jury. The juror in question answered honestly and simply. Subsequently, the judge asked, "Do any of you know any reason at all, perhaps something I haven't touched on in my voir dire, that would bear upon your qualities to serve as a fair and impartial juror?," to which no one responded. The defendant's attorney discovered during the jury's final instructions that one of the jurors was mildly mentally retarded, and filed for a reversal of the conviction.

A clinical psychologist later testified that the juror in question was a long-term resident of a group home and had an IQ of 66. In the psychologist's opinion, the juror would have had difficulty processing the information in the trial, due to "her shortened attention span and her inability to process testimony at a normal rate of speech." It was also revealed, however, that the juror in question worked 20 hours a week in a retail store, and had received several promotions and raises during the past two and a half years. The juror was also capable of getting to and from work using public transportation.

California Code of Civil Procedure, section 203, lists the factors that disqualify potential jurors. These include people who are not U.S. citizens; who do not live in the state or in the jurisdiction in which they are called to serve; who have been convicted of a felony; who are serving as grand jurors; or who are the subject of conservatorship. On these grounds, the judge denied the defendant's motion for a new trial, noting that none of these exclusions applied to the mentally retarded juror. The California Court of Appeal, however, ruled that the defendant had been denied due process "to a jury whose members are both impartial and mentally competent." The appellate court ruled that section 203 eliminates certain categories of people, but not all categories of people who may be unfit to serve.

This case raises several issues regarding the efficacy of the voir dire process, as well as the standards of "competence" and "incompetence" to be used in juror selection.

Ewing, C. P. (1995, July). Is IQ relevant to juror selection? *APA Monitor*, p. 16.

Evaluating the SAT

Many of the people in your classes will be first-year students and will have recently taken the Scholastic Aptitude Test (SAT). Your discussion of intelligence and mental abilities presents a good opportunity to introduce some strengths and weaknesses of the SAT testing program.

Critics of the SAT question its predictive validity and its fairness toward minorities, as well as the reliance on SAT scores (or other standardized tests) in college admission decisions. In his discussion of the use of standardized tests, Hargadon suggests that much of the controversy and confusion result from the complex techniques of test construction, the common failure to separate the issues of reliability and validity from the potential effects of test use on social issues, and a misconception of the actual role of test scores in college admission processes.

Linn evaluated the validity of the SAT and concluded that it has reasonable predictive validity for academic performance. The correlation between SAT scores and first-year grades is .41 (multiple correlation; verbal and quantitative tests). Because all students do not take the exam, range restriction makes this a conservative estimate. High school grades are better predictors (.52), as SAT critics claim, but the combination of SAT and grades is better still (.58). Also, test scores are objective, whereas high school grades can be influenced by biased teachers or differences in courses and school standards.

Linn also addressed the charge that the SAT is unfair (biased) against minorities. The test is not culture-free, nor is it independent of experiential effects. It predicts only the current ability of an individual to perform in a standard academic environment. However, the predictive validity is comparable for minorities and the white middle-class majority, and most schools use separate criteria for minorities, reducing the effect of bias.

The importance of SAT scores minimizes the impact of any test weaknesses. Although the SAT is often portrayed as the primary determinant of college admission, Hargadon found that many schools give it little emphasis. Only 48 percent of the responding institutions even require SAT (or ACT) scores. A high school transcript was the most common requirement (74 percent). High school performance was rated as very important by 65 percent of colleges requiring transcripts (84 percent of private and 77 percent of public four-year schools). Test scores were very important to 45 percent of the colleges requiring tests (55 percent of private and 63 percent of public four-year schools). Based on these data plus the number of schools that do not require test scores, Hargadon concluded that test scores do not play an unreasonably prominent role in college admissions decisions.

Hargadon, F. (1981). Tests and college admissions. *American Psychologist, 36*, 1112-1120.
Linn, R. L. (1982). Admissions testing on trial. *American Psychologist, 37*, 279-291.

Reprinted from Whitford, F. W. (1995). Instructor's resource manual for *Psychology: Principles and applications* by S. Worchel and W. Shebilske. Englewood Cliffs, NJ: Prentice Hall.

Birth Order and Intelligence

Birth order has been invoked to explain all manner of behavior, according to the pop psychology that crowds the bookstore shelves. Although some of the claims are false and some are wishful thinking, there is a ring of truth to the effects of one's family position on behavior. In particular, birth order has been used to explain some elements of intellectual performance.

Several studies have found that earlier-born children (in a family sequence) tend to perform better on aptitude and intelligence tests compared to later-born children. Why this is the case, however, remains somewhat a matter of debate. Several theories on the "nature" side of things, such as hormonal or other biological changes in slightly older mothers affecting later-borns, have been advanced and rejected. At present, the "nurture" side of the debate, emphasizing environmental influences, has captured the attention of researchers seeking to explain this outcome.

Robert Zajonc and Gregory Markus have offered an explanation. Their *confluence model* argues that children will attain higher intellectual achievements if they are raised in environments that provide greater intellectual stimulation, coming, in part, from parents and siblings. At first blush this theory would suggest that larger families should provide more of such opportunities, and further that later-born children should reap the rewards of the abundant intellectual stimulation of their numerous siblings. However, Zajonc and Markus made the opposite argument, that as family size increases the intellectual climate of the family decreases.

In the simplest case of two parents and a single child, the overall intellectual climate can be calculated based on a simple heuristic. If the parents each contribute 50 "intelligence units" (an arbitrary value used for illustration) and the infant contributes zero, the overall intellectual climate of the family would be 50 + 50 + 0 = 100 / 3 = 33. As the child grows his or her contribution to the family intellectual climate might increase by 3 points a year. After two years, if another child is born, the overall intellectual climate of the family has now changed to 50 + 50 + 6 + 0 = 106 / 4 = 27. If another sibling arrives two years after that, the equation changes to 50 + 50 + 12 + 6 + 0 = 118 / 5 = 24. In short, as more children arrive the overall intellectual climate decreases, given the contributions made by each family member, but only to a point. With extraordinarily large families (e.g., 10 or more children) a rise in overall climate can be seen in these calculations.

When applied to data, Zajonc and Markus' theory holds up remarkably well. For example, a reanalysis of data from a large Dutch study (Belmont & Marolla, 1973) generally confirmed the confluence model, with a few exceptions. First, there was an "only-child" effect, such that children with no siblings scored at about the same performance level as first-borns in families with four children. The confluence model should predict only-children to score highest, given that they enjoy the richest intellectual climate (based on the calculations). Second, there was a "last-born" effect, such that the last sibling's intellectual performance tended to drop dramatically. This is curious, given the slight rise in calculated scores as families become substantially larger.

Zajonc and Markus suggested that neither only-children nor last-borns get to be "teachers," which may account for the anomalies in the pattern of scores. Only children have no one to teach, and last children seem unlikely candidates for teaching their older siblings. This intriguing explanation has a ring of truth to it, and fits well with the available data.

So, how to plan a family to maximize intellectual development? Here the answer is not so clear. Only children may enjoy a rich intellectual climate, but succumb to the only-child effect. Up to a point, more children will reduce the overall intellectual climate. The strategy of spacing births out considerably, such as 5 or more years between two children to maximize the first child's contributions, may lead to the last-child effect. Although the confluence model makes a compelling case for explaining birth order effects, it remains silent on strategies for optimal family planning.

Belmont, L., & Marolla, F. (1973). Birth order, family size, and intelligence. *Science, 182,* 1096-1101.
Zajonc, R. B., & Markus, G. B. (1975). Birth order and intellectual development. *Psychological Review, 82,* 74-88.

Culture and the School Year

Chapter 8 discusses some differences in the academic performance of American, Japanese, and Chinese schoolchildren. To put these findings in context, here are the number of school days per year that different countries mandate for their students.

Country	Length of School Year
United States	180
Sweden	180
France	185
Finland	190
England	192
The Netherlands	200
Thailand	200
Russia	210
Germany	210
Japan	243

Adapted from Prentice Hall Sociology Transparency Series III, (1994).

Termites Show Intelligence

When intelligence testing was in its infancy there was a wide spectrum of unanswered questions. How should intelligence best be assessed? What was the stability of the intelligence quotient over time? What factors contributed to poor versus superior performance? How did geniuses differ from the rest of the population? To address some of these questions, Lewis Terman undertook in the early part of this century a longitudinal study of geniuses.

A group of some 250,000 elementary school students (who had been identified by their teachers as possibly gifted) formed the basis for Terman's initial screening. After administering intelligence tests Terman selected 857 boys and 671 girls (1528 students total) who had IQs in the superior range. Specifically, the mean IQ of these children was 150, with a low score of 135 and 80 students scoring above 170. These 8- to 12-year-olds were then observed carefully for the next few years.

One early finding was that, contrary to popular opinion, gifted children were not bookish, maladapted freaks. Rather, these children ("Termites," as they were later dubbed) were typically taller and broader than average children, and had many markers of physical prowess, such as superior hand grip strength, greater lung capacity, and earlier sexual maturity. Intrigued by these findings, Terman decided to extend his study to a very large-scale longitudinal design; so longitudinal, in fact, that it has continued for the past 60+ years, even long after Terman's death.

Some summary findings are these. First, in keeping with their childhood development, the Termites tended to have lower rates of childhood illnesses and accidents than the population as a whole, lower incidences of alcoholism and criminality, and lower death and accident rates than the rest of the population. Second, although these children tended to do better academically than their peers (as might be imagined), they were no better in non-academic arenas, such as physical education, art, or metal-shop. As a corollary, these children also did not burn out over time; their academic performance remained strong as 70% went on to complete university degrees. Third, this gifted group became well-off financially. Perhaps because of their education and suitability for a range of professions (e.g., physicians, lawyers, architects, executives) their median salary during the 1950s tended to be in the upper 1% of the population. Finally, when assessed later in life, the Termites also were a contented group. Overall they report feeling generally satisfied with their lives, again contrary to the notion that highly intelligent people are more susceptible to neuroses or psychological disturbances.

Terman's studies were not without criticism, much of it focused on his sometimes dicey emphasis on genetic components of intelligence. Nonetheless, this long-term study of genius has proven to be a once-in-a-lifetime glimpse into the lives of a very select group.

Terman, L. (Ed.) (1921-1959). *Genetic studies of genius* (Vols 1-5). Stanford, CA: Stanford University Press.

Intelligence Testing and Cultural Considerations

The specter of test bias has loomed over the intelligence testing enterprise virtually since its inception. The possible misuses, misinterpretations, or misapplications of intelligence tests hold legal, moral, and social implications. As awareness of these consequences increases, active steps have been taken to limit the influence of cultural, racial, or social factors that might bias a test's uses.

One well-known example of this approach is the System of Multicultural Pluralistic Assessment, or SOMPA. Developed by sociologist Jane Mercer during the 1970s, it is based on the assumption that all cultural groups have the same average potential. Differences between groups, therefore, may be more apparent than real: Those who do not perform well may not lack intelligence, but rather lack access to the cultural experiences of the test developers. More instructive may be within-groups differences, since within a shared cultural context there will still be individual differences in ability.

The SOMPA takes a multi-faceted approach to assessment by incorporating medical, social-system, and pluralistic components. The medical component seeks to identify any physical, biological, or medical disturbances that may contribute to intellectual performance. The social-system component examines a child's functioning in light of cultural and social norms. The pluralistic component trades on the subgroups that may prevail within a given culture. That is, the individual is compared not to the norms of the society at large, but to the experiences shared by a particular subgroup. The end result of this componential system is a broad-based reading of a child's functioning.

> Mercer, J. R. (1979). In defense of racially and culturally non-discriminatory assessment. *School Psychology Digest, 8*, 89-115.

demonstrations

Defining Intelligence

Although the study of intelligence has a long history in psychology, the textbook notes that its definition and measurement has been a matter of controversy. As part of its discussion of divergent views on intelligence, the text reviews research by Robert Sternberg and his colleagues (1981), which compares psychologists' perceptions and understanding of intelligence to definitions given by laypeople. The results indicated that people have well-defined concepts about intelligent behaviors and that most people (experts and laypeople alike) include practical problem solving ability and verbal ability in their definitions of intelligence. Laypersons, however, rated behaviors associated with social competencies highly, whereas experts were more likely to include behaviors related to practical intelligence (e.g., sizes up a situation well, knows how to achieve goals, aware of the world around him or her).

In this activity, you can replicate Sternberg et al.'s initial study by having your students list behaviors that are associated with academic and everyday intelligence. Ask your students to take out two sheets of paper. Tell them to label the first sheet "academic intelligence" and explain that they will have 5 minutes to list all of the behaviors that they can think of that are characteristic of academic intelligence. After completing this list, have them put this sheet aside. Now tell them to label the second sheet "everyday intelligence" and ask them to list behaviors that are characteristic of this type of intelligence. Instruct them not to go back to the previously completed list. After completing the exercise, ask your students to share some of the behaviors that they listed for each category. You can relate their responses to those reported by Sternberg and his colleagues and use their responses to stimulate discussion about the definition and measurement of intelligence.

Sternberg, R. J., Conway, B. E., Ketron, J. L., & Bernstein, M. (1981). *Journal of Personality and Social Psychology, 41,* 37-55.

Adapted from Hill, W. G. (1995). Instructor's resource manual for *Psychology* by S. F. Davis and J. J. Palladino. Englewood Cliffs, NJ: Prentice Hall.

Debate: Can Intelligence Be Increased?

Chapter 8 considers the determinants of intelligence and the ongoing debate between proponents of the heredity approach (who believe that intelligence is genetically determined) and the environment approach (who argue that intelligence depends at least in part on an individual's experience and environment). The important practical (and political) issue arising from this debate is whether compensatory programs such as the government's Head Start Program should be adopted in order to improve individuals' mental abilities. Not surprisingly, proponents of the heredity approach argue that such programs are a waste of time and resources given that intelligence is immutable, whereas proponents of the environment approach suggests that intelligence can be--and should be--trained. Use the debate procedures suggested at the beginning of this manual (or develop your own) and assign students to defend both answers to this question using articles from Issue 10 in *Taking Sides* and any other sources they deem appropriate. Note that this debate will invariably give rise to issues raised in the recent controversial best-selling book, *The Bell Curve*, which is also briefly discussed in the text.

Hernstein, R. J., & Murray, C. (1994). The Bell Curve: Intelligence and class structure in American life. New York: Free Press.

Slife, B. (1996). Taking sides: Clashing views on controversial psychological issues (9th ed.). Guilford, CT: Dushkin Publishing Group.

Debate: Is There a Racial Difference in Intelligence?

A debate related to that above is the more focused question of whether there are racial differences in intelligence. Issue 8 of the most recent *Taking Sides* provides a starting point for this volatile issue. J. Philippe Rushton argues that the correlation between brain size and intelligence can help explain his position that blacks are genetically predetermined to have lower intelligence levels, whereas Zack Cernovsky argues that the correlation is weak and the overall evidence is dubious, at best. In short, this debate topic, like the previous one, will help students examine issues raised in the text, such as the nature versus nurture argument and the role of culture in learning and intelligence.

Slife, B. (2000). Taking sides: Clashing views on controversial psychological issues (11th ed.). Guilford, CT: Dushkin Publishing Group.

Insight

Insight, the sudden understanding of a problem, is often considered to be a component of intelligence. You can demonstrate the "aha" feeling that insight inspires by presenting students with the problems in Handout 7-6, which are taken from the popular game, *MindTrap©*. Students are likely to exclaim with joy each time they experience the insight necessary to solve a particular problem.

Answers:

1. The letters should be arranged as follows: *one word*.
2. A desert is a region so arid that it supports little or no vegetation. This includes frozen deserts of the far north, where Abdullah made his crossing. Thus, he survived by eating ice and snow.
3. It is the shortest sentence in the English language that includes every letter of the alphabet.
4. The "pack on her back" was a pack of wild wolves.
5. The two of you must stand back to back.
6. There aren't any penguins in the Arctic (they are native to the Southern Hemisphere).

MindTrap Games, Inc. (1991). *MindTrap*. Norwalk, CT: Great American Puzzle Factory.

Remote Associates Test

Chapter 8 describes Mednick and Mednick's (1967) *Remotes Associates Test* (RAT) as one of the most popular and commonly-used measures of creativity. In this test, subjects are presented with a series of seemingly unrelated words and are asked to come up with a single word that effectively links the words. After discussing measures of creativity in class, give your students practice forming remote associations by presenting them with the word sets in Handout 8-2 (this can be photocopied and distributed to students or projected on an overhead). These word sets, which were suggested by Margaret Matlin (1994), are similar to items on the Mednicks' test; answers are given below. Interestingly, although early research by Mednick and Mednick (1967) suggested a positive relationship between RAT scores and creativity in job performance, later studies (e.g., Andrews, 1975) revealed that RAT scores predicted creativity only in ideal environments that fostered innovation and creativity (e.g., by encouraging and allowing for ingenuity, independence, and professional security). Currently, evidence for the relationship between the RAT and creativity is equivocal: people who score high on the RAT sometimes show superior creative achievement, and sometimes they don't.

Answers:

1. prince
2. dog
3. cold
4. glasses
5. club
6. boat
7. defense
8. black
9. pit
10. writer

Andrews, F. M. (1975). Social and psychological factors which influence the creative process. In I. A. Taylor & J. W. Getzels (Eds.), *Perspectives in creativity.* Chicago: Aldine.

Matlin, M. W. (1994). *Cognition* (3rd ed.). Fort Worth: Harcourt Brace.

Mednick, S. A., & Mednick, M. T. (1967). *Examiner's manual, Remote Associates Test.* Boston, MA: Houghton Mifflin.

Mental Hotfoot

In his book, *Brain Power: Learn to improve your thinking skills*, Karl Albrecht (1980) suggests using the game of mental hotfoot as a way to sharpen thinking and creativity skills. *Mental hotfoot* (a term coined by comedian George Carlin) is a variation on the remotes associations theme in that it involves coming up with novel ideas or phrases by combining or challenging well-known phrases. Carlin himself was fond of this brand of humor, having once asked, "Why are there small craft warnings, but no large craft warnings?" Albrecht suggests other possible "hotfeet" such as, "Why isn't there a special name for the tops of your feet?", "Does a sweeping generalization use a broom?", "If a rooster can crow, can a crow rooster?", and "Why aren't there divorce licenses, divorce ceremonies, divorce gowns, and divorce receptions?" As a fun and entertaining way to sharpen students' creativity skills, ask your students (either individually or in small groups) to play mental hotfoot and to generate as many novel phrases as they can, perhaps offering prizes for the most creative or humorous examples.

Albrecht, K. (1980). *Brain Power: Learn to improve your thinking skills.* Englewood Cliffs, NJ: Prentice-Hall.

What-if?

You might also consider asking your students to play *What-If*, another creativity-strengthening game recommended by Albrecht. In this game, the goal is to generate as many alternative possibilities in situations where conventional wisdom tells you they won't work. In other words, the goal is to be as imaginative as possible by loosening reality constraints and engaging in wild speculation. To start this game, one person says, "What if..." and then lets their imagination fill in the rest. For example, if one person says, "What if you had eyes in the back of your head?", others could respond by naming potential effects that this anatomical change would have. Possible responses include (a) hats would have to be redesigned, (b) one pair of eyes could rest while the other worked, (c) you wouldn't need rearview mirrors in cars, (d) you could tell if the person behind you was enjoying the movie, (e) teachers could keep an eye on their students while writing on the board, and so on. Albrecht suggests that trying this game with a number of different statements (e.g., What if people didn't sleep? What if we could read another's mind? What if all countries used the same money system?) should lead to noticeable improvement in imagination skills and the ability to associate.

Albrecht, K. (1980). *Brain Power: Learn to improve your thinking skills.* Englewood Cliffs, NJ: Prentice-Hall.

Divergent Thinking

Another common measure of creativity is divergent thinking, which occurs when individuals expand on the given facts in a problem in order to generate a number of diverse possible solutions. Bill Hill (1993) suggests challenging your students with a popular measure of divergent thinking, the Unusual Uses Test. Introduce your students to the brickyard problem by reading the following scenario:

> Imagine that you are a consultant for a brickyard that makes common red construction bricks and is having financial difficulty. The manager of the brickyard is interested in new uses for her product and has asked you to provide her with some. Spend a few minutes thinking about the problem and then write down as many new uses for the construction bricks that you can think of.

After students have had about 10 minutes to generate possible answers, have them exchange papers and count the number of unusual uses on each other's paper. Explain to students that a listed use must be both novel and appropriate. If they have a question as to how to score an item, tell them to call you over as a consultant. After the papers are returned, ask the students to share some of their uses with their classmates. You can use this exercise to generate a class discussion on the definition of creativity and the difficulties involved in evaluating creativity. This activity can also be used to compare individual versus group efforts in generating creative solutions (see Chapter 15). [Note: There are numerous possible variations on this demonstration. For example, you can ask students to think of several possible unusual uses for any common household object, such as a paperclip, hanger, toothpick, thimble, automobile tire, nail file, and so on.]

    Hill, W. G. (1995). Instructor's resource manual for *Psychology* by S. F. Davis and J. J. Palladino. Englewood Cliffs, NJ: Prentice Hall.

student assignments

Constructing a Multiple Intelligences Test

Chapter 8 discusses a variety of theorists (including Cattell, Guilford, Thurstone, Sternberg, and Gardner) who propose, in contrast to Spearman, that intelligence is composed of several distinct aptitudes or abilities rather than a single, general one. One way for students to gain a better understanding of the concept of multiple intelligences is to construct their own test. Lester Sdorow (1994) suggests that students find a relevant article in *Psych Abstracts* and use it, along with the background material in the text, to write a three-page paper proposing their own intelligence test. Students' tests should assess more than the abilities required to succeed academically. In addition, students should describe in their papers: (a) the rationale and components (i.e., distinct aptitudes or abilities) of the test, (b) how they would standardize it and determine its reliability and validity, (c) any similarities or differences to other intelligence tests (such as the Stanford-Binet, the WAIS-R, WISC-III, or even other multiple intelligence tests). Students will no doubt enjoy this opportunity to creatively apply course concepts, and will also be left with a better understanding of how tests are constructed.

>Sdorow, L. (1994). The Frankenstein course: Teaching assistants, laboratory exercises, and papers in introductory psychology. Paper presented at the Southwest Regional Conference for Teachers of Psychology, Fort Worth.

Intelligence and Mental Capacity in Film

Chapter 8 briefly discusses the extremes of intelligence, from mental retardation to giftedness. The two films described below expand on these topics and give students an opportunity to explore these extremes in much greater detail. *Charly* explores the world of mental retardation whereas *Little Man Tate* considers the question of how best to nourish genius. Depending on your interests, assign either of these films (or give students a choice) and ask students to write a short paper relating insights in the films to psychological principles covered in the text and lecture. You might ask students to supplement their discussion with an article or two from the mental retardation or giftedness literatures using *Psychological Abstracts*.

• *Charly* (1968). In this endearing and classic tale, Oscar-winner Cliff Robertson portrays a retarded man with a drive to learn so powerful that he agrees to an experimental surgical procedure in order to become smarter. When he gets his wish, he must struggle to adapt to the changes and newfound emotions that accompany his sharp increase in intelligence (CBS/Fox; 104 min).

• *Little Man Tate* (1991). Jodie Foster stars in this heartwrenching tale of an uneducated mother who knows she cannot provide the stimulating and enriched environment her genius son needs to thrive. This extremely well-done film depicts the boy's frustrating struggle to gain both the love and the academic stimulation he needs (Orion; 99 min).

video

ABC News/Prentice Hall Video Library

Contract to Get Parents Involved in a Child's Education (3:47 min, Series III). ABC's *World News Tonight* looks at a program in Stone Mountain, Georgia, that encourages parents to actively become involved in their children's education. Parents of students at Pine Ridge Elementary sign contracts agreeing to attend parent-teacher conferences, spend a minimum of 15 minutes reinforcing each day's lessons, and volunteer at the school.

Other Sources

Discovering Psychology, Part 16: Testing and Intelligence (1990, 30 min, ANN/CPB). Provides an overview of how tests are developed and used to assign values to different abilities and behaviors, with a particular focus on intelligence and personality.

Intelligence (1990, 30 min, IM). Discusses difficulties associated with the definition and measurement of intelligence, the development of intelligence tests, and the question of whether intelligence is fixed or variable.

May's Miracle: A Retarded Youth With A Gift For Music (28 min, FL). An "idiot savant"--blind, retarded, and suffering from cerebral palsy--nonetheless recreates complex piano pieces from memory.

Schools of Thought: Teaching Children in America and Japan (55 min, FHS). A comparison of Japanese and American educational systems forms the basis for answering questions such as why differences in education exist and how personal and cultural goals influence the education process.

Why Didn't I Think Of That? Creative Problem Solving (1990, 28 min, LS). This videotape invites audience participation as it presents brainteasers, analytic problems, and anagrams designed to spur creative solutions. Several principles of cognition are presented at an intuitive level, such as priming, mental imagery, and some Gestalt principles. An accompanying booklet includes summaries of the key points on the tape and solutions to the audience participation problems.

MULTIMEDIA

Web Investigations

Sex Differences in the Brain

This chapter presents some interesting, challenging, and perhaps infuriating observations about differences between women and men concerning intellectual functioning. Because we place so much value on intellectual functioning, these differences can quickly become topics for emotionally charged debates. Although gender differences in math and verbal abilities may be so slight as to be nonexistent, differences in spatial ability may be more meaningful. Additionally, more men than women fall at the extreme ranges of measured intellectual abilities. There is significant debate over how, when, or even *if* sex differences should be reported, especially when these differences are subject to routine misinterpretation by non-psychologists.

The *Web Investigations* for this chapter will allow your students to evaluate some supposed differences in intellectual abilities by reading an article by Doreen Kimura, who speculates about the origins of sex differences in cognitive and intellectual skills.

Making Connections

Theories of Intelligence

Q What is the difference between intelligence, aptitude, and ability?

A An ability is a skill that people already have and for which they need no additional training. An aptitude is a potential ability. Intelligence refers to a person's general intellectual ability, whether actual or potential.

Q How is Gardner's theory of multiple intelligences like Thurstone's theory of intelligence? How is it different?

A Gardner's theory is similar to Thurstone's in that both hold that intelligence is made up of several distinct abilities. However, the two theories identify different specific types of intelligence.

Q How does Spearman's theory of intelligence account for the fact that performance is not uniform across tasks, that people have strengths and weaknesses?

A According to Spearman's theory, differences in performance reflect differences in how the same underlying general intelligence reveals itself, not different abilities or types of intelligence.

Q Compare and contrast the major theories of intelligence discussed in this section.

A Spearman's view of general intelligence is the simplest of the formal theories of intelligence. Thurstone and Cattell attempted to identify the structure of mental abilities in more detail. Sternberg and Gardner's theories both emphasize practical abilities. But whereas Sternberg has designed mental tests to measure different aspects of intelligence, Gardner has relied more on anecdotal evidence.

Intelligence Tests

Q For what purpose did Binet and Simon develop their intelligence test?

A Binet and Simon developed their intelligence test to identify children who might have difficulty in school.

Q What three scores are provided by the WAIS and WISC?

A The WAIS and WISC provide scores for verbal skills, performance skills, and overall IQ.

Q How do group intelligence tests eliminate bias on the part of the examiner?

A Group intelligence tests eliminate examiner bias by eliminating personal interaction between the examiner and the test taker.

Q What is the principal way in which performance and culture-fair tests are alike?

A Both performance and culture-fair tests minimize or eliminate the use of language.

What Makes a Good Test?

Q How is a good test like a good alarm clock?

A A good test is like a good alarm clock in that it is reliable, meaning that scores on the test are dependable and consistent.

Q Name and define two kinds of validity measures.

A Two measures of validity are: (a) content validity, the extent to which test items represent the knowledge or skills being measured, and (b) criterion-related validity, the extent to which a test correlates with other accepted measures of what is being tested.

Q How can the use of intelligence test scores influence student achievement?

A The use of intelligence test scores can influence student achievement by causing administrators to label students as "slow" because of problems taking tests rather than innate ability.

What Determines Intelligence?

Q Describe Tryon's experiment on maze learning. What were his major findings?

A Tryon formed two groups of rats: one group that was good at running mazes ("maze-bright") and another group that was not ("maze-dull"). The brightest offspring of the bright rats were allowed to breed, and so were the dullest offspring of the dull rates. Within a few generations the difference between the two groups had widened considerably. While this experiment did not prove that heredity is more important than environment, it did demonstrate that a specific ability can be passed from one generation of rats to another.

Q Are the IQ scores of adopted children more like those of their biological mothers or their adoptive mothers? What does this suggest about the heritability of intelligence?

A The IQs of adopted children are more like those of their biological mothers than like those of their adoptive mothers. This suggests that genetic factors play a significant role in determining intelligence, but it does not rule out a role for environmental factors.

Q Explain how both heredity and environment are thought to be responsible for differences in IQ scores.

A Each person inherits certain mental capacities, but the development of those abilities depends on environmental influences. Thus, while an individual's IQ may be determined to a large extent by his or her genetic endowment, a significant percentage is determined by the nutrition and intellectual stimulation he or she receives in childhood.

Mental Ability and Human Diversity

Q Which sex has an advantage in tasks involving spatial ability? In verbal skills? How significant are sex differences in mental ability?

A Males apparently have an advantage in tasks involving spatial ability, but there are no gender differences in verbal ability. Overall, gender differences in mental ability are insignificant.

Q According to Stevenson, Asian students learn more and enjoy school more than American students. Why?

A According to Stevenson, Asian students learn more and enjoy school more than American students because they spend more time in school each day and have more frequent breaks, and because Asian students are more likely than American students to attribute success to effort rather than innate ability.

Extremes of Intelligence

Q How does the APA define mental retardation? What deficiencies must exist for a person to be classified as having mental retardation?

A The APA defines mental retardation as "significantly subaverage general intellectual functioning . . . that is accompanied by significant limitations in adaptive functioning." To be classified as mentally retarded, a person must have an IQ of 70 or less and be unable to perform the ordinary tasks of daily living.

Q How do current definitions of giftedness differ from older definitions?

A Current definitions of giftedness include such qualities as creativity and motivation in addition to superior intelligence.

Creativity

Q What features characterize creative work?

A Creative ideas and objects are novel and socially valued.

Q How is creativity measured? How reliable are such measures?

A Creativity is measured by means of open-ended questions; scores are based on the number and originality of the answers. These measures do not show a high degree of criterion-related validity.

Video Classics

Cattell on Intelligence

SYNOPSIS: Raymond B. Cattell discusses the concepts of fluid and crystallized intelligence. In this brief interview segment, Cattell notes the methodological basis for positing these two types of intelligence, and discusses some of the ways in which fluid and crystallized intelligence differ from one another.

Form a Hypothesis

Q Do you think that the traditional intelligence test is a measure of fluid intelligence or crystallized intelligence?

A Traditional intelligence tests are biased towards the assessment of crystallized intelligence, or our ability to recall fact and apply verbal skills.

Test your Understanding

Q What are some personal examples of fluid intelligence and crystallized intelligence for you?

A Examples will differ. Students will probably describe labeling and factual recall for crystallized intelligence and vivid examples of problem-solving for fluid intelligence.

Q Why do some intellectual abilities decline with age, while others do not?

A Some abilities may be influenced by aging, illness or injury. Others may actually be enhanced by the additional experience brought by growing older.

Thinking Critically

Q Why is the distinction between fluid and crystallized intelligence important?

A If only one dimension of intelligence is assessed, an incomplete picture of the progression of human intellectual function results and misleading conclusions, like the supposed decline in mental functioning with age, are likely.

Q What developmental changes are related to the fluid/crystallized distinction?

A Crystallized intelligence, stressing reasoning, verbal, and numerical ability, is most likely to be influenced by formal education such that increased education should increase crystallized intelligence. Fluid intelligence should be less susceptible to experience.

Mental Age Testing

SYNOPSIS: Children of three different ages are shown performing on a standardized intelligence test. The tasks and responses are appropriate to each age level, and they illustrate the growing sophistication in reasoning that comes with maturation. The crewcut kid from *Short-Term Memory* does well in this clip.

Form a Hypothesis

Q What type of language items do you think will be asked of a 2-year-old? 5-year-old? 8-year-old?

A In the video segment, the two-year old is asked to associate a use or purpose with its object by pointing. The five-year old is asked to describe the composition of common objects (e.g., "what is a chair made of?"). The eight-year old is asked to define and describe more abstract terms ("what does scorch mean?").

Test Your Understanding

Q Did you think any of the test items shown in the video were biased? If so, how?

A Yes. The items are appropriate to a middle-income child in the 1950's and 1960's. Children from other backgrounds, especially economically disadvantaged ones, may have difficulty identifying "what you would use to buy candy" or "what do you ride in?"

Q If a two-year-old child has an MA of 6, what is her IQ?

A As IQ = 100 X (MA / CA), her IQ is 300! Not bad!

Q If a five-year-old child has an MA of 5, what is his IQ?

A 100, or average for his age.

Q If an eight-year-old child has an MA of 6, what is his IQ?

A 75, a significantly below average IQ.

Thinking Critically

Q Why isn't the IQ representative of adult intelligence? How, then, can an adult's intelligence be measured?

A IQ in children is less predictive of adult IQ the farther from adulthood the child is when she or he is tested. Adult IQ can be tested by using an assessment appropriate to an adult age group.

Q Why do you suppose it has been necessary to make periodic revisions of the Stanford-Binet over the years?

A Some of the items have changed over the years, such as the automobile, coinage, and telephone illustrated in the segment with the two-year old. Additionally, the national trend towards early childhood education may mean that younger children are performing like older age peers, forcing periodic re-norming of the Stanford-Binet.

Web Links

1. http://www.surfaquarium.com/

This site highlights Howard Gardner's eight criteria for identifying an intelligence. The list of criteria and an explanation of each is provided. Ask your students to review this site and prepare a short report comparing and contrasting what it takes to make an "intelligence."

2. http://maple.lemoyne.edu/~hevern/psychref4-11.html

Psychological Testing, Assessment, and Psychometrics. This site focuses on intelligence, and provides links to other worthwhile sites.

3. http://www.thearc.org/

Provides thorough answers to common questions about mental retardation. Ask your students to visit this site as a starting point for discussing applied aspects of learning and memory.

4. http://home8.swipnet.se/~w-80790/Index.htm

This site explains IQ and offers the estimated intelligence quotient of several well-known geniuses. Useful for quick examples of the range of intelligence and the problems of estimating intelligence without sound psychometric techniques.

transparencies

Series V

8.1 *Some Age-related Tasks from Binet's 1911 Intelligence Test*
This transparency gives examples of tasks to be performed at the 3-, 7-, and 15-year levels.

8.2 *Mental Age, Chronological Age, and the Intelligence Quotient*
The relationship of these terms and the term "IQ" are explained. The intelligence quotient was first used in the 1916 Stanford-Binet Intelligence Scale developed by Lewis Terman and his colleagues at Stanford University. Today, almost all intelligence tests (including the current edition of the Stanford-Binet) report deviation IQ scores, which relate a person's measured intelligence to the normal distribution.

8.3 *Items Similar to Performance Subtests of the Wechsler Intelligence Scale*
Items similar to those from the Picture Arrangement and Block Design subtests of the WAIS-R and WISC-III are illustrated.

8.4 *Distribution of IQ Scores*
This graph presents the percentage of persons achieving different IQ scores. The "bell curve" is approximated.

8.5 *Correlations of IQ Scores of Persons with Varying Kinship*
This graph presents evidence for both hereditary and environmental influences on IQ. It is clear that persons with the greatest genetic similarity have the most similar IQs. Fraternal twins have the same proportion of shared inheritance as other siblings, but their IQs are more alike. This is thought to be due to the fact that, unlike other siblings, fraternal twins are the same age as their families experience different life events. Therefore the developmental environments of fraternal twins is more similar than that for other siblings. Also note that unrelated persons reared together have IQs that are more similar than unrelated persons reared apart.

8.6a *Gardner's Multiple Intelligences*
8.6b It has been argued that traditional conceptualizations of intelligence and the instruments for measuring IQ are too narrow in scope. Gardner (1983) has presented a model of multiple intelligences.

8.7 *Degrees of Severity/Characteristics of Intellectual Impairment*
This transparency provides information about IQ score ranges and functional abilities for persons with varying degrees of mental handicap (mental retardation).

Text Figures

    8-1 to 8-5.   *Intelligence Test Item*

    8-1.   *The Approximate Distribution of IQ Test Scores in the Population*

    8-2.   *Correlations of IQ Scores of Family Members*

Handout 8-1

Insight

Instructions: Give the correct answer for each of the following problems.

1. How would you rearrange the letters in the words *new door* to make one word? [Note: There is only one correct answer.]

2. It is impossible for anyone to survive longer than one week without drinking, yet Abdullah managed a ten-day desert crossing without finding water or bringing any along. How was this possible?

3. What is so unusual about the sentence below? (Aside from the fact that it doesn't make a lot of sense.)
    "Jackdaws love my big sphinx of quartz."

4. A well-known fashion designer, wanting to escape the hustle and bustle of the city, decided to spend a few days at a rural resort. After a day of relaxing, she went for a winter stroll to get some fresh air. That was the last time anyone saw her alive. The autopsy revealed that her death was due to the pack on her back. What was so deadly about this pack?

5. How can you stand behind your father while he is standing behind you?

6. Even if they are starving, natives living in the Arctic will never eat a penguin's egg. Why not?

Source: MindTrap Games, Inc. (1991). MindTrap. Norwalk, CT: Great American Puzzle Factory.

Handout 8-2

Finding Remote Associates

Instructions: For each set of three words, try to think of a fourth word that is related to all three words. For example, the words ROUGH, COLD, and BEER suggest the word DRAFT, because of the phrases, ROUGH DRAFT, COLD DRAFT, AND DRAFT BEER.

1	CHARMING	STUDENT	BEER
2	FOOD	CATCHER	HOT
3	BITTER	FEET	HEARTED
4	DARK	SHOT	SUN
5	CANADIAN	GOLF	SANDWICH
6	TUG	GRAVY	SHOW
7	ATTORNEY	SELF	SPENDING
8	MAGIC	PITCH	POWER
9	ARM	COAL	PEACH
10	TYPE	GHOST	STORY

Adapted from Matlin, M. W. (1994). Cognition (3rd ed.). Fort Worth: Harcourt Brace.

Chapter 9 Motivation and Emotion

chapter outline 236

learning objectives 238

lecture suggestions

    Fat Free? 239
    Weight and See 239
    More to Love 240
    Gender Differences in Sexuality 240
    Intersex at a Crossroads 241
    Peak Experiences 242
    Mood Awareness 242
    Contempt 244
    The Amazing Amygdala 245
    Miles of Smiles 245
    Le Docteur Duchenne 246
    Expression and Sensory Restriction 247
    Is Everybody Happy? 248
    👍 👆 ✌️ 🖖 👉 🖐️ 249

demonstrations and activities

    Gender Differences in Body Image 250
    Debate: Is Body Chemistry the Major Determinant of Eating? 250
    Debate: Do Evolutionary Factors Determine Sexual Behaviors? 250
    Guest Lecture: Sexual Orientation Panel Discussion 251
    Heterosexual Privilege 251
    Exploring the Motives of Everyday Behavior 252
    Identifying Human Motives Using Maslow's Hierarchy 252
    Smile When You Say That 252
    Channels of Communication 253
    Vocal Cues and Emotion 254
    Tiny Fast Faces 254
    Facial Expressions of Emotion 256

student assignments

    Exploring Cross-cultural Influences on Sexuality 257
    Experiencing Homophobia 257
    Icons of Emotional Expression 258
    Icons of Emotional Expression: International Version 258
    The Medium and the Message 259
    Motivation and Emotion in Film 260

video 261
multimedia 263
transparencies 271
handouts

    Body Attitude Questionnaire 273
    Identifying Human Motives 274

chapter outline

I. Perspectives on Motivation

    A. Instincts: Although once popular, several shortcomings led to its demise

    B. Drive-reduction theory: Needs ⊃ Drives ⊃ Drive reduction ⊃ Homeostasis

        1. Drive-reduction inadequate to explain all motivated behavior

    C. Arousal theory: Organisms seek an optimal level of arousal

        1. Yerkes-Dodson Law

    D. Intrinsic and extrinsic motivation

        1. Intrinsic: Desire to perform a behavior stems from the behavior performed

        2. Extrinsic: Desire to perform a behavior stems from wanting reward, avoiding punishment

II. Hunger and Thirst

    A. Biological factors: Hypothalamic "hunger center" and "satiety center" regulate food intake

    B. Cultural and environmental factors: Learning and social conditioning play a role in hunger

    C. Eating disorders and obesity: Anorexia and bulimia remain issues of concern, especially in Western society

III. Sex

    A. Sexual motivation

        1. Testosterone is a major biological influence for both men and women

        2. Genders differ in what they find arousing

    B. Sexual behavior

        1. Four stages of the human sexual response cycle: excitement, plateau, orgasm, resolution

    C. Sexual orientation

        1. Neither nature nor nurture alone has provided a satisfactory explanation

        2. Acquired ideas about morality, appropriateness, pleasurability affect sexual behavior

IV. Other Motives

    A. Exploration and curiosity: Rats and humans have a taste for the novel and unfamiliar

    B. Manipulation and contact: Motivation to experience things first-"hand"

        1. Harlow's studies of infant monkeys illustrate importance of contact

    C. Aggression: Intentionally inflicting physical or psychological harm on others

        1. Aggression seen by some as an instinct that seeks expression (Freud)

        2. Frustration-aggression hypothesis

        3. Most view aggression as a learned response

            a. Modeling plays a role in the acquisition of this response

        4. Aggression and culture

            a. The collectivist/individualist distinction may help explain violence within cultures

        5. Gender and aggression

            a. Although males are higher than females in aggressiveness, the reason is not clear

    D. Achievement: Work, mastery, competitiveness

    E. Affiliation: The need to be with others

    F. A hierarchy of motives

        1. Maslow's representation: Physiological, safety, belongingness, esteem, actualization needs

V. Emotions

    A. Basic emotions

        1. Plutchik proposes 8 basic emotions that vary in intensity

        2. Cross-cultural studies suggest universal recognition of primary emotions

    B. Happiness and well-being are related to goals and adaptability

    C. Theories of emotion

        1. Early theories of emotion: James-Lange and Cannon-Bard

            a. James-Lange theory: Stimuli ⊃ physiological changes ⊃ emotions result from changes

            b. Cannon-Bard theory: Stimuli ⊃ simultaneous biological changes & emotion experience

        2. Cognitive theories: Emotional experience depends on perception or judgment of situation

        3. Challenges to cognitive theory

            a. Zajonc: Preferences need no inferences, emotion comes before cognition

            b. Izard: Primacy of emotion tied to expression of emotion

                i. Refinement of James-Lange view

VI. Nonverbal Communication of Emotion

    A. Voice quality

        1. Verbal descriptions of emotional states may be impoverished

        2. Tone, pitch, other vocal qualities carry additional information

    B. Facial expression: Have a universal, evolutionarily adaptive character

    C. Body language: May convey broad affective information

    D. Personal space: Often culturally determined

    E. Explicit acts

        1. Gestures often convey specific affective information

        2. Actions may function as nonverbal messages

VII. Gender, Culture, and Emotion

    A. Gender and emotion: Men and women differ in some aspects of their emotional experience

    B. Culture and emotion

        1. Facial expressions of primary emotions are universal

            a. Substantial cross-cultural evidence supports this view

            b. Display rules are culture specific, and act to modify natural expression

learning objectives

After reading this chapter, students should be able to:

1. Describe several perspectives on motivation including: instincts, drive-reduction, arousal theory, and intrinsic/extrinsic motivation

2. Summarize the Yerkes-Dodson law.

3. Define motive and emotion and explain the roles of stimulus, behavior, and goals in motivation.

4. Identify the primary drives and their physiological bases.

5. Describe how hunger is controlled in the brain. Explain how external cues and experience influence hunger.

6. List the biological factors involved in the sex drive. Discuss psychological influences on sexual motivation. List the stages of the human sexual response cycle.

7. List the characteristics of the following stimulus motives: activity, exploration, curiosity, manipulation, and contact.

8. Define aggression. Discuss theories of aggressive behavior.

9. Explain why the need for achievement is so strong in some people.

10. Distinguish between the motives for power, affiliation, and achievement, and give an example of each.

11. Identify the five categories in Maslow's hierarchy of motives.

12. Describe and give an example of each of the three basic categories of emotions.

13. Explain how Plutchik categorized emotions.

14. Describe and differentiate among the James-Lange, Cannon-Bard, cognitive, and Izard's theories of emotion.

15. Identify several kinds of nonverbal communications. Give one example of each kind.

lecture suggestions

Fat Free?

The popular press has recently heralded the discovery of a so-called "magic bullet" for treating obesity. Dr. Jeffrey Friedman, a molecular geneticist at the Howard Hughes Medical Institute at Rockefeller University, led a team of researchers who successfully isolated the gene (called *ob*) that helps control body weight in mice. From this gene the researchers synthesized a protein hormone (called *leptin*) that, when injected into obese mice, caused them to lose 40 percent of their body weight within a month. Although the mice had access to ample food, Friedman reports that they simply chose to eat less. In addition to curbing the animals' appetites, leptin appeared to speed their metabolism as well. Moreover, the weight loss itself was solely from fat, and no adverse effects were observed.

Although the long term effects of leptin have yet to be studied, scientists and pharmaceutical companies are already anticipating applications to human weight loss. For example, it is known that humans produce a hormone similar to leptin. Pending human clinical trials, it is possible that leptin could be used to treat obesity and, along with sensible diet and exercise, also act to regulate weight in normal-weight individuals. In a testament to these potential applications, the pharmaceutical company Amgen has already paid Rockefeller University $20 million for a patent license, with the promise to pay many times that should the drug prove effective in treating human obesity.

Steps in that direction are already being made. Jay Erickson, also at the Howard Hughes center, recently identified the importance of one factor in producing the leptin-obesity link. Called neuropeptide Y (or NPY for short; see Chapter 2 of this manual, *Would you like fries with that peptide?*), it is one of several elements responsible for regulating weight gain.

Mice with a flawed ob gene don't produce leptin, and as a consequence they become obese. Erickson and his colleagues gave this natural process a head start by breeding mice that lacked the leptin gene but had the NPY gene intact. After 16 weeks these animals had eaten an average of 62 percent more than normal mice. With "NPY on the brain" and no leptin to keep it in check, the mice's unrestricted eating turned into a feeding frenzy. By comparison, those mice which were genetically engineered to lack both the leptin and NPY genes ate 35 percent more than a normal weight control group. Although there are several other factors that contribute to obesity, Friedman, Erickson, and their colleagues have taken significant steps in identifying the links among some primary components of obesity.

Kolata, G. (1995, July 27). Hormone trims fat, researchers discover. *Austin American Statesman*, pp. A1, A10.
Recer, P. (1996, December 6). At least in rats, chemical in brain linked to obesity. *Austin American-Statesman*, A3.
Staff. (1995, August 14). It's a fat accompli. *People*, p. 93.
Wade, N. (1997, June 24). Scientists suspect obesity caused by genetic defect. *Austin American-Statesman*, A12.
Watson, T. (1995, August 7). The new skinny on fat. *US News and World Report*, pp. 45-48.

Weight and See

Perceptions of body weight can play a role in the motivation to eat; from the perceptual distortions seen in anorexic patients, to the inexplicable way clothes seem to shrink at the waist, to the hesitancy to have one more doughnut as we look in the mirror. A recent study suggests, however, that culture may play a role in one's perceptions of weight and body image.

Researchers at the University of Arizona asked African-American and caucasian teenage girls to describe their version of an "ideal" girl. The white teens suggested someone blue-eyed, five feet seven inches tall, weighing between 100 and 110 pounds; in short, Barbie. The Black teens, in contrast, emphasized personal characteristics such as a sense of style, a nice personality, or having a good head on one's shoulders. When pressed for a physical description, most responded that fuller hips, large thighs, and a small waist were desirable.

The researchers also found that close to 90 percent of the white teens were dissatisfied with their weight, whereas 70 percent of the Black respondents were satisfied. In the case of the white teens, having weight as a central aspect of their self-views may promote increased social stress and unrealistic expectations about achieving some "body ideal." The African-American women, though satisfied with their bodies, may not be concerned enough about their weight, given their heightened risk of hypertension as adults. In either case, perceptions of one's body image are clearly influenced by personal, social, and cultural standards that may vary from one subculture to another.

Staff (1994, September/October). White weight. *Psychology Today*, p. 9.

More to Love

Mayok Mayen force-fed himself cow's milk blended with cow urine at a rate of 5 gallons a day for 12 weeks. Lying on a mat for most of the day, in an effort to avoid burning calories, he eventually became weak from inactivity and found it difficult to even speak. His heart became overworked by the huge weight gain, and he stopped counting the number of chins he'd developed. Some strange suicide ritual? A brain tumor gone haywire? Actually, these deliberate acts were in the service of Mayen's finding a mate.

In the cow-culture of Payiir, Sudan, bigger is better when it comes to mate selection. Eligible bachelors intentionally gorge themselves to obesity in an effort to attract women. The significance is that an obese man is thought to come from a very well-off family, one that can afford to spare the extra cow's milk to fatten a relative. (Big herds are an embarrassment of riches in this culture, as is singing of one's loved one as "a beautiful bull.") Judges look at both the girth and firmness of each bachelor's body, and the winner of this contest is held in high esteem by all concerned.

Mayen, by the way, was not victorious. Deng Wauor turned out to be taller, fatter, bulkier...and ultimately, more attractive.

Associated Press (1996, October 28). Tribe's women love the fat men. *Austin American-Statesman*, A25.

Gender Differences in Sexuality

A recent meta-analysis has examined the interplay of gender and sexuality. Mary Beth Oliver and Janet Shibley Hyde examined 177 sources that reported gender differences in a variety of sexual behaviors and attitudes. Their meta-analytic review concluded that:

❖ Between the 1960s and the 1980s, gender differences decreased for many behaviors. The authors credit this narrowing of the gap to a variety of factors, such as the availability of birth control pills (starting in 1960), the legalization of abortion, a rapidly rising divorce rate, and the AIDS and herpes epidemics (begun in the 1980s).

❖ There were two large gender differences in sexuality: Men reported a higher incidence of masturbation, and also held more permissive attitudes toward sex. For example, men were more likely than women to be accepting of premarital sex and to feel less guilty about engaging in it. Although attitudes towards masturbation did not differ between genders, 92 percent of men (compared to 52 percent of women) masturbate during the course of their lifetimes.

❖ Men and women show little difference in their attitudes toward homosexuality, although men are more likely to engage in homosexual acts.

❖ Men lose their virginity earlier than women, have sex more frequently, and report having more sexual partners over their lifetimes. The effect sizes for these differences were in the small to moderate range.

Oliver, M. B., & Hyde, J. S. (1993). Gender differences in sexuality: A meta-analysis. *Psychological Bulletin, 114*, 29-51.

Intersex at a Crossroads

Woman or man, female or male, girl or boy. Such is the common wisdom when distinctions between anatomy, gender, biological sex, and sexual orientation get blurred into a simple taxonomy of "one or the other." But nature is not always so cooperative to fit our classification schemes. For those individuals who, at birth, may not clearly be "one or the other," gender identity and gender development can be a complicated affair.

Fetal development typically follows one of two courses. Genetically female fetuses (having XX sex chromosomes) have gonads that mature into ovaries, whereas in genetically male fetuses (having XY sex chromosomes) the same gonads develop into testes. Although there is a "default" for any fetus to become anatomically female, the presence of testosterone in the XY baby - at the right time, and to the right tissues - causes the development of gender-appropriate sex organs.

However, about 1 baby in 2,000 (by experts' rough estimates) is born with sex organs that don't clearly fit either of the two categories. These *intersex* individuals can be classified into three groups. "True" *hermaphrodites* have both ovarian and testicular tissue, due many times to a chromosomal abnormality. *Female pseudohermaphrodites* are genetic females who have masculinized external sex organs, partly due to prenatal exposure to testosterone. Finally, *male pseudohermaphrodites* are genetically male but did not fully masculinize in the womb, due perhaps to a lack of necessary hormones or to tissues that failed to respond. (Nature is not always the culprit. Intersex individuals can be surgically produced, as when a botched circumcision leads to a medical decision to surgically fashion a damaged penis into a vagina.)

For 40 years the medical advice to parents of intersex babies was simple: Transform the child into an externally-identified female through a series of operations and hormone treatments, raise the child as a girl, and (in most cases) keep the entire process a secret. The notion that gender identity was primarily a social construct - raising an intersex child as a girl "makes" it a girl - drove these recommendations, and for quite some time they seemed appropriate. Currently the American Academy of Pediatrics recommends surgery within the first 15 months of life for children with ambiguous genitalia, and counsels that they can be raised successfully as members of either sex. (Modern surgical techniques have greatly improved the outcomes of genital reconstructions.) But these recommendations are based largely on intuition rather than data. Few long-term studies have examined the psychological development and adjustment of intersex people.

A case study by Milton Diamond and Keith Sigmundson followed the progress of John/Joan who, in 1963, was castrated after a bungled circumcision and raised as a girl. Interviewed in 1994 and 1995, John revealed a sense of constant discomfort throughout his years of being raised as "Joan." (In the late 1970s he had a sex-change operation and was surgically changed back to "John.") For example, Joan engaged in stereotypically male play activities and insisted on urinating standing up. She was seen by others (and herself) alternately as a tomboy, a mental patient, or a freak throughout her childhood and adolescence. A 1977 sex change operation, at age 14, finally brought with it a sense of "correctness," bolstered by a tearful confrontation with her parents that revealed the truth about her gender.

Similarly, a handful of studies that have looked at the physical and psychological adjustment of intersex individuals reveal that decreases in quality of life are most often due to complications from surgery. In short, genital transformations that look acceptable immediately after surgery may require years of additional treatment to stay that way, often with little improvement or few guarantees.

Several advocacy groups have convened to lobby the medical profession regarding the appropriateness of treatment for intersex individuals. To date the issue remains largely unresolved, and continues to be a matter of debate, judgment, and some measure of soul-searching.

Cowley, G. (May 19, 1997). Gender limbo. *Newsweek*, 64-66.

Gorman, C. (March 24, 1997). A boy without a penis. *Time*, 83.

Money, J. (1988). *Gay, straight, and in-between.* Oxford University Press.

Peak Experiences

Chapter 8 briefly discusses Maslow's hierarchy of needs and the humanistic concept of self-actualization. One of the defining elements self-actualization is having peak experiences, or experiences that can best be defined as mystic or profound in nature.

Humanism often suffers the criticism of being vague and untestable, and many of Maslow's descriptions of human activities certainly qualify. To the best of descriptive powers, then, peak experiences can be thought of as a kind of *oceanic feeling*. The individual at once feels focused yet open to unlimited experiences, powerful yet weak, ecstatic, and as though time and space have slowed or stopped. These feelings are apparently experienced without a specific link back to the self, so that the feeling, rather than the feeler, is the source of the experience. Peak experiences generally lead to the perception that something important has happened, possibly that can change one's direction in life. In general, peak experiences are a momentary loss or transcendence of the self, during which a kind of revelation is experienced.

Maslow thought that most people could have peak experiences, although they were more common among those who were self-actualized. Similarly, Maslow argued that a number of different circumstances could trigger peak experiences, from communing with nature to listening to classical music to insightfully solving a problem to orgasm. Apparently there is hope for us all, both to climb the hierarchy to self-actualization and to glimpse the infinite in a peak experience.

Maslow, A. H. (1976). *Religion, values, and peak experiences.* Harmondsworth, England: Penguin Books.

Mood Awareness

Emotional intelligence (a broad collection of abilities related to understanding and utilizing affect) and *alexithymia* (a stunted awareness of one's emotional states) have been "hot topics" recently in both the popular press and scientific circles. These notions share a common component, that awareness of one's moods and emotions can contribute to successful mood regulation. This idea has been pursued in a recent set of empirical studies.

Mood awareness refers to individual differences in attention directed toward one's mood states. It is measured by the Mood Awareness Scale (MAS; Swinkels & Giuliano, 1995), a reliable 10-item measure composed of two related but distinct dimensions: *mood labeling* and *mood monitoring*. Mood labeling refers to the ability to identify and categorize one's mood states, whereas mood monitoring refers to the tendency to focus on, evaluate, or scrutinize one's mood.

The processes of mood labeling and mood monitoring may be better understood by an analogy. There is a marked difference in the approaches used by a physician and by a hypochondriac when trying to assess states of health. The physician, because of training, experience, or insight, is usually successful in making an accurate diagnosis of an illness and recommending some course of treatment. In other words, the medical condition is diagnosed or categorized fairly readily, and steps are then taken to remedy the complaint (e.g., "take two aspirin and call me in the morning") or maintain the state of health (e.g., "keep jogging to work every day"). In contrast, hypochondriacs are quite concerned about the state of their physical health, and in fact may become preoccupied with keeping track of their health status. A process of monitoring physical symptoms and checking for the onset of illness may become an ongoing ritual. The problem, of course, is that although hypochondriacs may be vigilant in checking their health, they are apt to be misled many times about their condition. In other words, they check on their physical states often, but may not reach a satisfactory or final judgment about their health, concluding instead that they are suffering from some vague bodily complaint.

Several studies have demonstrated that labeling and monitoring exert different influences on other mood-relevant variables. For example, in comparison with low mood labelers, high mood labelers tend to seek and be satisfied with social support, experience positive affect, have higher levels of self-esteem, be extraverted, be less socially anxious or neurotic, and express greater global life satisfaction. High (as compared with low) mood monitors, by contrast, tend to experience more intense affective states, experience greater negative affect, have lower self-esteem, and report neurotic tendencies. Various other studies have investigated the role of mood awareness in: depression; self-views; reactions to life stress; self-reported physical symptoms; intelligence and cognitive abilities; and numerous other personality dimensions.

More importantly, mood monitoring and mood labeling play a role in the process of mood regulation. Most people are motivated to sustain a positive mood (mood maintenance) or change a negative one (mood repair), although monitors and labelers might be more or less successful at this task. One study (Swinkels & Giuliano, 1995, Study 4), for example, found that although high mood monitors agreed that their moods influenced their behavior and were important to them, they reported less success at regulating their negative mood states. Another study (Giuliano, 1995) found that the ability of mood labelers and mood monitors to repair their negative moods over time differed. High labelers were able to take relatively quick action to alter their mood states, whereas high monitors tended to wallow in their negative moods for a longer period of time.

The reason for these differences can be understood by returning to the medical analogy. The act of labeling something implies that it becomes identified or categorized for further use. The physician who has made an accurate diagnosis now knows the likely course and duration of the illness, the available treatments, and the number of subsequent office visits for which the patient can be billed. In this sense *mood labeling* should generally promote constructive thought and behavior in regard to one's feelings. A mood that is readily labeled is a mood that does not need to be dwelt upon in order to be understood: the mood state has been identified and the stage presumably is set for acting on that mood in some way.

In contrast, monitoring implies a certain degree of vigilance by an individual, which may or may not be productive. Like the hypochondriac who is nervously attuned to each twitch and tremor of his or her body, *mood monitoring* would imply a similar type of examination of or dwelling upon one's mood; for some, perhaps, to the point of unhealthfulness, but for most out of a simple concern with tracking the progress of one's feelings. The difficulty with mood monitoring, then, is that it may contribute to becoming absorbed in one's mood state, much like the overconcern with physical health experienced by the hypochondriac. The high mood monitor may check on his or her moods often, and be quite vigilant in doing so, yet may still remain a bit confused about the nature of the mood state. Just as the accuracy of the hypochondriac's diagnoses may be clouded by numerous false alarms or uncertainty about the nature of the discomfort, so too may the high mood monitor's judgments of his or her mood be clouded by too great an absorption in the mood state itself. In the case of bad moods, this absorption may produce prolonged negative affect.

Giuliano, T. A. (1995, August). Mood awareness predicts mood change over time. Presented at the 103rd Annual Convention of the American Psychological Association, New York.

Swinkels, A. (1993, August). Exploring the role of mood awareness in mood regulation. In D. Tice (Chair), *Self regulation of mood and emotion.* Symposium conducted at the 101st Annual Convention of the American Psychological Association, Toronto.

Swinkels, A., & Giuliano, T. A. (1995). The measurement and conceptualization of mood awareness: Monitoring and labeling one's mood states. *Personality and Social Psychology Bulletin, 21*, 934-949.

Swinkels, A., Giuliano, T. A., & Helweg-Larsen, M. (1996, August). Assessing mood awareness in diverse groups. Presented at the 104th Annual Convention of the American Psychological Association, Toronto.

Swinkels, A., & Giuliano, T. A. (1992a). Mood awareness and self-regulation. Presented at the Fourth Annual Convention of the American Psychological Society, San Diego, California.

Swinkels, A., & Giuliano, T. A. (1992b). [Mood clash: Negotiating interpersonal affect]. Unpublished research data.

Contempt

Happiness, sadness, anger, fear, surprise, and disgust have long been recognized as the six primary emotions. Their universality is based on several converging lines of evidence; strong cross-cultural agreement in both recognizing and producing facial expressions of these emotions (Ekman et al., 1987), specific anatomical configurations associated with these expressions (Ekman & Friesen, 1978), and autonomic nervous system activity that distinguishes between these emotional states (Ekman, Levenson, and Friesen, 1983). Although there have been some minor challenges to this universalist position (e.g., Ortony & Turner, 1990; Russell, 1994) the evidence clearly suggests that these six emotions enjoy a special status. That status should be shared, though, by a seventh emotion: *contempt*.

Throughout much of their research program Paul Ekman and Wally Friesen, as well as most other emotion researchers, studied disgust/contempt as one "emotion family." This decision was based on the similarity of the expressions (e.g., lip curls) and on the commonalities of their experience (e.g., aspects of avoidance, judgment, disdain). In the mid-1980s, however, Ekman and Friesen gathered evidence to suggest that contempt was better understood as its own emotion, with its own distinct set of expressions, apart from disgust. Citizens of Estonia, Germany, Greece, Hong Kong, Italy, Japan, Scotland, Turkey, the United States, and West Sumatra were shown three photographs of each of the six primary emotions, along with two photographs each of three prototypical contempt displays. These were 1) a tightening and slight raise of the corner of the upper lip unilaterally (e.g., the Elvis Presley or Johnny Rotten look); 2) the same expression performed bilaterally (i.e., both lip corners raised); and 3) raising the entire upper lip slightly, without tightening or raising the lip corners. Their judgment task was similar to that used in previous studies of universality, and, like previous studies, there was high agreement about what emotion was displayed for the six primary expressions.

Across the 10 countries there was considerable agreement that the unilateral lip curl was an expression of contempt. Seventy-five percent of the participants (summing across countries) judged this expression as showing contempt, whereas 36 percent and 19 percent agreed that the bilateral expression or upper-lip-raise, respectively, showed this emotion. In short, citizens from a variety of Western and non-Western cultures, holding a variety of attitudes about emotional expression, showed high rates of agreement for this facial expression. The researchers were able to further demonstrate that the contempt judgments were not confused with judgments of disgust (as the previous literature would suggest) or anger (an expression often misjudged as disgust). These findings were not immune to criticism (e.g., Izard & Haynes, 1988; Russell, 1991). However, these results have been replicated among the Minangkabau of West Sumatra (Ekman & Heider, 1988), and they show the promise of replication in future cross-cultural, anatomical, and physiological studies.

Ekman, P., & Friesen, W. V. (1978). *Facial Action Coding System: A technique for the measurement of facial movement.* Palo Alto, CA: Consulting Psychologists Press.

Ekman, P., & Friesen, W. V. (1986). A new pan-cultural facial expression of emotion. *Motivation and Emotion, 10,* 159-168.

Ekman, P., & Friesen, W. V. (1988). Who knows what about contempt: A reply to Izard and Haynes. *Motivation and Emotion, 12,* 17-22.

Ekman, P., Friesen, W. V., O'Sullivan, M., Chan, A., Diacoyanni-Tarlatzis, I., Heider, K., Krause, R., LeCompte, W. A., Pitcairn, T., Ricci-Bitti, P. E., Scherer, K., Tomita, M., & Tzavaras, A. (1987). Universals and cultural differences in the judgments of facial expressions of emotion. *Journal of Personality and Social Psychology, 53,* 712-717.

Ekman, P., & Heider, K. (1988). The universality of a contempt expression: A replication. *Motivation and Emotion, 12,* 303-308.

Ekman, P., Levenson, R. W., & Friesen, W. V. (1983). Autonomic nervous system activity distinguishes between emotions. *Science, 221,* 1208-1210.

Izard, C. E., & Haynes, O. M. (1988). On the form and universality of the contempt expression: A challenge to Ekman and Friesen's claim of discovery. *Motivation and Emotion, 12,* 1-16.

Ortony, A., & Turner, T. J. (1990). What's basic about basic emotions? *Psychological Review, 97,* 315-331.

Russell, J. A. (1991). The contempt expression and the relativity thesis. *Motivation and Emotion, 15,* 149-168.

Russell, J. A. (1994). Is there universal recognition of emotion from facial expression? A review of the cross-cultural studies. *Psychological Bulletin, 115,* 102-141.

The Amazing Amygdala

Scientists have long known that the limbic system is involved in emotional experience. In particular, the amygdala seems to play a crucial role in two different activities related to emotion.

David Zald, a researcher at the Veterans Affairs Medical Center in Minneapolis, led a research team that studied the relation between odors and emotional reactions. Zald asked 12 women to smell a variety of concoctions while undergoing repeated brain scans. Some of the odors were quite pleasant, such as the scents of flowers, fruits, or spices, whereas others ranged from garlic breath to motor oil, and a sulfurous stench crossing rotting vegetables with a sewer. The pleasant smells didn't trigger much of a reaction; only the right amygdala responded weakly. The most pungent odors, however, caused both amygdalae to respond swiftly and markedly, the equivalent of sending a "Yuck!" message to the rest of the brain. In fact, the anatomical link between the amygdala and brain centers responsible for processing olfactory sensations suggests a strong link between odor and affect. Pinpointing the amygdala's reaction may help explain why unpleasant odors can produce negative emotional reactions.

In a separate study, researchers also examined the amygdala's role in perceiving facial expressions of emotion. Researchers at the Salk Institute and the University of Iowa College of Medicine, led by Antonio Damasio, studied a remarkable woman identified as S.M. This 33-year-old was intelligent, cooperative, and had no difficulty remembering names and faces of acquaintances or people she recently met. When asked to pose an expression of fear on her face, however, S.M. found it impossible to do. Furrowing her brows and grimacing desperately, she was unable to display one of the primary emotions. Moreover, although S.M. could correctly identify expressions of happiness posed by others, she could not perceive fear in another person's facial expression. The cause of these difficulties seemed to be the destruction of cells in the amygdala due to disease. What it revealed to the research team was the importance of this particular limbic system component in recognizing and producing a very specific expression of emotion. What it reveals more generally is the evolutionary development of emotion. Fear, an emotion so crucial to survival, seems to have claimed its own niche in the brain.

Holtz, R. L. (December 24, 1994). Scientists find part of brain that reads facial expressions. *Austin American-Statesman*, A13.
Ritter, M. (February 9, 1997). Tests catch image of brain saying "Yech!" *Austin American-Statesman*, A22.

Miles of Smiles

The Mona Lisa has a famous one. Your dentist encourages you to preserve yours. Jimmy Carter got elected using his. What could be more beguiling, more disarming than a smile...and yet, more complicated?

Laypeople, and many scientists, would argue that a smile is a smile is a smile. Just as happiness is a pretty uncomplicated emotion, so too is its expression. Indeed, cross-cultural research has found that expressions of happiness are most easily and most accurately detected by members of a variety of cultures (Ekman, 1984). Yet research has also demonstrated that smiles come in many varieties, many of which signal particular internal states.

For example, the smile that accompanies enjoyment (once called a "felt" smile; see Ekman & Friesen, 1982, and Frank, Ekman, & Friesen, 1993) is characterized not only by the action of the *zygomatic major* muscle (which serves to pull the lip corners up and back) but more importantly is characterized by the action of the *obicularis oculi*. This muscle surrounds the eye and produces the slight squinting and "crow's feet" seen in the eye region when happiness is displayed. This particular smile of enjoyment has been dubbed the "Duchenne smile," in honor of G. B. Duchenne de Bologne, the French anatomist who originally postulated its existence (Duchenne, 1862/1990).

In other cases, different smiles, with different corresponding facial actions, can signal other affective states. For example, Paul Ekman, Wally Friesen, and Maureen O'Sullivan (1988) studied the smiles shown by nurses who either told the truth or lied about a videotape they were watching. Whereas the smile of enjoyment could be detected (using the Facial Action Coding System) when the nurses truthfully related their positive experiences, "masking" smiles could be measured when the nurses lied. These types of smiles showed the action of the *zygomaticus major*, but also contained facial muscle actions shown when negative emotions such as disgust, anger, or sadness, are displayed. If considered at a surface level, however ("Is this person smiling?"), the differences in the muscle actions would be difficult to detect by an untrained observer.

Ekman has also discussed the embarrassment smile, qualifier smile, coordination smile, Chaplin smile, dampened smile, miserable smile, compliance smile, and listener response smile as variants on this supposedly simple facial action (Ekman, 1985). The picture that emerges is that there is substantial research still called for, especially across cultures, to determine when a smile is just a smile.

> Duchenne, G. B. (1990). *The mechanism of human facial expression or an electro-physiological analysis of the expression of the emotions* (A. Cuthbertson, Trans.). Cambridge, England: Cambridge University Press. (Original work published 1862)
> Ekman, P. (1982). *Emotion in the human face* (2nd ed.). Cambridge, England: Cambridge University Press.
> Ekman, P. (1985). *Telling lies.* New York: Norton.
> Ekman, P., & Friesen, W. V. (1982). Felt, false, and miserable smiles. *Journal of Nonverbal Behavior, 6,* 238-252.
> Ekman, P., Friesen, W. V., & O'Sullivan, M. (1988). Smiles when lying. *Journal of Personality and Social Psychology, 54,* 414-420.
> Frank, M. G., Ekman, P., & Friesen, W. V. (1993). Behavioral markers and recognizability of the smile of enjoyment. *Journal of Personality and Social Psychology, 64,* 83-93.

Le Docteur Duchenne

Research on facial expressions of emotion seems to have a short history. The classic work of Paul Ekman and Wally Friesen, or the late Sylvan Tomkins, or Carroll Izard, took place largely during the 1960s (and continues today). However, a long tradition of studying facial expressions waxed and waned well before that time. For example, a few of the more well-known names associated with this kind of research include: Harold Schlosberg, who developed a scale for measuring facial expressions along two dimensions (1941, 1952); J. P. Guilford, whose interest in facial expressions fed and was fed by an interest in social intelligence (1929, 1930); E. G. Boring and Edward Titchener, certainly no slouches in the history of psychology, who developed a model for demonstrating facial expressions (1923); and most obviously, Charles Darwin, whose *Expression of the Emotions in Man and Animals* ushered in the evolutionary perspective adopted by Ekman, Tomkins, and Izard.

A forgotten name in this history, however, is one G. B. Duchenne de Bologne, a French anatomist who first postulated many of the actions of the facial muscles that produce emotional expressions. Duchenne's book, *Mécanisme de la Physionomie Humaine ou Analyse Électro-Physiologique de l'Expression des Passions, Applicable a la Pratique des Arts Plastiques*, was unique for its time in that it included over 100 photographic plates (illustrating various expressions), each of which had to be pasted into the book by hand. Consequently, few copies of this work were produced at the time, and until Cambridge University Press reissued the book in 1990, copies were available only in a select few libraries throughout the world.

Duchenne's methods for studying the face involved electrical stimulation of the various muscle groups, followed by photography to capture the resulting expression. The main object of his attention was a haggard, toothless, somewhat slow-witted elderly man who apparently did not object too strenuously to having electrical currents course through his face. As Duchenne remarks, "I was able to experiment on his face without causing him pain, to the extent that I could stimulate his individual muscles with as much precision and accuracy as if I were working with a still irritable cadaver" (1990, p. 43). The result of this experimentation was a detailed mapping of the facial musculature, the combinations that produced a variety of emotional and nonemotional expressions, and a corpus of the expressions themselves. This early work was a precursor to more sophisticated facial measurement systems, such as Ekman and Friesen's Facial Action Coding System (FACS; 1978), Izard's Maximally Discriminative Facial Coding System (MAX; 1979), or Hjortsjö's (1970) anatomical system.

Boring, E. G., & Titchener, E. B. (1923). A model for the demonstration of facial expression. *American Journal of Psychology, 34*, 471-485.

Darwin, C. (1872). *The expression of the emotions in man and animals.* London: John Murray.

Duchenne, G. B. (1990). *The mechanism of human facial expression or an electro-physiological analysis of the expression of the emotions* (A. Cuthbertson, Trans.). Cambridge, England: Cambridge University Press. (Original work published 1862)

Ekman, P., & Friesen, W. V. (1978). *Facial Action Coding System (FACS): A technique for the measurement of facial action.* Palo Alto, CA: Consulting Psychologists Press.

Guilford, J. P. (1929). An experiment in learning to read facial expression. *Journal of Abnormal and Social Psychology, 24*, 191-202.

Guilford, J. P., & Wilke, M. (1930). A new model for the demonstration of facial expressions. *American Journal of Psychology, 42*, 436-439.

Hjortsjö, C. H. (1970). *Man's face and mimic language.* Lund, Sweden: Student-Litteratur.

Izard, C. E. (1979). The maximally discriminative facial movement coding system (MAX). Unpublished manuscript. University of Delaware.

Schlosberg, H. (1941). A scale for the judgment of facial expressions. *Journal of Experimental Psychology, 29*, 497-510.

Schlosberg, H. (1952). The description of facial expressions in terms of two dimensions. *Journal of Experimental Psychology, 44*, 229-237.

Expression and Sensory Restriction

Chapter 8 briefly mentions that "children who are born deaf and blind use the same facial expressions as other children do to express the same emotions." This observation bolsters the universalist position on facial expressions and works against the culture-learning view. Because these children have limited avenues for social learning within a particular culture their facial expressions must reflect innate aspects of emotional experience.

This approach to the universalist/culture-specific debate actually got its start with Darwin. As was his custom, Darwin collected informal observations of behavior from colleagues around the world, and part of this evidence was that blind children seemed to "blush with shame" and show other expressions in a manner similar to sighted children. Empirical research on this topic was conducted well before the innate-versus-acquired debate developed in the 1960s. For example, Florence Goodenough observed a 10-year-old girl who had been blind and deaf from birth, noting that she would show surprise when something unexpected happened, display sadness when a favorite toy was taken from her, or laugh and smile when given pleasant things. Jane Thompson built upon this approach, photographing 26 blind children experiencing natural emotional states. When compared to photographs of sighted children in similar circumstances there was remarkable consistency of expression across the 7-week-old to 13-year-old children in the sample. Moreover, raters accurately judged the emotional expressions of both groups of children in about 70 percent of the photographs. Both Freedman and Fulcher continued these types of investigations in subsequent years.

Perhaps the most elaborate study of this type was conducted by Irenäus Eibl-Eibesfeldt, the well-known German ethologist, during the mid-1960s. Eibl-Eibesfeldt took motion pictures of three girls and two boys who were born deaf and blind, and one additional boy deaf and blind from the age of 1½. In addition these children, who suffered a variety of birth defects due to Thalidomide use by their mothers during pregnancy, represented a range of intelligence. Petra and Patrik both had very extensive brain damage (intelligence less than 2 deviations below normal), Beatrice and Heiko had deformed limbs and extensive brain damage (below normal range), and Sabine had no eyeballs and slight brain damage, and Harald, who had contracted meningitis at 18 months, was of average intelligence. After examining the films in slow motion and in thorough detail, Eibl-Eibesfeldt noted that in the case of each child smiling, crying, affection, embracing, frustration, conflict, pouting, distancing, surprise, and frowning could all be clearly seen and in a manner similar to expressions shown by sighted children.

Taken as a whole these studies form a nice complement to research supporting the universalist viewpoint. Eibl-Eibesfeldt's studies in particular demonstrate that even among children who are sensorily restricted, of substantially reduced mental capacity, and with deformed limbs--all factors that work against cultural learning of emotional expression--some innate capacities for expression are clearly exhibited.

Eibl-Eibesfeldt, I. (1970). *Love and hate.* New York: Holt Rinehart and Winston.

Eibl-Eibesfeldt, I. (1973). The expressive behaviour of the deaf-and-blind-born. In M. von Cranach & I. Vine (Eds.), *Social communication and movement* (pp. 163-194). London: Academic Press.

Fulcher, J. S. (1942). "Voluntary" facial expressions in blind and seeing children. *Archives of Psychology, 38*, Whole No. 272.

Freedman, D. G. (1964). Smiling in blind infants and the issue of innate versus acquired. *Journal of Child Psychology and Psychiatry, 5*, 171-184.

Goodenough, F. L. (1932). Expressions of the emotions in a blind-deaf child. *Journal of Abnormal and Social Psychology, 27*, 328-333.

Thompson, J. (1941). Development of facial expression of emotion in blind and seeing children. *Archives of Psychology, 37*, No. 264.

Is Everybody Happy?

Life...liberty...the pursuit of happiness. These goals seem as universal as...well, apple pie, to twist a phrase. But what makes us happy? The editors of *Psychology Today* asked four leading researchers of happiness, or *subjective well-being*, these questions: How do you define happiness? What are the best ways to get there? Who is happy, happier, happiest? What doesn't lead to happiness, that we mistakenly think will? Has the definition of happiness changed significantly over the last few decades? The experts submitted essays exploring these topics, and offered suggestions about the circumstances and experiences that contribute to happiness:

❖ John Reich, Arizona State University, emphasizes a sense of mastery. Our knowledge that we are the cause of the positive events in our lives (and that we can help prevent negative events from happening) contributes to our sense of subjective well-being. Hence, being able to cause positive events, and be successful at them, is an effective path to happiness. Contributing to this are first knowing what truly makes us happy, knowing how to create such events, and finally putting them into action.

❖ Ed Diener, University of Illinois, reminds us that frequency and intensity are the two primary dimensions underlying affectivity. Of those, however, it is the frequency of positive events that plays a more substantial role in producing happiness; in short, many minor pleasures will contribute more to subjective well-being than will the rush of haphazard, intense thrills. Diener also notes some correlates of subjective well-being. For example, women in Western cultures tend to experience more intense emotions than do men. Also, extraversion, self-esteem, and individualism tend to show strong positive associations with happiness. Finally, physical attractiveness and intelligence, long thought to be prime contributors to happiness, generally show only weak correlations with one's state of well-being.

❖ David Myers, Hope College, offers several suggestions for boosting happiness. These include acting happy, seeking work and leisure that are engaging, exercising, maintaining close relationships, pursuing realistic goals, and cultivating feelings of self-esteem, control, and optimism. Myers also advocates interdependence in producing well-being. Rather than the materialistic, individual-centered notions of happiness that prevail, a view of happiness borne from close relationships, meaningful interactions, and giving and receiving social support should be encouraged.

❖ Alex Michalos, University of Guelph, Ontario, suggests that maintaining a range of short-term and long-term goals can contribute to well-being. For example, the short-term pleasure of playing the drums can provide ongoing satisfaction, while the long-term goal of becoming a better professor propels anticipation and motivation. Michalos also points out that the catalog of pleasures seems to have remained unchanged over the years; healthy bodies, productive jobs, peace of mind, and family and friends continue to be mainstays in the pursuit of happiness.

Staff (1994, July/August). The road to happiness. *Psychology Today*, pp. 32-37.

The study of nonverbal gestures and their meaning has received extensive research attention in psychology, sociology, and communication. Through basic research we know a great deal about what gestures convey, how they are culturally variable, and how they act as cues to emotional and other internal states of a communicator. Roger Axtell, former international business executive and now professional speaker and author, has cataloged a variety of gestures and their appropriate uses in cultures around the world. His collection of examples shows clearly that an intended message may not always be communicated successfully. Some common miscommunicated meanings include:

❖ The "two-fingered salute." In most of the contemporary world flashing the index and middle finger in a "V" shape, palm outward, signifies "victory" or "peace" (depending on the vintage of the communicator). However, in England, Australia, and several other countries, a simple turn of the wrist (flashing the sign with the palm toward the communicator) changes this gesture to a highly insulting one: a two-fingered version of our "one-fingered salute."

❖ "The fig." Brazilians clench their fists with a thumb jutting between the index and middle fingers to signal good luck and help in warding off evil spirits. In Greece and Turkey, however, this same gesture is quite insulting, whereas in Holland and Tunisia it has sexual connotations.

❖ "Hook 'em Horns." Texans, especially Austinites, know that an outstretched index and pinky finger signal a cheer for the University of Texas Longhorns to do well on the playing field. This same gesture signals a curse in Africa, a good luck sign in Brazil, and an Italian chide that the recipient is being cuckolded.

❖ Signaling that someone is "crazy" can take on a variety of forms. In Germany it is done by rotating the forefingers back and forth around one's temples. Italians send the same message by tapping their hands to their foreheads. To complicate matters, in Holland a forefinger to the temple means "intelligent" whereas a forefinger to the forehead signals "crazy." The common North American gesture of a circular motion around the temple actually signals "There's a phone call" among Argentineans.

❖ "Nice job!" Flashing a "thumbs up" to a friend usually signals that the person has done well or that the communicator wishes good luck. In Australia, however, it is considered the equivalent of the "two-fingered salute" discussed above, whereas in Japan it signals "five," in Germany it indicates "one," and in Bangladesh it is considered obscene.

❖ "Pointing" is accomplished in North America and Europe by using the index finger. In Malaysia the thumb is preferred, whereas in Japan and China an open hand is used.

❖ The "hand sweep." Moving one's hand and arm across a table in a sweeping motion signals "someone is stealing" in Latin American countries. In Peru, this same gesture means "pay me."

❖ Extending the palm of the hand toward someone might be a way of saying "no more" or "no thanks." In Greece, however, it is an extremely insulting gesture mimicking shoving dirt (and other brown matter) into someone's face.

Axtell, R. E. (1991). Gestures: The do's and taboos of body language around the world. New York: Wiley.
Ekman, P., & Friesen, W. V. (1969). The repertoire of nonverbal behavior: Categories, origins, usage, and coding. Semiotica, 1, 49-98.
Ekman, P., & Friesen, W. V. (1972). Hand movements. Journal of Communication, 22, 353-374.

demonstrations

Gender Differences in Body Image

Eating disorders such as anorexia and bulimia have often been traced, at least in part, to people's perceptions (and misperceptions) of their body image. Caroline Schacht and her colleagues (1993) suggest the following exercise to help increase students' awareness of their own body image and also to explore gender differences in body image. Copy and distribute to your students Handout 9-1, which contains the Body Attitude Questionnaire. Explain to students that their responses are anonymous (and should contain no identifying information except gender) and thus they should try to respond as honestly and accurately as possible. After students have completed the questionnaire, collect their responses and either tally them on the board or share a sample of the responses with the class. Class discussion should focus on differences between the responses of men and women and the implications these differences have for self-esteem, gender identity, eating disorders, and sexual behavior. [See also the related *Lecture Suggestion* in this chapter.]

Schacht, D., Knox, D., & McCammon, S. L. (1993). Instructor's manual with test bank to accompany *Choices in sexuality* by S. L. McCammon, D. Knox, and C. Schacht. Minneapolis/St. Paul: West Publishing Company. (Originally adapted from an idea submitted to the authors by Clayton Hewitt, Middlesex Community College, Middletown, Connecticut).

Debate: Is Body Chemistry the Major Determinant of Eating Behavior?

Chapter 8 notes that hunger, a primary motive, is driven by a biological need for nutrition yet is also influenced by cues in the environment. Although both physiological and environmental factors undoubtedly play a role in eating behavior, there is some debate about the relative influence of these two variables. On the one hand are scientists who argue that eating behavior (including food preferences, eating disorders, and weight problems) is primarily determined by neurochemicals in the brain. On the other hand are scientists who stress that psychological factors (e.g., stress, social norms) play a crucial role in eating behavior as well. This debate has a variety of interesting implications that range from understanding the causes of eating disorders and obesity to how they should best be treated to how the stigma attached to being overweight might be changed. Use the debate procedures suggested at the beginning of this manual (or develop your own) and assign students to research and defend both sides of this issue. *Taking Sides* contains excellent articles both pro and con on this topic (see Issue 2), or you may want to assign articles of your own (or students') choosing.

Slife, B. (1994). *Taking sides: Clashing views on controversial psychological issues* (8th ed.). Guilford, CT: Dushkin Publishing Group.

Debate: Do Evolutionary and Genetic Factors Determine Our Sexual Behaviors?

Evolutionary psychology is a theme that runs throughout the textbook, and is particularly relevant in Chapter 8. Reproductive success forms a large part of the evolutionary perspective, and in turn sexual relations form the basis of reproductive success. But the forces that drive our sexual behaviors are far from agreed upon. In particular, the role of evolutionary or genetic factors in shaping our sexuality has become a matter of some debate. One argument suggests that an evolutionary perspective can help explain complex behaviors such as monogamy, mate selection, and child-rearing. A different perspective suggests that evolutionary explanations ignore the advantages of more proximal explanations for the same behavior. Issue 5 of *Taking Sides* provides a starting point for your students to explore this topic and formulate arguments on both sides of this debate.

Slife, B. (2000). *Taking sides: Clashing views on controversial psychological issues* (11th ed.). Guilford, CT: Dushkin Publishing Group.

Guest Lecture: Sexual Orientation Panel Discussion

Any discussion of diversity would be incomplete without a consideration of sexual orientation. Gays, lesbians, and bisexuals are often discriminated against, yet their status as recipients of discrimination has historically been overlooked. For a powerful and unforgettable class discussion, arrange for a discussion panel of gays, lesbians, and bisexuals to come and speak to your class. Your campus may have a gay and lesbian student organization that could provide you with potential panelists, or your city or community may have such a group. Many big cities, for example, have a Gay, Lesbian, and Bisexual Speakers Bureau that supplies presenters to a variety of organizations; check your local yellow pages. Panelists typically share personal stories (e.g., how they came out to friends and relatives, experiences with homophobia or harassment) and discuss a wide variety of topics, including religious issues, gay relationships, parenting aspirations, and what life is generally like for a gay, lesbian, or bisexual. Much of the time in these sessions is usually spent in a question and answer session, and students really appreciate the chance to ask a wide variety of questions and get honest, first-hand answers. Students typically find these discussions to be enlightening and of great interest, and both panelists and students report them to be helpful in reducing prejudicial attitudes.

Anne Dineen suggests a few helpful tips to keep in mind. (1) Plan ahead; contact speakers well in advance of the presentation, and be sure to inform them of relevant issues that have been discussed and how their presentation might best fit in with your course. (2) Try to have an equal number of males and females on the panel (and from a variety of occupations, if possible). (3) Be sure to allot plenty of time for questions; one recommended format is to have panel members tell their personal stories at the beginning of the session and then use the remainder of the period for questions and discussions. And finally, (4) Have your students read beforehand the information about gay, lesbians, and bisexuals presented in Handout 9-1.

Dineen, A. (1995). The use of sexual orientation panel discussions in the teaching of psychology. Paper presented at the 17th National Institute on the Teaching of Psychology, St. Petersburg Beach.

Heterosexual Privilege

Much more subtle than outright hostility toward gays and lesbians but damaging nonetheless are heterosexist attitudes. Because our society is predominately heterosexual, many people take being in the majority, and the rewards and privileges it affords, for granted. Homosexuals, who as members of the minority do not wield much social and political power, do not have this luxury. Many of the most basic privileges denied to homosexuals are taken for granted by heterosexuals: being able to talk openly about one's partner without fear of recrimination or abuse, being able to publicly display affection toward one's partner, obtaining employment benefits from a partner's job, serving openly in the military or corporate settings, being able to legally document a relationship commitment or to adopt children, and even being able to engage in private sexual behavior without fear of criminal penalties. For most homosexuals, simply taking one's relationship partner to a party or having that person's picture on one's desk is a social privilege that is denied. Heterosexism is a somewhat controversial but intriguing topic to explore with your students. To aid in the discussion, photocopy and distribute to students (or project on a transparency) Handout 9-2, which contains a humorous and widely-circulated scale developed by Martin Rochlin. This scale turns the tables on the usual question of "What causes *homosexuality*?" and in doing so illustrates how hypocritical and one-sided attitudes toward gays, lesbians, and bisexuals often are. Rochlin has been using this popular questionnaire in lectures and in conferences as a consciousness-raising tool since 1972.

Simoni, J. M. (1996). Confronting heterosexism in the teaching of psychology. *Teaching of Psychology, 23*, 220-226.

Exploring the Motives of Everyday Behavior

The text discusses several different categories of motives, including biological motives or drives (such as hunger, thirst, and sex), stimulus motives (such as exploration and curiosity, manipulation, and contact) and learned motives (including aggression, achievement, affiliation, and power). Bill Hill (1995) suggests an activity that is designed to get students to explore these various sources of motivation by examining their own behavior. Ask students to take out a sheet of paper and to write down 25 specific things that they did over the last 24 hours. For example, they might write down items such as getting out of bed, walking to class, having lunch, watching TV, or brushing their teeth. After giving them about 5 minutes to complete their list, explain that you now want them to categorize their behaviors into one of the three types or sources of motivation, biological, stimulus, or learned. When they have completed this task, lead the class in a discussion of the difficulties they may have had in identifying the motive for some of the behaviors, asking class members to share some behaviors they had difficulty categorizing.

Hill, W. G. (1995). Instructor's resource manual for *Psychology* by S. F. Davis and J. J. Palladino. Englewood Cliffs, NJ: Prentice Hall.

Identifying Human Motives Using Maslow's Hierarchy

Gray and Gerrard (1981) described an activity that helps student identify behaviors that are be related to different levels of Abraham Maslow's hierarchy of needs. After you've discussed Maslow's hierarchy, photocopy and distribute to students copies of Handout 9-3 and go over the instructions with them. Give students about 5 minutes to complete the exercise and then ask volunteers to share their responses (correct answers are given below). You can then use the students' responses to help clarify and elaborate on Maslow's theory.

Answers to the Motives Questionnaire:

1. Psychological Need
2. Belonging Need
3. Self-actualization Need
4. Esteem Need
5. Safety Need
6. Esteem Need
7. Esteem Need

Gray, W. A., & Gerrard, B. A. (1981). Understanding yourself and others: A student activity book of psychological experiments and activities. New York: Harper & Row.

Smile When You Say That

Chapter 8 includes a brief discussion of language and emotion, focusing on cultural differences for describing affective states. But language and emotion are linked in another way, one that capitalizes on the metaphors we use for feeling states.

Several researchers, such as linguist George Lakoff, cognitive psychologist Andrew Ortony, or social psychologist Klaus Scherer, have noted the bond between the experience of emotion and the way we describe it to others. As just one example, when we're *angry* we feel ready to *blow up*, our *blood is boiling*, and we need to *let off steam*. In other words, we're likely to do a *slow burn* whenever we're *hot under the collar*. Understandably, we'd have a *short fuse* if we were *hotheaded*, although eventually we'd *simmer down* once we'd stopped *fuming*. These metaphors are not accidental; the internal experience of anger is marked by a kind of agitated increase in internal pressure, much like the lid of a boiling pot bouncing up and down on a hot stove. In fact, George Lakoff and Zoltán Kövecses have detailed the many metaphors we use for anger. Anger is an internal pressure (*bursting a blood vessel; eyes popping out*), a particular area of the visible spectrum (*seeing red; red in the face*), an interference (*can't see straight; blind with rage*), an explosion (*hit the roof; blew my top; flipped my lid*), a dangerous animal (*snarling; hackles up; bite my head off*), and, apparently, a precursor to insanity (*fit to be tied; tearing my hair out; climbing the walls; foaming at the mouth; driving me crazy*). The same can be said for other emotions: The metaphors we use for fear, sadness, happiness, surprise, and disgust try to capture the internal experience of those emotions.

Have your students generate examples such as those just listed. As a start, consider how and when we talk about being *cool, calm, and collected*, or what *gag me with a spoon* is meant to convey, or why we're *frozen* with fear, *dumb* with surprise, and *jumping* for joy. To make the activity more involved, have students work in small groups to categorize the metaphors within each emotion, as Lakoff and Kövecses did for anger.

This activity can be a nice lead-in to talking about cultural similarities and differences in emotional experience (i.e., ask your bilingual students for other similar idioms and their meanings), or about the physiological components of emotion. It's difficult to measure exactly what the body's doing when various emotions are experienced, but our language can give us some insights: *Boiling blood* is unlikely to describe the experience of great happiness!

Lakoff, G., & Johnson, M. (1980). *Metaphors we live by*. Chicago: University of Chicago Press.
Lakoff, G, & Kövecses, Z. (1983). The cognitive model of anger inherent in American English. *Berkeley Cognitive Science Report, 10*.
Ortony, A., Clore, G. L., & Collins, A. (1988). *The cognitive structure of emotions*. Cambridge: Cambridge University Press.

Channels of Communication

Nonverbal behavior is often taken for granted, probably because it occurs so effortlessly in our interactions that we fail to notice it. It provides such a valuable aspect of communication, however, that it is definitely noticed when it is missing. You can illustrate the importance of nonverbal behavior to your students with a simple demonstration.

Start by drawing a simple dichotomy between verbal channels of communication and nonverbal channels. The verbal channel is easy; it is the words used, or perhaps a transcript of them. Ask your students to list the nonverbal channels of communication as you write them on the blackboard. The first response will usually be a generic "body language," but tell them to be more specific; body language is a catch-all term incorporating many nonverbal channels. In short order you should find that students list facial expressions, eye contact, vocal cues (mainly tone of voice), and gestures, and with a little prodding they will add touch, interpersonal distance, speech dysfluencies, posture, gait, or appearance (such as hair or clothing style) as ways of communicating nonverbally. Seeing the board fill up with one verbal means of communication and 5 to 8 nonverbal channels will illustrate clearly the importance of nonverbal behavior.

After generating these ways of communicating, illustrate what kind of information each adds to a message. This will take some acting on your part, but it is easy to master with a little practice. Start by saying a very emphatic message ("I'm absolutely thrilled to be here today!") while keeping all other channels of communication constant. In other words, hold your body perfectly still (arms at your side), keep a neutral facial expression, and say the words in a monotone. It should be clear that although the verbal channel is quite enthusiastic, the nonverbal channels belie the impact of the message. Next repeat the message, adding the appropriate vocal inflections and tone cues, but keeping all other channels constant. Add a happy facial expression in the next iteration, and finally repeat the gushing message with inflection, a happy face, and a broad sweep of your arms. Your students will get the idea that words actually "say" very little; most of this message is carried by other channels.

A variation on this idea is suggested by Richmond and McCroskey, focusing on the vocal channel. You can demonstrate this yourself or by enlisting the help of 4 or 5 students willing to ham it up in front of the class. Consider the following phrases: "Gee, thanks," "This turned out to be a fine day," "I just love it when you do that," "Way to go, dude," "I would like nothing better," "Wow, this is fun," "Wonderful," "That's my favorite," "Truly awesome," "Real nice," "This stinks," and "Rhonda's a real winner, isn't she?" Ask your students to say each phrase using a variety of vocal styles, and have the class comment on the change in meaning that results. In each case the most obvious difference will come from the use of sarcasm, where the vocal inflection runs opposite to the verbal content. But many of these phrases (as well as others you might generate that are more specific to your university or to your class) can carry other meanings as well. For example, "Real nice" can convey sarcasm, sincerity, or sexuality depending on how it is delivered. Like the facial expression demonstration described earlier, these are fun and easy ways to introduce the topic of nonverbal behavior.

Richmond, V. P., & McCroskey, J. C. (1995). *Nonverbal behavior in interpersonal relations* (3rd ed.). Needham Heights, MA: Allyn and Bacon.

Vocal Cues and Emotion

Several of your students have probably heard "I love you" said to them in a way that meant anything *but* the connotation of those words. Words are the meat and potatoes of oral communication, but paralanguage adds the spice. "I love you" could be the prelude to a breakup, a response made out of fear, a drunken slur between friends, a statement of empathy, or the expression of a genuine sentiment. Vocal cues, such as inflection, tone, speech rate, or pitch, convey much of the meaning behind words.

Your students can demonstrate this with a simple exercise, borrowed from Richmond and McCroskey. Ask students to stand at the front of class in pairs, and tell them that their job is to communicate different emotional states to one another. (You might have one pair demonstrate this for the rest of the class, or use different pairs of people for different sets of emotions, or have partners within a pair trade-off.) Here are the rules. First, the students must stand back-to-back, facing away from one another. Second, the person communicating the emotion is allowed to use only one statement: "These pretzels are making me thirsty." Hearing this phrase only, it is the partner's job to guess each of the following emotions:

anger	excitement	dejection	disgust	joy
concern	affection	protection	pleasure	sadness
fear	sympathy	love	frustration	hate

Given the restrictions of the rules, students often are surprised to find that they guess any of the emotions correctly; in fact, they'll probably identify a significant number of them. That's because the vocal expression of emotion is found in paralinguistic cues rather than the actual speech content. Studies of content-free filtered speech demonstrate that nervousness, anger, sadness, and happiness are the easiest emotions to detect from vocal cues alone, whereas surprise, fear, and love are much more difficult. Have students keep track of the number and type of emotions successfully communicated, and use this as a basis for discussing paralanguage.

Richmond, V. P., & McCroskey, J. C. (1995). *Nonverbal behavior in interpersonal relations* (3rd ed.). Needham Heights, MA: Allyn and Bacon.

Tiny Fast Faces

Collecting people's judgments of facial expressions of emotion in the laboratory is a fairly easy task. Typically, subjects are given clearly visible depictions of faces and ample time to make their judgments. In real life, however, facial expressions must often be judged from greater distances or with very little time. This demonstration examines how recognition accuracy is affected when image size or image duration are changed.

To prepare this demonstration you'll need pictures of facial expressions. One source is Ekman and Friesen's *Unmasking the Face*; pages 175 to 201 contain photographs of facial expressions. Additional sources include textbooks, newspapers or magazines, or posed photographs taken of friends and colleagues. Be sure that the six primary emotions expressed are clear and accurately portrayed.

To demonstrate the effects of image size on judgments use a photocopier to successively reduce the pictures to half-size, quarter-size, or as many increments as you'd like. Next, make transparencies of all the facial expressions and bring them to class. From here you can make the procedure as simple or elaborate as you'd like. For instance, at the simple end you might present one example of each facial expression at original, half-, and quarter-size, varied randomly across the 18 presentations (6 depictions x 3 sizes). More elaborate strategies would include using more image sizes and/or more depictions of each expression. (Ultra-elaborate strategies would involve complete counterbalancing using a double-reverse, triple-hammerlock design...) Be sure to keep the exposure time relatively constant. Your students' task is to simply identify which of the six primary emotions (happiness, sadness, fear, anger, disgust, or surprise) is depicted in each case.

If your students are like the subjects in Paul Ekman, Karen Brattesani, Maureen O'Sullivan, and Wally Friesen's experiment they should have little trouble identifying the faces. These researchers varied image size between one-fifth that of a normal human face to twice the area of a typical human face, and found that little information was lost when subjects viewed the small facial expressions. Similarly, Joe Hager and Paul Ekman demonstrated that at distances between the observer and expressor of 30, 35, 40, or 45 meters, observers could maintain high rates of accuracy. However, this was especially true for the positive affects of happiness and surprise. Interestingly, a man's expression of anger was judged equally well as the positive affects, even at 45 meters. Extrapolating from the data Hager and Ekman estimated that recognition accuracy could be maintained at distances up to 100 meters, beyond the range that hand-propelled weapons could be thrown.

To demonstrate the effects of image duration on judgments choose one set of pictures (i.e., the full-size set or perhaps the half-size set). The presentation of the faces can again be as simple or elaborate as you'd like. At the elaborate end, for example, you could purchase Ekman's *Pictures of Facial Affect* (a set of more than 100 slides of facial expressions) and display them using a timer-driven slide projector. At the simple end, you can re-use the transparencies and develop a quick wrist to cover and uncover the overheads rapidly! In any event, present a series of expressions with a very short duration and have students identify the expressions. If your students are like the subjects in Gilles Kirouac and François Doré's experiment their accuracy should be quite good. Kirouac and Doré varied exposures between 10 and 50 milliseconds and found that 1) as duration increased, accuracy increased; 2) at 40 msec accuracy rates were already in the 60 to 80 percent range, and 3) happiness showed the highest accuracy (about 83 percent) at 30, 40, or 50 msec, whereas disgust showed comparatively worse accuracy (about 60 percent). An earlier study by these authors found accuracy rates in the 80 to 90 percent range using a 10-second exposure time. In short (literally!), brief exposures do not seem to hinder recognition of facial expressions of emotion.

Of course, your students may not be like the subjects in any of these experiments. Examine their accuracy rates for different types of presentations. Discuss with your students why some facial expressions remain easy to identify even from far away or with short durations. What adaptive significance might this have? Why is it more adaptive to be able to recognize the "all is well" message of a smile or the "I'm going to kill you" message of anger from a greater distance, than it is the "I'm in distress" message of a sadness expression?

Hager, J. C., & Ekman, P. (1979). Long-distance transmission of facial affect signals. *Ethology and Sociobiology, 1,* 77-82.

Ekman, P. (1976). *Pictures of facial affect.* Palo Alto, CA: Consulting Psychologists Press.

Ekman, P., Brattesani, K. A., O'Sullivan, M., & Friesen, W. V. (1979). Does image size affect judgments of the face? *Journal of Nonverbal Behavior, 4,* 57-61.

Ekman, P., & Friesen, W. V. (1975). *Unmasking the face.* Englewood Cliffs, NJ: Prentice Hall.

Kirouac, G., & Doré, F. Y. (1984). Judgment of facial expressions of emotion as a function of exposure time. *Perceptual and Motor Skills, 59,* 147-150.

Facial Expressions of Emotion

For a lively and crowd-pleasing introduction to facial expressions of emotion, perform the following demonstration in your class. Prior to class, write each of the following emotions (along with the given number) on 12 separate index cards.

1. Happiness
2. Desire
3. Surprise
4. Jealousy
5. Disgust
6. Pride
7. Sadness
8. Love
9. Fear
10. Disappointment
11. Anger
12. Relief

After you begin your lecture on emotional expression, explain that you are going to conduct a live demonstration of facial expressions, and that you need 12 students to volunteer to *pose* or *send* emotions while the rest of the class attempts to *receive* or *decode* them. Solicit 12 student volunteers who aren't shy about posing facial expressions in front of the class (preferably expressive or outspoken people who will "ham it up"), and randomly distribute to each an index card containing the target emotion that they are to pose. Instruct the remainder of the class to number a blank sheet of paper from 1 to 12 and tell them to try to accurately decode the emotion being posed in the facial expression of each volunteer. Remind student senders that they are restricted to facial expressions only, and caution them not to use verbal (e.g., sighs or groans) or postural cues (e.g., slumping) in sending their emotion.

When your 12 volunteers are ready, have them pose their emotions one-by-one (in numerical order), leaving enough time for class members to clearly see each emotion and record their responses. After going through all expressions once, have each volunteer again pose their target expression (this time getting the crowd to share their guesses) and then reveal the correct response. Student should correct their own guesses and count the number of responses correct out of 12. After all volunteers have revealed their target emotion, dismiss them to this seats (preferably with a thundering round of applause to show your appreciation!). Then, review the results with your class and discussion their implications. For each emotion, ask for a show of hands for students who interpreted it correctly. How accurate were their guesses? Were some emotions easier to decode or understand than others? Were some emotions easier to send or pose than others? You should find that students were more accurate at decoding the odd-numbered emotions than the even-numbered ones. Similarly, many volunteers often grumble or show discomfort when trying to send the even-numbered emotions. This is because the odd-numbered emotions (happiness, surprise, disgust, sadness, fear, and anger) are primary emotions associated with universally recognized facial expressions, whereas the others are idiosyncratic and not universally recognizable. Discussion can focus on the origins of universal expressions, accuracy in sending and receiving emotional expressions (including a consideration of gender differences), the role of empathy in understanding others' emotional reactions, and the difficulty and quality of posed vs. spontaneous facial expressions. This exercise can also be introduced in Chapter 16, which considers evidence for the universality of facial expressions in more detail.

Whitford, F. W. (1995). Instructor's resource manual to accompany *Psychology: Principles and applications*, by S. Worchel and W. Shebilske. Englewood Cliffs, NJ: Prentice Hall.

student assignments

Exploring Cross-Cultural Influences on Sexuality

Chapter 8 notes that although human sexual behavior is somewhat affected by hormones and other biological factors, it is profoundly dependent on learning and experience. Nowhere is this more apparent that when one considers the tremendous variation in sexual behavior around the world. Simply put, what is considered *normal* in one culture might be considered *natural* in another, and it is often the case that the same behaviors that are prohibited in one culture are tolerated in another and even expected in yet a third culture. Cross-cultural variations in sexual customs include variations in behaviors, attitudes, and sanctions related to premarital and extramarital sex, incest, menstruation, homosexual behavior, gender roles, contraception use, prostitution, sodomy and oral sex, abortion, polygamy, genital mutilation, public nudity, child molestation, sterilization, interracial sex, transvestitism, and in what people find sexually arousing. For this assignment, ask students to write a research report exploring cross-cultural influences on sexuality. Students should either (a) select one major aspect of sexuality (e.g., childbirth practices, homosexuality, genital mutilation) and discuss how this aspect varies across several different cultures (and why this is the case) or (b) select one culture and discuss a broad range of sexually-related topics in that culture, noting the role and functions that sexuality plays in the lives of people from that culture. If you have time, you might allow students to give oral presentations of their findings to the rest of the class for extra credit.

Schacht, D., Knox, D., & McCammon, S. L. (1993). Instructor's manual with test bank to accompany *Choices in sexuality* by S. L. McCammon, D. Knox, and C. Schacht. Minneapolis/St. Paul: West Publishing Company.

Experiencing Homophobia

Being tolerant and accepting of diversity is somewhat easier to do in principle than in practice, a point made in the *Reducing Prejudice* section of Chapter 15. Research reported in that section also suggests that making people more mindful of people who are different from us may lessen our prejudice of those groups. Indeed, one way to become more mindful of others is to "wear their shoes" for a day or two. Along these lines, Sandra Caron suggests that students can gain valuable insight into the homophobia experienced by gays and lesbians by engaging in any of the simple activities suggested below. Caron stresses that students should resist the temptation to "explain away" their behavior (i.e., if they are perceived as being gay or lesbian) as a class exercise because gays and lesbians do not have this option. Afterward, students should write a short paper about their experience, describing the reactions they received from others as well as their own responses to these reactions. Activities suggested by Caron include: (a) having students carry around a gay-themed book (e.g., *On Being Gay*, by Brian McNaught) or magazine (e.g., *The Advocate*; *Ten Percent*) for a few days, reading it in public (e.g., the library, student union) and leaving it in plain view at home, (b) wearing openly and visibly a button that symbolizes gay pride (e.g., a pink triangle, a rainbow flag, or some pro-gay message such as "Stop Homophobia") and explaining what it means to anyone who asks, (c) publicly challenging (and keeping written notes about) any homophobic jokes or comments made by friends, relatives, strangers, or the media, and (d) attending (with a same sex friend, if possible) some advertised gay and lesbian event (e.g., a speech or rally) and telling everyone you know that you are going.

Schacht, D., Knox, D., & McCammon, S. L. (1993). Instructor's manual with test bank to accompany *Choices in Sexuality* by S. L. McCammon, D. Knox, and C. Schacht. Minneapolis/St. Paul: West Publishing Company.

Icons of Emotional Expression

Examples of universal facial expressions of happiness, sadness, anger, fear, surprise, and disgust, posed on human faces, are scattered throughout Chapter 9. For this assignment, have your students collect examples of these expressions that stand as icons. In other words, ask them to find facial symbols for these six primary emotions from artwork, graphic design, the popular press, and whatever other sources they can find.

Here are some examples of such icons:

- Kabuki masks used in traditional Japanese Noh theater
- Clown faces
- Emoticons used when sending email: :)   :(:| :\   :o   ;>
- The yellow "Have a nice day" smiley button of the 1970s
- "Mr. Yuk," a green anti-smiley sticker warning young children of poisons
- Caricatures
- Warpaint

In each case an emotion is expressed using a minimum of information. For example, a clown's painted face is typically little more than two arching lines above the eyes and lines extending the mouth corners, yet it very clearly expresses happiness. The simplest icon for surprise - two dots for eyes and a circle below them - is recognized immediately.

In completing this assignment have your students focus on questions such as these: What is the minimum amount of information needed to convey an emotion on the face? Do the elements of the icons correspond to the muscle patterns identified by research psychologists? What evolutionary significance is there to being able to identify emotional expressions quickly and accurately? Why are these icons successful for their specific task (e.g., entertainment, warning, advertising)? Your criteria for judging the success of this project should include the creativeness with which students collected icons. For example, students who gathered icons for several different emotions from several different sources should be rewarded more than students who picked only a few obvious examples. Look for themes: Are the examples primarily from art? From advertising? Reward students not for the sheer number of examples they can assemble but for the depth of their thinking regarding the meaning behind the icons.

Icons of Emotional Expression: International Version

As an extension of the previous assignment, discuss with your students the trend in Japanese emoticons. They are more complex (and, finally, in the correct orientation!) than the winks, nods, and leers your students might be familiar with, and they reveal aspects of nonverbal communication in Japanese culture.

- *Basic Smiley Face*   (^_^)   and *Double-byte Smiley*   (^__^)

Keyboards still lack a horizontal character that represents a simple curving smile. The Japanese alternative, however, substitutes a straight line, suggesting that a knowledge of the context in which the message is presented is crucial to understanding the sender's intent.

- *Girl's Smile*   (^.^)

This symbol is more traditionally Japanese, denoting the tendency for girls and young women to cover their mouths when laughing or to smile without baring their teeth.

o *Banzai Smiley* \\(^_^)/   or   \\(^o^)/

These more elaborate emoticons depict someone expressing joy with outstretched arms raised in victory.

o *Cold Sweat* (^ ^;)
o *Excuse Me*   (^o^;>)

Display rules often limit the expression of negative emotions in Japanese culture, such as anger or sadness. The two emoticons depicted above perhaps put the onus of negative affect on the sender. In the first, a bead of cold sweat drips down the "face" of someone who may be nervous, embarrassed, or apologetic. The second symbol depicts someone with his or her hand behind the head (note the "greater-than" bent elbow). An embarrassed or apologetic person may sometimes scratch the back of his or her head.

Your students may be intrigued by these depictions of emotional expressions. They might even find that the cross-cultural communication they allow is *Exciting*   (*^o^*).

(Many more emoticons, expressing both emotions and non-emotions, can be found at the following internet sites:

http://www.computeruser.com/resources/dictionary/emoticons.html
http://www.netlingo.com/smiley.cfm
http://www.muller-godschalk.com/emoticon.html
http://www.windweaver.com/emoticon.htm
http://www.ccim.com/emote.htm

Pollack, A. (1996, August 17). Japanese turn e-mail 'smiley faces' right side up. *Austin American-Statesman*, C1, C5.

The Medium and the Message

Studies of the expression of emotion tend to focus on the face, and for good reason. Although posture and gestures can also communicate, the emotional information they provide tends to be rather gross and undifferentiated. Standing with one's arms crossed, for example, can convey a negative emotional state, but whether it is boredom, impatience, anger, sadness, or fatigue is up for grabs. The face, in comparison, can signal very specific information about specific emotional states.

But what happens when that medium for communication changes? We recognize that facial expressions can change, but how do changes in the face itself affect the clarity of the expressions conveyed? Paul Ekman has written about *static facial features*, or physiognomic characteristics that give the face a perpetual type of look. Some people with particularly pronounced brows, for example, may appear to have an angry expression even when their faces are at rest, or someone with a jowly lower face may appear sad even when he or she isn't. Medical advances, of course, have made it possible to do something about jowls, crow's feet, and unflattering noses, and that is the basis of this assignment.

Have your students investigate this question by collecting examples of famous faces that have changed dramatically. For example, Michael Jackson, Roseanne, Phyllis Diller, and Joan Rivers have all admitted that they've undergone plastic surgery (in some cases, quite extensively). How has this modification to the communication channel (i.e., the face itself) changed the communication of the message (i.e., the facial expressions of emotion)? For example, if one were to look at a photograph of Michael Jackson posing an expression of happiness (i.e., smiling) from 10 years ago, and a similar photograph of him taken recently, what differences would be immediately apparent? Does the expression seem more intense? Better-defined? What about the interaction of the *obicularis oculi* around the eyes and the *zygomaticus major* around the mouth, comparing nipped-n-tucked to pre-nipped-n-tucked? In short, how has changing static facial features changed the interpretation of facial expressions of emotion?

A similar effect can be had by having your students examine photographs of themselves, their parents, or family friends taken recently and taken some time earlier (e.g., 5 or 10 years ago). There should be some changes to static facial features which in turn may affect the expression of emotion. It may be easier for students to collect a greater variety of facial expressions (representing the six primary emotions) from this source.

What your students might conclude is that in some cases the change is very minor, whereas in others it is more dramatic. If they were to examine photographs of themselves taken 5 years ago and taken recently, for example, the most striking differences would no doubt be due to basic maturational processes; baby fat is lost, facial features become more mature, and so on. In the cases of plastic surgery the differences should be more pronounced; let's face it, Roseanne looks like an entirely different person! (and so too might her emotional expressions seem quite different). This assignment will help students to disentangle static facial elements from the emotional expressions themselves, and to see how some elements of expression are truly universal.

Ekman, P., & Friesen, W. V. (1975). *Unmasking the face*. Englewood Cliffs, NJ: Prentice Hall.

Motivation and Emotion in Film

Listed below are several excellent films that can provide students with the opportunity to apply some of the topics discussed in Chapter 8, including hunger and eating, aggression, and of course, Maslow's hierarchy of motives. Ask your students to select one of these films (or, if you prefer, you can assign one of your choosing) and to write a thought paper discussing how motivational concepts from the text and lecture apply to the film.

• *A Clockwork Orange* (1971). Malcolm McDowell stars in this surrealistic glimpse into the future as Alex, a violent, cold-blooded thrill-seeking killer. Once captured by authorities for perpetrating numerous rapes, tortures, and beatings, he is psychologically reprogrammed to become nauseated when he witnesses violence. This film, which is replete with raw aggression and violence, can be analyzed at two different levels: (a) Where do the motives to aggress originate? and (b) What are the consequences (according to social learning theory) of viewing violent movies such as this one? Also psychologically relevant are the intriguing scenes of classical conditioning (Warner; 137 min).

• *Eating* (1990). A group of Southern California women (played by Nelly Allard, Frances Bergen, Mary Crosby, Lisa Richards, Gwen Welles, and Dapha Kastner) gathered for a birthday party talk about themselves and their favorite subject --eating -- while lounging around the poolside. Henry Jaglom's unusual but very entertaining film explores the physical, sensual, and psychological aspects of eating in glorious detail (Paramount Home Video; 110 min).

• *Gaby: A True Story* (1981). Uplifting true story of Gabriela Brimmer (played by Liv Ullman), a young woman born with severe cerebral palsy which affected nearly her entire body--but not her brain. Gaby's titanic struggle to overcome physical limitations, emotional pain, and societal obstacles on the way to becoming a famous writer is an inspirational demonstration of both the need-drive-response model of motivation and Maslow's hierarchy of motives (Columbia/TriStar; 115 min).

• *The Karate Kid* (1984). Ralph Macchio stars as the new kid in town who is bullied around by a gang of local street toughs. Forced to defend himself, he learns karate from his apartment complex's Japanese gardener (Pat Morita), a self-actualized elderly gent whose teaching prowess and gracious approach to life help Daniel climb Maslow's pyramid of motives. Provides a dramatic enactment of Maslow's hierarchy; students should have no problem identifying scenes that illustrate each level (Columbia/TriStar; 126 min).

video

ABC News/Prentice Hall Video Library

Sex for Sale (14 min, Series III). It's been called the world's oldest profession, but as this *20/20* segment shows, prostitution is becoming more professional every year. There is a move afoot in several quarters to legalize prostitution; this video segment examines the issues involved in that decision.

So Angry You Could Die (11 min, Series III). This *20/20* segment presents people on the edge, and some who are well past it. A variety of stress-related illnesses are linked to anger (and its inappropriate expression); this brief video piece explores ways to ward them off by reducing hostile responses to the world.

You Have to Be Perfect (10 min, Series III). What happens when "good enough" isn't good enough? This *20/20* segment looks at a handful of people for whom the quest for perfection has taken on life-altering proportions. The psychological, behavioral, and health consequences of perfectionism are explored from a series of first-person accounts.

Other Sources

Advertising Alcohol: Calling the Shots (30 min, CAM). A critical unveiling of the persuasion tactics used by the alcohol industry.

An Anorexic's Tale: The Brief Life of Catherine (80 min, FHS). The docu-drama explores Catherine Dunbar's unsuccessful struggle with an eating disorder. A 7-year downward spiral led from obsession to addiction to death at 40 pounds.

Body Language: An Introduction to Nonverbal Communication (1994, 25 min, LS). This video presents an overview of kinesics, personal distance, eye contact, and the interpretation of gestures. Cross-cultural nonverbal miscommunication is also examined (in the spirit of Roger Axtell's book mentioned in the lecture suggestion above). An accompanying booklet includes summaries of the key points on the tape and suggestions for further activities. This video is very well produced, although the pacing and level of presentation may make it more appropriate for use in a high school or community college course.

Crime and Human Nature (28 min, FHS). It's a small step from discussing "motives for aggression" to discussing "crime and human nature." This video facilitates that discussion as host Phil Donahue asks anthropologist Ashley Montagu and others to share their thoughts on this subject.

Date Rape (52 min, FHS). This docu-drama takes the viewer from start to finish in the investigation and criminal proceedings of a rape, using both actors and real-life law enforcement officials. This powerful demonstration shows the legal, emotional, and interpersonal impact of this crime.

The Differences Between Men and Women (23 min, FHS). Nature versus nurture is invoked to examine (and sometimes explain) the behavioral and cognitive differences between women and men. A discussion of recent research on sex differences in the brain is also included.

Discovering Psychology, Part 12: Motivation and Emotion (1990, 30 min, ANN/CPB). Distinguishes between emotion and motivation and describes how they interact. Biological and psychological aspects of motivation are examined through research on sexual behavior and optimistic beliefs.

Dying To Be Thin (28 min, FHS). A young woman obsessed with the desire to be thin is profiled; repeated hospitalization and years of therapy have begun to offer solutions. The general problems of bulimia and anorexia are presented.

Emotion (1990, 28 min, IM). The universality of emotional expressions is demonstrated by Paul Ekman, including a discussion of his general research program. Carol Tavris discusses the nature of anger and effective ways to manage and deal with that emotion.

Face Value (38 min, FLI). Cross-cultural comparisons of facial expressions of emotion are presented, and the link between the physiology of the face and emotion is explored.

The Impact of Violence on Children (28 min, FHS). This recent film could be used as an "applied" example when discussing aggression. The presentation looks at sources of violence that affect children and causes of that violence.

The Interpersonal Perception Task (40 min, UC). Thirty brief video segments are presented, and viewers must decode the nonverbal behavior in each. Themes of deception, status, kinship, intimacy, and competition are represented. More information can be found in Costanzo, M., & Archer, D., 1991, A method for teaching about verbal and nonverbal communication, *Teaching of Psychology, 18*, 223-226.

Motivation (1990, 30 min, IM). Examines factors influencing motivation including curiosity, need for achievement, and intrinsic and extrinsic rewards. The program also addresses cognitive, learning, and biological theories of motivation and summarizes Maslow's hierarchy.

Questions About Behavior (24 min, PENN). Illustrates the role of instincts in behavior through Niko Tinbergen's research with the male stickleback fish.

Pleasure (23 min, FHS). The many paths to pleasure are traveled, including exercise, sex, pain, effort, and the pleasures of the senses.

Rape: An Act of Hate (30 min, FHS). The history, mythology, causes, and consequences of rape are the topic of this video. Interviews with survivors, case workers, and legal experts provide a range of viewpoints.

Sex Hormones and Sexual Destiny (26 min, FHS). Examines the role of hormones on "masculine" and "feminine" behavior, sex differences in brain structure, and environmental influences on male and female behavior.

Street Gangs of Los Angeles (44 min, FHS). As a manifestation of aggression and aggressive motives, gang life comes chillingly close to home in this video. A look at the thrills and dangers of hanging with a set in the gang capital of the U.S.

The Truth About Lies (60 min, PBS). Deception in childhood, in the family, in daily interactions, and at a national level. From the *Bill Moyers: The Public Mind* series.

Violence By and Against Latinos (28 min, FHS). In the context of a recent drive-by shooting, efforts to help school-age victims of crime in understanding their fear and insecurity are discussed. The effects of the Los Angeles riots on various immigrant groups are also considered.

multimedia

Live! Psych

Module	Title	Book Page #
9.1	Name That Emotion!	p. 351

Screen 1 introduces the idea that facial expression is an important nonverbal communication tool we use in our everyday social interactions. In Screen 2, students click and drag emotional labels to the corresponding facial expressions, such as surprise, disgust, happiness, sadness, anger and fear.

Web Investigations

Exploring Academic Dishonesty

Prior to reading this chapter, if someone asked your students "Why do we eat?" they probably would have responded, "Because we are hungry, of course!" Now they know that we eat because the activity of hunger centers in the hypothalamus, contributing to our subjective sense of being hungry. However, other factors enter into the motivation mix, including olfactory cues, emotional states, social influences and cultural factors. Even "simple" acts like eating often have a complex web of factors that influence them. Such is the nature of motivation, or "...forces that arouse the organism and direct its behavior towards a goal." Psychology has attempted to understand these forces throughout its history, especially for actions we find problematic or troubling. For example, a more complete understanding of why individuals aggress might lead to effective ways to reduce the rates of aggression in our society.

One problematic activity on college and university campuses is cheating. Although cheating on exams and papers is an activity that should be discouraged, the forces that contribute to cheating offer insights into the phenomenon of motivation. It is an interesting issue to examine, because although most individuals condemn cheating and many institutions have serious sanctions against it, some students nonetheless cheat. This *Web Investigation* examines these issues and asks your students to evaluate definitions of cheating and to assess various measures for dealing with academic dishonesty.

Making Connections

Perspectives on Motivation

Q How does instinctive behavior differ from learned behavior?

A Instinctive behavior is inborn and is characteristic of an entire species, whereas learned behavior is acquired and may differ from one individual to another.

Q What is homeostasis?

A Homeostasis is a state of balance in which bodily needs have been satisfied.

Q According to arousal theory, what motivates behavior?

A According to arousal theory, behavior is motivated by the desire to maintain an optimum level of arousal at any given time.

Q How do intrinsic and extrinsic motivation differ?

A Intrinsic motivation comes from an activity that is engaged in for its own sake. Extrinsic motivation comes from an outside source and is provided as a consequence of an activity.

Hunger and Thirst

Q Explain the biological processes involved in the experience of hunger.

A Hunger occurs in response to three sets of stimuli: (a) changes in the blood levels of glucose that signal the need for food; (b) signals from receptors in the stomach that sense how much food is present; and (c) a hormone released by the small intestine. These stimuli are interpreted by centers in the hypothalamus that control eating behavior.

Q Describe some ways in which culture influences the perception of hunger.

A Culture influences the perception of hunger by establishing specific times when it is appropriate to eat and identifying particular foods that are "good" or "bad."

Q What are the differences between bulimia and anorexia nervosa?

A Anorexia is characterized by refusal to eat, whereas bulimia is characterized by binge eating followed by self-induced vomiting.

Q Describe how both internal and external cues regulate thirst.

A Internal cues regulate thirst by signaling the need to replace fluid both within and outside the cells. External cues such as seasonal customs and weather conditions can also stimulate thirst.

Sex

Q Briefly describe the biological factors that affect the human sex drive.

A The biological factors that affect the sex drive include (a) the hormone testosterone, which plays a role in sexual development, the differentiation of male and female sex organs, and establishing patterns or sexual behavior; (b) pheromones, substances that influence sexual attraction; and (c) the limbic system, which is involved in sexual excitement.

Q Explain how culture and experience affect the human sex drive.

A Culture affects the sex drive by guiding a person's view of sexual attractiveness. Experience plays a role because different people learn to be stimulated by different environmental conditions.

Q What is known about the origins of homosexuality?

A The causes of homosexuality are unclear. There is some evidence that genetic factors may play a role and that there are differences between the brains of homosexual and heterosexual men. On the other hand, the argument that sexual orientation is determined by early socialization is supported by cross-cultural research. It is likely that both biological and environmental factors play a role.

Other Motives

Q What is curiosity? What factors cause this motive to vary in humans?

A Curiosity is the desire to know something. It varies according to an individual's creativity and his or her familiarity with events and circumstances.

Q What evidence supports the existence of a need for contact?

A Evidence of the need for contact can be seen in experiments showing that when forced to choose between contact and food, baby monkeys will choose contact. Other evidence comes from the fact that premature infants who are held gain weight faster than those who are seldom touched.

Q What does it mean to state that the interpretation of what is aggressive depends on a person's culture and gender?

A Culture establishes norms and values, and these influence whether a person will view a particular action as aggressive. Gender plays a role because males are more likely than females to behave aggressively.

Q Describe the characteristics of people with strong achievement motivation.

A People with strong achievement motivation are fast learners, relish unique and challenging tasks, are self-confident, willingly take on responsibility, and do not readily bow to social pressures.

Q What evidence suggests that the affiliation motive has an evolutionary basis?

A Evidence that the need for affiliation has an evolutionary basis may be seen in the fact that cues that signal danger, such as illness or catastrophe, appear to increase the desire to be with others. Moreover, children who stay with adults instead of wandering away are more likely to survive and ultimately reproduce.

Q According to Maslow, what needs must be met first?

A According to Maslow, basic needs related to survival must be met before higher needs can be addressed.

Emotion

Q What is the difference between primary and secondary emotions?

A Primary emotions are shared by all people regardless of culture; secondary emotions are found in one or more cultures but not in all cultures.

Q Summarize the main tenets of Zajonc's theory of emotions.

A According to Zajonc, feelings occur before cognition. We respond immediately to situations and then invent explanations to label our feelings.

Communication of Emotion

Q Give an example of how voice quality can express emotion.

A Voice quality can express emotion by emphasizing words that would not be stressed in normal speech.

Q What do children born deaf and blind reveal about facial expressions?

A Deaf and blind children exhibit the same facial expressions as other children, showing that these expressions are innate, not learned.

Q Define personal space.

A Personal space is the distance people maintain between themselves and others.

Q How accurate are our estimates of our skill at interpreting nonverbal skills?

A We tend to overestimate our ability to interpret nonverbal cues.

Gender and Culture and Emotion

Q Describe some basic differences and similarities in the expression of emotion in men and women.

A While men and women may experience similar degrees of emotional arousal, men are more likely to inhibit the expression of their emotions. Men and women also tend to react to the same situation with different emotions. In addition, whereas men turn their anger outward, women are more likely to turn it against themselves.

Q What is the "universalist" position, and what is its opposite?

A The universalist position holds that in all cultures the fact looks the same whenever certain emotions are expressed. Its opposite is the culture-learning position, which holds that facial expressions of emotion are learned and therefore may differ from one culture to another.

Video Classics

Skinner on Needs and Motives

SYNOPSIS: In this interview segment B. F. Skinner discusses how reinforcement affects needs and how various motives can be explained. Predictably, Skinner argues that concepts such as achievement motivation can be accounted for by Behaviorist principles. This clip provides a good illustration of Skinner's commitment to the operant conditioning paradigm.

Form a Hypothesis

Q How do you suppose B.F. Skinner would explain achievement motivation?

A Skinner rejects the concept of need, which underlies McClelland's formulation of need for achievement. Rather, Skinner views achievement motivation as the consequence of selective reinforcement such that acts that would otherwise obtain reinforcement become reinforcing themselves. In other words according to Skinner, people achieve not because of a need or drive, but because achieving is a learned (secondary) reinforcer.

Test Your Understanding

Q Behaviorists seek to influence motivation through the use of rewards and punishments. Reinforcement has been used successfully in the classroom to raise students' achievement behaviors. What are various schedules of reinforcement?

A There are fixed interval, fixed ratio, variable interval and variable ratio schedules. In a fixed schedule, the rules of administration do not change from reinforcer to reinforcer, so a fixed ratio schedule counts the number of behaviors to determine after which behavior a reinforcer is delivered while a fixed interval marks the passage of time before reinforcer eligibility occurs. Variable schedules change the rules of administration from reinforcer to reinforcer but otherwise function like ratio and interval schedules.

Q According to Skinner, how can employers make workers motivated to be highly productive?

A Skinner would put workers on a schedule of reinforcement that promotes productivity. This would ordinarily be a variable ratio schedule, in which a worker would get reinforced after producing 4 items, 15 items, 3 items, 24 items, etc.

Q How do behavioral psychologists and industrial psychologists differ in their assumptions about achievement motivation?

A In general, a behavioral psychologist would examine the environment to create conditions that promote achievement. An industrial psychologist might take a more "clinical" view in that she or he would examine how the individual thought about achievement, what achievement experience she or he experienced, etc. to better understand the individual.

Q According to Skinner, what is the role of reinforcement in achievement?

A It's everything to Skinner. We can reinforce someone to achieve and arrange the contingencies such that the behavior of achieving becomes reinforcing in its own right.

Thinking Critically

Q How do individuals with a high need for achievement differ from those who have a low need?

A High need for achievement individuals typically come from backgrounds in which achievement was valued, expected, and rewarded. They enjoy moderate challenges with a moderate chance of success and tasks that provide accurate feedback about their accomplishments.

Q How has the Thematic Apperception Test (TAT) been used to assess the need for achievement?

A High need for achievement individuals provide stories in response to TAT stimuli that stress accomplishment and success under challenging circumstances.

Skinner on Emotion

SYNOPSIS: Skinner continues his discussion of mysterious internal states by considering the construct of emotion. Not surprisingly, Skinner argues that these things we call emotions are in reality poorly-understood physiological states subject to reinforcement. Skinner incorrectly foresees that distinguishing emotions based on patterns of physiological responses will never succeed (cf. Ekman, Levenson, & Friesen, 1983).

Form a Hypothesis

Q Do you think B.F. Skinner would say emotion is a useful concept? Why or why not?

A No. As a reference to an internal state, Skinner would avoid using the term as it is commonly used. However, Skinner might examine emotional behavior to identify what changes it causes in the social environment and the consequences of these changes.

Test Your Understanding

Q How does Skinner define emotion?

A Skinner offers two definitions in the video segment. Emotion is "an imagined internal state supposed to account for behavior," (his characterization of traditional definitions of emotion. Skinner then defines emotion as a "change in the probability of certain behaviors, defined by certain probabilities."

Q How does Skinner define anger, fear, and love?

A Anger is a change in our likelihood of attacking another. Fear is an increased probability of running away. Love is an increased probability of doing good to another.

Thinking Critically

Q Is Skinner accurate in his characterization of emotion? Why or why not?

A Although Skinner is correct to draw attention to the interpersonal consequences of emotional expression, he neglects the consequences that emotional states have for the individual. People who are happy approach situations more optimistically while sad individuals are less responsive to some of the demands of the environment. Further, research indicates that we tend to seek situations that are consistent with our emotional state. So, emotions do have some causal influence beyond that characterized by Skinner.

Terrycloth Comfort

SYNOPSIS: This silent footage from Harlow's classic experiments on infant monkey attachment summarizes the basic findings regarding terrycloth versus wire surrogate mothers. Although both surrogates provided food (from embedded bottles), the infants preferred the comforts of the terrycloth surrogate. Be warned: when the freaky drumming bear toy makes its appearance, you may become as frightened as the monkey.

Form a Hypothesis

Q Do you think that the newborn monkeys will prefer the cloth "mother" or the wire "mother"?

A Individual monkeys will spend the bulk of their time on the cloth mother, seeking the lactating wire mother only to nurse.

Test your Understanding

Q The newborn monkeys spent almost all of their time with the terrycloth surrogate mother. The wire mother was identical to the cloth mother in all respects except for the ability to provide "contact comfort." Newborn monkeys showed a clear preference for "contact comfort" over food, regardless of the feeding situation. Harlow concluded that contact comfort, not nursing, was the primary variable determining affection for the mother. How do early experiences affect development?

A Harlow reported that infant monkeys deprived of contact comfort were "neurotic" adolescents and adults engaging in fearful behavior and social isolation. Later researchers would report the importance of secure attachment to adult social behavior.

Q What different styles of attachment did Mary Ainsworth identify in her strange-situation test?

A When a stranger entered a room after a child's mother left to return later, children showed three types of reactions. In the avoidant attachment pattern, the child ignores the mother when she is present and shows minimal distress to the stranger. In the resistant attachment pattern, the child shows ambivalence towards the mother and resists attachment when she returns. If she uses the mother for comfort, the child may attempt to pull away after a brief period of time. In the secure attachment pattern, the child shows a preference for the mother when present and may be friendly to the stranger, relying on the mother for security in the strange situation.

Thinking Critically

Q How important is this first relationship?

A Although there is still some debate about the importance of attachment and bonding, most would accept that promoting attachment is sound advice.

Q Does a secure attachment with a mother or father provide a foundation for good relationships with others later in life?

A Yes. There seems to be some advantages enjoyed by securely attached children. Some research shows that securely attached children are viewed more positively during their school years than their avoidant or resistant counterparts.

Interview with Carl Rogers

SYNOPSIS: Rogers discusses gardening, with particular emphasis on growing begonias. Really. But he uses it as a metaphor for concepts such as need for achievement, motivation, striving, and so on. Rogers suggests that relying on these higher-order concepts misleads us from a more basic-level notion: begonias grow because they want to maximize their begonia-ness. The garden's bounty provides a valuable lesson for humanity.

Form a Hypothesis

Q What do you predict Carl Rogers will say is the central aspect of all motivation?

A For Rogers, the central tendency for all motivation is enhancement of the organism. In humans, this tendency is the drive towards self-actualization.

Test Your Understanding

Q How does the humanistic approach to motivation differ from the general theories of motivation (drive theory, arousal theory, and incentive theory)?

A Although in drive, arousal, and incentive theories individuals behave to reduce a drive state, control their arousal levels, or obtain incentives, humanistic approaches assume that the fundamental tendency is the growth of the individual. Achieving one's potential lies at the core of humanistic approaches.

Q How does Maslow's hierarchy relate to human motivation?

A Maslow theorizes that basic needs related to biological survival are met first. Once these are met, individuals are motivated by social and individual well-being. Self-actualization motivates individuals only when 'lower' needs are met.

Thinking Critically

Q According to Abraham Maslow, human beings are motivated to fulfill a hierarchy of needs. What are these needs?

A The progression is: physiological→safety→belongingness→esteem→self-actualization.

Q What need is at the top of Maslow's pyramid?

A Self-actualization.

Web Links

1. http://www.vanguard.edu/faculty/ddegelman/amoebaweb/index.cfm?doc_id=860

AmoebaWeb: Emotion and Motivation. This site presents web resources related to motivation and emotion. Lots of mixed topics, but a good starting place for a variety of viewpoints.

2. http://www.carleton.ca/~tpychyl/

Procrastination Research Group. A history of procrastination, intervention strategies, and related links. Ask your students to visit this site sometime, and tell them you'll make up an assignment some day that you'll collect…later.

3. http://www.popcouncil.org/gfd/scoer/scandrh.html

This website presents research on sexual coercion and reproductive health. Students with questions about these sensitive topics might gather information here in a nonthreatening, anonymous way.

4. http://mambo.ucsc.edu/

Facial Analysis. This site offers pictures, descriptions, and theories of facial expressions of emotion. Follow the mambo.ucsc links to hook up with the larger community of nonverbal behavior researchers.

transparencies

Series V

67. *Maslow's Hierarchy of Needs*
Maslow's steps toward self-actualization are illustrated.

68. *The Yerkes-Dodson Law*
The relationship between arousal and performance is shown.

69. *Three Components of Emotion*
The elements of emotional experience are depicted.

70. *Plutchik's Theory of Emotions*
Plutchik's emotion solid is shown in this transparency.

71. *Theories of Emotion*
James-Lange, Cannon-Bard, and the cognitive theory of emotions are compared.

Text Figures

	9-1.	*Yerkes-Dodson Law*
	9-2.	*Rising Obesity Among American Youth*
	9-3.	*Human Sexual Response*
	9-4.	*Maslow's Hierarchy of Needs*
	9-5.	*Plutchik's Eight Basic Categories of Emotion*
	9-6.	*Plutchik's Three-Dimensional Model of the Eight Basic Emotions*
	9-7.	*Display of Anger in Animal and Human*
	9-8.	*Name That Face*
	9-9.	*The Three Major Theories of Emotion*
	9-10.	*The "Brow-Raise" Greeting*
	9-11.	*Emotion and Brain Activity in Men and Women*

Handout 9-1

Body Attitude Questionnaire

Instructions: The following questions assess your attitudes and perceptions of your body image. Please answer each question as honestly and as accurately as possible. All your responses will remain anonymous, so please do not put any identifying information (except gender) on this questionnaire.

I. My Gender is: (circle one)   Female   Male

II. For each of the following aspects of your body, indicate your satisfaction by writing the appropriate abbreviation in the blank next to the item. Use the following code:

    Very Satisfied **(VS)**
    Satisfied **(S)**
    Unsatisfied **(U)**
    Very Unsatisfied **(VU)**

_____ weight	_____ height	_____ skin
_____ buttocks	_____ abdomen	_____ face
_____ hair	_____ genitals	_____ breasts
_____ hands	_____ arms	_____ legs

III. Complete the following sentences:

1. My best physical feature(s) is (are)...

2. My worst physical feature(s) is (are)...

3. To use my body athletically makes me feel...

4. When I see myself nude in the mirror, my reaction is...

5. To be seen nude by others makes me feel...

6. In general, a word or phrase which best describes my feelings about my body is...

7. If I am engaged in sexual relations, I feel _____ about my body.

Adapted from Schacht, D., Knox, D., & McCammon, S. L. (1993). Instructor's manual with test bank to accompany Choices in sexuality by S. L. McCammon, D. Knox, and C. Schacht. Minneapolis/St. Paul: West Publishing Company. (Originally adapted from an idea submitted to the authors by Clayton Hewitt, Middlesex Community College, Middletown, Connecticut).

Handout 9-2

Identifying Human Motives

Instructions: Identify the specific motive illustrated in the following examples by placing the appropriate abbreviation in the blank next to the item. Use the following code:

Maslow's Hierarchy of Needs:

Self-actualization Needs (SA)
Esteem Needs (ESTEEM)
Belonging Needs (BELONG)
Safety Needs (SAFE)
Biological Needs (BIO)

_____ 1. "Have I got a terrible headache. It's really splitting."

_____ 2. "It gets lonely in my apartment on the weekends. My roommate goes to visit her parents and most of my neighbors are away too."

_____ 3. "I feel really bored by this course. It's a lot like the one I took last year. I was hoping it would be more challenging."

_____ 4. "He really makes me furious. I'm tired of his put-downs! Who does he think he is anyway?"

_____ 5. "Uh, listen, do you mind if we don't go into that nightclub? I hear that some tough types hang out there and that someone got beaten up there last week."

_____ 6. "Hey, guess what? I just got an A+ on my term paper. Pretty good, eh?"

_____ 7. "I've decided to leave home and get an apartment of my own. My parents are upset, but I just want to make it on my own."

Originally appeared in Gray, W. A., & Gerrard, B. A. (1981). *Understanding yourself and others: A student activity book of psychological experiments and activities.* New York: Harper & Row. Used by permission of Prentice Hall.

Chapter 10 Lifespan Development

chapter outline 276

learning objectives 279

lecture suggestions

    Infant Memories? 280
    Object Permanence Changes 280
    Hormones and Toy Preferences 281
    The Consequences of Sexual Abuse 281
    Talk That Talk, Baby 282
    A Picture is Worth a Thousand Words 282
    Gender Roles and Parenting 283
    Is the Potential for Divorce Genetic? 283
    Theories of Physical Aging 284
    The Benefits of Control 285
    Predicting Alzheimer's Disease 286

demonstrations and activities

    Guest Lecturer: Registered Childbirth Educator 287
    Show and Tell 287
    Using Children's Books to Illustrate Developmental Principles 287
    Using Homemade Videotapes 288
    Constructing a Life Line 288
    Illustrating Piagetian Concepts 289
    Moral Development 290
    Debate: Is Television Bad for Children? 290
    Hello Mother, Hello Father 290
    Guest Lecture: Adult Relationships 291
    Adolescence Is 291
    Development Across the Lifespan 291
    Exploring Societal Attitudes about Aging 292
    "Wearing the Shoes" of the Elderly 292

student assignments

    Naturalistic Observation 294
    Constructing a Moral Development Quiz 294
    Dear Daughter/Dear Son 294
    Youth Sports Participation 295
    Media Influences on Gender-Role Development 295
    Adolescence in Film: *The Breakfast Club* 296
    Adolescence and Identity Development 296
    Aging in Film: *To Dance With the White Dog* 297
    Keeping a Psychology Journal 297

video 298

multimedia 302

handout

    Development Across the Lifespan 312

chapter outline

I. Methods in Developmental Psychology
    A. Cross-sectional study: Comparing people of different ages at about the same time
        1. Cohort: A group of people born during the same historical time period
    B. Longitudinal study: Evaluating the same group of people at different points in their lives
    C. Biographical study: Reconstructing people's past through interviews and inference

II. Prenatal Development
    A. Fertilized egg ⊃ Embryo ⊃ Fetus
    B. Critical period when fetus can be affected by teratogens
        1. Fetal alcohol syndrome

III. The Newborn Baby
    A. Reflexes: Rooting, sucking, swallowing, grasping, stepping
    B. Temperament: Easy, difficult, slow-to-warm-up, shy
        1. Infant temperament may predict later disposition
    C. Perceptual abilities
        1. Vision: Newborns are nearsighted
        2. Depth perception
            a. Visual cliff research
        3. Other senses

IV. Infancy and Childhood
    A. Physical development
    B. Motor development
        1. Developmental norms
        2. Maturation: biological processes that unfold as a person grows older
    C. Cognitive development
        1. Piaget's stages of cognitive development
            a. Sensory-motor stage (Birth to 2 years)
            b. Preoperational stage (2 to 7 years)
            c. Concrete operations (7 to 11 years)
            d. Formal operations (11 to 15 years)
        2. Criticisms of Piaget's theory
            a. Refinements and clarifications added to Piaget's original observations
    D. Moral development
        1. Preconventional, conventional, postconventional levels of moral reasoning
    E. Language development: Cooing, babbling, holophrases

1. Theories of language development
    a. Skinner's reinforcement view
    b. Chomsky's language acquisition device
2. Bilingualism and development of a second language

F. Social development
   1. Parent-child relationships in infancy: Development of attachment
       a. Imprinting in nonhuman animals; attachment in humans
       b. Development of autonomy is important
       c. Steps toward socialization
   2. Parent-child relationships in childhood
       a. Authoritarian, permissive, authoritative parenting styles
   3. Relationships with other children: Solitary, parallel, and cooperative play styles
   4. Children in dual-career families

G. Sex-role development
   1. Development of gender identity, gender constancy, gender-role awareness, and sex-typed behavior

H. Television and children: Television's effects on aggression, intellectual development unclear

V. Adolescence

A. Physical changes
   1. Sexual development: Puberty and menarche
   2. Early and late developers
   3. Adolescent sexual activity
   4. Teenage pregnancy and childbearing

B. Cognitive changes
   1. Imaginary audience
   2. Personal fable

C. Personality and social development
   1. How "stormy and stressful" is adolescence?
   2. Forming an identity: Identity achievement, foreclosure, moratorium, identity diffusion
   3. Relationships with peers
   4. Relationships with parents

D. Some problems of adolescence
   1. Declines in self-esteem
   2. Depression and suicide
   3. Youth violence

VI. Adulthood

A. Love, partnerships, and parenting
   1. Forming partnerships

       2. Parenthood

       3. Ending a relationship

   B. The world of work

       1. Dual-career families

       2. Children in dual-career families

   C. Cognitive changes

   D. Personality changes

       1. Midlife crises or midlife transitions?

   E. The "change of life"

VII. Late Adulthood

   A. Physical changes

   B. Social development

       1. Retirement

       2. Sexual behavior

   C. Cognitive changes

       1. Alzheimer's disease

   D. Facing the end of life

       1. Stages of dying

           a. Denial

           b. Anger

           c. Bargaining

           d. Depression

           e. Acceptance

       2. Widowhood

learning objectives

After reading this chapter, students should be able to:

1. Describe research methods used in developmental psychology.

2. Describe the sequential stages of prenatal development.

3. Describe the physical and motor development of the newborn baby, infant, and child.

4. Describe the perceptual development of a baby. How does object perception change? What are some of the factors influencing depth perception in infants?

5. List and describe the four stages of Piaget's theory of cognitive development. Define terms such as object permanence and assimilation.

6. List four factors associated with the social development of a child.

7. List and describe the stages of Kohlberg's theory of moral development.

8. Trace language development from infancy through age 5.

9. Explain critical periods in language development.

10. Explain the importance of secure attachments between a caregiver and child. Describe attachment styles.

11. Summarize the important physical changes that the adolescent undergoes during puberty.

12. Describe the cognitive development of adolescents.

13. Describe the sequence of social development from the start of adolescence though young adulthood.

14. Identify the central concerns and crises that characterize the young, middle, and late adulthood stages.

15. Summarize the physiological changes that people undergo as they age.

16. Identify the changes in cognitive development that people undergo as they age.

17. Summarize the differences in the ways men and women in young, middle, and later adulthood approach friendship, marriage, sexuality, parenthood, divorce, death of a spouse, and work.

18. Identify Elisabeth Kübler-Ross' five sequential stages though which people pass as they react to their own impending death.

lecture suggestions

Infant Memories?

The current consensus on childhood memory is that it's generally inaccessible (see Chapter 6, "Why you don't remember your first birthday party"). However, recent research that draws on a distinction between different memory processes sheds light on how infants form memories, and what may become of those memories in later life.

Declarative memory, or the capacity for calling to mind specific events or facts, differs from procedural memory, or the skills and knowledge that come to mind with little effort. Laraine McDonough, of the University of California at San Diego, drew upon that distinction in an experiment involving normal and brain damaged adults (who were unable to retain memories for more than a few minutes). McDonough showed the adults a sequence of behaviors that formed a causal chain (for example turning on a hair dryer, holding a balloon in front of it, and then manipulating the balloon's movements by moving the dryer), and a sequence that was arbitrarily ordered (for example, folding a piece of paper, cutting it, then drawing a star on the paper). The following day, the research participants were given the same sets of objects and asked first to handle them as they wished, and then to imitate what the researcher had done. Although the healthy participants correctly imitated the researcher's behavior (even while using the objects as they wished), the brain damaged volunteers performed at about the same level as others who had been given the objects with no prior instructions or behaviors to imitate. The conclusion reached by McDonough about this *deferred imitation* ability was that it must rely on declarative memory; the amnesiac volunteers were unable to call to mind the specific facts and events necessary to perform the task, although they could generally work with the objects appropriately.

McDonough and Jean Mandler then performed a subsequent experiment on deferred imitation, using 11-month-olds as subjects. These infants also saw a causal sequence (shaking a bead in a box to make a rattle) and an arbitrary sequence (putting a bracelet on a teddy bear and then brushing the bear's hair). Both one day later and three months later the babies were able to accurately imitate the causal sequence but had forgotten the arbitrary sequence.

Whether these outcomes provide evidence for conscious memory recall by infants is a matter of debate. They may shed light on the loss of infant memories in adulthood. If declarative memory is at work, it is unlikely that as adults we would retain information based on specific events experienced in childhood. This is particularly true given that brain connections are radically shaped, pruned, and lost during early childhood. This research at least provides a glimpse of the capacities of infants to store and retrieve information.

Bower, B. (1995). Conscious memories may emerge in infants. *Science News, 148*, 86.

Object Permanence Changes

Infants often fail to search for a hidden object until approximately one year of age, which suggested to Piaget that the infant lacked the concept of object permanence. Flavell, Miller, and Miller, however, noted that recent research suggests infants may have a greater understanding of object permanence earlier than Piaget assumed. The belief that object permanence does not stabilize until the end of the first year may have been the result of Piaget's methodology. That is, his observations were based upon the child's ability to perform certain motor behaviors that do not appear until later in development. Flavell and his colleagues noted, however, that a failure to perform a search for the object does not necessarily mean that the child lacks the concept of object permanence. Researchers have developed several techniques that visually present situations that are either possible or impossible given the rules of object permanence. Based upon observations of the reactions of infants to these presentations, the results indicated that infants as young as 3 to 4 months exhibited surprise reactions when situations were presented that were impossible given the rules of object permanence. Such findings suggest that the concept of object permanence may appear much earlier than originally proposed by Piaget.

Flavell, J. H., Miller, P. H., & Miller, S. A. (1993). *Cognitive development* (3rd ed.). Englewood Cliffs, NJ: Prentice Hall.

Reprinted from Hill, W. G. (1995). Instructor's resource manual for *Psychology* by S. F. Davis and J. J. Palladino. Englewood Cliffs, NJ: Prentice Hall.

Hormones and Toy Preferences

An early characteristic of gender role stereotypes is the preference for playing with sex-typed toys. Studies of individuals with the genetic disorder congenital adrenal hyperplasis (CAH), a condition characterized by high levels of adrenal androgens during prenatal development, reveal that CAH women exhibit traditional male characteristics (for example, more active and rougher play, a preference for masculine activities, and a greater spatial ability than their female relative). Most studies of this type, however rely on interview data rather than direct observation.

To remedy this methodological shortcoming, Berenbaum and Hines studied 37 children (26 girls and 11 boys) with CAH and 33 unaffected male and female relatives, all between the ages of 3 and 8. The dependent variable, toy preference, was measured as the amount of time spent playing with either masculine (e.g., helicopter, cars, construction blocks), feminine (e.g., dolls, kitchen supplies, toy telephone), or neutral toys (e.g., books, board games, jigsaw puzzle). Although the control girls and boys showed large differences in toy preferences along sex-typed lines, CAH girls showed a significant preference for masculine toys (compared to the control girls) and also played with feminine toys less often than did the controls. Parental surveys and medical data indicated that these results could not be attributed to differential treatment or disease factors. The researchers concluded that "Although the data are consistent with an androgen influence on sex-typed toy choices, it is not necessary that hormones have a direct influence on these choices. Hormones may affect toy choices indirectly, perhaps through an influence on activity level, motor skills, abilities, or temperament" (p. 205).

Berenbaum, S. A., & Hines, M. (1992). Early androgens are related to childhood sex-typed toy preferences. *Psychological Science, 3,* 203-206.

Adapted from Hill, W. G. (1995). Instructor's resource manual for *Psychology* by S. F. Davis and J. J. Palladino. Englewood Cliffs, NJ: Prentice Hall.

The Consequences of Sexual Abuse

Two independent studies reported at the 1995 meeting of the American Psychiatric Association found evidence that severe childhood sexual abuse leaves a permanent mark on the brain. The researchers in both cases used magnetic resonance imaging (MRI) to examine the hippocampus, a brain structure involved in organizing memory, in groups of women. The studies found that the hippocampal volume of women who had suffered severe sexual abuse as children was smaller than that of women who were comparable in age, but who had not been abused. Both groups of women were recruited from the same women's health clinic, where they were receiving general care.

The research teams suggest that this cerebral alteration may predispose people to experience dissociation and to develop the symptoms of post-traumatic stress disorder (PTSD). Other investigators have reported similar reductions in hippocampal volume among Vietnam combat veterans suffering from PTSD. However, the point at which the reduction takes place is not clear, especially given that many adults who develop PTSD have experienced prior traumas.

If the severe traumas of childhood sexual abuse or combat release stress hormones that harm the hippocampus, it may account in part for the fragmented memories experienced by many people suffering from PTSD. However, it is also known that many trauma survivors display no memory disruptions, dissociation, or symptoms of PTSD. This has led some researchers to speculate that a genetic predisposition to react strongly to extreme stress may also be implicated, especially in men. Further research will hopefully clarify this link between behavior and brain.

Bower, B. (1995). Child sex abuse leaves mark on brain. *Science News, 147,* 340.

Talk That Talk, Baby

"Does baby want to play with the beads?! Do yoooooouuuu want to play with the beeeeeaaaaads? Yes you doooooo!! Yes you dooooooooo, don't yooouuuuuuuu?!!" The high-pitched, drawn-out baby talk that new babies seem to find mesmerizing and new parents seem to find necessary may have a deeper significance than previously suspected. That semi-annoying tendency to repeatedly accentuate vowel sounds may serve an important function in language development, and may have a universal component.

Patricia Kuhl, a neuroscientist at the University of Washington, studied mothers in Sweden, Russia, and Seattle as they talked to their infants. Swedish, Russian, and English have substantially different vowel systems, yet the vowel sounds that are common to each language--"ee," "ah," and "oo"--were the same sounds that were unintentionally accentuated in the mothers' speech. These parents did not accentuate all sounds or raise the pitch of all words, as might someone pretending to speak "baby talk." Rather, acoustic profiles of some 2,363 words across all three groups revealed that just these important vowels were exaggerated, and, according to Kuhl, for good reason. By providing an infant with unambiguous examples of what vowel sounds belong together, the task of language acquisition is presumably made that much easier. To a 5-month-old learning to enunciate vowel sounds this can be an important boost.

Some intriguing unanswered questions remain, however. First, although Kuhl and her associates have demonstrated the type of input given to these infants, it's not known what babies do with this information or how and when learning takes place. If an adult did not exaggerate vowel sounds, for example, it's not clear whether there would be a negative effect on an infant's learning or simply no effect at all. Second, the universality of this effect suggests a biological basis for knowing how to talk to an infant. "Ee," "ah," and "oo" are in fact sounds common to all human languages. Why they are spontaneously stressed under certain circumstances hints at an important adaptive tendency.

Neergaard, L. (1997, August 1). Baby talk contributes to an infant's learning. *Austin American-Statesman,* A19.

A Picture is Worth a Thousand Words

Young children sometimes have difficulty recalling information. A recent study suggests that drawing can enhance children's memories for events.

Sarnia Butler, of the University of Otago in Dunedin, New Zealand, led a study involving 5- and 6-year-olds who took a field trip to a fire station. While there the children clambered on the fire engines, watched drills performed by the firefighters, tried on the firefighting gear, and even watched as one of their chaperones slid down the firepole, much to the displeasure of the tour leader, who reprimanded her. (This event, and several others, were prearranged ahead of time.) Both one day and one month later, the children were asked about their outing. Those children who were asked to draw and describe the events of that day--how they got there, what they saw, the events that transpired--accurately reported much more information than those children who were simply asked to tell what happened. This effect was not observed among 3- to 4-year-olds, although among both groups drawing did not appear to increase errors in recall.

This research indicates that memory for pleasant events may be increased by coupling words and pictures. It remains to be seen whether the same effect would hold for negative events. If so, this technique may hold promise for boosting children's recall of abuse, incest, or other traumatic events.

Staff (1995). Kids draw on their memories. *Science News, 148,* 111.

Gender Roles and Parenting

Diana Baumrind noted that some researchers have suggested that androgynous individuals may assume a more authoritative parenting style, exhibiting more flexibility and competence as parents. In order to test this hypothesis, she examined parenting and child behaviors as a function of degree of sex-typing. Data were gathered on 9-year-old children and their parents using naturalistic and structured observations, interviews, tests (including the Bem Sex Role Inventory), and self-reports.

Overall, Baumrind found that there were no differences in parenting styles between androgynous and nonadrogynous women. Androgynous men, however, tended to be more similar to women in their approach to childrearing. In addition, she found that androgynous men were also more unconventional and autonomous in their overall lifestyle patterns. Furthermore, androgynous parents were more child-centered (responsive to the child), less demanding, and less authoritative in their parenting practices. Corresponding to their general attitude, sex-typed fathers tended to be firm, demanding, and positively reinforcing with their children, while sex-typed mothers were more loving and responsive. Baumrind also reported that both male and female children of sex-typed parents were somewhat more competent on several social and cognitive tasks, and females were more assertive. Baumrind concluded that her results indicated that assumptions by some researchers of advantages associated with androgynous parents with respect to childrearing and development may not be correct.

Baumrind, D. (1982). Are androgynous individuals more effective persons and parents? *Child Development, 53*, 44-75.

Reprinted from Hill, W. G. (1995). Instructor's resource manual for *Psychology* by S. F. Davis and J. J. Palladino. Englewood Cliffs, NJ: Prentice Hall.

Is the Potential for Divorce Genetic?

McGue and Lykken noted that one of the strongest predictors of divorce is a family background that includes parental divorce. Although most researchers have attributed this effect to environmental factors such as social modeling, McGue and Lykken investigated potential genetic factors. Using subjects from the Minnesota Twin Registry, they obtained survey information on marital history from 722 same-sex monozygotic twins, 794 same-sex dizygotic twins, their parents, and their spouse's parents. They reported that the concordance rate for divorce was significantly higher for monozygotic twins than for dizygotic twins. Based upon their results, they estimated that the predicted divorce rate for a hypothetical marriage between two monozygotic twins with divorced parents and a divorced co-twin would be 77.5%, while the predicted divorce rate for a marriage between two monozygotic twins with a background of no familial divorce would be 5.3%. The researchers concluded that their "data suggest that cultural factors influence the threshold for divorce while, within a given culture, variations in underlying aggregate risk are strongly influenced by genetic factors" (p. 372). They do, however, emphasize that genetic factors may be mediated by personality factors such as personal values and the individual's capacity for happiness.

McGue, M., & Lykken, D. T. (1992). Genetic influence on risk of divorce. *Psychological Science, 3*, 368-373.

Reprinted from Hill, W. G. (1995). Instructor's resource manual for *Psychology* by S. F. Davis and J. J. Palladino. Englewood Cliffs, NJ: Prentice Hall.

Theories of Physical Aging

Growing old, it's been said, sure beats the alternative. The process of aging may be inevitable, but at least the mechanisms of aging can be understood with some degree of certainty.

Wear and Tear Theories

This general class of theories proposes that the human body is analogous to a machine in that our parts begin to wear down and malfunction as they age. Although this seems to make sense and may apply to some body systems (e.g., elbow or knee problems experienced by athletes), it fails to account for the fact that the body's systems are continuously engaged in repairing and replacing damaged tissue. In addition, it does not explain why continued use or exertion of body systems, such as that associated with routine exercise, actually improves functioning.

Accumulation Theories

This group of theories focuses on explanations of aging that are the result of problems at the cellular level. One theory attributes aging to an accumulation of cellular reproduction errors. For example, the aging of the skin may be the result of increasing errors in cellular reproduction due to damage in cellular DNA from exposure to the sun and other toxic substances. Another accumulation theory is the metabolic waste theory. This theory suggests that aging results from the accumulation of undisposed waste products in the cells. Waste accumulation, however, seems to result from changes in the body's ability to remove waste and thus may be more of a symptom of aging than a cause. A third accumulation theory attributes aging to the buildup of fibrous proteins (collagen and elastin) in the body. The buildup of these proteins is associated with external aspects of aging such as wrinkles and sagging skin.

Immune System Malfunction

Another theory focuses on the potential contribution of declines in immune system functioning with age. For example, research has demonstrated that the ability of the immune system to produce antibodies begins to decline after adolescence. Some studies also have suggested that the immune system may lose its ability to detect and destroy slightly mutated cells, allowing them to reproduce and accumulate in the body. The autoimmune theory of aging, however, suggests that the immune system loses its ability to differentiate between normal and abnormal cells, resulting in the destruction of healthy cells.

Genetic Clock

This approach suggests that cells are preprogrammed to survive and reproduce for a specific period, after which they begin to degenerate and die. Based upon studies of human cell regeneration limits, researchers estimate that the maximum human life span would be between 110 and 120 years.

Berger, K. S. (1994). *The developing person through the life span* (3rd ed.). New York: Worth.
Hayslip, B., Jr., & Panek, P. E. (1993). *Adult development and aging* (2nd ed.). New York: HarperCollins.

Adapted from Hill, W. G. (1995). Instructor's resource manual for *Psychology* by S. F. Davis and J. J. Palladino. Englewood Cliffs, NJ: Prentice Hall.

The Benefits of Control

A sad reality of aging in the United States is that the elderly are sometimes demoted to the status of "second-class citizens." Consigned to nursing homes due to frailty, hardship, or the indifference of family members, the elderly often find themselves in an environment not of their choosing and inconsistent with their previous lifestyles. Consequently, they may feel unable to control, predict, or determine their outcomes, even on a day to day basis. A classic study by Ellen Langer and Judy Rodin, did much to illustrate the benefits to the elderly of being in control.

Langer and Rodin enlisted the cooperation of the Arden House nursing home in Connecticut to perform an intervention using its residents. Those who lived on the four floors of the Arden House were all from similar backgrounds, of similar states of health, and generally assigned to floors and rooms on a random basis. Langer and Rodin therefore randomly chose the residents of one floor to receive an *increased responsibility* treatment, leaving the residents of another floor as a comparison group.

Both groups attended information meetings led by the director of the facility, who worked in cooperation with the researchers. However, the increased responsibility residents were told that they should take charge of arranging their room as they wished, making their complaints known to the director, and scheduling the activities they wished to participate in. For example, these residents were told of upcoming movies to be shown on a Thursday and Friday night, and were asked to indicate their preference for attending. Similarly, these residents each selected a small houseplant to care for and were told that it would be their responsibility to tend to its needs. In contrast, the residents of the comparison group were given slightly different information. They were also told that their comfort and happiness were of primary importance, although the director stated that it was the staff's responsibility to make sure that happened. As an example, the houseplants given to this group would be watered and tended to by the nurses. And although they too heard about the upcoming "nights at the movies," they were informed that they would be told which night they could attend. In short, Langer and Rodin manipulated the amount of responsibility the two groups had for their own outcomes.

All the residents had completed a questionnaire on their satisfaction with the living arrangements a week prior to the director's presentation. A similar questionnaire was completed three weeks after the talk. The increased responsibility residents reported being happier and more active (compared to the control group) on the second questionnaire, which was complemented by interviewer's ratings of increased alertness for this same group. Furthermore, nurses (who remained uninformed about each residents experimental status) rated the increased responsibility residents as showing greater general improvement and as spending more time visiting other residents, talking to staff, and visiting with guests, and significantly less time simply sitting and watching the staff. Interestingly, more members of the responsibility group attended the film that was shown, and although 10 "responsibility residents" entered a jelly bean guessing contest that night, only 1 member of the comparison group did.

Finally, the most provocative difference was in the mortality rate of the two groups of residents: Thirty percent of the comparison group had died during the 18-month interval between the original study and a subsequent follow-up visit, compared to only fifteen percent of the increased responsibility participants. Although other factors surely played a role, this "ultimate DV" provides startlingly evidence of the importance of control in our daily lives.

Langer, E. J., & Rodin, J. (1976). The effects of choice and enhanced personal responsibility for the aged: A field experiment in an institutional setting. *Journal of Personality and Social Psychology, 34*, 191-198.

Predicting Alzheimer's Disease

Alzheimer's disease tragically afflicts many elderly people each year, resulting in a gradual deterioration of memory, reasoning ability, and personality. Even more disturbing is that the diagnosis of Alzheimer's can only be made conclusively upon autopsy, when the plaques and tangles in the brain, characteristic of the disorder, can be confirmed. Recently, however, the results of an archival study have suggested that linguistic markers may predict Alzheimer's with some degree of accuracy.

David Snowdon, an epidemiologist at the University of Kentucky, led a research team that examined the writings of 93 nuns. In the 1930s, when these women entered a Milwaukee convent, they composed brief autobiographical essays, which subsequently were scored by Snowdon's team for linguistic markers such as the density of ideas or grammatical complexity. For example, a nun who might have written "I plan to give my all to God" probably would score low on such measures, whereas a nun who composed the beatitude "I long to linger in the sweet garden of Christ, rejoicing in the splendor that He is and thanking Him daily for His abundances" might not win a literature contest, but certainly shows a greater degree of complexity in her writing. All of the nuns lived under highly similar conditions. Sixty years later, however, those nuns who scored low on the psycholinguistic markers were more prone to develop Alzheimer's. Of the 14 nuns who had died, in fact, five had low idea density scores, and all five had Alzheimer's disease.

What this reveals about the course of Alzheimer's is still something of a mystery. It may be, for example, that as young women these nuns were already showing signs of the disorder, suggesting that Alzheimer's develops slowly and insidiously over a prolonged period of time. Studies showing that some forms of Alzheimer's can afflict people in their 20s complement this idea. An alternative, however, is that linguistic skills may offer some "immunity" to the development of Alzheimer's, much as the adage "use it or lose it" suggests. Perhaps those nuns with more highly developed linguistic ability were better able to stave off the effects of this disorder. As with most studies of this nature, the causality of events remains murky. Other archival data, or other markers of ability (such as mathematics scores, or measures of reasoning or memory) may shed more light on this encouraging line of research.

Indeed, Snowdon and his associates have imposed on the generous nuns of the School Sisters of Notre Dame one more time. The research team has recently discovered an important link between strokes and declines in mental abilities seen in Alzheimer's patients. Among 61 deceased nuns whose brains all clearly showed signs of Alzheimer's, 19 seemed in life to have escaped the confusion, dementia, and mental deterioration so characteristic of the disease. In one case, a 101-year-old nun remained, by all accounts, as sharp as a tack, even though her brain was a battlefield of plaques, tangles, and gaping holes. The key was that she, like 18 of the others, had not suffered from strokes during old age. In fact, only 57% of stroke-free nuns developed Alzheimer's, compared to 93% of nuns who had a history of ministrokes. In an additional comparison, Snowdon looked at the brains of 41 nuns who did not have Alzheimer's-like brains but who had suffered strokes; these women had no significant decrease in their overall mental competence.

An avenue for treatment suggests itself. By preventing strokes it may be possible to delay the onset of symptoms in Alzheimer's patients. The "double-whammy" of dealing with two brain diseases in a single individual may be halved, providing substantial comfort to those dealing with Alzheimer's.

Nash, J. M. (March 24, 1997). Medicine. *Time*, 80-82.
Rogers, A. (1996, March 4). The weight of words: Can writing style predict dementia? *Newsweek*, 55.

demonstrations

Guest Lecturer: Registered Childbirth Educator

An engaging and memorable way to expand upon the text's discussion of prenatal development is to invite a registered childbirth educator to your class. You should have no problem locating a qualified speaker through the local yellow pages (e.g., under childbirth education, clinics, hospitals, or birthing centers), or if you prefer, you can ask family or friends for a recommendation. As experts in prenatal development, these educators often have access to terrific visual aids (including, for example, pictures of a fetus at various stages, models of the uterus, etc.) and are also likely to share interesting anecdotes from their own experiences. Besides describing the stages of prenatal development, they can discuss a variety of important issue in pregnancy and childbirth, such as the effects of drugs and toxins on the unborn baby (e.g., fetal alcohol syndrome, smoking and pregnancy), the importance of proper nutrition on development, options in reproductive technology, uses of prenatal screening tests (e.g., ultrasound, amniocentesis), and the merits of breast versus bottle feeding. Students--many of whom will be future parents--are likely to appreciate this lively, entertaining, and unforgettable presentation.

Show & Tell

Beers (1987) noted that the topic of developmental psychology often generates a desire to share personal experiences on the part of students and proposed the activity described below as a means to formalize the sharing process. Ask your students to bring to a designated class period some physical artifact from their childhood that has special meaning to them (for example, a picture, toy, craft or school project). Prior to the class, they should think about how the artifact relates to a developmental concept that has been discussed in class or the textbook and be prepared to describe the relationship. Beers suggested that you can either organize the presentation of different artifacts chronologically or have the students present them to each other in small groups, with each group selecting the best example for presentation to the entire class. Beers warns that you should be careful to make sure that the presentations focus on developmental stages, not simply anecdotal experiences. She also suggested that this activity is a good opportunity to discuss how psychologists can use artifactual evidence to study development.

Beers, S. E. (1987). "Show and tell" for developmental psychology. In V. P. Makosky, L. G. Whittemore, & A. M. Rogers (Eds.), *Activities handbook for the teaching of psychology: Vol. 2* (pp. 93-94). Washington, DC: American Psychological Association.

Reprinted from Hill, W. G. (1995). Instructor's resource manual for *Psychology* by S. F. Davis and J. J. Palladino. Englewood Cliffs, NJ: Prentice Hall.

Using Children's Books to Illustrate Developmental Principles

As a variation on the above assignment, bring a variety of children's books to class and use them to illustrate developmental principles. Children's books make excellent teaching tools because they apply a tremendous range of principles in developmental psychology. Implicit in most books, for example, are important lessons that attempt to strengthen children's development in some way. Popular topics include moral development (e.g., lying, stealing), coping with adversity and stress (e.g., death, divorce), techniques to advance cognitive and intellectual skills, issues of identity development and self-esteem, physical development and change (e.g., potty training), social and relationship issues (e.g., how to share, how to get along with others), coping with fears (e.g., of the dark), tolerance of diversity (e.g., racial, gender, and religious differences), gender role development, and so on. If you have a limited number of books available, you can describe them to the class and solicit student comments as you go through them. If you have several books available, divide your students into small groups, distribute two or three books to each, and have them identify the relevant developmental concepts applicable to each. Then, to stimulate class discussion, you can allow groups to take turns making short presentations and soliciting student comments and questions.

Using Homemade Videotapes to Teach Developmental Concepts

It is often difficult to illustrate developmental processes that occur in infancy and childhood in the classroom. One technique that is often suggested is to bring infants or children to the classroom for in-class demonstrations. Although this "live" demonstration is appealing, it has several problems such as locating infants or young children to use each time you teach the course, conflicts between your class schedule and the child's schedule, and uncooperative or shy children. Although there are many good commercially produced videos of topics related to infant and child development (see the list at the end of this chapter), several authors have advocated the use of homemade videos (Poole, 1986; Silvestro, 1979; Trnavsky & Willey, 1984). A major advantage of homemade videos is the ability to develop brief teaching modules that address specific concepts which you are interested in covering in your course. Rather than edited videotapes illustrating specific developmental issues, Poole (1986) suggested using unedited videos and having the students analyze the video for illustrations of concepts that have been discussed in class. Poole (1986), Silvestro (1979), and Trnavsky and Willey (1984) provide specific guidelines and suggestions for developing your own instructional videotapes.

Poole, D. A. (1986). Laboratories and demonstrations in child development with unedited videotapes. *Teaching of Psychology, 13*, 212-214.

Silvestro, J. R. (1979). Use of video-cassette summaries of childhood in teaching developmental psychology. *Teaching of Psychology, 6*, 171-172.

Trnavsky, P., & Willey, D. L. (1984). Developing instructional videotapes. *Teaching of Psychology, 11*, 169-170.

Reprinted from Hill, W. G. (1995). Instructor's resource manual for *Psychology* by S. F. Davis and J. J. Palladino. Englewood Cliffs, NJ: Prentice Hall.

Constructing a Life Line to Illustrate Erikson's Stages of Development

Peggy Brick suggests giving students the opportunity to actively explore Erikson's stages of development in their own lives by constructing a "life line." After discussing the eight stages of Erikson's theory, ask students to take out a piece of paper, turn it lengthwise, and draw a line across the middle of the page. Tell them to put their birth date on the far left and a projected date of death on the far right. Then have them put the current date a few inches down the line from their birth date. Now instruct them to list several important events during the childhood and adolescence between their birth date and the current date. For example, they might list an accident, a family move, a birthday party, their first day of elementary or high school, or a special holiday memory. After giving them a few minutes to list these events, ask them to consider the future and to list things that they would like to accomplish during early, middle, and late adulthood, including what their retirement will be like and what they want to do before they die. Brick suggests pairing students to let them discuss their time lines and then leading the class in a discussion of what they learned from the activity. During the discussion, ask students to focus on how the events or accomplishments that they listed reflect aspects of Erikson's theory.

Brick, P. (1981). The life cycle. In L. T. Benjamin, Jr. & K. D. Lowman (Eds.), *Activities handbook for the teaching of psychology* (pp. 128-130). Washington, DC: American Psychological Association.

Illustrating Piagetian Concepts

Harper (1979) described two activities that can be used to illustrate Piagetian concepts with adult students. His demonstrations, which focus on the processes of assimilation, accommodation, and equilibration, are described below. Holbrook (1992) also described a demonstration that can be used to illustrate concepts related to conservation.

Assimilation and Accommodation. Harper (1987) suggested a demonstration that illustrates the Piagetian concepts of assimilation and accommodation. In the first activity, you distribute lollipops to the class and ask them to eat them. After the students have begun to eat them, point out that the lollipop tends to elicit the schema of sucking, illustrating how an object is assimilated into an existing schema. Harper also suggested that you can note that the differences in how individuals consume the lollipop (such as biting or rolling the lollipop around in their mouth) reflect elaborations on the basic schema. You can then ask your students to provide additional examples of the assimilation and accommodation of innate, reflexive schemas in other everyday activities.

Equilibration and Concept Acquisition. Another demonstration suggested by Harper (1987) introduces a novel object in order to demonstrate the process of equilibration and its relationship to concept formation as experienced by a young child. Without telling the students the name or function of the object, pretend to remove an imaginary object called a "gloquex" (pronounced glocks) from a box and place it on a table. Tell the students that you have just removed a device from the box that weighs about 10 kg and is 60 mm X 30 mm X 30 mm in size. Then proceed to pretend to plug it in and let it warm up. At this point, if students do not begin spontaneously asking questions about the object, encourage them to do so. Harper (1987) noted that some common questions and possible answers might include:

1. What is it called? A gloquex.
2. What does it do? The gloquex counteracts negative electromagnetic waves (i.e., bad vibes) often encountered by instructors in the classroom.
3. How does it work? An inversely reciprocating frimfram bollixes any waves entering the aperture.
4. What is it made of? Hyperventilated case hardened mollox.
5. Why can't I see it? You can't? (followed by an incredulous look; or alternatively) It's clear.

Following the questions, give students a test on their knowledge and understanding of the gloquex. After the test, point out to the students how their responses are similar to those of a child learning a new concept. That is, they know the name, general purpose, and that the gloquex belongs to the category of objects known as machines, but not much else. Because the gloquex does not easily fit into an existing schema, the students' responses will often use descriptions based upon comparisons to previously experienced objects (attempts at assimilation). Ask your students to discuss how their behavior with respect to the gloquex may be similar to that of an 18-month-old child learning about concepts such as dog or bird.

Harper, G. F. (1979). Introducing Piagetian concepts through the use of familiar and novel illustrations. *Teaching of Psychology, 6,* 58-59.

Holbrook, J. E. (1992). Bringing Piaget's preoperational thought to the minds of adults: A classroom demonstration. *Teaching of Psychology, 19,* 169-170.

Reprinted from Hill, W. G. (1995). Instructor's resource manual for *Psychology* by S. F. Davis and J. J. Palladino. Englewood Cliffs, NJ: Prentice Hall.

Moral Development

The text introduces Kohlberg's stages of moral development by presenting the famous Heinz dilemma. Vandendorpe (1990) suggests supplementing this discussion with two other moral dilemmas that seem to be more realistic and relevant to undergraduates. Ask your class to consider two important dilemmas--exceeding the 65-mph speed limit and cheating in school--and have them generate every reason they can imagine both for and against these behaviors. Then, divide the class into small groups and have them classify each reason according to its level of morality for Kohlberg's theory. Groups should then decide what rationale they would use for each dilemma that would be effective in encouraging moral growth in adolescents.

Vandendorpe, M. M. (1990). Three tasks of adolescence: Cognitive, moral, social. In V. P. Makosky, C. C. Sileo, L. G. Whittemore, C. P. Landry, & M. L. Skutley (Eds.), *Activities handbook for the teaching of psychology: Vol. 3* (pp. 126-127). Washington, DC: American Psychological Association.

Debate: Is Television Bad for Children?

Chapter 9 discusses the powerful and influential role that television plays in children's daily lives. At the heart of this issue lies the controversy over whether excessive TV viewing by children is harmful to their intellectual development and/or promotes aggressive behavior. There is no easy answer, as proponents on both sides of the issue cite a variety of studies to support their cause. Thus, while some argue that viewing violent TV is correlated with aggressive behavior, others contend that there is no relationship or even that viewing prosocial programs can lead to an increase in helpful behavior. Similarly, although research shows no correlation between the amount of television viewed and IQ, others suggest that television prevents children from engaging in other intellectually challenging activities. Your students will likely have strong opinions on this issue and will enjoy the chance to explore the controversy in greater depth. Use the debate procedures suggested at the beginning of this manual (or develop your own) and assign students to research and defend both sides of this issue. *Taking Sides* contains excellent articles both pro and con on this topic (see Issue 6), or you may want to assign articles of your own (or students') choosing. Be prepared for a lively (and loud) debate!

Slife, B. (2000). *Taking sides: Clashing views on controversial psychological issues* (11th ed.). Guilford, CT: Dushkin Publishing Group.

Hello Mother, Hello Father

Here's a simple demonstration gathered from the Teaching in Psychology (TIPS) computer bulletin board. Ask your students two simple questions: "What does it mean to father a child?" and "What does it mean to mother a child?" Chances are that responses to the first question will focus on biological aspects of reproduction; "being a sperm donor," "impregnating a woman," or "having sex." Responses to the second question typically emphasize nurturance or prolonged commitment; "raising a child," "showing attention," or "being supportive" are likely offerings. Discuss with your students why they hold these views and why they responded to the questions differently. This is an opportunity to discuss sex role stereotypes, gender roles, and some issues of early adulthood. If your students are a particularly enlightened bunch there may be no difference in their responses to the two questions. In that case discuss what led to their egalitarian outlooks, or why other people might respond differently.

Guest Lecture: Adult Relationships

To stimulate class discussion and present students with a variety of perspectives, assemble a discussion panel of couples who have lived together various lengths of time. For example, you might invite a newlywed pair, a gay couple, a middle-aged couple, and a couple married more than 25 years to discuss their relationships. Topics might include the types of problems that arose in their relationship and how they were dealt with, ways in which their partners have been important to them during the relationship, prospects for the future, and other developmental issues they've faced together. If there are any married students in your class you might invite them to participate as well.

A few helpful tips to keep in mind. (1) Plan ahead; contact speakers well in advance of the presentation, and be sure to inform them of relevant issues that have been discussed and how their presentation might best fit in with your course. (2) Try to have men and women from a variety of backgrounds and occupations, if possible. (3) Be sure to allot plenty of time for questions; one recommended format is to have panel members tell their personal stories at the beginning of the session and then use the remainder of the period for questions and discussion. Use this activity as an opportunity for students to ask questions and gather information about long-term relationships at various stages of development.

Adolescence Is...

Marilyn Coleman suggests a "popcorn" method for identifying generalizations about adolescence. Ask your students to call out the first thoughts that come to mind when they hear the word "adolescent." Write their responses on the board, allowing ample time for students to share their thoughts. Discuss the patterns that emerge from this list. Is adolescence seen primarily as a carefree time? A time of stress? What themes come up repeatedly in your students' perceptions? Most of your students will be in the late stages of adolescence and will have reflections and memories firmly in mind. Use this discussion to link their experiences to the topics covered in Chapter 11.

Adapted from Coleman, M. (1992). *Instructor's manual to accompany Human Development* (6th ed.). Englewood Cliffs, NJ: Prentice Hall.

Development Across the Lifespan

Freda Rebelsky (1981) described an activity designed to illustrate stereotypes concerning people's attitudes, beliefs, and behavior across the lifespan. Photocopy and distribute copies of Handout 10-1 and go over the instructions with your students. Tell them to think of three words that seem descriptive of each decade and to write the words on the corresponding blank line next to each decade. As an example, for the sixth decade they should think of a hypothetical person who is between the ages of 50 and 59 and ask themselves what words come to mind when trying to describe that person's life. After giving students about 15 minutes to complete this task, ask them to designate the decades that they found the easiest and hardest to generate words for by putting the letters E and H by the respective decades. Then ask the students to discuss aloud which decades they found easiest and hardest to describe and tabulate the results on the board.

Rebelsky noted that you will rarely get an equal distribution across all decades and can use the results to generate a discussion of why some decades were easier or harder than others. You can also ask students to volunteer some of their responses for the various decades. What words were most commonly associated with certain decades and why? What similarities and differences were there, and how do these reflect common stereotypes associated with particular age groups? Were there some decades for which descriptions or association were uniform? Were there some decades that were associated with very diverse responses? Rebelsky also notes that you could modify the instructions and have half of the class do the activity while thinking of a female, while the other half think of a male. This would allow students to explore variations in perceived experiences based on the sex of the hypothetical individual. If you have a relatively equal distribution of males and females in your class, you could further analyze how these differences depend on the sex of the student (e.g., are opposite-sex perceptions of experience, such as a female describing what life is like for a male, different from same-sex perceptions, such as a female describing what life is like for a female)?

> Rebelsky, F. G. (1981). Life span development. In L. T. Benjamin, Jr. & K. D. Lowman (Eds.), *Activities handbook for the teaching of psychology* (pp. 131-132). Washington, DC: American Psychological Association.

Exploring Societal Attitudes about Aging

An excellent way to explore societal attitudes about aging is to observe how the elderly are reflected in a variety of media. About two weeks before your coverage of Chapter 9, ask students to begin gathering greeting cards, magazine and newspaper articles, cartoons, or examples of advertising that illustrate society's attitudes about aging. On the day of your discussion, collect student samples. Then, after introducing the topic of aging, divide your class into small groups and randomly distribute to each group several of the samples (making sure each group gets a variety of different sources). In their discussion, groups should note the major stereotypes about aging portrayed in these examples. Give the groups about 15 minutes for discussion, and then reconvene the class and have each group present their findings to the larger group. What common themes seem to run throughout the various portrayals? Are all stereotypes about the elderly negative (e.g., sedentary, senile, set in their ways, crabby, physically deteriorated), or are there positive stereotypes (e.g., wise, mature, respected) as well? Why do such stereotypes persist? Do students know people who do not fit these stereotypes? Can they make any suggestions for combating these negative portrayals? Have these stereotypes had any impact on students' attitudes about growing older? That is, are they looking forward to this time, or are they dreading it? Are there steps they can take now to make things more positive when they get older?

If you have time, you might also discuss portrayals of the elderly on television, comparing current or recent shows that are centered around older characters (e.g., *Golden Girls*, *Matlock*, *Murder She Wrote*) to those in which older characters play a more secondary role (e.g., George's parents on *Seinfeld*). Similarly, you might consider whether or not there is a double standard with respect to aging. In other words, are the effects of aging (at least in terms of people's perceptions) more negative for one sex than the other? Many people feel, for example, that gray hair is distinguishing on a man but just plain "old" on a woman. Also, several Hollywood actresses have recently complained that their choice of roles decrease drastically when they get older, but that the opposite is true for male actors. Is there evidence for this kind of double standard? Students are likely to enjoy this exercise, which is a humorous and thought provoking way to create a better understanding of ageism.

"Wearing the Shoes" of the Elderly

Students often have difficulty understanding or appreciating the sensory losses that sometimes accompany aging. Herbert Shore (1976), who designed a training program to help people who work with the elderly better understand sensory losses, suggests several simple and effective simulations, some of which can be experienced in class, and some of which might best be done out of class.

Hearing. According to Shore, hearing loss is one of the most problematic sensory impairments for the elderly because the lack of clarity and understanding can lead to suspiciousness and paranoia. Hearing losses can be simulated by having students wear ear plugs, ear muffs, or by simply putting their fingers in their ears when trying to understand what is being said. Shore also recommends the "Unfair Hearing Test" in which students try to comprehend a list of words that have been tape-recorded with slight decibel distortions and with frequencies filtered out.

Vision. Changes in the lenses can be simulated by having students wear underwater goggles. In addition, taping yellow cellophane on the goggles can help simulate changes in color perception. Blindness can be simulated by having the student wear a blindfold while trying to perform a simple task such as tying their shoelaces. In addition, you may want to take the blindfolded student on a "blind walk" so that they can experience dependency on a companion. Finally, losses in peripheral vision can be simulated by taping pieces of paper on the sides of glasses.

Taste. Taste loss commonly experienced by the elderly can be simulated by camouflaging the texture of food by chopping, pureeing, or liquefying it (or by using commercial baby foods) and then having a volunteer eat it while blindfolded and wearing a nose clip.

Kinesthesia. Difficulty in mobility can be simulated by wrapping an ace bandage around the student's knee or elbow to simulate stiffness in joints. Other physical disabilities, such as those brought about by a stroke or other injury, can be simulated by writing with the opposite hand, walking on crutches, using a cane, or relying a wheelchair for a day.

Touch. Losses in tactile sensitivity can be simulated by applying rubber cement or paraffin to a finger. You can also have students try to identify common objects (that are out of view) while wearing mittens or plastic baggies on their hands.

Shore, H. (1976). Designing a training program for understanding sensory losses in aging. *The Gerontologist, 16*, 157-165.

student assignments

Naturalistic Observation

After students are well versed in the theories of development, ask them to make unobtrusive observations of children at play. Observations should be relatively informal so that students are watching children as they engage in a variety of activities in natural settings. Potentially rich settings include classrooms, daycare centers or preschools, churches, parks, Little League baseball games, playgrounds, video arcades, and shopping malls. [Note that student observers should be unobtrusive so they don't unintentionally influence children's behavior, and that they should secure permission if they are observing on private property.] Ask students to write a 2 to 4-page paper describing their observations and to include a discussion of how principles from the text and lecture apply to their observations. For best results, students should narrow their focus and identify their goals and expectations prior to observation. For example, are they going to explore variation in physical ability and motor development? Focus on evidence of cognitive development (in terms of Piaget's stages)? Examine issues related to social development (play in groups, sharing, competition, same versus mixed-sex play)? If student observers are able to get within hearing distance, they might also relate principles of language development to children's conversations (e.g., identifying babbling, holophrases, use of intonations, overgeneralizations, motherese).

Constructing a Moral Development Quiz

Using the Heinz dilemma presented in the text as a model, ask each student to generate and bring to the next class one or two dilemmas that would be especially relevant to adolescents. During class, collect students' dilemmas and go over them with your students, critiquing them and selecting the best examples from the group. After class, compile the best examples and type up a survey that includes the dilemmas along with instructions for how to respond. Then, distribute two copies of the survey to your students and ask each to give the survey to two adolescents. Preferably, the adolescents would be different on some dimension, such as age or sex. Students should try to keep as accurate a record of their subjects' responses as possible, and should also try to determine the level of moral development based on those responses. During the next class session, you can collate the data and read several interesting responses. This should spark an involving class discussion in which students compare responses (including information about the age and sex of subjects) and interpret them in terms of Kohlberg's stages.

Adapted from Siaw, S., & Clark, M. (1995). Instructor's resource guide to accompany *Child Psychology: The modern science* (2nd ed.). New York: John Wiley & Sons.

Dear Daughter/Dear Son

Ellen Junn (1989) describes an innovative exercise from her course on parenting and family relations that can be readily adapted and simplified for an introductory psychology course. For this assignment, Junn suggests having students write semi-autobiographical letters as a way of exploring developmental issues from a more concrete and personal perspective. Tell your students that you want them to write a letter to a future (or if they already have one, actual) child on his or her 18th birthday. You should assure students that their letters are confidential and are not meant to elicit overly private or emotional events in their lives. According to Junn, students should give the following questions careful consideration in their letter: (a) When or why did you decide to have the child? (b) What are the most important qualities for a parent to have and why? (c) What personal qualities do you possess that might facilitate or interfere with your ability to be a good parent? (d) What qualities do you hope your child will possess and why? Students should also mention specific strategies that they can use as a parent to foster growth in terms of physical, motor, cognitive, moral, social, personality, and sex-role development, relying on concepts presented in the text and lecture. Junn notes that this assignment increases the sensitivity of students to their own attitudes and beliefs about child development and parenting. In addition, it promotes understanding and application of course material to a personally relevant task. Junn also described a similar assignment asking students to write a letter to their parents.

Junn, E. N. (1989). "Dear Mom and Dad": Using personal letters to enhance students' understanding of developmental issues. *Teaching of Psychology, 16*, 135-138.

Youth Sports Participation

Each year, a large number of children between the ages of 6 and 12 participate in youth sports, including soccer, basketball, baseball, softball, football, swimming, and kickball. What is the impact of these sports on kids' development, social skills, and self-esteem? Is the impact primarily a positive one, or are there negative aspects as well? Ask your students to consider this issue by writing a short research paper addressing participation in youth sports and its consequences. The report can focus on a number of factors, such as how sports participation contributes to physical, cognitive, social, moral, or personality development. Students may also want to explore more specific issues relevant to participation, such as (a) What role should parents play in helping their children get the maximum benefit out of participation? (b) What role should coaches play, and what goals should they teach their players? (c) Are there some sports that seem to be better or worse than others for encouraging certain kind of development? (d) Which sports would students encourage their own kids to play? (e) Are the consequences of participation different for kids who are naturally athletic compared to those with less athletic ability? (f) What factors predict success in sports? and (g) How does participation influence kids' self-esteem and ability to get along with others? Many of your students will themselves have participated in sports, and they should feel free to include their own experiences in their report as well. Students should enjoy researching this important and timely issue, as it is a decision that the majority of them will face someday as parents.

Media Influences on Gender-Role Development

One activity that is consistently popular with students is to have them explore a variety of media for views of sex-role development, gender identity, and the portrayal of gender stereotypes. Books (including children's books as well as books aimed at parents), movies, videos, newspapers, magazines (including children's magazines), and advertisements are all suitable subjects for analysis. After gathering a variety of sources, students should write a short paper applying principles from the text and lecture to their examples. What common themes or stereotypes are found throughout? Are there many instances of sex-typed behavior? Are there certain kinds of media that break stereotypic portrayals? What influence will these portrayals likely have on the development of gender identity and gender role awareness in children? If available, it might be particularly instructive to compare older media sources (e.g., magazines or books that are 10-15 years old) with current ones. Which stereotypes seem to be firmly rooted in our culture and resistant to change? In what ways have stereotypes changed in the past decade? Because television is such an influential medium, particularly with respect to children, your students might also consider gender portrayals in various types of programming, comparing and contrasting children's educational shows (e.g., *Barney, Sesame Street*), cartoons (e.g., *Animaniacs*), action shows (e.g., *Power Rangers*), and situation comedies (e.g., *Full House*). Students' papers can also form the basis for a lively class discussion on this important topic.

Adapted from Siaw, S., & Clark, M. (1995). Instructor's resource guide to accompany *Child psychology: The modern science* (2nd ed.). New York: John Wiley & Sons.

Adolescence in Film: *The Breakfast Club*

John Hughes' wildly popular 1985 film gave birth to the infamous "brat pack" of actors and actresses and set the standard by which all teen movies were evaluated for several years. Molly Ringwald, Ally Sheedy, Emilio Estevez, Anthony Michael Hall, and Judd Nelson star as five totally different high school kids (a princess, a kooky introvert, a jock, a nerd, and a delinquent, respectively) who get to know each other while thrown together during an all-day Saturday detention session. This film gives credence to the "storm and stress" view of adolescence discussed in Chapter 9. Also included are compelling insights into adolescent struggles with identity formation, moral reasoning, self-esteem, sexual activity, and peer and parent relationships. Although it is likely that many of your students have already seen this film, ask them to watch it again, this time with an eye toward applying psychological principles from Chapter 9 to the key issues of adolescence portrayed in the movie (MCA/Universal; 92 min).

Adolescence and Identity Development: A Personal Exploration

An excellent and involving way for students to consider the topic of adolescent development is to apply theory and research in this area to their own experiences. For this assignment, ask your students to write a thoughtful, reflective paper exploring aspects of their own identity formation during adolescence. Students should be given latitude to address whatever issues they feel are important and to include personal experiences at their discretion. It is important to assure students that their papers will be strictly confidential and that they do not have to reveal any sensitive information about themselves. Although there need not be firm guidelines for this assignment, you might suggest the following questions as potential issues for discussion:

1. Describe five positive and five negative characteristics you had as an adolescent. How did you come to be aware of your positive characteristics? Your negative characteristics? How did you overcome the negative aspects of your personality?
2. What were your typical concerns during early, middle, and late adolescence? How did you deal with these concerns?
3. Can you think of one or more events that happened during your high-school years that marked a turning point in your life, that had a profound influence on your personality? In other words, was there an event that caused you to feel that you were crossing some boundary or somehow growing up and developing into a different, more mature person? Looking back, how do you feel about it now?
4. What were you peer relationships like? How did they affect your life? How did your peer relationships change throughout adolescence?
5. What was your relationship with your parents like? Describe some of the positive and negative aspects. What were the major issues in this relationship? How has your relationship with your parents changed?
6. How would you generally characterize your adolescence? Was it difficult? Does it support the "storm and stress" view of adolescence? What were your fears, anxieties, and hopes?
7. Can you think of personal instances which support David Elkind's fallacies of adolescent thinking, *imaginary audience* and *personal fable*? Do these concepts apply to your thoughts and behaviors at that time?
8. How did your peers influence you with respect to alcohol and tobacco use? What information about smoking, drugs, and sexual behavior did you receive from school? What influenced your own decisions about these matters?

Adapted from Siaw, S., & Clark, M. (1995). Instructor's resource guide to accompany *Child psychology: The modern science* (2nd ed.). New York: John Wiley & Sons.

Aging in Film: *To Dance With the White Dog*

In this 1993 made-for-TV movie, Hume Cronyn portrays an elderly man struggling to go on after the death of his beloved wife (Jessica Tandy). In poor health and terribly lonely, he befriends a stray white dog that protects and loves him. This extremely well-done film provides an honest portrayal of aging, loneliness, and death, and should give students remarkable insights into the mind and experience of an elderly person as well as ample material for a paper assignment (Republic; 98 min).

Keeping a Psychology Journal

In order to increase the personal relevance of material covered in class, you may require students to keep an on-going psychology journal for the duration of the course. The primary purpose of the journal is to encourage students to connect the facts, concepts, and principles that they acquire from the course to their own personal experiences. The journal adds a personal dimension to the course and provides an opportunity to apply course concepts to daily experiences (Hettich, 1990). The following writing prompts are a useful starting point. Additional suggestions for writing prompts are included in other chapters.

1. Draw a line down your paper and mark off the years since you were born. To the left of your time-line mark events in your life that you find personally meaningful (e.g., graduation from high school, first kiss, moving to a new city, parents' divorce, special teachers, etc.). To the right of the line fill in the major stage theories from the chapters on development (Piaget, Kohlberg, and Erikson). Write a paragraph at the bottom about how you feel about this assignment; did you learn anything about yourself?

    Hettich, P. (1976). The journal: An autobiographical approach to learning. *Teaching of Psychology, 3*(2), 60-63.
    Hettich, P. (1980). The journal revisited. *Teaching of Psychology, 7*(2), 105-106.
    Hettich, P. (1990). Journal writing: Old fare or nouvelle cuisine? *Teaching of Psychology, 17*(1), 36-63.

video

ABC News/Prentice Hall Video Library

A Pill to Improve Failing Memory as We Age (3:43 min, Series III). This clip from ABC's *World News Tonight* looks at research conducted by Cortex, a California firm. Using animal models, researchers at Cortex have developed a pill that helps information be retained 30 to 40% longer than normal. Human trials are underway in Europe, and work in America with Alzheimer's patients is soon to begin.

Building Brains (12:41 min, Series III). The developmental changes that take place during the first three years of life are remarkable, particularly those changes that occur in the brain. This *Nightline* segment focuses on the importance of early stimulation, training, and education for "building" better brains.

Contract to Get Parents Involved in a Child's Education (3:47 min, Series III). ABC's *World News Tonight* looks at a program in Stone Mountain, Georgia, that encourages parents to actively become involved in their children's education. Parents of students at Pine Ridge Elementary sign contracts agreeing to attend parent-teacher conferences, spend a minimum of 15 minutes reinforcing each day's lessons, and volunteer at the school.

Pushover Parents (14 min, Series III). Parenting can be a joy or it can be a nightmare. This 20/20 segment is not about joy. Children throwing tantrums, children out of control, parents without control--it's all here in this examination of what parents can do to regain control over their offspring.

The Value of a Wife (6 min, Series III). Gary Wendt is the CEO of a successful business. His wife, Lorna, agreed through 30 years of marriage to adopt the role of primary caregiver and household manager. Now that Gary and Lorna are divorcing a sticky issue has arisen; what is the value of Lorna's contribution to their partnership? Gary says it's $11.5 million, but Lorna contends it's at least half of Gary's $90 million net worth. This 20/20 segment sorts out the issues involved.

What's the Oldest A Woman Should Be Giving Birth? (8:40 min, Series III). Technology--from egg donation to in-vitro fertilization to surrogate parenting--has provided hope to countless women who have difficulty conceiving a child. In this case technology has helped a 63-year-old woman give birth. This *Nightline* segment looks at the moral and medical issues surrounding decisions that some see as "defying nature."

Other Sources

7 Up - 14 Up - 21 Up - 28 Up - 35 Up - 42 Up (various years; PBS). Noted director Michael Apted has followed the lives of two groups of British school children; those "to the manor born" and those of the working class. Starting from age 7 (in 1964) and continuing through adulthood, we glimpse the changes their lives have undergone. Later films contain clips from earlier films; these are a "must-see."

7 Up in the Soviet Union (1990, 68 min, IM). Like the Apted films mentioned above, this video presents a portrait of life for 20 seven-year-olds in the former Soviet Union.

Adolescence: Crisis or Change (1991, 60 min, IM). The sometimes slow development of autonomy during adolescence and its consequences--peer relationships, vocational decisions, individuation are examined.

Adolescent Development (1990, 30 min, IM). A broad overview of the changes experienced during adolescence is presented.

The Adult Years: Continuity and Change--The Fountain of Youth (28 min, PENN). Discusses research on biological theories of aging and their ethical implications.

The Aging Process (19 min, FHS). Summarizes the effects of aging on the mind and body and explores the "damage" and "cell clock" theories of aging. Behaviors that are related to longevity and health are also discussed.

Babywatching (50 min, FHS). Desmond Morris provides a baby's-eye-view of the world as he explores psychological and anthropological issues of development in a variety of cultures.

Character Formation in Different Cultures (8-part series, PENN). Based on the work of Margaret Mead and Gregory Bateson, several parts of the series examine an aspect of the relationship between culture and personality development in Bali and New Guinea. Segments include *Bathing Babies in Three Cultures* (11 min), *Childhood Rivalry in Bali and New Guinea* (17 min), *First Days in the Life of a New Guinea Baby* (20 min), *Karba's First Years: A Study of Balinese Childhood* (21 min), and *A Balinese Family* (20 min).

A Child Grows: The First Year (25 min, LS). The first 365 days of a child's life are a time of remarkable growth and development. This video, aimed at a lay audience, examines some of those changes. Follow up with *Toddlers: The Second Year of Life.*

Child's Play (1990, 24 min, IM). This BBC production looks at the theories of Piaget and George Herbert Mead in regard to the importance of play in development.

Cognitive Development (30 min, IM). Using examples of the child's cognitive skills at various stages, the program provides an overview of Piaget's theory and also addresses aspects being questioned by other researchers.

Developmental Phases Before and After Birth (30 min, FHS). Examines physical and psychological development from conception through the first year. Based upon cross-cultural similarities, differences are attributed to the quality if the mother-child relationship.

Discovering Psychology, Part 5: The Developing Child (1990, 30 min, ANN/CPB). Explores the contributions of heredity and environment to early development.

Discovering Psychology, Part 18: Maturing and Aging (1990, 30 min, ANN/CPB). Explores physical and psychological aspects of aging, and society's reactions to the aging process.

The Elementary Mind (1992, 30 min, IM). Robert Sternberg and Rochel Gelman discuss Piaget's views of memory, cognition, and intelligence. Also shown are experiments related to developing cognition.

Erik Erikson: A Life's Work (38 min, IM). Erik Erikson discusses his stage theory of psychosocial development.

The First 365 Days in the Life of a Child (Thirteen 28 min programs, FHS). A 13-part series examining developmental milestones for the newborn and at the end of each of the child's first

12 months. The first segment on the newborn may be particularly useful as a supplement for the discussion in this chapter.

The First Year of Life (28 min, FHS). Examines newborn sensory and cognitive abilities and how they contribute to its interactions with its environment and the development of individuality during the first year.

Family Influences (1992, 30 min, IM). Authoritative, permissive, authoritarian, and uninvolved parenting styles form the basis for this presentation of how family background influences people's views of themselves and others.

Florence and Robin: Lesbian Parenthood (52 min, FHS). Like any other couple, Robin and Florence would like to have a baby. Their lesbianism, however, presents obstacles to achieving their goals in a society that has conflicting attitudes about parenting. An informative film.

The Development of the Human Brain (46 min, PENN). Describes the development of the brain from conception to age eight.

Gender Socialization (1993, 60 min, IM). The impact of gender roles on self-esteem, behavior, and world views is considered.

Growing Old in a New Age (1993, 13 parts, 60 min each, ANN/CPB). This recent series looks at the physical and psychological consequences of growing older. Included in separate programs are topics such as sexuality and intimacy, intergenerational communication, illness and disability, myths and realities of aging, death and dying, and trends in the aging process as we become an older society.

The Infant Mind (1992, 30 min, IM). Piaget's views on infant cognition are presented and challenged. Recent research reveals that many cognitive operations appear earlier than previously believed.

The Influence of the Family (1991, 60 min, IM). An examination of how complex family interactions affect childhood development. Data on discipline styles, birth order, and various family structures are presented.

Make a Wish (5 min, PENN). Auditory and visual simulations allow the viewer to experience sensory loss associated with aging.

The Mind: Development (60 min, PBS). Focusing on particular brain cells, this program (part of a 9-part series) examines brain development from conception to age six.

Moral Development (30 min, IM). Examines a number of theories of moral development including Kohlberg, Piaget, social learning, and psychoanalytic.

Notable Contributors to the Psychology of Personality Series: Dr. Jean Piaget with Dr. Barbet Inhelder, Part 1 (40 min, PENN). Piaget and Inhelder summarize the stages of cognitive development and discuss traditional notions of motivation, learning, and perception from American psychology.

Play and Imagination (1992, 30 min, IM). The development of play, and its relation to social, cognitive, and emotional skills, is the topic of this video. Comparisons of Mexican and American mothers and their children reveal cultural differences in play.

Preschoolers: How Three and Four Year Olds Develop (24 min, LS). A companion to *A Child Grows: The First Year* and *Toddlers: The Second Year of Life*, this video looks at cognitive and social developmental milestones during the third and fourth years of life from an intuitive perspective.

The Psychological Development of the Child (8 parts, 21-28 min each, FHS). This series considers topics such as physical and psychological development before birth, the development of self-identity, and parent-child/world-child relationships.

Seasons of Life (1990, 5 parts, 60 min, ANN/CPB). This 5-part series is divided into programs that examine infancy and childhood, childhood and adolescence, early adulthood, middle adulthood, and late adulthood.

Sex and Marriage (1994, 30 min, IM). The variety of opinions and customs related to marriage, courtship, and sex across cultures is examined.

Sex Roles: Charting the Complexity of Development (1991, 60 min, IM). Freudian, social-learning, and cognitive-developmental approaches to understanding sex roles are presented.

Teenage Relationships (1992, 30 min, IM). The development of adolescent relationships, from peers to friends to love, forms the basis of this video.

Teenage Mind and Body (1992, 30 min, IM). Focuses on adolescent cognitive and physical development, including discussions of formal operational thought and moral development.

Time to Grow: Part 2, Contexts of Development (28 min, PENN). Discusses the interaction of genetic, social, economic, and cultural factors that contribute to child development.

Time to Grow: Part 17, The Elementary Mind (28 min, PENN). Examines the changes in intellectual abilities during middle childhood and their impact on later learning. The program also includes a discussion of intelligence and its measurement.

Toddlers: The Second Year of Life (26 min, LS). How terrible are the terrible two's? This video, aimed at a lay audience, addresses that question by looking at the developmental milestones of the second year of life. Follow this with *Preschoolers: How Three and Four Year Olds Develop*.

multimedia

Live! Psych

Module	Title	Book Page #
10.1	Evolutionary Psychology and the Evolution of Visual Preferences	p. 372

Screen 1 introduces the study of evolutionary psychology. Screen 2 introduces Robert Fantz' 1961 study of visual preferences in newborns. Student interacts with the screen by clicking on each disk to learn the amount of time newborns spent gazing at the various disks. Screen 3 presents the findings. Fantz found that infants spent more time looking at a human face more than any of the other patterns. Screen 4 introduces Mark Johnson's 1991 study of newborn orientation toward the face. Screen 5 presents the findings. The researchers found that the infants tracked the facelike pattern more than they did the scrambled and blank patterns. Screen 6 introduces Andrew Meltzoff and Keith Moore's 1983 study of infant imitation. The student clicks to see how babies responded when the adult researcher made gestures. Screen 7 presents the findings. The researchers found that newborns not only look at faces but often mimic gestures.

10.2   Piaget's Theory of Cognitive Development   p. 378

The first of these five screens present an overview of Piaget's cognitive stages of development. Import this screen to introduce each stage and the corresponding age range. You may also use this screen to discuss how the developmental processes of assimilation, accommodation, and equilibration enable individuals to progress from one cognitive stage to the next. Screens 2 through 5 may be used to identify and describe key cognitive milestones in each stage of development. Screen 2 identifies object permanence and separation anxiety as two key cognitive milestones during the sensorimotor stage. Screen 3 identifies symbolic representation and egocentricity as the cognitive milestones of the preoperational stage. Screen 4 identifies the ability to conserve as the major achievement of the concrete operational stage. Screen 5 identifies abstract reasoning and hypothetical thinking as characterizing the formal operational stage.

Principle of Conservation   p. 378

Import this screen to introduce Piaget's classic experiments of conservation. Discuss how this ability to conserve marks the transition from the preoperational to the concrete operational stages of development. Use this screen to compare and contrast the limitations of the preoperational and concrete operational child.

Conservation of Volume   p. 378

Import Screens 1 and 2 to view a simulation of a conservation of volume experiment.

Conservation of Mass   p. 378

Import Screens 1 and 2 to view a simulation of a conservation of mass experiment.

Web Investigations

Tick Tock Goes the Social and Biological Clock

In this activity important biological events, such as birth, puberty, or the birth of a first child, are related to the culturally-prescribed timing for important social events, such as college attendance, marriage, and parental leave from work. Our bodies pull us in some ways, our cultures pull us in others; this exercise explores the overlap between the two.

Making Connections

Methods in Developmental Psychology

Q What is the essential difference between cross-sectional and longitudinal studies?

A A cross-sectional study observes or tests people of different ages at the same point in time. A longitudinal study tests the same people two or more times, as they grow older.

Q What is a cohort?

A A cohort is all people born at the same time, such as all Americans born in 1960.

Prenatal Development

Q What is the difference between an embryo and a fetus?

A An embryo is the name given to the developing child from the period of about two weeks after conception, when the cells begin to differentiate, until three months after conception.

Q What is a critical period?

A A critical period is the developmental stage during which a particular toxin is most likely to harm an embryo or fetus.

Q Give three examples of teratogens.

A Teratogens include infectious agents, such as the viruses that cause rubella and AIDS, as well as alcohol, nicotine, and many legal and illegal drugs.

The Newborn Baby

Q What reflexes are present at or shortly after birth?

A The rooting, sucking, swallowing, grasping, and stepping reflexes are present at birth.

Q What evidence suggests the existence of innate temperamental differences in humans?

A Evidence that temperamental differences are innate may be seen in differences in the behaviors exhibited by babies from different cultures, which may be due to differences in genetic predispositions.

Q Describe the visual abilities of newborns.

A Newborns can see most clearly when objects are 8 to 10 inches from them. They prefer patterns with clear contrasts and find human faces particularly interesting; they can distinguish between their mother's face and that of a stranger.

Infancy and Childhood

Q Describe the general pattern of physical growth in infants and children.

A Children grow rapidly in their first year, but that growth takes place in fits and starts. Growth slows during the second year and gradually until adolescence. In the early years the head grows faster than the rest of the body, but after age 2 head growth slows and the rest of the body grows faster. While head growth is complete by age 10, the body continues to grow for several years after that.

Q How do internal and external factors interact to promote motor development?

A The biological processes referred to as maturation make possible the development of various motor skills, but the child's own activities also play a role. The child must experiment with a new skill and practice it before it becomes established.

Q Discuss current criticisms of Piaget's theory of cognitive development.

A The findings of much contemporary research have cast doubt on some aspects of Piaget's theory. It appears that infants have a more sophisticated understanding of the world than Piaget assumed, and there is evidence that social interaction plays a greater role in cognitive development than Piaget acknowledged. In addition, the interests and experiences of the individual child may influence cognitive development in ways that Piaget's theory cannot account for.

Q According to Gilligan, how does girls' moral development differ from boys'?

A According to Gilligan, girls are more likely to base their moral judgments on criteria of caring about others and maintaining relationships, whereas boys tend to base their moral judgments solely on abstract concepts of justice.

Q Briefly describe the process of language development.

A Language development begins with cooing and proceeds to babbling, which gradually begins to show signs of intonation. By around age 1 infants can use intonation to indicate commands and questions, and show signs of understanding what is said to them. The first word is uttered at this time. During the next few months the child builds a vocabulary of one-word sentences called holophrases. During the second year children attempt to learn the names of objects around them, and during the third year they begin to form two- and three-word sentences. After age 3 language production increases rapidly: By age 5 or 6 most children of a vocabulary of over 2,500 words and can construct sentences of 6 to 8 words.

Q What is attachment, and why is it important?

A Attachment is the emotional bond formed by an infant to its caregivers. It is essential to the development of basic trust, which enables infants to begin exploring their environment and develop a sense of independence or autonomy.

Q What evidence suggests that watching TV is linked to violent behavior?

A Evidence that watching violent TV programs is linked to violent behavior can be seen in the fact that children who frequently watch such programs are more aggressive than other children. According to social learning theory, these children are imitating models that they have observed being rewarded for violent behaviors.

Adolescence

Q Briefly describe the major physical changes of adolescence.

A The most obvious physical change of adolescence is the growth spurt, a rapid increase in height and weight. The hands, feet, arms, and legs lengthen; the torso grows; boys' chests broaden; and girls' hips widen. In addition, the chin and nose become more prominent and the lips fuller.

Q Define the two common fallacies of adolescent thinking.

A The two common fallacies of adolescent thinking are (a) the imaginary audience, teenagers' tendency to feel that they are constantly being observed and judged by others, and (b) the personal fable, adolescents' unrealistic sense of their own uniqueness.

Q Describe the process of identity formation during adolescence.

A Identity formation occurs when an adolescent integrates a number of different roles into a coherent whole. It requires a period of intense self-exploration called an identity crisis.

Q Discuss some causes of low self-esteem during adolescence.

A Low self-esteem during adolescence may be caused by concerns about physical appearance, problems in school, and, in girls, negative feelings about being female.

Adulthood

Q Describe some of the problems that commonly affect intimate relationships.

A When couples have children, the demands of the children may leave them with less time or energy for each other. Parenthood may also heighten conflicts between pursuit of careers and responsibilities at home.

Q What are some reasons that the world of work presents more problems today than in the past?

A The world of work is more complex than in the past, requiring a choice among many more possible careers. And because more women are working outside the home than ever before, problems like discrimination and sexual harassment are more common. Pressures are also created by the need to balance the demands of career and family and to find quality child care.

Q What cognitive changes occur in adulthood?

A In adulthood people's thinking becomes more flexible and practical.

Q How is Erikson's idea of generativity related to the midlife crisis?

A Generativity refers to the ability to continue being productive and creative. A person who experiences a midlife crisis must resolve it successfully in order to achieve generativity and not stagnate.

Q What changes are part of the "change of life"?

A The "change of life" refers to the decline in the function of the reproductive organs that occurs during middle age. In women this takes the form of menopause, the cessation of menstruation, accompanied by a sharp drop in the production of estrogen. In men it takes the form of a gradual decline in testosterone.

Late Adulthood

Q Describe the physical changes that accompany normal aging.

A In a person who is aging normally, the hair thins and turns white or gray; the skin wrinkles; bones become more fragile; muscles lose power; joints stiffen; circulation slows; blood pressure rises; energy declines; body shape and posture change; the reproductive organs atrophy; reaction times become slower; and the senses become less acute.

Q What important social changes occur during late adulthood, and what are their consequences?

A In late adulthood a person starts to interact with fewer other people and to perform social roles. Behavior becomes less influenced by social rules and expectations, and in time the person accepts the fact that there is a limit to social involvement. These changes do not necessarily entail a psychological disengagement from the social world.

Q Describe the course of Alzheimer's disease. How common is this condition?

A Alzheimer's disease begins with minor memory losses. As it progresses, personality changes may occur in which the person first becomes emotionally withdrawn and later suffers from delusions. In time victims of Alzheimer's become confused, lose the ability to speak, and can no longer care for themselves or recognize family members.

Q What are the five stages of dying?

A According to Kubler-Ross, the five stages of dying are denial, anger, bargaining, depression, and acceptance.

Video Classics

The Visual Cliff

SYNOPSIS: This clip demonstrates the basic experimental paradigm of visual cliff research. Several infants are shown on the visual cliff apparatus, with pinwheels and mothers and other inducements present. They behave as babies on a visual cliff typically behave. This vintage footage will give your students a sense of what the original research looked like.

Form a Hypothesis

Q Do you think the babies will crawl to their mothers at the deep end, in other words, will they crawl out over the cliff?

A If the perception of depth is inborn, the infants should refuse to crawl over the cliff.

Test Your Understanding

Q Because infants cannot tell us whether they perceive depth, the visual cliff was devised. What are other methods a psychologist could use to study infant development?

A Infants can be shaped through operant conditioning to respond to a target stimulus with a head turn but to withhold the head turn when other stimuli are presented. If the infant turns to look at, or better hear a stimulus, she or he must perceive it.

Q Most babies would crawl to their mothers when the mothers called from the shallow end. But despite mothers' calling and coaxing, most babies did not crawl out over the cliff. They clearly demonstrated their perception of the steepness of the drop. Why do you suppose that the researchers used infants who were between 6 and 14 months old?

A Younger infants would not be able to crawl and therefore would not be able to demonstrate through their behavior that they had perceived the drop.

Thinking Critically

Q Do you think that the results of the study prove that the ability to perceive depth is innate rather than learned? Why or why not?

A Although impressive, infants who can crawl have had approximately six months of experience before being tested. We cannot rule out that depth perception develops through these earlier experiences.

Q How are infants younger than 6 months tested on the visual cliff?

A They could be placed on the deep end of the cliff and monitored for signs of emotional distress, such as crying and fussing.

Q What sensory abilities are inborn or develop very early in life?

A All sensory systems are inborn. Repeated interactions with the physical world give rise to enhancement of sensory acuity and the ability to perceive ('interpret') sensory stimulation.

Piaget on Child Development

SYNOPSIS: Jean Piaget is interviewed regarding his ideas about early childhood development. He provides detailed answers...in French. Happily, a British voice-over interpreter clears things up for those of us who failed French in high school. The sensorimotor period, development of self-awareness in the infant, and other basic Piagetian concepts are discussed as the man himself wields his pipe emphatically.

Form a Hypothesis

Q What cognitive stage of development undergoes the most rapid change?

A Sensorimotor period. In this stage, the child moves from virtually nonexistent self-awareness to an understanding of himself or herself as an agent of action.

Test Your Knowledge

Q What are criticisms of Piaget's theory of cognitive development?

A Not all developmental psychologists agree that development occurs following discontinuous stages. The ages established for each stage may be too late, e.g., children can accomplish tasks earlier than Piaget asserted. The theory may be culture-bound in that it applies more reliably to children in Western cultures.

Q Does cognitive development progress through a series of distinct stages or is it gradual?

A Evidence exists for both assertions. However, evidence seems to be mounting to support the notion that cognitive development is a continuous process.

Thinking Critically

Q What cognitive achievements and limitations characterize each stage of cognitive development?

A
Sensorimotor stage;
    Achievement: development of first mental representations
    Limitations: absence of object permanence and representational thought

Preoperational stage;
    Achievement: language and concept development
    Limitation: egocentrism

Concrete-Operational stage;
    Achievement: ability to mentally manipulate internal representations of objects
    Limitation: inability to manipulate abstract concepts

Formal-Operational stage;
    Achievement: ability to manipulate abstract ideas and formal relationships
    Limitations: theoretically, none.

Interview with Barbel Inhelder

SYNOPSIS: The distinction between performance and competence is the topic of this video clip. Inhelder suggests that standardized intelligence tests measure intellectual performance (especially as it relates to tasks in school), whereas the assessment of competence (i.e., the potential or ability to perform a task) yields different and complementary information about an individual.

Form a Hypothesis

Q How is the Stanford-Binet related to the Piagetian theory of cognitive development?

A According to Inhelder, the Stanford-Binet assesses an individual's ability to perform. A Piagetian analysis would note what a child could accomplish, whether or not she or he performs at that level.

Test Your Knowledge

Q What is the distinction between performance and competence? According to Dr. Inhelder, which is more important to know about a child—performance or competence?

A In this context, performance refers to what a child does on a test of intelligence. Competence reflects a child's 'possibilities', what she or he is capable of. It is important to assess competence as many factors may interfere with performance and could reflect correctable conditions.

Q Why is intelligence measured?

A Intelligence is measured to estimate competence or potential.

Thinking Critically

Q How was IQ originally defined? How is it defined today?

A IQ used to reflect a child's absolute limit in terms of intellectual development. Today, IQ is viewed as establishing a range of potential within which an environment can promote intellectual development.

Web Links

1. http://classweb.gmu.edu/awinsler/div7/homepage.shtml

APA's Division 7 (Developmental Psychology) homepage. This site provides links that both you and your students will find valuable as you discuss this topic.

2. http://server.bmod.athabascau.ca/html/aupr/developmental.htm

Psychology Center: Developmental Psychology. Numerous links to sites related to developmental psychology. Ask your students to pick a timeframe in lifespan development (i.e., adolescence, old age, infancy) and explore 2 or 3 relevant links from this site. A brief report on what they found would be in order.

3. http://www.ecdgroup.com

International resources in support of young children and their families are the focus here.

.4. http://maple.lemoyne.edu/~hevern/psychref4-4.html
PsychREF: Developmental Psychology. This site provides links to other resources regarding childhood and adolescence. Your younger students may find some of the adolescent material still quite relevant.

5. http://education.indiana.edu/cas/

ADOL: Adolescence Directory OnLine. A resource guide for teens, counselors, educators, health practitioners, and researchers of adolescent issues.

transparencies

Series V

60. *The Direction of Movement in Speech Production and Comprehension*
This diagram shows a linear model of the relationship between meaning, sentences, morphemes, and phonemes.

61. *Milestones in Language Development*
This transparency presents information about the average age when different milestones in language development are attained. Children often depart from these averages.

62. *Vocabulary Size and Age*
This graph illustrates the dramatic increase in vocabulary in normal language development.

72. *The Twenty-Three Pairs of Chromosomes Found in Every Normal Human Cell*
Just what it sounds like.

73. *Transmission of Eye Color by Dominant and Recessive Genes*
The four possible combinations of eye-color genes in a parents' offspring are depicted.

74. *Longitudinal and Cross-Sectional Research*
This transparency contrasts these two research designs.

75. *Milestones in Motor Development*
The average ages and variations in age for motor development are shown.

76. *Piaget's Periods of Cognitive Development*
The four periods of development and their associated age ranges are depicted.

77. *Piaget's Tests of Conservation*
Conservation of volume and number are illustrated in this transparency.

78. *Growth According to Age and Gender*
This graph shows height and weight charts for boys and girls of different ages.

79. *Marcia's Model of Identity Formation*
Identity achievement, identity foreclosure, identity diffusion, and moratorium are shown.

80. *A Life Span Profile of Influences*
The relative strength of age-graded, history-graded, and nonnormative influences is shown.

81. *Fluid and Crystallized Intelligence*
This transparency shows the changes in fluid and crystallized intelligence over the lifespan.

82. *Stages of Confronting Death*
The traditional stages of confronting death are shown in this transparency.

85. *Erikson's Eight Stages of Personality Development*
Each stage and its associated crisis is shown.

Handout 10-1

Development Across the Lifespan

Instructions: Choose three words that are descriptive of each decade below and write your responses on the blank next to each one. To do this task, you should think of a hypothetical person from each decade (e.g., a person who is between the ages of 50 and 59) and write the words that come to mind when thinking of that person and what their life is like.

DECADE	DESCRIPTORS
0 - 9	_____
10 - 19	_____
20 - 29	_____
30 - 39	_____
40 - 49	_____
50 - 59	_____
60 - 69	_____
70 - 79	_____
80 - 89	_____
90 - 99	_____

Adapted from Rebelsky, F. G. (1981). Life span development. In L. T. Benjamin, Jr. & K. D. Lowman (Eds.), *Activities handbook for the teaching of psychology* (pp. 131-132). Washington, DC: American Psychological Association.

Chapter 11 Personality

chapter outline 314

learning objectives 317

lecture suggestions

    Freud, Skinner, Rogers 318
    Introverts and Extraverts 319
    Archetypes 320
    The Study of Bumps On the Head 320
    Gender Differences in Personality 321
    Hippocratic Oafs 322
    Allport on Personality Development 322
    L P Q R T 323

demonstrations and activities

    Defining Personality 324
    A Jungian Exploration of the Personal Unconscious 324
    Constructing a Life Line 325
    Just For Fun: The Hidden Brain Damage Scale 325
    Using Projective Tests in Personality Assessment 325
    Doodling as a Projective Technique 326
    The Sentence Completion Test 326
    Identifying Defense Mechanisms 326
    Role Playing Defense Mechanisms 327

student assignments

    Personality Collage 328
    Applying Personality Theories to TV Characters 328

video 329

multimedia 331

transparencies 338

handouts

    Defining Your Personal View of Personality 339
    Exploring the Personal Unconscious 340
    Jungian Complex Indicators 341
    Hidden Brain Damage Scale 342
    Doodling Exercise 343
    Analysis Guidelines for Doodles 344
    Sentence Completion Test 345
    Sentence Completion Test Scoring Guidelines 348

chapter outline

I. The Case of Jaylene Smith
A case study of a young woman is presented as a theme throughout the chapter

II. Psychodynamic Theories
Personality is the result of unconscious, often sexual, motivations and conflicts

A. Sigmund Freud
1. How personality is structured
    a. Id, ego, superego
    b. Pleasure principle, reality principle, ego ideal
2. Defense mechanisms
    a. Denial: Refusing to acknowledge a painful reality
    b. Repression: Banishing uncomfortable thoughts from consciousness
    c. Projection: Attributing one's motives, feelings, wishes to others
    d. Identification: Taking on characteristics of someone else
    e. Regression: Reverting to behaviors and defenses inappropriate to one's age
    f. Intellectualization: Thinking abstractly about problems or stresses
    g. Reaction formation: Expressing exaggerated forms of beliefs opposite to one's own
    h. Displacement: Shifting repressed motives to a less-powerful source
    i. Sublimation: Redirecting repressed motives to socially acceptable channels
3. How personality develops
    a. Libido: Energy generated by the sexual instinct
    b. Oral, anal, phallic, latency, genital stages of personality development
        i. Oedipus and Electra complexes during phallic stage

B. Carl Jung
1. Personal unconscious contains repressed thoughts, experiences, ideas
2. Introvert, extravert, rational, irrational summarize people's basic natures

C. Alfred Adler
1. Compensation of shortcomings impels positive striving toward perfection
    a. Inferiority complex: A fixation that produces emotional stagnation

D. Karen Horney
1. Anxiety is a stronger motive than Freud's sexual energy
    a. Neurotic trends help in coping with anxiety
        i. Submission, aggression, detachment are examples

E. Erik Erikson
1. Eight stages of development and associated conflicts
    a. Trust versus mistrust

        b. Autonomy versus shame and doubt
        c. Initiative versus guilt
        d. Industry versus inferiority
        e. Identity versus role confusion
        f. Intimacy versus isolation
        g. Generativity versus stagnation
        h. Integrity versus despair
  F. A psychodynamic view of Jaylene Smith
  G. Evaluating psychodynamic theories
    1. Psychodynamic theory is difficult to evaluate, although widely known
        a. Some criticisms of culture-bound nature of ideas
        b. Some criticisms of unscientific nature of ideas
        c. Some experimental support for some ideas

III. Humanistic Personality Theories

Personality theories that assert the fundamental goodness and strivings of people

  A. Carl Rogers
    1. Actualizing and self-actualizing tendencies shape development
    2. Fully functioning persons are "on track" to actualization
        a. Unconditional positive regard helps the process
        b. Conditional positive regard limits the process
  B. A humanistic view of Jaylene Smith
  C. Evaluating humanistic theories
    1. Humanism is largely unscientific and empirically untestable

IV. Trait Theories

Categorizing and describing individual differences in personality

  A. Development of trait theories
    1. Early approaches identified thousands of traits
    2. Cattell's use of factor analysis produces 16 main dimensions
  B. The Big 5 approach seems to capture primary dimensions of personality
    1. Extraversion, Agreeableness, Conscientiousness, Emotional stability, Openness to experience
    2. Are the Big Five traits universal?
  C. A trait view of Jaylene Smith
  D. Evaluating trait theories
    1. Traits only offer description, no explanation
    2. Traits represent populations, not individuals
    3. Traits may not capture the complexity of human behavior

V. Cognitive Social-Learning Theories

Roots of personality in thought, action, and response to environment

A. Locus of control and self-efficacy
1. Expectancies produce effects on behavior in a given situation
2. Locus of control influences approach to situations
3. Self-efficacy: Feeling that one can meet one's goals
4. Performance standard: Standard to rate adequacy of behavior

B. A cognitive-social learning view of Jaylene Smith

C. Evaluating cognitive social-learning theories
1. Avoids extremes of case studies, trait theories
2. Empirically testable
3. Hold promise for explaining a wide range of behavior

VI. Personality Assessment

A. The personal interview
1. Structured or unstructured interviews can gather a wealth of information

B. Direct observation
1. Direct observation or videotape can capture person/environment interaction

C. Objective tests
1. Tests administered and scored in a standardized way
    a. 16 Personality Factor Questionnaire
    b. Minnesota Multiphasic Personality Inventory

D. Projective tests
1. Ambiguous or unstructured material that elicits a variety of responses
    a. Rorschach inkblot technique
    b. Thematic Apperception Test

learning objectives

After reading this chapter, students should be able to:

1. Define personality.

2. Summarize the interaction among Freud's id, ego, and superego.

3. List and describe Freud's five stages of psychosexual development.

4. Describe all of the defense mechanisms.

5. Differentiate between the theories of Jung, Adler, Horney, and Erikson.

6. Identify Erik Erikson's eight stages of personality development.

7. Contrast Carol Rogers' humanistic theory with Freudian theory.

8. Explain trait theory and list the traits of the Big Five model.

9. Compare cognitive social-learning theories to other views of personality.

10. Describe the four basic tools psychologists use to measure personality.

11. List two objective tests and their uses. List the advantages and disadvantage of objective tests.

12. Discuss the advantages of projective tests. Explain how the Rorschach Test and the Thematic Apperception Test are administered.

lecture suggestions

Freud, Skinner, Rogers

Sigmund Freud, B. F. Skinner, and Carl Rogers were arguably three of the most influential personality theorists. Each took as his aim a greater understanding of human nature, although each adopted a distinct perspective on personality. Robert Nye has summarized some of these differences among these three thinkers.

Views of Basic Human Nature

Freud's psychoanalytic view of human nature is rather pessimistic. Driven by primitive urges, humans are little more than controlled savages seeking to satisfy sexual and aggressive pleasures. The internal conflicts between id, ego, and superego only serve to exacerbate the turmoil at the root of personality. This dark view is in sharp contrast to Rogers' humanism, which starts from the perspective that humans are basically good and continually striving to be even better. Motivations for growth, creativity, and fulfillment pepper Rogers' optimistic stance on human nature. With Freud pessimistic and Rogers optimistic, Skinner is left somewhat neutral on human nature. True to his behaviorist approach, Skinner would have difficulty supporting notions of either internal turmoil or internal motives for fulfillment. Although Skinner acknowledged that genetic factors were important in determining which behaviors were emitted (and eventually reinforced), he saw environment as exerting a stronger effect on shaping behavior.

Views of Personality Development

Freud's psychosexual stages and their associated milestones and conflicts were key to his overall view of human nature. Personality, like most human qualities, developed slowly over time. Rogers agreed with this general notion of personality as changing and unfolding, but stressed the positive aspects of growth fueled by unconditional positive regard. Skinner also endorsed the notion of change, but emphasized humans as behavior emitters. The changes in "personality" over time are actually due to changes in behaviors, their consequences, and various response contingencies.

Views of Maladjustment and Therapy

All three theorists saw a link between personality and maladjustment. Conflicts among unconscious desires and the strain of internal tensions produce maladjustment from Freud's perspective. The goal of therapy was to uncover the hidden roots of current problems. Rogers thought otherwise. The interruption or stunting of actualization processes, due largely to receiving conditional regard from ourselves and from others, was responsible for maladjustment. The goal of therapy was to point out sources of unconditional positive regard and to orient the person back to a path of growth and personal fulfillment. "Neurotic," "psychotic," and "actualized" would be hard pressed to find a home in Skinner's psychology. Environments cause maladaptive behaviors, such as when undesirable behaviors are reinforced or there is a history of excessive punishment. The goal of therapy is to change or reapply reinforcement schedules to correct the current maladaptive behaviors.

Views on the Study of Human Behavior

None of these thinkers particularly endorsed traditional experimental procedures. Although Skinner did perform numerous quantitative, controlled, laboratory studies, he disdained theorizing and avoided statistical tests. Freud based his views on qualitative, subjective judgments of individuals, and he drew his inspiration as much from literature, art, and society as he did the clinic. Rogers perhaps held the most balanced view. Although he endorsed objective, quantitative studies of behavior, he also advocated the use of subjective knowledge and phenomenological knowledge. His own work relied heavily on these latter two approaches.

Views of Society

Civilization and Its Discontents summarizes Freud's view of society. Primitive sexual and aggressive instincts are not likely to find free expression in most civilizations, although society can ease this conflict by providing avenues for sublimating these desires. A balance of expression and sublimation within an evolving society would complement Freud's view of human nature. *Walden Two* might summarize Skinner's view of society, although *Beyond Freedom and Dignity* could serve equally well. Because society controls the behavior of its members it needs to be constructed thoughtfully and efficiently. Reinforcement of some behaviors and the extinction of others will eventually benefit all members of a society. Finally, any number of Rogers' writings hold clues to his view of society's role in daily life. Rogers felt that societies were generally too restrictive and static, and that most social institutions worked against growth and development of the individual. Freedom for alternative lifestyles and opportunities for creative outlets are important elements of a Rogerian world.

Nye, R. D. (1996). Three psychologies: Perspectives from Freud, Skinner, and Rogers (5th ed.). Pacific Grove, CA: Brooks/Cole.

Introverts and Extraverts

The introversion/extraversion dimension has been a mainstay of trait approaches to personality. In one form or another it has found a home in the thinking of everyone from Hippocrates to Hans Eysenck to devotees of the Big Five. As such, considerable energy has been spent cataloging the factors that distinguish introverts from extraverts, such as that introverts tend to salivate more than extraverts when lemon juice is placed in their mouth. Here are a few more examples, drawn from Bem P. Allen:

Eye-blink Conditioning

Introverts demonstrate faster classical conditioning because they are more easily aroused. Using an eye-blink conditioning procedure, Eysenck and Levey (1972) found that introverts exhibited greater conditioning and were able to be conditioned with weaker stimuli than were extraverts.

Reactions to Bad News

Fremont, Means, and Means (1970) administered a task that required students to learn a digit-symbol code. After the learning phase, they were either told that they had scored higher or lower than average or given no feedback at all. They were then immediately given a test of anxiety. Introverts showed significantly higher anxiety than extraverts after receiving negative feedback, but did not differ under any of the other conditions.

Drug Effects

Hans Eysenck (1962) suggested that depressants like alcohol would increase extraverted-like behavior, while stimulants like coffee or tobacco would increase introverted-like behavior. His hypothesis has received some support. Jones (1974) found that the effect of alcohol was greater on extraverts than introverts, while Gupta and Kaur (1978) found that the stimulant dextroamphetamine enhanced the effectiveness of extraverts while inhibiting that of introverts. Allen (1994) noted that one explanation of hyperactivity in children is that they are underaroused, much like extraverts. Therefore, administering the stimulant Ritalin may act to make them more like introverts, thus increasing their attention and responsiveness.

Allen, B. P. (1994). *Personality theories*. Boston: Allyn and Bacon.

Reprinted from Hill, W. G. (1995). Instructor's resource manual for *Psychology* by S. F. Davis and J. J. Palladino. Englewood Cliffs, NJ: Prentice Hall.

Archetypes

Chapter 10 briefly mentions some of Jung's better-known archetypes, such as anima/animus or the persona. These denizens of the collective unconscious are joined by a number of other archetypes.

- *The Hero.* From world leaders to mythic gods to gargantuan sandwiches, the hero represents someone who rises to the occasion to conquer and vanquish with great might. Often the hero is a relatively weak individual, but one who connects to powerful internal forces. Herein lies a blueprint for the development of one's own sense of individuality.

- *The Trickster.* This archetype is often seen as a collective shadow figure representing the underdeveloped or inferior traits of individuals. In mythology (such as many Native American folktales) the trickster is often dull-witted but someone who typically produces positive outcomes.

- *Great Mother.* The Virgin Mary, the Hindu goddess Kali, fertility symbols, Henry Moore sculptures, "Mother Earth," myths and legends of motherhood...these are all reflections of our archetype of one who ushers us into existence and nurtures us.

- *Spiritual Father.* Our image and sense of fathers is tied to spirituality. An obvious link, established well before Jung, is found in many Judeo-Christian religions.

- *Mandala.* The archetype of order. Examples of this are plentiful both within and across cultures. Circles, squares, fractal forms, swastikas, wheels, yin-yang, crosses, and numbers are a few examples.

- *Transformation.* Journeys to the self, whether in mythology, dreams, or symbols, represent transformation. From Diogenes' search for an honest person to someone's life-altering revelation, transformation plays a role in human development and growth.

Jung, C. G. (1968). *Alchemical studies* (R. F. C. Hull, Trans.). Princeton, NJ: Princeton University Press.
Jung, C. G. (1969). *Four archetypes: Mother, rebirth, spirit, trickster* (R. F. C. Hull, Trans.). Princeton, NJ: Princeton University Press.

The Study of Bumps on the Head

Franz Joseph Gall (1758-1828) was a skilled brain anatomist whose descriptions of the brain's gray and white matter, cerebral commissures, and contralateral innervation remain an important part of the knowledge base of neurology and psychology. Also, Gall was among the first to discuss the relationship between brain and behavior. Unlike the dualism of Descartes, Gall's view asserted that the mind was located in the brain. His studies of the brains of animals and of people of various ages and types indicated that cognitive abilities are based on the amount and placement of healthy cortical tissue, and that greater amounts of cortical tissue are usually associated with superior functioning. This field was named *phrenology*. An additional important aspect of Gall's view was that personality characteristics and abilities are determined by independent, genetically determined, neurologically distinct structures (Fodor, 1983). Gall postulated 27 faculties, including amativeness (sexual behavior), acquisitiveness, reverence, verbal memory, marvelousness, love of the picturesque, defensiveness, and number.

Gall's neuroanatomy research and "faculty" theory led to the notion of phrenology. Unfortunately, it is phrenology for which Gall is remembered best and as a result, ridiculed. His true accomplishments have been buried under the quackery of phrenology, even though it was his followers, rather than Gall himself, who were responsible for the worst sins of phrenology (Fodor, 1983). What's more, Gall's theories are often misrepresented or misunderstood by critics and modern historians.

Phrenology, as developed by Gall and his followers such as Spurzheim and Combe, asserted that (1) the mind is located in the brain; (2) mental abilities are determined by innate faculties that are located in specific parts of the brain; (3) the size of the brain devoted to a faculty indicates the strength of that faculty; (4) the shape and external characteristics of the skull at particular locations reflect the brain beneath those locations; and (5) examination of the head/skull allows a description of the individual's personality and abilities (Kurtz, 1985). These ideas supposedly were stimulated by Gall's boyhood observation that several of his classmates who were not generally more intelligent, but who were more scholastically successful because of their superior memory abilities, all had large, bulging eyes (Fancher, 1979), and were furthered by Gall's later anatomical research. Through the study of many individuals, Gall and his associates mapped the regions of the skull they believed corresponded to each of the 27 faculties. For example, Gall's boyhood observation led to the hypothesis that verbal memory ability is reflected in the region of the cortex lying immediately behind the eyes: The brain is overdeveloped at that location when ability is great, and causes the eyes to protrude. Gall's interactions with a "Passionate Widow" revealed a large, hot neck, which he interpreted as a sign that the cerebellum at the lower back of the brain was the seat of sexual behavior ("amativeness") (Fancher, 1979, p. 48).

Phrenology has been attacked on several points. First, the skull does not accurately reflect the underlying brain. Thus, even if the size of the brain at specific locations did indicate the strength of the corresponding faculty, the skull's topology would be worthless for determining this. Second, although certain abilities do seem to be localized in specific parts of the brain (e.g., speech production at Broca's area), the amount of brain tissue does not reflect the level of the ability. Also, the 27 faculties are poorly chosen and described. Many are ill-defined, and others are usually considered to be the result of the combination of several other abilities, not independent faculties. A third major problem was the rather unscientific methods of research used to "confirm" the theory. Gall and his associates reportedly cited only cases that supported the theory, while ignoring or explaining away negative results (Fancher, 1979). Gall employed the concept of "balancing actions" by one or more of the 27 faculties when the characteristics of the skull did not match the characteristics of the subject. As Fancher (1979) points out, with 27 factors involved, Gall could explain just about any result. Theories that do not allow any chance of disconfirmation are not good scientific theories.

Although most of the scientific community quickly savaged Gall and phrenology, phrenology retained great popularity among the general public. By 1832 there were 29 phrenology societies in Great Britain, and several journals devoted to phrenology were being published there and in America. Eventually, however, the interest in phrenology dissipated, and today phrenology receives attention only as a quaint example of pseudoscience. Kurtz lists three primary criteria for pseudoscience: (1) Stringent experimental methods are not routinely employed in the research; (2) There is no testable, coherent conceptual framework; and (3) Claims of confirmation are made even though questionable methods were used. By these criteria, phrenology is a pseudoscience, not merely an incorrect theory.

Fancher, R. E. (1979). *Pioneers of psychology.* New York: Norton. Pp. 43-58.
Fodor, J. A. (1983). *The modularity of mind.* Cambridge, MA: MIT Press/Bradford Books. Pp. 14-23.
Kurtz, P. (1985). Is parapsychology a science? In P. Kurtz (Ed.), *A skeptic's handbook of parapsychology.* Buffalo, NY: Prometheus Books.
Robinson, D. N. (1982). Cerebral plurality and the unity of self. *American Psychologist, 37,* 904-910.

Reprinted from Whitford, F. W. (1995). Instructor's resource manual for *Psychology: Principles and applications* by S. Worchel and W. Shebilske. Englewood Cliffs, NJ: Prentice Hall.

Gender Differences in Personality

Personality can be assessed in a variety of ways, from the musings of Freud to laboratory approaches linking traits and behaviors to the use of scales such as the MMPI, CPI, NEO, or 16PF. Alan Feingold of Yale University recently conducted four meta-analytic reviews of gender differences in personality, drawing both on the vast literature in this area (between 1958 and 1992) and on normative data generated by well-known personality inventories (between 1940 and 1992). In so doing he replicated and extended the findings of earlier reviews of gender differences, such as the work of Eleanor Maccoby and Carol Jacklin (1974; discussed in the text in Chapter 16) and Judy Hall (1984; see Chapter 16).

Gender differences of note were that men tended to be more assertive than women and tended to have slightly higher self-esteem. Women were higher than men in the areas of trust, extraversion, anxiety, and "tender-mindedness" or nurturance. Feingold found that the magnitude of sex differences did not appreciably differ as a function of age, educational level, years in which the data were collected, or nations (U.S. versus non-U.S.). This suggests some stability to the dimensions measured and probably more so to the measurement process itself. No consistent differences between the sexes were found for traits such as social anxiety, reflectiveness, locus of control, impulsiveness, activity, or orderliness.

Feingold, A. (1994). Gender differences in personality: A meta-analysis. *Psychological Bulletin, 116*, 429-456.
Hall, J. A. (1984). *Nonverbal sex differences*. Baltimore: Johns Hopkins University Press.
Maccoby, E. E., & Jacklin, C. N. (1974). *The psychology of sex differences*. Stanford, CA: Stanford University Press.

Hippocratic Oafs

Hippocrates' four-humors theory may be the oldest constitutional theory of personality. Hippocrates (460-377 B.C.) postulated the operation of four fluids or *humors* within the body, imbalances or excesses of which would have emotional as well as physical consequences. This chart shows the four humors, the condition created by too much of each, and their respective emotions:

Humor ⇨	Blood	Yellow Bile	Black Bile	Phlegm
Condition ⇨	Sanguinity	Biliousness	Melancholia	Phlegmatic
Emotion ⇨	Cheerfulness	Anger	Sadness	Lethargy

The Hippocratic theory of personality popularized the practice of bloodletting--opening a vein or applying leeches to "drain off" excessive amounts of the troublesome humor. In medieval Europe, it was common for barber-surgeons (whose professional practice relied on sharp instruments like knives and razors) to advertise their bloodletting services by posting a sign depicting a pale human arm traced with a crimson spiral of blood. (Remember that a largely illiterate culture required signs with pictures rather than words.) The lasting legacy of the bloodletters is the modern barber pole, a highly stylized version of the white arm with the bloody red stripe, advertising the services within.

Adapted from Whitford, F. W. (1995). Instructor's resource manual for *Psychology: Principles and applications* by S. Worchel and W. Shebilske. Englewood Cliffs, NJ: Prentice Hall.

Allport on Personality Development

To many people, Gordon Allport's claim to fame in the personality literature was his compendium of some 18,000 trait terms used to describe people and their personality characteristics. (In fact, some see his contribution as one of pure stamina, to have counted all those words!) Clearly Allport was a seminal figure in both personality and social psychology, and his contributions are well established through his work on prejudice, social cognition, the transmission of rumor, religiosity, the nature of the self, and writings on the history of psychology.

What is sometimes lost in these contributions is Allport's theory of the development of personality. Overshadowed by better-known approaches, such as those of Freud or Erikson, Allport's ideas in this area have languished somewhat. Nonetheless, he is unique in several respects. First, unlike Freud, Allport argued for a certain core unity to personality; rather than warring id, ego, and superego, Allport thought that with maturation came a unity of interests, traits, biological predispositions, and so on. Second, Allport thought that his stages were somewhat arbitrary. Unlike Erikson or Piaget, he believed that the stages of personality development may occur at different times for different people, and that the development of any single individual would actually be an uninterrupted, continuous process. Finally, Allport thought that personality developed from a foundation of heredity, mainly an infant's activity level and temperament.

Bodily sense is the first stage of development in infancy, followed by *self-identity*. The child learns what different sensations and experiences are like, and begins to develop a sense of existence as an independent agent. From age 2 to 3 *ego-enhancement* takes place, characterized by building self-esteem. *Ego-extensions*, as when a child begins to identify his or her toys, his or her parents, or other personal belongings, mark the next stage. *Self-image* refers to the process of evaluating our present self and considering future aspirations; children age 4 to 6 are capable of forming these future goals. From age 6 to 12 the child is a *rational agent*: solving problems, doing schoolwork, planning activities, and so forth., Rather than a Freudian period of conflicted sexuality and general inner turmoil, Allport saw these years as a time of developing adaptive functions. *Propriate striving*, beginning in adolescence, is marked by the development of a life ideology or sense of directedness. Finally, adults achieve the status of *self as knower*, whereby they integrate the previous aspects of development into a unified whole.

Allport, G. W. (1937). *Personality: A psychological interpretation*. New York: Henry Holt.
Allport, G. W., & Odbert, H. S. (1936). Trait-names: A psycholexical study. *Psychological Monographs, 47*, No. 211.
Cloninger, S. C. (1993). *Theories of personality: Understanding persons*. Englewood Cliffs, NJ: Prentice Hall.

L P Q R T

Raymond Cattell's view of personality and methods of assessing it are mentioned briefly in Chapter 10. Cattell was somewhat unique in advocating a variety of approaches to the study of traits. Some of his contemporaries adopted a strictly statistical approach, others pursued a purely theoretical approach, while others opted for a largely content-based approach to assessment and still others used criterion-keying methods. Although Cattell used factor analysis primarily, he relied on a range of data and a combination of techniques.

L-data, or data from a person's *life record*, represents the activities and events of people's daily lives over an extended period. Much like keeping a diary, Cattell's research participants might report on their social contacts, their states of health, the organizations they've joined, mishaps or illnesses experienced, and so on. The key to this approach is to gather lots of evidence from lots of realms over time. Q-data, from *questionnaires*, represents a more typical personality assessment approach. Here research participants would supply responses to standardized measures, such as the MMPI or Cattell's own 16PF. Because of the limitations typically associated with questionnaire responses (e.g., response biases, lack of insight or knowledge about the self, social desirability) these data are not used as the sole source of information about a person. Rather, T-data, or data derived from *tests*, are relied on to supplement Q-data. Here an individual's personality dimensions are assessed without the person's knowledge of which aspects of behavior are being measured, as when direct observation is used or projective techniques are applied.

This mass of data can then be examined using either *R-technique* or *P-technique* factor analysis. R-technique involves analyzing the responses of multiple individuals, primarily to identify clusters of traits or commonalties among behaviors. P-technique involves tracing the strength of traits over a period of time for single individuals. The parallels to idiographic versus nomothetic approaches to understanding behavior, or between-subjects versus within-subjects experimental designs, are clear. Cattell was an early advocate of unifying these various approaches to understanding people.

A brief historical note: Contrary to popular opinion, Raymond Cattell did not inspire the famous Lucky Strike cigarette ad ("**L**ucky **S**trike **M**eans **F**ine **T**obacco").

Cattell, R. B. (1950). Personality: A systematic, theoretical, and factual study. New York: McGraw-Hill.
Cattell, R. B. (1973). Personality and mood by questionnaire. San Francisco: Jossey-Bass.
Hergenhahn, B. R. (1994). An introduction to theories of personality (4th ed.). Englewood Cliffs, NJ: Prentice Hall.

demonstrations

Defining Personality

The textbook defines a variety of personality theories, some of which may or may not correspond to students' personal theories of personality. Kerber (1987) described an activity designed to allow students to consider their personal theory of personality and how it relates to the theories described in the textbook as a means of introducing the major theoretical approaches. After a brief introduction to the concept of personality, distribute the questionnaire in Handout 11-1 and go over the instructions. Kerber designed the list of items on the questionnaire so that they included "concepts associated with each of five major approaches to personality: psychoanalytic (childhood experiences, unconscious motives, sexual instincts); humanistic (conscious awareness, the self, subjective feelings); cognitive (interpretations of experience, organization of reality, expectations); trait (temperament, abilities, enduring characteristics); and learning (external environment, rewards and punishments, observable behavior)." After the students have completed the questionnaire, ask them to share and explain their choices. You should point that the items represent different theories and which theories most closely match their personal theory as indicated by their item selections. Kerber also suggested collecting the questionnaires and summarizing the class data so that individuals can compare their choices to the entire class. Kerber noted that this activity is effective in introducing the concept of personality, providing an overview of personality theories, and exploring the notion of personal theories of personality and their possible functions in behavior.

Kerber, K. W. (1987). What is personality? A personal appraisal. In V. P. Makosky, L. G. Whittemore, & A. M. Rogers (Eds.), *Activities handbook for the teaching of psychology: Vol. 2* (pp. 182-184). Washington, DC: American Psychological Association.

Reprinted from Hill, W. G. (1995). Instructor's resource manual for *Psychology* by S. F. Davis and J. J. Palladino. Englewood Cliffs, NJ: Prentice Hall.

A Jungian Exploration of the Personal Unconscious

As noted in the text, Carl Jung proposed two distinct levels of the unconscious, a *collective* unconscious (consisting of all the memories and behavior patterns inherited from past generations) and the *personal* unconscious (consisting of repressed thoughts, forgotten experiences, and undeveloped ideas). Jung further argued that the personal unconscious contains clusters of emotionally important thoughts called *complexes*. These complexes--which can be thought of as personally disturbing collections of ideas connected by a common theme--exert a disproportionate amount of influence on our behavior because the overriding theme of the complex tends to recur over and over again throughout our lives. For example, a person with a "power" complex will spend a disproportionate amount of time on activities either directly or indirectly (symbolically) related to the issue or idea of power. Jung felt that it was crucial to identify and deal with complexes because they consumed a great deal of psychic energy and inhibited psychological growth.

To study complexes, Jung used word-association tests in which he read patients a list of words and asked them to respond with the first word that came to mind. Besides measuring response time and breathing rate, he also examined subjects' responses for *complex indicators*, or factors that indicated the presence of a complex. Hergenhahn (1994) suggests that you can readily demonstrate Jung's test and notion of complexes by giving students the following word-association test. Ask students to number a blank sheet of paper from 1 to 20, and explain to them that you will read aloud a list of 20 words and that they should respond as quickly as they can with the first word that comes to mind. Then, slowly read the list of 20 words presented on the following page.

1. death	6. pity	11. unjust	16. anxiety
2. to sin	7. stupid	12. family	17. to abuse
3. money	8. book	13. friend	18. ridicule
4. pride	9. sad	14. happiness	19. pure
5. journey	10. to marry	15. lie	20. to beat

After you've read the list, allow students to score their responses by projecting a transparency of Handouts 11-2a and 11-2b, which contain the original word list as well as a number of complex indicators identified by Jung. Students should try to determine whether their responses show any indication of a complex, and if so, they should try to describe the content of the complex. Student volunteers can share their interpretations, and this exercise should stimulate a discussion of the significance of complexes as well as the validity of this kind of test for identifying them.

Hergenhahn, B. R. (1994). *An introduction to theories of personality (4th ed.).* Englewood Cliffs, NJ: Prentice Hall.

Constructing a Life Line to Illustrate Erikson's Stages of Development

Peggy Brick (1981) suggests giving students the opportunity to actively explore Erikson's stages of development in their own lives by constructing a "life line." After discussing the eight stages of Erikson's theory, ask students to take out a piece of paper, turn it lengthwise, and draw a line across the middle of the page. Tell them to put their birth date on the far left and a projected date of death on the far right. Then have them put the current date a few inches down the line from their birth date. Now instruct them to list several important events during the childhood and adolescence between their birth date and the current date. For example, they might list an accident, a family move, a birthday party, their first day of elementary or high school, or a special holiday memory. After giving them a few minutes to list these events, ask them to consider the future and to list things that they would like to accomplish during early, middle, and late adulthood, including what their retirement will be like and what they want to do before they die. Brick suggests pairing students to let them discuss their time lines and then leading the class in a discussion of what they learned from the activity. During the discussion, ask students to focus on how the events or accomplishments that they listed reflect aspects of Erikson's theory.

Brick, P. (1981). The life cycle. In L. T. Benjamin, Jr. & K. D. Lowman (Eds.), *Activities handbook for the teaching of psychology* (pp. 128-130). Washington, DC: American Psychological Association.

Just for Fun: The Hidden Brain Damage Scale

For a humorous diversion during your coverage of personality assessment, distribute to your students Dan Wegner's (1979) Hidden Brain Damage Scale, a tongue-in-cheek measure of personality. The scale is reproduced in Handout 11-3.

Wegner, D. M., Vallacher, R. R., & Gilbert, C. (1979). The Hidden Brain Damage Scale. *American Psychologist, 34,* 192-193.

Using Projective Tests in Personality Assessment

Students will often have a better appreciation for projective methods of personality assessment after they have completed one themselves. Divide students into small groups (4 to 6) and distribute to each group a card from the Thematic Apperception Test (or some other ambiguous picture if the TAT is not available). Then, ask individual group members to write a story about the picture. After students have composed their stories, reconvene the groups and ask them to share their stories, comparing similarities and differences, and generating hypotheses to explain differences. Halonen (1986) notes that this exercise helps students to understand that there are several different ways of perceiving the same stimulus and makes them more tolerate of multiple perspectives (i.e., acknowledging other perspectives as "different" rather than "wrong"). This exercise can also be used as a launching point for a discussion of the validity of projective tests.

Halonen, J. S. (1986). *Teaching critical thinking in psychology.* Milwaukee: Alverno Productions.

Doodling as a Projective Technique

A similar demonstration can be conducted by using a doodling exercise suggested by Gardner (1981). Gardner noted that some psychologists have become interested in examining doodles as a means of understanding personality characteristics. Presumably, people will unconsciously project aspects of their personality, attitudes towards themselves, and attitudes toward the world in their doodles. Prior to discussing projective tests, distribute Handout 11-4 to your students and give them a few minutes "to doodle." After they have finished, project on a transparency Gardner's analysis guidelines, which are reproduced in Handout 11-5. Using the guidelines, have the students make a list of the personality characteristics evidenced in their doodles. Ask students the following questions: Is your personality assessment accurate? What might be some shortcomings in using doodles to assess personality? How is this method similar to and different from that of other projective tests discussed in the textbook? Be sure to caution your students not to take their results too seriously. Point out that this is not a standardized test that has been evaluated by a trained professional. Note that it is simply an activity designed to help them better understand projective assessment techniques.

Gardner, R. M. (1980). *Exercises for general psychology.* Minneapolis, MN: Burgess Publishing.

Reprinted from Hill, W. G. (1995). Instructor's resource manual for *Psychology* by S. F. Davis and J. J. Palladino. Englewood Cliffs, NJ: Prentice Hall.

The Sentence Completion Test

Another activity described by Gardner that is effective in demonstrating projective assessment methods uses the sentence completion test. Gardner's Sentence Completion Test (1980) is reproduced in Handout 11-6. After the students have completed the test, distribute the scoring guidelines provided in Handout 11-7 and have them score their own tests. Gardner (1980) suggested having students discuss the following questions: Which items were the most difficult to complete and why? Does your score correspond to your own assessment of your level of adjustment? What are some cautions that should be considered when interpreting the results? You could also ask the students how their responses may vary as a function of situational or dispositional factors. You should also point out that tests like these are usually administered to large numbers of people in order to develop norms to which individual scores are compared. Caution your students not to take their results too seriously since this is not a standardized test that has been evaluated by a trained professional. Note that it is simply an activity designed to help them better understand projective assessment techniques.

Gardner, R. M. (1980). *Exercises for general psychology.* Minneapolis, MN: Burgess Publishing.

Reprinted from Hill, W. G. (1995). Instructor's resource manual for *Psychology* by S. F. Davis and J. J. Palladino. Englewood Cliffs, NJ: Prentice Hall.

Identifying Defense Mechanisms

Although students intuitively understand the Freudian defense mechanisms used in defensive coping, they often have trouble distinguishing among them in practice. Handout 11-8 contains several real world examples that illustrate the 9 defense mechanisms discussed in the text: denial, repression, projection, identification, regression, intellectualization, reaction formation, displacement, and sublimation. After you have reviewed these defense mechanisms in class, test your students' ability to apply what they've learned by having them complete the exercise in Handout 11-8. Be sure to go over the correct answers with students, which are presented below.

1. G (Reaction Formation)
2. H (Displacement)

11. I (Sublimation)
12. B (Repression)

3. D (Identification)
4. I (Sublimation)
5. C (Projection)
6. F (Intellectualization)
7. A (Denial)
8. C (Projection)
9. I (Sublimation)
10. H (Displacement)
13. A (Denial)
14. H (Displacement)
15. C (Projection)
16. E (Regression)
17. G (Reaction Formation)
18. D (Identification)
19. B (Repression)
20. E (Regression)

Role Playing Defense Mechanisms

For a more interactive demonstration of defense mechanisms, try the following exercise suggested by Jack Grieder. Ask for eight volunteers (preferably 4 women and 4 men) who are willing to role-play various defense mechanisms for the class. Assign them (Grieder suggests in mixed-sexed pairs) to portray two defense mechanisms each and send them into the hall to prepare their skits. During that time (about 10 to 15 minutes), list the defense mechanisms on the board and briefly describe each to the class. Call the volunteers back into the class and have them perform their skits. Students in the audience should try to correctly identify the defense mechanism being portrayed in each skit. Discussion should center around the place of defense mechanisms in personality theory and the role of defense mechanisms in normal functioning. When are defense mechanisms useful? When are they harmful? Which mechanisms are used more than others? Students may also be willing to share personal examples of defense mechanisms they (or someone they know) have used recently.

Grieder, J. J. (1987). Defense mechanisms. In L. T. Benjamin & K. D. Lowman (Eds.), *Activities handbook for the teaching of psychology* (p. 182. Washington, DC: American Psychological Association.

student assignments

Personality Collage

Randy E. Osborne (1994) suggests an exercise that not only helps students to explore their personality but also illustrates the differences between the way they view themselves and the way they are viewed by others. Instruct students to create a personality collage that best represents "who they really are." To form their collage, students should use headlines and clippings from newspapers and magazines, photographs, advertisements, cartoons, and any other material they deem appropriate and paste them onto a half sheet of posterboard. Students should then give the other half of the posterboard to someone who knows them very well (e.g., a relative, close friend, or relationship partner) and ask that person to create a personality collage that best represents the student. Note that this person should *not* see the student's own collage beforehand.

When both collages are completed, students are required to compare the two collages and write a short thought paper pondering the similarities and differences. Some issues that Osborne suggests should be addressed in the paper are: What are some of the major themes about yourself that are depicted in your collage? What are the major similarities and differences between your version and your partner's version? How did the differences make you feel? What have they taught you about yourself and/or your partner that you didn't already know? Would you want to eliminate these differences? What key elements from the theories discussed in the text or lecture apply to the collages? Finally, Osborne notes that lively class discussions are typically generated by this exercise, as students voluntarily share their reactions to the collages. In one interesting case, Osborne reports that a mother and daughter in his class were able to resolve many of the conflicts in their relationship by discussing the discrepancies that surfaced from their mutual collages.

Osborne, R. E. (1994). What do you see when you look at me?: What we can learn from the way others see us. Paper presented at the 17th National Institute on the Teaching of Psychology, St. Petersburg Beach, FL.

Applying Personality Theories to TV Characters

James Polyson (1983) suggests an engaging exercise that asks students to apply principles in personality theory to the behavior of a television character. After giving students an overview of the major personality theories, ask them to think of a potentially interesting TV character to focus on (perhaps a favorite character, or one with a particularly vivid or unique personality). Once they've selected a character, they should focus on a *specific* episode of the TV show that features that character. Then, they should write a short (2 to 3-page) essay in which they first briefly describe the circumstances and plot of the episode, and then devote the remainder of their essay to explaining that character's behavior in terms of one of the major personality theories (i.e., psychodynamic, humanistic, trait, or cognitive social-learning). Other guidelines explain to students that (a) they can use more than one theoretical approach if they'd like, (b) that they are not restricted to characters with negative or maladaptive personalities (i.e., "healthy" characters can be interesting, too), and (c) that they should feel free to be creative and original in their application of the theory. Student papers are typically very insightful and thoughtful and tend to cover the gamut of personality theories and character types. The most recent set of papers contained creative analyses of characters from *E.R., Cheers, Seinfeld, Friends, Melrose Place, The Simpsons*, and several daytime soap operas. Students react very positively to this assignment and indicate that it is a valuable learning experience--not only is it helpful in clarifying some of the more abstract constructs in many personality theories, but it also helps them to see the application of these theories to actual human behavior.

Polyson, J. (1983). Student essays about TV characters: A tool for understanding personality theories. *Teaching of Psychology, 10*, 103-104.

video

Discovering Psychology, Part 15: The Self (1990, 30 min., ANN/CPB). Explores the motivational and emotional effects of beliefs about oneself.

Discovering Psychology, Part 16: Testing and Intelligence (1990, 30 min., ANN/CPB). Provides an overview of how tests are developed and used to assign values to different abilities and behaviors, with a particular focus on intelligence and personality.

Carl Gustav Jung: An Introduction (60 min, FHS). This video looks at Jung from inside and out. A tour of the environment where he lived and worked is complemented by images of his memories, dreams, and fantasies. Part of the series *The Psychology of Jung: Passions of the Soul.*

Erik Erikson: A Life's Work (1992, 38 min, IM). Erikson's colleague, Margaret Brenman-Gibson, discusses his stage theory of personality development and other facets of his theories.

Mind and Matter (60 min, FHS). Yin and yang get their due as this video explores the relationships between mind and matter, physics and psychology, conscious and unconscious, and feeling and thinking. Part of the series *The Psychology of Jung: Passions of the Soul.*

Notable Contributors to the Psychology of Personality--Carl Rogers, Part 1 (50 min, PENN). Rogers discusses his views on motivation, perception, learning, and the self as well as his development of client-centered therapy.

Notable Contributors to the Psychology of Personality--Discussion With Dr. Carl Jung: Introversion-Extroversion and Other Contributions (36 min, PENN). Jung discusses his differences with Freud and describes basic concepts of his theory such as introversion-extroversion and archetypes.

Notable Contributors to the Psychology of Personality--Hans Eysenck (32 min, PENN). Eysenck outlines aspects of introverted and extraverted personality types, his criticisms of psychoanalytic theory, and the advantages of a behavioral approach to personality.

Personality (1990, 30 min, IM). Provides an overview of psychoanalytic, social-learning, humanistic, biological, and behavioral theories of personality. The film also addresses the trait approach and the issue of consistency.

Psychological Defenses, Parts 1 & 2 (45 min each, IM). Using dramatizations, Part 1 explains the levels of consciousness proposed by Freud and illustrates the defense mechanisms of repression, denial, and regression. Part 2 discusses the additional defense mechanisms of projection, rationalization, identification, displacement, reaction formation, and sublimation.

Self-Knowledge (60 min, FHS). Interviews with various Jungians (an analyst, a religious historian, a Gnostic bishop) form the basis for addressing the question of self-knowledge. Part of the series *The Psychology of Jung: Passions of the Soul.*

Symbols and Symbolism (60 min, FHS). Jung's views on mythology, symbolism, and magic cast a mystic glow across this video. Part of the series *The Psychology of Jung: Passions of the Soul.*

Theories of Personality (1994, 20 min, IM). Psychoanalytic, humanist, social-learning, cognitive, and trait theories of personality are presented through discussions with clinical and research psychologists.

---
multimedia

Live! Psych

Module	Title	Book Page #
11.1	Personality and Heritability	p. 437

Screen 1 displays the big five personality factors. The construct of personality is defined. Import this screen to learn more about the big five. Student clicks on each factor for a description of each personality trait. Screen 2 introduces the heritability statistic used by behavioral geneticists to determine the percentage of the variability of a trait within a group that is attributable to genetic factors.

Twin Studies — p. 437

Screen 1 displays a table for measuring the effects of nature and nurture. Two methods for sorting out influences of heredity and environment are the study of twins and the study of adopted children. The objective of the twin study and the adoption study is displayed, and key comparisons are made. Screen 2 provides an animation for identical twins which shows a single sperm cell penetrating the ovum and after fertilization has occurred and the zygote splitting in half. Screen 3 provides an animation for fraternal twins, which shows two separate sperm cells fertilizing with two separate egg cells. Screen 4 introduces the identical twins reared apart studies and explains that the assumption behind these studies is that identical twins share the same heredity, but if reared apart they would be subject to different environmental influences. Screen 5 displays a correlation table on 11 characteristics based on results of the University of Minnesota Study of Twins Reared Apart research. Researchers determined that the correlations are similar whether the identical twins were reared apart or together. The small differences suggest that genetic factors play a strong role in determining these personality characteristics. Screen 6 shows that the scores of identical twins have a correlation of about 50 percent, while those of fraternal twins have a correlation of only about 15 to 20 percent, suggesting that variation on the big five personality traits might be strongly influenced by genetic inheritance.

Adoption Studies — p. 437

Screen 1 provides an animation linking an adopted child to biological parents (shared genes) and animation linking adopted child to adoptive parents (shared environment). Screen 2 displays a bar graph showing the IQ correlations found in the Texas Adoption Project. Student clicks on each of the pairs to study IQ correlations.

Web Investigations

Investigating Graphology: Is the Writing on the Wall?

People have tried to read personality from faces, from bumpy heads, from Ts and Fs blackened with a Number 2 pencil. They've also tried to determine personality from handwriting. Graphology has its adherents, but this critical thinking exercise by Diane Halpern challenges students to examine the evidence with a discerning eye. This interactive demonstration fits nicely with discussions of the Barnum Effect and a general consideration of how to assess personality validly and reliably. It's a good exercise.

Making Connections

Psychoanalytic Theories

Q What are the key components of Freud's theory of the structure and development of personality?

A According to Freud, the personality is formed around three structures: the id, which consists of unconscious urges and desires and operates according to the pleasure principle; the ego, which controls all thinking and reasoning and operates by the reality principle; and the superego, which acts as a moral watchdog. Personality development occurs in stages based on the way in which we satisfy the sexual instinct. Those stages are oral (birth to 18 months), anal (18 months to 3-1/2 years), phallic (ages 3 to 5 or 6), latency (ages 5 or 6 to 12 or 13), and genital (from puberty on).

Q What are the major differences between Jung's theory and Freud's?

A Whereas Freud stressed sexual instincts, Jung stressed rational and spiritual qualities. Also, while Freud considered development to be shaped in childhood, Jung believed psychic development comes to fruition during middle age.

Q Explain Adler's theory of compensation.

A Adler's theory of compensation is based on the idea that personality develops through the individual's attempt to overcome physical weaknesses. In a broader version of the theory, people seek to overcome feelings of inferiority that may or may not have a basis in reality.

Q What influence did Horney's emphasis on cultural forces have on her view of personality?

A Horney's emphasis on culture rather than anatomy led to an optimistic understanding of personality in which personality characteristics can be changed if a person's social status and roles are changed.

Q Why was the quality of parent-child relationships so important to Erikson?

A The quality of parent-child relationships was important to Erikson because parents can help the child feel competent and valuable and thus develop a secure sense of identity.

Humanistic Personality Theories

Q According to Rogers, what effect does conditional positive regard have on a developing child?

A According to Rogers, conditional positive regard causes a tendency to change one's self-concept so as to become more like the person one is expected to be. As a result, one's self-concept is less well matched with one's inborn capacities.

Q What criticisms have been offered of humanistic theory?

A Humanistic theories have been criticized for their lack of scientific evidence and rigor. It is also claimed that they take an overly optimistic view of human beings, that they foster self-centeredness, and that they reflect Western rather than universal values.

Trait Theories

Q How did trait theory originate?

A Trait theory originated when Allport and Odbert went through the dictionary and found nearly 18,000 words that might refer to personality traits. Other psychologists used factor analysis to identify distinct clusters of traits.

Q What are the Big Five?

A The Big Five traits are extroversion, agreeableness, conscientiousness, emotional stability, and culture or openness.

Q Explain two major criticisms of trait theory.

A Trait theories have been criticized because they are primarily descriptive and do not try to explain the causes of basic dimensions of personality. Also, the traits identified through factor analysis represent statistical properties of populations and may not be applicable to individuals. Some critics argue that it is dangerous to reduce the diversity of human nature to just a few traits.

Cognitive-Social Learning Theory

Q According to social learning theory, how does a person develop expectancies?

A People develop expectancies on the basis of the environmental feedback that follows particular behaviors.

Q What evidence suggests that cognitive-social learning theories can accurately explain and predict behavior?

A Research evidence shows that temperament remains stable over time and that children develop a habitual explanatory style by age 8. Other research has found that expectancies can have a significant effect on behavior.

Personality Assessment

Q What is the difference between structured and unstructured personal interviews?

A In a structured interview, the interviewer adheres to a set format. In an unstructured interview, the interviewer is free to decide what questions to ask.

Q What are the benefits of systematic observation?

A Systematic observation allows psychologists to look at aspects of personality as they are expressed in real life.

Q What are the most important objective tests used for assessing personality? What are they used for?

A The most important objective tests for assessing personality are the Sixteen Personality Factor Questionnaire, which provides scores on each of 16 traits, and the Minnesota Multiphasic Personality Inventory, which is used in diagnosing psychiatric disorders and to differentiate among normal personality dimensions.

Q What are the advantages of projective tests? the disadvantages?

A Advantages of projective tests are that they can be taken in a relaxed atmosphere and the responses are unlikely to be faked. A disadvantage is that their accuracy and usefulness depend largely on the skill of the examiner.

Video Classics

Allport on Traits

SYNOPSIS: Gordon Allport is interviewed about the distinctions between primary, secondary, central, and cardinal traits. Allport discusses each in turn and notes how they help define a trait view of personality.

Form a Hypothesis

Q How do you think Gordon Allport distinguishes between cardinal traits and central traits?

A For Allport, a cardinal trait is the distinguishing trait of the individual. It is a trait from which other traits and attitudes may be inferred. Central traits are more in number. They offer themes for development and experience, but show less integration than cardinal traits.

Test Your Understanding

Q What are common traits?

A Common traits are traits shared by many individuals.

Q What are individual traits?

A Individual traits are personal and idiosyncratic.

Thinking Critically

Q According to Allport, what are the building blocks of personality?

A Traits are the building blocks, which are stable characteristics that distinguish each individual.

Q Most researchers agree that the five-factor model best characterizes individual differences in personality. What are the "big five" and how would you describe each?

A Neuroticism: nervousness, emotional instability, and a tendency to worry
Extroversion: sociability, interest in others
Openness: imagination, curiosity, aesthetic orientation
Agreeableness: pleasant nature, charity, empathy
Conscientiousness: reliability, doing things correctly

Q An important contribution of trait psychology is the construction of personality inventories. What is the most widely used personality inventory?

A This depends on one's application. The NEO Personality Inventory Revised consists of 240 items that measure the Big Five traits. It is common in nonclinical assessment of personality traits. The Minnesota Multiphasic Personality Inventory is probably the most widely used measure to assess clinically important orientations, such as hypochondriasis is, depression, and psychopathic deviate tendencies.

Jung at Heart

SYNOPSIS: Carl Jung was a neo-Freudian theorist who agreed with Freud that human behavior is influenced by the unconscious, but he disagreed with Freud on two points in particular. First, there exists not only a personal unconscious but also a collective unconscious, a kind of memory bank that stores images and ideas that humans have accumulated over the course of evolution. Because of this evolutionary history, certain common themes appear in cultural myths and legends throughout the world. Jung coined the term archetypes to refer to these universal tendencies to perceive things in a certain way. Second, Jung argued that people strive for more than just the satisfaction of biological drives. At the age of forty or so, people undergo a midlife transition and spiritual concerns become more important.

Form a Hypothesis

Q How do you think Carl Jung's meaning of the unconscious differs from Sigmund Freud's?

A Jung separated the unconscious into a personal unconscious, unique to the individual, but capable of limited perception. Jung viewed the collective unconscious as a shared entity containing memories common to all human beings by fact of their humanness. Freud viewed the unconscious as a more private structure, filled with repressed personal memories and conflicts.

Test Your Understanding

Q Although Carl Jung proposed a competing theory, he agreed with many Freudian concepts. On what points does Jung agree with Freud?

A As the video segment notes, Jung and Freud would agree on at least two points concerning the unconscious. First, humans have limited objective awareness of the unconscious. Second, people often react without knowing why they reacted as they did; presumably, this reaction is attributable to the influence of the unconscious.

Thinking Critically

Q How did Carl Jung seek to change Freud's theory of psychoanalysis?

A Jung and Freud parted company on the issue of infant sexuality. For Freud, sexuality was the driving force underlying personality. For Jung, the development of personality was motivated by forces other than sexual and could continue throughout life.

Q Who are other neo-Freudian theorists?

A Alfred Adler, who emphasized ones personal struggle to overcome feelings of inferiority, Karen Horney who emphasized persons struggles with basic anxiety, our reaction to a competitive modern culture were two prominent neo-Freudians.

Q What projective personality tests have been developed to allow people to "project" unconscious needs, wishes, and conflicts onto ambiguous stimuli?

A The Rorschach Inkblot Test is the classic projective assessment. Also used is the Thematic Apperception Test, which consists of stimuli to which the subject tells a story.

Interview with Erik Erikson

SYNOPSIS: Erikson discusses the developmental stage of intimacy versus isolation. He notes that intimacy refers not only to friendship, love, and sexuality, but also the deeper notion of fusing one's identity with another. He argues that this is the basis for a lasting interpersonal relationship.

Form a Hypothesis

Q What do you think Erikson means by "intimacy?"

A Erikson defines intimacy as "the ability to fundamentally identify with another without losing ones sense of self."

Test Your Understanding

Q Why does Erikson say some marriages don't work?

A Erickson sees intimacy as key to a successful marriage. Marriages often fail when people marry seeking intimacy because the ability to be intimate is a prerequisite for marital success.

Q What happens if intimacy is not developed?

A Although not addressed in the video segment, marital strife is more likely in the absence of intimacy.

Thinking Critically

Q What are the eight psychosocial stages of development? What psychosocial stages unfold during adolescence and adulthood?

A Infancy: Trust vs. mistrust
Childhood: Autonomy vs. Shame and Doubt / Initiative vs. Guilt / Industry vs. Inferiority
Adolescence: Identity vs. Role Confusion
Young Adulthood Intimacy vs. Isolation
Middle Adulthood: Generativity vs. Stagnation
Late Adulthood: Integrity vs. Despair

Web Links

1. http://www.learner.org/exhibits/personality/

What makes us who we are? Find out here, with descriptions and exhibits of personality as it relates to reputation, behavior, thoughts, and feelings.

2. http://www.personalityresearch.org/

Great Ideas in Personality. This site provides links to a variety of research programs in attachment theory, basic emotions, behavior genetics, personality disorders, the five-factor model, psychoanalysis, and much more. Start here when rewriting your personality lecture presentations.

3. http://ksi.cpsc.ucalgary.ca/PCP/PCP.html

Personal Construct Psychology. *That* PCP, not the other one from Chapter 4. Visit here for information about the theory and related conferences.

4. http://www.philosophy.ucf.edu/pi.html

This site provides bibliographies and texts relevant to concepts of the person, self, and personal identity. Point your students here as a starting point for their short papers on personality theory.

5. http://plaza.interport.net/nypsan/freudarc.html

Sigmund Freud and the Freud Archives. Links to Internet resources about Freud's works and writings about Freud. IF you like Freud, you'll like this.

6. http://www.wynja.com/personality/top.html

Personality and consciousness. That's pretty much it.

7. http://maple.lemoyne.edu/~hevern/psychref4-11.html

Testing, assessment, and psychometrics; explore the empirical side of personality measurement.

transparencies

Series V

83a. *"Big Five" Dimensions of Personality*
83b This two-part transparency identifies and describes the dimensions of this trait approach.

84. *Freud's Structure of Personality*
The relationships between consciousness, preconsciousness, and the unconscious are depicted.

85. *Erikson's Eight Stages of Personality Development*
Each stage and its associated crisis is shown.

86. *Bandura's Model of Reciprocal Determinism*
The interacting influences of the person, environment, and behavior are illustrated in this transparency.

Text Figures

11-1.	*Relationship of the Id, Ego, and Superego*
11-2.	*Rorschach Inkblots*
11-3.	*Sample Items from the Thematic Apperception Test*

Handout 11-1

Defining Your Personal View of Personality

Instructions: Listed below are some concepts that may be important to you in the way that you think about your own personality and the personalities of the people around you. Think about each item and check three items that are the most important regarding your personal view of human personality.

___	external environment	___	the self
___	temperament	___	unconscious motives
___	interpretation of experience	___	observable behavior
___	conscious awareness	___	enduring characteristics
___	childhood experiences	___	expectations
___	rewards and punishments	___	subjective feelings
___	abilities	___	sexual instincts
___	organization of reality		

IN THE SPACE BELOW, EXPLAIN WHY YOU CHOSE THE THREE ITEMS THAT YOU CHECKED.

Adapted from Kerber, K. W. (1987). What is personality? A personal appraisal. In V. P. Makosky, L. G. Whittemore, & A. M. Rogers (Eds.), Activities handbook for the teaching of psychology: Vol. 2 (pp. 182-184). Washington, DC: American Psychological Association.

Handout 11-2a

Exploring the Personal Unconscious

Original Word List

1. death
2. to sin
3. money
4. pride
5. journey
6. pity
7. stupid
8. book
9. sad
10. to marry
11. unjust
12. family
13. friend
14. happiness
15. lie
16. anxiety
17. to abuse
18. ridicule
19. pure
20. to beat

Jungian *Complex* Indicators

1. displaying longer-than-average reaction time to a stimulus word
2. repeating the stimulus word back as a response
3. failing to respond at all
4. using expressive bodily reactions, such as laughing, increased breathing rate, or increased conductivity of the skin
5. stammering
6. continuing to respond to a previously used stimulus word
7. reacting meaninglessly (e.g., with made-up words)
8. reacting superficially with a word that sounds like the stimulus word (e.g., die-lie)
9. responding with more than one word
10. misunderstanding the stimulus as some other word

Reprinted from Hergenhahn, B. R. (1994). An introduction to theories of personality (4th ed.). Englewood Cliffs, NJ: Prentice Hall. Used by permission of Prentice Hall.

Handout 11-3

Hidden Brain Damage Scale

Please respond TRUE or FALSE to each of the following items.

_____ 1. People tell me one thing one day and out the other.
_____ 2. I can't unclasp my hands.
_____ 3. I can wear my shirts as pants.
_____ 4. I feel as much like I did yesterday as I do today.
_____ 5. I always lick the fronts of postage stamps.
_____ 6. I often mistake my hands for food.
_____ 7. I'd rather eat soap than little stones.
_____ 8. I never liked room temperature.
_____ 9. I line my pockets with hot cheese.
_____ 10. My throat is closer than it seems.
_____ 11. I can smell my nose hairs.
_____ 12. I'm being followed by boxer shorts.
_____ 13. Most things are better eaten than forgotten.
_____ 14. Likes and dislikes are among my favorites.
_____ 15. Pudding without raisins is no pudding at all.
_____ 16. My patio is covered with a killer frost.
_____ 17. I've lost all sensation in my shirt.
_____ 18. I try to swallow at least three times a day.
_____ 19. My best friend is a social worker.
_____ 20. I've always known when to close my eyes.
_____ 21. My squirrels don't know where I am tonight.
_____ 22. Little can be said for Luxembourg.
_____ 23. No napkin is sanitary enough for me.
_____ 24. I walk this way because I have to.
_____ 25. Walls impede my progress.
_____ 26. I can't find all of my marmots.
_____ 27. There's only one thing for me.
_____ 28. My uncle is as stupid as paste.
_____ 29. I can pet animals by the mouthful.
_____ 30. My toes are numbered.
_____ 31. Man's reach should exceed his overbite.
_____ 32. People tell me I'm deaf.
_____ 33. My beaver won't go near the water.
_____ 34. I can find my ears, but I have to look.
_____ 35. I'd rather go to work than sit outside.
_____ 36. Armenians are comical in full battle dress.
_____ 37. I don't like any of my loved ones.

Note: The Hidden Brain Damage Scale stands alone as the only psychometric instrument capable of predicting preference for pimento loaf. Although a true-false format is recommended, many test-takers opt for the response of getting tangled up in the drapery.

Wegner, D. M., Vallacher, R. R., & Gilbert, C. (1979). The Hidden Brain Damage Scale. *American Psychologist, 34,* 192-193. Copyright © 1979 by the American Psychological Association. Reprinted with permission.

Handout 11-4

Doodling Exercise

Instructions: In the four boxes below you are to add to the diagrams in any way you wish. Note that in the fourth box there is no design and you are to make any design you wish in that box.

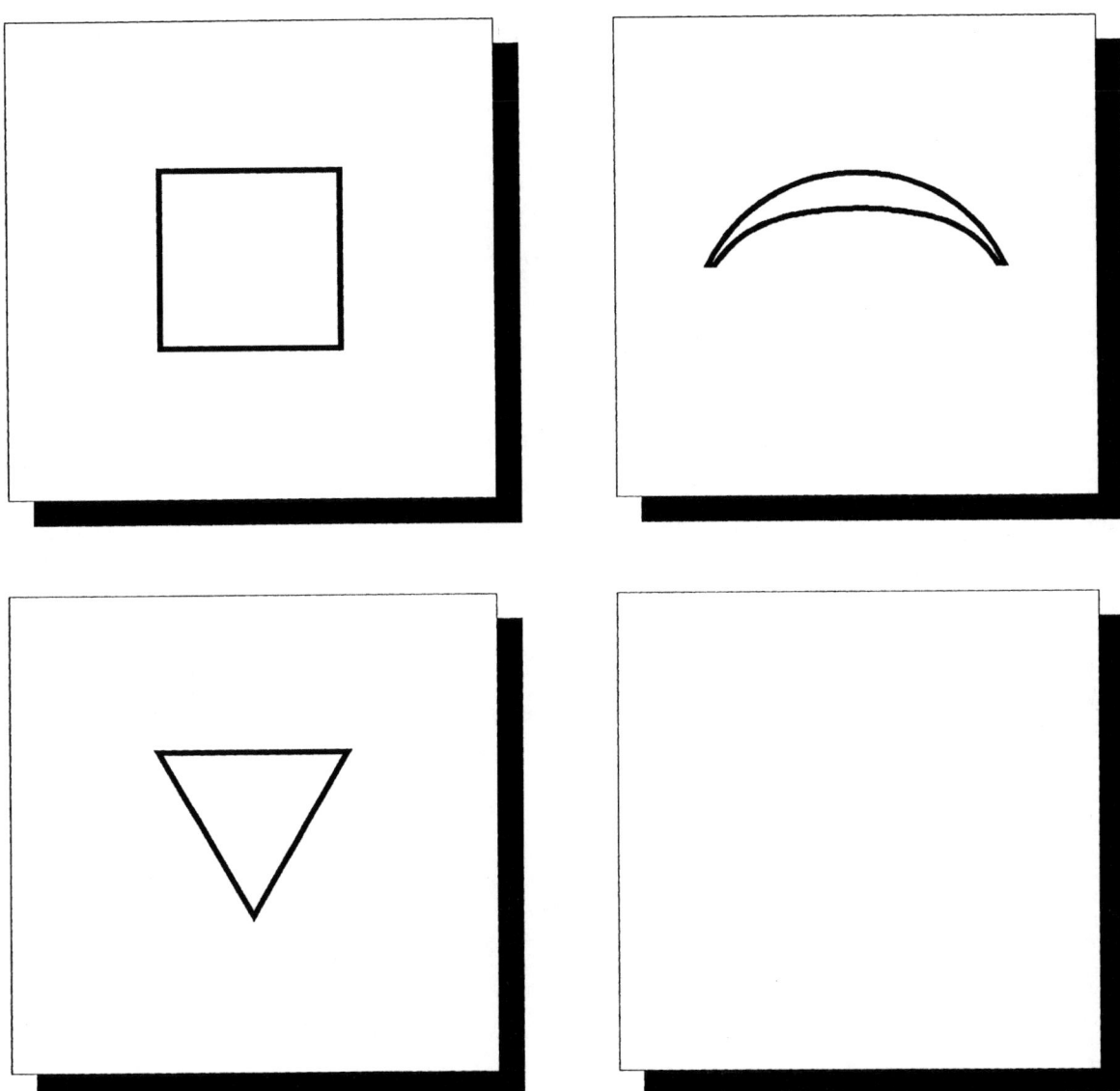

Chapter 11 ■ *Page 343* ■ Personality

Handout 11-5

Analysis Guidelines for Doodles

Psychologists have correlated certain aspects of doodles with personality characteristics as measured by various assessment techniques. They have found the following to be highly correlated:

1. Square objects denote masculinity, while round objects denote femininity.
2. Objects with sharp protrusions indicate feelings of aggression.
3. Precise dimensions, neatness, and order suggest an intense need to have order in their lives, often to the point of being obsessive-compulsive.
4. Sharpness and clarity of form indicate high intelligence.
5. Numerous circles or circular strokes indicates that the person is dependent on others, non-assertive, or effeminate.
6. People who shade doodles with crossing vertical and horizontal lines are typically obsessive personality types.
7. Multiple edges with few curving lines suggest that the person is overtly aggressive and poorly adjusted.
8. Filling in (shading) of letters, circles, etc. is associated with a person who is obsessive-compulsive, tidy, neat, or usually very controlled.
9. Houses indicate a feeling of security.
10. Animals:
    - Well integrated and adjusted people often draw pictures of common domesticated animals such as dogs, cats, horses, etc.
    - Phobic patients tend to draw bugs, spiders, and mice.
    - Large animals are often drawn by males who feel the need to be more masculine.
11. Boats may indicate a fixation or dependency on one's mother.
12. Drawing of people with long necks are related to feelings of dependency.
13. Drawings displaying a high level of creativity and imagination usually reflect a person with creative potential.

Adapted from R. M. Gardner (1980). *Exercises for general psychology.* Minneapolis, MN: Burgess Publishing. Reprinted by permission of Prentice Hall

Handout 11-6

Sentence Completion Test

Instructions: Finish each of the following sentences in any way you wish. You will not hand this sheet in.

1. I secretly wish _____
2. What worries me is _____
3. Secretly, I need _____
4. In the evening _____
5. My mom _____
6. I want _____
7. My college courses _____
8. I fear _____
9. I get angry when _____
10. Men _____
11. Tomorrow _____
12. My best friend _____
13. My nerves _____
14. I have fantasies about _____
15. For sure _____
16. Higher education _____
17. Getting married _____
18. If only I could _____
19. My dad _____
20. People _____
21. I would eventually like to _____
22. My dad thinks my mom _____
23. I wish I could forget _____
24. Many of my friends _____
25. My biggest wish _____
26. My best friend doesn't know _____
27. I don't know why _____
28. My mother and I _____

29. I feel like _____

30. I really hope _____

31. A decade from now I _____

32. My dream _____

33. After I'm married _____

34. Going on dates _____

35. My family _____

36. The thing that bothers me most about myself is _____

37. When I was younger _____

38. It is hard for me to _____

39. The opposite sex _____

40. A friend _____

41. Sex _____

42. Compared to my friends, I _____

43. My mom thinks my dad _____

44. Sometimes I _____

45. I would be truly happy if _____

46. My looks are _____

47. Even though it is silly _____

48. Women _____

49. My father and I _____

50. Mothers should _____

Adapted from R. M. Gardner (1980). *Exercises for general psychology.* Minneapolis, MN: Burgess Publishing. Reprinted by permission of Prentice Hall

Handout 11-7

Sentence Completion Test Scoring Guidelines

Score your completed sentences as follows:

P ⇨   If your response indicates a positive, humorous, or hopeful attitude.
C ⇨   If your response indicates conflict, antagonism, pessimism, emotional disturbance.
N ⇨   If your response is neutral; that is, it is not clearly positive or conflictive.

The following examples show how a response might be scored:

Boys _____
P ⇨   are friendly, are easy to get along with, are nice, are swell, are good sports, are considerate, are fun at a party, are good friends, are okay, etc.
C ⇨   are a pain in the neck, get on my nerves, can't be trusted, bother me, give me a headache, think they are superior, are rude, are stupid, etc.
N ⇨   are human beings, are taller than girls, are stronger than girls, are the opposite sex, are the same sex, etc.

Evaluate each of your responses and categorize it as a "P," "C," or "N" response. Record the total number of each of these types of responses below.

P =

C =

N =

Compute your total score by adding 50 to the number of C responses and subtract from this sum the number of P responses. Do not mark omissions if there are any.

Total Score =

INTERPRETATION

Scores can range from 0 to 100. A low score below 50 would indicate that you have a generally positive outlook on life and that you view life optimistically. A high score about 50 indicates that your outlook on life is somewhat negative and that you view life rather pessimistically.

Adapted from R. M. Gardner (1980). *Exercises for general psychology*. Minneapolis, MN: Burgess Publishing. Reprinted by permission of Prentice Hall.

Handout 11-8

Identifying Defense Mechanisms

Instructions: Identify the defense mechanism illustrated in the following examples by placing the appropriate letter in the blank next to each item. Use the following code.

    A. Denial   F. Intellectualization
    B. Repression   G. Reaction Formation
    C. Projection   H. Displacement
    D. Identification   I. Sublimation
    E. Regression

_____ 1. Mark never stops ranting about the dangers of pornography. He gives endless examples of smut he has seen in movies and on television, and spends a lot of time hanging around porno houses to get even more examples.

_____ 2. Chad always teases and annoys his kid brother Nathan after he himself is bullied and picked on by his older brother Sam.

_____ 3. Although verbally and physically abused by his cell guard, Shane actually admires his captor and even imitates him on occasion.

_____ 4. Judy, who has always been aggressive and fiercely competitive, becomes captain of her college soccer team.

_____ 5. Diane, who keeps accusing Sam of being in love with her, probably has secret desires for Sam.

_____ 6. Theresa, who has recently been diagnosed with cancer, spends all of her time in the library becoming an expert in cancer research.

_____ 7. Despite overwhelming evidence and a murder conviction, Jay's mother refused to believe that her son could actually take the life of another human being.

_____ 8. Brett, who is extremely hard to convince in arguments, complains that all of his friends are stubborn.

_____ 9. Even as a child Lisa was always impulsive and engaged in risky behavior. Perhaps not surprisingly, she grew up to become a famous race car driver.

_____ 10. Roger, a major league pitcher, often "beans" (i.e., hits with a pitch) the next batter after someone has hit a home run against him.

_____ 11. After an unsuccessful attempt at a sexual relationship, Pete began devoting most of his energies toward church activities.

_____ 12. Wendy was embarrassed because somehow she kept forgetting to keep her appointments with the dentist.

_____ 13. Amanda broke off her relationship with Jack, but Jack still talks and acts as if they are still dating.

_____ 14. After her new baby sister came home from the hospital, her parents discovered that Susie had dismembered her favorite doll.

_____ 15. Amy, who has had many extramarital affairs, begins to accuse her husband Dan of being unfaithful.

_____ 16. Larry began wetting his pants again after the birth of his baby brother.

_____ 17. Todd, who is unsure about his own sexuality, frequently make homophobic and gay-bashing remarks.

_____ 18. Brad's father acts like a big shot around town because Brad is the star quarterback of his high school football team.

_____ 19. Two years after breaking off his relationship with Julie, Rick fails to even recognize her at a cocktail party.

_____ 20. At the first sign of any problems or trouble in his life, Bill immediately runs to his parents to bail him out.

Chapter 12 Stress and Health Psychology

chapter outline 351

learning objectives 353

lecture suggestions

    Japan's "Prig Syndrome" 354
    Smokin' in the Boys' Room 355
    The Ah-choo Blues 355
    (Don't) Smoke! Smoke! Smoke! That Cigarette 356
    DSM and PMS 356
    Stress Management and Medicine 357
    The Control Process 358
    Talk To Me 358
    Rub-A-Dub-Don't 359
    A Burdened Heart 360
    Adhering to Medical Advice 361

demonstrations and activities

    Defining Stress 362
    Lifestyle Awareness Triangle 362
    Assessing Student Worries 362
    Type A Behavior Patterns 363
    Guest Lecture: Promoting a Healthy Lifestyle 363
    Culture and Health 364

student assignments

    Evaluating Self-Help Books 365
    AIDS in Film 365

video 367

multimedia 369

transparencies 374

handouts

    Worries Survey 376

chapter outline

I. Sources of Stress
- A. Life changes: Social Readjustment Rating Scale assesses major life changes
- B. Everyday hassles: Daily hassles, annoyances, and irritations contribute to experiencing stress
    1. Pressure: Intensifying, changing, or speeding up one's behavior or performance
    2. Frustration: Being prevented from reaching one's goals
        a. Delays
        b. Lack of resources
        c. Losses
        d. Failure
        e. Discrimination
    3. Conflict: Simultaneous incompatible demands, opportunities, goals, needs
        a. Approach/approach conflict: Simultaneous attraction to two goals
        b. Avoidance/avoidance conflict: Presentation of two undesired or threatening possibilities
        c. Approach/avoidance conflict: Attraction and repulsion to the same goal
- C. Stress and individual differences
    1. Hardiness and resilience
    2. Self-imposed stress

II. Coping With Stress
- A. Direct coping: Action taken to change an uncomfortable situation
    1. Confrontation: Acknowledging a stressful situation directly and initiating coping
    2. Compromise: Choosing a more realistic goal when an ideal goal cannot be met
    3. Withdrawal: Avoiding a situation when other options are not practical
- B. Defensive coping
    1. Defense mechanisms represent one way of summarizing defensive coping
    2. Self-deception is substituted for stress
- C. Socioeconomic and gender differences
    1. The challenging aspects of lower-class life may produce greater stress
    2. Under many circumstances women and men seem equally affected by stress

III. Stress and Health
- A. The biology of stress
    1. Cannon's "fight or flight" notion
    2. Selye's general adaptation syndrome
        a. Alarm reaction
        b. Resistance

        c. Exhaustion
- B. Stress and heart disease: The Type A behavior pattern shows links to coronary heart disease
- C. Stress and the immune system
    1. Psychoneuroimmunology shows stress can suppress immune functioning
- D. Staying healthy / Methods of reducing stress
    1. Calm down
    2. Reach out
    3. Religion and altruism
    4. Learn to cope effectively
    5. Coping with stress at college

IV. Adopt a Healthy Life Style
- A. Diet
- B. Exercise
- C. Quit smoking
- D. Avoid high risk behaviors

V. Extreme Stress
- A. Sources of extreme stress
    1. Unemployment and underemployment
    2. Divorce and separation
    3. Bereavement
    4. Catastrophes: A sequence of reactions to disasters
        a. Shock stage
        b. Suggestible stage
        c. Recovery stage
    5. Combat and other threatening personal attacks
- B. Post-traumatic stress disorder is receiving increasing recognition

VI. The Well-Adjusted Person
- A. "Healthy," "normal," "well-" adjustment a matter of debate
    1. Issues of conformity versus nonconformity predominate
- B. Evaluating adjustment
    1. Does the action meet the adjustive demands?
    2. Does the action meet the individual's needs?
    3. Is the action compatible with the well-being of others?

learning objectives

After reading this chapter, students should be able to:

1. Define adjustment and stress. Identify sources of stress.

2. Describe the nature of pressure, frustration, conflict, anxiety, and identify situations that produce each one.

3. Identify five basic sources of frustration.

4. Give examples of each of the following: approach/approach conflict; avoidance/avoidance conflict; approach/avoidance conflict; double approach/avoidance conflict.

5. Distinguish between direct coping and defensive coping.

6. Identify and characterize three ways that people cope directly.

7. Discuss the psychological and physiological effects of stress on people using the stages of Seyle's general adaptation syndrome.

8. Identify five sources of extreme stress.

9. Describe post-traumatic stress disorder and identify three situations that are associated with devoloping the disorder.

10. Discuss the opposing views of what characterizes a well-adjusted individual.

lecture suggestions

Japan's "Prig Syndrome"

A wave of panic is sweeping Japan, and it's not from a tsunami. Actually, it's not much of a panic either, but it is a growing concern: prig syndrome. Japanese citizens are increasingly worried about the perceived dirt, germs, and infections they might receive from others.

Traditionally, Japan has emphasized cleanliness, regard for others, and proper etiquette. In a country about the size of the state of California, yet home to a population half that of the United States, order and ritual are important to maintain peaceful coexistence. For example, Japanese citizens honor good grooming and a neat appearance. Bathing is a ritual in Japan, as is removing one's shoes before entering someone's home. It is also common practice for those suffering from colds to wear face masks on the streets and subways, so as not to infect others. And money, a common gift on celebratory occasions, is typically ironed so that it will be clean and crisp for the honoree. These types of behaviors highlight the premium placed on tidiness.

Some argue that this emphasis has gone too far. Popular Japanese magazines have for several years written about "prig syndrome," referring to an individual's perceptions that others are dirty. The syndrome appears to predominate among young female office workers, who fear that they can catch "cooties" from their older male coworkers. As an example of prig syndrome, many people use tissues while they hold public telephones away from their ear, fearing infection from the previous user. Some subway riders get tossed around on their daily commute, rather than touch the subway strap to support themselves. Pens, envelopes, money, and other items that come into frequent public contact are also handled with suspicion by some. In fact, some Karaoke bars keep personal microphones behind the counter for their regular customers, so that the danger of catching germs from someone else's sing-a-long is minimized!

The captains of industry have responded to the problem. Pentel has introduced a line of pens and pencils with an antiseptic chemical soaked in the barrel to kill bacteria. Stationery, bicycle handles, origami paper, and even tambourines and maracas are available with the same treatment. In addition, it is possible to buy fax machines, computer disks, telephones, and dishwashers that have a similar sanitary coating. Hitachi Ltd. has taken a different approach. Since many Japanese see money as a source of potential contamination, the company has developed an automated teller machine that irons and sanitizes the bills before dispensing them.

According to psychiatrist Toru Sekiya, who treats people with prig syndrome, the reason for the obsession with sanitation stems from Japan's declining birth rate. Children, being rarer than before, are overprotected, and parents tend to react with alarm to every childhood cut, scrape, and bruise. For some patients Sekiya recommends separating mothers and offspring, and sending the children to dormitories where they can get used to living with other people. As a national concern, however, prig syndrome will require a national treatment: Changes in attitudes and childhood education may be the only effective remedy.

Pollack, A. (1995, July 28). Japan escalates war on bacteria with new gadgets. *Austin American-Statesman*, p. A12.

Smokin' in the Boys' Room

Stanley Schachter is well known for his research on affiliation, attribution and arousal, and obesity and food intake. Less well known, however, are his investigations of urinary pH and cigarette smoking. Although the findings are somewhat controversial, Schachter's reductionist explanation for smoking is a good illustration of the dogged pursuit of an idea and where it can lead.

Schachter began by reviewing and conducting studies that demonstrated that smoking does not necessarily calm the smoker or improve his or her mood. Rather, not smoking (or insufficient nicotine consumption) makes smokers feel worse on a number of dimensions, such as irritability, anxiety, or annoyance. When stressed, then, smoking should increase (as anecdotal and experimental evidence suggests it does), but stress alone can't account for cigarette consumption: Smokers are neither more nor less calm than nonsmokers. Schachter reasoned that stress must play a different role, such as reducing the available supply of nicotine. Because of an addiction to nicotine, smokers under stress may be trying to regulate their nicotine intake.

Schachter's chain of reasoning was correct. Under stress nicotine leaves the body more rapidly, due to increased acidity (pH) of the smoker's urine. Turning that pharmacological effect around, it should be true that the pH of urine affects the rate of smoking, a small but reliable effect that Schachter and his colleagues were able to demonstrate. In one experiment, for example, thirteen smokers received alternate doses of placebo or vitamin C and acidulin (to increase acidity). Smokers kept track of their number of daily cigarettes. During periods when the smokers took the acidifying agents, cigarette consumption increased 20 percent, compared to the placebo periods. In another experiment, both stress and pH levels were manipulated. Participants were exposed to either a high or low stress situation 50 minutes after ingesting either a placebo or bicarbonate of soda. The bicarbonate's action is such that it quickly elevates urinary pH and then stabilizes it at a highly alkaline level. High stress participants were more edgy than low stress participants, regardless of what they had ingested. However, in the high stress/placebo group, stress should acidify urine, whereas in the high stress/bicarbonate group it should not (given the high alkaline concentration). Schachter and his colleagues found, in fact, that participants in the high stress/placebo group took significantly more puffs on available cigarettes, whereas among the bicarbonate participants stress did not affect smoking. In these and similar studies, the effects of stress on smoking seem driven by the body's need to replenish nicotine.

Grunberg, N. E. (1987). Cigarette smoking and money: Developing new research lines. In N. E. Grunberg, R. E. Nisbett, J. Rodin, & J. E. Singer (Eds.), *A distinctive approach to psychological research: The influence of Stanley Schachter* (pp. 206-222). Hillsdale, NJ: Lawrence Erlbaum.

Kozlowski, L. T. (1987). Observations, demonstrations, and applications: Research on cigarettes, coffee, walking, and sense-of-direction. In N. E. Grunberg, R. E. Nisbett, J. Rodin, & J. E. Singer (Eds.), *A distinctive approach to psychological research: The influence of Stanley Schachter* (pp. 187-205). Hillsdale, NJ: Lawrence Erlbaum.

Schachter, S. (1977). Nicotine regulation in light and heavy smokers. *Journal of Experimental Psychology: General, 106*, 5-12.

Schachter, S. (1980). Non-psychological explanations of behavior. In L. Festinger (Ed.), *Retrospections on social psychology* (pp. 131-157). New York: Oxford University Press.

Schachter, S. (1982). Recidivism and self-cure of smoking and obesity. *American Psychologist, 37*, 436-444.

The Ah-choo Blues

Allergy sufferers have a new reason to cry: Recent research suggests that people with seasonal allergies may also have a predisposition toward depression.

Roughly 20 to 25 percent of all Americans suffer from seasonal allergies, such as ragweed, Cedar fever, or hayfever. Although they won't cause major clinical depression by themselves, such allergies may initiate depression's symptoms, such as emotional withdrawal, fatigue, irritability, or mood swings. Paul S. Marshall, a neuropsychologist at the Hennepin County (Minneapolis) Medical Center, reports that the reason has to do with neurotransmitters. Acetylcholine and norepinephrine normally counter each other's activity in the nervous system. Allergies may cause an imbalance in this neurotransmitter action, which in turn may initiate depressive behavior, particularly during stressful periods or intensive allergic responses. Given this link, depression may influence allergies as well. Those people with mild allergies during childhood may experience more severe allergies only after a period of depression during their mid-twenties. Eventually, the allergy-depression link (especially when compounded by stress) may further alter the brain's neurochemical balance.

Staff (1993, May/June). God bless you-depress you. *Psychology Today,* p. 9.

(Don't) Smoke! Smoke! Smoke! That Cigarette

The percentage of black teenagers in the United States who smoke cigarettes has dropped dramatically, according to recent national surveys. Only about 5 percent of black high school seniors in 1994 reported smoking on a daily basis, compared to 23 percent of their white high school counterparts. Black teenagers also reported a lower incidence of using chewing tobacco. These data were collected in the annual survey Monitoring the Future, sponsored by the Institute for Social Research at the University of Michigan.

Although these findings are encouraging, explaining them has vexed scientists at a number of institutions. Researchers from the U.S. Centers for Disease Control and Prevention, the National Institutes of Health, and the University of Michigan agree that there is a downward trend, but are at a loss to explain why. For example, the results seem to be independent of factors such as differences in disposable income between blacks and whites, religiousness, parents' dropout rates, or the teenagers' dropout rates. Moreover, black teens do not appear to have merely dropped cigarettes in favor of other drug use.

Focus groups conducted by Sherry Mills, an epidemiologist at the National Institutes of Health National Cancer Institute, may provide some avenues for future research. Black teens reported that they knew of the dangers of cigarettes from lessons learned in school, from their parents, and from various public service announcements. However, the same teens who eschewed cigarette smoking engaged in other risky behaviors, such as not wearing seat belts or engaging in unprotected sex. Some boys volunteered that they identified with athletes who did not smoke, and viewed athletic scholarships as a ticket to college. Some girls noted that they had no desire to maintain a waif-like body (see Chapter 10 in this manual, "Weight and See"), and therefore did not see cigarettes as a means of appetite suppression. Many of the reasons offered, however, could equally pertain to white and black teen smokers. What factors predict their differential cigarette consumption remain to be found.

Goldstein, A. (1995, September 2). Black youths smoking less, study says. *Austin American Statesman,* p. A35.

DSM and PMS

The *Diagnostic and Statistical Manual of Mental Disorders-IV* (DSM) adds premenstrual syndrome (PMS) as an identifiable disorder. However, Australian psychologist Elizabeth Harding disagrees not only with its inclusion in the DSM, but also with the existence of PMS.

Harding asked 101 University of Melbourne employees to keep a daily diary of stress and health for 10 weeks. Although 40 percent of the participants reported experiencing PMS, not one reported mood changes over two consecutive cycles that met the diagnostic criteria set forth in the DSM. Participants were as likely to report PMS whether they showed occasional menstrual mood change, postmenstrual mood change, or no change at all. Although 18 percent of the women studied did show marked premenstrual mood change, it was not significantly different from the mood changes reported by women who had reached menopause or who had undergone hysterectomies.

Harding contends that the PMS label provides a socially sanctioned outlet for women to be irritable upon occasion. The real problem, however, may be more widespread. Harding reported that 25 percent of the women in her study demonstrated chronic negative affect, or generalized, persistent feelings of unhappiness. Harding suggests that teaching coping skills, relaxation exercises, and stress management may be more productive avenues for reducing negative affect, allowing women to express themselves at any time of the month.

Staff (1994, September/October). PMS or SOS? *Psychology Today*, p. 8.

Stress Management and Medicine

Stress management can involve the reduction of either chronic stress or acute stress. Ludwick-Rosenthal and Neufeld reviewed the research on acute stress, with a particular focus on stress management in individuals undergoing aversive medical procedures. In this review four major techniques are described and evaluated: Information, relaxation, cognitive-behavioral, and modeling techniques.

The first technique, providing information about the impending aversive procedure, was stimulated by research that indicated that postoperative recovery was improved when patients were informed about the procedure and preoperative fear was kept to a minimum (Janis, 1958). Information can be procedural (the upcoming sequence of events is described) or sensory (the common sensations associated with the procedure are described). Theoretically, providing information increases the patient's feeling of control and therefore reduces the level of stress.

The effectiveness of the information technique itself is unclear, as is the relative effectiveness of procedural and sensory information. The greatest effect usually involves behavioral ratings of discomfort; self-report measures of anxiety do not reliably show an effect. However, methodological problems, such as a lack of control over the total information a subject receives and less-than-ideal control groups for comparison, prevent us from drawing firm conclusions about the information technique's effectiveness. Still, its failure to affect measures of anxiety seriously limits practical value.

The second common type of technique involves a variety of cognitive-behavioral manipulations, among them distraction, attention focusing, and positive self-statements. Ludwick-Rosenthal and Neufeld conclude that these techniques are generally effective in both behavioral ratings and self-report of anxiety. However, they note that manipulations designed to increase the person's perceived level of control over the situation have not been effective.

The third type of stress-management procedure is relaxation techniques, most commonly progressive muscle relaxation. This technique is based on the idea that anxiety and relaxation are mutually exclusive. Significant reductions in self-reported anxiety and behavioral indices of stress were obtained in most of the studies reviewed, but some caution is warranted because of the possibility of artifacts.

The fourth technique, modeling, assumes that the person will learn to cope well by watching others do so. Thus patients are shown a film of people undergoing the procedure and coping effectively. Again, significant effects were found. Self-reported anxiety was reduced, as were behavioral and psychophysiological measures. But, as the authors point out, because this technique often involves components of other techniques, it is difficult to determine the origin of the stress-reduction effect.

When the four techniques are compared for relative effectiveness, the cognitive-behavioral and modeling techniques seemed to produce greater effects.

Janis, I. L. (1958). Psychological stress: Psychoanalytic and behavioral studies of surgical patients. New York: Wiley.
Ludwick-Rosenthal, R., & Neufeld, R. W. J. (1988). Stress management during noxious medical procedures: An evaluative review of outcome studies. Psychological Bulletin, 104, 326-342.

Reprinted from Whitford, F. W. (1995). Instructor's resource manual for Psychology: Principles and applications by S. Worchel & W. Shebilske. Englewood Cliffs, NJ: Prentice Hall.

The Control Process

Chapter 11 discusses different strategies for dealing with stress, focusing on direct coping, defensive coping, and defense mechanisms. A broader approach to understanding people's reactions to stress involves understanding their sense of control. In Chapter 10 of this manual Langer and Rodin's study of control was discussed (see "The Benefits of Control"). Here we examine specific control strategies and their effects on adjustment to stressful events, as outlined by Susan Fiske and Shelley Taylor.

- *Behavior control.* This strategy involves taking concrete steps to reduce the unpleasantness of a negative event. For example, if your next door neighbor insists on playing his Wayne Newton albums at maximum volume, you might shut the doors and windows or forcibly turn down the volume knob on his stereo. This kind of very direct control will typically alleviate the stress associated with the aversive event. However, actual (or perceived) behavior control can also help reduce stress prior to the anxiety-provoking event, or at least increase tolerance of the event when it occurs.

- *Cognitive control.* Cognitive control means thinking about the unpleasant event differently or reevaluating the nonaversive aspects of the event. This strategy seems to help adjustment at all levels of the event; prior, during, and after.

- *Decision control.* Being able to make decisions about the onset, timing, or type of aversive event can be helpful if the outcomes of the decision are favorable. If the results of the decision are unfavorable, the effects on adjustment are unclear. For example, someone who is able to select between two types of root canals may enjoy improved adjustment after the success of the procedure (and, presumably, the decision to elect that procedure).

- *Information control.* The goal here is to gather information about a potentially stressful event, such as the sensations likely to be experienced, the duration or timing of the event, or its cause. For example, a debtor preparing for a tax audit might seek as much information as possible about the procedures, questions asked, documents required, and so forth. Information about sensations ("Will it hurt?") and procedures ("What comes next?") reliably reduce stress, although information about causes has equivocal effects.

- *Retrospective control.* This strategy involves believing that one could have controlled an aversive event that has already happened. For example, a robbery victim may replay the events of the crime to identify what went wrong ("I shouldn't have been there") or what could have prevented it ("I should know better than to flash my $100 bills in public"). Presumably this reflection confers a sense of control to the individual that should work against the event's recurrence; however, the few experiments examining this strategy have been equivocal.

- *Secondary control.* This technique involves aligning one's behavior with the environment, rather than trying to bring the environment under one's control. "Riding it out," "Going with the flow," "Joining rather than beating," or placing oneself in the hands of experts typify this approach. When direct control is not possible, this strategy may help to improve adjustment.

Fiske, S. T., & Taylor, S. E. (1991). *Social cognition* (2nd ed.). New York: McGraw-Hill.

Talk To Me

Jamie Pennebaker, of Southern Methodist University, has published numerous studies over the past decade exploring the benefits of confiding in others. A clear picture has emerged: Confession is good for mind, body, and soul.

Pennebaker and his colleagues Janice Kiecolt-Glaser and Ronald Glaser (1988) asked students to write about either traumatic events in their lives (preferably, stressors that they had not previously discussed with others) or trivial topics for four consecutive days. Prior to the experiment the research participants provided self-reports of their mood, and blood pressure, heart rate, and immunological assays were also collected. These same dependent measures were collected after the writing project, and the assays were also collected 6 weeks after the experiment. The researchers found that the experimental group indeed wrote about rather consequential topics, although they did not enjoy immediate benefits of confession; after writing these participants reported feeling worse than did the control group. However, longer-term benefits were noted. Although measures of autonomic arousal did not distinguish the two groups, students who had confided made fewer subsequent visits to the campus health center and had better immunological functioning than did members of the control group. Moreover, greater improvement in immunological functioning was found for those participants who wrote about previously undisclosed events rather than stressful events that had previously been discussed with others.

Similar benefits were enjoyed by spouses of suicide and accidental-death victims. Pennebaker and Robin O'Heeron (1984) asked nineteen spouses to complete surveys regarding their health and coping one year after their partners' deaths. Results showed that the more these volunteers had discussed their spouses' deaths with friends and loved ones, and the less they had ruminated on the tragic events, the fewer health problems they reported. Importantly, this effect did not depend on the number of friends the spouses reported having. Rather than being a function of the availability of social support, these benefits seem to be a function of confession.

What produces these benefits? Inhibition is hard work. The act of not confiding or ruminating on an aversive event is physiologically taxing (and mentally stressful; see "The Psychology of Mental Control" in Chapter 8 of this manual). Over time, the cumulative stress placed on the body increases the long-term probability of stress-related illness. Confiding, talking, and writing about an event, on the other hand, provides meaning and a new understanding. By organizing and assimilating the experience, a person may become habituated to the event and gradually dull the sharp edges of the experience; over time the information can be cognitively consolidated much like other, less traumatic memories. Language itself may help in this regard. When called upon to summarize a traumatic event in words, language forces a certain structure; the relatively slow process of writing sequencing and temporal organization. What were previously harrowing images are often reduced to a comparatively small set of words. Finally, confession helps to externalize an event. By writing in a diary or confiding to a friend we are able to distance ourselves somewhat from a traumatic event. Once the memory of an event has been committed to paper there is less need to mentally rehearse the event, and thus it is robbed of some of its power to torment us.

Pennebaker, J. W. (1990). Opening up: The healing power of confiding in others. New York: Morrow.
Pennebaker, J. W., & O'Heeron, R. C. (1984). Confiding in others and illness rate among spouses of suicide and accidental-death victims. Journal of Abnormal Psychology, 93, 473-476.
Pennebaker, J. W., Hughes, C. F., & O'Heeron, R. C. (1987). The psychophysiology of confession: Linking inhibitory and psychosomatic processes. Journal of Personality and Social Psychology, 52, 781-793.
Pennebaker, J. W., Kiecolt-Glaser, J., & Glaser, R. (1988). Disclosure of traumas and immune function: Health implications for psychotherapy. Journal of Consulting and Clinical Psychology, 56, 239-245.

Rub-A-Dub-Don't

A recent study conducted by the survey firm Wirthlin Worldwide is useful for discussing research methods (particularly unobtrusive observation), health concerns (particularly the spread of disease), and the correspondence between attitudes and behaviors (particularly their weak link). It may also cause your students to think twice before shaking hands with someone.

Bayer Corporation and the Public Health Committee of the American Society for Microbiology sponsored a study of hand washing in public restrooms. Researchers from the survey group hid in stalls or pretended to comb their hair while they observed over 6,000 men and women in five large cities. Their observations revealed that many people prefer a "get up and go" strategy, failing to wash their hands after using the restroom facilities. In New York's Penn Station, for example, only 60% of restroom users washed after relieving themselves. Similar rates were found in other cities: 64% of restroom users washed at a Braves game in Atlanta, 69% washed in San Francisco's Golden Gate Park, 71% used soap and water in a New Orleans casino, and a laudable 78% washed their hands after using the toilet at

Chicago's Navy Pier. In general, women washed their hands more often than men did--74% compared to 61%--although this trend was slightly reversed in New York and New Orleans.

As part of the research project, Wirthlin Worldwide also conducted a telephone poll asking people about their hand washing habits. Of the 1,004 adults surveyed, a full 94% claimed to always wash their hands after using a public restroom. Although that's a comforting perception to cling to, keep in mind that a friendly wave may be healthier than a firm handshake.

Haney, D. Q. (January 12, 1997). Many don't wash hands, study shows. *Austin American-Statesman*, A5.

A Burdened Heart

An example relevant to health psychology can illuminate the problem of inferring causality from correlation. For quite some time it's been known in the medical community that a link exists between depression and heart disease. For example, large epidemiological surveys typically find that 1½ to 3 percent of the population is depressed at any given time. Among patients with heart disease, however, the rate is closer to 18%. Similarly, about 1 in 6 people in the general population has an episode of major depression during their lifetimes, compared to about 50% of people with heart disease. Finally, a Canadian study revealed that of 222 patients who had suffered heart attacks, those who were depressed were four times as likely to die within the next 6 months.

Amassing this evidence is one thing, but explaining it is quite another. One possibility is that heart disease is the result of biochemical changes that take place in depressed people, such as the secretion of stress hormones. An alternative explanation is that people who are depressed lack the cognitive, motivational, or emotional wherewithal to look after their health or take medications, leaving them more vulnerable to heart diseases such as arrythmias or heart attacks.

A large-scale study by William Eaton at the Johns Hopkins School of Hygiene and Public Health suggests that the causal arrow points from depression to heart disease, but with a few stops along the way. Eaton and his colleagues studied 1,551 people in the Baltimore area who were free from heart disease in 1981. Those who were depressed were four times as likely to have a heart attack in the next 14 years, compared to those who were not depressed. In fact, depression was as strong a predictor of heart disease as was elevated levels of blood cholesterol. The physiological changes that take place in depressed people seem to be the culprits. For example, depressed people's hearts beat faster, their heart rate does not adjust well to changes in activities, and they tend to have elevated blood pressure; these factors in combination produce stress on the heart. Moreover, many depressed people are in a state of hyperarousal due to the secretion of cortisol; they sleep less, eat less, and although they feel mopey and lethargic their fight-or-flight system is set on HIGH. Cortisol also prompts the accumulation of abdominal fat, which in turn elevates the risk of heart disease. In sum, the well-known biochemical changes that take place in depression can increase a person's vulnerability to heart disease.

What's called for is a study demonstrating that therapeutic interventions can reduce the risk of heart disease among depressed people. Such a study has begun, sponsored by the National Heart, Lung, and Blood Institute. It's results could help make sense of this potentially deadly correlation.

Kolata, G. (February 16, 1997). Heartsick, sick heart: Deciphering the link. *Austin American-Statesman*, J1, J5.

Adhering to Medical Advice

One factor that positively influences health is locating a doctor with whom you are able to communicate. Communication, however, is only the first step. Assuming that the doctor's advice is accurate, you must also follow that advice. Research indicates that the rate of adherence to medical advice averages only about 50%, with somewhat higher rates associated with treatments that are designed to cure as opposed to prevent an illness. These rates are relatively consistent regardless of whether the situation involves keeping an appointment with a doctor, taking medication, or staying on a dietary or exercise regimen.

Three general factors influence adherence to medical advice: characteristics of the disease and treatment, the person, and the relationship with medical personnel. Low adherence rates are often associated with treatments of long duration, more complex treatments (e.g., requiring a number of different medications), and negative interactions with medical personnel (e.g., poor communication, delays in getting an appointment, and delays in the waiting room). Increased rates of adherence are often related to a personal perception of the severity of the illness, strong social support, a personal belief in the efficacy of the treatment, clear, specific information from medical personnel about the illness and the reasons for a particular treatment regimen, and personal characteristics of medical personnel such as friendliness, warmth, and a caring attitude. Finally, adherence does not seem to be related to disease severity as defined solely by medical personnel, severity of treatment side-effects, personality traits, and demographic characteristics (at least when measured independently) such as age, gender, race, or educational level.

Cognitive-behavioral techniques seem to be the most effective in increasing adherence. For example, strategies such as prompts to remind patients, tailoring the regimen to the individual's daily habits and activities, a graduated implementation of the regimen, and a contingency contract between the patient and medical personnel help to boost adherence.

Brannon, L., & Feist, J. (1992). *Health psychology: An introduction to behavior and health* (2nd ed.). Belmont, CA: Wadsworth.

Taylor, S. E. (1995). *Health psychology* (3rd ed.). New York: Random House.

Adapted from Hill, W. G. (1995). Instructor's resource manual for *Psychology* by S. F. Davis and J. J. Palladino. Englewood Cliffs, NJ: Prentice Hall.

demonstrations

Defining Stress

The text notes that the perception of an event as stressful varies across individuals, and that not all events perceived as stressful are negative. This exercise is designed to assist students in exploring their own definition of stress and comparing their perspectives to those of their classmates. After you have briefly introduced the topic of stress, ask students to take out two sheets of paper. Tell students that you want them to list specific situations or hassles that they have experienced as being stressful in a negative way. After about 5 minutes, tell them to stop and that you now want them to list events or situations that they would categorize as examples of positive stress. After completing the second list, ask students to share items from each list. You may find that some items listed as an example of positive stress for one student were listed as an example of negative stress for another student. The items listed by students can serve as the basis for a discussion concerning the variability in individual perceptions of whether an event is stressful. You may also want to have students compare their responses to the top ten hassles obtained by Kanner, Coyne, Schaefer, and Lazarus (1981) when they administered the Hassles Scale. In descending order, the top ten hassles were: weight concerns, family health problems, rising prices of common necessities, home maintenance, too many things to do, lost or misplaced items, yard work or outside home maintenance, money management issues related to investments, property, or taxes, crime, and one's physical appearance.

Kanner, A. D., Coyne, J. C., Schaefer, C., & Lazarus, R. S. (1981). Comparison of two modes of stress measurement: Daily hassles and uplifts versus major life events. *Journal of Behavioral Medicine, 4*, 1-39.

Adapted from Hill, W. G. (1995). Instructor's resource manual for *Psychology* by S. F. Davis and J. J. Palladino. Englewood Cliffs, NJ: Prentice Hall.

Lifestyle Awareness Triangle

Gary Piggrem (1994) suggests having students draw a "lifestyle triangle" to help them visualize the stress in their lives. The three sides of the triangle should represent (a) school and/or work, (b) leisure/recreational activities, and (c) relationships with others. The length of each side should accurately reflect the amount of time and energy spent on this aspect, so that longer sides represent more time and energy expended. Ask your students to draw two lifestyle triangles, one representing their *ideal* triangle (i.e., how they wished their triangle looked), and one representing their *actual* triangle (i.e., the way it really looks). In general, bigger discrepancies between the two triangles reflect greater perceived stress experienced by students. Piggrem notes that sometimes the school/work side of a triangle is so long that the other sides can't possible connect with each other! Discuss with students the implications of the triangles they have drawn (perhaps volunteers would be willing to share their depictions) and brainstorm ways that they can change their behavior so that their actual triangle can become more like their ideal triangle--which should ultimately reduce some of the stress in their lives.

Piggrem, G. (1994). Instructor's manual for *Abnormal psychology in a changing world* (2nd ed.) by J. S. Nevid, S. A. Rathus, and B. Greene. Englewood Cliffs, NJ: Prentice Hall.

Assessing Student Worries

Although many textbooks address the definition and measurement of stress, McDaniel and Eison (1987) pointed out that few address the notion of worries, probably because there is little research on this abstract concept. Worry can be generally defined as a pattern of thoughts that are often uncontrollable, negative, and reflect fears. As a means of generating class discussion on the topic and its relationship to stress, administer a condensed version of Eison and McDaniel's (1985) Worries Survey, which can be found in Handout 12-1. Ask students to place a check mark next to the items that they occasionally or regularly worry about. You can then use their responses to discuss the most common worries and concerns of college students (i.e., by tallying positive responses to each item on the board). Your students can also gain some insight into their own worries by noting categories that seem to be of particular concern. The seven categories represented by this scale are school (items 1, 6, 18), romance and relationships (2, 11, 19), health and appearance (3, 7, 12), career development (4, 13, 15), social acceptance (8, 16, 20), money (9, 14, 17), and time (5, 10, 21).

>Eison, J., & McDaniel, P. S. (1985). The development of a student worry survey. Unpublished manuscript.
>McDaniel, P. S., & Eison, J. (1986). Assessing student worries. In V. P. Makosky, L. G. Whittemore, & A. M. Rogers (Eds.), *Activities handbook for the teaching of psychology: Vol. 2* (pp. 241-245). Washington, DC: American Psychological Association.

Type A Behavior Patterns

After lecturing on the Type A behavior pattern, you can use an activity described by Eagleston (1987) to help increase your students' understanding of Type A behavior. You should note to your students that people exhibiting Type A behavior "engage in a set of observable behaviors that can be grouped into three areas: (a) excessive competitiveness and achievement orientation, (b) time urgency and impatience, and (c) easily aroused anger and hostility" (Eagleston, 1987). After writing these three areas on the board, divide students into small groups and tell each group to develop a list of specific and observable behaviors representing each of the areas. After about 10 minutes, ask the groups to share their behaviors and have the class develop a consensus list of behaviors. The ensuing class discussion will help facilitate an understanding of the characteristics associated with Type A behavior. Eagleston suggested that you may want to compare the student generated checklist with those available in Chesney, Eagleston, and Rosenman (1980) and Friedman and Ulmer (1984). Eagleston also proposed having students use their checklist to observe and record the behavior of a friend, relative, or even themselves over a set period.

>Chesney, M., Eagleston, J. R., & Rosenman, R. (1980). The Type A structured interview: A behavioral assessment in the rough. *Journal of Behavioral Assessment, 2,* 225-272.
>Eagleston, J. R. (1987). Understanding the Type A behavior pattern. In V. P. Makosky, L. G. Whittemore, & A. M. Rogers (Eds.), *Activities handbook for the teaching of psychology: Vol. 2* (pp. 166-168). Washington, DC: American Psychological Association.
>Friedman, M., & Ulmer, D. (1984). *Treating Type A behavior and your heart.* New York: Knopf.

>Reprinted from Hill, W. G. (1995). Instructor's resource manual for *Psychology* by S. F. Davis and J. J. Palladino. Englewood Cliffs, NJ: Prentice Hall.

Guest Lecture: Promoting a Healthy Lifestyle

The health psychology chapter provides the perfect opportunity to give your students practical information about important and timely health-related topics. Listed below are several potential topics on which a health expert might lecture, any of which should make for an excellent, engaging, and beneficial presentation.

Diet and Nutrition. Invite a registered dietitian or other nutrition expert to your class to discuss the role of diet and nutrition in health. Although more and more adults are taking an interest in their diets as part of an overall trend toward health consciousness, myths and misconceptions abound. As part of his or her presentation, ask your guest lecturer to address student concerns and help them separate fact from fiction when it comes to nutrition. Relevant issues for discussion include the role of fat and cholesterol in diet, the relationship between alcohol and heart disease, the risks and benefits of taking vitamin supplements, the relationship between fresh vegetable consumption and cancer risk, vegetarianism, food additives, the problems of yo-yo dieting, and how to read the new government labels. Your expert might also address the proper place in the diet for salt, caffeine, fiber, water, and carbohydrates.

Stress Management. Arrange for a representative from the counseling center or health center to discuss stress management with the class. Your students may not be aware of the counseling services that your college or university provides. A guest speaker can teach students a variety of useful techniques (e.g., relaxation, time management, social support) that will help them successfully manage and cope with stress, especially near the end of the semester when they need it most.

AIDS and STDs. Alternatively, a health counselor might talk frankly with students about AIDS and other sexually transmitted diseases. Although college students like to think they're not vulnerable to sexually transmitted diseases, the evidence is to the contrary: STDs have reached near-epidemic proportions at many colleges and universities. Again, student myths and misconceptions should be addressed, and ways to prevent the spread of these diseases (such as safer sex practices, and increased communication between sexual partners) can be explored.

Culture and Health

Many of the health attitudes and behaviors taken for granted in the United States are less common in other countries. For example, the city of Los Angeles recently enacted a ban on smoking in restaurants, and several other cities are following suit. This would no doubt seem bizarre in many European countries, where the general concept of "smoking sections" and "no smoking sections" in public places has yet to be appreciated. Similarly, because many fitness-conscious Americans are concerned with getting an optimal level of exercise, it is not uncommon (particularly in the early morning and late afternoon) to see men and women jogging around parks, lakes, and on neighborhood streets throughout the United States. In Europe, however, jogging American tourists--especially females--are occasionally greeted with quizzical looks, as if to say, "What are you running from?"

It is clear, then, that culture plays an important role in health behavior (see Triandis, 1994, for a review). Differences in life expectancy, which can range from 40 to 50 years in underdeveloped or poor countries to 70 to 80 years in developed or rich countries, can be traced to cultural difference in diet, levels of stress, access to health care, and relationships with others. Interestingly, not all health outcomes favor rich or industrialized countries. Many poorer countries have better diets (and lower rates of heart disease) than richer countries, since affluence is related to the consumption of meat and other fatty foods. Even among industrialized countries there are important differences. For example, life expectancy is higher in Scandinavian countries than in the United States (because of greater access to health care), and rates of alcoholism and stress are both lower in collectivist countries (e.g., Japan), in which people depend on others and have a large family support network, than they are in individualistic countries (e.g., the United States), which emphasize individualism and self-reliance over dependence on others.

Ask your students to share their experiences as travelers or as members of another culture regarding the diversity of health attitudes and health practices. Use examples of smoking, alcohol, regular exercise, consumption of high cholesterol or fatty foods, preventive health care, attitudes toward leisure time and vacation, and relationships with others. What types of cultural norms might be driving these various practices? What role does the media play in shaping general health attitudes?

Triandis, H. C. (1994). *Culture and social behavior.* New York: McGraw-Hill.

student assignments

Evaluating Self-Help Books

This assignment, which calls for students to review and evaluate a popular self-help book of their choice, serves three primary purposes: (a) it gives students an opportunity to gather information about some area of concern in their lives, (b) it allows them to apply principles of health and well-being from the text and lecture, and (c) it encourages them to take a critical look at the burgeoning field of "bibliotherapy." Students should begin by browsing the local book store and selecting a self-help book of interest to them. Those who haven't already spent some time in the self-help section of the bookstore may be surprised at the number and variety of books available. Many books are relevant to self-improvement and tell readers "How To" do just about anything, such as lose weight, quit smoking, eat a healthier diet, be more assertive, get along with others, have higher self-esteem, become more organized and so on. Others suggest they can help readers cope with any number of problems, including depression, anxiety, stress, phobias, codependency, a relationship breakup, and grief, to name a few. Because some of these topics are more sensitive than others, you should advise students not to choose a topic that is uncomfortable for them, and you should also assure them that you will keep their papers confidential and anonymous.

Students should begin their paper by reviewing the author's general theoretical stance as well as the basic techniques or strategies suggested in the book. They should then evaluate the author's advice in terms of their own experience. Did the book provide an accurate basis for self-diagnosis and for checking your progress? Were the techniques in the book clearly articulated and easy to follow? In general, how useful was the book in terms of solving the target problem? Students should also include in their paper a discussion of any principles from the text or lecture that are applied in the book. Finally, students should step back and evaluate the book from a scientific perspective. Does the author offer any empirical support to substantiate his or her claims? Has the book been tested in a clinical setting? In general, how accurate do the claims made in the title or content of the book appear to be?

Randy Smith (1995) in his critical look at bibliotherapy notes that although self-help books have their advantages (e.g., consumers can be educated about psychotherapy; in some cases potential problems can be prevented) and disadvantages (e.g., people can improperly diagnosis their condition, or become discouraged if the book fails to solve the problem), their biggest problem is often a lack of scientific evidence to support the authors' claims. Nonetheless, it is likely that not all self-help books are a waste of time, just as not all self-help books are beneficial. After the papers are turned in, conduct a class discussion exploring some of the issues mentioned above. Hopefully, some students will be willing to share their experiences (both positive and negative) and shed some light on this timely topic.

Smith, R. A. (1995). Challenging your preconceptions: Thinking critically about psychology. Pacific Grove, CA: Brooks/Cole.

AIDS in Film

No discussion of health psychology would be complete without a discussion of one of the fastest growing (yet preventable) health crises of our time: AIDS. Despite heavy publicity in the last decade, studies reveal that even as college students begin to finally understand how the AIDS virus is transmitted, they feel invulnerable to it and continue to engage in risky sexual behavior. In addition, depending on your location many of your students may not have ever been "touched" by AIDS (i.e., they may not have known anyone personally with the disease). To give your students a better understanding of this horrible disease, have your students write a reaction paper to one of the two superb films listed below. What did they learned about AIDS and its victims that they didn't already know? Did they have any misconceptions that were cleared up by the film? Do they have better insight into and empathy for the suffering of AIDS victims? What suggestions do they have for getting the message across to teenagers and college students to engage in safe sex?

• *And the Band Played On* (1993). Matthew Modine heads an all-star cast in this excellent made-for-cable movie that dramatizes the story of the AIDS epidemic. The story chronicles the initial discovery of the disease by the Centers for Disease Control, the failure of the blood bank industry to take proper precautions, efforts in the gay community to adopt safer sex and to shut down bathhouses, and the long, uphill battle to convince the government and the public of the severity of the problem, with many intriguing subplots in between (HBO; 140 min). Based on the book by the late Randy Shilts.

Shilts, R. (1987). And the Band Played On: Politics, People, and the AIDS Epidemic. New York: St. Martin's Press.

• *Longtime companion* (1990). Bruce Davison stars in this highly-acclaimed film that follows a close-knit group of gay men in New York City in the early days of AIDS. The affecting and sensitive film reveals the increasingly devastating and personal consequences of the disease, as each of the men individually becomes affected by it in one way or another (Vidmark; 100 min).

video

ABC News/Prentice Hall Video Library

The Breaking Point (15 min, Series III). Shannon Faulkner, Kim Messer, and Jeannie Mentavlos may not be household names, but their experiences have secured them a place in history. Faulkner was the first woman admitted to The Citadel, that bastion of all-male tradition, followed closely by Messer and Mentavlos. This *20/20* segment focuses on Messer's experiences while there and the forces that drove her out.

So Angry You Could Die (11 min, Series III). This *20/20* segment presents people on the edge, and some who are well past it. A variety of stress-related illnesses are linked to anger (and its inappropriate expression); this brief video piece explores ways to ward them off by reducing hostile responses to the world.

What's the Oldest A Woman Should Be Giving Birth? (8:40 min, Series III). Technology--from egg donation to in-vitro fertilization to surrogate parenting--has provided hope to countless women who have difficulty conceiving a child. In this case technology has helped a 63-year-old woman give birth. This *Nightline* segment looks at the moral and medical issues surrounding decisions that some see as "defying nature."

Other Sources

AIDS: No-Nonsense Answers (10 min, FHS). This short film presents the facts about AIDS in a straightforward manner. You'd probably be surprised at how little your students know about a disease that has been rampant for most of their lifetimes. This film will provide a much-needed education.

AIDS Research: The Story So Far (57 min, FHS). Stunning computer graphics and top production values make this an engaging treatment of how HIV works, how AIDS develops, and what can be done to treat the disease.

And The Band Played On (1993, 120 min, HBO). A recent dramatization of Randy Shilts' account of the AIDS epidemic. A good source of background knowledge for discussing the early detection and spread of the disease, and the ignorance that surrounded it.

Anorexia and Bulimia (19 min, FHS). Explores the causes and symptoms of anorexia nervosa and bulimia and their effects on the cardiovascular and central nervous systems.

Beyond the Ashes (1992, 24 min, IMP). A documentary about the fires that ravaged the Berkeley and Oakland hills, and the psychological impact of those events.

Cigarettes: Who Profits, Who Dies? (49 min, FHS). Former cigarette models now dying of cancer...international tactics that American tobacco companies use to boost overseas sales in the face of a flagging local market...persuasion leading to addiction. The grim realities of cigarette use are presented in this unflinching video.

Discovering Psychology, Part 23: Health, Mind, and Behavior (1990. 30 min, ANN/CPB). This video examines mind-body relationships, risk factors for physical and psychological distress, and the general work of health psychologists.

Emotion and Illness (30 min, FHS). The relation between psychology and immunology is examined, focusing on women with cancer.

The Healing Mind (1991, 58 min, IM). Psychoneuroimmunology is the topic of this video, which looks at how mind and body interact to produce healthful states.

Health and Lifestyles: Positive Approaches to Well-Being (28 min, UIOWA). The role of nutrition, weight control, exercise, and stress management in promoting health is explored.

Health, Stress, and Coping (1990, 28 min, IM). This videotape in the series *Psychology: The Study of Human Behavior* presents recent findings on the psychological aspects of health and their relationship with stress, coping, and other factors. Selye's General Adaptation Syndrome is discussed by Norman Cousins and various experts in the field of health behavior.

Managing Stress (19 min, FHS). The distinction between eustress and distress forms the basis for this discussion of what stress is and how it affects mind and body.

Post-Traumatic Stress Disorder (26 min, FHS). Using several case studies, the causes and effects of post-traumatic stress disorder are discussed.

Reducing Stress (19 min, FHS). Discusses a variety of physical problems that have been related to stress and techniques for stress reduction. Also explores post-traumatic stress disorder.

Smoking: Time to Quit (18 min, FHS). The motivation to quit smoking is discussed, but motivation is sometimes not enough; this program also offers concrete tips for kicking the habit.

Stress (23 min, FHS). Stress in all its forms is discussed: The tension that lets bridges stand, the forces that produce frustration in our lives, the chronic hassles that lead to illness.

Stress (26 min, FHS). The focus of this program is actually stress management. Noted researchers and clinicians offer effective strategies for dealing with sources of stress in daily life.

Stress and Immune Function (26 min, FHS). Cancer, herpes, respiratory functions, and autoimmune disorders have been linked to stress. This video looks at how and why that happens, and what to do about it.

Stress Reduction Strategies That Work (1990, 30 min, IM). Current information on how people react to stress and techniques for reducing stress symptoms. Includes interviews with physicians.

The World of Abnormal Psychology, Part 2: The Nature of Stress (1992, 60 min, ANN/CPB). Examines the occurrence of stress in a variety of situations, its long-term effects, and techniques for reducing stress.

The World of Abnormal Psychology, Part 4: Psychological Factors and Physical Illness (1992, 60 min, ANN/CPB). Explores the relationship between emotion and health and how psychological treatments can improve one's well-being.

multimedia

Live! Psych

Module	Title	Book Page #
12.1	The Sympathetic Nervous System Response to Stress	p. 464

Screen 1 shows how the sympathetic nervous system prepares the body for "fight-or-flight." Screen 2 explains how stress triggers the release of adrenaline and other stress hormones into the bloodstream, and these hormones weaken the immune system by suppressing lymphocyte activity.

12.2	General Adaptation Syndrome	p. 466

In Screen 1, stress is defined and Hans Selye, the pioneer of the study of physiological responses is introduced. Screen 2 explains that Selye observed that people respond in similar ways to all events they perceive as stressful or threatening, regardless of whether they are physiological or psychological. A graph outlines the three-stage process by which the body responds to stress, which Selye called the general adaptation syndrome.

Alarm Stage — p. 466

Screen 1 has sound effects of a speeding car with a screeching sound and highlights the alarm stage. Screen 2 explains that when you are exposed to a stressor, the hypothalamus reacts by organizing a generalized response that affects organs throughout your body. Collectively, these are known as "fight or flight" responses. The hypothalamus activates the sympathetic nervous system, causing the adrenal glands to release the stress hormones. The student clicks on the labels of the human body to see how the different parts of the body respond to a stressor. Screen 3 shows the human body and the effects of the different parts of the body after the stressful situation ends and the parasympathetic nervous system takes over and restores the body to its premobilized calm state.

Resistance Stage — p. 466

In Screen 1, a graph displays this second stage, in which we mobilize all of our physiological resources to cope with the stressor. Screen 2 presents an animation of the internal physiological changes during the resistance stage.

Exhaustion Stage — p. 466

In Screen 1, a graph displays exhaustion, the third stage of the general adaptation syndrome. A bar graph shows relative risks of catching a cold under various levels of stress. Ways to manage stress are discussed.

12.3	The Immune System	p. 468

Screen 1 illustrates pathways to illness. In Screen 2, the student clicks on different body parts on the human body to learn about the search-and-destroy nature of lymphocytes. Screen 3 presents an animated graphic to identify two major systems related to the central nervous system and involved in the body's response to stress: the HPA axis and the sympathetic nervous system.

Web Investigations

Investigating Gangs and Behavior

Your students might not immediately think of gangs as a health issue, yet most medical authorities note that behavioral factors, such as poor diet, lack of exercise, addictive behaviors, and unsafe acts, are major *preventable* sources of illness in our society. Certainly gangs promote several of these unhealthy factors, including addiction and risky criminal conduct. Gangs use violence to defend their territories, commit revenge on rival groups, and to keep wayward members in line with the group's authority. Often, these practices involve handguns with lethal consequences. Moreover, gangs represent a significant source of stress for members of a community who are subjected to their presence. Clearly, ours would be a healthier society that would enjoy a higher quality of life without the deleterious influence of gangs.

But gangs exist for reasons beyond the illegal and unhealthy behaviors they frequently promote. Understanding why individuals join gangs is at the core of efforts to prevent gangs or to reduce their influence. This *Web Investigation* provides an overview of the functions and activities of gangs.

Making Connections

Sources of Stress

Q Why can positive life changes cause stress?

A Positive life changes cause stress because they require us to change or adapt in order to meet our needs.

Q Name the three most common types of everyday hassles.

A The three most common types of everyday hassles are pressure, frustration, and conflict.

Q What are the main types of conflict?

A The main types of conflict are approach/approach conflict, avoidance/avoidance conflict, and approach/avoidance conflict.

Q Explain the differences between hardy and resilient individuals on the one hand, and anxious individuals on the other, in terms of their appraisal of situations.

A Hardy and resilient individuals tend to view a stressful situation as an opportunity. They are open to change and internally motivated, and view difficult demands from the environment as challenging. Anxious individuals view the same situations as intimidating.

Coping with Stress

Q How is direct coping different from defensive coping?

A Direct coping consists of intentional efforts to change an uncomfortable situation. It is problem-oriented and focuses on the immediate issue. Defense coping consists of various forms of self-deception that are emotion oriented and do not change the actual situation.

Q Can defensive coping be adaptive? When is it maladaptive?

A Defensive coping can be adaptive when it reduces anxiety and thus allows for a higher level of adaptation than would otherwise be possible. It is maladaptive when it interferes with a person's ability to deal directly with a problem or creates new problems.

Q What situational factors explain different styles of coping among the poor? Among men and women?

A Situational factors affecting the way the poor cope with stress include substandard housing, high rates of crime and unemployment, and poor schools. While there are no clear gender differences in coping with stress, there is some evidence that men and women use different coping strategies in some situations. Men are more likely to turn to alcohol, while women are more likely to ruminate about the problem.

Stress and Health

Q What are the three stages of Selye's General Adaptation Syndrome? At which stage does stress begin to take a toll on health?

A The stages of the general adaptation syndrome are alarm reaction, resistance, and exhaustion. Stress may begin to take a toll on health if the second stage is prolonged.

Q Both an aggressive Type A personality and depression can contribute to heart disease; explain how this happens in terms of the physiology of stress.

A Type A behavior and depression both can contribute to heart disease by keeping the body in a constant state of arousal, which damages the heart and blood vessels.

Q How does stress affect the immune system? Name at least one mental, physical, and social activity that can reduce stress.

A Stress affects the immune system by reducing the production of lymphocytes (white blood cells), which are essential in fighting disease. You can reduce stress by staying calm, exercising, and reaching out to family and friends.

Extreme Stress

Q What do the different forms of extreme stress discussed here have in common?

A All forms of extreme stress cause a radical departure from everyday life, such that a person cannot carry on as before and may never fully recover.

Q Who is most likely to develop post-traumatic stress disorder?

A Women are more likely than men to develop post traumatic stress disorder.

The Well-Adjusted Person

Q How do realistic actions that meet the demands of the situation and the individual's needs, as well as contribute to the well-being of others, lead to self-actualization?

A Realistic actions lead to self-actualization because they allow people to enhance their own growth and fulfillment while minimizing escapism, inner conflict, and the stress caused by hurting others.

Video Classics

Carl Rogers on the Self

SYNOPSIS: Rogers distinguishes between the self and the organism. One's organism (the physical body and all its attributes) may behave differently from one's self (which encompasses self-views, self-concept, and self-esteem), as illustrated by Rogers in the case of a pedophile. Maladjustment comes in part from a static, unchanging self in response to changes in the organism.

Form a Hypothesis

Q What would Carl Rogers say leads to maladjustment?

A Rogers views maladjustment as a "collision" between ones assessment of themselves and ones standards.

Test Your Understanding

Q What is self-actualization?

A For Rogers, self-actualization is a near total awareness of what is going on with themselves and their environments. They have a continued commitment to grow and evolve, be open to experience, trust their judgment, live in harmony with others, and will live in the present.

Q According to Rogers, how does maladjustment occur?

A These standards are established by "conditions of worth", rules and expectations established by our parents for offering us affection.

Thinking Critically

Q What are three traits that make up the hardiness personality style? How do these traits relate to self-actualization?

A Hardiness is characterized by commitment, challenge, and control. Hardy individuals have a sense that they can control their situation, that they are committed to values, and that they experience stressful events as a challenge, not a threat. The self-actualized individual should embody hardiness, especially considering commitment and challenge.

Web Links

1. http://www.teachhealth.com

Health Education: stress, depression, anxiety, drug use, and sleep problems are just some of the topics you'll find here.

2. http://maple.lemoyne.edu/~hevern/psychref4-7.html

PsychREF: Clinical and Behavioral Medicine. This site provides links to other sites on general health, AIDS, well-being, dieting and obesity, sleep and sleep disorders, sports and exercise, and relaxation. Point your students here for basic references for a brief in-class report on a health-related topic of their choice.

3. http://www.ncptsd.org/

National center for PTSD. A useful site for information about this specific condition.

4. http://www.imt.net/~randolfi/StressPage.html

Stress Management and Emotional Wellness Page. This site includes links, a discussion forum, and information about maximizing health and performance, managing stress, and enhancing one's emotional well-being.

transparencies

Series V

87a. *Types of Conflict*
87b Approach/approach/ approach/avoidance, avoidance/avoidance, and double approach/avoidance conflicts are illustrated.

88. *Physiological Responses to a Stressor*
This transparency shows how the sympathetic nervous system and the endocrine system react to a potential stressor.

89. *Selye's General Adaptation Syndrome*
Alarm, resistance, and exhaustion stages are depicted.

90a. *Psychological Defense Mechanisms*
90b Unconscious defenses are illustrated in this two-part transparency.

91. *Frequency of Various Coping Strategies by Adults*
This transparency presents the results of a survey about the types of strategies and frequency of such strategies used by adults to cope with stress.

Text Figures

- 12-1. *Appraising Stress*
- 12-2. *The Physiological Response to Stres*
- 12-3. *Mental Trauma in Societies at War*

Handout 12-1

Worries Survey

Instructions: Below is a list of common worries taken from interviews and surveys with individuals like yourself. Please read each statement carefully and place a check mark in the blank next to the items about which you worry occasionally or regularly. Please answer honestly and candidly without spending too much time thinking about any one item.

_____ 1. I worry about being able to get into the classes I need or want.

_____ 2. I worry about spending more time alone than I prefer (e.g., not having someone to date or friends to spend time with).

_____ 3. I worry about maintaining a desirable body weight.

_____ 4. I worry about whether I have really chosen the right major.

_____ 5. I worry about having too much to do and too little time to do it.

_____ 6. I worry about not studying effectively.

_____ 7. I worry about not being able to break bad habits (e.g., quit smoking or drinking, etc.).

_____ 8. I worry about being liked by my friends.

_____ 9. I worry about not having enough money for both essentials and recreation.

_____ 10. I worry about spending too little time with people I care about.

_____ 11. I worry about making existing relationships (e.g., marriage, or other relationships) successful.

_____ 12. I worry about not eating properly and/or exercising regularly.

_____ 13. I worry about not being successful in my major.

_____ 14. I worry about not having enough money to pay for my education.

_____ 15. I worry about finding a job in my major field upon graduation.

_____ 16. I worry about getting along with my professors.

_____ 17. I worry about not knowing how to manage money wisely.

_____ 18. I worry about my grades.

_____ 19. I worry about coping with the ending of a serious relationship.

_____ 20. I worry about being a good family member.

_____ 21. I worry about not having enough time, quiet time, for myself.

Adapted with permission from McDaniel & Eison (1985). Assessing student worries. In V. P. Makosky, L. G. Whittemore, & A. M. Rogers (Eds.), *Activities handbook for the teaching of psychology: Vol. 2* (pp. 241-245). Copyright ©1987 by the American Psychological Association. Reprinted with permission.

Chapter 13 Psychological Disorders

chapter outline 378

learning objectives 381

lecture suggestions

    Parameters of Mental Illness 382
    Viral Infection and Schizophrenia 383
    A Unique Sexual History 383
    Mental Disorders and the Criminal Justice System 384
    Once More, With Feeling 385
    A Filtering Cigarette Can Ease Schizophrenic Symptoms 385
    Catching Madness in the Act 386
    Uncommon Psychiatric Syndromes 386
    Cross-Cultural Comparisons of Mental Illness 388
    Autism 389
    Impulse Control Disorders 389
    Art and Mental Illness 390
    Thought Disorders and Delusions 391

demonstrations and activities

    Defining Abnormal Behavior 393
    Gender Stereotypes and Mental Illness 393
    The Obsessive-Compulsive Test 394
    Debate: Does Multiple Personality Disorder Really Exist? 394
    Debate: Is Schizophrenia a Biological Disorder? 395
    Demonstrating Schizophrenia 395
    Diagnosing Mental Disorders 396
    The Client 396
    Trick or Treat 396

student assignments

    Abnormal Psychology in Literature: *The Eden Express* 397
    Abnormal Psychology in Film 397

video 399

multimedia 404

transparencies 410

handouts

    Mental Health Questionnaire, Forms A, B, and C 411, 412, 413
    Obsessive-Compulsive Test 414
    Diagnosing Mental Disorders 415

chapter outline

I. Perspectives on Psychological Disorders
- A. What causes psychological disorders?
    1. View of society: non-conformity to the social order
    2. View of Individual: personal discomfort and lack of well-being
    3. View of Mental Health: poor life functioning
- B. Historical Views of Psychological Disorders
    1. Supernatural views: Disorders the result of demons, possession, supernatural powers
    2. Naturalistic views: Beginnings in ancient Greece with Hippocrates
- C. Theories of the nature, causes, and treatment of psychological disorders
    1. The biological model: Psychological disorders have a biochemical or physiological basis
    2. The psychoanalytic model: Psychological disorders are the result of unconscious conflicts
    3. The cognitive-behavioral model: Disorders are the result of learning maladaptive responses
    4. The diathesis-stress model and systems theory
        - a. Diathesis-stress model:
            - i. Those biologically disposed to mental illness show disorder under stress
        - b. Systems approach
            - i. Risk factors combine to produce psychological disorders
                - Also called the biopsychosocial model of psychological disorders
- D. Classifying psychological disorders
    1. The Diagnostic and Statistical Manual (4th edition) typically used
- E. The prevalence of psychological disorders

II. Mental Illness and the Law
- A. Insanity: a legal term used to indicate whether an individual can understand the difference between right and wrong.
- B. Competence: a legal term used to indicate whether an individual can understand the charges against them and assist in the defense against the charges.

III. Mood Disorders
- A. Depression: Sadness, lack of interest, feelings of worthlessness
    1. Clinical depression versus "normal" depression
    2. Major depressive disorder versus dysthymia
- B. Mania and bipolar disorder: Euphoria, extreme activity, distractedness, excessive talkativeness
- C. Causes of mood disorders
    1. Biological factors: Both genetics and neurotransmitters play a role
    2. Social factors: Interpersonal difficulties play a role

3. Psychological factors: Cognitive distortions play a role
       D. Suicide
IV. Anxiety Disorders
   A. Specific phobias: Intense fears associated with specific circumstances, objects
      1. Social phobias: Excessive fears associated with social situations
      2. Agoraphobia: Intense fear of crowding and public places
   B. Panic disorder: Recurrent panic attacks of fear without cause
   C. Other anxiety disorders
      1. Generalized anxiety disorder: Prolonged vague but intense fears without focus
      2. Obsessive-compulsive disorder: Driven to disturbing thoughts or rituals
   D. Causes of anxiety disorders
V. Psychosomatic and Somatoform Disorders
   A. Psychosomatic: Psychological factors play a role in producing real physical disorders
   B. Somatoform: Physical symptoms persist without any identifiable physical cause
      1. Somatization disorder: Recurrent vague somatic complaints without physical cause
      2. Conversion disorders: Dramatic disability with no physical cause
      3. Hypochondriasis: Interpreting insignificant symptoms as serious illness
      4. Body dysmorphic disorder: Preoccupation with imagined ugliness
   C. Causes of somatiform disorders
VI. Dissociative Disorders and Fugue
   A. Dissociative amnesia: Loss of memory without organic cause
   B. Dissociative identity disorder: Multiple personality disorder
   C. Depersonalization disorder: Person suddenly feels strangely changed or different
   D. Causes of dissociative disorders
VII. Sexual Disorders
   A. Sexual dysfunction
      1. Erectile disorder or disfunction and female sexual arousal disorder
      2. Sexual desire disorders
      3. Orgasmic disorders
      4. Premature ejaculation and vaginismus
   B. Paraphilias
      1. Fetishism: Nonhuman object preferred for sexual arousal
      2. Voyeurism: Desire to watch others having sexual relations
      3. Exhibitionism: Compulsion to expose one's genitals in public
      4. Frotteurism: Achieving sexual arousal by rubbing or touching a nonconsenting person
      5. Transvestic fetishism: Sexual gratification through wearing opposite sex's clothing
      6. Sexual sadism: Sexual gratification through humiliating or harming a partner
      7. Sexual masochism: Sexual gratification through pain

8. Pedophilia: Sexual relations with or persistant sexual fantasies about children

C. Gender-Identity Disorders

1. Gender identity disorder in children

VIII. Personality Disorders

A. Types of personality disorders

1. Schizoid: Inability or desire to form social relationships

2. Paranoid: Inappropriately suspicious of others and their motives

3. Dependent: Inability to make decisions or act independently

4. Avoidant: Marked social anxiety leading to isolation

5. Narcissistic: Displaying a grandiose sense of self-importance

6. Borderline: Marked instability in self-image, mood, relationships

B. Antisocial personality disorder

1. Showing little sense of remorse while lying, cheating, stealing

C. Causes of antisocial personality disorder

IX. Schizophrenic Disorders

A. Common psychotic symptoms

1. Hallucinations, delusions, language disruptions

B. Types of schizophrenic disorders

1. Disorganized: Bizarre, childlike behavior predominates

2. Catatonic: Disturbed motor behavior most notable symptom

3. Paranoid: Extreme suspiciousness and bizarre, complex delusions

4. Undifferentiated: Clear symptoms that don't meet criteria for other subtypes

C. Causes of schizophrenia

X. Childhood Disorders

A. Attention deficit/hyperactivity disorder (AD/HD)

B. Autistic disorder

XI. Gender and Cultural Differences in Psychological Disorders

A. Gender differences

1. Women tend to have higher rates of disorders than do men

a. Especially true of mood and anxiety disorders

b. Both biology and socialization seem to contribute

i. Explanations still a matter of debate

B. Cultural differences

learning objectives

After reading this chapter, students should be able to:

1. Distinguish among the standards for defining psychological disorders from the view of society, the individual, and the mental-health professional.

2. Summarize historical attitudes toward psychological disorders.

3. State the four current models of psychological disorders and explain the diathesis-stress model.

4. Explain how the DSM-IV classifies mental disorders.

5. Distinguish between the two basic kinds of mood disorders and how they may interact with each other.

6. Describe and compare the anxiety disorders.

7. Recognize the characteristics of the psychosomatic disorders and the somatoform disorders.

8. Characterize three different types of dissociative disorders.

9. Define and give examples of the sexual disorders.

10. Define gender-identity disorders.

11. Define personality disorder. Describe four kinds of personality disorders.

12. Describe four types of schizophrenic disorders and identify possible causes of the disorder.

13. List characteristics of children with attention-deficit/hyperactivity disorder and autism.

lecture suggestions

Parameters of Mental Illness

A research team at the University of Michigan conducted the National Comorbidity Study, the first study to administer a structured psychiatric interview on a national scale. The study revealed that nearly one-half of all Americans between the ages of 15 and 54 have experienced an episode of psychiatric disorder at some time in their lives. Moreover, 30 percent of them have experienced a disorder within the past year. Altogether, about 5.2 million Americans account for 90 percent of all episodes of severe mental illness each year.

Comorbidity, or the clustering of psychiatric illnesses in a single person, presents a challenge to accurate diagnosis and treatment. Because a single individual may present aspects of several disorders, it may be difficult to simultaneously and effectively identify or treat them all. Comorbidity was definitely revealed in the survey. Fifty-six percent of people with a history of one psychiatric disturbance also showed a range of other disorders.

The survey revealed some surprising findings as well. For example, blacks have a lower incidence of anxiety and substance abuse than whites, even though blacks typically face generally inferior financial and economic conditions. Also, perhaps counterintuitively, it was found that Americans living in rural areas were just as likely as their urban fellows to suffer from either year-long or lifetime psychiatric disorders.

The survey also found other demographic trends:

- The rates of almost all psychiatric disorders decline with increasing income and education. An exception is lifelong substance abuse, which tends to be significantly higher among the middle-education group.

- People between the ages of 25 and 34 experience the highest overall rates of mental illness. Beyond that range, rates of mental illness tend to decline with age.

- Seventeen percent of the population have experienced one or more episodes of major depression at some point in their lives.

- Women seem to suffer from anxiety disorders and affective disorders, whereas men show higher rates of substance abuse and antisocial disorders. Lifelong substance abuse disorders and lifelong antisocial personality disorders also tended to be highest in the West, whereas lifelong anxiety disorders were highest in the Northeast.

- Although one sixth of the population suffers from one or more lifetime psychiatric disorders, only 40 percent ever receive psychiatric care.

Staff (1994, July/August). The culture of distress. *Psychology Today*, pp. 14-15.

Viral Infection and Schizophrenia

A recent theory about the cause of schizophrenia argues that viral infections play a critical role in the onset of the disorder. Research has demonstrated that viral infections may spread to the central nervous system by moving along nerves. The viral hypothesis proposes that infant respiratory viruses may infect the brain by traveling along the maxillary nerve and trigeminal ganglion. The virus would remain dormant, however, until activated either by hormones released during puberty or another viral infection during early adulthood. Schizophrenia researcher E. Fuller Torrey noted that this hypothesis may explain the finding that schizophrenia tends to be more common among individuals born during the spring and winter months. These are also periods during which there is a high incidence of upper respiratory infections. In addition, he also noted that the higher rate of birth complications found among schizophrenics may indicate the possibility of slight brain damage due to anoxia that makes them more susceptible to brain infections.

Torrey, E. F. (1991). A viral-anatomical explanation of schizophrenia. *Schizophrenia Bulletin, 17,* 15-18.

Adapted from Hill, W. G. (1995). Instructor's resource manual for *Psychology* by S. F. Davis and J. J. Palladino. Englewood Cliffs, NJ: Prentice Hall.

A Unique Sexual History

Wardell Pomeroy was an associate of Alfred Kinsey, and along with Clyde Martin they published *Sexual Behavior in the Human Male*, a landmark study of human sexuality. Kinsey of course went on to publish other collections of his research on sexuality, but Pomeroy relates one episode that stands out from the rest of the research. In his book *Dr. Kinsey and the Institute for Sex Research*, Pomeroy relates a tale of the longest interview they ever conducted.

> When we got the record after a long drive to take his history, it astounded even us, who had heard everything. This man had had homosexual relations with 600 preadolescent males, heterosexual relations with 200 preadolescent females, intercourse with countless adults of both sexes, with animals of many species, and besides had employed elaborate techniques of masturbation. He had set down a family tree going back to his grandparents, and of thirty-three family members he had sexual contacts with seventeen. His grandmother introduced him to sexual intercourse, and his first homosexual experience was with his father. If this sounds like *Tobacco Road* or *God's Little Acre*, I will add that he was a college graduate who held a responsible government job. . .
>
> At the time we saw him, this man was sixty-three years old, quiet, soft-spoken, self-effacing--a rather unobtrusive fellow. It took us seventeen hours to get his history. . . .
>
> At one point in his history taking he said he was able to masturbate to ejaculation in ten seconds from a flaccid start. Kinsey and I, knowing how long it took everyone else, expressed our disbelief, whereupon our subject calmly demonstrated it to us. . . .It was the only sexual demonstration among the 18,000 subjects who gave their histories (pp. 122-123).

Kinsey, A. C., Pomeroy, W. B., & Martin, C. E. (1948). *Sexual behavior in the human male.* Philadelphia: Saunders.
Pomeroy, W. B. (1972). *Dr. Kinsey and the Institute for Sex Research.* London: Thomas Nelson and Sons.

Mental Disorders and The Criminal Justice System

Mental disorders complicate the workings of the criminal justice system. When a crime is committed by someone with a possible mental disorder, should that person be held accountable for his or her actions and sent to prison, or not held accountable and given treatment instead? Can the person's condition be determined accurately enough to evaluate accountability and make reasonable decisions concerning his or her need for treatment?

Insanity is a legal rather than a psychological concept. People judged to be insane are not held liable for their actions. The formal concept of insanity dates to 1843 and the M'Naughten decision. While attempting to assassinate the British prime minister, Daniel M'Naughten killed the prime minister's secretary. He was found not guilty due to insanity. The court established a definition of insanity, the M'Naughten Rule, which stated that a person should be found to be insane if "the party accused was laboring under such a defect of reason, from disease of the mind, as not to know the nature and quality of the act he was doing; or if he did know it, that he did not know he was doing what was wrong" (M'Naughten case, 1843, cited in Shapiro, 1985). Here the requirement stressed a loss of cognitive capacity.

A new standard, the American Law Institute Rule (ALI Rule), was adopted by all federal courts and many state courts after the Brawner decision in 1972. This definition allows an insanity judgment when at the time of the crime the person lacked "substantial capacity either to appreciate the criminality (wrongfulness) of his conduct or to conform his conduct to the requirements of the law" (Shapiro, 1985). Here either the cognitive deficiency of the M'Naughten Rule or an inability to control one's behavior are required.

Although in obvious cases of insanity the public may be willing to substitute treatment for punishment, many insanity defenses are viewed with suspicion or outrage. For example, when John Hinkley, who shot then-President Ronald Reagan, was found not guilty by reason of insanity and subject only to commitment for treatment, some Americans were outraged. Hinkley did not appear to be seriously disturbed to the average person, and the verdict raised questions about the appropriateness of the insanity definition as well as the accuracy of the forensic psychiatrists' judgment. Hinkley won a court decision in 2004 which allowed him to begin taking supervised overnight trips outside the treatment facility, and most legal commentators believe that he will ultimately be released back into society.

The public's suspicions are not without foundation. Each side in a trial usually presents expert witnesses to support its case, and these witnesses contradict each other. Moreover, experts have been fooled by people able to fake a mental disorder, as apparently happened in the case of Kenneth Bianchi, the so-called Hillside Strangler. Bianchi claimed to have multiple personalities, and several psychiatrists agreed with him. Eventually evidence was presented that strongly suggested that he was faking, and Bianchi dropped his claim of having multiple personalities and pled guilty. In another case Edmund Kemper III killed eight people after being released from a mental hospital, where he had been committed as the result of a successful insanity defense in the murder of his grandparents.

Finally, there is the popular perception that the insanity defense is frequently used with success and often with questionable foundation. Actually, less than 1 percent of felony cases involve an insanity plea (Holden, 1983), and only 2 percent of those are successful (Monahan & Loftus, 1982). But it is true that some cases are questionable. Insanity pleas have been based on premenstrual syndrome, epilepsy, and even junk food diets (Pollack, 1984). For example, Dan White, who killed the mayor of San Francisco, was found guilty on the lesser charge of manslaughter based on his "Twinkie Defense."

Holden, C. (1983). Insanity defense reexamined. *Science, 222,* 994-995.
Monahan, J., & Loftus, E. (1982). The psychology of law. *American Review of Psychology.* Palo Alto, CA: Stanford University Press.
Pollack, P. (1984). The epilepsy defense. *Atlantic Monthly,* May, 20-28.
Sarason, I. G., & Sarason, B. R. (1995). *Abnormal Psychology,* 8th ed. Upper Saddle River, NJ: Prentice Hall.
Shapiro, D. C. (1985). Insanity and the assessment of criminal responsibility. In C. P. Ewing (Ed.), *Psychology, psychiatry, and the law: A clinical and forensic handbook.* Sarasota, FL: Professional Resource Exchange.

Reprinted from Whitford, F. W. (1995). Instructor's resource manual for *Psychology: Principles and applications* by S. Worchel and W. Shebilske. Englewood Cliffs, NJ: Prentice Hall.

Once More, With Feeling

"I'd better check......one more time.....just let me make sure.....I'd better go back...." In isolation these comments might come from anyone wondering whether the headlights are turned off on the car. But as the mantra of people suffering from obsessive-compulsive disorder these thoughts plague their daily lives. Whether its washing one's hands 25 times a day or checking to make sure the stove burner is off every hour on the hour, OCD can severely hobble one's peace of mind.

More rightly, it may be a piece of brain that produces these intrusive thoughts. UCLA's Jeffrey Schwartz and his colleagues used PET scans to study the brains of obsessive-compulsive patients. They found that the orbital cortex, the part of the brain responsible for sensing when something is amiss, seemed to be stuck on ACTIVE. For example, when most of us notice that the dishes in the sink need washing, our caudate nucleus clicks on to signal us to respond. If the caudate nucleus misfires, the orbital cortex in turn becomes perpetually engaged. The result, according to psychiatrist Schwartz, is that the thought that something needs to be checked or fixed or is yet-to-be done doesn't go away.

To remedy this, Schwartz and his colleagues propose the use of behavioral modification and cognitive therapy. When an intrusive thought makes its appearance, OCD patients are trained to relabel the thought for what it is: an obsession. They next attribute that obsession to a biochemical imbalance in their brain. Finally, patients focus on some constructive activity, such as paying the bills or weeding the garden, for 15 minutes, to allow their stuck caudate nucleus to become unstuck and shift to other thoughts. This technique has had limited success, with only 12 of 18 OCD patients reporting substantial relief from their intrusive thoughts. When it is successful the evidence is clear: PET scans show a much more subdued caudate nucleus after 8 to 12 weekly therapy sessions, combined with the relabeling and refocusing done by the patient at home. In the final analysis, it may indeed be that a piece of mind alters a piece of brain to restore peace of mind.

Begley, S., & Biddle, N. A. (1996, February 26). For the obsessed, the mind can fix the brain. *Newsweek*, 60.

A Filtering Cigarette Can Ease Schizophrenic Symptoms

It's been noted that among psychotic patients, schizophrenics are often the heaviest smokers. New research may hold an answer to why this is the case, as well as suggest avenues for treating this devastating mental illness.

A research team led by Robert Freedman of the Denver Veterans Affairs Medical Center discovered something that apparently many people with schizophrenia had known for some time: A long drag can bring brief relief to information overload. Freedman identified a gene linked to the inherited trait of being able to filter out sources of stimulation, such as a dripping water faucet or the buzz of a fluorescent light bulb. Although most people can achieve this selective attention quite readily, it is often difficult for schizophrenics to reduce the stimulation of the external world. The researchers also linked the gene to a brain receptor site which appears to be stimulated by nicotine. In short, ingesting nicotine can trigger a momentary increase in the ability to filter information.

Although the research team has not yet identified the genetic mutation that would cause the link between this particular schizophrenic characteristic and the nicotine receptor gene, there is some evidence in support of this line of research. Clozapine, for example, is a psychoactive drug that appears to help the information filtering problem in schizophrenics, and many patients report smoking fewer cigarettes while on the drug. Clozapine's exact mechanism is unknown, but in conjunction with genetic research new treatment options may be found. At the very least, friends and family members may be more understanding of why a schizophrenic person is so reluctant to kick the habit.

Neergaard, L. (January 21, 1997). Scientists find link between schizophrenia gene, nicotine. *Austin American-Statesman*, A2.

Catching Madness In the Act

David Silbersweig and Emily Stern, of the Cornell Medical Center in New York, received some popular press recently. One reason was because of a new technique they developed for capturing PET scans of very short durations. The other reason was because of how they applied the technique. Silbersweig and Stern, along with colleagues in London, were able to use PET technology to capture an image of the schizophrenic brain in the process of hallucinating.

Six volunteers agreed to provide this rare glimpse to the researchers. All experienced hallucinations; one patient, for example, heard voices that bellowed "How horrible!" or "Don't act stupid!" whereas another was tormented by images of rolling, decapitated heads that shouted orders to him. Once in the PET scanner, patients pressed a button to indicate the onset of hearing hallucinatory voices and pressed it again when the experience stopped. The PET scans revealed that the structures active during this period were deep inside the brain. For example the hippocampus, thalamus, and striatum seemed abuzz with activity; these structures usually integrate emotion, memory, and perception, suggesting that a miswired neural circuitry may be implicated in schizophrenia. Importantly, none of the brain structures that should have activated did. For example, there was no significant activity in the prefrontal cortex, suggesting that the reality-monitoring functions of the prefrontal lobe were not at work. Furthermore, when a control group heard actual voices PET scans revealed that the auditory cortex was activated, and none of the deep structures were.

The immediate application of these results, and to some extent, their exact interpretation, is not clear. At a minimum they suggest that schizophrenia may involve more than simply a chemical disruption; indeed, 5 of the 6 patients in the study obtained no relief from standard medication. Further research may reveal whether aberrant brain circuitry is present and where it might be; eventually, a surgical intervention may be used in treating schizophrenia. For now, researchers are satisfied to have gained a new tool for shedding light on a very private and very scary event.

Begley, S. (1995, November 20). Lights of madness. *Newsweek*, 76-77.

Uncommon Psychiatric Syndromes

Chapter 12 presents a thorough overview of the major DSM-IV classes of disorders and the specific disorders that represent them. Your students may be interested to hear about more unusual cases of mental disturbances, to give a context to the presentation of psychological disorders.

David Enoch and Sir William Trethowan (1991) have published a handbook of psychiatric disorders that are at the outposts of mental disturbance. Although some of them are increasingly discussed in textbooks and the popular press (e.g., Tourette's syndrome) and others border on anthropological and social analyses (e.g., possession and exorcism), many are worth presenting to illustrate the extremes of psychopathology.

Capgras' Syndrome

In 1923 Capgras and Reboul-Lachaux described a syndrome in which a patient believes that a person close to him or her has been replaced by an exact double. The syndrome typically accompanies other functional psychoses (such as schizophrenia or affective disorders), although it tends to be the dominating feature. In such cases the misidentification is quite specific; the patient acknowledges the striking resemblance of a loved one but insists the person is a duplicate. The syndrome is also seen in concert with some organic disorders, where it is characterized by more confusion about the misidentification. To date there has been no reliable link between experiencing Capgras' syndrome and being a devotee of the science fiction classic *Invasion of the Body Snatchers*.

Capgras' syndrome is often placed in a family of Delusional Misidentification Syndromes which include other similar disorders. For example, the *illusion of Fregoli* (named for a famous stage actor and presented by Courbon and Fail in 1927) finds the patient convinced that his or her persecutors are changing faces, so that the person's spouse, doctor, coworker, or mail carrier are alternately presented as that same one person. Courbon also described the *illusion of intermetamorphosis* in which a patient believes that those in his or her surroundings are changing from one to another; Bob becomes Mitch, Mitch becomes Roger, and Roger becomes Bob. The *subjective doubles syndrome* involves a patient's conviction that others have been transformed into the patient; this was described by Christadoulou in 1978. Finally, *reduplicative paramnesia*, described by Pick in 1903 and regarded as a neurological syndrome, involves the perception that a physical location has been duplicated.

Ekbom's Syndrome

Ekbom's syndrome, or *delusional parasitosis*, refers to patients who suffer delusions of infestation. Those afflicted believe quite certainly that lice, maggots, insects, or other small vermin are living on them, in their skin, or in some cases in their bodies.

Although reference is made to delusional parasitosis during the late 1800's, Ekbom first thoroughly described the manifestations of the delusion in 1937. By most accounts the syndrome is very rare; one study estimated that 3 cases were seen in 1,869 psychiatric admissions over 18½ years. Among those suffering from it, however, it appears to be rather intractable once established.

Munchausen Syndrome

Munchausen syndrome by proxy has received increasing attention by practitioners and researchers as a form of child endangerment. It involves a caregiver's persistent fabrication of medical symptoms and signs in the person cared for (typically a mother/child relationship), leading to illness, endangerment, and unnecessary invasive or hazardous treatments. Munchausen syndrome itself refers to such behavior in a single individual. The patient is usually admitted to a hospital presenting some acute illness that has a dramatic but plausible origin. It is subsequently discovered that the history is riddled with falsehoods, and that the patient has similarly deceived the staff of several other hospitals. Patients often discharge themselves against medical advice, often after arguing about a course of treatment or after some medical intervention has been initiated.

The key elements in both of these manifestations are the presence of physical symptoms that are self-induced (or other-induced, in the case of proxy), and pathological lying reminiscent of Baron Munchausen, a renowned teller of tall tales. Some illustrative cases include:

- Acute abdominal disturbances: A young nurse swallowed a dinner fork on six separate occasions to necessitate gastrostomy each time; she eventually died as a result of this practice.

- Hemorraghic disturbances: Patients have pricked their fingers and contaminated the wounds with urine, or used an animal spleen to simulate a blood clot in the mouth.

- Neurological disturbances: Some patients have undergone craniotomy or prefrontal leucotomy as a result of their presentations.

- Respiratory disturbances: Some patients have inserted needles into their chests; others have ingested infected sputum from other patients.

Other patients repeatedly swallow safety pins or needles; some self-inflict stab wounds or purposely irritate scabs and blisters to prevent healing and promote infection.

Folie á deux

The DSM lists folie á deux ("insanity of two") as *shared paranoid disorder*, characterized by a person developing persecutory delusions as a result of a close relationship with another person who already has such a disorder. The first full account of the disorder was provided by Lasègue and Falret who described seven cases in 1877. Although they concentrated on "psychosis by association" in sisters, folie á deux describes the case when any two (or more; folie á trois, folie á quatre, folie á famille, have been described) persons in close association with one another develop delusional ideation. Variants include *folie imposée* (the patient with the primary psychosis is dominant in the relationship), *folie simultanée* (delusions occur simultaneously but independently in the two parties), and *folie communiquée* (the second party initially develops delusions similar to those of the first, then develops a unique delusional system independently). Separation of the two delusional participants is usually the first step in treating this disorder; in many cases separation produces marked recovery in the recipient of the delusion.

Enoch, M.D., & Trethowan, W. (1991). *Uncommon psychiatric syndromes* (3rd ed.). Oxford, UK: Butterworth-Heinemann, Ltd.

Cross-Cultural Comparisons of Mental Illness

At various times we have been said to be living in the "Age of Anxiety," the "Age of Alienation," or the "Age of Insanity." These descriptions are more figural than literal, meant to capture the spirit of a particular time. But their underlying theme contains a particular bias. In most cases, these "Ages of Whatever" are meant to describe the conditions in developed, Westernized societies. A more provocative question is this: How do approaches to and descriptions or rates of Psychological Disorders compare across societies? Researchers are beginning to address this topic more enthusiastically; Thomas Oltmanns and Bob Emery have discussed two studies that provide some interesting comparisons.

Jane Murphy, a Harvard anthropologist, lived with the Inuit of Alaska and the Yoruba of tropical Nigeria during the 1970s. She collected reports from native healers among the Yoruba and from a key Inuit informant about the lives of the respective, relatively small cultures. Particular attention was devoted to descriptions of Psychological Disorders. Both cultures recognized behaviors as "crazy," such as hearing voices when no one is nearby, talking in peculiar ways that don't make sense to others, or behaving in bizarre or erratic ways. The parallels with the Western notion of schizophrenia are obvious and striking. However, some of these descriptions could also be applied to the behavior of shamans within these cultures. Both the Inuit and the Yoruba distinguish between the "craziness" of the shaman and the behaviors just described. In the case of the shaman, it is a controlled or purposeful "craziness;" the shaman is able to voluntarily control his actions and direct them toward a particular goal (e.g., healing a sick member of the group).

A more recent study was initiated by the World Health Organization. Some 1200 hospitalized psychiatric patients in nine countries (Columbia, Czechoslovakia, Denmark, England, India, Nigeria, Taiwan, Russia, and the United States) were studied. In each setting the frequency of schizophrenia was approximately the same, despite obvious cultural differences (i.e., developing nations, such as India or Nigeria, versus developed countries, such as Denmark or the U.S.). Like Murphy's earlier study, the WHO study found some cross-cultural variation in the description, behaviors, and subtypes used to define schizophrenia.

These studies suggest that rather than being a Westernized concept, severe forms of mental illness (such as schizophrenia) have some cross-cultural commonality to them.

Jablensky, A., Sartorius, N., Ernberg, G., Anker, M., Korten, A., Cooper, J. E., Day, R., & Bertelsen, A. (1992). Schizophrenia: Manifestations, incidence, and course in different cultures: A World Health Organization ten-country study. *Psychological Medicine*, Monograph Supplement 20, 1-97.

Murphy, J. M. (1976). Psychiatric labeling in cross-cultural perspective. *Science*.

Oltmanns, T. F., & Emery, R. E. (1995). *Abnormal psychology*. Englewood Cliffs, NJ: Prentice Hall.

Autism

Autism is one of several disorders that are first diagnosed in infancy or early childhood. Although the DSM-IV noted that it only occurs at a rate of 2 to 5 cases per 10,000, it is probably one of the most well-known childhood disorders due to its frequent portrayal in movies and television programs.

The general characteristics of autism described in the DSM-IV include severe deficits in reciprocal social interactions, communication disorders, and restricted activity and interest levels. Autistic children often will be withdrawn from others, failing to engage in social play or even to recognize the presence or needs of others. They often fail to initiate interactions with others and do not engage in reciprocal social and emotional behavior. Language development is either delayed or totally absent. When language is used, it is often repetitive (e.g., repeating words or phrases without meaning) or idiosyncratic rather than meaningful. Behavior also tends to be restricted and repetitive. Autistic children will tend to focus intensely on one or more patterns of behavior that are performed in a stereotyped, repetitive manner (e.g., rocking, preoccupations with a very specific interest, organizing objects repeatedly in a specific pattern). Their behaviors are also often very ritualized and inflexible, and they will get very upset if the behavioral pattern is disturbed or changed. They may also exhibit self-injurious behaviors such as hitting themselves or biting body parts. There may also be a perceptual preoccupation with particular objects, parts of objects, or movement.

The rate of this disorder is four to five times higher in males, and there appears to be a genetic factor involved since higher rates are found among siblings (American Psychiatric Association, 1994). Cognitive explanations of autism suggest that the disorder may be related to an inability to comprehend sounds, a tendency toward stimulus overselectivity, or an inability to engage in abstract thinking. The majority of treatment approaches tend to focus on controlling symptoms through behavior modification or drug treatments. Although there may be some improvement, social and communication problems often continue into adolescence and adulthood.

American Psychiatric Association. (1994). *Diagnostic and statistical manual of mental disorders* (4th ed.). Washington, DC: Author.

Comer, R. J. (1992). *Abnormal psychology*. New York: W. H. Freeman.

Reprinted from Hill, W. G. (1995). Instructor's resource manual for *Psychology* by S. F. Davis and J. J. Palladino. Englewood Cliffs, NJ: Prentice Hall.

Impulse Control Disorders

"Self-control disorders" can encompass a range of pathologies, from eating disorders to criminal acts to aggressive outbursts. A better-defined subset of this classification is impulse control disorders, which are characterized by three essential features: an inability to not act on impulses that are harmful to the actor or to others; a compelling pressure to act experienced just before the behavior takes place; a sense of pleasure or gratification upon completing the behavior. Several well-known, and a few more obscure, disorders meet these criteria.

❖ *Kleptomania*. This disorder is characterized by a desire to steal, rather than a desire to acquire. Kleptomaniacs are less interested in what they steal than in the act itself. Although most laypeople have heard of this disorder and would think it somewhat prevalent, it is most often seen clinically in the context of other disorders. This suggests that kleptomania may be a symptom of some other disorder, one that is perhaps biologically based. Evidence supporting this conclusion is that Prozac, which increased serotonin activity, has been found to be helpful is treating kleptomania.

❖ *Pathological gambling*. When does the neighborhood poker game turn pathological? When Lenny has one too many beers and starts to belly dance on the table. Besides that, though, "Lotto fever," being obsessed with "hitting it big" at the track, entering every office football pool, or playing the dollar slots for 9 straight hours in Vegas may be signs of an impulse control disorder. Pathological gambling is debilitating financially, psychologically, and interpersonally. Betting becomes the focus of existence for these gamblers, which in turn becomes financially draining when the big wins turn to big losses, which places stress on family and loved ones; the prevalence of drinking, smoking, eating disorders, and suicide attempts among spouses of pathological gamblers has been estimated to be inordinately high. Pathological gambling is usually associated with the presence of other disorders, such as narcissistic, antisocial, or aggressive personality disorders, low tolerance for boredom, and proneness to addiction. Treatment usually follows a behaviorist approach, relying on aversive therapy or imaginal desensitization.

❖ *Trichotillomania.* This rare disorder involves an irresistible urge to pull out one's hair. Beyond a simple eyebrow pluck or desire for electrolysis, people with trichotillomania acquire bald patches, lost eyelashes, missing armpit or pubic hair, and in extreme cases may swallow the hair after pulling it out, leading to a range of other harmful consequences. This disorder may be linked to obsessive-compulsive disorder, although trichotillomaniacs tend to suffer from other disorders, such as mood, anxiety, eating, or substance abuse disorders. Behavioral treatments seem effective in reducing the frequency of hair pulling.

❖ *Pyromania.* This impulse control disorder refers to the compelling and intense desire to prepare, start, or watch fires. It is a relatively rare disorder; even among fire starters, only 2 to 3 percent would be considered pyromaniacs. The disorder often gets its start in childhood, and although it has been linked to sexual paraphilias there has been little systematic research exploring this connection. Pyromania is seen in conjunction with other disorders, however. David Berkowitz, the Son of Sam serial killer, set more than 2,000 fires in New York City during the 1970s.

❖ *Intermittent explosive disorder.* This disorder is characterized by sudden, brief bouts of extreme rage. Like most impulse control disorders, the difficulty lies in suppressing a common inclination; many of us feel enraged from time to time, but are able to control our tempers or channel our aggressive impulses elsewhere. Biological origins of intermittent explosive disorder seem most likely. Serotonin, insulin, and norepinephrine deficits have all been implicated, and a link to epilepsy is being explored.

❖ *Sexual impulsivity.* Frequent and indiscriminate sexual activity is the hallmark of this disorder. People who are sexually impulsive often come from family backgrounds where excessive guilt, sexual abuse, or restrictive attitudes toward sex predominated. One pathological reaction to this environment would be sexual aversion; sexual impulsivity may be a reaction at the opposite extreme.

Halgin, R. P., & Whitbourne, S. K. (1994). *Abnormal psychology: The human experience of psychological disorders.* Fort Worth: Harcourt Brace.

Art and Mental Illness

The link between creativity and madness has piqued the imagination of scholars, artists, and laypeople alike. There has been a spate of recent research and popular books exploring this presumed fine line. However, another aspect of this link seems to increasingly vie for popular attention. *Outsider art*, or art produced by people on the fringes of society, has become the "hot ticket" among critics and collectors within recent years.

The term "outsider art" has been broadly applied to works produced by transients, the criminally insane, artwork by the mentally ill, art that can be found primarily in thrift stores, art produced in isolation and discovered only upon the artist's death, art that at one time would have qualified as a "primitive" style (e.g., the work of Grandma Moses), as well as work that typically conveys a singular, often idiosyncratic view of mundane subjects. (This multiplicity of definitions no doubt reflects the premium and price tag currently put on this type of work; where the "outside" boundary lies is often determined by a buyer and seller.) In this regard, the work of Rev. Howard Finster (who painted the cover of the Talking Heads album *Little Creatures*) or anything done on velvet (from Elvis to large-eyed weeping children to clowns) would qualify. Better known examples would include Munch's *The Scream,* Louis Wain's famous paintings of cats (which grew more bizarre as his schizophrenia progressed), or much of the work of Van Gogh.

At one time, however, "outsider art" referred exclusively to the works of the mentally ill (*inter alios,* the criminally insane). *Art brut,* or art of the insane, actually has enjoyed popularity for a number of decades in underground circles. The paintings of convicted serial killer John Wayne Gacy, for example, were quietly acquired by various collectors before his execution. (After his death a single collector acquired all he could for the express purpose of publicly destroying them.) There have also been exhibitions of such work in several respected galleries, as well as a collection housed at the Musée de l'Art Brut in Lausanne.

Without arguing their merits or value, it is nonetheless fascinating to study art brut for what it reveals about the psychological state of the person producing it. In some instances it easily reflects the turmoil experienced by a moderately depressed person or someone suffering from an anxiety disorder. In other cases it is art that is unusual, yet doesn't seem to map onto a tidy diagnosis. At the Landers Clinic in Gugging, Austria, for example, there is an artists' wing dedicated exclusively to a handful of patients. These painters and a sole poet have produced artwork that has been shown worldwide and has been acquired by collectors for handsome prices (all profits are maintained in trust funds for the artists). In the opinion of the ward's director, Johann Feilacher, had these patients not become ill they nonetheless would have been talented artists. In this sense art brut becomes the work of artists who happen to be mentally ill, rather than a mentally ill person's artistic products.

The many meanings of art brut discussed in this lecture suggestion can be shared with your students to stimulate discussion. You might address the link between creativity and madness, explore the definition of what constitutes art brut, or discuss the therapeutic and diagnostic value of having patients express themselves in this way. If possible, share with your students some of this work. A convenient source of art produced by the mentally ill is *Schizophrenia Bulletin.* Each issue of this journal features cover artwork and brief commentary by a schizophrenic patient.

Prinzhorn (1995). *Artistry of the mentally ill.* New York: Springer-Verlag.
Staff (1994, November/December). When out is in. *Psychology Today,* p. 13.
Theoz, M. (1976). *Art brut.* New York: Rizzoli Press.
Tuchman, M. (1992). *Parallel visions: Modern artists and outsider art* (LACMA Exhibition). Princeton University Press.
Weinberg, S. (1995, August 6). Portraits of the mental patient as inspired artist. *The New York Times Magazine,* pp. 42-43.
Weiss, A. S. (1992). *Shattered forms: Art brut, phantasms, modernism.* Albany, NY: SUNY Press.

Thought Disorders and Delusions

Delusional or disordered thought is a hallmark of many forms of mental illness, especially schizophrenia. Some of the more common delusions (false beliefs that are inconsistent with the thinker's background or level of intelligence) and thought disorders (disrupted patterns of cognition, language, or logic) have been summarized by Richard Halgin and Susan Whitbourne.

Delusions

❖ *Persecution.* The belief that another person or group is trying to harm the individual or his or her loved ones. An example might be believing that General Motors is maintaining a file on your activities and is plotting to destroy your homestead.

❖ *Grandeur.* These delusions can be either specific or somewhat vague. For example, believing that you are Abraham Lincoln is a rather focused delusion, whereas believing that you are someone who has been preordained to have an important role in history is more diffuse. Delusions of grandeur in general involve an exaggerated view of one's own importance.

❖ *Somatic.* These beliefs involve a preoccupation with one's body, especially that some disease or disorder is present. Mistakenly believing that tape worms are gnawing away your stomach lining would be a somatic delusion. (Compare with Ekbom's psychosis, discussed above.)

❖ *Nihilism.* The delusion that the world, others, and/or oneself is nonexistent. A spooky sense of unreality or believing that one is "living in a dream" often accompanies this delusion.

❖ *Reference.* Delusions of reference are beliefs that the behaviors of others or certain events have been targeted specifically toward oneself. Believing that the storyline of Melrose Place has been taken (literally) from your own life would be an example.

❖ *Thought broadcasting.* The notion that one's thoughts are being broadcast to everyone in the vicinity. For example, you might believe that your mental rehearsal of your grocery list can be heard by your coworkers around you.

❖ *Thought insertion.* The idea that thoughts are being inserted into one's mind by outside forces. David Berkowitz, the Son of Sam, reportedly believed that his thoughts were being implanted in his mind by his neighbor's dog.

Thought Disorders

❖ *Incoherence.* This thought disturbance is probably the best known among laypeople. Incoherence involves speech that is incomprehensible or lacking in meaning and structure, such as saying, "The sheep are on the roof because twelve is New Jersey" when asked one's name.

❖ *Flight of ideas.* Here speech is intelligible, but marked by a fast pace and rapid acceleration, often with abrupt changes of topic. Flight of ideas has the quality of a speaker ready to burst forth with a spew of sentences.

❖ *Loosening of associations.* A cognitive disruption characterized by an illogical, unfocused, or vague train of thought. When asked how you are feeling, replying "Healthy, wealthy, and wise. Three wise men run the bank, you know; they have the wealth of nations" might be an example.

❖ *Neologisms.* The invention of new words or distortion of existing ones, often to match some self-perceived meaning. Describing the "wretchedivism" of your "tetramatic" lifestyle would be an example.

❖ *Clanging.* In this thought disorder the sounds of words, rather than their meaning, determines the content of one's speech. For example, you might respond "The note in the till, by the goat eating swill, sank the boat on the hill" when asked how you arrived at the psychiatric clinic.

❖ *Circumstantiality.* Speech filled with unnecessary, tedious, and inconsequential detail, leading to rambling descriptions of events or responses to questions. It's late at night, now, when I'm trying to think of an example of this, although this morning when I woke up I felt as though today would be a productive day of writing. While I was eating my Cap'n Crunch, as a matter of fact, that thought occurred to me. Especially when I was pouring my milk, which is always nonfat. Traci and I try to cut down on our fat intake wherever possible. I think the milk came from Safeway, but I can't remember. Anyway, by now you get the idea...

❖ *Perseveration.* Not clanging, but *clinging* to the same idea, word, phrase, or sound repeatedly. "I must stop writing. I must stop writing. I have to finish this. I must stop writing. I have to finish this writing. I must stop" would be an example.

Halgin, R. P., & Whitbourne, S. K. (1994). *Abnormal psychology: The human experience of psychological disorders.* Fort Worth: Harcourt Brace.

demonstrations

Defining Abnormal Behavior

The text notes that psychologists use several criteria to distinguish between normal and abnormal behavior, including statistical rarity, interference with day-to-day functioning, personal distress, and social norms. Students often have their own definitions of abnormality that may or may not be related to these criteria. The following exercise, adapted from one proposed by Gardner (1976), is designed to enable students to explore their own definition of psychology and its relationship to these criteria. First ask your students to list and then share synonyms for mental illness, explaining the origin of any unusual terms. Next, divide the class into small groups and have half of the groups construct a definition of abnormality or mental illness while the remainder are to define normal or mentally healthy behavior. Tell the students that their definitions should not include any of the synonyms generated in the first part of the exercise. After about 10 to 15 minutes, have group spokespersons share their definitions. You can relate the group definitions to the various criteria described in the textbook. Also, have your students discuss the difficulties they had in generating appropriate definitions for abnormality or normality without recourse to using synonyms.

Gardner, J. M. (1976). The myth of mental illness game: Sick is just a four letter word. *Teaching of Psychology, 3*, 213-214.

Reprinted from Hill, W. G. (1995). Instructor's resource manual for *Psychology* by S. F. Davis and J. J. Palladino. Englewood Cliffs, NJ: Prentice Hall.

Gender Stereotypes and Labeling Mental Illness

Broverman et al. (1970) reported the results of a study of clinically-trained experts (i.e., psychiatrists, clinical psychologists, social workers) that investigated characteristics associated with mental health for a female, male, and average adult (sex not specified). The results showed that the characteristics associated with a healthy individual (sex unspecified) were more likely to resemble those characteristics associated with mental health for a male than for a female. The following exercise was designed to replicate the Broverman et al. results in class (Anonymous, 1981). The questionnaires to be used in the exercise are reproduced in Handout 13-1; versions a, b, and c ask students to rate the characteristics of a healthy male, female, and average adult, respectively. Randomly distribute the three versions of the questionnaire to your students without revealing that they are getting different forms. After they have completed the questionnaire, count the number of times that each phrase was selected for each target person. Ask the students if their results are similar to those of Broverman et al. That is, are items selected for a person similar to those for a male? Do items selected for a female differ from those chosen for a person and a male? If your students' results differ from those of Broverman et al., have them discuss why. Some possibilities may be changes in societal attitudes since the original study, the class size may be too small to produce differences, or that students' beliefs and attitudes are different from those of professionals. Finally, have your students consider the effects of gender stereotypes on diagnosis and treatment. You could also relate the issue of gender stereotypes to the criticisms raised about the sexism inherent in Freud's theory.

Anonymous. (1981). Sex role stereotypes and mental health. In L. T. Benjamin, Jr. & K. D. Lowman (Eds.), *Activities handbook for the teaching of psychology* (pp. 141-142). Washington, DC: American Psychological Association.
Broverman, I. K., Broverman, D. M., Clarkson, F. E., Rosenkrantz, P. S., & Vogel, S. R. (1970). Sex role stereotypes and clinical judgments of mental health. *Journal of Consulting and Clinical Psychology, 34*, 1-7.

Adapted from Hill, W. G. (1995). Instructor's resource manual for *Psychology* by S. F. Davis and J. J. Palladino. Englewood Cliffs, NJ: Prentice Hall.

The Obsessive-Compulsive Test

One of the types of anxiety disorders described in the Chapter 13 is obsessive-compulsive disorder. The text points out that all of us experience occasional obsessive thoughts. However, in the obsessive-compulsive disorder these thoughts and their related behaviors are often uncontrollable and generate high anxiety. Gardner (1980) provided a test designed to measure obsessive-compulsive thoughts and behaviors, reproduced in Handout 13-2, that you can administer in class. After students have completed the test, instruct them to add the total value of the circled numbers. Gardner's proposed scoring and interpretation of results are as follows:

25 - 45	*Not obsessive-compulsive*
46 - 55	*Mildly obsessive-compulsive*--it is adaptive and generally beneficial
56 - 70	*Moderately obsessive-compulsive*--although still adaptive, you experience short periods of high tension
71 - 100	*Severely obsessive-compulsive*--although adaptive, you may be insecure and hard-driving, experiencing extended periods of high tension

Because Gardner didn't provide any information concerning the development of this test, you should emphasize that this exercise is simply meant to help the student understand obsessive-compulsive behavior, and it is not meant to be used as a diagnostic tool. For example, you may want to have the students discuss test construction issues related to ambiguity in the wording and interpretation of some of the test items. You can also use the test as the basis for a discussion of variations between normal and abnormal levels of obsessive-compulsive behavior.

Gardner, R. M. (1980). *Exercises for general psychology*. Minneapolis, MN: Burgess Publishing.

Adapted from Hill, W. G. (1995). Instructor's resource manual for *Psychology* by S. F. Davis and J. J. Palladino. Englewood Cliffs, NJ: Prentice Hall.

Debate: Does Multiple Personality Disorder Really Exist?

Because of famous presentations depicted in the news media and in popular film, your students will likely be fascinated by dissociative identity disorder (also known as multiple personality disorder). Chapter 13 highlights the controversial nature of this disorder by explaining that whereas some clinicians and researchers argue that it is a genuine disorder that develops as a coping mechanism in response to severe abuse, others suggest that it is a feigned or role-played disorder whose incidence has dramatically increased as a result of media publicity. Is multiple personality disorder real? Does research provide compelling support for psychological and physiological changes between different personalities? Are multiple personalities discovered in hypnosis sessions, or are they in fact created by such sessions? Is the recent explosion in the number of reported cases of multiple personality disorder due to better diagnostic criteria or to greater media publicity? Encourage your students to explore the answer to these questions by considering the scientific evidence and arguments in a debate format. Assign students to research this issue and to be prepared to defend either side. Excellent background resources for this discussion can be found in *Seeing Both Sides*, a compendium of debates in abnormal psychology. Chapter 8 in this excellent book contains both pro and con viewpoints on this controversial topic, and students should be encouraged to find more recent sources from journal articles and from the popular media.

Lilienfeld, S. O. (1995). *Seeing both sides: Classic controversies in abnormal psychology*. Pacific Grove, CA: Brooks/Cole.

Debate: Is Schizophrenia a Biological Disorder?

Several psychological disorders once thought to have social or behavioral origins are now known to have strong biological bases. There's compelling evidence that affective disorders, for example, have a substantial biological foundation. Similar arguments have been made for the biological basis of schizophrenia, although not without dissent. A debate exists regarding the extent to which schizophrenia can be classified as a biological disorder. Those on one side of the issue argue that as the links between mind and brain become increasingly clear the biological origins of schizophrenia will similarly manifest themselves. Those in opposition to this view assert that a focus on biology excludes other potentially important contributors to mental disorders. Issue 10 in Taking Sides provides a starting point for your students to investigate this debate topic.

Slife, B. (2000). *Taking sides: Clashing views on controversial psychological issues* (11th ed.). Guilford, CT: Dushkin Publishing Group.

Demonstrating Schizophrenia

Timothy Osberg described a demonstration that is effective in simulating the bizarre verbalizations and thoughts of a schizophrenic. Prior to discussing schizophrenia and without warning, deliver the monologue shown below. Osberg suggested practicing it beforehand to increase its spontaneity and using either blunted or inappropriate affect during its presentation. After students have gotten over their reactions to the monologue, explain that it was meant to illustrate the language, thought processes, and affect of schizophrenia. Ask the students to share what they were thinking during the monologue. Osberg suggested using their responses to generate a discussion of how people might respond to schizophrenics and how these responses might be perceived by the schizophrenic. After describing some of the disturbances of thought and language characteristic of schizophrenia, Osberg suggested showing an overhead transparency of the monologue and asking students to identify examples of these disturbances in the monologue. The "Disordered Monologue," as originally written by Osberg (1992, p. 47), is given below.

> Okay class, we've finished our discussion of mood disorders. Before I go on I'd like to tell you about some personal experiences I've been having lately. You see I've [pause] been involved in high abstract [pause] type of contract [pause] which I might try to distract [pause] from your gaze [pause] if it were a new craze [pause] but the sun god has put me into it [pause] the planet of the lost star [pause] is before you know [pause] and so you'd better not try to be as if you were one with him [pause] always fails because one and one makes three [pause] and that is the word for three [pause] which must be like the tiger after his prey [pause] and the zommon is not common [pause] it is a zommon's zommon. [pause] But really class, [holding your head and pausing] what do you think about what I am thinking about right now? You can hear my thoughts can't you? I'm thinking I'm crazy and I know you [point to a student] put that thought in my mind. You put that thought there! Or could it be that the dentist did as I thought? She did! I thought she put that radio transmitter into my brain when I had the Novocain! She's making me think this way and she's stealing my thoughts!

Osberg, T. M. (1992). The disordered monologue: A classroom demonstration of the symptoms of schizophrenia. *Teaching of Psychology, 19*, 47-48.

Reprinted from Hill, W. G. (1995). Instructor's resource manual for *Psychology* by S. F. Davis and J. J. Palladino. Englewood Cliffs, NJ: Prentice Hall.

Diagnosing Mental Disorders

After you've reviewed the psychological disorders in Chapter 12, test your students' ability to apply their knowledge to realistic case studies. Handout 13-3 contains several scenarios that depict a wide range of disorders discussed in the text. Photocopy and distribute copies of the handout to students (this will also make an excellent study tool for the exam) and have them write their diagnoses on the handout. Be sure to go over the answers with students, and to discuss any confusing similarities between related disorders. The correct answers are given below.

1. Paranoid Schizophrenia
2. Body Dysmorphic Disorder
3. Autistic Disorder
4. Borderline Personality Disorder
5. Specific Phobia (claustrophobia)
6. Dissociative Fugue
7. Post-Traumatic Stress Disorder
8. Frotteurism
9. Dependent Personality Disorder
10. Panic Attack/Disorder
11. Depersonalization Disorder
12. Agoraphobia
13. Major Depression
14. Obsessive-Compulsive Disorder
15. Somatization Disorder

The Client

In this exercise (described by Halonen, 1986), you (or a guest actor, if you prefer) play the role of a client with some undisclosed psychological disorder that class members must try to accurately diagnose. On the assigned day (which should be after you have covered the broad spectrum of psychological disorders), tell students at the start of class that you are a client entering a clinician's office for the first time and that you want them (as the therapists) to interview you in order to make a diagnosis. From that point on, you should sit quietly and respond only to their questions; in other words, they should derive a diagnosis based on your verbal answers rather than from any active behavior on your part. Instruct students beforehand that you will stop the exercise (and play teacher again) only when they have agreed on a diagnosis and can provide evidence to support their conclusions. Because disorders vary in how easily they are identified, you may want to try this exercise more than once, once with a relatively clear-cut disorder and once with a more ambiguous one.

Halonen, J. S. (1986). *Teaching critical thinking in psychology.* Milwaukee: Alverno Productions.

Trick or Treat:
Using Costumes to Portray a Psychological Disorder

Halonen (1986) suggests an entertaining but educational way to explore student's understanding of psychological disorder. For this exercise, ask students to volunteer to come to the next class in a costume that will nonverbally portray a disorder discussed in the text or lecture. Then, during that class period (preferably sometime near Halloween, if you can swing it), all students participate in trying to diagnose the disorders. Clever examples reported by Halonen include a narcissist (e.g., a student strapped to a full-length mirror) and a hypochondriac (e.g., a student carrying a medicine chest). A benefit of this exercise is that students learn about the disorders not only by diagnosing them, but also in trying to accurately portray them. Because of the deviant nature of the assignment, Halonen suggests making this an optional exercise, perhaps by awarding bonus points for successful portrayals.

Halonen, J. S. (1986). *Teaching critical thinking in psychology.* Milwaukee: Alverno Productions.

student assignments

Abnormal Psychology in Literature:
The Eden Express

Michael Gorman (1984) suggests that Mark Vonnegut's *The Eden Express* (an autobiographical account of the author's schizophrenic breakdown) provides an excellent opportunity for students to apply abnormal psychology principles from the text and lecture to a real case study. After your students have read the book, ask them to write a paper describing the cause and cure of Vonnegut's schizophrenia in terms of the different theoretical perspectives of psychological disorder. Gorman notes that although Vonnegut himself attributes his illness to biomedical factors, there is also evidence to support behavioral, humanistic, and psychoanalytic theories if one looks hard enough. Importantly, in trying to apply the different perspectives, students should learn the relative strengths and weaknesses of each perspective and also acknowledge the importance of multiple perspectives in explaining complex behavior.

Gorman, M. E. (1984). Using the Eden Express to teach introductory psychology. *Teaching of Psychology, 11*, 39-40.
Vonnegut, M. (1975). *The Eden Express.* New York: Bantam Books.

Abnormal Psychology in Film

Abnormal behavior is a consistently popular subject for feature films; practically every disorder ever discovered has been portrayed at one time or another. For this assignment, ask students to write a paper analyzing a character's illness in terms of the theoretical perspectives (e.g., biological, psychoanalytic, cognitive-behavioral, biopsychosocial) presented in Chapter 13. Students should include in their paper a description of the character's diagnosis in terms of the DSM-IV and a discussion of which perspective of mental illness best explains the development of the character's symptoms. If applicable, students should describe any treatment received by the character and also comment on whether they would recommend a similar or different treatment. All of the films suggested below contain excellent depictions of psychological disorder and should make good choices for this assignment. Note that a few of the films are also noteworthy for their portrayal of the therapeutic process; thus, these are listed in the next chapter as well.

Adapted from Chrisler, J. C. (1990). Novels as case-study materials for psychology students. *Teaching of Psychology, 17,* 55-57.

• *Henry: Portrait of a Serial Killer* (1990). Michael Rooker stars in this fascinating but grisly look into the life of a serial killer (loosely based on real-life Texas murderer Henry Lee Lucas). This unpleasant movie, although not exploitative, depicts several scenes of rapes and murders and includes the gruesome reactions of Henry and his roommate. This movie is not for everyone, and should most certainly be optional. Nonetheless, if you think your students can stomach the violence, they will get some incredible insights into the workings of the mind of an individual with antisocial personality disorder (MPI; 90 min).

• *Clean, Shaven* (1995). Peter Greene stars in this haunting, disturbing look at the world through the eyes of a schizophrenic. Writer/director Lodge Kerrigan masterfully captures the disorientation, confusion, and paranoia of the protagonist's world as he searches fitfully for his daughter. Along the way we share his frustrations at simple tasks such as making a sandwich or pouring sugar in his coffee. We also witness his self-mutilation as he tries to pry a misperceived transmitter/receiver set from his scalp and thumb. A good film for generating discussion. (Orion Home Video; 80 min).

• *One Flew Over the Cuckoo's Nest* (1975). Jack Nicholson stars in this moving drama as Randall P. McMurphy, a rebellious prisoner who stirs things up in a mental hospital after his transfer there. In going head to head with the authoritarian Nurse Ratchet, he revives the spirit of the other patients who have been browbeaten into submission by the institution. Although somewhat dated and stereotypical, this surprisingly entertaining film portrays a wide variety of deviant behavior and also highlights controversial therapeutic techniques (e.g., prefrontal lobotomy, electroconvulsive therapy), depicts the often inhumane conditions in mental institutions, and contains fascinating character studies of McMurphy and the other patients (HBO; 129 min). [Note: This film could also be assigned in the personality chapter as a fascinating case study of the character of sane misfit McMurphy.]

> Kesey, K. (1975). *One flew over the cuckoo's nest*. New York: New American Library.

• *Sybil* (1977). Sally Field won an Emmy for her performance in this made-for-TV drama that depicts the story of a woman with 17 different personalities. Although at times disturbing, it convincingly portrays the relatively rare condition of multiple personality disorder (also referred to as "dissociative identity disorder"). Importantly, it depicts Sybil's adoption of different personalities as an adaptive response to an unbearably abusive childhood, and in doing so provides valuable insights into a unique therapeutic relationship (CBS/Fox; 122 min). Based on the book by Flor Schreiber.

> Schreiber, F. (1974). *Sybil*. New York: Warner.

video

ABC News/Prentice Hall Video Library

Depression: Beyond the Darkness (47 min, Series III). This entire *20/20* program focuses on depression. Several first-person accounts from people of all ages who have struggled with depression are given, as are comments from their relationship partners, psychiatrists, and other mental-health professionals. This segment provides a fine example of depression from the perspective of the depressed.

Journey to Tragedy (20 min, Series III). The case of Hedda Nussbaum and Joel Steinberg made national headlines several years ago. Their daughter, Lisa, had been beaten into a fatal coma by Steinberg. However, Nussbaum also was abused at the hands of Steinberg, a fact that played a pivotal role in the couple's trial and sentencing. In this *PrimeTime Live* segment Nussbaum reveals the details of her relationship and her suffering.

Other Sources

> Several of the videos listed in Chapter 14 (Therapy) may be suitable for use in the present context (Psychological Disorders). The titles are not duplicated here.

A Is For Autism (12 min, FHS). This short film is nonetheless impactful as it presents words, drawings, and music provided by autistic people. A rare glimpse into an uncharted world.

Advertising Alcohol: Calling the Shots (30 min, CAM). A critical unveiling of the persuasion tactics used by the alcohol industry.

An Anorexic's Tale: The Brief Life of Catherine (80 min, FHS). The docu-drama explores Catherine Dunbar's unsuccessful struggle with an eating disorder. A 7-year downward spiral led from obsession to addiction to death at 40 pounds.

Anorexia and Bulimia (19 min, FHS). Anorexia, bulimia, and their addictive natures are considered in this video. A nutritionist illustrates the extremes to which people with eating disorders commonly go.

Assessment and Diagnosis of Childhood Psychopathology (26 min, PENN). The focus is on disorders of childhood, although this film provides an overview of assessment techniques in general.

Autism (30 min, FHS). This film provides a fascinating look at Temple Grandin, a 44-year-old Ph.D. who grew up autistic. She talks about her experiences and the importance of early, structured treatment.

Autism: A World Apart (52 min, FHS). Three autistic people, aged 2, 4, and 18, are introduced in the discussion of autism, the treatments available, and its effects on the family.

Biology, Brain, and Behavior: Seasonal Affective Disorder (25 min, PENN). Describes the characteristics of seasonal affective disorder, the effectiveness of light treatments, and biological factors that may contribute to its occurrence.

Case Study of a Multiple Personality (30 min, PENN). Chris Sizemore, "Eve" of multiple-personality fame, is interviewed in this presentation of Cleckley and Thigpen's case study and treatment regimen.

Childhood Depression (19 min, FHS). Depression is often overlooked or misdiagnosed among children. This video profiles a 3-year-old and his parents, all of whom have depression.

The Compulsive Mind (28 min, FHS). A woman suffering from an intense fear of contamination is the focus of this program. Her rituals are discussed, as are the biochemical factors that play a role in OCD.

The Compulsive Mind: Tourette's Syndrome/OCD (19 min, FHS). A man with Tourette's Syndrome is profiled, with a focus on how medication helps relieve his symptoms. The general biochemical basis of OCD is also discussed.

Coping With Phobias (28 min, FHS). The hows, whys, and whats of phobias are addressed, with special attention given to the fear of flying. Strategies for treating phobias are also considered.

Depression (19 min, FHS). Basic definitions are the focus of this film; what separates transient from chronic depression, how levels of severity are determined, and what courses of treatment are appropriate.

Depression: Beyond the Blues (19 min, FHS). A portrait of depression: A psychiatrist explains causes, symptoms, and remedies; a young woman talks about her feelings after her father's suicide; two people who attempted suicide discuss what drove them to it.

Depression: Beyond the Darkness (50 min, IM). Describes misconceptions about depression, biological and cognitive theories as to its cause, and cognitive, drug, and ECT treatments.

Depression: Biology of the Blues (26 min, FHS). Focuses on biological factors related to the occurrence of depression.

Deviance (1991, 30 min, IM). Deviance comes in all forms, from minor eccentricities to more severe destructive behaviors. The historical, social, and cultural realities of deviance across this spectrum are examined, and explanations are offered.

The Diagnosis and Treatment of Attention Deficit Disorder in Children (27 min, FHS). ADD is an increasingly recognized disorder that calls for effective, efficient treatment. Some approaches to dealing with ADD are suggested in this film.

Discovering Psychology, Part 14: The Mind Hidden and Divided (1990, 30 min., ANN/CPB). Examines the influence of the subconscious mind on thought and behavior. The segment on multiple personalities is relevant to this chapter.

Discovering Psychology, Part 21: Psychopathology (1990, 30 min., ANN/CPB). Summarizes the symptoms and causes of schizophrenia, phobias, and affective disorders.

Dying To Be Thin (28 min, FHS). A young woman obsessed with the desire to be thin is profiled; repeated hospitalization and years of therapy have begun to offer solutions. The general problems of bulimia and anorexia are presented.

Eating Disorders (26 min, FHS). The personality profiles of likely anorexics are considered in this overview of anorexia.

Explaining Social Deviance (1995, 10 parts, 45 min each, IM). The sociological perspective on deviance is offered in this multi-part lecture series. Various clips might be used to enhance your presentation of these issues.

Getting Anxious (30 min, IM). Describes the anxiety disorders of phobias, obsessive-compulsive disorder, and panic attacks as well as evaluating drug, cognitive-behavioral, and behavior modification treatments.

Losing the Thread: The Experience of Psychosis (1992, 54 min, IM). The film presents what textbooks alone cannot; a vivid, first person account of what it is like to experience a psychotic break with reality. Rachel Corday, who has dealt with intermittent psychosis over 25 years, discusses her experiences.

Madness: Brainwaves (60 min, PBS). Examines the biological explanations and treatments from the 18th century to the present, including ECT, psychosurgery, and drug therapies.

Madness: The Talking Cure (60 min, PBS). Describes the historical development of psychotherapies, focusing particularly on Freudian-based therapies.

Madness: In Two Minds (60 min, PBS). Explores research demonstrating a biological basis for schizophrenia and the relationship of schizophrenia to societal, family, or mental trauma.

Madness: To Define True Madness (60 min, PBS). Examines attitudes toward mental illness throughout the history of Western culture. Interviews with patients and scenes of diagnosis and treatment are designed to aid in understanding what it means to be mentally ill.

The Many Faces of Marsha (1991, 48 min, IM). A woman with 200 personalities is the focus of this discussion of multiple personality disorder.

Mental Illness (23 min, FHS). Phobias, anxiety, and schizophrenia are the focus of this overview of common forms of mental illness.

The Mind: Depression (60 min, PBS). Using footage of and interviews with people suffering from depression and bipolar disorder, this program distinguishes between normal mood variations and severe depression and explores causes of severe depression.

The Mind of a Serial Killer (60 min, FHS). The FBI psychological profiles division is itself profiled in this PBS-produced account of how psychological puzzles are fit together to solve crimes.

The Mind vs. the Brain: Has Freud Slipped? (27 min, FHS). The long-standing notion, often popularized by Freud, that the origins of mental illness are in environment and experience is being increasingly challenged. This film looks at the biological underpinnings of several forms of mental illness.

Mysteries of the Mind (58 min, FHS). Alcoholism, mood disorders, obsessive-compulsive disorder, and affective disorders are explored from neurochemical and biological perspectives.

Obsessive-Compulsive Disorder (24 min, FHS). Focuses on the biological factors related to the obsessive-compulsive disorder and related drug treatments.

Panic! (27 min, FHS). Focuses on extreme anxiety disorders such as panic attacks and agoraphobia, possible biological causes of these disorders, and treatments using drugs, cognitive therapy, and systematic desensitization.

Post-Traumatic Stress Disorder (26 min, FHS). Using several case studies, the causes and effects of post-traumatic stress disorder are discussed.

Prisoners of the Brain (58 min, IM). Presents research linking imbalances in brain chemistry to various disorders, focusing primarily on how and why antipsychotic drugs work with schizophrenia.

Psychopath (30 min, PENN). This video provides a case history of a patient diagnosed with antisocial personality disorder.

Psychotic Disorders: Schizophrenia (30 min, IM). An examination of the symptoms of schizophrenia, current causal explanations, and treatments.

Schizophrenia (28 min, FHS). Phil Donahue hosts this discussion of the causes, prevalence, and symptoms of schizophrenia, with insightful comments from E. Fuller Torrey.

Schizophrenia: Out of Mind (52 min, FHS). The schizophrenic's world is revealed through glimpses of patients, parents, friends, family, doctors, and staff.

Schizophrenia: The Voices Within, the Community Without (19 min, FHS). In addition to describing symptoms and treatments using psychotropic drugs, this program focuses on deinstitutionalization of schizophrenics and related problems.

Serious Depression (28 min, FHS). A broad overview of serious depression. The rates among women and men (and why they are imbalanced), the causes (including biochemical factors), and the available treatments (such as ECT) are presented.

Sex and Money (1990, 50 min, IM). John Money, noted sexologist, discusses gender identity and transexuality in this German film, presented with subtitles.

Sexual Dysfunction (19 min, FHS). The psychological underpinnings of various forms of sexual dysfunction are the focus.

Suicide: The Teenager's Perspective (26 min, FHS). The stress of teenage life, and the promise for relief and support from peers, are important factors in determining suicide attempts among teenagers. This program offers solutions for help before it is too late.

Suicide: The Parent's Perspective (26 min, FHS). Grief, guilt, and bereavement are a thoroughly unpleasant combination. This program helps parents listen to their teenagers in a proactive, mutually-beneficial way.

The Treatment of Attention Deficit Disorder in Adults (27 min, FHS). ADD is often considered an exclusively childhood disorder; however, adult sufferers need treatment as well. The use of biofeedback, growing in popularity as a treatment choice, is discussed among other options.

Unmasking Depression (28 min, FHS). Four adults talk about the suffering they endured through the depths of depression, and explain what they did to overcome it.

What is Normal? (30 min, IM). Explores the question of what distinguishes normal from abnormal and the classification of Psychological Disorders using the DSM, including criticisms of the DSM.

When Panic Strikes (19 min, FHS). This close captioned film considers the difficulties in accurately diagnosing and treating panic disorder, using a young woman's experiences as an illustrative case.

Women and Depression: When the Blues Won't Go Away (28 min, FHS). American women suffer a high rate of depression; this film examines why, presenting a positive, hopeful approach to understanding a potentially debilitating problem.

The World of Abnormal Psychology, Part 1: Looking at Abnormal Behavior (1992, 60 min, ANN/CPB). Provides an overview of different types of psychological disorders and the theories used to explain and treat them.

The World of Abnormal Psychology, Part 3: The Anxiety Disorders (1992, 60 min, ANN/CPB). Examines two of the more common anxiety disorders, panic with agoraphobia and generalized anxiety disorder, and treatments for them.

The World of Abnormal Psychology, Part 5: Personality Disorders (1992, 60 min, ANN/CPB). Describes the narcissistic, antisocial, borderline, and obsessive-compulsive disorders and issues related to their diagnosis and treatment.

The World of Abnormal Psychology, Part 6: Substance Abuse Disorders (1992, 60 min, ANN/CPB). Discusses the abuse of alcohol, cigarettes, and cocaine, their health costs and dangers, and techniques for overcoming these addictions.

The World of Abnormal Psychology, Part 7: Sexual Disorders (1992, 60 min, ANN/CPB). Using a case study approach, this program examines the assessment and treatment of sexual disorders over the last 25 years.

The World of Abnormal Psychology, Part 8: Mood Disorders (1992, 60 min, ANN/CPB). Describes psychological and biological approaches to explaining and treating depression and bipolar disorder.

The World of Abnormal Psychology, Part 9: The Schizophrenias (1992, 60 min, ANN/CPB). Explores the symptoms, treatment, and myths associated with schizophrenia.

The World of Abnormal Psychology, Part 10: Organic Mental Disorders (1992, 60 min, ANN/CPB). Examines organic mental disorders related to head injury, alcohol abuse, and Alzheimer's disease.

The World of Abnormal Psychology, Part 11: Behavior Disorders of Childhood (1992, 60 min, ANN/CPB). Describes several disorders that occur in childhood including attention deficit hyperactivity disorder, conduct disorder, separation anxiety disorder, and autism.

multimedia

Web Investigations

Recognizing Mood Disorders

Students can explore affective disorders from the perspective of a clinician, by diagnosing six sample patients and getting feedback on their diagnoses. This activity also includes audio clips of patients with bipolar disorder and depression, so students can hear some of the speech patterns associated with these disorders. This activity can be linked to several of the other online resources discussed in this chapter and the next, making them a fine basis for a substantial report on affective disorders.

Making Connections

Perspectives on Psychological Disorders

Q What is the distinction between the supernatural view of mental disorder and the naturalistic view?

A The supernatural view saw madness as a sign that spirits had possessed a person; the naturalistic view maintained that madness was like any other sickness--a natural event arising from natural causes.

Q Explain how the biological, psychoanalytic, cognitive-behavioral, and systems approaches account for mental disorders.

A The biological model of psychological disorders holds that abnormal behavior is caused by physiological malfunction. The psychoanalytic model views behavior disorders as symbolic expressions of unconscious internal conflicts, generally traceable to the early years of life. The cognitive-behavioral model suggests that, like all behavior, abnormal behavior is the result of learning. The systems approach examines how biological, psychological, and social risk factors combine to produce psychological disorders.

Q What is the major goal of the DSM-IV?

A The major goal of the DSM is to provide careful descriptions of symptoms of different disorders in order to make possible consistent diagnosis.

Q What does it mean to say that some mental illnesses may be characterized as lifestyle diseases?

A Some mental illnesses may be characterized as lifestyle diseases because they are normal psychological reactions to significant biological changes.

Mood Disorders

Q What is the difference between clinical depression and "normal" feelings of depression that most people experience?

A Clinical depression differs from "normal" depression because it is serious, lasting, and well beyond the typical reaction to a stressful life event.

Q What is bipolar disorder? How does it differ from depression?

A Bipolar disorder is a mood disorder in which periods of mania and depression alternate, sometimes with periods of normal mood intervening. It differs from depression because it involves changes of mood, whereas depression is characterized by a constant state of sadness.

Q What evidence suggests that cognitive distortions may lead to the development of depression?

A Evidence that cognitive distortions may lead to the development of depression can be seen in the fact that people with negative cognitive styles are at higher risk of developing depression than those with more positive cognitive styles.

Anxiety Disorders

Q What is a specific phobia? What are some common examples of specific phobias?

A A specific phobia is an intense, paralyzing fear of a specific object or situation, such as snakes, blood, or heights.

Q Explain how panic attacks can lead to the development of specific phobias.

A Panic attacks can lead to the development of specific phobias because they become associated with the situations in which they occur, leading the sufferer to attempt to prevent a recurrence by avoiding such situations at all costs.

Q What is obsessive-compulsive disorder? What function does it serve?

A Obsessive-compulsive disorder is characterized by involuntary thoughts that recur despite the person's attempts to stop them, together with repetitive behaviors that the person feels compelled to perform. These behaviors apparently serve to reduce anxiety.

Q How would an evolutionary psychologist explain the development of phobias?

A An evolutionary psychologist would say that phobias evolved over time as humans learned which objects or situations in their environment were harmful and which ones were not.

Psychosomatic and Somatoform Disorders

Q How do psychological factors lead to the development of psychosomatic disorders?

A Psychological factors such as stress and anxiety lead to the development of psychosomatic disorders by altering body chemistry, the functioning of bodily organs, and the body's immune system.

Q How do psychologists distinguish between somatoform disorders and real physical disorders?

A Somatoform disorders differ from real physical disorders in that they have no organic cause and may serve to resolve a conflict or relieve the patient of the need to confront a difficult situation.

Q Summarize the psychoanalytic and cognitive explanations of somatoform disorders.

A The psychoanalytic explanation of somatoform disorders suggests that they are related to traumatic experiences buried in a patient's past and serve to prevent the patient from acting out forbidden desires (primary gain) while allowing him or her to avoid an unpleasant activity (secondary gain). The cognitive explanation focuses on the idea of secondary gain, proposing that the patient's behavior is being rewarded in some way, such as enabling the person to avoid facing unpleasant or stressful situations.

Dissociative Disorders

Q What are some common causes of dissociative amnesia?

A Dissociative amnesia may occur as a reaction to intolerable experiences such as war or rape.

Q What is dissociative identity disorder?

A Dissociative identity disorder, or multiple personality, is a disorder in which a person has several distinct personalities that emerge at different times.

Q How is depersonalization disorder distinguished from normal feelings of loss of control?

A Depersonalization disorder differs from normal feelings of loss of control in that it is a long-term problem that may impair normal social functioning.

Q What is now known about the causes of dissociative disorders?

A Little is known about the causes of dissociative disorders, but there is evidence that biological factors play a role in some cases.

Sexual Disorders

Q What are the most common types of sexual disorders in men and women?

A The most common types of sexual disorders are erectile disorder and female sexual arousal disorder.

Q What is a paraphilia? What are the most common types?

A A paraphilia involves the use of unconventional sex objects or situations to obtain sexual arousal. Common paraphilias include fetishism, voyeurism, and exhibitionism.

Q What evidence suggests that gender-identity disorders are biologically based?

A Evidence that gender-identity disorders are biologically based may be seen in the fact that these disorders are often apparent from early childhood.

Personality Disorders

Q What characteristics define a personality disorder? Give an example.

A Personality disorders are characterized by inflexible and maladaptive ways of thinking and behaving that are so exaggerated and rigid that they cause serious distress to the individual and create problems for others. An example is paranoid personality disorder.

Q Why is the prevalence of antisocial personality disorder high among prison inmates?

A The prevalence of antisocial personality disorder is high among prison inmates because people with this disorder tend to lie, steal, cheat, and show little sense of responsibility, and therefore account for a good deal of crime and violence.

Q What theories account for the development of antisocial personality disorder?

A Possible causes of antisocial personality include an autonomic nervous system that is less responsive to stress; damage to the prefrontal region of the brain during infancy; emotional deprivation in early childhood; and rejection by parents. Cognitive theorists suggest that moral development may be arrested among children who are emotionally rejected and inadequately disciplined.

Schizophrenic Disorders

Q What are the major types of schizophrenic disorders?

A The major types of schizophrenic disorders are disorganized schizophrenia, catatonic schizophrenia, paranoid schizophrenia, and undifferentiated schizophrenia.

Q What is known about the cause of schizophrenia?

A Studies indicate that a biological predisposition to schizophrenia may be inherited. Part of the problem may lie in excessive amounts of dopamine in the central nervous system; pathology in various structures of the brain may also play a role. Environmental factors must also play a role in the development of schizophrenia, but it is not clear exactly how these factors operate. According to the systems model, genetic factors predispose some people to schizophrenia, and family interaction and life stress activate the predisposition.

Childhood Disorders

Q What are the symptoms of AD/HD?

A Children with AD/HD are easily distracted, often fidgety and impulsive, and almost constantly in motion.

Q What is known about the causes of autism?

A It is not known what causes autism, but some causes of mental retardation also seem to increase the risk of autism. There is considerable evidence that genetic factors play a role in causing the disorder.

Gender and Cultural Differences in Psychological Disorders

Q How do differences in socialization affect gender differences in prevalence of mental disorders?

A Differences in socialization affect gender differences in the prevalence of mental disorders because women are socialized to feel that it is acceptable to discuss emotional difficulties and seek professional help.

Q What effect does culture have on prevalence of mental disorders?

A Culture affects the prevalence of mental disorders because some disorders are found only in particular cultural groups.

Video Classics

Three Faces of Eve

SYNOPSIS: Chris Sizemore (a.k.a. Eve) is interviewed by Dr. Thigpen, who along with Dr. Cleckley, diagnosed her multiple personality disorder. Eve White, Eve Black, and Jane each discuss what life will be like after their personality reintegration. This clip is highly recommended.

Form a Hypothesis

Q What do you think are common symptoms of Dissociative Identity Disorder (DID)?

A DID involves distinct personalities, identities, mannerisms, etc. Sometimes, a personality may not know about another personality residing in the DID individual.

Test Your Understanding

Q What were the three personalities of Eve?

A Eve White, the "good" personality, Eve Black, the pleasure-seeking "bad" personality and Jane, a combination of the two.

Q What is DID normally preceded by?

A Current theorization suggests that DID occurs in response to childhood trauma or abuse. The children learn to deal with abuse by dissociating themselves, directing the abuse to a personality of which they have no knowledge.

Thinking Critically

Q What is the new name for "multiple personality disorder"?

A Dissociative Identity Disorder, a name that better conveys current theorization about the origins of "multiple personality."

Web Links

1. http://www.mhnet.org/

Mental Health Net. Comprehensive descriptions of the symptoms and treatment of mental disorders are presented here. Brush up on your DSM-IV categories and information about a variety of conditions as you prepare your classroom discussions.

2. http://www.save.org/

SAVE: Suicide Awareness / Voices of Education. The symptoms, misconceptions, and prevention of suicide is the focus here.

3. http://www.psycom.net/depression.central.html

Dr. Ivan's Depression Central. See Dr. Ivan for links related to depression and other mood disorders.

4. http://www.algy.com/anxiety/

The Anxiety Panic Internet Resource. Anxiety disorders and their treatment are highlighted here. Students interested in this topic may use this site as a starting point for further research.

5. http://phobialist.com/

The Phobia List. Don't be afraid; explore it to find information about a variety of phobias and their treatments. Use this as a class exercise, like a "phobia bee," to quiz students on various phobias and what they entail.

6. http://www.ocfoundation.org/indright.htm

Obsessive-Compulsive Foundation. This site explains the symptomotology of OCD and effective treatments, and offers resources for support. Visit this site 85 times a day.

7. http://www.trauma-pages.com/

This website provides links to descriptions of trauma, trauma articles, and information about disasters. A good site for "applied" aspects of psychological disturbance.

transparencies

Series V

90a. *Psychological Defense Mechanisms*
90b Unconscious defenses are illustrated in this two-part transparency.

92. *Criteria for Abnormality*
Four criteria for abnormality are identified and defined.

93. *Orientation of Psychologists*
This pie chart presents the results of a survey of 422 practicing clinical and counseling psychologists who were asked to state their theoretical orientation.

94. *Where People Turn for Help*
This transparency lists the sources of support in people's lives.

95. *Duration of Therapy and Improvement*
The strength of the relationship between reported improvement and duration of therapy, as found in the Consumer Reports study.

96. *Major Perspectives on Therapy*
Insight, behavior, cognitive, group, and biological therapies are represented.

Text Figures

13-1.   Gender and Race Differences in the Suicide Rate Across the Life Span

13-2.   Sexual Dysfunction in the United States

Handout 13-1a

Mental Health Questionnaire

Instructions: Think of a normal adult male. Check each item below that describes a "mature, healthy, socially competent adult male."

_____ not at all aggressive	_____ easily influenced
_____ conceited about appearance	_____ very objective
_____ very ambitious	_____ very self-confident
_____ almost always acts as a leader	_____ has difficulty making decisions
_____ very independent	_____ dependent
_____ does not hide emotions at all	_____ likes math and science very much
_____ sneaky	_____ very direct
_____ very active	_____ very passive
_____ very logical	_____ knows the way of the world
_____ not at all competitive	_____ excitable in a minor crisis
_____ feelings easily hurt	_____ very adventurous
_____ not at all emotional	_____ very submissive
_____ very strong need for security	_____ not uncomfortable about being aggressive

Adapted from Anonymous, 1981, "Sex role stereotypes and mental health," in L. T. Benjamin, Jr. & K. D. Lowman (Eds.), Activities handbook for the teaching of psychology (pp. 141-142). Copyright ©1981 by the American Psychological Association. Adapted with permission.

Handout 13-1b

Mental Health Questionnaire

Instructions: Think of a normal adult female. Check each item below that describes a "mature, healthy, socially competent adult female."

_____ not at all aggressive

_____ conceited about appearance

_____ very ambitious

_____ almost always acts as a leader

_____ very independent

_____ does not hide emotions at all

_____ sneaky

_____ very active

_____ very logical

_____ not at all competitive

_____ feelings easily hurt

_____ not at all emotional

_____ very strong need for security

_____ easily influenced

_____ very objective

_____ very self-confident

_____ has difficulty making decisions

_____ dependent

_____ likes math and science very much

_____ very direct

_____ very passive

_____ knows the way of the world

_____ excitable in a minor crisis

_____ very adventurous

_____ very submissive

_____ not uncomfortable about being aggressive

Adapted from Anonymous, 1981, "Sex role stereotypes and mental health," in L. T. Benjamin, Jr. & K. D. Lowman (Eds.), Activities handbook for the teaching of psychology (pp. 141-142). Copyright ©1981 by the American Psychological Association. Adapted with permission.

Handout 13-1c

Mental Health Questionnaire

Instructions: Think of a normal, average adult. Check each item below that describes a "mature, healthy, socially competent adult."

_____ not at all aggressive	_____ easily influenced
_____ conceited about appearance	_____ very objective
_____ very ambitious	_____ very self-confident
_____ almost always acts as a leader	_____ has difficulty making decisions
_____ very independent	_____ dependent
_____ does not hide emotions at all	_____ likes math and science very much
_____ sneaky	_____ very direct
_____ very active	_____ very passive
_____ very logical	_____ knows the way of the world
_____ not at all competitive	_____ excitable in a minor crisis
_____ feelings easily hurt	_____ very adventurous
_____ not at all emotional	_____ very submissive
_____ very strong need for security	_____ not uncomfortable about being aggressive

Adapted from Anonymous, 1981, "Sex role stereotypes and mental health," in L. T. Benjamin, Jr. & K. D. Lowman (Eds.), Activities handbook for the teaching of psychology (pp. 141-142). Copyright ©1981 by the American Psychological Association. Adapted with permission.

Handout 13-2

Obsessive-Compulsive Test

Instructions: Read each of the statements below and ask yourself if they apply to you. For each question, mark whether these statements apply to you using this scale:

1--none or a little of the time
2--some of the time
3--a good part of the time
4--most or all of the time

1 2 3 4   I prefer things to be done my way.

1 2 3 4   I am critical of people who don't live up to my standards or expectations.

1 2 3 4   I stick to my principles, no matter what.

1 2 3 4   I am upset by changes in the environment or in the behavior of people.

1 2 3 4   I am meticulous and fussy about my possessions.

1 2 3 4   I get upset if I don't finish a task.

1 2 3 4   I insist on full value for everything I purchase.

1 2 3 4   I like everything I do to be perfect.

1 2 3 4   I follow an exact routine for everyday tasks.

1 2 3 4   I do things precisely to the last detail.

1 2 3 4   I get tense when my day's schedule is upset.

1 2 3 4   I plan my time so that I won't be late.

1 2 3 4   It bothers me when my surroundings are not clean and tidy.

1 2 3 4   I make lists for my activities.

1 2 3 4   I think that I worry about minor aches and pains.

1 2 3 4   I like to be prepared for any emergency.

1 2 3 4   I am strict about fulfilling every one of my obligations.

1 2 3 4   I think that I expect worthy moral standards in others.

1 2 3 4   I am badly shaken when someone takes advantage of me.

1 2 3 4   I get upset when people do not replace things exactly as I left them.

1 2 3 4   I keep used or old things because they might be useful.

1 2 3 4   I think that I am sexually inhibited.

1 2 3 4   I find myself working rather than relaxing.

1 2 3 4   I prefer being a private person.

1 2 3 4   I like to budget myself carefully and live on a cash-and-serve basis.

Adapted from R. M. Gardner, *Exercises for general psychology*. Reprinted by permission of Prentice Hall, Copyright 1980.

Handout 13-3

Diagnosing Mental Disorders

Instructions: For each of the following case studies, play the role of a clinician and make the most accurate diagnosis possible from the given information. Write your response in the blank space beneath each description.

1. If you interacted with Scott briefly, you might think that he is normal. However, once he told you about the government's plot against him and how he was going to be rescued by some alien friends, you would start to suspect that he is disordered.

2. Matthew, although a good-looking guy, is so preoccupied with what he thinks is his large, unsightly nose that he is unable to realistically evaluate his own looks and often talks with his hands in front of his face. He will likely have plastic surgery some day.

3. As a baby, Charlie resisted being held and showed no interest in human stimulation. Usually passive, he sometimes played with his wind-up toys but did not respond to his name being called and showed outbursts of temper if someone moved even one of his little cars from where he had placed it.

4. Shannon's moods seem to swing abruptly, and she often seems unable to control her impulses. She has had many sexual encounters and often complains of boredom, though she is seldom alone and often caught up in very intense, stormy relationships. Her friends are on edge around her because of her Jekyll-Hyde behavior.

5. Emmit, who has just suffered a serious knee injury, cannot undergo an MRI because he has an irrational fear of narrow, enclosed places.

6. Frank awoke one morning and suddenly realized that he had another name and a family in another state. He had no idea how he came to be living his present life.

7. Although Karina was not personally injured in the earthquake, the experience was a terrifying one and her house was badly damaged. She has frequent nightmares about earthquakes, and even when awake she sometimes gets flashes as if she's reliving the experience. The slightest noise or movement around her causes her heart to pound rapidly.

8. Roger loves to go to the mall on Saturdays, when it is most crowded, because there are lots of opportunities for him to rub up against women without them knowing it. Few activities make Roger as sexually aroused as this one.

9. Although Elaine is a kind, considerate person, she has trouble making decisions by herself. She leans heavily on her friends and family for advice, even for seemingly trivial decisions.

10. While teaching her class one day, Theresa suddenly begins having difficulty breathing. Her heart starts pounding wildly, and she feels weak and dizzy. She feels as if she's having a heart attack and is honestly afraid that she's going to die in the next minute or two. (Assume that Theresa is not having a heart attack).

11. Although Jack is enjoying watching the football game, he feels oddly detached, as though he is watching himself and his actions from outside of his own body. Because this has happened several times recently, Jack is startled for fear that he will totally lose control of his thoughts and behavior.

12. Sarah has an unrealistic fear of shopping in crowded stores and walking through crowded streets. She has begun to spend more and more time home alone in order to avoid the panicky feeling she gets when she goes out in public.

13. Sam's friends are starting to worry about him. Normally energetic and fun-loving, Sam has become withdrawn and sullen. He has lost weight, is constantly tired, and hasn't been showing up to lacrosse practice or to his fraternity meetings. In his conversations with others, he expresses feelings of doubt and unworthiness, and seems to be entertaining suicidal thoughts.

14. Because Amy feels "dirty" a lot of the time, she spends much of her day at the sink, washing and rewashing her hands hundreds of times until they are red and raw.

15. Joan has seen several specialists and undergone numerous diagnostic tests to determine the cause of her recurring headaches and episodes of dizziness. The doctors are perplexed and can seem to find no physiological cause for Joan's symptoms.

Chapter 14 Therapies

chapter outline 418

learning objectives 421

lecture suggestions

    EMDR 422
    Culture and Therapy 423
    Tech-no-phobia 423
    Treatments for Tourette's Syndrome 424
    Facilitated Communication 424
    A Brief History of Convulsive Therapies 425
    Ch-Ch-Ch-Changes 426
    On Being Sane in Insane Places 426
    How Can I Find a Good Therapist? 427

demonstrations and activities

    Suggesting Treatments for Abnormal Behavior 429
    The Client, Part II 430
    Role-playing Client-centered Therapy 430
    Systematic Desensitization 431
    Irrational Beliefs 431
    Debate: Does Psychotherapy Really Work? 432
    Debate: Is the *Consumer Reports* Conclusion Valid? 432
    Debate: Is Insight Necessary for Behavior Change? 433
    Debate: Should Psychologists Be Allowed to Prescribe Drugs? 433
    Debate: Have Antidepressant Drugs Proven Effective? 434
    Debate: Is Electroconvulsive Therapy Safe and Effective? 434

student assignments

    Interviewing Mental-health Professionals 435
    Psychotherapy in Film 435

video 437

multimedia 440

transparencies 445

handout

    Treating Psychological Disorders 446

chapter outline

I. Insight Therapies
  A. Psychoanalysis
    1. Psychological problems are symptoms of repressed inner conflicts
      a. Analyst's task is to bring these hidden conflicts to conscious awareness
    2. Free association used to produce a stream of consciousness
      a. These verbalizations offer insight into the unconscious mind
    3. Analyst remains an impartial sounding board for much of early part of therapy
      a. Positive or negative transference may occur
    4. Analyst's growing active interpretation promotes insight
      a. The patient comes to gain insight into repressed feelings and memories
        i. The process of working through old conflicts begins
    5. Classic psychoanalysis requires substantial investments of time and money
      a. Patients must be motivated and highly verbal
  B. Client-centered therapy
    1. Clients (not "patients") strive to become fully-functioning individuals
    2. Therapist provides unconditional positive regard in a nondirective atmosphere
  C. Gestalt therapy
    1. Emphasizes wholeness of the person
      a. An attempt to reawaken clients to emotions and sensations
        i. Deals emphatically with the here-and-now
          - Encounter groups
          - Empty chair technique
  D. Recent developments
    1. Short-term psychodynamic psychotherapy has become increasingly popular

II. Behavior Therapies
  A. Objective is to teach people new and more productive behaviors
  B. Using classical conditioning techniques
    1. Desensitization, extinction, and flooding
      a. Systematic desensitization
        i. Gradually associating a new response (relaxation) with fearful stimulus
        ii. Hierarchy of fears is established
        iii. Former response eventually extinguished
      b. Aversive conditioning
        i. Pairing an unwanted behavior with a painful or undesirable stimulus
  C. Operant conditioning
    1. Behavior contracting: Therapist and client agree on reinforcements for achieving set goals
    2. Token economy: Tokens earned for desired behaviors exchanged for other desired items

  D. Modeling
    1. Desired behaviors are learned by watching others perform them

III. Cognitive Therapies
  A. Stress-inoculation therapy
    1. Coping in stressful situations improved by learning more adaptive self-talk
  B. Rational-emotive therapy
    1. Therapist's directive approach disabuses client of irrational beliefs
  C. Beck's cognitive therapy
    1. Identifying and changing inappropriately negative patterns of thought

IV. Group Therapies
  A. Family therapy
    1. Client and family are seen in therapy
    2. Attempt to work with the family unit for mutual benefit
    3. Goals: Improved communication, heightened empathy, shared responsibilities
  B. Couple therapy
    1. Troubled couples improve problems of communication and interaction
      a. Empathy training
      b. Behavioral techniques
      c. Cognitive techniques
  C. Self-help groups
    1. Groups structured around common problems can provide a substantial benefit

V. Effectiveness of Psychotherapy
  A. Does psychotherapy work?
    1. Being in *some* therapy seems to be better than nothing, for most disorders
  B. Which type of therapy is best for which disorder?
    1. It depends
      a. Cognitive, insight, and behavioral therapies all have their strengths
      b. Therapists relying more and more on an ecelectic approach to treatment

VI. Biological Treatments
  A. Drug therapies
    1. Antipsychotic drugs
      a. Very effective for positive symptoms (hallucinations)
      b. Less effective for negative symptoms (social withdrawal)
      c. Operate by blocking dopamine receptors
    2. Antidepressant drugs
      a. MAO inhibitors, tricyclics produce serious side effects
      b. Prozac's introduction hailed as a wonder drug
        i. Acts on serotonin uptake
        ii. Effectiveness and side effects still controversial
    3. Lithium

        a. Used in treatment of bipolar disorder
    4. Other medications
        A. Psychostimulants heighten alertness and arousal
            1. Often used to treat hyperactivity
        B. Antianxiety medications produce calm and mild euphoria
            2. Valium, others, used to treat general tension and anxiety
  B. Electroconvulsive therapy
    1. Currently used for treating prolonged or severe depression
    2. An electrical current is passed through the brain, producing convulsions
        a. Unilateral ECT: Current introduced to one side of the brain only
    3. Memory impairment, confusion, are potential side effects
    4. Reasons for effectiveness remain obscure
  C. Psychosurgery
    1. Prefrontal lobotomy severs connections to deeper centers of the brain
    2. Once popular, lobotomy rarely used today

VII. Institutionalization and Its Alternatives
  A. Deinstitutionalization
    1. Policy of treating mentally ill within the larger community or halfway houses
    2. Although a fine idea, in practice it has proved less than stellar
  B. Alternative forms of treatment
  C. Prevention
    1. Primary prevention
    2. Secondary prevention
    3. Tertiary prevention

VIII. Gender and Cultural Differences in Treatment
  A. Gender differences
    1. Women are more likely than men to be in treatment
    2. Women also disproportionately receive drug prescriptions for treatment
  B. Cultural differences
    1. Seen through the lens of another culture, some behaviors may not be in need of "treatment"

learning objectives

After reading this chapter, students should be able to:

1. Differentiate between insight therapies, behavior therapies, cognitive therapies, and group therapies.

2. Discuss the criticisms of psychoanalysis.

3. Explain how client-centered and rational-emotive therapists interpret causes of emotional problems. Describe the therapeutic techniques of each approach.

4. Summarize the behavioral therapist's interpretation of disorders. Describe aversive conditioning, desensitization, and modeling.

5. Describe stress-inoculation therapy, Beck's cognitive therapy, and Gestalt therapy.

6. List the advantages and disadvantages of group therapies. Identify five current approaches to group therapy.

7. Discuss the effectiveness of psychotherapy.

8. Outline the available biological treatments and discuss the advantages and disadvantages of each.

9. Summarize the inadequacies of institutionalization. List the alternatives to institutionalization.

10. Explain the differences between primary, secondary, and tertiary prevention.

11. Discuss possible areas of misunderstanding when there are cultural differences in therapy.

lecture suggestions

EMDR

Eye Movement Desensitization and Reprocessing (EMDR), developed by Francine Shapiro in 1987, has generated considerable attention in recent years. Heralded by many as a simple, effective treatment for anxiety disorders, especially post-traumatic stress disorder, it is practiced by an increasing number of clinicians across the country. However, EMDR has also been labeled the "trend du jour of psychotherapy," "the next fad," and a "snake oil cure." Undeniably it is a controversial technique that has attracted the attention of a large segment of the psychology community.

EMDR involves clients conjuring an image associated with a traumatic event, and then performing rapid left-right eye movements while tracking an object waved in front of their eyes by a therapist. Advocates of the technique report that relief is experienced quickly, and that typical sessions take little time to complete. The appeal of EMDR is widespread. Both the American Psychological Association and the American Psychological Society have presented symposia on the topic at their recent conventions. EMDR also has been practiced in Bosnia by a team of psychologists organized by therapist Geoffrey White. Many therapists report using the technique for a number of complaints, including phobias, panic disorder, hyperactivity, addictions, eating disorders, or depression.

Although Shapiro and others claim a substantial base of research findings supporting the effectiveness of EMDR, critics argue that the evidence is largely anecdotal and based on individual case studies. Many therapists and researchers alike are concerned about the rush to use a technique that they feel is largely unvalidated by carefully controlled studies; this concern is compounded by the application of EMDR by some practitioners to a wide range of disorders. Of the "research" conducted to date, clients' self-evaluations ("I feel so much better!"), often spurred by strong suggestions ("We can do it again until you feel better"), constitute the main measures of improvement. There is a lack of evidence, however, for any reduction in physiological or behavioral anxiety. To complicate the issue further, there is no solid claim from any source as to why EMDR works, assuming that it does. There is both conjecture and evidence to suggest that tapping one's fingers, following suggestions, listening to auditory tones, or merely distracting oneself away from the traumatic image produce equivalent levels of success. If so, the essential role of eye movement seems suspect.

EMDR may be a miracle cure, a marketing phenomenon, or perhaps a little of both. It is clear that in the coming years the community of researchers and practitioners will devote considerable attention to determining the value of this controversial technique.

Cavaliere, F. (1995, August). Team works to quell stress in Bosnia. *APA Monitor*, p. 8.
Lazrove, S. (1995, August). EMDR-facilitated abreaction in dissociative identity disorder. Paper presented at the Annual Convention of the American Psychological Association, New York City.
Marano, H. E. (1994, July/August). Wave of the future. *Psychology Today*, pp. 22-25.
Tolin, D. F., Montgomery, R. W., Kleinknecht, R. A., & Lohr, J. M. (1995). An evaluation of eye movement desensitization and reprocessing. In S. Knapp, L. VandeCreek, & T. L. Jackson (Eds.), *Innovations in clinical practice*, Vol. 15.

Culture and Therapy

Psychotherapy is often viewed from a decidedly Western standpoint. Many of the techniques and assumptions about therapy have developed within a particular cultural framework. There can be considerable variability across cultures, however, in treating similar disorders.

Although several therapies practiced in other cultures might be considered unusual from a Western perspective, most emphasize Western-type attitudes about therapy (such as assisting the client in gaining personal insight). An example of an insight-based therapy is *Morita therapy*, which is used in Japan to treat some forms of anxiety disorders. This therapy initially requires clients to stay in bed and inactive for up to two weeks. In the next phase clients can engage in some light activity, but must still remain socially isolated. Near the end of the therapeutic process, they will receive lectures focusing on issues related to self-control and egocentrism before returning to normal social activities.

Therapies employed in some cultures also use drugs or other activities designed to produce altered states of consciousness. These approaches reflect the assumption that the altered state will reveal the causes of and potential treatments for the problem. An example of this type of technique is practiced by the zar cult, a group that is found in some countries in the Middle East. The term *zar* is used to refer both to the psychological problem and the spirit that is believed to cause the problem. Treatment involves both the client (who is most often a woman) and therapist entering a dissociative state in order to identify which spirit caused the problem and an appropriate treatment.

Prince, R. (1980). Variations in psychotherapeutic procedures. In H. C. Triandis & J. G. Draguns (Eds.), *Handbook of cross-cultural psychology, Vol. 6: Psychopathology* (pp. 291-350). Boston: Allyn and Bacon.

Adapted from Hill, W. G. (1995). Instructor's resource manual for *Psychology* by S. F. Davis and J. J. Palladino. Englewood Cliffs, NJ: Prentice Hall.

Tech-no-phobia

The fear of heights experienced by acrophobics is no small matter; tall buildings, airplane rides, bridges, even stepladders may present a paralyzing challenge. A new therapeutic approach, however, can help to lessen the anxiety experienced by acrophobics.

Ralph Lamsen, of the Kaiser Permanente Medical Group, uses virtual reality to desensitize acrophobes to their fear. The virtual world experienced through the helmet, glove, and handgrip presents a series of challenges relevant to the phobic situation. For example, clients are presented with a plank they must cross, an experience that usually produces elevated heart rate and blood pressure. Clients are encouraged to progress at a comfortable pace, staying at the edge of the plank until ready. After successfully navigating this virtual hurdle, clients are then presented with a bridge they must cross. Typically, once clients "return" to the plank, desensitization has taken place and their blood pressure and heart rate have returned to normal. A virtual reality session of this sort takes about 40 minutes to complete.

Among the more than 60 clients who have participated in this therapy, over 90 percent successfully rode a real-world glass elevator up fifteen stories and completed self-determined tasks, such as driving across the Golden Gate Bridge or cleaning roof gutters. In addition, the benefits of the therapy appeared to persist after three months.

Staff (1994, November/December). Virtual therapy. *Psychology Today*, p. 20.

Treatments for Tourette's Syndrome

Tourette's syndrome is an organic disorder related to abnormalities in the basal ganglia and can be regulated through drugs that are dopamine antagonists. In addition to (or instead of) drug treatments, several behavioral treatments are also employed to treat this disorder.

Peterson and Azrin published a review of the effectiveness of available drug and behavioral treatments, noting that three drugs have been used in the treatment of Tourette's syndrome: haloperidol (the most common drug of choice), pimozide, and clonidine. While haloperidol and pimozide have been demonstrated to produce between a 34 percent and 67 percent reduction in tics, clonidine only produces about a 10 percent reduction in motor tics and may increase vocal tics. Behavioral treatments for Tourette's syndrome include: massed negative practice (having the patient perform the tic rapidly and intensely for extended periods in order to produce reactive inhibition), contingency management (attempting to modify tic frequency through either positive reinforcement or punishment), relaxation techniques focusing on the muscles associated with a tic, self-monitoring of tic frequency and intensity, and habit reversal (training competing muscular responses). Habit reversal seems to be the most effective technique, with studies reporting up to a 90 percent reduction in motor tic frequency. The other behavioral techniques tend to produce reductions of up to 50 percent, but these reductions may be temporary.

Drugs are often the treatment of choice because they have the advantage of taking less time to produce an improvement. A major disadvantage of drug treatments, however, is that the drugs produce adverse side effects in between 50 percent to 85 percent of the patients, often resulting in the discontinuation of drug use. Although behavioral treatments are more difficult to use and are more time consuming, they can be effective without the problem of side effects associated with drugs. These conclusions should be evaluated in light of some difficulties associated with studying the effectiveness of therapies for Tourette's syndrome. Specifically, studies vary in how they assess treatment outcome, are based on small samples, or fail to do adequate follow-up evaluations. Although some studies (particularly those using behavioral treatments) use objective frequency counts of motor and vocal tics, many studies simply rely on subjective ratings of frequency, intensity, and severity.

Peterson, A. L., & Azrin, N. H. (1993). Behavioral and pharmacological treatments for Tourette syndrome: A review. *Applied & Preventive Psychology, 2,* 231-242.

Reprinted from Whitford, F. W. (1995). Instructor's resource manual for *Psychology: Principles and applications* by S. Worchel & W. Shebilske. Englewood Cliffs, NJ: Prentice Hall.

Facilitated Communication

Like EMDR, facilitated communication has been touted as the "next therapeutic breakthrough." Developed in Australia by Rosemary Crossley for use with cerebral palsy patients, this technique involves helping those who can't otherwise communicate. Australian special educator Douglas Biklen introduced the technique to the United States and urged its use for people with autism.

Facilitated communication, as described by Thomas Oltmann and Bob Emery, involves a trained facilitator who supports the arms and hands of the palsy sufferer or autistic person, enabling that person to communicate more effectively using a keyboard to type replies. Biklen and others suggest that this technique illuminates the world of autistic people, showing them to be insightful, intelligent, aware, and sometimes, victims of traumatic abuse. Biklen's claims are based on case studies which he says show solid proof of the technique's effectiveness. Critics of the technique argue that it is little more than an outlet for facilitators to advance whatever therapeutic agenda they might have. The only thing communicated, critics say, is whatever the facilitator wants to type.

While rhetoric flies back and forth, what is called for is a controlled study of facilitated communication. Eberlin, McConnachie, Igel, and Volpe provided such a test. Twenty-one adolescents diagnosed with autism and ten facilitators who were enthusiastic about the technique were studied. In the baseline condition of the experiment, the autistic adolescents were asked a variety of factual and personal questions and allowed to communicate as best they could using any available means. A special typewriter with the letters arranged alphabetically was available, or the adolescents could give a verbal or gestural response. In the pretest condition the adolescents were asked the same questions as in the baseline, but were encouraged to respond with the help of a facilitator, who remained uninformed about the questions asked. The third condition allowed the adolescents to freely respond to questions with the help of a facilitator who had been trained for 20 hours and who saw and heard the questions being asked. Finally, a posttest condition enlisted trained facilitators in answering identical questions to those of the pretest.

The results of this experiment showed that responses to the questions were *worse* during facilitated communication (in either the pretest or posttest) than they had been during the baseline period. For example, only 3 participants were able to answer at least one personal question correctly with the help of a facilitator, whereas 14 of 21 adolescents were able to respond correctly during the unassisted baseline. Moreover, findings during the free response condition cast doubt on the workings of facilitated communication. One respondent, who was able to communicate only by using two manual signs, typed "EMOTION ZOMETHIN* FEEL EXPREZ" when asked to define emotion. Without the earlier baseline information, this response would indeed have seemed impressive. In this experimental context, however, it smacks of something much less noble.

Biklen, D. (1992). Autism orthodoxy versus free speech: A reply to Cummins and Prior. *Harvard Educational Review, 62*, 242-256.
Crossley, R., & McDonald, A. (1980). *Annie's coming out.* New York: Penguin.
Eberlin, M., McConnachie, G., Igel, S., & Volpe, L. (1993). Facilitated communication: A failure to replicate the phenomenon. *Journal of Autism and Developmental Disorders, 23*, 507-530.
Oltmanns, T. F., & Emery, R. E. (1995). *Abnormal psychology.* Englewood Cliffs, NJ: Prentice Hall.

A Brief History of Convulsive Therapies

Electroconvulsive therapy (ECT) is a topic that guarantees lively classroom debate. Some background on the development of convulsive techniques will enrich your discussion.

❖ Julius Wagner-Jauregg (1857-1940) noticed that improvements in mental illness often followed a severe fever. Beginning in 1886 he induced fevers in the mentally ill, using at turns tuberculin, typhus vaccine, and tertian malaria. In 1917 nine patients with general paresis were treated by injecting blood from patients experiencing active malaria; three recovered, three showed temporary relief, and three showed no improvement. In 1927 Wagner-Jauregg won the Nobel Prize for Medicine based on this type of work.

❖ Manfred Sakel (1900-1957) in 1933 reported success using insulin coma and insulin subcoma therapy to treat schizophrenia. Sakel concluded that the repeated induction of hypoglycemia, typically accompanied by coma and convulsions, produced beneficial effects. With the advent of chlorpromazine in the early 1950s and subsequent clinical comparisons, insulin coma therapy quickly fell from favor.

❖ Laszlo Meduna (1896-1964), a Hungarian psychiatrist, is credited as the founder of modern convulsive therapy. A somewhat popular notion in Meduna's time was that schizophrenic processes were helpful in treating epilepsy, leading some researchers to unsuccessfully transfuse the blood of schizophrenics to treat those with epilepsy. Meduna sought to demonstrate the reverse, believing that there was a fundamental antagonism between epileptic processes and schizophrenic processes. Accordingly, he tried camphor, pentylenetetrazol, and carbon dioxide to induce seizures in his patients.

❖ Ugo Cerletti's (1877-1963) contribution to this sequence of events was to advocate the use of electroshock. In 1938, after a series of studies using nonhuman animals, Cerletti applied electroshock to a 19-year-old man found wandering the streets of Rome in a psychotic state. The patient received 11 electroshock applications, and was reported to be "cured" after 1 year and able to return to his former job. Electroshock methods were introduced to the United States in 1939, although the *Journal of the American Medical Association* published editorials warning of the possibility of electrocution.

❖ After World War II interest in convulsive therapies increased, although concern was growing over complications associated with the techniques. For example, both pentylenetetrazol and electrical inductions produced death, panic, fear, fractures, memory loss, postseizure delirium, spontaneous seizures, and cardiovascular disorders. By 1950, then, muscle paralysis and anesthesia were commonly used when inducing seizures. More recent developments include localizing the placement of electrodes to one side of the head, and modifying the amount of electricity or frequency of treatments.

Fink, M. (1979). *Convulsive therapy: Theory and practice* (pp. 5-17). New York: Raven Press.

Ch-Ch-Ch-Changes

"The more that things change, the more they stay the same." This pithy observation may serve to make us look erudite after a few beers at the bar, but for many people it doesn't ring true. From plastic surgery to career changes to relocating hearth and home, people seek change because it *isn't* the same old thing. What can and cannot change, however, is another matter. Looking over the research, psychologist Martin Seligman sketches traits, disorders, and behavior patterns that seem more or less resistant to change.

Panic	Curable
Specific Phobias	Almost Curable
Sexual Dysfunctions	Marked Relief
Social Phobia	Moderate Relief
Agoraphobia	Moderate Relief
Depression	Moderate Relief
Sex Role Change	Moderate Relief
Obsessive-Compulsive Disorder	Moderate Mild Relief
Sexual Preferences	Moderate Mild Change
Anger	Mild Moderate Relief
Everyday Anxiety	Mild Moderate Relief
Alcoholism	Mild Relief
Overweight	Temporary Change
Post-traumatic Stress Disorder	Marginal Relief
Sexual Orientation	Probably Unchangeable
Sexual Identity	Probably Unchangeable

Seligman, M. E. P. (1994, May/June). What you can change and what you cannot change. *Psychology Today*, pp. 35-41, 70, 72-74, 84. Used by permission.

On Being Sane in Insane Places

One of the more controversial articles published about mental hospitals is Rosenhan's "On Being Sane in Insane Places." This account describes how 8 sane people gained admission to 12 different mental hospitals by complaining to the admissions office that they had been hearing voices that said, "Empty, hollow, and thud." The pseudo-patients behaved normally during the rest of the admission interview and throughout their hospitalization. Although all of them were eventually released from the mental hospitals, with the length of the hospitalization ranging from 7 to 52 days, all were released with the stigmatizing label "schizophrenia in remission."

The most shocking aspect of the study concerns the experiences the pseudo-patients had while in the mental hospitals. In brief, they received almost no attention from the doctors, nurses, or even attendants, and they were sedated with over 2,000 pills (which they flushed down the toilets, as did many real patients). The few interactions they had with the staff were usually antitherapeutic. For example, Rosenhan describe how doctors ignored patients, as in the following exchange:

Pseudo-patient: Pardon me, Dr. X. Could you tell me when I am eligible for grounds privileges?

Physician: Good morning, Brett. How are you today? (Moves off without waiting for a response.)

In summing up the study, Rosenhan noted that the pseudo-patients experienced very strong feelings of powerlessness and depersonalization, leading to the conclusion that many mental hospitals are actually detrimental to the patients' mental health. The flaws of the mental hospitals described in Rosenhan's article are not unavoidable, as evidenced by the hospital system described by Polak, Deever, and Kirby (1977). For example, in a southwest Denver inpatient hospital alternative system, clients are diagnosed at home rather than in the hospital. Staff offices have been eliminated, leading to greatly increased patient-staff interaction. To avoid depersonalization, patients are often placed and treated in the homes of carefully screened families rather than in a large, impersonal hospital. Also, the daily cost of such treatment is considerably less than the standard rate in hospitals. All of this indicates that it is possible to develop a workable, cost-efficient alternative to psychiatric hospitals.

> Polak, P. R., Deever, S., & Kirby, M. W. (1977). On treating the insane in sane places. *Journal of Community Psychology, 5*, 380-387.
> Rosenhan, D. L. (1973). On being sane in insane places. *Science, 179*, 250-258.
> Rosenhan, D. L. (1975). The contextual nature of psychiatric diagnosis. *Journal of Abnormal Psychology, 84*, 442-452.
> Slife, B. (1998). *Taking sides: Clashing views on controversial psychological issues* (10th ed., Issue 14). Guilford, CT: Dushkin Publishing Group.
> Spitzer, R. L. (1975). On pseudoscience in science, logic in remission, and psychiatric diagnosis: A critique of D. L. Rosenhan's "On being sane in insane places." *Journal of Abnormal Psychology, 84*, 442-452.
> Spitzer, R. L. (1976). More on pseudoscience in science and the case for psychiatric diagnosis: A critique of D. L. Rosenhan's "On being sane in insane places" and "The contextual nature of psychiatric diagnosis." *Archives of General Psychiatry, 33*, 459-470.

> Reprinted from Whitford, F. W. (1995). Instructor's resource manual for *Psychology: Principles and applications* by S. Worchel & W. Shebilske. Englewood Cliffs, NJ: Prentice Hall.

How Can I Find a Good Therapist?

Surprisingly, people do not go for counseling because they suffer from the disorders typically described in psychology textbooks, such as phobias, dissociative disorders, and schizophrenia. The most common complaints therapists hear are: "I'm depressed; I feel overwhelmed, anxious all the time; I'm having interpersonal difficulties; I feel worthless, perhaps even suicidal." To a lesser degree, therapists hear complaints about sexual problems, problems at work, fears, and obsessive-compulsive problems. Although common problems of living are often eliminated simply by the passage of time or through the support of friends or family, people with little available social support should consider professional therapy.

There are many places to begin a search for a professional therapist: One could write to the American Psychiatric Association, if a psychiatrist (e.g., someone who could prescribe drugs) is desired, or to other professional groups, such as the Association of Behavior Therapists. Librarians can help locate the addresses of organizations. Referrals can be obtained from one's family physician or local mental-health department. Finally, friends and relatives can be consulted, though this approach may not be as effective as the others.

People considering therapy should know that there is no such thing as the "best" therapist because satisfaction with a particular therapy depends on what is desired. Decisions between group and individual therapy and between long-term and short-term treatment depend on several factors: Group therapy is often cheaper, for example, but traditional psychoanalysis cannot be done either in groups or in the short term. Also, there is the question of whether the therapist should be directive or not (for those who favor talking out problems, a client-centered therapist might be best). What type of professional would be most appropriate? A psychiatrist or a psychologist, a social worker, a psychiatric nurse, a pastoral counselor? One big difference among these therapists is in the type and length of training they have received and the fees they charge. It should be noted that studies have shown that paying a lot for therapy does not necessarily make that therapy any more effective than free or inexpensive treatment (Yoken & Berman, 1984). There are still other factors to consider: Is a therapy that focuses on the past or on present concerns desired? Would there be better rapport with a male or a female therapist? Various consumer guides to counseling offer more detail on how to find a therapist (e.g., Kovel, 1976).

Regardless of the particular therapeutic orientation chosen, people need a therapist with whom they feel comfortable. In fact, this may be the single most important factor in determining the success of therapy. A therapist whose personality is seriously abrasive or otherwise unpleasant, who does not welcome questions, or who suggests sexual intimacy should be avoided. But although warmth, empathy, and genuineness may be necessary ingredients of successful therapy, they are not sufficient. Whenever possible, clear goals should be specified. Many therapists today enter into a written contract with their clients in order to provide unambiguous goals and conditions.

Kovel, J. (1976). A complete guide to therapy: From psychoanalysis to behavior modification. New York: Pantheon Books.

Yoken, C., & Berman, J. S. (1984). Does paying a fee for psychotherapy alter the effectiveness of treatment? Journal of Consulting and Clinical Psychology, 52, 254-260.

demonstrations

Suggesting Treatments for Abnormal Behavior

Handout 14-1 presents several case studies of abnormal behavior. Distribute the handout to your students, and ask them to work either individually or in small groups to recommend an appropriate therapy for the case in question. In doing so have them concentrate on (a) what the nature of the disturbance seems to be, (b) a likely diagnosis of the disorder (to refresh their memory for material from Chapter 13), (c) a prognosis for the duration or the severity of the disturbance if left untreated, and (d) one or two therapeutic approaches that would seem to be warranted by the evidence and would be effective in addressing the problem. Encourage your students to be specific; rather than stating "We'd use a behavioral approach," instruct them to specify whether they would use systematic desensitization, token economy, and so on.

You may use this exercise as a basis for a number of discussion topics. For example, by focusing more on the duration and outcomes of the disorders you can highlight the issue of whether psychotherapy is effective. Alternatively, if your students recommend different approaches to treating the same problem, as a class discuss the issues of how therapists decide on a course of treatment, how one's training affects one's approach to administering therapy, or how an accurate diagnosis is necessary for recommending a course of treatment. Finally, if students seem to be in agreement about what type of therapy to pursue in a particular case, talk about notions of "matching" therapies to disorders (e.g., behavioral approaches seem most effective for phobias; biological treatments might be best for affective disorders).

Listed below are some probable therapeutic strategies, although your students may recommend and defend other reasonable alternatives.

1. Madge is definitely actively psychotic, probably schizophrenic. Antipsychotic medication would be called for as one course of treatment, and possibly institutionalization (at least short-term), given her current living arrangements and lack of friends or relatives to supervise her.

2. Bipolar disorder. Biological approaches such as the use of Lithium might be warranted.

3. Phobia. Although the childhood trauma/sadistic brother angle might suggest a psychoanalytic approach, this seems to be a case for systematic desensitization.

4. A range of difficulties, although probably *not* alcoholism (Dan) *nor* depression (Lisa). The miscommunication and dysfunctionality present suggest family therapy.

5. Cindy seems to have low self-esteem, maybe a little depression, but it's all more apparent than real. Her unrealistic, overly-negative thinking, in light of disconfirming evidence, suggests that some kind of cognitive therapy such as RET is called for.

Example 2 drawn from W. A. Gray & B. A. Gerrard (1981). Understanding yourself and others: A student activity book of psychological experiments and activities. New York: Harper and Row.

The Client, Part II

This exercise is an elaboration of one suggested in the previous chapter. If you did not play "The Client" in the last chapter, this exercise is good practice for diagnosing mental disorders and also a good introduction to different therapeutic perspectives. If you did the exercise in the previous chapter, students will already be familiar with the diagnosis portion and you will only need to explain the variation on the rules.

Recall that for "The Client," you (or a guest actor) play the role of a client with an undisclosed psychological disorder that class members must try to accurately diagnose. The premise is that you are a client entering a clinician's office for the first time and that you want them (as the therapists) to interview you in order to assess your problem. At that point, you sit quietly and answer student questions until they agree on a diagnosis.

In this version, you again portray a client with a mental disorder, but this time groups of students are assigned to role play psychologists from different theoretical orientations. For example, groups of students could represent the psychoanalytic, client-centered, cognitive, and behavioral approaches. Although the goal is generally the same (i.e., to make an accurate diagnosis), students should try to confine their questions to their assigned perspective (e.g., behaviorists should not ask about childhood traumas). In addition, groups should--from within their assigned perspective--offer a plausible explanation for the development of the client's symptoms and also suggest a plan for treatment. Because this assignment is more difficult and involved than the previous one, it is wise to give students time to meet in their groups so they can discuss their theoretical perspective and come up with a cohesive strategy for questions and diagnosis.

Adapted from Halonen, J. S. (1986). *Teaching critical thinking in psychology*. Milwaukee: Alverno Productions.

Role-Playing Client-Centered Therapy

William Balch suggests using a role-playing exercise to demonstrate techniques of client-centered therapy. Ask student volunteers to take on the role of Pat, a conflicted young person, and various other people who provide her with directive, specific advice. (The roles of the various players are described below.) If you have clinical training or are comfortable with the client-centered approach, you may assume the role of the therapist who remains nondirective and facilitates Pat's self-discovery. Better yet, you might ask a representative from the counseling center to play the role of the therapist. Have your students and the participants discuss the exercise and their insights into this approach to therapy.

Pat: She is enrolled in a difficult pre-medical program, and her grades are beginning to drop sharply. Pat is not sure she wants to be a doctor, and is considering enrolling in a nearby school of art and design. The deadline for applications is drawing near. Pat has also been having problems with her dating partner, Lee. [*Note*: Pat may be either a woman or a man.]

Lee (Pat's relationship partner): Lee thinks that Pat has been selfishly preoccupied with her own concerns, and that she hasn't been invested in their relationship. Lee has threatened to break off their relationship unless Pat starts showing some attention. [*Note*: Lee should remain an off-stage presence, whose feelings toward and relationship to Pat are known by the audience and the acting members. Lee may be either a woman or a man.]

Pat's Father: A struggling insurance salesperson, Pat's father thinks that he himself could have been a physician had he applied himself more in school. His advice to Pat is to simply pull herself together and work harder. He is opposed to Pat's idea of going to art school, and thinks she can become a fine doctor.

Pat's Mother: Although she was told by her own English teacher that she had a real talent for writing, Pat's mother never pursued it and instead was content to remain at home while her husband worked. She is sympathetic to Pat's desire to attend art school, but is worried Pat might make the same mistake she did; submitting to pressure to enter a long-term romantic relationship at too young an age.

Pat's Best Friend, Rene: Rene dropped out of high school and is working in a blue-collar job as a stock clerk. Her advice to Pat is to leave medical school, art school, and the whole middle-class values trip behind, get a job, and earn enough to make a living.

Pat's Therapist: The therapist uses client-centered techniques to help Pat determine what her own thoughts and feelings are. The therapist avoids telling Pat what to do, although Pat hopes the therapist has some answers for her.

> Balch, W. (1983). The use of role-playing in a classroom demonstration of client-centered therapy. *Teaching of Psychology, 10*, 173-174.

Systematic Desensitization

The textbook discusses the technique of systematic desensitization, which is frequently used to treat persons suffering from phobias. This technique basically occurs in three phases: identifying a procedure that is effective in reducing the person's anxiety, developing a hierarchy for the phobic object or event, and progressively presenting items in the hierarchy through either in vivo or imaginal graduated exposure while the individual practices the relaxation technique. In this exercise, divide the class into small groups and have them develop a systematic desensitization treatment for a phobia. Since the textbook uses snakes as its example, you should select another phobia that is somewhat concrete and familiar to the students (for example, visiting the dentist to get a filling or a fear of the water). In order to facilitate the discussion after the exercise, all groups should be assigned the same phobic object or situation. After you have briefly explained the phobia, instruct the groups to do the following: (a) decide upon and justify the type of relaxation techniques to be used by your client, (b) construct a complete hierarchy of scenes related to the phobia, and (c) based upon their relaxation technique and hierarchy, decide whether to use in vivo or imaginal graduated exposure and be prepared to justify their choice. Give the groups approximately 15 or 20 minutes to complete their tasks and then ask each group to describe its treatment program. Class discussion can focus on the differences and similarities in treatment programs.

> Reprinted from Hill, W. G. (1995). Instructor's resource manual for *Psychology* by S. F. Davis and J. J. Palladino. Englewood Cliffs, NJ: Prentice Hall.

Irrational Beliefs

The textbook describes Rational Emotive Therapy, which is based on Albert Ellis's assumption that maladaptive emotions result from irrational, inconsistent, and unsupported beliefs. For example, the tendency to "catastrophize" events or dwell on worse-case scenarios can lead one to imagine all kinds of sources, durations, and consequences for negative events. In order to encourage students to think about irrational beliefs and how they relate to behavior, ask your students to write down examples of irrational beliefs and how they might contribute to maladaptive emotional and behavioral patterns. Albert Ellis and Robert Harper have outlined some common irrational beliefs, such as: You must have love and approval from all the significant people in your life; You must be thoroughly competent, adequate, and achieving; You have little ability to change or control your feelings; It's horrible and terrible when things don't turn out the way you want them to.

Students sometimes endorse these same kinds of irrational beliefs. For example, your students are likely to have generated statements similar to the ones given below. If your students are hesitant to share their thoughts, read some of them and ask if anyone has thought this way: "I have to get A's on every test and in every class or I will be a failure;" "If I don't make it into (law school/medical school/graduate school/business school) my future will be ruined;" "My parents will only love me if I do well in school;" "If I don't get accepted into Sorority X I won't have any friends;" "I can't get a date because I am unlikable;" "The professor doesn't like me because she knows I'm unintelligent."

Ask some students if they would be willing to share some of their beliefs (either ones they've fallen prey to personally or the more general examples they listed earlier) and allow the other class members to analyze them. The analysis should focus on how the examples incorporate absolutist and dogmatic statements, or whether there are fundamental, unseen flaws to the reasoning. In discussing the therapeutic aspects of dealing with irrational beliefs, you might rely on the textbook's suggestions for correcting distorted thinking.

Ellis, A., & Harper, R.A. (1975). *A new guide to rational living.* Englewood Cliffs, NJ: Prentice Hall.

Adapted from Hill, W. G. (1995). Instructor's resource manual for *Psychology* by S. F. Davis and J. J. Palladino. Englewood Cliffs, NJ: Prentice Hall.

Debate: Does Psychotherapy Really Work?

Although experts generally agree that psychotherapy is a worthwhile and effective treatment for many types of psychological disorders, a deeper exploration into this ostensibly self-evident conclusion can yield insights into the different approaches to psychotherapy as well as the methods used to evaluate their success. For example, at least in certain critics' minds there is still some question as to whether psychotherapy is significantly more effective than either nontreatment or a placebo. Another crucial question to be answered is whether some forms of psychotherapy (e.g., insight, cognitive, behavioral) are generally more effective than others or whether some forms of therapy are particularly well-suited to treating certain people or types of problems. Ask your students to explore these questions in more depth by considering the scientific evidence and arguments in a debate format. Assign students to research this issue and to be prepared to defend either side. Chapter 12 in *Seeing Both Sides* presents both pro and con viewpoints on this controversial topic; students could also be encouraged to find additional recent sources from journal articles and from the popular media.

Lilienfeld, S. O. (1995). *Seeing both sides: Classic controversies in abnormal psychology.* Pacific Grove, CA: Brooks/Cole.

Debate: Is the *Consumer Reports* Conclusion Valid?

When *Consumer Reports* published the results of its large-scale survey on the effectiveness of psychotherapy it sparked considerable debate among methodologists, practitioners, researchers, and laypeople alike. The survey found that psychotherapy was generally effective, among other conclusions. The methodology used to gather data and reach this conclusion, however, has sparked a lively exchange. On the one hand, several researchers have argued that the *Consumer Reports* approach, while showing some limitations, nonetheless extends available methodologies and offers a new approach to addressing this topic. On the other hand are those who question the validity of the *Consumer Reports* survey methods and advocate experimental techniques for addressing the issue of psychotherapy effectiveness. Arguments on both sides are presented in Issue 1 of *Taking Sides*.

Slife, B. (2000). *Taking sides: Clashing views on controversial psychological issues* (11^h ed.). Guilford, CT: Dushkin Publishing Group.

Debate: Is Insight Necessary for Behavior Change?

Although there are a variety of therapies currently practiced (over 200, by most estimates, not including new self-help books that appear almost daily) there is a fundamental difference of opinion between two of them. Insight therapists, such as those who adopt a psychodynamic, client-centered, or Gestalt approach, argue that long-lasting behavior change can only be attained after a patient has achieved some degree of insight into the root of his or her problem. Without that, only the symptoms of the problem are treated, leaving the problem to linger and leaving open the possibility of symptom substitution. Behaviorally-oriented therapists, in contrast, argue that treating the behavior is treating the problem and that deep insight is not necessary. Long-lasting behavior change can be achieved by restructuring reward contingencies, extinguishing maladaptive behaviors, and modifying the environment. Have your students adopt one of these positions, research the question more fully, and present their arguments to one another in the debate format suggested at the beginning of this manual.

Atlas, G. D. (1995). Instructor's resource manual for *Abnormal Psychology* by T. F. Oltmanns and R. E. Emery. Englewood Cliffs, NJ: Prentice Hall.

Debate: Should Psychologists Be Able to Prescribe Drugs?

One of the distinguishing characteristics between clinical psychologists and psychiatrists is that psychiatrists can prescribe drug treatments because of their medical training. Some psychologists, however, are beginning to advocate the ability to prescribe psychotropic medication.

For example, Ronald Fox has argued that prescribing drugs is a logical extension of psychological practice. The ability of psychologists to provide help for the client should not be limited by restrictions on the therapeutic techniques that they can employ. Research clearly demonstrates that many psychological disorders have biomedical aspects that require drug treatments, and psychologists should be able to take advantage of the rapid and direct intervention available through drug treatments when it is necessary for the welfare of the client. Fox also indicated that providing psychologists with prescription privileges is in the public interest because it can contribute to an increased availability of health services. Finally, Fox believes that general practitioners are often less adequately trained than psychologists to evaluate the responses to and effectiveness of psychotropic medication. Based upon his experience, Fox indicated that many general practitioners often either prescribe dosages that are either insufficient or excessive for the condition being treated.

Even among psychologists, however, there is disagreement on the issue of prescription privileges. For example, DeNelsky argued that prescription privileges could have a negative impact on the practice of psychology. He stated that one of the current advantages of clinical psychology is that it is clearly distinguished from psychiatry by its emphasis on psychotherapy over drug-based treatments. An ability to prescribe drugs may contribute to an eventual blurring of the distinction between psychiatry and clinical psychology, with clinical psychology shifting away from approaches that emphasize personal change and growth in favor of the quick solution provided by drug treatments. DeNelsky also argued that prescription privileges would require major changes in the content and length of training in order to address basic physiology, neuroanatomy, and pharmacology. Finally, DeNelsky believes that efforts to gain prescription privileges will be financially costly and potentially harmful to psychology because of strong resistance by the medical community.

This issue involves legislative, training, procedural, and practical aspects, and it is not clear how these will be resolved to the mutual satisfaction of all parties involved. It is clear, however, that this issue will command considerable attention in the years to come.

DeNelsky, G. Y. (1991). Prescription privileges for psychologists: The case against. *Professional Psychology: Research and Practice, 22,* 188-193.

Fox, R. E. (1988). Prescription privileges: Their implications for the practice of psychology. *Psychotherapy, 25,* 501-507.

Slife, B. (2000). *Taking sides: Clashing views on controversial psychological issues* (11th ed.). Guilford, CT: Dushkin Publishing Group.

Adapted from Hill, W. G. (1995). Instructor's resource manual for *Psychology* by S. F. Davis and J. J. Palladino. Englewood Cliffs, NJ: Prentice Hall.

Debate:
Have Antidepressant Drugs Proven to be Effective?

With the advent of Prozac and related antidepressant medications a new era in treating affective disorders was heralded. No longer was depression seen as a necessarily debilitating condition, but rather as a disorder that could be effectively treated and substantially alleviated. But the response to antidepressant medication has not been uniformly optimistic. Although many extol the virtues of antidepressant drugs, others counter that their effectiveness is mixed (at best) and that studies examining the issue have had significant flaws. Arguments from both perspectives on this controversial topic are presented in Issue 13 of *Taking Sides*.

Slife, B. (2000). *Taking sides: Clashing views on controversial psychological issues* (11th ed.). Guilford, CT: Dushkin Publishing Group.

Debate:
Is Electroconvulsive Therapy Safe and Effective?

Chapter 13 briefly discusses electroconvulsive therapy as a form of biological treatment for psychological disorder. Our experience has been that students are well versed in the horrors of ECT but have never been exposed to arguments that it is an effective (and safe) alternative treatment for severe conditions when other methods have failed. One great way to expose your students to *both* sides of this controversial issue (and to allow them to make up their minds based on available evidence) is to hold a debate on this fascinating and complex topic. Use the debate procedures suggested at the beginning of this manual (or develop your own) and assign students to research and defend both sides of this issue. Both *Taking Sides* (see Issue 15) and *Seeing Both Sides* (see Chapter 16) contain excellent articles supporting the pro and con positions on this topic.

Lilienfeld, S. O. (1995). Seeing both sides: Classic controversies in abnormal psychology. Pacific Grove, CA: Brooks/Cole.

Slife, B. (1994). Taking sides: Clashing views on controversial psychological issues (8th ed.). Guilford, CT: Dushkin Publishing Group.

student assignments

Interviewing Mental-health Professionals

This assignment gives your students first-hand knowledge about careers in therapeutic settings. Have your students interview a mental-health professional and either write a brief report about their conversation or present the information in class for discussion. The interviewee could be a member of your school's counseling center, a psychiatric case worker, a clinician, a psychiatrist, a clinical psychologist in private practice, a social worker, a staff member at the local Veteran's Administration hospital, a director of a halfway house, or a doctor at a state or private hospital. The structure of the interview should include (a) information about the professional's education and training, (b) years of experience on the job, (c) memorable or difficult cases and the solutions used to work with that person, (d) day-to-day responsibilities, (e) pay range, (f) job satisfaction, and (g) information about how and why the professional chose this career path. If your students are able to interview a range of professionals, you could devote class time to comparing the responses given by different workers to the same questions. Many undergraduates are attracted to psychology because they want to be involved in administering therapy; this exercise may prove enlightening to them as a glimpse into the real world of mental-health professionals.

Psychotherapy in Film

This assignment gives students an opportunity to explore the psychotherapeutic relationship in great depth as it is portrayed on screen. In this paper, students should analyze a character's illness and treatment from the perspective of a psychotherapist. Students should include in their discussion (a) the character's diagnosis in terms of the DSM-IV, (b) a brief discussion of the apparent etiology of the character's symptoms, and (c) an in-depth analysis of the treatment prescribed for the character in terms of the theoretical perspectives described in Chapter 14--psychoanalytic, client-centered, gestalt, and behavior therapy. Which perspective(s) is(are) being represented in the film? Does the treatment seem to be effective? What are the advantages and disadvantages of this approach? What, if any, alternative approach would the student recommend?

Adapted from Chrisler, J. C. (1990). Novels as case-study materials for psychology students. *Teaching of Psychology, 17*, 55-57.

❖ *David and Lisa* (1962). Featuring Keir Dullea and Howard Da Silva, this low-budget, independent gem presents a sensitive, realistic portrayal of two emotionally scarred teenagers and the painfully slow therapy that enables them to learn how to trust. Two therapy alliances are followed: one with David (who is neurotic) and his psychiatrist Dr. Swinford, and another with Lisa (who is schizophrenic) and, ironically, David acting as her therapist/friend. Yields powerful insights into disorder and therapy (Columbia/TriStar; 94 min). Also available as a book.

Rubin, T. (1986). *Lisa and David*. Mattituck, NY: Amereon.

❖ *One Flew Over the Cuckoo's Nest* (1975). Jack Nicholson stars in this moving drama as Randall P. McMurphy, a rebellious prisoner who stirs things up in a mental hospital after his transfer there. In going head to head with the authoritarian Nurse Ratchet, he revives the spirit of the other patients who have been browbeaten into submission by the institution. Although somewhat dated and stereotypical, this surprisingly entertaining film portrays a wide variety of deviant behavior and also highlights controversial therapeutic techniques (e.g., prefrontal lobotomy, electroconvulsive therapy), depicts the often inhumane conditions in mental institutions, and contains fascinating character studies of McMurphy and the other patients. [Note: This film could also be assigned in the personality chapter as a fascinating case study of the character of sane misfit McMurphy.]

Kesey, K. (1975). *One flew over the cuckoo's nest*. New York: New American Library.

❖ *Ordinary People* (1980). An academy-award winning film starring Donald Sutherland, Mary Tyler Moore, Judd Hirsch, and Timothy Hutton. This powerhouse drama deals with many issues relevant to the introductory course, including suicide, depression, dysfunctional families, emotions, death and bereavement, and so on. But its treatment of the psychotherapeutic process is the most impressive of all. It tells the story of the Jarretts, a family devastated by the death of an older son in a boating accident. The family's well-ordered suburban veneer effectively denies its unresolved grief until the suicide attempt of the surviving son, Conrad. There are seven therapy scenes that not only give the film its structure and dramatic arc, but also provide one of the most positively illustrated portrayals of psychotherapy ever put on film. The reference for the book, which is also excellent, is given below (Paramount; 124 min).

Guest, J. (1982). *Ordinary People*. New York: Ballantine.

❖ *Sybil* (1977). Sally Field won an Emmy for her performance in this made-for-TV drama that depicts the story of a woman with 17 different personalities. Although at times disturbing, it convincingly portrays the relatively rare condition of multiple personality disorder (also referred to as "dissociative identity disorder"). Importantly, it depicts Sybil's adoption of different personalities as an adaptive response to an unbearably abusive childhood, and in doing so provides valuable insights into a unique therapeutic relationship (CBS/Fox; 122 min). Based on the book by Flor Schreiber.

Schreiber, F. (1974). *Sybil*. New York: Warner.

❖ *Girl, Interrupted* (1999). Winonna Rider, Angelina Jolie, and Whoopi Goldberg star in a portrayal of Susanna Kaysen's short stay in a mental hospital to cure her 'borderline personality' disorder. Set in the late 1960's, Winona Ryder effectively portrays Kaysen. Throughout the film, writer James Mangold's exploration of Kaysen's changing emotions and attempts to understand her `illness' is captivating. (Columbia Pictures; 122 min).

Kaysen, S. (1974). *Girl, Interrupted*. New York: Vintage.

video

ABC News/Prentice Hall Video Library

Depression: Beyond the Darkness (47 min, Series III). This entire *20/20* program focuses on depression. Several first-person accounts from people of all ages who have struggled with depression are given, as are comments from their relationship partners, psychiatrists, and other mental-health professionals. This segment provides a fine example of depression from the perspective of the depressed.

Other Sources

> Several of the videos listed in Chapter 13 (Psychological Disorders) may be suitable for use in the present context (Therapies). The titles are not duplicated here.

Abnormal Behavior: A Mental Hospital (28 min, CRM). A look at life in a modern mental institution. Schizophrenics are interviewed, and an ECT session is observed.

APA Psychotherapy Series (1995, 12 parts, APA). This series of training tapes is designed for therapists seeking insight into other methods and techniques, and students new to psychotherapy seeking basic training. However, individual tapes might be useful in a classroom context to illustrate typical therapy sessions. Individual tapes focus on multimodal, feminist, ethnocultural, client-centered, cognitive-behavior, cognitive-affective, and short-term dynamic therapies, as well as psychoanalytic therapy with schizophrenics and individual therapy using a family systems approach.

Approaches to Therapy (1990, 30 min, IM). A single client is seen engaged in psychodynamic, humanistic, and cognitive-behavioral therapies. Differences among the sessions are discussed by experts, who also offer tips for choosing a therapist.

Asylum: Hospitals for the Criminally Insane (1993, 30 min, IM). Patients at a facility for the criminally insane talk about their lives, their crimes, and the treatment they are receiving. The complex questions of crime and competence are addressed.

Basic Interviewing Skills for Psychologists (1991, 51 min, IM). What to do, and more importantly what *not* to do, when interviewing clients is reviewed in this film.

Behavior Modification (45 min, IM). Provides an overview of behavior modification techniques and discusses how they are used to break habits, overcome anxiety, and teach social skills.

Committed in Error: The Mental-health System Gone Mad (52 min, FHS). Sixty-six years is a long time to be incarcerated in a mental-health institution, especially if there's nothing wrong with you. Find out the details of this real-life case in this video.

Depression: Back From the Bottom (28 min, FHS). Summarizes the symptoms of and various treatments for depression. The discussion of ECT distinguishes between its old and new forms and how ECT may affect brain biochemistry.

Depression: Medication Uses and Side Effects (10 min, IM). Describes various drugs used to treat depression and their potential side effects.

Discovering Psychology, Part 22: Psychotherapy (1990, 30 min., ANN/CPB). Psychodynamic, humanistic, behavioral, cognitive, and biomedical treatments for mental illness are portrayed in recreations and some footage from actual therapy sessions.

The Law and Persons With Mental Disability (1992, 6 parts, 35 min each, IM). This multi-part series examines a range of questions related to involuntary civil commitment. Issues such as individual's rights, the rights of the community, tort law, and the right to refuse treatment are considered.

Meanings of Madness: The Institution of Insanity (23 min, PENN). Examines the development of psychiatric care from the English county asylum system to the present, relating the development of treatments to social values, economics, and scientific progress.

Meanings of Madness: The Medicine Man (25 min, PENN). Explores medical approaches explaining mental illness and how they impact diagnosis and treatment.

Meanings of Madness: Rights and Rituals (23 min, PENN). Discusses a variety of issues related to the treatment of the mentally ill, including management of the mentally ill, certification issues, long-term institutionalization, and the community mental-health movement.

Medicine at the Crossroads: Disordered States (60 min, PBS). Examines the history of psychiatric medicine and explores the relationship of treatment to one's cultural and social context through illustrations of treatments used in several different cultures.

Mistreating the Mentally Ill (56 min, FHS). Japan, Egypt, India, and the U.S. are the focus of how various cultures see mental illness and what they offer to treat it. Financial shortfalls aside, the indifference of society often contributes to a lack of proper care for the seriously mentally ill.

No Place To Go (1993, 21 min, IM). The U.S. faces a crisis in integrating deinstitutionalized mental patients into the community. So does Canada, and this film looks at the issues and problems facing mentally ill homeless people.

Notable Contributors to the Psychology of Personality--Carl Rogers, Part 1 (50 min, PENN). Rogers discusses his views on motivation, perception, learning, and the self as well as his development of client-centered therapy.

Prisoners of Childhood: Exploring the Inner Child (1992, 52 min, IM). Inner children are popular these days, and more are being born all the time. Five actors work with a therapist in this video to bring to light lost feelings from their childhood.

Race and Psychiatry (25 min, FHS). Are the needs of all members of society equally well met by mental-health professionals? The issue of racism in mental-health care is explored in this video.

Therapy Choices (1990, 30 min, IM). Family-systems therapy, group psychotherapy, and self-help are examined. Clients and experts share their views.

Titticutt Follies (85 min, Grove Press). A chilling look at life in a prison for the criminally insane, circa early 1960s. Some of it is depressing, some of it is quite graphic, all of it is worth seeing. This film was heavily censored in the greater Boston area for quite some time.

Token Economy: Behaviorism Applied (23 min, IM). Skinner explains the basics of positive reinforcement and punishment and discusses applications using a token economy.

Treating Tourette's and Other Mental Illnesses (24 min, FHS). Dopamine--what it is, how it works, and how it contributes to Tourette's Syndrome and other disorders--is the focus of this program.

The World of Abnormal Psychology, Part 12: Psychotherapies (1992, 60 min, ANN/CPB). Psychodynamic, cognitive-behavioral, Gestalt, couples, and group therapy sessions involve the viewer as an observer.

The World of Abnormal Psychology, Part 13: An Ounce of Prevention (1992, 60 min, ANN/CPB). A tour of several treatment programs that are working to reduce the known risk factors for mental illness. Their stories provide hope and encouragement for the effective treatment of the mentally ill.

You Don't Have to Feel Fright, Dear: An Interview With Dr. Albert Ellis (28 min, PENN). Ellis discusses the basic principles of rational emotive therapy and contrasts them with Freudian-based therapies.

multimedia

Web Investigations

Investigating Sex Differences in Depression

Tom Ludwig summarizes the research on sex differences in depression, noting the prevalence of the disorder and its cross-cultural occurrence. In this Learning Activity students can take an online Self-Rating Depression Scale and compare their results with averages for their gender and the nation. This activity can be linked with *Depression's Double Standard*, discussed below. You might ask students to write a short reflection paper after visiting this site, being sensitive to the content and your students' remarks. Also remind them of the limits of self-diagnosis.

Making Connections

Insight Therapies

Q Describe the techniques and goals of classical psychoanalysis.

A Psychoanalysis is designed to bring hidden feelings to conscious awareness so that the person can deal with them more effectively. One way of doing so is through free association, a process in which the client discloses whatever thoughts or fantasies come to mind without editing or otherwise inhibiting them. Another technique is transference, in which the client comes to transfer feelings held toward authority figures from childhood to the analyst. The desired outcome is insight, or awareness of feelings, memories, and actions from the past that were unconscious but were exerting a strong influence on the person's present feelings and behavior.

Q Compare client-centered therapy to psychoanalysis.

A In contrast to psychoanalysis, client-centered therapy is nondirective; the therapist does not analyze the client's feelings but instead asks the client to interpret his or her statements. In addition, client-centered therapy focuses on current feelings rather than on unconscious feelings with roots in the distant past.

Q Describe the major techniques of Gestalt therapy.

A The techniques of Gestalt therapy include encouraging people to "own their feelings" by talking in an active rather than a passive way, and the empty chair technique, in which clients are asked to speak to an imaginary part of themselves.

Q Discuss some recent developments in psychotherapy.

A Recent developments in psychotherapy include time-limited treatment and more problem- or symptom-oriented therapies.

Behavior Therapies

Q Describe three behavioral therapy techniques that rely on classical conditioning.

A Behavioral therapy techniques that rely on classical conditioning include systematic desensitization (gradually associating a new response with stimuli that have been causing anxiety); flooding (exposing the person to the feared stimulus at full intensity and for a prolonged period); and aversive conditioning (teaching clients to associate pain and discomfort with the behavior that they want to unlearn).

Q How does behavior contracting help people reduce undesirable behavior?

A Behavior contracting helps people reduce undesirable behaviors by providing reinforcement when the person behaves in the desired manner.

Q For what types of conditions are modeling techniques used?

A Modeling techniques are used to reduce common phobias and to help people with mental retardation learn job skills. In combination with positive reinforcement, they can help people with schizophrenia learn appropriate behavior.

Cognitive Therapies

Q Explain how stress-inoculation therapy works.

A Stress-inoculation therapy works by leading the client to replace negative, anxiety-evoking thoughts with positive, "coping" thoughts.

Q What is the basic premise of rational-emotive therapy?

A The basic premise of rational-emotive therapy is that most people in need of therapy hold a set of irrational and self-defeating beliefs.

Q Explain the differences between rational-emotive therapy and Beck's cognitive therapy.

A Beck's cognitive therapy differs from rational-emotive therapy in that the therapist is much less challenging and confrontational, trying to help the client examine each dysfunctional thought in a supportive but objective manner.

Group Therapies

Q How do self-help groups prevent psychological disorders?

A Self-help groups prevent psychological disorders by providing social support to people who are near the limits of their ability to cope with life stresses.

Q In what circumstances is family therapy appropriate?

A Family therapy is appropriate when there are problems between husband and wife or parents or children, or when a person's progress in individual therapy is slowed because family members have trouble adjusting to the person's improvement.

Q What techniques do couple therapists use?

A Techniques used by couple therapists include empathy training (teaching each member of the couple to share inner feelings and understand the partner's feelings), behavioral techniques such as scheduling exchanges of benefits, and cognitive marital therapy (helping partners recognize ways in which they have been misinterpreting each other's communications).

Effectiveness of Psychotherapy

Q What evidence suggests that psychotherapy is effective in most cases?

A Evidence that psychotherapy is effective in most cases comes from studies that have averaged the results of a large number of individual studies and found that psychotherapy works best for relatively mild disorders and for people who really want to change.

Q What is an empirically supported therapy? Why is this concept important?

A An empirically supported therapy is one that has been shown to be effective through controlled research. This concept is important because it can help therapists decide on the most appropriate therapy for a specific disorder.

Biological Treatments

Q What are the most important types of drug therapies, and what conditions do they treat?

A The most important types of drug therapies are antipsychotic drugs (for symptoms of schizophrenia), antidepressant drugs (for depression), and lithium (for bipolar disorder).

Q How is electroconvulsive therapy performed, and what is it used for?

A Electroconvulsive therapy is used for cases of severe depression that do not respond to other forms of therapy. An electrical current is passed through one side of the brain, producing a brief convulsion followed by a temporary loss of consciousness.

Q For what conditions is psychosurgery used?

A Psychosurgery is used as a last resort in severe cases of psychosis, epilepsy, obsessive-compulsive disorder, and pain in a terminal illness.

Institutionalization and Its Alternatives

Q What are the causes and the effects of deinstitutionalization?

A Deinstitutionalization resulted from the advent of antipsychotic drugs, which made it possible to treat mentally ill patients in the community. However, many ex-patients are poorly prepared to live in the community and receive little assistance. As a result, they have stopped taking the drugs that made their release possible and have again become psychotic, often ending up homeless and living on the streets.

Q What alternative forms of treatment are available for mental illness, and why are these options seldom used?

A Alternative forms of treatment include living at home, with training to cope with daily activities; hostels offering therapy and crisis intervention; day-care treatment; visits from public-health nurses combined with medication; and intensive outpatient counseling combined with medication.

Q Define and give examples of primary, secondary, and tertiary prevention.

A Primary prevention consists of efforts to improve the environment so that new cases of mental disorders do not develop; an example is providing family planning services. Secondary prevention involves identifying groups that are at high risk for mental disorders and intervening before the disorders develop, for example, by providing services such as suicide hot lines. Tertiary prevention is designed to help people adjust to community life after release from a mental hospital, and may take the form of halfway houses where patients live during a period of transition between hospitalization and full integration into the community.

Gender and Cultural Differences in Treatment

Q In what ways do men and women receive similar treatment for psychological disorders? In what ways do treatments differ?

A Men and women receive similar treatment for psychological disorders, but that treatment tends to encourage women to adopt male-oriented views of what is normal or appropriate and to adjust to their surroundings passively. Treatments differ in that women are more likely to be treated with drug therapies.

Q What does it mean to say that our ideas about normal behavior are culture bound?

A Our ideas about normal behavior are culture bound because each culture includes specific norms of behavior that are learned by members of that culture. These norms often differ from one culture to another and must be interpreted carefully to prevent misunderstandings.

Video Classics

Carl Rogers on Therapy

SYNOPSIS: Kindly Carl Rogers discusses three attributes a therapist should exhibit for successful work with a client: genuineness, unconditional acceptance of the client, and empathy. This interview segment does a good job of summarizing Rogers' basic position on client-centered therapy.

Form a Hypothesis

Q What conditions do you think are important to the counselor relationship in person-centered therapy?

A Rogers describes three: Genuineness, acceptance, and empathic understanding.

Test Your Knowledge

Q How does Carl Rogers define empathy? Unconditional positive regard? Reflection?

A Empathy is understanding a client and communicating that understanding to the client. Unconditional positive regard is demonstrating acceptance of the individual, regardless of what she or he may say or do. Reflection is the communication of accurate empathy to the client.

Q According to Rogers, who is ultimately responsible for making positive changes?

A Rogers used the term "client-centered therapy" to change the therapeutic relationship from one in which a patient consulted an expert to one in which a client takes an active role in their own development.

Thinking Critically

Q What two types of humanistic therapy have had a marked effect on clinical practice?

A Certainly, client-centered therapy is one. Gestalt therapy, intended to help people become more authentic in their day-to-day interactions is the other as evidenced by the number of personal growth groups it has motivated.

Web Links

1. http://maple.lemoyne.edu/~hevern/psychref4-1.html

PsychREF: Clinical Psychology and Psychiatry. This installment of PsychREF provides many links to sites on psychodynamic psychotherapy, law and psychology, creative arts therapies, forensic psychology, and many other counseling-related topics.

2. http://www.shef.ac.uk/~psysc/psastud/index.html

Psychoanalytic Studies. Find an electronic journal from the Centre for Psychotherapeutic Studies, University of Sheffield, right here.

3. http://www.enabling.org/ia/gestalt/gerhards/archive.html

Gestalt Archive of the International Society for Gestalt Theory and Applications. Visit this site for information about this approach to therapy. Make sure you see the whole thing before trying to understand it.

4. http://www.yalom.com

Irving Yalom – Group Therapy. Provides students with a better understanding of group therapy, focusing mainly on Yalom.

5. http://maple.lemoyne.edu/~hevern/psychref4-2.html

PsychREF: Psychopharmacology and Psychotherapy (Medications). Direct your students here for a look at the biological approach to therapy.

transparencies

Series V

90a. *Psychological Defense Mechanisms*
90b Unconscious defenses are illustrated in this two-part transparency.

92. *Criteria for Abnormality*
Four criteria for abnormality are identified and defined.

93. *Orientation of Psychologists*
This pie chart presents the results of a survey of 422 practicing clinical and counseling psychologists who were asked to state their theoretical orientation.

94. *Where People Turn for Help*
This transparency lists the sources of support in people's lives.

95. *Duration of Therapy and Improvement*
The strength of the relationship between reported improvement and duration of therapy, as found in the Consumer Reports study.

96. *Major Perspectives on Therapy*
Insight, behavior, cognitive, group, and biological therapies are represented.

Text Figures

Summary Table	*Major Perspectives on Therapy*
14-1.	*Duration of Therapy and Improvement*
14-2.	*How Do the SSRI's Work?*
14-3.	*Use of Psychiatric Medications Among Preschoolers*

Handout 14.1

Treating Psychological Disorders

Instructions. Given below are short descriptions of abnormal behaviors. For each case you should decide (a) what the root of the problem seems to be, (b) a diagnosis of the disorder (drawing on your knowledge of material from Chapter 13), (c) a prognosis for the duration or the severity of the disturbance if it is left untreated, and (d) the type of therapy you would recommend. Be specific: Rather than recommending "a behavioral approach" state whether you would use systematic desensitization, aversive conditioning, a token economy, and so on.

1) "Madge" was found wandering the streets of New Jersey. She was brought to the attention of a licensed clinical social worker because she would routinely stand in automobile traffic and scream obscenities at the top of her lungs to no one in particular. During one of "Madge's" rare lucid moments, she told the social worker that she lived in a garbage dumpster and that she obeyed voices who commanded her to do the things she did. A search by police and news agencies for friends or relatives proved futile; no one seemed to know who "Madge" was, she seemed to have nowhere to go, and her disordered thinking was becoming more and more bizarre.

2) Kurt's mood swings were unpredictable and excessive in nature. One time he was hyperactive and extremely elated with accelerated speech and a flight of ideas which, at times, seemed incoherent. During this period he worked feverishly day and night on an important novel that "had to be started and finished that week." Months later, Kurt experienced a sad period, during which he could not get out of bed for more than minutes at a time. He would not see any friends for a period of some weeks until he slowly came out of it and seemed to be normal again (for a while). Sometimes Kurt felt so dejected and agitated that he contemplated suicide.

3) Gwen has had an intense fear of dogs since she was a child. When she was 4 years old her older brother forced her to approach a large sleeping dog who was chained in a yard. Although she escaped being bitten, the dog's loud angry barking and frantic movements, coupled with her crying and agitation, left their mark on her. Now, as an adult, she is still wary of being around dogs and feels apprehensive and anxious whenever she sees a dog on the street. Visits to friends who keep pets have been severely cut off; Gwen never drops by unannounced for fear that the dog might be free in the house. On the rare occasions when she does visit the animals must be kept chained out of sight in the backyard.

4) Dan's drinking had become more frequent over the past 6 months. Although he didn't drink to the point of becoming grossly incapacitated and was careful to never drink and drive, it was clear that his time in the bar after work had increased and that his daily cocktail had become three or four. Dan blamed his recent problems at work for his "need to unwind," and also cited difficulties with his wife, Sharon. According to Dan, when he tried to discuss his stress with Sharon she seemed distant and uninterested, or dismissed his problems as minor. She seemed much more concerned about their daughter, Lisa, and her increasing moodiness.

5) Cindy feels as though she is a failure. Although her college GPA is a respectable 3.7 she feels as though she should be doing much better. She is concerned about her parents' views of her. Even though they call, visit, and send care packages often, Cindy is sure they do so because they know she is incapable of caring for herself. When a recent short-term relationship fizzled out Cindy blamed her own inability to maintain a witty conversation as the cause of the break-up. Although several other people have since asked her out, she is nervous about accepting because she knows if things don't go well she won't ever get a second chance.

Chapter 15 Social Psychology

chapter outline 448

learning objectives 451

lecture suggestions

    Bad Guys Wear Black 452
    Explaining Correspondence Bias 452
    "Can I Ask You a Simple Question?" 453
    It's A Small World After All 454
    Jonestown: A Study in Social Psychology Change 455
    What Do You Think You're Doing? 456
    Similarity and Attraction Revisited 457
    Miss America Meets the Smurfs 458
    A Peg and A Grasshopper 460
    An Eight-Ball and A Cockroach 460
    Social Perception and Social Goals 461

demonstrations and activities

    The Actor-Observer Effect 462
    The Self-Serving Bias 462
    Identifying Persuasion Techniques 463
    Gender Stereotypes in Advertising 463
    Inducing Cognitive Dissonance 464
    Demonstrating Obedience 465
    Deindividuation 465
    Demonstrating Group Polarization 466
    Is This Sexual Harassment? 466
    Group Processes 467

student assignments

    Lookin' for Love 468
    Sometimes You Gotta Break the Rules 468
    Social Psychology in Literature: *Erewhon* 469
    Gender Roles in Film: *Tootsie* 469
    Ethnicity and Subculture in Film: *Boyz in the Hood* 469
    Social Psychology in Film 469

video 471

multimedia 474

transparencies 480

handouts

    Trait Identification Questionnaire 481
    Who Will Survive? 482

chapter outline

I. Social Cognition
  A. Impression formation
    1. Schemata
      a. Relying on schemas speeds information processing in the social world
        i. Schematic processing aids encoding and recall of person information
      b. Primacy effect
        i. Earlier information about a person carries more weight in impression
      c. Self-fulfilling prophecies
        i. Expectations about another elicit behavior confirming the expectations
    2. Stereotypes
      a. A type of schema about members of a social category
      b. Stereotypes may contribute to self-fulfilling prophecies
  B. Attribution
    1. Explaining behavior
      a. Behavior may be attributed to internal or external causes
      b. Three kinds of information help us assign causality
        i. Distinctiveness: Is there anything unique about these circumstances?
        ii. Consistency: Does the person act the same way in other situations?
        iii. Consensus: Do other people act this way in this situation?
    2. Biases in attribution
      a. The correspondence bias (fundamental attribution error)
        i. Overestimating dispositional causes of another person's behavior
        ii. Failing to adequately account for the effects of the situation
      b. Defensive attribution
        i. Our successes attributed to internal causes, failures to external causes
      c. Just world hypothesis
        i. Good things happen to good people, bad things happen to bad people
    3. Attribution across cultures
      a. Internal/external distinctions a markedly Western phenomenon
  C. Interpersonal attraction
    1. Proximity: Closer proximity predicts greater attraction
    2. Physical attractiveness: We ascribe other positive qualities to the physically attractive
    3. Similarity: A much stronger predictor of attraction than "opposites attracting"
    4. Exchange: We are attracted to those with whom we exchange rewards

        a. Equity: We are satisfied with whom we share an equitable relationship

    5. Intimacy: Reciprocity of self-disclosure facilitates development of intimacy

II. Attitudes

  A. The nature of attitudes

    1. Three components

        a. Evaluative beliefs about the attitude object

        b. Feelings toward the attitude object

        c. Behavioral tendencies toward the attitude object

    2. Attitudes and behaviors

        a. Relatively weak link between attitudes and behavior can be strengthened

            i. Measure attitudes and behavior at comparable levels

            ii. Consider additional predictors of behavior

        b. Self-monitoring as a personality trait relevant to this link

            i. High self-monitors may override privately held attitudes with behavior

                - Focus on meeting the demands of the situation

    3. Attitude development

        a. Family, peers, and media contribute to attitude formation

  B. Prejudice and discrimination

    1. Prejudice: Unfair, intolerant, or unfavorable attitudes toward a group of people

        a. Prejudicial beliefs trade strongly on stereotypes

        b. Discrimination: Unfair behavior toward a group of people

    2. Sources of prejudice

        a. Frustration-aggression hypothesis

        b. Authoritarian personality

        c. Modern racism and institutional racism

    3. Reducing prejudice

        a. Recategorization, controlled processing, improved contact between groups

            i. Contact hypothesis

                - Members of opposing groups must have equal status

                - One-on-one contact necessary

                - Contact improves under cooperation, rather than competition

                - Social norms should encourage contact

  C. Attitude change

    1. The process of persuasion

    2. The communication model

        a. Source, message, medium, audience

        b. Fear, discrepancy, commitment

    3. Cognitive dissonance theory

III. Social Influence
  A. Cultural influence
   1. Cultural truisms: Beliefs accepted by members of a culture as unerringly true
  B. Cultural assimilators
  C. Conformity
   1. Cultural norms influence conformity
   2. Asch studies demonstrate power of conformity
   3. Conformity across cultures
    a. Asch-type studies show diversity in results when repeated in other cultural contexts
  D. Compliance: Foot-in-the-door, lowball, door-in-the-face techniques
  E. Obedience: Milgram's studies demonstrate extremes of destructive obedience

IV. Social Action
  A. Deindividuation: The anonymity produced by being stripped of identity
  B. Helping behavior
   1. Altruism: Helping not motivated by personal gain
   2. Situational Variables
    a. Bystander effect: Helping decreases as crowd size increases
   3. Personal Characteristics
   4. Altruism and the Holocaust
   5. Helping behavior across cultures: Collectivism predicts greater likelihood of offering help
  C. Group decision making
   1. Group polarization: Group discussion leads attitudes to be more extreme
   2. The effectiveness of the group: Task, size, cohesiveness important determinants
   3. Leadership: Great Person and Zeitgeist approaches gave way to transactional view
   4. Leadership across cultures: Individualism/collectivism is predictive here, as well
  D. Organizational behavior
   1. Productivity: The Hawthorne effect
   2. Communication and responsibility

learning objectives

After reading this chapter, students should be able to:

1. Describe the process by which we form first impressions of other people. Identify three factors that influence person perception.

2. Explain three aspects of attribution and explain attribution errors.

3. Explain the dynamics of interpersonal attraction.

4. Identify the components of attitudes. Discuss the relationship between attitude and behavior.

5. Explain how attitudes are acquired.

6. Explain the origin of prejudice and discrimination and how prejudice can be reduced.

7. Discuss the dynamics of attitude change and the process of persuasion.

8. Explain the theory of cognitive dissonance. List ways to reduce cognitive dissonance.

9. Define risky shift and polarization. Summarize the conditions under which groups are effective and ineffective in solving problems.

10. Explain how culture, conformity, compliance, and obedience exert social influence.

11. Identify the four types of social action discussed in this chapter.

12. Discuss helping behavior by making reference to situational characteristics, personal characteristics, and cultural influences on altruism.

13. Identify the theories of leadership discussed in this chapter.

14. Discuss the concerns of organizational behavior and the role of the industrial/organizational psychologist.

lecture suggestions

Bad Guys Wear Black

Tom Gilovich, at Cornell University, has distinguished himself as a creative researcher in both social and cognitive psychology, and as an avid sports fan. He has combined these interests in a set of multimethod studies examining some causes of aggression.

Mark Frank and Gilovich started with the observation that almost universally black is seen as a color of evil and death. From mourning rituals to cowboy hats to heavy-metal music to being "blacklisted," "blackmailed," or "blackballed," cultures as diverse as the U.S., Germany, Hong Kong, Denmark, India, and tribes of Central Africa agree that black has negative connotations. To explore this phenomenon, Frank and Gilovich looked at the association between black and badness among teams in the National Football League (NFL) and National Hockey League (NHL).

Using archival records for the period between 1970 and 1986, the researchers calculated the number of yards penalized among the NFL teams and the number of minutes spent in the penalty box among the NHL teams as a measure of aggressiveness. These penalties were then compared between teams whose uniforms were primarily black (in the NFL: Pittsburgh Steelers, Oakland Raiders, New Orleans Saints, Cincinnati Bengals, and Chicago Bears, although the Bears actually wear dark blue uniforms; in the NHL: Pittsburgh Penguins, Vancouver Canucks, Philadelphia Flyers, Boston Bruins, and Chicago Blackhawks) and teams whose uniforms were not. Frank and Gilovich found that the black-clad teams reliably were more aggressive. As a further test, the researchers also identified two NHL teams (Pittsburgh and Vancouver) who had switched uniform colors from nonblack to black some time during their history. Following the switch, penalty minutes increased for these teams. However, this was not a mere effect of new fabric; when the New Jersey Devils moved from Colorado their uniforms changed from blue-and-gold to red-and-green, although there was no reliable change in the number of penalty minutes after the switch.

To explain these findings, Frank and Gilovich suggest that both self-perception and social perception are at work. When donning a black uniform, one may see oneself as tougher, meaner, and more aggressive, and so act in ways consistent with that self-perception. However, referees may also perceive players in dark uniforms as tougher, meaner, and more aggressive than they actually are (given the strong cultural association between black and badness), and so assess more penalties. To explore these explanations the researchers performed laboratory experiments. In one study college students and referees watched staged football games between teams wearing black or white uniforms. Both the students and the referees awarded more penalties to a team when it wore black. In a second experiment, students wore either white or black uniforms before participating in an athletic competition. Given their choice between aggressive and nonaggressive games, students wearing black reliably chose aggressive activities.

Frank, M. G., & Gilovich, T. (1988). The dark side of self- and social perception: Black uniforms and aggression in professional sports. *Journal of Personality and Social Psychology, 54,* 74-85.

Explaining Correspondence Bias

The correspondence bias, sometimes called the fundamental attribution error, has intrigued social psychologists for decades. It refers to the tendency of social perceivers to overestimate the dispositional causes of an actor's behavior, or, conversely, to fail to adequately take the effects of the situation into account. That the correspondence bias can take place has been established; *why* this uneven assignment of causality takes place has not. Although several explanations have been offered, no satisfactory explanation of correspondence bias has been agreed upon.

Dan Gilbert has addressed this question and offers a compelling explanation for the correspondence bias. Rather than being a unitary process, the act of inferring another's traits, attitudes, or attributes is a multi-stage process. First, some *categorization* of the behavior takes place ("Nick is yelling at Reggie"), followed by a *characterization* of the behavior ("Nick is a hostile fellow"), and then a *correction* of the inference that takes into account information about situational constraints ("But Reggie just punched and insulted Nick"). When these processes are allowed to run to completion, people ought not to commit the correspondence bias; their initial characterizations (trait inferences) of behavior can be corrected by the application of situational information. The problem is that the three stages do not involve the same amount of mental work. Categorization and characterization are relatively automatic, effortless tasks, but the process of correction is a more controlled, effortful process. Disruptions to this sequence of events, then, are more likely to affect the correction stage, because disruptions will usurp the cognitive resources needed to adequately correct for the effects of the situation. Specifically, when made cognitively busy (doing simultaneous mental tasks) social perceivers should be unable to adequately correct their initial characterizations, and so be left with attributions heavily weighted toward the actor's dispositions.

To test this process Gilbert and his colleagues showed research participants videotapes of a very anxious woman. The viewers were told that the woman was discussing anxiety-provoking topics, such as her sexual fantasies and public embarrassments she had endured. Most participants categorized the behavior as anxiousness, characterized the woman as suffering from manifest anxiety, but then corrected their attribution to account for the situation. However, when subjects were asked to simultaneously perform another, resource-consuming task (i.e., memorizing the discussion topics prompting the woman's anxiety as they scrolled across the bottom of the video screen) they were unable to correct their initial attributions, and were left committing the correspondence bias. These cognitively busy participants believed that the woman actually was dispositionally anxious. Ironically, the information that could have been used to correct that judgment (memorizing the discussion topics) was the very information that limited their ability to correct their judgments.

These effects of cognitive busyness have been demonstrated in a number of domains. For example, the cognitively busy act of trying to ingratiate oneself to someone leads a misbegotten perception of the individual. Hearing either a pro-choice or anti-abortion speech while simultaneously trying to think of a reply usurps resources vital to correction. And when the process is disrupted earlier (by making the categorization or characterization stages effortful) similar results obtain. Moving from the lab to the real world, the explanation offered for the correspondence bias is clear. Social perception is a cognitively demanding task; without the resources needed for correction, we may be left with mistaken, trait-based ascriptions about the individual.

Gilbert, D. T., McNulty, S. E., Giuliano, T. A., & Benson, E. J. (1992). Blurry words and fuzzy deeds: The attribution of obscure behavior. *Journal of Personality and Social Psychology, 62*, 18-25.

Gilbert, D. T., Pelham, B. W., & Krull, D. S. (1988). On cognitive busyness: When person perceivers meet persons perceived, *Journal of Personality and Social Psychology, 54*, 733-740.

"Can I Ask You A Simple Question?"

Sociobiological views of courtship, close relationships, and sexual activity paint very different pictures of men's and women's behaviors. The claim is that men will follow a reproductive strategy that allows them to impregnate a maximum number of women with a minimum amount of investment, whereas women, because of greater investment of resources in carrying and caring for a limited number of offspring, should be more selective in their reproductive choices. This sociobiological sketch predicts different outcomes for men's and women's willingness to engage in casual sex, a notion tested by Russell Clark and Elaine Hatfield in a series of field experiments.

In 1978 and 1982 male and female experimental confederates, all of average attractiveness, approached attractive strangers of the opposite sex on a college campus and said, "I've been noticing you around campus. I find you very attractive." This was followed by one of three straightforward requests: "Would you go out with me tonight?," "Would you come over to my apartment tonight?," or "Would you go to bed with me tonight?" Men and women responded to the request for a date about equally; in one study

50 percent of men and 56 percent of women agreed, and in another study 50 percent of both sexes agreed. A noticeable difference was found for the sex request. In two experiments 75 percent and 69 percent of the men agreed to the request for sex compared to far fewer of the women. In fact, a common response among these men was along the lines of, "Why do we have to wait until later?"

Clark repeated this experiment in the late 1980s to determine if concern brought about by the AIDS epidemic would substantially alter participants' responses. Given heightened social awareness of the dangers of HIV and AIDS, and practices that lead to infection, one's willingness to engage in casual sex with a total stranger should be reduced dramatically. The results, however, revealed very little change from the earlier studies. Among the women, 44 percent agreed to a date, 14 percent agreed to return to the confederate's apartment, and none agreed to the request to go to bed. Among men, however, 69 percent agreed to a date, 50 percent agreed to return to the woman's apartment, and 69 percent agreed to casual sex with the woman. Both men and women offered similar reasons for turning down the requests, the most prevalent (for both sexes) being that they were currently involved with a dating partner. Among the men who complied with the requests, 79 percent responded immediately with some variation of "Where and when?", with the remaining 21 percent simply asking for the confederate's telephone number or directions to her house.

Competing explanations for these findings, such as men's and women's differential perceptions of danger in dating a stranger or returning to that person's apartment, were lessened by a close examination of participants' reasons for compliance or noncompliance. It seems, then, that there is merit to the sociobiological explanation for reproductive strategies. It also seems, however, that collegians may need to exercise greater care in the dating choices they make.

Clark, R. D., III (1990) The impact of AIDS on gender differences in willingness to engage in casual sex. *Journal of Applied Social Psychology, 20,* 771-782.

Clark, R. D., III, & Hatfield, E. (1989). Gender differences in receptivity to sexual offers. *Journal of Psychology and Human Sexuality, 2,* 39-55.

It's A Small World After All

Most students and professors recognize Stanley Milgram's name in connection with his famous studies of obedience. Few realize, however, that Milgram was responsible for exploring a number of other fascinating social phenomena. These include conformity (confederates staring upwards at nothing), psychological maps, the lost-letter technique of attitude measurement (stamped envelopes addressed to Medical Research Associates versus Friends of the Communist Party), intrusion into waiting lines, television's effects on aggression (including a study manipulating the nationally-seen drama *Medical Center*), and an exploration of cyranoids (humans carefully trained to parrot surreptitious messages from others). Among the many creative avenues Milgram pursued is the small world problem.

Building on the earlier work of Ithiel de Sola Pool and others, Milgram posed a simple question: Given any two people in the world, what are the odds that they will know each other? The mathematics of answering this question quickly reveal a related question: If Person X and Person Y do not know each other directly, how many intermediate links in an acquaintance network would it take to bring the two together? That is, X may not know Y, but Person X knows Person Z, who in turn knows Person Q, who in turn knows Person W, who in turn knows Person C, and C knows Person Y quite well.

When most people are posed this question they assume that the links between X and Y must be very great or, to put it another way, the chances must be quite slim that X and Y can be linked easily. (As an aside, Milgram also found that most people believed very few others were capable of following orders encouraging destructive obedience; folk wisdom has not fared well in Milgram's research!) To put the question to experimental test, Milgram asked a group of women and men from all walks of life to try to pass a message to a target person, someone living in the United States and chosen arbitrarily. Participants were instructed to transmit the message to someone else who was more likely to know the target than did the participant. This process would be repeated (always among people who knew each other on a first-name basis) until the message was received by the target.

Milgram found that the number of links required to accomplish this task typically varied between 3 and 10, with a median of 5.5. That is, on the average it took about 6 links to move a message between two previously unacquainted people. The mechanics of this phenomenon involve a dizzying array of variables--the social circles one moves in, intuition about who might best know the target person, willingness to cooperate in transmitting the message, racial or cohort differences, and so on. But the results are clear and quite counterintuitive: Despite our far-flung, fast-paced culture, it really is a small world.

The small world problem has since inspired mathematicians, sociologists, linguists, and epidemiologists to investigate its parameters, and even served as the theme for the play *Six Degrees of Separation*.

Kochen, M. (Ed.) (1989). *The small world*. Norwood, New Jersey: Ablex.
Korte, C., & Milgram, S. (1970). Acquaintance networks between racial groups: Application of the small world method. *Journal of Personality and Social Psychology, 15*, 101-108.
Milgram, S. (1992). *The individual in a social world* (2nd ed.). New York: McGraw-Hill.
Travers, J., & Milgram, S. (1969). An experimental study of the small world problem. *Sociometry, 32*, 425-443.

Jonestown: A Study in Social Psychology Change

In 1978 over 900 people died at the People's Temple of Jonestown in Guyana. At the urging of Jim Jones, the founder of the church who had led his followers from the United States to this isolated settlement in South America, parents poisoned their children and then themselves. Afterward one question was voiced repeatedly: How could 900 people be induced to commit suicide? As Neal Osherow points out, the events at Jonestown can be understood in terms of basic social-psychological concepts.

As Stanley Milgram's research has shown, people will perform extreme acts under the instructions of an authority figure, particularly when no one else rebels. In Jonestown dissent was severely punished, both physically and through public humiliation. Because of informers, no one felt free to voice complaints to anyone else. This served to isolate people and to promote the feeling that no one else had doubts. Also, the members had been asked to commit less extreme acts in the past, followed by demands that were gradually increased. This "foot in the door" technique (Freedman & Fraser, 1966) contributes to compliance and to self-justification of that compliance.

Jim Jones also utilized excellent techniques of persuasion. Members were gradually indoctrinated through long sermons and taught to distrust contradictory views, while at the same time outside information was reduced. Moreover, a jargon developed that masked the true meaning of statements. These factors, coupled with the prohibition of dissent, resulted in members blaming apparent discrepancies on their own inadequacy rather than on that of the church or Jim Jones.

One of the most puzzling aspects of this case was that many of the church members had no desire to leave, believed in Jim Jones to the end, and committed suicide quite willingly. As Jeanne Mills, a defector from the Temple, writes, "I am faced with an unanswerable question: 'If the church was so bad, why did you and your family stay so long?'" This possibility can be answered through the concept of cognitive dissonance. As their participation expanded, members were required to sacrifice personal property and family relationships and to experience a host of undesirable events. Making such sacrifices would be irrational if the church and Jim Jones were bad. To reconcile the dissonance between the sacrifice and the worth of the church, members maintained the attitude that the church was good. As the sacrifices increased, so did their belief in the church. By the time Jim Jones called for mass suicide, many members were totally committed to him and the church, so their obedience was not too surprising.

Although the events of Jonestown provide a wealth of examples of conformity, compliance, and obedience, they may seem somewhat remote to your students. After all, many of the people in your classes may not have been born when the 1978 events took place. To bring the principles behind the events to the present, discuss how groups such as the Branch Davidians near Waco, Texas, the religious cultists who met their deaths in Switzerland in 1995, the mass suicide of the Heaven's Gate cult, or the members of the Japanese sect Aum Shinrikyo might have operated under similar conditions.

Festinger, L. (1957). *A theory of cognitive dissonance.* Stanford, CA: Stanford University Press.
Freedman, J. L., & Fraser, S. C. (1966). Compliance without pressure: The foot-in-the-door technique. *Journal of Personality and Social Psychology, 4*, 195-202.
Milgram, S. (1963). Behavioral study of obedience. *Journal of Abnormal and Social Psychology, 67*, 371-378.
Mills, J. (1979). *Six years with God.* New York: A & W Publishers.
Osherow, N. (1984). Making sense of the nonsensical: An analysis of Jonestown. In E. Aronson (Ed.), *Reading about the Social Animal*, 4th ed. New York: Freeman.

What Do You Think You're Doing?

A large part of social behavior involves asking the simple question, "What is that person doing?" A large part of self-perception relies on being able to answer the question, "What am I doing?" Dan Wegner and Robin Vallacher have proposed the theory of action identification to address how people might answer both these questions.

Actions are fundamentally ambiguous, in that they can be described in any number of ways. My actions in composing this paragraph, for example, could be identified as "writing," "assembling words," "offering suggestions," "doing what's necessary to get paid," "describing an idea," "typing letters of the alphabet," or "changing thoughts into pixels." Action identification theory starts with this observation, and the related idea that act identities can be arranged in a hierarchy. For any given action there are higher-level and lower-level explanations, although "high" and "low" are comparative terms defined by their relation to one another; thus "writing" is a higher-level identification than "typing letters of the alphabet," but lower than "offering suggestions." The theory goes on to state that when more than one act identity is available to a person, people tend to describe their behavior at relatively higher levels. However, when an action is performed poorly under one identity, the individual will adopt a lower-level identification for the action. When "offering suggestions" leads to incoherent writing, I might re-identify my actions as "typing actual English-language words." Tasks that are novel, difficult, or complex often prompt this retreat to a lower-level identification (Wegner, Vallacher, Macomber, Wood, & Arps, 1984).

From these simple postulates come two very intriguing predictions. First, the theory predicts the control of action. Adjusting between higher and lower level identities for the same action promotes the efficient execution of the task. Identifying at too high a level ("Finish this chapter") provides an inadequate guide for controlling behavior, whereas identifying at too low a level ("spell everything correctly") leads to premature disintegration of the action. Second, the theory predicts the emergence of new action. When people are forced to move from a higher level to a lower level of identification, there comes with the switch a revised understanding of their behavior and the establishment of new courses of action. When actions are maintained at a high level of identification, the emergence of new action is unlikely.

Action identification theory has been applied in a number of domains and empirical tests have supported its propositions. For example, Wegner, Vallacher, and Dizadji (1983) constructed a hierarchy of 50 identifications for the act of "drinking alcoholic beverages," along with instructions to rate each identification on a 1-7 scale according to how well it described the act. The survey was administered to a group of undergraduates (whose experiences with drinking varied widely) and to a group of inpatients at the Chicago Alcohol Treatment Center (who had a great deal of experience with alcohol consumption). A factor analysis revealed six factors that characterized the identifications: "rewarding myself," "getting drunk," "overcoming boredom," "relieving tension," "hurting myself," and a collection of relatively low-level identities, such as *lifting a glass, swallowing liquid,* or *experiencing a taste*. Further analyses revealed that the inpatient sample tended to identify this action at higher levels, such as "relieving tension" or "hurting myself," whereas the college sample opted for lower-level identifications. In other words, people who have performed the act infrequently tend to identify it in terms of its details, whereas those who are proficient skip the details and rush headlong toward more encompassing identities. It is precisely these higher-level identities that may make suppression of the act difficult.

In another case, however, lower-level identities sometimes were called for to successfully complete the task at hand. Participants delivered a speech to either an easy-to-persuade audience or a difficult-to-persuade audience, while thinking about their actions in either high-level (effects and implications) or low-level (mechanical details of the action) terms. Speakers made fewer speech errors when the task was identified at a high level and was personally easy, and when the task was personally difficult and identified at a low level. Identifying the action at the appropriate level produced better performance of the action.

Finally, the emergence of action can be seen in a study by Wegner, Vallacher, Macomber, Wood, and Arps (1984). Participants were invited to the laboratory to drink coffee (which was decaffeinated, unbeknownst to them). Some participants drank from a regular coffee cup, whereas others drank from a contraption meant to spur them to lower-level identifications. When the coffee cup was mounted on a tin can weighted with rocks, participants indeed had to retreat to identifications such as "moving my arm" or "bringing the cup to my lips." All participants then completed a questionnaire designed to bring them to a higher-level identification of the act. Some participants completed items suggesting coffee drinking could be seen as "making myself seek stimulation" whereas others had the identity of coffee drinking as "making myself avoid stimulation." The researchers predicted that those participants who drank from the disruptive cups (and consequently identified at a lower level) would emerge with the new high-level identification suggested by their questionnaire. This prediction was confirmed. Participants listened to music for an 8-minute period and were told to adjust the headphone volume knob to whatever level suited them. Those low-level identifiers who received the "seek stimulation" act identification reliably turned the volume up, just as their counterparts in the "avoid stimulation" condition reduced the volume. Those participants who had already identified "drinking coffee" at a high level showed no such tendencies. In short, the level of action identification predicted the emergence of new action.

Vallacher, R. R., & Wegner, D. M. (1985). *A theory of action identification*, Hillsdale, NJ: Erlbaum.
Vallacher, R. R., & Wegner, D. M. (1987). What do people think they're doing? Action identification and human behavior. *Psychological Review, 94*, 3-15.
Vallacher, R. R., Wegner, D. M., & Somoza, M. P. (1989). That's easy for you to say: Action identification and speech fluency. *Journal of Personality and Social Psychology, 56*, 199-208.
Wegner, D. M., Vallacher, R. R., & Dizadji, D. (1989). Do alcoholics know what they're doing? Identifications of the act of drinking. *Basic and Applied Social Psychology, 10*, 197-210.
Wegner, D. M., Vallacher, R. R., Macomber, G., Wood, R., & Arps, K. (1984). The emergence of action. *Journal of Personality and Social Psychology, 46*, 269-279.

Similarity and Attraction Revisited

Similarity--of attitudes, background, goals, beliefs, interests, values--has been shown to be a powerful predictor of interpersonal attraction. Robert Zajonc and his colleagues have investigated similarity and relationships from a slightly different perspective, with fascinating results.

Zajonc and his coworkers solicited photographs from couples in Michigan and Wisconsin who had lived together for 25 years. These couples were asked to supply photos taken when they were first involved with one another and more recently, after this long period of time together; many couples provided shots from their wedding and from their 25th anniversary. The photographs were cropped so that only the faces of the men and women were visible. This was done so that other cues such as clothing styles or background scenes were not visible. The shots of these men and women were then presented to groups of judges, whose task was a relatively simple one. Presented with the photo of a young woman, for example, and an array of 6 photographs of young men, participants were asked to simply match "who went with whom," or to identify the woman's spouse from the array of men. (The other combinations--male targets and female options, photos of the older partners, and so on--were also represented in the experimental design.)

As an antecedent of interpersonal attraction, the similarity thesis might predict that couples resembled one another early in their relationship, thereby drawing them together. This is not what Zajonc found, however. Raters were no better than chance at matching couples based on their young photographs. They were quite accurate, however, in matching the older photographs. At levels better than chance, participants could tell who resembled whom after 25 years of marriage. This couldn't be due to artifactual cues (scenes in the background, quality of the images) or methods of presentation, as these elements were carefully controlled. The conclusion is inescapable; these couples grew to look like one another in facial resemblance after years of marriage.

Zajonc offers some suggestions as to why this might occur. First, diet could reasonably be implicated. Couples tend to adopt the same dietary habits, so it is possible that years of eating high- or low-fat diets could lead to similar fatty deposits in the face, in turn producing greater physical resemblance. However, a rank correlation between weight and age failed to support this notion. Another possibility is that environmental factors could have played a role. Twenty-five years of living in Texas, for example, could produce the leathery skin cues that distinguish one couple from another hailing from the Minnesota tundra. However, all participants came from the same Midwestern background, limiting the impact of environmental as well as income, cohort, or socioeconomic factors.

The explanation preferred by Zajonc and his colleagues is based on empathic responding and its effects on facial musculature. Most couples share some modicum of empathy for one another. The joys and sorrows of one partner typically are matched in the expression of the other partner, such that when one spouse beams with news of a pleasant event the other spouse responds in kind, grinning from ear to ear. This matching of facial actions--expressions of happiness at another's happiness, sadness at a partner's sorrow, and all points in between--multiplied by 25 years, may indeed etch the kinds of muscular and skin tone changes that produce greater resemblance. Bolstering this explanation, Zajonc found that when the original partners who supplied the photographs were surveyed, those who bore the greatest resemblance (and hence, who were likely to have experienced greater empathic responding) rated themselves as more satisfied with their relationships.

Besides being a novel take on the similarity thesis, Zajonc's study has important implications for your students. Ask them to conjure an image of the person they're currently dating or interested in. Concentrate on it......mull it over.....take a good long look: Do they *really* want to look like that person 25 years from now?!

Zajonc, R. B., Adelmann, P. K., Murphy, S. T., & Niedenthal, P. M. (1987). Convergence in the physical appearance of spouses. *Motivation and Emotion, 11,* 335-346.

Miss America Meets the Smurfs

Chapter 14 briefly discusses the role of physical attractiveness in interpersonal relations, although a consideration of what people find attractive is omitted. Michael Cunningham and his colleagues offer some sociobiological suggestions as to what the sexes find attractive in one another.

Cunningham assembled a collection of photographs of women taken from college yearbooks and from Miss Universe contestants, and asked college men to rate the women's attractiveness. The experimenters also took physiognomic measurements of the women's faces, assessing such dimensions as midface length, nostril width, pupil width, facial length, separation of eyes, width of smile, width of face at cheekbones, width of face at mouth, height of forehead, width of cheeks, thickness of upper lip, and so on. Women who possessed certain features usually associated with children (e.g., small chin, small nose, relatively large eyes widely spaced) were rated as highly attractive. Also attractive were prominent cheekbones and narrow cheeks, as well as high eyebrows and a wide smile. There was also some cross-cultural generality, given that the Miss Universe contestants came from a range of countries and in fact had been selected for their attractiveness by a multinational panel.

Cunningham explains these preferences for features using a sociobiological approach. Indicators of neotany (i.e., relatively childlike features) may signal that the bearer is friendly, fertile, and healthy, as well as elicit responses for caregiving and affection. (The Smurfs, Bambi, E.T., Snuggles the Fabric Soft Bear, and black velvet paintings of children with large, dewy eyes have all capitalized on this effect.) Indicators of maturity (such as high cheekbones), when combined with neonate features, may signal that the woman is at an optimal age for mating. Indicators of expressiveness (such as large eyes and wide smiles) may cue sociability and receptiveness. Although all three sets of indicators were present in the judgments made by the college men, neonate features predominated.

A subsequent study examined the attractiveness choices of women judging men. Following the same strategy, Cunningham and his colleagues asked college women to rate the attractiveness of photographs of men taken from college yearbooks. When later compared to physiognomic measurements, it seemed women followed a multiple-motive strategy. Although women found the neotenous feature of large eyes to be attractive, they were also drawn by maturity cues (such as prominent cheekbones and a large chin) and expressive features (such as a big smile and high-status clothing). These multiple motives suggest that women seek an optimal combination of features, altogether signaling fitness for reproduction and capacity to provide for needs.

Cunningham, M. R. (1986). Measuring the physical in physical attractiveness: Quasi-experiments on the sociobiology of female facial beauty, *Journal of Personality and Social Psychology, 50,* 925-935.

Cunningham, M. R., Barbee, A. P., & Pike, C. L. (1990). What do women want? Facialmetric assessment of multiple motives in the perception of male facial physical attractiveness, *Journal of Personality and Social Psychology, 59,* 61-72.

A Peg and a Grasshopper

What do a peg and a grasshopper have in common? Cognitive dissonance. Chapter 14 discusses dissonance theory in regard to cognitive consistency and attitude change. Two classic studies will illuminate dissonance theory further.

Leon Festinger and James M. Carlsmith provided one of the first, and one of the best, demonstrations of the induced compliance paradigm for studying cognitive dissonance. Seventy-one college men reported for a two-hour experiment on "measures of performance." With little fanfare the participants were asked to use one hand to remove 12 spools from a tray, and then refill it. This mundane task lasted about half an hour, only to be followed by an equally mundane task. Participants were presented with an array of 48 pegs sunk into a board, and asked to move each of them a quarter-turn at a time, until they were returned to their original position. After half an hour of this, all participants were quite bored, frustrated, and in a fairly negative mood; precisely the condition Festinger and Carlsmith wanted them in.

All participants were then told that there was a second part to the study. At this point, they were informed, a confederate usually came in to convince the next waiting subject of how fun, exciting, and interesting the tasks were. The participants are told that, unfortunately, this person hadn't shown up today, and so they were asked if they would be willing to do this job. Half the participants were told they would be paid $1 for their help, whereas the remainder were to be given $20 for their assistance. All participants agreed to help, conveyed the information to the waiting subject, and as they were leaving their attitudes toward the experiment were measured. In keeping with the predictions of dissonance theory, those participants who had been paid $1 reported enjoying the task much more than those who had been paid $20. Given that their behavior could not be revoked, and that $1 was an insufficient justification for telling the lie, the only option available to reduce dissonance was to bring their attitudes in line with their behavior.

Phil Zimbardo and his colleagues extended this work on induced compliance in a novel way. ROTC members, military reservists, and college students took part in a study of novel foods. Cast as a study relevant to the "new mobile military," participants were informed that the study sought to determine liking for fried grasshoppers. The procedures and information were delivered in one of two ways. In the "Mr. Nice" condition, the experimenter warmly greeted the participants and appeared sensitive to their needs, and interacted well with his coworkers. "Mr. Nasty," on the other hand, was gruff and surly, and berated his assistants. Although many participants ate at least one grasshopper, those in the "Mr. Nasty" condition professed much greater liking for grasshoppers as food. The dissonance produced between disliking grasshoppers and eating them could not be reduced by recourse to the experimenter; after all, he was a jerk. The only avenue available to the participants was to bring their attitudes in line with their behavior.

Festinger, L., & Carlsmith, J. M. (1959). Cognitive consequences of forced compliance. *Journal of Abnormal and Social Psychology, 58*, 203-210.

Zimbardo, P. G., Weisenberg, M., Firestone, I., & Levy, B. (1965). Communicator effectiveness in producing public conformity and private attitude change. *Journal of Personality, 33*, 233-255.

An Eight-Ball and a Cockroach

What do an eight-ball and a cockroach have in common? Social facilitation. What do social facilitation and social inhibition have in common? Robert Zajonc. These riddles may sound bizarre, but there is a theme that connects them. It's the story of social facilitation, a cornerstone of social psychology.

Norman Triplett is reported to have conducted the first social psychology experiment in 1897 on a topic of some concern to social psychologists: What happens to an individual's behavior when other people are watching it transpire? Triplett thought that task performance should be improved (i.e., the presence of others makes us do better at the task), and demonstrated it through his observations of racing cyclists and children reeling in fishing line. Social facilitation, as this effect came to be called, seemed entrenched in social psychology....until Floyd Allport came along. Gordon's older brother, among others, promoted the idea of social inhibition, or that the presence of others should hinder the task performance of an individual. In short, social facilitation and social inhibition were at loggerheads for much of the ensuing history of social psychology....until Robert Zajonc came along. Zajonc proposed that arousal was the mechanism underlying both facilitation and inhibition. The presence of other people is arousing, because of evaluation apprehension, audience effects, and so on. What we do with that heightened arousal, however, is a function of the task at hand. If the task is well-learned, dominant, easy, or something we're good at, the arousal produced by the presence of others should cause us to do better at the task, thus producing a social facilitation effect. However, if the task is novel, difficult, poorly learned, or not high in our repertoire, the arousal produced by the presence of others should cause us to perform the task worse, thus producing a social inhibition effect.

Zajonc was instrumental in synthesizing these competing viewpoints. But what about the 8-ball? In a novel extension of this theory, James Michaels and his colleagues examined social facilitation in the poolroom. Players in a college student union were identified as either above average (making at least two-thirds of their shots) or below average (making no more than one-third of their shots) by a team of raters. The research team of four students then walked to the table to watch the players shoot. In the presence of others the above average players improved their performance, moving from about 70 percent of their shots made (when not observed) to about 80 percent; social facilitation was at work. Those players who were below average suffered the effects of social inhibition. Their accuracy dropped from about 36 percent to 24 percent of shots made when a crowd was watching.

So where do the cockroaches figure in? In probably the most novel extension of all Zajonc demonstrated that facilitation and inhibition were not limited to humans. He placed cockroaches on either runways (a simple task) or in mazes (a complex task) and measured their running speed when either alone or in the presence of a gallery of other roaches. Supporting previous research, the presence of other roaches did indeed facilitate performance on the runway task whereas it hampered performance in the mazes. This same effect has been demonstrated in other species, suggesting that an arousal-based explanation is correct. Now, if only the roaches would get off the pool table...

Michaels, J. W., Blommel, J. M., Brocato, R. M., Linkous, R. A., & Rowe, J. S. (1982). Social facilitation and inhibition in natural setting. *Replications in Social Psychology, 2*, 21-24.

Zajonc, R. B. (1968). Social facilitation in cockroaches. In E. C. Simmel, R. A. Hoppe, & G. A. Milton (Eds.), *Social facilitation and imitative behavior.* Boston: Allyn and Bacon.

Zajonc, R. B., Heingartner, A., & Herman, E. M. (1969). Social enhancement and impairment of performance in the cockroach, *Journal of Personality and Social Psychology, 13*, 82-92.

Social Perception and Social Goals

Chapter 14 discusses cultural differences in attribution, focusing on ways in which different cultures may subscribe more or less to the attribution tendencies of Americans. Doug Krull has recently demonstrated that the inferential goals of the perceiver determine the types of attributions made about the perceived, and his research suggests a link to a broader cultural context.

Western views of the attribution process, and particularly the correspondence bias, emphasize determining "what the person is like." Fritz Heider is often held responsible for this emphasis, although actually he only suggested that people might be more interested in ascertaining an individual's dispositions as a shortcut to determining the person's behavior patterns. Clearly, attributions can be made about situations, although until recently no one studying the attribution process has devoted much attention to this issue.

Krull gave some of his participants/perceivers the goal of estimating a target's disposition. Following the stages of social perception, perceivers first characterized the target as having dispositional characteristics that correspond to the behavior observed, then corrected that estimate for situational contributions to the behavior. Other research participants, however, were given the explicit goal of inferring a situation based on the target's behavior. These perceivers first characterized the situation as corresponding to the behavior, then adjusted this estimate for the contribution of the target's disposition. In short, we are not inexorably bound to draw dispositional inferences about those we encounter; when our goal is to understand situations (rather then persons), we can do so in a manner that parallels more conventional attribution processes.

Cultures vary in the degree to which they endorse individualism or collectivism. It is not surprising that Western cultures, which embrace an individualistic viewpoint, have generated research supporting the correspondence bias of overestimating dispositional causes of behavior. When attention is focused primarily on individuals, it is likely that our goal will be to match dispositions to a given behavior. Among cultures that are more collectivist, however, we may see an emphasis on inferring situations based on behavior. Such cultures are more likely to view the actions of an individual as part of the overall stream of behavior; therefore, the attribution process within these cultures may be quite different, and along the lines that Krull has demonstrated.

Krull, D. S. (1993). Does the grist change the mill? The effect of the perceiver's inferential goal on the process of social inference, *Personality and Social Psychology Bulletin, 19,* 340-348.

demonstrations

The Actor-Observer Effect

Chapter 14 notes that although we tend to attribute others' behavior to personal or dispositional factors, we typically attribute our own behavior to situational factors. This well-known attribution bias, better known as the actor-observer effect, can be readily demonstrated in class by using an activity suggested by Mary Kite. Photocopy and distribute two copies of Handout 15-1 to each student. Ask them to fill out the questionnaire twice, once for a well-known celebrity (e.g., Katie Couric, Michael Jackson, Heather Locklear, Michael Jordan, etc.) and once for themselves. After students have completed both questionnaires, ask them to count the number of times they chose "depends on the situation" for themselves versus for the well-known celebrity. If your results are consistent with the actor-observer effect (they almost always are), you should find that students are much more willing to ascribe a trait to someone else than they are for themselves. Ask them to explain why this is the case (e.g., they see themselves behaving in a variety of different situations, whereas they typically only see the celebrities' on-camera persona). You can also expand this demonstration by having students complete the questionnaire using their best friend as the target person; this will nicely demonstrate that attributions are affected by the degree to which we know someone personally.

Kite, M. E. (1991). Observer biases in the classroom. *Teaching of Psychology, 18,* 161-164.

The Self-Serving Bias

The text describes "defensive attribution" as the tendency to attribute our successes to internal or personal factors but to attribute our failures to situational factors beyond our control. Also known as the "self-serving bias," this bias accounts for the consistent human tendency to take credit for success but to deny responsibility for failure (e.g., doing well on an exam because of innate brilliance or studying hard versus failing an exam because it was unfair or tricky; winning a game because of athletic prowess versus losing a game because "the referees were blind"). Dunn (1989) notes that students often have trouble recognizing the self-serving attributional bias in their own behavior, especially when it extends beyond the internal-external dimension related to success and failure on a particular task. To illustrate this bias to your students in a context other than task success or failure, try the following exercise suggested by Dunn. At the end of the class period prior to the one in which you'll introduce the self-serving bias, tell students that during the next class you will be talking about the self-concept and that you want to collect some data to use in that discussion. Ask them to take out a sheet of paper and to draw a line down the middle. Tell them to label one column "strengths" and the other "weaknesses" and then to list their personal strengths and weaknesses. Emphasize that their responses are anonymous and that they should not put their name on the sheet. Collect the sheets and before the next class compute the mean number of strengths and weaknesses listed. Your students should consistently list more strengths than weaknesses. You can then use these results to generate a discussion of the self-serving bias, including the processes that might contribute to its occurrence and its potential positive and/or negative effects on behavior. Dunn also suggested that you could perform this exercise simply by having students verbally volunteer strengths and weaknesses and recording their responses on the board. If you use this public method, Dunn cautioned to be sure to point out that the variety of responses may be limited by which students participated and self-presentational concerns present in a public setting.

Dunn, D. S. (1989). Demonstrating a self-serving bias. *Teaching of Psychology, 16,* 21-22.

Identifying Persuasion Techniques

Makosky (1985) argued that most introductory textbooks tend to focus on persuasion issues such as communicator attributes, whether the message is one- or two-sided, and aspects of the audience like attention and prior opinions concerning the message. She noted, however, that advertising makes use of additional persuasion techniques that may not be included in the textbook. Therefore, she proposed an exercise designed to expose the student to common techniques used in advertising. The techniques suggested for discussion and analysis by Makosky (1985) were:

1. an *appeal to or creation of needs*--Makosky suggested describing this technique through reference to Maslow's hierarchy of needs (biological, safety and security, belonging and love, self-esteem and status, cognitive, aesthetic, and self-actualization).

2. *social and prestige suggestion*--these are techniques based on the premise that you should buy or do something because many others do so (social suggestion) or some well-known person makes a recommendation (prestige suggestion).

3. *loaded words and images*--Makosky noted that these tend to be more subtle techniques, including the use of attractive people in the advertisement, images of positive social situations associated with a product, or incorporating "buzzwords" such as "natural" for food and beauty products.

Using the techniques of persuasion described above, you need to find a set of advertisements that illustrate one or more of the types. The advertisements can either be recorded television commercials, print advertisements made into slides (or photocopied and made into packets), or both. After reviewing the types of persuasion techniques using several sample advertisements, hand out an answer sheet numbered 1 to 20 with the three types of persuasion listed next to each number. Tell the students that you are going to show them a series of 20 advertisements, and they are to indicate which types of persuasion, if any, are depicted in each by circling the name of the stereotype. After showing the advertisements, go over and discuss the students' responses to each. Makosky also suggested several variations such as examining the types of persuasion techniques used as a function of the cost of the magazine (expensive versus cheap) and the intended audience (male or female).

Makosky, V. P. (1985). Identifying major techniques of persuasion. *Teaching of Psychology*, 12, 42-43.

Reprinted from Hill, W. G. (1995). Instructor's resource manual for *Psychology* by S. F. Davis and J. J. Palladino. Englewood Cliffs, NJ: Prentice Hall.

Gender Stereotypes in Advertising

You might also explore with your students the role advertisements play in the development and perpetuation of gender-role stereotypes. Jones (1991) noted that an analysis of advertisements by Goffman (1976) found numerous instances of subtle stereotyping including:

1. *functional ranking* - the tendency to depict men in executive roles and as more functional when collaborating with women,
2. *relative size* - the tendency to depict men as taller and larger than women, except when women are clearly superior in social status,
3. *ritualization of subordination* - an overabundance of images of women lying on floors and beds or as objects of men's mock assaults,
4. *the feminine touch* - the tendency to show women cradling and caressing the surface of objects with their fingers, and
5. *family* - fathers depicted as physically distant from their families or as relating primarily to sons, and mothers depicted as relating primarily to daughters.

Using the types of stereotyping listed above, you need to find a set of advertisements that illustrate one or more of the types and preferably have them made into slides (or, if your class is relatively small, you can make photocopied packets of the ads and use them in future classes). Jones indicated that she found it relatively easy to find examples in magazines such as *Cosmopolitan, Glamour, Newsweek,* and *Vogue.* She also recommended combining advertisements from the 1950s with more current advertisements to allow the comparisons of different trends in gender stereotyping over time. You can also include advertisements that illustrate nontraditional or innovative gender-role portrayals as well as ads that do not incorporate gender stereotypes at all. After reviewing Goffman's types of gender stereotyping (it is best to write them on the board) and providing several sample advertisements, ask students to take out a blank sheet of paper and number it from 1 to 20. Tell students that you are going to show them a series of 20 advertisements, and they are to indicate which types of gender stereotyping, if any, are depicted in each ad. After showing the advertisements, go over them and discuss students' responses to each. Jones suggested that class discussion can focus on how advertisements influence gender stereotypes as well as changes in stereotypes over time (if you included advertisements from the 1950s), and how other sources (such as television or the workplace) contribute to gender stereotyping.

Basow, S. A. (1986). *Gender stereotypes: Traditions and alternatives.* Pacific Grove, CA: Brooks/Cole.
Jones, M. (1991). Gender stereotyping in advertisements. *Teaching of Psychology, 18,* 231-233.

Adapted from Hill, W. G. (1995). Instructor's resource manual for *Psychology* by S. F. Davis and J. J. Palladino. Englewood Cliffs, NJ: Prentice Hall.

Inducing Cognitive Dissonance

Carkenord and Bullington (1993) suggest a simple exercise that helps students better understand the phenomenon of cognitive dissonance by experiencing it first-hand in class. In this exercise, cognitive dissonance is induced by comparing students' attitudes and behaviors on a variety of social issues. Prior to your discussion of cognitive dissonance, draw a 5-point Likert scale on the board ranging from (1) *strongly disagree* to (5) *strongly agree.* Then, ask students to take out a blank piece of paper and to indicate the extent to which they agree or disagree with a series of statements that you will read aloud (by writing a number from 1 to 5 corresponding to the scale). Carkenord and Bullington suggest using the following statements:

1. World hunger is a serious problem that needs attention.
2. Our country needs to address the growing number of homeless.
3. The right to vote is one of the most valuable rights of American citizens.
4. Our government should spend less money on nuclear weapons and more on helping citizens better their lives.

Then, ask students to turn their papers over and to answer the next series of questions by responding "Yes" or "No" according to whether they "perform the behavior on a regular basis." This series of behavioral questions corresponds to the previous attitudinal items:

1. Do you personally do anything to lessen world hunger (e.g., donate money or food or write your representative)?
2. Do you personally do anything to help the homeless (e.g., volunteer at a homeless shelter or donate money)?
3. Did you vote in the last election for which you were eligible?
4. Do you personally convey your feelings to the government (e.g., by writing your representative or by participating in protests/marches)?

After students have completed both series of questions, have them back to Side 1 and ask them (by a show of hands) how many agreed or strongly agreed with attitudinal Item 1. Next, ask them to turn their papers over and to raise their hands if they responded "Yes" to the corresponding behavioral item. Repeat this process for all four questions. Students generally get the point of this exercise very quickly. In most cases, a majority of students will agree with or show positive attitudes toward the issue, but only a small minority will actually report behavior consistent with those attitudes. Carkenord and Bullington suggest that the discussion should focus on (a) how these inconsistencies made students feel, (b) formal definitions for consonance and dissonance, (c) research on cognitive dissonance (including Festinger and Carlsmith's famous study), and (d) strategies for reducing dissonance.

Carkenord, D. M., & Bullington, J. (1993). Bringing cognitive dissonance to the classroom. *Teaching of Psychology, 20*, 41-43.

Demonstrating Obedience

William Hunter (1981) noted that many students have difficulty believing the results of Milgram's study on obedience to authority. He proposed a simple demonstration designed to illustrate in a more personal manner the concept of obedience. Prior to discussing obedience and the Milgram studies, you should enter the classroom and make sure that everyone is seated. Then go through a series of increasingly bizarre requests with your students. Examples of possible requests are given below (feel free to substitute or add your own ideas here):

- ask students to switch seats with another student
- have everyone remove their shoes and place them in a pile at the front of the room
- ask students to take off their watch and exchange it with one other person
- ask students to do jumping jacks in order to loosen up
- ask students to rub their tummy while patting their head (and vice-versa)
- ask students to do the wave (this one is actually very neat in a large class)
- ask students to quack like a duck or to sing a silly song
- ask students to come up with a class cheer (e.g., "We've got spirit yes we do, we've got spirit how 'bout you?") and yell it in unison several times as loud as they can

End your session with a big round of applause, and then, after everyone has returned to their seat, ask them why they complied with the sequence of behaviors you requested of them. Once students recognize that they responded to requests made by an authority figure (i.e., because you are the professor), Hunter suggests focusing the discussion on issues such as attributes of authority figures, why we obey authority, whether we should always obey authority, how a person gets authority, and what society would be like without authority. This exercise is a real crowd-pleaser; besides being invigorating and entertaining, it helps students relate the seemingly unreal circumstances of the Milgram experiment to their own real-life experiences. It also tends to cure the "I would never obey an authority without good reason" feeling that students often have when hearing about Milgram's results for the first time.

Hunter, W. J. (1981). Obedience to authority. In L. T. Benjamin, Jr. & K. D. Lowman (Eds.), *Activities handbook for the teaching of psychology* (pp. 149-150). Washington, DC: American Psychological Association.

Deindividuation

David Dodd describes a highly effective and entertaining exercise that illustrates the concept of deindividuation discussed in the text. According to Dodd, the object of this exercise is to demonstrate that even normal, well-adjusted college students are capable of deviant, antisocial behavior given the right situational conditions (e.g., feelings of anonymity and nonresponsibility). Have your students respond anonymously to the following question:

> If you could be totally invisible for 24 hours and were completely assured that you would not be detected or held responsible for your actions, what would you do?

Ask students to record their responses on a blank sheet of paper (they should disguise their handwriting by printing neatly) and to fold their papers before turning them in. Collect students' answers and randomly select several to read aloud. At this point, students will react excitedly in anticipation of the results. Indeed, laughter usually erupts as common themes emerge, including criminal acts ("rob a bank" is often the single most popular response), sexual acts, and spying or eavesdropping. Although occasional charitable responses (e.g., resolving wars, ending world hunger) are revealed, antisocial acts typical outnumber prosocial ones. Dodd also likes to point out to his classes that the average number of antisocial responses given by his college students (36%) is no different than the number of antisocial responses given by inmates at a maximum security prison where he once taught.

Dodd, D. (1985). Robbers in the classroom: A deindividuation exercise. *Teaching of Psychology, 12*, 89-91.

Demonstrating Group Polarization

Peter Gray (1993) suggests a simple exercise that readily demonstrates the group polarization effect. Before lecturing on group decision making in Chapter 14, have your students declare on a Likert scale how strongly they agree or disagree with some statement or idea (Gray suggests the idea that the next exam should be essay rather than multiple choice). Collect the responses and divide students into like-minded groups for a short, 5-minute discussion. After the group discussion, have students rate their agreement with the proposition again on the same Likert scale. The results should be consistent with group polarization: those who initially agreed should agree more strongly after group discussion, and those who initially disagreed should disagree even more strongly after group discussion. According to Gray, asking your students to speculate about the causes of the effect should generate the same explanations generated by psychologists over the years (i.e., that members are exposed to new, persuasive arguments, and that members gradually take a more extreme position in order to be viewed positively by others). An added benefit is that, in addition to learning the group polarization effect in a memorable way, students learn that they can successfully "think like psychologists" in generating plausible explanations for observed events.

Gray, P. (1993). Engaging students' intellects: The immersion approach to critical thinking in psychological instruction. *Teaching of Psychology, 20*, 68-74.

Is This Sexual Harassment?

A discussion of leadership unfortunately brings with it a discussion of when leadership fails. Robin Warshaw, writing in *Exec* magazine, presents several cases brought before public hearing examiners. Share these with your students and use them as a basis for discussing the definition and identification of sexual harassment and it's relation to leadership and group processes.

Case 1: Several employees of the Securities and Exchange Commission, including supervisors, were having romantic affairs with one another. This included holding frequent parties and leaving the office during the day to go drinking. A female attorney who did not participate in these activities claimed that she was harassed by the environment in which she had to work, and additionally charged that women who had affairs with male supervisors were rewarded with promotions and bonuses. The woman admitted that no one had pressured her for sex, nor had she been denied any promotions because she didn't participate in the activities of the others.

Ruling and Analysis: A judge ruled that although the woman was not harassed on a *quid pro quo* basis, the SEC office was nonetheless an offensive work environment. She was awarded back pay, a promotion, and her choice of two jobs. Although socializing at the office routinely takes place, the Carnival of the Senses set up in the SEC office went beyond the bounds of typical social interaction.

Case 2: A severe snowstorm sent workers at a Virginia corporation home early. A female word-processing technician needed a ride, and a male engineer (for whom she'd done some work) readily offered to take her in his four-wheel drive vehicle. When they arrived at her apartment the man entered with her and, according to him, only kissed her. The woman charged that he tried to kiss and fondle her, despite her protestations. She complained to her employer, who reprimanded the man and warned him that he would be fired if he did anything like that in the future.

Ruling and Analysis: Was this simply a case of a clumsy but mild-intentioned man looking for companionship? Doubtful. The woman's attorneys demonstrated in court that the corporation had received similar complaints about similar behavior involving this man. The employer made an out-of-court settlement after the court ruled that the company had a legal responsibility to prevent such actions from happening. According to Louise Fitzgerald of the University of Illinois at Champaign, this type of predatory unwanted attention is common; 15% of working women in one of Fitzgerald's research studies had been the object of unwanted kissing, grabbing, touching, or fondling.

Case 3: Obscene cartoons depicting a female coworker (by name) engaged in various sex acts were posted in the men's room of her office building. These remained in the public bathroom for a week, even after the company's chief executive had seen them. They were removed only after he learned that the woman was upset about the cartoons.

Ruling and Analysis: The court determined that the cartoons were "highly offensive" and an impediment to the woman's dealing "with fellow employees and clients in a professional manner." The matter could have been helped had the cartoons been taken down immediately, but male allies of women are often rare in work settings. Men may feel they are breaking ranks or not being "one of the boys." This particular situation was made worse by the company's chief executive's ignorance and inaction. The employer paid the woman's full salary and psychiatric bills until she found a new job.

Warshaw, R. (1993). Is *this* sexual harassment? *Exec, Summer*, 62-65.

Group Processes

Gardner (1980) proposed an activity that can be used to demonstrate several of the principles related to group processes and decision making described in the text. After randomly dividing the class into groups of five or six students each, instruct the groups to take a few minutes and select a leader. Next, distribute the problem scenario described by Gardner (reproduced in Handout 15-2) and go over the basic problem and instructions with the groups. After the groups have had sufficient time to arrive at their solution, lead the class in a discussion focusing on characteristics of group processes and decision making by having them analyze how their groups arrived at a decision. As part of your discussion, group members should explore: how they selected a group leader (e.g., Was the leader task-oriented or relationship-oriented?), how difficult it was to make a decision, whether everyone agreed with the final decision or whether there were conformity pressures added, whether there was any evidence of group polarization or Groupthink, and how they arrived at their final decision (e.g., Did a few individuals dominate the discussion? Were concessions made?).

Gardner, R. M. (1980). *Exercises for general psychology*. Minneapolis, MN: Burgess Publishing.

Reprinted from Hill, W. G. (1995). Instructor's resource manual for *Psychology* by S. F. Davis and J. J. Palladino. Englewood Cliffs, NJ: Prentice Hall.

student assignments

Lookin' For Love

Chapter 14 mentions some of the antecedents of interpersonal attraction, such as similarity, proximity, and physical attractiveness. This assignment gives your students experience at spotting these antecedents at work in real life. Have your students scan the personal ads of your local newspaper or weekly circular for evidence that everyday laypeople use the antecedents social psychologists have identified as being predictors of interpersonal attraction. The procedure for this brief written assignment can be as informal or elaborate as you'd like to make it. For example, we've had success by simply asking students to scan the ads and identify the most common antecedents used (similarity tends to be far and away most common: "I'm XYandZ, looking for same;" "I like this-n-that, hope you do too;" "Are you just like me? Let's meet"). From there students discuss any patterns that they see, such as gender differences in the qualities advertised by the seeker and/or looked for in a partner, or differences in heterosexual versus homosexual ads, or simply examples of the different antecedents and what makes them effective. A more elaborate project might involve taking a random sample of ads and content analyzing them for common themes. In the past we've had students voluntarily compute statistics on an entire page of ads, giving frequencies for the number of times similarity, proximity, or physical characteristics were mentioned, by whom, for whom, and in what context. Personal ads are essentially archival data, and as such they can be analyzed with as much or as little sophistication as your students can handle. Regardless of the approach you adopt, have your students look at the Big Picture. Rather than merely listing examples of cute or clever ads, ask them to focus on what these ads reveal about lay conceptions of what works and what doesn't when looking for love.

Sometimes You Gotta Break the Rules

Social norms are the invisible glue that keeps societies together. As implicit rules for social behavior, norms are really only noticed when they are violated. This assignment asks your students to do just that: Break a social norm that everyone typically obeys.

Explain to students that they should observe a variety of social norms in action for a few days, then choose one to violate. They should break the norm several times, rather than once, and in a variety of settings involving different people. Examples of some norm violations are: sitting right next to a stranger in an otherwise empty movie theater; violating gender roles, such as a man wearing a dress; raising both hands simultaneously to ask a professor a question; looking at other riders rather than the floor numbers in an elevator; singing out loud in public; conspicuously taking more than the maximum number of items to the grocery express check-out lane; impinging on someone's personal space; asking a stranger to take her or his seat on the bus; being excessively helpful or excessively disclosive in response to a stranger's simple request.

Be clear about some ground rules. First, students should not do anything illegal, unethical, dangerous, or obnoxious; pointless antics that waste other people's time or money, or that might be threatening to others, are not allowed. Second, students should give a clear definition of what the norm is, and how their behavior would violate it; there are lots of bizarre behaviors students could perform, but many of them would not violate any implicit social rule. Third, students may want to run their ideas by you before they engage in the behavior, to get an objective opinion about the first two points. In their written reports on this project students should address these questions: What were the reactions of other people as you broke the norm? How did you feel as you broke the norm? What function does the norm serve in society? How does it keep interaction flowing smoothly? What might have happened if you violated this norm in a different culture or subculture?

Social Psychology in Literature: *Erewhon*

Don Osborn (1990) recommends the use of the novel *Erewhon* to demonstrate the universality of social psychological insights. Samuel Butler's (1972/1983) utopian tale of a sheep farmer who stumbles upon a strange and mysterious land populated by beautiful natives provides the backdrop for numerous social psychological principles, including interpersonal attraction, similarity, causal attribution, cognitive consistency, and the importance of values, among others. For this assignment, ask your students to read *Erewhon* and then to write a short paper applying as many of the social psychological principles from the text and lecture as they can.

Butler, S. (1983). *Erewhon*. New York: Penguin books. (Original work published in 1872).

Osborn, D. R. (1990). Samuel Butler's *Erewhon* as social psychology. *Teaching of Psychology, 17*, 115-117.

Gender Roles in Film: *Tootsie*

Dustin Hoffman stars in this hilarious 1982 comedy as a struggling actor who, unable to find work as a man, masquerades as a woman in order to land a part on a daytime soap opera. When he gets the part, he is forced to play the role of a woman full time, both on screen and off. Although this premise is not a new one, it makes for good comedy and yields several interesting insights about differences between the sexes. Ask your students to write a paper revealing these insights; they should have no problem discussing numerous instances in the film and how they relate to gender roles and gender stereotypes. For example, what stereotypes are depicted in the film? In what ways (nonverbal as well as verbal) is *Michael's* behavior different from *Dorothy's*? What does Michael's portrayal of Dorothy reveal about how men view women? How do examples from the film map onto real-world gender differences (as revealed by research) in behavior? (Columbia/TriStar; 116 min)

Ethnicity and Subculture in Film: *Boyz in the Hood*

John Singleton (1991) directed Cuba Gooding and Larry Fishburne in this emotionally charged portrayal of a father's attempt to keep his oldest son out of trouble in South Central Los Angeles. This insightful film painfully yet clearly depicts the poverty, crime, and gangs that come with living in the inner city, and in doing so humanizes for the rest of us the struggle faced by the young, urban poor. It also effectively shows diversity within the tough African-American neighborhood, as we see examples of people trying, with honor and dignity, to make a better life for themselves. As a thought-provoking assignment, ask your students to watch this film (perhaps again; many will have already seen it) and to write a paper relating it to the concepts discussed in Chapter 16. In addition, students should try to make some kind of larger statement about the societal-level factors influencing this community. What kind of attributions do students make for the struggles of the urban poor? Can they identify any of the structural conditions that may prevent young Black males from "making it" (e.g., a long history of discrimination; living in constant fear of the threat of violence; lack of economic opportunities)? Would they describe these young men's sense of ethnic identity as positive or negative? What kind of role models are available in this subculture? (Columbia/TriStar; 112 min)

Social Psychology in Film

There are a number of films, both classic and recent, that contain many of the major social psychological themes covered in Chapter 14. As a fun and enlightening paper assignment, ask students to apply social psychological concepts from the text and lecture to any one of the terrific films suggested below.

• *Defending Your Life* (1991). Meryl Streep and Albert Brooks star in this hilarious comedy as two recently-deceased souls who are called upon to defend their lives in order to be sent to heaven.

Attribution theory, social comparison, and interpersonal attraction are central social psychological principles in this film (Paramount; 112 min).

• *Europa, Europa* (1983). A foreign film (based on a true story) about a 13-year-old Jewish boy's fight to escape from the Nazis during World War II. Highly acclaimed, and highly engrossing. Prejudice and discrimination, attitude change, and cognitive dissonance are a few of the many relevant concepts (Orion; 115 min).

• *Guess Who's Coming to Dinner?* (1967). Spencer Tracy, Katherine Hepburn, Sidney Poitier, and Katherine Houghton star in this academy award-winning film about interracial dating. When an African-American man is invited by an upper class White woman to her politically liberal family home, her parents discover that it isn't always easy to "practice what you preach." Impression formation, attitude change, stereotypes, and prejudice play a central role in this excellent film. A must see (Columbia/TriStar; 108 min).

• *Lords of Discipline* (1986). David Keith stars in this engaging drama that chronicles the operations of a secret society within a young men's military academy. Conformity and obedience, hostility and aggression, and intergroup conflict are central, social psychological principles in this film, among others (Paramount; 116 min).

• *Twelve Angry Men* (1957). Henry Fonda stars in this tense, compelling courtroom drama in which jurors must decide the fate of a boy accused of murdering his father. As the lone not-guilty vote in a seemingly cut-and-dried case, he gradually and methodically builds a case to win over the other jurors. This engrossing film provides excellent coverage of conformity, attitude change, and group decision making (MGM/UA; 93 min).

video

ABC News/Prentice Hall Video Library

The Breaking Point (15 min, Series III). Shannon Faulkner, Kim Messer, and Jeannie Mentavlos may not be household names, but their experiences have secured them a place in history. Faulkner was the first woman admitted to The Citadel, that bastion of all-male tradition, followed closely by Messer and Mentavlos. This *20/20* segment focuses on Messer's experiences while there and the forces that drove her out.

Don't Get Me Involved (12 min, Series III). This complicated tale revolves around a simple beginning; the failure to offer help when it is clearly called for. 20/20's Deborah Roberts interviews the principal actors in this account of death and indifference.

Other Sources

The Adult Years: Continuity and Change Series--Love and Marriage (28 min, PENN). Describes "six integral elements of love" and examines how they change during the lifespan.

Beyond Macho (26 min, HUMSCI). Examines men's changing roles in society, with emphasis on the "suburban househusband." Looks generally at sex roles in transition.

Biculturalism and Acculturation Among Latinos (28 min, FHS). Conflict over retaining traditional Latino cultural values versus assimilating into U.S. culture is presented. Common misperceptions about Latinos in the United States are examined.

Conformity, Obedience, and Dissent (1990, 30 min, IM). Explores research on why people conform, obey, and dissent, including Milgram's obedience study, the Asch studies, studies on styles of leadership and dissent, and studies on the Groupthink phenomenon.

Dear Lisa: A Letter to My Sister (1991, 45 min, IM). Interviews with 13 women of different ages, races, and backgrounds highlight this look at the forces that shape gender socialization. Footage from the 1960s illustrates the sex-typed culture that once was, and hopefully is diminishing.

Discovering Psychology, Part 17: Sex and Gender (1990, 30 min, ANN/CPB). Examines psychological differences between men and women and how societal values impact sex roles.

Discovering Psychology, Part 19: The Power of the Situation (1990, 30 min, ANN/CPB). Examines the role of situational factors in influencing our beliefs and behavior.

Discovering Psychology, Part 20: Constructing Social Reality (1990, 30 min, ANN/CPB). Explores how mental processes affect our interpretation of reality and interactions with society.

Face Value: Perceptions of Beauty (26 min, FHS). Sociobiological explanations take center stage in this discussion of universals in perceptions of beauty. Novel tests of this idea are presented, and opposing viewpoints are considered.

Gender and Relationships (1990, 30 min, IM). Love, sex, and everything in between are discussed in this film. Examines the forces that conspire to produce attraction, liking, and love.

Gender Socialization (1993, 60 min, IM). The impact of gender roles on self-esteem, behavior, and world views is considered.

Group Dynamics: Why Good People Make Bad Decisions (1994, 17 min, LS). A group of high school students team up to complete a class project. Along the way they discover the dynamics of Groupthink, social roles, and interpersonal expectations. An accompanying booklet includes summaries of the key points on the tape and suggestions for further activities. This video is very well produced, although the pacing and level of presentation may make it more appropriate for use in a high school or community college course.

Groupthink (Revised Edition) (22 min, PENN). Discusses the symptoms of Groupthink proposed by Irving Janis, provides illustrations of group decision making, and explains the role of effective leadership in avoiding Groupthink.

History of Anti-Semitism: The Longest Hatred (150 min, FHS). Traces anti-Semitism from its earliest manifestations in antiquity to the recent ominous outbreaks in Germany, Russia, and elsewhere.

The Idea of Gender (1995, 60 min, IM). The evolution of notions of gender in Europe and America during the past 200 years is discussed by Stanford professor James Sheehan.

Invisible Persuaders: The Battle For Your Mind (1994, 22 min, LS). This video explores unrecognized aspects of persuasion, such as why vacuum cleaners are noisy (people think they are more powerful than quieter models) or how packaging affects purchase (movie theater candy yields the same volume as store-bought, yet comes in a much bigger container). The scarcity principle, mere exposure, and other social psychological concepts are discussed in an intuitive way. An accompanying booklet includes summaries of the key points on the tape and suggestions for further activities.

Obedience (45 min, PENN). Documentary film of Stanley Milgram's classical study on obedience to authority using original footage and interviews.

Racial and Sexual Stereotyping (28 min, FHS). Phil Donahue leads the discussion of how prejudicial attitudes are perpetuated from one generation to the next. The teenage panelists discuss their hopes and concerns.

Quiet Rage: The Stanford Prison Experiment (1990, 50 min, IM). This update of Zimbardo's well-known study mixes recent hindsights with footage from the original event. A slick production, worth seeing.

Sexual Stereotypes in the Media: Superman and the Bride (37 min, FHS). Using examples from films, TV, and the print media, this program illustrates the pervasive nature of sexual stereotypes.

Social Psychology (1990, 30 min, IM). A broad overview of social psychology, including attitudes and prejudice, group behavior, and the power of social roles.

Social Psychology Series: Aggression (30 min, PENN). Presents research that emphasizes the role of learning in the occurrence of aggression and describes possible methods for controlling aggression.

Social Psychology Series: Communication - Negotiation and Persuasion (30 min, PENN). Describes and demonstrates verbal and nonverbal factors that influence the behaviors and attitudes of others.

Social Psychology Series: Communication - Social Cognition and Attributions (30 min, PENN). Discusses research on how we perceive others, wish to be perceived by others, interpret communications, and attribute causes to behavior. Also includes an overview of research methods used by social psychologists.

Social Psychology Series: Conformity (30 min, PENN). Examines the advantages and disadvantages of conforming in various situations as well as factors that influence the likelihood of conformity.

Social Psychology Series: Friendship (30 min, PENN). Examines the factors that contribute to the formation of friendships and the characteristics of friendships, including differences between male and female friendships.

Social Psychology Series: Group Decision Making and Leadership (30 min, PENN). Describes the strategies and interpersonal interactions, including the function of leadership, that impact group decision making in various situations.

Social Psychology Series: Helping and Prosocial Behavior (30 min, PENN). Explores why people help others, including the roles of reciprocity and social responsibility.

Social Psychology Series: Prejudice (30 min, PENN). Using dramatizations, the relationship of stereotypes and emotions to prejudice are examined. Methods of reducing discrimination are also discussed.

multimedia

Live! Psych

Module	Title	Book Page #
15.1	Attribution Theory	p. 566

Screen 1 explains that we may attribute people's behavior to internal causes or external causes. Screen 2 defines attribution theory. Screen 3 presents an animated graphic of the three types of information we use to make an internal or external attribution for a behavior: consensus, distinctiveness, and consistency. Screen 4 presents an animated graphic examining the importance of consistency in attributing behavior. Screen 5 is an interactive figure. Students click on each type of information to learn more about these three types of information.

Attribution Biases — p. 566

Screen 1 explains and illustrates the fundamental attributional error. Screen 2 explains and illustrates the self-serving bias.

15.2 Origins of Prejudice — p. 576

Screen 1 provides an interactive table. Students click on each source of prejudice: psychological, social, economic, and cultural sources to learn more about examples of each source of prejudice. Psychological sources include low self-esteem, anxiety, and insecurity. Social sources include groupthink, conformity, parental messages, and societal messages. Economic sources include the majority's desire to preserve its status as well as competition for jobs, power, and resources. Finally, cultural sources include ethnocentrism, desire for group identity, and the justification of war.

Cycle of Distrust — p. 576

This concept animates the cycle of distrust that perpetuates prejudice.

15.3 Solomon Asch's Classic Conformity Study — p. 583

In this concept, students participate in a simulation of Asch's conformity study. In Screen 1, students are told that they are going to be a participant in a visual perception study. In Screen 2, the student participates in the study. The experimenter shows all participants a pair of cards. One card has a standard line and the other has three different comparison lines. The student is asked to decide which of the three comparison lines are the same length as the standard line on three different trials. Screen 3 explains the results of the study.

Factors Influencing Conformity — p. 583

In this concept, students explore factors that influence conformity using an interactive table. Both situational factors and individuals factors influence the effects of conformity on our behavior. Screen 2 presents an animated graph, by pointing out the peak of conformity at seven confederates and the decline with larger group sizes. Import this screen to demonstrate that people are most likely to conform if seven other participants gave the same response and that larger groups seem to weaken the effect. Screen 3 presents an animated bar graph to show that a single dissenter reduces the pressure to conform by 80 percent. Screen 4 presents an animated bar graph showing that when the task is difficult or poorly defined, conformity tends to be higher. Screen 5 presents a picture showing that we are more likely to conform when the group consists of people who are similar to us. Screen 6 shows that we are more likely to conform to a group we are attracted to. Screen 7 shows that we are more likely to conform when one or more members are perceived as having a higher status as in a group of physicians. Screen 8 shows that conformity increases when an individual wants to be accepted by the group. Screen 9 shows that the culture you live in could affect your willingness to conform to group norms.

Web Investigations

Predicting Our Own Social Behavior

Janet Swim and Laurie Hyers asked female students how they would react to a sexist remark made by a male member of their group. The responses of the subjects showed the action of social influence, persuasion, and conformity. Your students can examine the research and indicate online how they would react in a similar situation. Use this exercise as a starting point for discussing several topics in social psychology, including social influence, prejudice and sexism, or person perception.

Making Connections

Social Cognition

Q How do schemata and stereotypes affect our impressions of other people.

A Schemata and stereotypes affect our impressions of other people by leading us to categorize them according to a few surface characteristics.

Q What is attribution theory, and how does it account for our social cognitions?

A Attribution theory deals with how we decide whether to attribute a given behavior to causes inside or outside the person. It affects our social cognitions because we tend to attribute the behavior of others to causes within themselves and not to pay enough attention to the circumstances in which the behavior occurs.

Q What are the major ways in which social psychologists explain interpersonal attraction?

A Social psychologists have found that interpersonal attraction is related to proximity, physical attractiveness, similarity, and equitable exchange.

Attitudes

Q What are the components of attitudes? How do attitudes affect behavior?

A The components of attitudes are evaluative beliefs about the object, feelings about the object, and behavior tendencies toward the object. Attitudes affect behavior because they may be positive or negative and thus cause us to behave in positive or negative ways toward particular objects, people, or events. However, people who rate highly on self-monitoring are likely to override their attitudes in order to behave in accordance with others' expectations.

Q What strategies can reduce prejudice and discrimination?

A Strategies for reducing prejudice and discrimination include recategorization (expanding our schema for a particular group), controlled processing (training ourselves to be more mindful of people who differ from us), and improving contact between groups.

Q What approaches do social psychologists use to explain the process of attitude change?

A Social psychologists explain attitude change by means of the communication model of persuasion, which focuses on the source, the message, the medium of communication, and characteristics of the audience. According to the cognitive dissonance model, attitudes may also be changed when new actions contradict preexisting attitudes, creating cognitive dissonance.

Social Influence

Q What are social norms? How are they reinforced?

A Social norms are culturally shared ideas or expectations about how to behave or not to behave. They are reinforced by conditioning, in which a person is rewarded or punished for particular behaviors and thus learns to do what is expected in various situations.

Q How can cultural assimilators help us to remain broadminded about culture?

A Cultural assimilators encourage us to be open-minded by seeking to understand the reasons for the behavior of members of other cultures.

Q What situational variables affect conformity?

A Conformity is affected by the size of the group, the degree of unanimity in the group, and the nature of the task.

Q What is compliance? What techniques enhance compliance?

A Compliance is a change of behavior in response to an explicit request. It can be enhanced by the foot-in-the-door effect, the lowball procedure, and the door-in-the-face effect.

Q What explanations have been offered to explain obedience?

A Obedience has been explained as stemming from (a) respect for people in power, (b) trust in people in authority, or (c) failure to perceive the situation correctly.

Social Action

Q What factors explain mob violence?

A Mob violence is explained by deindividuation, in which people lose their personal sense of responsibility in a group, and the snowball effect, in which people who have been persuaded to behave in a certain way convince others, who will convince still others until the group becomes a mob.

Q What factors explain helping behavior? Under what circumstances are people most likely to behave altruistically?

A Helping behavior is explained by variables inherent in the situation and grounded in the individual. People are more likely to behave altruistically when there are few passive bystanders, when the situation is unambiguous, when the individual feels a sense of personal responsibility, and when the individual is in a good mood and does not fear embarrassment.

Q Under what circumstances are groups more effective than individuals at making decisions?

A Groups are more effective than individuals at making decisions when the requirements of the task match the skills of the group, the group's members interact efficiently, the group is large enough to include people with the skills needed to solve the problem, and the group's morale is high.

Q What topics do I/O psychologists study?

A I/O psychologists study the influence on human interaction of large, complex organizational settings, with special emphasis on behavior in the workplace.

Video Classics

Obedience to Authority

SYNOPSIS: This video segment is taken from Milgram's original footage of his experiments on obedience. The camera focuses on a "teacher" delivering shocks to a "learner," and shows the teacher's growing agitation as the shock intensity increases.

Form a Hypothesis

Q What percentage of subjects do you predict delivered shock all the way up to 450 volts—"DANGER: SEVERE SHOCK"?

A Although lay predictions of those who would dutifully proceed to the 450-volt level typically fall under 10%, fully 65% of the subjects obeyed.

Test Your Understanding

Q Sixty-five percent of the subjects followed the experimenter's orders and delivered the highest level of shock to the learner. What would you have done if you were a subject in this experiment? Why?

A Students may answer truthfully. More likely, they will indicate that they would have terminated the procedures before the 450-volt level.

Q What factors in this situation contributed to such a high degree of obedience?

A Obedience was enhanced by the status of the institution sponsoring the research, the presence of the researcher in the room with the teacher, and the prosocial nature of the research cover story ("a study of the effects of punishment on learning"). Moreover, the individuals in the study had no doubt received many years of socialization to obey as members of their culture.

Q How did Milgram deceive his subjects? How could this experiment be harmful to subjects? When can deception in research be justified?

A Milgram informed subjects that he was studying punishment's effects on learning. Subjects could have been harmed immediately by the stress induced by the procedures and on a longer-term basis as they reflected on their obedient conduct. Deception in research is justified only when the safety and comfort of the subject is not unduly jeopardized <u>and</u> when other nondeceptive techniques cannot be employed.

Q Suppose you are on a research panel to approve or reject Milgram's study of obedience today. Would you approve or reject his study? On what ethical guidelines do you base your answer?

A Approve: Because the benefits to society outweighed the comparatively minor inconvenience to the subject.

Reject: The stress experienced by subjects was too extreme to justify the beneficial outcome to society.

Thinking Critically

Q This experiment demonstrates how other people can influence our behavior. Can you cite examples of how people have complied with authority at any cost in our society's history? Why do you think people obey orders from authority figures?

A Contemporary examples include death squads in South America and ethnic cleansing in the former Yugoslavia. People probably obey when they are trained to do so, the authority promotes a feeling of vulnerability in the individual and when the authority assumes moral responsibility for the victimization committed by the obedient.

The Bystander Effect

SYNOPSIS: A very young John Darley and Bibb Latane recreate their "smoke filled room" experiment to illustrate people's responses during an emergency. This video segment shows what happens when one person versus three people are in the presence of a presumed emergency, and also includes narration from Latane regarding the origin and interpretation of the bystander effect.

Form a Hypothesis

Q Do you think people will be less likely to make an emergency interpretation of an event if they are in the presence of other people or if they are alone?

A Latané and Darley's research demonstrates that this interpretation is <u>less</u> likely in the presence of others, especially if the other witnesses are nonchalant or demonstrating confusion concerning how they should behave.

Test Your Understanding

Q Latané and Darley found that 55 percent of the subjects in the alone condition reported the smoke within the first two minutes, whereas 12 percent of the subjects who were in the presence of others did so. What factors inhibit a response to an emergency?

A The presence of others may reduce the personal responsibility felt by any one individual for the well being of the victim. Additionally, others tend to behave in ways that reduce emergency attributions, e.g., hiding one's concern or panic in the presence of others.

Q What characteristics of the victim, the bystanders, and the situation make helping most likely to occur?

A When victims are helpless, attractive, and nonthreatening, assistance is more likely. Bystanders can facilitate helping by clearly declaring that an emergency is underway and instructing others how to respond. Situations that are unambiguous (e.g., a building fire) are more likely to generate assistance than ambiguous situations (an argument between a couple).

Thinking Critically

Q What is bystander effect and what was its role in the case of Kitty Genovese?

A The bystander effect refers to reduced helping when there are multiple potential helpers. In the Genovese case, individuals failed to respond because they assumed that others had already done so.

Q What are the five steps of the decision-making process in emergency interpretation?

A Awareness / Interpretation as an Emergency / Assume Responsibility / Select Course of Action /

Implementation of Action

Web Links

1. http://www.socialpsychology.org/

The Social Psychology Network. This could easily be the only resource you'll ever need for information about social psychology on the Internet. Scott Plous has done an incredible job of assembling more resources than you can visit in a week. Highly recommended.

2. http://www.socialpsychology.org/social.htm

Social Psychology Network links by subtopic. Actually, SPN also has links for Introductory Psychology, I/O psychology, and other topics, so exploring the ones on this page is only the beginning.

3. http://psych.athabascau.ca/html/aupr/psycres.shtml

Psychology Centre: Social and Cultural Psychology.

4. http://maple.lemoyne.edu/~hevern/psychref4-6a.html

PsychREF: Industrial/Organizational Psychology. This site applies social psychology to the workplace. Interested students will find a great deal of I/O information here.

transparencies

Series V

97. *Asch's Experiment on Conformity*
A depiction of Asch's line-judging experiment.

98. *Biases in the Attribution Process*
Various attributional biases are identified and explained.

99. *Milgram's Experiment on Obedience*
The details of Milgram's procedure are presented.

100. *The Bystander Effect*
Components of why people fail to offer help are illustrated in this transparency.

Text Figures

15-1. *Racial Attitudes in the United States*

15-2. *Asch's Experiment on Conformity*

Handout 15-1

Trait Identification Questionnaire

Instructions: Listed below are 20 pairs of opposite traits. For each pair, indicate which of the traits is most characteristic of _____ (YOU / A WELL-KNOWN CELEBRITY) by circling the trait. If neither trait is most characteristic, indicate that by circling "depends on the situation."

Serious	Lighthearted	Depends on the situation
Subjective	Analytic	Depends on the situation
Future Oriented	Present Oriented	Depends on the situation
Energetic	Relaxed	Depends on the situation
Unassuming	Self-assertive	Depends on the situation
Lenient	Firm	Depends on the situation
Reserved	Emotionally Expressive	Depends on the situation
Dignified	Casual	Depends on the situation
Realistic	Idealistic	Depends on the situation
Intense	Calm	Depends on the situation
Skeptical	Trusting	Depends on the situation
Quiet	Talkative	Depends on the situation
Cultivated	Natural	Depends on the situation
Sensitive	Tough-minded	Depends on the situation
Steady	Flexible	Depends on the situation
Self-sufficient	Sociable	Depends on the situation
Dominant	Submissive	Depends on the situation
Cautious	Bold	Depends on the situation
Uninhibited	Self-controlled	Depends on the situation
Conscientious	Happy-go-lucky	Depends on the situation

Adapted from Kite, M. E. (1991). Observer biases in the classroom. *Teaching of Psychology, 18*, 161-164.

Handout 15-2

Who Will Survive?

A group of 15 individuals are traveling in a space ship on their way to colonize a distant planet that is presently void of any intelligent life but that has an environment which could easily support humans. There is a sudden malfunction in the oxygen-replenishing equipment on the ship that cannot be repaired. It can now only supply oxygen for a maximum of 8 people. If the 15 continue to breathe the air, they will exhaust the oxygen and all will die before reaching the planet. Therefore, 7 people must be eliminated so that the remaining 8 can survive to colonize the planet. Your group is to decide which 7 are to be eliminated. This must be a unanimous decision by the group. Majority rule or voting is not allowed. The descriptions of the 15 people in the space ship are listed on the next page. Assume that this is the only information you have on these individuals. List below the 7 persons who were eliminated and briefly list the reasons for the decision.

1. _____

    Reason:

2. _____

    Reason:

3. _____

    Reason:

4. _____

    Reason:

5. _____

    Reason:

6. _____

    Reason:

7. _____

    Reason:

Name	Age	Description
Sarah Jansen	34	Divorced, unable to have children. Advanced degree in education, excellent teacher.
Bonnie Jansen	9	4th grade, good health, average student. Mrs. Jansen's daughter.
Susan Adams	31	Unmarried, beginning nursing student, does not date men.
Sam Markus	25	Interested in electronics. Comes from very poor background. Married with pregnant wife. Introvert who likes to be left alone.
Ruth Markus	20	Wife of Mr. Markus. Six months pregnant. College graduate in art. Having marital problems.
Father Crimble	40	Catholic priest. Good health. A Socialist who is active in liberal politics.
Dr. Joe Perkins	68	Medical doctor. History of heart problems but is currently practicing medicine.
Dr. Ed Miller	38	Ph.D. in psychology. University professor. 1 child. Recently divorced.
Michael Miller	11	Son of Dr. Miller. Physically healthy but mentally retarded with IQ around 75.
Jean Majors	21	Former beauty queen. High school drop-out. Likes to work with children.
June Hart	42	Women's rights activist, college educated in nursing. Divorced, no children.
Tom Stein	27	Atheist, history of emotional problems. Last year medical student.
Cynthia Allen	25	Reformed prostitute. Divorced, one infant child. Unable to have more children.
Lisa Allen	1	Infant daughter of Cynthia Allen. Nursing, good health.
John Watson	19	Sophomore college student, average grades, undecided on a major.

Adapted from R. M. Gardner, *Exercises for general psychology*. Reprinted by permission of Prentice Hall, Copyright 1980.